Visual C# 2010 Recipes

A Problem-Solution Approach

Allen Jones and Adam Freeman

Apress®

Visual C# 2010 Recipes: A Problem-Solution Approach

ISBN-13 (pbk): 978-1-4302-2525-6

ISBN-13 (electronic): 978-1-4302-2526-3

Printed and bound in the United States of America 9 8 7 6 5 4 3 2 1

Distributed to the book trade worldwide by Springer-Verlag New York, Inc., 233 Spring Street, 6th Floor, New York, NY 10013. Phone 1-800-SPRINGER, fax 201-348-4505, e-mail orders-ny@springer-sbm.com, or visit www.springeronline.com.

For information on translations, please e-mail rights@apress.com, or visit www.apress.com.

Apress and friends of ED books may be purchased in bulk for academic, corporate, or promotional use. eBook versions and licenses are also available for most titles. For more information, reference our Special Bulk Sales–eBook Licensing web page at www.apress.com/info/bulksales.

The source code for this book is available to readers at www.apress.com.

For my lovely wife Lena, and our three wonderful girls, Anya, Alexia, and Angelina. I love you all.

—Allen Jones

For my wife, Jacqui Griffyth, who I love a great deal.

—Adam Freeman

Contents at a Glance

Contents

About the Authors

Allen Jones has a master's degree in software engineering from Oxford University and 20 years industry experience covering a wide range of IT disciplines. He has spent the last ten years leading the development of innovative commercial software solutions in areas such as security, content management, trading, portfolio management, strategic planning, and real-time search. Allen is a partner at QuantumBlack, a design and technology studio that applies visual analytics to help organizations make faster decisions and smarter investments, and earn new revenues.

Adam Freeman is an experienced IT professional who has held senior positions at a range of companies, most recently as chief technology officer and chief operating officer of a global bank. He started his career in programming and still finds it one of the most engaging and interesting ways to spend a day.

About the Technical Reviewer

Mark Collins has developed software for over 25 years, mostly using the Microsoft stack. He has served many roles, including development manager, architect, team lead, database administrator, and project manager. He has extensive experience in retail (point-of-sale and inventory) and customer relationship management (CRM) solutions. Mark currently serves as a senior software engineer for a nonprofit organization, providing a custom CRM, mail processing, and fulfillment system.

Acknowledgments

We would like to thank everyone at Apress for working so hard to bring this book to print. In particular, we would like to thank Anne Collett and Jonathan Hassell. We would also like to thank Damon Larson and Mark Collins, whose respective efforts as copy editor and technical reviewer made this book far better than it would have been without them.

Allen Jones
Adam Freeman

Introduction

Mastering the development of Microsoft .NET Framework applications in C# is less about knowing the C# language and more about knowing how to use the functionality of the .NET Framework class library most effectively. *Visual C# 2010 Recipes* explores the breadth of the .NET Framework class library and provides specific solutions to common and interesting programming problems. Each solution (or recipe) is presented in a succinct problem/solution format, and most are accompanied by working code samples.

Visual C# 2010 Recipes is not intended to teach you how to program, nor to teach you C#. However, if you have even the most rudimentary experience programming applications built on the .NET Framework using C#, you will find this book to be an invaluable resource.

Ideally, when you are facing a problem, this book will contain a recipe that provides the solution, or at least it will point you in the right direction. Even if you just want to broaden your knowledge of the .NET Framework class library, *Visual C# 2010 Recipes* is the perfect resource to assist you.

However, you cannot become proficient with C# and the classes in the .NET Framework class library merely by reading about them. Rather, you must use them and experiment with them by writing code, code, and more code. The structure and content of this book and the real-world applicability of the solutions it provides offer the perfect starting point from which to kick-start your own experimentation.

Allen Jones
Adam Freeman

CHAPTER 1

Application Development

This chapter covers some of the fundamental activities you will need to perform when developing your C# solutions. The recipes in this chapter describe how to do the following:

- Use the C# command-line compiler to build console and Windows Forms applications (recipes 1-1 and 1-2)
- Create and use code modules and libraries (recipes 1-3 and 1-4)
- Access command-line arguments from within your applications (recipe 1-5)
- Use compiler directives and attributes to selectively include code at build time (recipe 1-6)
- Access program elements built in other languages whose names conflict with C# keywords (recipe 1-7)
- Give assemblies strong names and verify strong-named assemblies (recipes 1-8, 1-9, 1-10, and 1-11)
- Sign an assembly with a Microsoft Authenticode digital signature (recipes 1-12 and 1-13)
- Manage the shared assemblies that are stored in the global assembly cache (recipe 1-14)
- Prevent people from decompiling your assembly (recipe 1-15)
- Manipulate the appearance of the console (recipe 1-16)
- Create static, anonymous, and dynamically expandable types (recipes 1-17, 1-18, and 1-19)
- Define automatically implemented properties (recipe 1-20)
- Overload an operator and implement a custom conversion operator (recipes 1-21 and 1-22)
- Handle an event with an anonymous function (recipe 1-23)
- Implement a customer indexer (recipe 1-24)

■ **Note** All the tools discussed in this chapter ship with the Microsoft .NET Framework or the .NET Framework software development kit (SDK). The tools that are part of the .NET Framework are in the main directory for the version of the framework you are running. For example, they are in the directory `C:\WINDOWS\Microsoft.NET\Framework\v4.0` (or `C:\WINDOWS\Microsoft.NET\Framework64\v4.0` for 64-bit systems) if you install version 4.0 of the .NET Framework to the default location. The .NET installation process automatically adds this directory to your environment path. The tools provided with the SDK are in the `Bin` subdirectory of the directory in which you install the SDK, which is `C:\Program Files\Microsoft SDKs\Windows\v7.0a\bin` (or `C:\Program Files(x86)\Microsoft SDKs\Windows\v7.0a\bin` on a 64-bit system) if you chose the default path during the installation of Microsoft Visual Studio 2010. This directory is *not* added to your path automatically, so you must manually edit your path in order to have easy access to these tools. Most of the tools support short and long forms of the command-line switches that control their functionality. This chapter always shows the long form, which is more informative but requires additional typing. For the shortened form of each switch, see the tool's documentation in the .NET Framework SDK.

1-1. Create a Console Application from the Command Line

Problem

You need to use the C# command-line compiler to build an application that does not require a Windows graphical user interface (GUI) but instead displays output to, and reads input from, the Windows command prompt (console).

Solution

In one of your classes, ensure you implement a `static` method named `Main` with one of the following signatures:

```
public static void Main();
public static void Main(string[] args);
public static int Main();
public static int Main(string[] args);
```

Build your application using the C# compiler (`csc.exe`) by running the following command (where `HelloWorld.cs` is the name of your source code file):

```
csc /target:exe HelloWorld.cs
```

■ **Note** If you own Visual Studio, you will most often use the Console Application project template to create new console applications. However, for small applications, it is often just as easy to use the command-line compiler. It is also useful to know how to build console applications from the command line if you are ever working on a machine without Visual Studio and want to create a quick utility to automate some task.

How It Works

By default, the C# compiler will build a console application unless you specify otherwise. For this reason, it's not necessary to specify the `/target:exe` switch, but doing so makes your intention clearer, which is useful if you are creating build scripts that will be used by others.

To build a console application consisting of more than one source code file, you must specify all the source files as arguments to the compiler. For example, the following command builds an application named `MyFirstApp.exe` from two source files named `HelloWorld.cs` and `ConsoleUtils.cs`:

```
csc /target:exe /main:HelloWorld /out:MyFirstApp.exe HelloWorld.cs ConsoleUtils.cs
```

The `/out` switch allows you to specify the name of the compiled assembly. Otherwise, the assembly is named after the first source file listed—`HelloWorld.cs` in the example. If classes in both the `HelloWorld` and `ConsoleUtils` files contain `Main` methods, the compiler cannot automatically determine which method represents the correct entry point for the assembly. Therefore, you must use the compiler's `/main` switch to identify the name of the class that contains the correct entry point for your application. When using the `/main` switch, you must provide the fully qualified class name (including the namespace); otherwise, you will get a CS1555 compilation error: "Could not find 'HelloWorld' specified for Main method."

If you have a lot of C# code source files to compile, you should use a response file. This simple text file contains the command-line arguments for `csc.exe`. When you call `csc.exe`, you give the name of this response file as a single parameter prefixed by the @ character—for example:

```
csc @commands.rsp
```

To achieve the equivalent of the previous example, `commands.rsp` would contain this:

```
/target:exe /main:HelloWorld /out:MyFirstApp.exe HelloWorld.cs ConsoleUtils.cs
```

The Code

The following code lists a class named `ConsoleUtils` that is defined in a file named `ConsoleUtils.cs`:

```
using System;

namespace Apress.VisualCSharpRecipes.Chapter01
{
    public class ConsoleUtils
    {
        // A method to display a prompt and read a response from the console.
```

```
        public static string ReadString(string msg)
        {
            Console.Write(msg);
            return Console.ReadLine();
        }

        // A method to display a message to the console.
        public static void WriteString(string msg)
        {
            Console.WriteLine(msg);
        }

        // Main method used for testing ConsoleUtility methods.
        public static void Main()
        {
            // Prompt the reader to enter a name.
            string name = ReadString("Please enter your name : ");

            // Welcome the reader to Visual C# 2010 Recipes.
            WriteString("Welcome to Visual C# 2010 Recipes, " + name);
        }
    }
}
```

The `HelloWorld` class listed next uses the `ConsoleUtils` class to display the message "Hello, world" to the console (`HelloWorld` is contained in the `HelloWorld.cs` file):

```
using System;

namespace Apress.VisualCSharpRecipes.Chapter01
{
    class HelloWorld
    {
        public static void Main()
        {
            ConsoleUtils.WriteString("Hello, world");

            Console.WriteLine("\nMain method complete. Press Enter.");
            Console.ReadLine();
        }
    }
}
```

Usage

To build `HelloWorld.exe` from the two source files, use the following command:

```
csc /target:exe /main:Apress.VisualCSharpRecipes.Chapter01.HelloWorld
/out:HelloWorld.exe ConsoleUtils.cs HelloWorld.cs
```

1-2. Create a Windows-Based Application from the Command Line

Problem

You need to use the C# command-line compiler to build an application that provides a Windows Forms–based GUI.

Solution

Create a class that extends the `System.Windows.Forms.Form` class. (This will be your application's main form.) In one of your classes, ensure you implement a `static` method named `Main`. In the `Main` method, create an instance of your main form class and pass it to the `static` method `Run` of the `System.Windows.Forms.Application` class. Build your application using the command-line C# compiler, and specify the `/target:winexe` compiler switch.

■ **Note** If you own Visual Studio, you will most often use the Windows Application project template to create new Windows Forms–based applications. Building large GUI-based applications is a time-consuming undertaking that involves the correct instantiation, configuration, and wiring up of many forms and controls. Visual Studio automates much of the work associated with building graphical applications. Trying to build a large graphical application without the aid of tools such as Visual Studio will take you much longer, be extremely tedious, and result in a greater chance of bugs in your code. However, it is also useful to know the essentials required to create a Windows-based application using the command line in case you are ever working on a machine without Visual Studio and want to create a quick utility to automate some task or get input from a user. In order to build a WPF application from the command line, you must use the MSBuild tool—see the MSBuild reference in the .NET Framework documentation.

How It Works

Building an application that provides a simple Windows GUI is a world away from developing a full-fledged Windows-based application. However, you must perform certain tasks regardless of whether you are writing the Windows equivalent of Hello World or the next version of Microsoft Word, including the following:

- For each form you need in your application, create a class that extends the `System.Windows.Forms.Form` class.
- In each of your form classes, declare members that represent the controls that will be on that form, such as buttons, labels, lists, and text boxes. These members should be declared `private` or at least `protected` so that other program elements cannot access them directly. If you need to expose the methods or properties of these controls, implement the necessary members in your form class, providing indirect and controlled access to the contained controls.
- Declare methods in your form class that will handle events raised by the controls contained by the form, such as button clicks or key presses when a text box is the active control. These methods should be `private` or `protected` and follow the standard .NET `event pattern` (described in recipe 13-11). It's in these methods (or methods called by these methods) where you will define the bulk of your application's functionality.
- Declare a constructor for your form class that instantiates each of the form's controls and configures their initial state (size, color, position, content, and so on). The constructor should also wire up the appropriate event handler methods of your class to the events of each control.
- Declare a `static` method named `Main`—usually as a member of your application's main form class. This method is the entry point for your application, and it can have the same signatures as those mentioned in recipe 1-1. In the `Main` method, call `Application.EnableVisualStyles` to allow Windows theme support, create an instance of your application's main form, and pass it as an argument to the `static` `Application.Run` method. The `Run` method makes your main form visible and starts a standard Windows message loop on the current thread, which passes the user input (key presses, mouse clicks, and so on) to your application form as events.

The Code

The `Recipe01-02` class shown in the following code listing is a simple Windows Forms application that demonstrates the techniques just listed. When run, it prompts a user to enter a name and then displays a message box welcoming the user to `Visual C# 2010 Recipes`.

```
using System;
using System.Windows.Forms;

namespace Apress.VisualCSharpRecipes.Chapter01
{
    class Recipe01_02 : Form
    {
        // Private members to hold references to the form's controls.
        private Label label1;
        private TextBox textBox1;
        private Button button1;

        // Constructor used to create an instance of the form and configure
```

```
// the form's controls.
public Recipe01_02()
{
    // Instantiate the controls used on the form.
    this.label1 = new Label();
    this.textBox1 = new TextBox();
    this.button1 = new Button();

    // Suspend the layout logic of the form while we configure and
    // position the controls.
    this.SuspendLayout();

    // Configure label1, which displays the user prompt.
    this.label1.Location = new System.Drawing.Point(16, 36);
    this.label1.Name = "label1";
    this.label1.Size = new System.Drawing.Size(148, 16);
    this.label1.TabIndex = 0;
    this.label1.Text = "Please enter your name:";

    // Configure textBox1, which accepts the user input.
    this.textBox1.Location = new System.Drawing.Point(172, 32);
    this.textBox1.Name = "textBox1";
    this.textBox1.TabIndex = 1;
    this.textBox1.Text = "";

    // Configure button1, which the user clicks to enter a name.
    this.button1.Location = new System.Drawing.Point(109, 80);
    this.button1.Name = "button1";
    this.button1.TabIndex = 2;
    this.button1.Text = "Enter";
    this.button1.Click += new System.EventHandler(this.button1_Click);

    // Configure WelcomeForm, and add controls.
    this.ClientSize = new System.Drawing.Size(292, 126);
    this.Controls.Add(this.button1);
    this.Controls.Add(this.textBox1);
    this.Controls.Add(this.label1);
    this.Name = "form1";
    this.Text = "Visual C# 2010 Recipes";

    // Resume the layout logic of the form now that all controls are
    // configured.
    this.ResumeLayout(false);
}

// Event handler called when the user clicks the Enter button on the
// form.
private void button1_Click(object sender, System.EventArgs e)
{
    // Write debug message to the console.
    System.Console.WriteLine("User entered: " + textBox1.Text);
```

```
            // Display welcome as a message box.
            MessageBox.Show("Welcome to Visual C# 2010 Recipes, "
                + textBox1.Text, "Visual C# 2010 Recipes");
        }

        // Application entry point, creates an instance of the form, and begins
        // running a standard message loop on the current thread. The message
        // loop feeds the application with input from the user as events.
        [STAThread]
        public static void Main()
        {
            Application.EnableVisualStyles();
            Application.Run(new Recipe01_02());
        }
    }
}
```

Usage

To build the Recipe01-02 class into an application, use this command:

```
csc /target:winexe Recipe01-02.cs
```

The /target:winexe switch tells the compiler that you are building a Windows-based application. As a result, the compiler builds the executable in such a way that no console is created when you run your application. If you use the /target:exe switch to build a Windows Forms application instead of /target:winexe, your application will still work correctly, but you will have a console window visible while the application is running. Although this is undesirable for production-quality software, the console window is useful if you want to write debug and logging information while you're developing and testing your Windows Forms application. You can write to this console using the Write and WriteLine methods of the System.Console class.

Figure 1-1 shows the WelcomeForm.exe application greeting a user named Rupert. This version of the application is built using the /target:exe compiler switch.

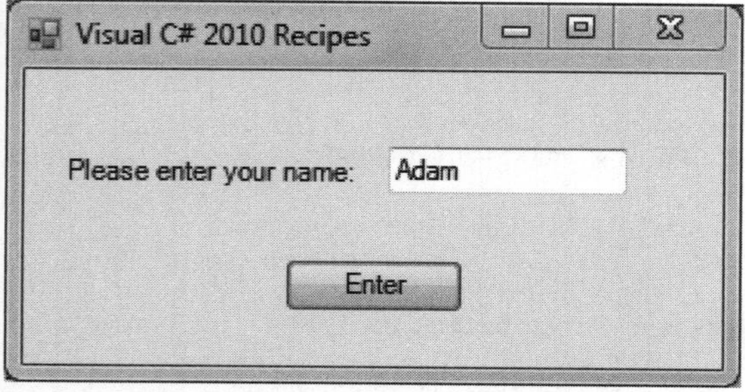

Figure 1-1. A simple Windows Forms application

1-3. Create and Use a Code Module

Problem

You need to do one or more of the following:

- Improve your application's performance and memory efficiency by ensuring that the runtime loads rarely used types only when they are required
- Compile types written in C# to a form you can build into assemblies being developed in other .NET languages
- Use types developed in another language and build them into your C# assemblies

Solution

Build your C# source code into a module by using the command-line compiler and specifying the `/target:module` compiler switch. To incorporate an existing module into your assembly, use the `/addmodule` compiler switch.

How It Works

Modules are the building blocks of .NET assemblies. Modules consist of a single file that contains the following:

- Microsoft Intermediate Language (MSIL) code created from your source code during compilation
- Metadata describing the types contained in the module
- Resources, such as icons and string tables, used by the types in the module

Assemblies consist of one or more modules and an assembly manifest. When a single module exists, the module and assembly manifest are usually built into a single file for convenience. When more than one module exists, the assembly represents a logical grouping of more than one file that you must deploy as a complete unit. In these situations, the assembly manifest is either contained in a separate file or built into one of the modules.

By building an assembly from multiple modules, you complicate the management and deployment of the assembly, but under some circumstances, modules offer significant benefits:

- The runtime will load a module only when the types defined in the module are required. Therefore, where you have a set of types that your application uses rarely, you can partition them into a separate module that the runtime will load only if necessary. This offers the following benefits:
    - Improving performance, especially if your application is loaded across a network
    - Minimizing the use of memory

- The ability to use many different languages to write applications that run on the Common Language Runtime (CLR) is a great strength of the .NET Framework. However, the C# compiler can't compile your Microsoft Visual Basic .NET or COBOL .NET code for inclusion in your assembly. To use code written in another language, you can compile it into a separate assembly and reference it. But if you want it to be an integral part of your assembly, then you must build it into a module. Similarly, if you want to allow others to include your code as an integral part of their assemblies, you must compile your code as modules. When you use modules, because the code becomes part of the same assembly, members marked as `internal` or `protected internal` are accessible, whereas they would not be if the code had been accessed from an external assembly.

Usage

To compile a source file named `ConsoleUtils.cs` (see recipe 1-1 for the contents) into a module, use the command `csc /target:module ConsoleUtils.cs`. The result is the creation of a file named `ConsoleUtils.netmodule`. The `netmodule` extension is the default extension for modules, and the filename is the same as the name of the C# source file.

You can also build modules from multiple source files, which results in a single file (module) containing the MSIL and metadata for all types contained in all the source files. The command `csc /target:module ConsoleUtils.cs WindowsUtils.cs` compiles two source files named `ConsoleUtils.cs` and `WindowsUtils.cs` to create the module named `ConsoleUtils.netmodule`. The module is named after the first source file listed unless you override the name with the `/out` compiler switch. For example, the command `csc /target:module /out:Utilities.netmodule ConsoleUtils.cs WindowsUtils.cs` creates a module named `Utilities.netmodule`.

To build an assembly consisting of multiple modules, you must use the `/addmodule` compiler switch. To build an executable named `MyFirstApp.exe` from two modules named `WindowsUtils.netmodule` and `ConsoleUtils.netmodule` and two source files named `SourceOne.cs` and `SourceTwo.cs`, use the command `csc /out:MyFirstApp.exe /target:exe /addmodule:WindowsUtils.netmodule,ConsoleUtils.netmodule SourceOne.cs SourceTwo.cs`. This command will result in an assembly consisting of the following files:

- `MyFirstApp.exe`, which contains the assembly manifest as well as the MSIL for the types declared in the `SourceOne.cs` and `SourceTwo.cs` source files
- `ConsoleUtils.netmodule` and `WindowsUtils.netmodule`, which are now integral components of the multifile assembly but are unchanged by this compilation process

---

■ **Caution** If you attempt to run an assembly (such as `MyFirstApp.exe`) without any required netmodules present, a `System.IO.FileNotFoundException` is thrown the first time any code tries to use types defined in the missing code module. This is a significant concern because the missing modules will not be identified until runtime. You must be careful when deploying multifile assemblies.

1-4. Create and Use a Code Library from the Command Line

Problem

You need to build a set of functionality into a reusable code library so that multiple applications can reference and reuse it.

Solution

Build your library using the command-line C# compiler, and specify the `/target:library` compiler switch. To reference the library, use the `/reference` compiler switch when you build your application, and specify the names of the required libraries.

How It Works

Recipe 1-1 showed you how to build an application named `MyFirstApp.exe` from the two source files `ConsoleUtils.cs` and `HelloWorld.cs`. The `ConsoleUtils.cs` file contains the `ConsoleUtils` class, which provides methods to simplify interaction with the Windows console. If you were to extend the functionality of the `ConsoleUtils` class, you could add functionality useful to many applications. Instead of including the source code for `ConsoleUtils` in every application, you could build it into a library and deploy it independently, making the functionality accessible to many applications.

Usage

To build the `ConsoleUtils.cs` file into a library, use the command `csc /target:library ConsoleUtils.cs`. This will produce a library file named `ConsoleUtils.dll`. To build a library from multiple source files, list the name of each file at the end of the command. You can also specify the name of the library using the `/out` compiler switch; otherwise, the library is named after the first source file listed. For example, to build a library named `MyFirstLibrary.dll` from two source files named `ConsoleUtils.cs` and `WindowsUtils.cs`, use the command `csc /out:MyFirstLibrary.dll /target:library ConsoleUtils.cs WindowsUtils.cs`.

Before distributing your library, you might consider strongly naming it so that nobody can modify your assembly and pass it off as being the original. Strongly naming your library also allows people to install it into the Global Assembly Cache (GAC), which makes reuse much easier. (Recipe 1-9 describes how to strongly name your assembly, and recipe 1-14 describes how to install a strongly named assembly into the GAC.) You might also consider signing your library with an Authenticode signature, which allows users to confirm you are the publisher of the assembly—see recipe 1-12 for details on signing assemblies with Authenticode.

To compile an assembly that relies on types declared within external libraries, you must tell the compiler which libraries are referenced using the `/reference` compiler switch. For example, to compile the `HelloWorld.cs` source file (from recipe 1-1) if the `ConsoleUtils` class is contained in the `ConsoleUtils.dll` library, use the command `csc /reference:ConsoleUtils.dll HelloWorld.cs`. Remember these four points:

- If you reference more than one library, separate each library name with a comma or semicolon, but don't include any spaces. For example, use `/reference:ConsoleUtils.dll,WindowsUtils.dll`.
- If the libraries aren't in the same directory as the source code, use the `/lib` switch on the compiler to specify the additional directories where the compiler should look for libraries. For example, use `/lib:c:\CommonLibraries,c:\Dev\ThirdPartyLibs`.
- Note that additional directories can be relative to the source folder. Don't forget that at runtime, the generated assembly must be in the same folder as the application that needs it except if you deploy it into the GAC.
- If the library you need to reference is a multifile assembly, reference the file that contains the assembly manifest. (For information about multifile assemblies, see recipe 1-3.)

1-5. Access Command-Line Arguments

Problem

You need to access the arguments that were specified on the command line when your application was executed.

Solution

Use a signature for your `Main` method that exposes the command-line arguments as a `string` array. Alternatively, access the command-line arguments from anywhere in your code using the `static` members of the `System.Environment` class.

How It Works

Declaring your application's `Main` method with one of the following signatures provides access to the command-line arguments as a `string` array:

```
public static void Main(string[] args);
public static int Main(string[] args);
```

At runtime, the `args` argument will contain a string for each value entered on the command line after your application's name. Unlike C and C++, the application's name is not included in the array of arguments.

If you need access to the command-line arguments at places in your code other than the `Main` method, you can use the `System.Environment` class, which provides two `static` members that return information about the command line: `CommandLine` and `GetCommandLineArgs`.

The `CommandLine` property returns a `string` containing the full command line that launched the current process. Depending on the operating system on which the application is running, path information might precede the application name—older versions of Windows, such as Windows 98 and Windows ME, include this information. The GetCommandLineArgs method returns a string array containing the command-line arguments. This array can be processed in the same way as the string array passed to the Main method, as discussed at the start of this section. Unlike the array passed to the Main method, the first element in the array returned by the GetCommandLineArgs method is the file name of the application.

The Code

To demonstrate the access of command-line arguments, the Main method in the following example steps through each of the command-line arguments passed to it and displays them to the console. The example then accesses the command line directly through the Environment class.

```
using System;
namespace Apress.VisualCSharpRecipes.Chapter01
{
    class Recipe01_05
    {
        public static void Main(string[] args)
        {
            // Step through the command-line arguments.
            foreach (string s in args)
            {
                Console.WriteLine(s);
            }

            // Alternatively, access the command-line arguments directly.
            Console.WriteLine(Environment.CommandLine);

            foreach (string s in Environment.GetCommandLineArgs())
            {
                Console.WriteLine(s);
            }

            // Wait to continue.
            Console.WriteLine("\nMain method complete. Press Enter.");
            Console.ReadLine();
        }
    }
}
```

Usage

If you execute the Recipe01-05 example using the following command:

```
Recipe01-05 "one \"two\"    three" four 'five    six'
```

the application will generate the following output on the console:

```
one "two"    three

four

'five

six'

Recipe01-05  "one \"two\"    three" four 'five    six'

Recipe01-05

one "two"    three

four

'five

six'


Main method complete. Press Enter.
```

Notice that the use of double quotes (") results in more than one word being treated as a single argument, although single quotes (') do not. Also, you can include double quotes in an argument by escaping them with the backslash character (\). Finally, notice that all spaces are stripped from the command line unless they are enclosed in double quotes.

1-6. Include Code Selectively at Build Time

Problem

You need to selectively include and exclude sections of source code from your compiled assembly.

Solution

Use the `#if`, `#elif`, `#else`, and `#endif` preprocessor directives to identify blocks of code that should be conditionally included in your compiled assembly. Use the `System.Diagnostics.ConditionalAttribute` attribute to define methods that should be called conditionally only. Control the inclusion of the conditional code using the `#define` and `#undef` directives in your code, or use the `/define` switch when you run the C# compiler from the command line.

How It Works

If you need your application to function differently depending on factors such as the platform or environment on which it runs, you can build runtime checks into the logic of your code that trigger the variations in operation. However, such an approach can bloat your code and affect performance, especially if many variations need to be supported or many locations exist where evaluations need to be made.

An alternative approach is to build multiple versions of your application to support the different target platforms and environments. Although this approach overcomes the problems of code bloat and performance degradation, it would be an untenable solution if you had to maintain different source code for each version, so C# provides features that allow you to build customized versions of your application from a single code base.

The `#if`, `#elif`, `#else`, and `#endif` preprocessor directives allow you to identify blocks of code that the compiler should include in your assembly only if specified symbols are defined at compile time. Symbols function as on/off switches; they don't have values—either the symbol is defined or it is not. The `#if..#endif` construct evaluates `#if` and `#elif` clauses only until it finds one that evaluates to true, meaning that if you define multiple symbols (`winXP` and `win7`, for example), the order of your clauses is important. The compiler includes only the code in the clause that evaluates to true. If no clause evaluates to true, the compiler includes the code in the `#else` clause.

You can also use logical operators to base conditional compilation on more than one symbol. Table 1-1 summarizes the supported operators.

Table 1-1. *Logical Operators Supported by the #if..#endif Directive*

Operator	Example	Description
`==`	`#if winXP == true`	Equality. Evaluates to true if the symbol `winXP` is defined. Equivalent to `#if winXP`.
`!=`	`#if winXP != true`	Inequality. Evaluates to true if the symbol `winXP` is *not* defined. Equivalent to `#if !winXP`.
`&&`	`#if winXP && release`	`Logical AND. Evaluates to true only if the symbols winXP` *and* `release are defined.`
`||`	`#if winXP || release`	Logical OR. Evaluates to true if either of the symbols `winXP` *or* `release` are defined.
`()`	`#if (winXP || win7) && release`	Parentheses allow you to group expressions. Evaluates to true if the symbols `winXP` *or* `win7` are defined *and* the symbol `release` is defined.

■ **Caution** You must be careful not to overuse conditional compilation directives and not to make your conditional expressions too complex; otherwise, your code can quickly become confusing and unmanageable—especially as your projects become larger.

To define a symbol, you can either include a #define directive in your code or use the /define compiler switch. Symbols defined using #define are active until the end of the file in which they are defined. Symbols defined using the /define compiler switch are active in all source files that are being compiled. To undefine a symbol defined using the /define compiler switch, C# provides the #undef directive, which is useful if you want to ensure a symbol is not defined in specific source files. All #define and #undef directives must appear at the top of your source file before any code, including any using directives. Symbols are case-sensitive.

A less flexible but more elegant alternative to the #if preprocessor directive is the attribute System.Diagnostics.ConditionalAttribute. If you apply ConditionalAttribute to a method, the compiler will ignore any calls to the method if the symbol specified by ConditionalAttribute is not defined at the calling point.

Using ConditionalAttribute centralizes your conditional compilation logic on the method declaration and means you can freely include calls to conditional methods without littering your code with #if directives. However, because the compiler literally removes calls to the conditional method from your code, your code can't have dependencies on return values from the conditional method. This means you can apply ConditionalAttribute only to methods that return void and do not use "out" modifiers on their arguments.

The Code

In this example, the code assigns a different value to the local variable platformName based on whether the winXP, win2000, winNT, or Win98 symbols are defined. The head of the code defines the symbols win2000 and release (not used in this example) and undefines the win98 symbol in case it was defined on the compiler command line. In addition, the ConditionalAttribute specifies that calls to the DumpState method should be included in an assembly only if the symbol DEBUG is defined during compilation.

```
#define win7
#define release
#undef  win2000

using System;
using System.Diagnostics;

namespace Apress.VisualCSharpRecipes.Chapter01
{
    class Recipe01_06
    {
        [Conditional("DEBUG")]
        public static void DumpState()
        {
```

```
            Console.WriteLine("Dump some state...");
        }

        public static void Main()
        {
            // Declare a string to contain the platform name
            string platformName;

            #if winXP       // Compiling for Windows XP
                platformName = "Microsoft Windows XP";
            #elif win2000   // Compiling for Windows 2000
                platformName = "Microsoft Windows 2000";
            #elif win7     // Compiling for Windows 7
                platformName = "Microsoft Windows 7";
            #else           // Unknown platform specified
                platformName = "Unknown";
            #endif

            Console.WriteLine(platformName);

            // Call the conditional DumpState method.
            DumpState();

            // Wait to continue.
            Console.WriteLine("\nMain method complete. Press Enter.");
            Console.Read();
        }
    }
}
```

Usage

To build the example and define the symbols `winXP` and `DEBUG` (not used in this example), use the command `csc /define:winXP;DEBUG ConditionalExample.cs`.

Notes

You can apply multiple `ConditionalAttribute` instances to a method in order to produce logical OR behavior. Calls to the following version of the `DumpState` method will be compiled only if the `DEBUG` or `TEST` symbols are defined:

```
[System.Diagnostics.Conditional("DEBUG")]
[System.Diagnostics.Conditional("TEST")]
public static void DumpState() {//...}
```

Achieving logical AND behavior is not as clean and involves the use of an intermediate conditional method, quickly leading to overly complex code that is hard to understand and maintain. The following is a quick example that requires the definition of both the `DEBUG` and `TEST` symbols for the `DumpState` functionality (contained in `DumpState2`) to be called:

```
[System.Diagnostics.Conditional("DEBUG")]
public static void DumpState() {
    DumpState2();
}

[System.Diagnostics.Conditional("TEST")]
public static void DumpState2() {//...}
```

■ **Note** The `Debug` and `Trace` classes from the `System.Diagnostics` namespace use `ConditionalAttribute` on many of their methods. The methods of the `Debug` class are conditional on the definition of the symbol `DEBUG`, and the methods of the `Trace` class are conditional on the definition of the symbol `TRACE`.

1-7. Access a Program Element That Has the Same Name As a Keyword

Problem

You need to access a member of a type, but the type or member name is the same as a C# keyword.

Solution

Prefix all instances of the identifier name in your code with the at sign (@).

How It Works

The .NET Framework allows you to use software components developed in other .NET languages from within your C# applications. Each language has its own set of keywords (or reserved words) and imposes different restrictions on the names programmers can assign to program elements such as types, members, and variables. Therefore, it is possible that a programmer developing a component in another language will inadvertently use a C# keyword as the name of a program element. The at sign (@) enables you to use a C# keyword as an identifier and overcome these possible naming conflicts.

The Code

The following code fragment instantiates an object of type `operator` (perhaps a telephone operator) and sets its `volatile` property to `true`—both `operator` and `volatile` are C# keywords:

```
// Instantiate an operator object.
@operator Operator1 = new @operator();
```

```
// Set the operator's volatile property.
Operator1.@volatile = true;
```

1-8. Create and Manage Strongly Named Key Pairs

Problem

You need to create public and private keys (a key pair) so that you can assign strong names to your assemblies.

Solution

Use the Strong Name tool (`sn.exe`) to generate a key pair and store the keys in a file or cryptographic service provider (CSP) key container.

■ **Note** A CSP is an element of the Win32 CryptoAPI that provides services such as encryption, decryption, and digital signature generation. CSPs also provide key container facilities, which use strong encryption and operating system security to protect any cryptographic keys stored in the container. A detailed discussion of CSPs and CryptoAPI is beyond the scope of this book. All you need to know for this recipe is that you can store your cryptographic keys in a CSP key container and be relatively confident that it is secure as long as nobody knows your Windows password. Refer to the CryptoAPI information in the platform SDK documentation for complete details.

How It Works

To generate a new key pair and store the keys in the file named `MyKeys.snk`, execute the command `sn -k MyKeys.snk`. (`.snk` is the usual extension given to files containing strongly named keys.) The generated file contains both your public and private keys. You can extract the public key using the command `sn -p MyKeys.snk MyPublicKey.snk`, which will create `MyPublicKey.snk` containing only the public key. Once you have this file in hands, you can view the public key using the command `sn -tp MyPublicKey.snk`, which will generate output similar to the (abbreviated) listing shown here:

```
Microsoft (R) .NET Framework Strong Name Utility  Version 2.0.50727.42

Copyright (C) Microsoft Corporation. All rights reserved.


Public key is

070200000024000052534132000400000100010002b4ef3c2bbd6478802b64d0dd3f2e7c65ee

6478802b63cb894a782f3a1adbb46d3ee5ec5577e7dccc818937e964cbe997c12076c19f2d7

ad179f15f7dccca6c6b72a


Public key token is 2a1d3326445fc02a
```

The public key token shown at the end of the listing is the last 8 bytes of a cryptographic hash code computed from the public key. Because the public key is so long, .NET uses the public key token for display purposes and as a compact mechanism for other assemblies to reference your public key. (Recipes 11-14 and 11-15 discuss cryptographic hash codes.)

As the name suggests, you don't need to keep the public key (or public key token) secret. When you strongly name your assembly (discussed in recipe 1-9), the compiler uses your private key to generate a digital signature (an encrypted hash code) of the assembly's manifest. The compiler embeds the digital signature and your public key in the assembly so that any consumer of the assembly can verify the digital signature.

Keeping your private key secret is imperative. People with access to your private key can alter your assembly and create a new strong name—leaving your customers unaware that they are using modified code. No mechanism exists to repudiate compromised strongly named keys. If your private key is compromised, you must generate new keys and distribute new versions of your assemblies that are strongly named using the new keys. You must also notify your customers about the compromised keys and explain to them which versions of your public key to trust—in all, a very costly exercise in terms of both money and credibility. You can protect your private key in many ways; the approach you use will depend on several factors.

■ **Tip** Commonly, a small group of trusted individuals (the *signing authority*) has responsibility for the security of your company's strongly named signing keys and is responsible for signing all assemblies just prior to their final release. The ability to delay-sign an assembly (discussed in recipe 1-11) facilitates this model and avoids the need to distribute private keys to all development team members.

One feature provided by the Strong Name tool to simplify the security of strongly named keys is the use of CSP key containers. Once you have generated a key pair to a file, you can install the keys into a key container and delete the file. For example, to store the key pair contained in the file `MyKeys.snk` to a CSP container named `StrongNameKeys`, use the command `sn -i MyKeys.snk StrongNameKeys`. (Recipe 1-9 explains how to use strongly named keys stored in a CSP key container.)

An important aspect of CSP key containers is that they include user-based containers and machine-based containers. Windows security ensures each user can access only their own user-based key containers. However, any user of a machine can access a machine-based container.

By default, the Strong Name tool uses machine-based key containers, meaning that anybody who can log onto your machine and who knows the name of your key container can sign an assembly with your strongly named keys. To change the Strong Name tool to use user-based containers, use the command `sn -m n`, and to switch to machine-based stores, use the command `sn -m y`. The command `sn -m` will display whether the Strong Name tool is currently configured to use machine-based or user-based containers.

To delete the strongly named keys from the `StrongNameKeys` container (as well as delete the container), use the command `sn -d StrongNameKeys`.

■ **Tip** You may need to start the command line with administrator privileges to use these tools, depending on the configuration of your system. Right-click the Command Prompt item in the Start menu and select "Run as administrator."

1-9. Give an Assembly a Strong Name

Problem

You need to give an assembly a strong name for several reasons:

- So it has a unique identity, which allows people to assign specific permissions to the assembly when configuring code access security policy
- So it can't be modified and passed off as your original assembly
- So it supports versioning and version policy
- So it can be installed in the GAC and shared across multiple applications

Solution

When you build your assembly using the command-line C# compiler, use the `/keyfile` or `/keycontainer` compiler switches to specify the location of your strongly named key pair. Use assembly-level attributes to specify optional information such as the version number and culture for your assembly. The compiler will strongly name your assembly as part of the compilation process.

■ **Note** If you are using Visual Studio, you can configure your assembly to be strongly named by opening the project properties, selecting the Signing tab, and checking the Sign the Assembly box. You will need to specify the location of the file where your strongly named keys are stored—Visual Studio does not allow you to specify the name of a key container.

How It Works

To strongly named an assembly using the C# compiler, you need the following:

- A strongly named key pair contained either in a file or a CSP key container. (Recipe 1-8 discusses how to create strongly named key pairs.)
- Compiler switches to specify the location where the compiler can obtain your strongly named key pair:
    - If your key pair is in a file, use the `/keyfile` compiler switch and provide the name of the file where the keys are stored. For example, use `/keyfile:MyKeyFile.snk`.
    - If your key pair is in a CSP container, use the `/keycontainer` compiler switch and provide the name of the CSP key container where the keys are stored. For example, use `/keycontainer:MyKeyContainer`.
- To optionally specify the culture that your assembly supports by applying the attribute `System.Reflection.AssemblyCultureAttribute` to the assembly. (You can't specify a culture for executable assemblies because executable assemblies support only the neutral culture.)
- To optionally specify the version of your assembly by applying the attribute `System.Reflection.AssemblyVersionAttribute` to the assembly.

The Code

The executable code that follows (from a file named `Recipe01-09.cs`) shows how to use the optional attributes (shown in bold text) to specify the culture and the version for the assembly:

```
using System;
using System.Reflection;

[assembly:AssemblyCulture("")]
[assembly:AssemblyVersion("1.1.0.5")]

namespace Recipe01_09
{
    class Recipe01_09
    {
```

```
        public static void Main()
        {
            Console.WriteLine("Welcome to Visual C# 2010 Recipes");

            // Wait to continue.
            Console.WriteLine("\nMain method complete. Press Enter.");
            Console.Read();
        }
    }
}
```

Usage

To create a strongly named assembly from the example code, create the strongly named keys and store them in a file named `MyKeyFile` using the command `sn -k MyKeyFile.snk`. Then install the keys into the CSP container named `MyKeys` using the command `sn -i MyKeyFile.snk MyKeys`. You can now compile the file into a strongly named assembly using the command `csc /keycontainer:MyKeys Recipe01-09.cs`.

1-10. Verify That a Strongly Named Assembly Has Not Been Modified

Problem

You need to verify that a strongly named assembly has not been modified after it was built.

Solution

Use the Strong Name tool (`sn.exe`) to verify the assembly's strong name.

How It Works

Whenever the .NET runtime loads a strongly named assembly, the runtime extracts the encrypted hash code that's embedded in the assembly and decrypts it with the public key, which is also embedded in the assembly. The runtime then calculates the hash code of the assembly manifest and compares it to the decrypted hash code. This verification process will identify whether the assembly has changed after compilation.

If an executable assembly fails strong name verification, the runtime will display an error message or an error dialog box (depending on whether the application is a console or Windows application). If executing code tries to load an assembly that fails verification, the runtime will throw a `System.IO.FileLoadException` with the message "Strong name validation failed," which you should handle appropriately.

As well as generating and managing strongly named keys (discussed in recipe 1-8), the Strong Name tool allows you to verify strongly named assemblies. To verify that the strongly named assembly `Recipe01-09.exe` is unchanged, use the command `sn -vf Recipe01-09.exe`. The `-v` switch requests the

Strong Name tool to verify the strong name of the specified assembly, and the `-f` switch forces strong name verification even if it has been previously disabled for the specified assembly. (You can disable strong name verification for specific assemblies using the `-Vr` switch, as in `sn -Vr Recipe01-09.exe`; see recipe 1-11 for details about why you would disable strong name verification.)

■ **Tip** You may need to start the command line with administrator privileges to use this tool, depending on the configuration of your system. Right-click the Command Prompt item in the Start menu and select "Run as administrator."

If the assembly passes strong name verification, you will see the following output:

```
Microsoft (R) .NET Framework Strong Name Utility  Version 2.0.50727.42
Copyright (C) Microsoft Corporation. All rights reserved.


Assembly 'Recipe01-09.exe' is valid
```

However, if the assembly has been modified, you will see this message:

```
Microsoft (R) .NET Framework Strong Name Utility  Version 2.0.50727.42
Copyright (C) Microsoft Corporation. All rights reserved.


Failed to verify assembly --
Strong name validation failed for assembly 'Recipe01-09.exe'.
```

1-11. Delay-Sign an Assembly

Problem

You need to create a strongly named assembly, but you don't want to give all members of your development team access to the private key component of your strongly named key pair.

Solution

Extract and distribute the public key component of your strongly named key pair. Follow the instructions in recipe 1-9 that describe how to give your assembly a strong name. In addition, specify the `/delaysign` switch when you compile your assembly. Disable strong name verification for the assembly using the `-Vr` switch of the Strong Name tool (`sn.exe`).

■ **Note** If you are using Visual Studio, you can configure your strongly named assembly to be delay-signed by opening the project properties, selecting the Signing tab, and checking the Delay Sign Only box.

How It Works

Assemblies that reference strongly named assemblies contain the public key token of the referenced assemblies. This means the referenced assembly must be strongly named before it can be referenced. In a development environment in which assemblies are regularly rebuilt, this would require every developer and tester to have access to your strongly named key pair—a major security risk.

Instead of distributing the private key component of your strongly named key pair to all members of the development team, the .NET Framework provides a mechanism called *delay-signing*, with which you can partially strongly name an assembly. The partially strongly named assembly contains the public key and the public key token (required by referencing assemblies) but contains only a placeholder for the signature that would normally be generated using the private key.

After development is complete, the signing authority (who has responsibility for the security and use of your strongly named key pair) re-signs the delay-signed assembly to complete its strong name. The signature is calculated using the private key and embedded in the assembly, making the assembly ready for distribution.

To delay-sign an assembly, you need access only to the public key component of your strongly named key pair. No security risk is associated with distributing the public key, and the signing authority should make the public key freely available to all developers. To extract the public key component from a strongly named key file named `MyKeyFile.snk` and write it to a file named `MyPublicKey.snk`, use the command `sn -p MyKeyFile.snk MyPublicKey.snk`. If you store your strongly named key pair in a CSP key container named `MyKeys`, extract the public key to a file named `MyPublicKey.snk` using the command `sn -pc MyKeys MyPublicKey.snk`.

Once you have a key file containing the public key, you build the delay-signed assembly using the command-line C# compiler by specifying the `/delaysign` compiler switch. For example, to build a delay-signed assembly from a source file named `Recipe01-11`, use this command:

```
csc /delaysign /keyfile:MyPublicKey.snk Recipe01-11.cs
```

When the runtime tries to load a delay-signed assembly, the runtime will identify the assembly as strongly named and will attempt to verify the assembly, as discussed in recipe 1-10. Because it doesn't have a digital signature, you must configure the runtime on the local machine to stop verifying the assembly's strong name using the command `sn -Vr Recipe01-11.exe`. Note that you need to do so on every machine on which you want to run your application.

■ **Tip** When using delay-signed assemblies, it's often useful to be able to compare different builds of the same assembly to ensure they differ only by their signatures. This is possible only if a delay-signed assembly has been re-signed using the `-R` switch of the Strong Name tool. To compare the two assemblies, use the command `sn -D assembly1 assembly2`.

Once development is complete, you need to re-sign the assembly to complete the assembly's strong name. The Strong Name tool allows you to do this without changing your source code or recompiling the assembly; however, you must have access to the private key component of the strongly named key pair. To re-sign an assembly named `Recipe01-11.exe` with a key pair contained in the file `MyKeys.snk`, use the command `sn -R Recipe01-11.exe MyKeys.snk`. If the keys are stored in a CSP key container named MyKeys, use the command `sn -Rc Recipe01-11.exe MyKeys`.

Once you have re-signed the assembly, you should turn strong name verification for that assembly back on using the `-Vu` switch of the Strong Name tool, as in `sn -Vu Recipe01-11.exe`. To enable verification for all assemblies for which you have disabled strong name verification, use the command `sn -Vx`. You can list the assemblies for which verification is disabled using the command `sn -Vl`.

■ **Note** If you are using the .NET Framework 1.0 or 1.1, the command-line C# compiler does not support the `/delaysign` compiler switch. Instead, you must use the `System.Reflection.AssemblyDelaySignAttribute` assembly-level attributes within your code to specify that you want the assembly delay-signed. Alternatively, use the Assembly Linker tool (`al.exe`), which does support the `/delaysign` switch. Refer to the Assembly Linker information in the .NET Framework SDK documentation for more details.

1-12. Sign an Assembly with an Authenticode Digital Signature

Problem

You need to sign an assembly with Authenticode so that users of the assembly can be certain you are its publisher and the assembly is unchanged after signing.

Solution

Use the Sign Tool (`signtool.exe`) to sign the assembly with your software publisher certificate (SPC).

How It Works

Strong names provide a unique identity for an assembly as well as proof of the assembly's integrity, but they provide no proof as to the publisher of the assembly. The .NET Framework allows you to use Authenticode technology to sign your assemblies. This enables consumers of your assemblies to confirm that you are the publisher, as well as confirm the integrity of the assembly. Authenticode signatures also act as evidence for the signed assembly, which people can use when configuring code access security policy.

To sign your assembly with an Authenticode signature, you need an SPC issued by a recognized *certificate authority (CA)*. A CA is a company entrusted to issue SPCs (along with many other types of certificates) for use by individuals or companies. Before issuing a certificate, the CA is responsible for confirming that the requesters are who they claim to be and also for making sure the requestors sign contracts to ensure they don't misuse the certificates that the CA issues them.

To obtain an SPC, you should view the Microsoft Root Certificate Program Members list at `http://msdn.microsoft.com/library/default.asp?url=/library/en-us/dnsecure/html/rootcertprog.asp`. Here you will find a list of CAs, many of whom can issue you an SPC. For testing purposes, you can create a test certificate using the process described in recipe 1-13. However, you can't distribute your software signed with this test certificate. Because a test SPC isn't issued by a trusted CA, most responsible users won't trust assemblies signed with it.

Some CAs will issue your SPC as a Personal Information Exchange file, which has a `.pfx` suffix—this is the file format that is needed to sign an assembly. Some CAs, however, will issue you with two files (either a private key file (`.pvk`) and an SPC (`.spc`) file or a private key file and a certificate file (with a `.cer` suffix)—if this is the case, you will have to convert your files to the PFX format—see the following usage details for instructions.

Once you have a PFX file, you use the Sign Tool to Authenticode-sign your assembly. The Sign Tool creates a digital signature of the assembly using the private key component of your SPC and embeds the signature and the public part of your SPC in your assembly (including your public key). When verifying your assembly, the consumer decrypts the encrypted hash code using your public key, recalculates the hash of the assembly, and compares the two hash codes to ensure they are the same. As long as the two hash codes match, the consumer can be certain that you signed the assembly and that it has not changed since you signed it.

Usage

If your CA has not issued you with a Personal Information Exchange (PFX) file, then the first step is to convert your certificate to the correct format using the `pnk2pfx.exe` tool. If you have received a PVK file and a CER file, then you should type the following at the command prompt:

```
pvk2pfx -pvk MyPrivateKey.pvk -spc MyCertificate.cer -pfx MyCertificate.pfx
```

If you have received a PVK file and an SPC file, then type the following command:

```
pvk2pfx -pvk MyPrivateKey.pvk -spc MyCertificate.spc -pfx MyCertificate.pfx
```

Both of these commands create the `MyCertificate.pfx` file. To sign an assembly, you type the following command at the command prompt:

```
signtool sign -f MyCertificate.pfx MyAssembly.exe
```

1-13. Create and Trust a Test Software Publisher Certificate

Problem

You need to create an SPC to allow you to test the Authenticode signing of an assembly.

Solution

Use the Certificate Creation tool (`makecert.exe`) to create a test X.509 certificate and the `pvk2pfx.exe` tool to generate a PFX file from this X.509 certificate. Trust the root test certificate using the Set Registry tool (`setreg.exe`).

How It Works

To create a test SPC for a software publisher named Allen Jones, create an X.509 certificate using the Certificate Creation tool. The command `makecert -n "CN=Allen Jones" -sk MyKeys TestCertificate.cer` creates a file named `TestCertificate.cer` containing an X.509 certificate and stores the associated private key in a CSP key container named `MyKeys` (which is automatically created if it does not exist). Alternatively, you can write the private key to a file by substituting the `-sk` switch with `-sv`. For example, to write the private key to a file named `PrivateKeys.pvk`, use the command `makecert -n " CN=Allen Jones" -sv PrivateKey.pvk TestCertificate.cer`. If you write your private key to a file, the Certificate Creation tool will prompt you to provide a password with which to protect the private key file (see Figure 1-2).

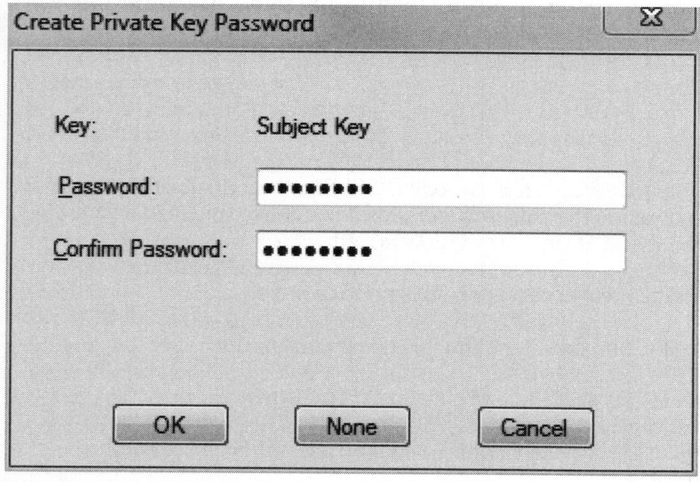

Figure 1-2. *The Certificate Creation tool requests a password when creating file-based private keys.*

The Certificate Creation tool supports many arguments, and Table 1-2 lists some of the more useful ones. You should consult the .NET Framework SDK documentation for full coverage of the Certificate Creation tool.

Table 1-2. *Commonly Used Switches of the Certificate Creation Tool*

Switch	Description
`-e`	Specifies the date when the certificate becomes invalid.
`-m`	Specifies the duration in months that the certificate remains valid.
`-n`	Specifies an X.500 name to associate with the certificate. This is the name of the software publisher that people will see when they view details of the SPC you create.
`-sk`	Specifies the name of the CSP key store in which to store the private key.
`-ss`	Specifies the name of the certificate store where the Certificate Creation tool should store the generated X.509 certificate.
`-sv`	Specifies the name of the file in which to store the private key.

Once you have created your X.509 certificate with the Certificate Creation tool, you need to convert it to a PFX file with the `pvk2pfx.exe` tool—this copies the public and private key information contained in the PVK and CER files into a PFX file. To convert the certificate `TestCertificate.cer` to a PFX file, use the following command:

```
pvk2pfx -pvk PrivateKey.pvk -spc TestCertificate.cer -pfx TestCertificate.pfx
```

The final step before you can use your test SPC is to trust the root test CA, which is the default issuer of the test certificate. The Set Registry tool (`setreg.exe`) makes this a simple task with the command `setreg 1 true`. When you have finished using your test SPC, you must remove trust of the root test CA using the command `setreg 1 false`. You can now Authenticode sign assemblies with your test SPC using the process described in recipe 1-12.

1-14. Manage the Global Assembly Cache

Problem

You need to add or remove assemblies from the GAC.

Solution

Use the Global Assembly Cache tool (`gacutil.exe`) from the command line to view the contents of the GAC as well as to add and remove assemblies.

How It Works

Before you can install an assembly in the GAC, the assembly must have a strong name; see recipe 1-9 for details on how to strongly name your assemblies. To install an assembly named `SomeAssembly.dll` into the GAC, use the command `gacutil /i SomeAssembly.dll`. You can install different versions of the same assembly in the GAC side by side to meet the versioning requirements of different applications.

To uninstall the `SomeAssembly.dll` assembly from the GAC, use the command `gacutil /u SomeAssembly`. Notice that you don't use the `.dll` extension to refer to the assembly once it's installed in the GAC. This will uninstall all assemblies with the specified name. To uninstall a particular version, specify the version along with the assembly name; for example, use `gacutil /u SomeAssembly,Version=1.0.0.5`.

To view the assemblies installed in the GAC, use the command `gacutil /l`. This will produce a long list of all the assemblies installed in the GAC, as well as a list of assemblies that have been precompiled to binary form and installed in the `ngen` cache. To avoid searching through this list to determine whether a particular assembly is installed in the GAC, use the command `gacutil /l SomeAssembly`.

■ **Note** The .NET Framework uses the GAC only at runtime; the C# compiler won't look in the GAC to resolve any external references that your assembly references. During development, the C# compiler must be able to access a local copy of any referenced shared assemblies. You can either copy the shared assembly to the same directory as your source code or use the `/lib` switch of the C# compiler to specify the directory where the compiler can find the required assemblies.

1-15. Prevent People from Decompiling Your Code

Problem

You want to ensure people can't decompile your .NET assemblies.

Solution

Build server-based solutions where possible so that people don't have access to your assemblies. If you must distribute assemblies, you have no way to stop people from decompiling them. The best you can do is use obfuscation and components compiled to native code to make your assemblies more difficult to decompile.

How It Works

Because .NET assemblies consist of a standardized, platform-independent set of instruction codes and metadata that describes the types contained in the assembly, they are relatively easy to decompile. This allows decompilers to generate source code that is close to your original code with ease, which can be problematic if your code contains proprietary information or algorithms that you want to keep secret.

The only way to ensure that people can't decompile your assemblies is to stop people from getting your assemblies in the first place. Where possible, implement server-based solutions such as Microsoft ASP.NET applications and web services. With the security correctly configured on your server, nobody will be able to access your assemblies, and therefore they won't be able to decompile them.

When building a server solution is not appropriate, you have the following two options:

- Use an obfuscator to make it difficult to understand your code once it is decompiled. Some versions of Visual Studio include the Community Edition of an obfuscator named Dotfuscator, which can be started by selecting Dotfuscator Software Services from the Visual Studio 2010 Tools menu. Obfuscators use a variety of techniques to make your assembly difficult to decompile; principal among these techniques are
    - Renaming of `private` methods and fields in such a way that it's difficult to read and understand the purpose of your code
    - Inserting control flow statements to make the logic of your application difficult to follow
- Build the parts of your application that you want to keep secret in native DLLs or COM objects, and then call them from your managed application using P/Invoke or COM Interop. (See Chapter 12 for recipes that show you how to call unmanaged code.)

Neither approach will stop a skilled and determined person from reverse engineering your code, but both approaches will make the job significantly more difficult and deter most casual observers.

■ **Note** The risks of application decompilation aren't specific to C# or .NET. A determined person can reverse engineer any software if they have the time and the skill.

1-16. Manipulate the Appearance of the Console

Problem

You want to control the visual appearance of the Windows console.

Solution

Use the `static` properties and methods of the `System.Console` class.

How It Works

The .NET Framework gives you a high degree of control over the appearance and operation of the Windows console. Table 1-3 describes the properties and methods of the `Console` class that you can use to control the console's appearance.

Table 1-3. *Properties and Methods to Control the Appearance of the Console*

Member	Description
Properties	
`BackgroundColor`	Gets and sets the background color of the console using one of the values from the `System.ConsoleColor` enumeration. Only new text written to the console will appear in this color. To make the entire console this color, call the method `Clear` after you have configured the `BackgroundColor` property.
`BufferHeight`	Gets and sets the buffer height in terms of rows.
`BufferWidth`	Gets and sets the buffer width in terms of columns.
`CursorLeft`	Gets and sets the column position of the cursor within the buffer.
`CursorSize`	Gets and sets the height of the cursor as a percentage of a character cell.
`CursorTop`	Gets and sets the row position of the cursor within the buffer.
`CursorVisible`	Gets and sets whether the cursor is visible.
`ForegroundColor`	Gets and sets the text color of the console using one of the values from the `System.ConsoleColor` enumeration. Only new text written to the console will appear in this color. To make the entire console this color, call the method `Clear` after you have configured the `ForegroundColor` property.
`LargestWindowHeight`	Returns the largest possible number of rows based on the current font and screen resolution.
`LargestWindowWidth`	Returns the largest possible number of columns based on the current font and screen resolution.
`Title`	Gets and sets text shown in the title bar.

Member	Description
`WindowHeight`	Gets and sets the width in terms of character rows.
`WindowWidth`	Gets and sets the width in terms of character columns.
Methods	
`Clear`	Clears the console.
`ResetColor`	Sets the foreground and background colors to their default values as configured within Windows.
`SetWindowSize`	Sets the width and height in terms of columns and rows.

The Code

The following example demonstrates how to use the properties and methods of the `Console` class to dynamically change the appearance of the Windows console:

```
using System;

namespace Apress.VisualCSharpRecipes.Chapter01
{
    public class Recipe01_16
    {
        static void Main(string[] args)
        {
            // Display the standard console.
            Console.Title = "Standard Console";
            Console.WriteLine("Press Enter to change the console's appearance.");
            Console.ReadLine();

            // Change the console appearance and redisplay.
            Console.Title = "Colored Text";
            Console.ForegroundColor = ConsoleColor.Red;
            Console.BackgroundColor = ConsoleColor.Green;
            Console.WriteLine("Press Enter to change the console's appearance.");
            Console.ReadLine();

            // Change the console appearance and redisplay.
            Console.Title = "Cleared / Colored Console";
            Console.ForegroundColor = ConsoleColor.Blue;
            Console.BackgroundColor = ConsoleColor.Yellow;
            Console.Clear();
            Console.WriteLine("Press Enter to change the console's appearance.");
            Console.ReadLine();
```

```
            // Change the console appearance and redisplay.
            Console.Title = "Resized Console";
            Console.ResetColor();
            Console.Clear();
            Console.SetWindowSize(100, 50);
            Console.BufferHeight = 500;
            Console.BufferWidth = 100;
            Console.CursorLeft = 20;
            Console.CursorSize = 50;
            Console.CursorTop = 20;
            Console.CursorVisible = false;
            Console.WriteLine("Main method complete. Press Enter.");
            Console.ReadLine();
        }
    }
}
```

1-17. Create a Static Class

Problem

You need to create a class that contains only static members.

Solution

Add the `static` keyword to your class declaration.

How It Works

A static class can contain only static members. You cannot instantiate the class using a constructor and you must refer to the members through the class name. The compiler will warn you if you add an instance member in the class (i.e., one that does not have the static keyword in its declaration)—you will still be able to use the static class, but the non-static methods will be inaccessible.

The Code

The following example defines a static class and calls the method and property it contains:

```
using System;

namespace Apress.VisualCSharpRecipes.Chapter01
{
    public static class MyStaticClass
    {
```

```
        public static string getMessage()
        {
            return "This is a static member";
        }

        public static string StaticProperty
        {
            get;
            set;
        }

    }

    public class Recipe01_16
    {
        static void Main(string[] args)
        {
            // Call the static method and print out the result.
            Console.WriteLine(MyStaticClass.getMessage());

            // Set and get the property.
            MyStaticClass.StaticProperty = "this is the property value";
            Console.WriteLine(MyStaticClass.StaticProperty);

            Console.WriteLine("Main method complete. Press Enter.");
            Console.ReadLine();
        }
    }
}
```

1-18. Create an Anonymous Type

Problem

You need to use an anonymous type for short-term data manipulation.

Solution

Declare a variable using the special type `var`, and then define the type's content using the `new` keyword.

How It Works

Anonymous types are convenient C# features that allow you to encapsulate a set of properties into a single object without having to define a type beforehand. The types of the properties you define in an anonymous type are inferred by the compiler and are read-only. The following fragment creates an anonymous type with two properties—a `string` and an `int`.

```
var anon = new {
    Name = "Adam Freeman",
    Age = 37;
};
```

The values of the properties can be accessed by calling **anon.Name** and **anon.Age**.

Anonymous types have some limitations. The properties are read-only, only properties (and not methods) can be defined, and their scope is limited to the method in which they are created—they cannot be passed as arguments to other methods. Anonymous types are often used in conjunction with LINQ—see Chapter 16 for LINQ recipes.

The Code

The following example creates an anonymous type that itself contains a nested anonymous type, and then prints out the various fields:

```
using System;

namespace Apress.VisualCSharpRecipes.Chapter01
{

    public class Recipe01_18
    {
        static void Main(string[] args)
        {

            // Create an anoymous type.
            var joe = new {
                Name = "Joe Smith",
                Age  = 42,
                Family = new {
                    Father = "Pa Smith",
                    Mother = "Ma Smith",
                    Brother = "Pete Smith"
                },
            };

            // Access the members of the anonymous type.
            Console.WriteLine("Name: {0}", joe.Name);
            Console.WriteLine("Age: {0}", joe.Age);
            Console.WriteLine("Father: {0}", joe.Family.Father);
            Console.WriteLine("Mother: {0}", joe.Family.Mother);
            Console.WriteLine("Brother: {0}", joe.Family.Brother);

            Console.WriteLine("Main method complete. Press Enter.");
            Console.ReadLine();
        }
    }
}
```

Running the example gives the following results:

```
Name: Joe Smith

Age: 42

Father: Pa Smith

Mother: Ma Smith

Brother: Pete Smith

Main method complete. Press Enter.
```

1-19. Create an ExpandoObject Dynamic Type

Problem

You need to create a type to contain a set of read-write properties.

Solution

Use the `System.Dynamic.ExpandoObject` class.

How It Works

In the previous recipe, we showed you how to encapsulate a set of properties using an anonymous type. One of the limitations of anonymous types is that the encapsulated properties are read-only. You can achieve a similar effect, but with properties that can be modified, using the `System.Dynamic.ExpandoObject` class.

The `ExpandoObject` is part of the dynamic language support introduced in.NET 4.0. Chapter 13 includes a recipe for using dynamic types more generally, but much of the functionality that the dynamic language support provides is not intended for use in C#. The most important thing to remember about dynamic types is that the calls you make to them in your code are not checked by the compiler, and you will not be able to see the impact of any misspelled method, parameter, property, or type name until your code is executed.

The `ExpandoObject` is useful because you can dynamically add properties just by assigning values to them. For example, the following fragment creates a new instance of `ExpandoObject` and creates a new property called `Name` with a value of `Joe Smith`.

```
dynamic expando = new ExpandoObject();
expando.Name = "Joe Smith";
```

We can get or set the value of the `Name` property as for any other type. Note that we have declared the instance of `ExpandoObject` using the `dynamic` keyword—if you declare the variable as an instance of `ExpandoObject` (by calling `ExpandoObject expando = new ExpandoObject()`, for example), then you will not be able to add any properties. You can define properties of any type, including other instances of `ExpandoObject`—see the example code for this recipe for an illustration of this.

The Code

The following example creates an `ExpandoObject` and writes out the property values:

```
using System;
using System.Dynamic;

namespace Apress.VisualCSharpRecipes.Chapter01
{
    public class Recipe01_19
    {
        static void Main(string[] args)
        {
            // Create the expando.
            dynamic expando = new ExpandoObject();
            expando.Name = "Joe Smith";
            expando.Age = 42;
            expando.Family = new ExpandoObject();
            expando.Family.Father = "Pa Smith";
            expando.Family.Mother = "Ma Smith";
            expando.Family.Brother = "Pete Smith";

            // Access the members of the dynamic type.
            Console.WriteLine("Name: {0}", expando.Name);
            Console.WriteLine("Age: {0}", expando.Age);
            Console.WriteLine("Father: {0}", expando.Family.Father);
            Console.WriteLine("Mother: {0}", expando.Family.Mother);
            Console.WriteLine("Brother: {0}", expando.Family.Brother);

            // Change a value.
            expando.Age = 44;
            // Add a new property.
            expando.Family.Sister = "Kathy Smith";

            Console.WriteLine("\nModified Values");
            Console.WriteLine("Age: {0}", expando.Age);
            Console.WriteLine("Sister: {0}", expando.Family.Sister);

            Console.WriteLine("Main method complete. Press Enter.");
            Console.ReadLine();
        }
    }
}
```

1-20. Define an Automatically Implemented Property

Problem

You want to declare a property that requires no logic in its accessors.

Solution

Use an automatically implemented property and allow the runtime to manage the underlying variable on your behalf.

How It Works

Many properties are defined simply to hold values and require no logic to process values in the accessors—for these cases, the standard pattern of defining a backing variable in the parent class and mapping access to it via the accessors is inelegant. For such properties, you can use the automatic implementation feature, where the compiler creates the backing instance and you do not need to provide any code in the accessors at all. The following fragment demonstrates an auto-implemented `string` property:

```
public string MyAutoImplementedProperty
{
   get;
   set;
}
```

The compile will generate an error if you do not specify both the get and set accessors, but otherwise automatically implemented properties can be used in just the same way as the regular kind.

The Code

The following example defines two static, automatically implemented properties and prints out the default values of each of them. Values are then assigned and read back out again.

```
using System;

namespace Apress.VisualCSharpRecipes.Chapter01
{
    public class Recipe01_20
    {
        // Define a static string property.
        static string MyStaticProperty
        {
            get;
            set;
        }


        static int MyStaticIntProperty
        {
            get;
            set;
        }

        static void Main(string[] args)
        {
            // Write out the default values.
            Console.WriteLine("Default property values");
            Console.WriteLine("Default string property value: {0}", MyStaticProperty);
            Console.WriteLine("Default int property value: {0}", MyStaticIntProperty);

            // Set the property values.
            MyStaticProperty = "Hello, World";
            MyStaticIntProperty = 32;

            // Write out the changed values.
            Console.WriteLine("\nProperty values");
            Console.WriteLine("String property value: {0}", MyStaticProperty);
            Console.WriteLine("Int property value: {0}", MyStaticIntProperty);

            Console.WriteLine("\nMain method complete. Press Enter.");
            Console.ReadLine();
        }
    }
}
```

Running the program gives the following result:

```
Default property values

Default string property value:

Default int property value: 0


Property values

String property value: Hello, World

Int property value: 32


Main method complete. Press Enter.
```

1-21. Overload an Operator

Problem

You want to be able to use your types with the standard operators (+, -, *, etc.).

Solution

Overload one or more operators by defining static methods with the operator symbol as the method name and using the `operator` keyword in the method declaration.

How It Works

To implement operators in your classes, you simply define static methods to overload the operator you want to use—for example, the following fragment shows the declaration of a method that implements the addition operator (+) to be used when adding together two instances of the type **`Word`**:

```
public static string operator +(Word w1, Word w2)
```

Adding and implementing this method to the `Word` class allows us to define what happens when we use the addition operator on two instances of the `Word` type:

```
string result = word1 + word2;
```

Notice that the result of our addition is a `string`—you can return any type you choose. You can also define the behavior for when operators are applied on different types, such as the following, which declares a method that overrides the operator for when an instance of `Word` and an `int` are added together:

```
public static Word operator +(Word w, int i)
```

The following fragment allows us to use the operator like this:

```
Word newword = word1 + 7;
```

Note that the order of the arguments is important—the previous fragment defines the behavior for a `Word + int` operation, but not `int + Word` (i.e., the same types, but with their order reversed). We would need to define another method to support both orderings.

See the code for this recipe for an example of how to use these operators and implementations for the operator overloads we have referred to. You can override the following operators:

+, -, *, /, %, &, |, ^, <<, >>

The Code

The following example defines the type `Word`, which has two overridden addition operators: one that inserts a space in between words when they are added together, and another for adding an `int` value to a word.

```
using System;
using System.Collections.Generic;
using System.Linq;
using System.Text;
using System.Dynamic;

namespace Apress.VisualCSharpRecipes.Chapter01
{
    public class Word
    {
        public string Text
        {
            get;
            set;
        }

        public static string operator +(Word w1, Word w2)
        {
            return w1.Text + " " + w2.Text;
        }

        public static Word operator +(Word w, int i)
        {
```

```
            return new Word() { Text = w.Text + i.ToString()};
        }

        public override string ToString()
        {
            return Text;
        }
    }

    public class Recipe01_21
    {
        static void Main(string[] args)
        {

            // Create two word instances.
            Word word1 = new Word() { Text = "Hello" };
            Word word2 = new Word() { Text = "World" };

            // Print out the values.
            Console.WriteLine("Word1: {0}", word1);
            Console.WriteLine("Word2: {0}", word2);
            Console.WriteLine("Added together: {0}", word1 + word2);
            Console.WriteLine("Added with int: {0}", word1 + 7);

            Console.WriteLine("\nMain method complete. Press Enter.");
            Console.ReadLine();
        }
    }
}
```

Running the example produces the following results:

```
Word1: Hello

Word2: World

Added together: Hello World

Added with int: Hello7



Main method complete. Press Enter.
```

1-22. Define a Conversion Operator

Problem

You need to be able to convert from one type to another.

Solution

Implement `implicit` or `explicit` conversion operator methods.

How It Works

You can specify how your type is converted to other types and, equally, how other types are converted to your type, by declaring conversion operators in your class. A conversion operator is a static method that is named for the type that you wish to convert to and that has the type you wish to convert from. For example, the following method fragment is a conversion operator from the `Word` type (taken from the code for this recipe) that converts an instance of `string` to an instance of `Word`:

```
public static explicit operator Word(string str)
{
    return new Word() { Text = str };
}
```

Defining this member in the `Word` class allows us to perform conversions such as the following:

```
Word word = (Word)"Hello";
```

Note that we have had to explicitly cast the string to `Word`—this is because our conversion operator included the `explicit` keyword. You can enable implicit conversion by using the `implicit` keyword, such as this:

```
public static implicit operator Word(string str)
{
    return new Word() { Text = str };
}
```

With the `implicit` keyword, now both of the following statements would compile:

```
Word word = (Word)"Hello";
Word word = "Hello";
```

Conversion operators must always be static, and you must choose between an explicit and an implicit conversion—you cannot define different conversion operators for the same pair of types but with different keywords.

The Code

The following example defines and demonstrates implicit and explicit conversion operators for the **Word** type.

```
using System;

namespace Apress.VisualCSharpRecipes.Chapter01
{
    public class Word
    {
        public string Text
        {
            get;
            set;
        }

        public static explicit operator Word(string str)
        {
            return new Word() { Text = str };
        }

        public static implicit operator string(Word w)
        {
            return w.Text;
        }

        public static explicit operator int(Word w)
        {
            return w.Text.Length;
        }

        public override string ToString()
        {
            return Text;
        }
    }

    public class Recipe01_22
    {
        static void Main(string[] args)
        {

            // Create a word instance.
            Word word1 = new Word() { Text = "Hello"};

            // Implicitly convert the word to a string.
            string str1 = word1;
            // Explicitly convert the word to a string.
            string str2 = (string)word1;
```

```
            Console.WriteLine("{0} - {1}", str1, str2);

            // Convert a string to a word.
            Word word2 = (Word)"Hello";

            // Convert a word to an int.
            int count = (int)word2;

            Console.WriteLine("Length of {0} = {1}", word2.ToString(), count);

            Console.WriteLine("\nMain method complete. Press Enter.");
            Console.ReadLine();
        }
    }
}
```

1-23. Handle an Event with an Anonymous Function

Problem

You need to handle an event, but don't want to define a method in your class to do so.

Solution

Use an anonymous delegate or a lambda expression.

How It Works

You can create a delegate for an event handler anonymously, meaning that you do not have to define a separate method for the delegate to call. To add an anonymous delegate, pass the method arguments to the `delegate` keyword and implement the method body between braces. The following fragment demonstrates how to register for an event using an anonymous delegate:

```
MyEvent += new EventHandler(delegate(object sender, EventArgs eventargs)
{
   ...implement method body...
});
```

Anonymous delegates simplify source code where you do not need to share an implementation between handlers and where you do not need to unregister for the event—you cannot unregister because you do not have a reference to unregister with when using anonymous delegates.

You can also handle events using a lambda expression, which is another form of the anonymous function. Lambda expressions use the lambda operator, =>, which is read as "goes to." On the left of the expression, you list names for the variables that will be passed to your expression, and to the right, you write the code that you want to execute, referring to the variables you defined as required. The following fragment shows how to use a lambda expression to handle an event:

```
MyEvent += new EventHandler((sender, eventargs) =>
{
   ... implment method, referring to sender and eventargs if required...
});
```

With a lambda expression, the compiler works out what the types of the variables on the left of the "goes to" sign should be, so you need only specify the names that you want to use.

The Code

The following example uses a named method to handle an event and illustrates how to do the same thing using an anonymous delegate and a lambda expression:

```
using System;

namespace Apress.VisualCSharpRecipes.Chapter01
{
    public class Recipe01_23
    {
        public static EventHandler MyEvent;

        static void Main(string[] args)
        {
            // Use a named method to register for the event.
            MyEvent += new EventHandler(EventHandlerMethod);

            // Use an anonymous delegate to register for the event.
            MyEvent += new EventHandler(delegate(object sender, EventArgs eventargs)
            {
                Console.WriteLine("Anonymous delegate called");
            });

            // Use a lamda expression to register for the event.
            MyEvent += new EventHandler((sender, eventargs) =>
            {
                Console.WriteLine("Lamda expression called");
            });

            Console.WriteLine("Raising the event");
            MyEvent.Invoke(new object(), new EventArgs());

            Console.WriteLine("\nMain method complete. Press Enter.");
            Console.ReadLine();
        }
```

```
        static void EventHandlerMethod(object sender, EventArgs args)
        {
            Console.WriteLine("Named method called");
        }
    }
}
```

1-24. Implement a Custom Indexer

Problem

You need to be able to access data in your custom type like an array.

Solution

Implement a custom indexer.

How It Works

You can enable array-style indexing for you class by implementing a custom indexer. A custom indexer is like a property, but the name of the property is the keyword `this`. You can choose any type to be used as the index and any type to return as the result—the code for this recipe illustrates a custom indexer that uses a string for the index and returns a custom type.

The Code

The following example demonstrates a class, `WeatherForecast`, which uses a custom string indexer in order to perform calculations on the fly in order to generate a result:

```
using System;
using System.Collections.Generic;
using System.Linq;

namespace Apress.VisualCSharpRecipes.Chapter01
{
    public class WeatherReport
    {
        public int DayOfWeek
        {
            get;
            set;
        }
```

```
    public int DailyTemp
    {
        get;
        set;
    }

    public int AveTempSoFar
    {
        get;
        set;
    }
}

public class WeatherForecast
{
    private int[] temps = { 54, 63, 61, 55, 61, 63, 58 };
    IList<string> daysOfWeek = new List<string>()
        {"Monday", "Tuesday", "Wednesday",
        "Thursday", "Friday", "Saturday", "Sunday"};

    public WeatherReport this[string dow]
    {
        get
        {
            // Get the day of the week index.
            int dayindex = daysOfWeek.IndexOf(dow);
            return new WeatherReport()
            {
                DayOfWeek = dayindex,
                DailyTemp = temps[dayindex],
                AveTempSoFar = calculateTempSoFar(dayindex)
            };
        }
        set
        {
            temps[daysOfWeek.IndexOf(dow)] = value.DailyTemp;
        }
    }

    private int calculateTempSoFar(int dayofweek)
    {
        int[] subset = new int[dayofweek + 1];
        Array.Copy(temps, 0, subset, 0, dayofweek + 1);
        return (int)subset.Average();
    }
}

public class Recipe01_24
{
    static void Main(string[] args)
    {
```

```
            // Create a new weather forecast.
            WeatherForecast forecast = new WeatherForecast();

            // Use the indexer to obtain forecast values and write them out.
            string[] days = {"Monday", "Thursday", "Tuesday", "Saturday"};
            foreach (string day in days)
            {
                WeatherReport report = forecast[day];
                Console.WriteLine("Day: {0} DayIndex {1}, Temp: {2} Ave {3}", day,
                    report.DayOfWeek, report.DailyTemp, report.AveTempSoFar);
            }

            // Change one of the temperatures.
            forecast["Tuesday"] = new WeatherReport()
            {
                DailyTemp = 34
            };

            // Repeat the loop.
            Console.WriteLine("\nModified results...");
            foreach (string day in days)
            {
                WeatherReport report = forecast[day];
                Console.WriteLine("Day: {0} DayIndex {1}, Temp: {2} Ave {3}", day,
                    report.DayOfWeek, report.DailyTemp, report.AveTempSoFar);
            }

            Console.WriteLine("\nMain method complete. Press Enter.");
            Console.ReadLine();
        }
    }
}
```

Running the program gives the following results:

```
Day: Monday DayIndex 0, Temp: 54 Ave 54

Day: Thursday DayIndex 3, Temp: 55 Ave 58

Day: Tuesday DayIndex 1, Temp: 63 Ave 58

Day: Saturday DayIndex 5, Temp: 63 Ave 59


Modified results...

Day: Monday DayIndex 0, Temp: 54 Ave 54

Day: Thursday DayIndex 3, Temp: 55 Ave 51

Day: Tuesday DayIndex 1, Temp: 34 Ave 44

Day: Saturday DayIndex 5, Temp: 63 Ave 54


Main method complete. Press Enter
```

CHAPTER 2

■ ■ ■

Data Manipulation

Most applications need to manipulate some form of data. The Microsoft .NET Framework provides many techniques that simplify or improve the efficiency of common data manipulation tasks. The recipes in this chapter describe how to do the following:

- Manipulate the contents of strings efficiently to avoid the overhead of automatic string creation due to the immutability of strings (recipe 2-1)
- Represent basic data types using different encoding schemes or as byte arrays to allow you to share data with external systems (recipes 2-2, 2-3, and 2-4)
- Validate user input and manipulate string values using regular expressions (recipes 2-5 and 2-6)
- Create `System.DateTime` objects from string values, such as those that a user might enter, and display `DateTime` objects as formatted strings (recipe 2-7)
- Mathematically manipulate `DateTime` objects in order to compare dates or add/subtract periods of time from a date (recipe 2-8)
- Sort the contents of an array or an `ArrayList` collection (recipe 2-9)
- Copy the contents of a collection to an array (recipe 2-10)
- Use the standard generic collection classes to instantiate a strongly typed collection (recipe 2-11)
- Use generics to define your own general-purpose container or collection class that will be strongly typed when it is used (recipe 2-12)
- Serialize object state and persist it to a file (recipes 2-13 and 2-14)
- Read user input from the Windows console (recipe 2-15)
- Use large integer values (recipe 2-16)
- Select elements from an array or collection (recipe 2-17)
- Remove duplicate entries from an array or collection (recipe 2-18)

2-1. Manipulate the Contents of a String Efficiently

Problem

You need to manipulate the contents of a String object and want to avoid the overhead of automatic String creation caused by the immutability of String objects.

Solution

Use the System.Text.StringBuilder class to perform the manipulations and convert the result to a String object using the StringBuilder.ToString method.

How It Works

String objects in .NET are immutable, meaning that once created their content cannot be changed. For example, if you build a string by concatenating a number of characters or smaller strings, the Common Language Runtime (CLR) will create a completely new String object whenever you add a new element to the end of the existing string. This can result in significant overhead if your application performs frequent string manipulation.

The StringBuilder class offers a solution by providing a character buffer and allowing you to manipulate its contents without the runtime creating a new object as a result of every change. You can create a new StringBuilder object that is empty or initialized with the content of an existing String object. You can manipulate the content of the StringBuilder object using overloaded methods that allow you to insert and append string representations of different data types. At any time, you can obtain a String representation of the current content of the StringBuilder object by calling StringBuilder.ToString.

Two important properties of StringBuilder control its behavior as you append new data: Capacity and Length. Capacity represents the size of the StringBuilder buffer, and Length represents the length of the buffer's current content. If you append new data that results in the number of characters in the StringBuilder object (Length) exceeding the capacity of the StringBuilder object (Capacity), StringBuilder must allocate a new buffer to hold the data. The size of this new buffer is double the size of the previous Capacity value. Used carelessly, this buffer reallocation can negate much of the benefit of using StringBuilder. If you know the length of data you need to work with, or know an upper limit, you can avoid unnecessary buffer reallocation by specifying the capacity at creation time or setting the Capacity property manually. Note that 16 is the default Capacity property setting. When setting the Capacity and Length properties, be aware of the following behavior:

- If you set Capacity to a value less than the value of Length, the Capacity property throws the exception System.ArgumentOutOfRangeException. The same exception is also thrown if you try to raise the Capacity setting above the value of the MaxCapacity property. This should not be a problem unless you want to allocate more that 2 gigabytes (GB).
- If you set Length to a value less than the length of the current content, the content is truncated.

- If you set Length to a value greater than the length of the current content, the buffer is padded with spaces to the specified length. Setting Length to a value greater than Capacity automatically adjusts the Capacity value to be the same as the new Length value.

The Code

The ReverseString method shown in the following example demonstrates the use of the StringBuilder class to reverse a string. If you did not use the StringBuilder class to perform this operation, it would be significantly more expensive in terms of resource utilization, especially as the input string is made longer. The method creates a StringBuilder object of the correct capacity to ensure that no buffer reallocation is required during the reversal operation.

```
using System;
using System.Text;

namespace Apress.VisualCSharpRecipes.Chapter02
{
    class Recipe02_01
    {
        public static string ReverseString(string str)
        {
            // Make sure we have a reversible string.
            if (str == null || str.Length <= 1)
            {
                return str;
            }

            // Create a StringBuilder object with the required capacity.
            StringBuilder revStr = new StringBuilder(str.Length);

            // Loop backward through the source string one character at a time and
            // append each character to StringBuilder.
            for (int count = str.Length - 1; count > -1; count--)
            {
                revStr.Append(str[count]);
            }

            // Return the reversed string.
            return revStr.ToString();
        }

        public static void Main()
        {
            Console.WriteLine(ReverseString("Madam Im Adam"));

            Console.WriteLine(ReverseString(
              "The quick brown fox jumped over the lazy dog."));
```

```
            // Wait to continue.
            Console.WriteLine("\nMain method complete. Press Enter");
            Console.ReadLine();
        }
    }
}
```

2-2. Encode a String Using Alternate Character Encoding

Problem

You need to exchange character data with systems that use character-encoding schemes other than UTF-16, which is the character-encoding scheme used internally by the CLR.

Solution

Use the `System.Text.Encoding` class and its subclasses to convert characters between different encoding schemes.

How It Works

Unicode is not the only character-encoding scheme, nor is UTF-16 the only way to represent Unicode characters. When your application needs to exchange character data with external systems (particularly legacy systems) through an array of bytes, you may need to convert character data between UTF-16 and the encoding scheme supported by the other system.

The abstract class `Encoding` and its concrete subclasses provide the functionality to convert characters to and from a variety of encoding schemes. Each subclass instance supports the conversion of characters between UTF-16 and one other encoding scheme. You obtain instances of the encoding-specific classes using the static factory method `Encoding.GetEncoding`, which accepts either the name or the code page number of the required encoding scheme.

Table 2-1 lists some commonly used character-encoding schemes and the code page number you must pass to the `GetEncoding` method to create an instance of the appropriate encoding class. The table also shows static properties of the `Encoding` class that provide shortcuts for obtaining the most commonly used types of encoding objects.

Table 2-1. Character-Encoding Classes

Encoding Scheme	Class	Create Using
ASCII	ASCIIEncoding	GetEncoding(20127) or the ASCII property
Default	Encoding	GetEncoding(0) or the Default property
UTF-7	UTF7Encoding	GetEncoding(65000) or the UTF7 property
UTF-8	UTF8Encoding	GetEncoding(65001) or the UTF8 property
UTF-16 (big-endian)	UnicodeEncoding	GetEncoding(1201) or the BigEndianUnicode property
UTF-16 (little-endian)	UnicodeEncoding	GetEncoding(1200) or the Unicode property
Windows OS	Encoding	GetEncoding(1252)

Once you have an Encoding object of the appropriate type, you convert a UTF-16–encoded Unicode string to a byte array of encoded characters using the GetBytes method. Conversely, you convert a byte array of encoded characters to a string using the GetString method.

The Code

The following example demonstrates the use of some encoding classes:

```
using System;
using System.IO;
using System.Text;

namespace Apress.VisualCSharpRecipes.Chapter02
{
    class Recipe02_02
    {
        public static void Main()
        {
            // Create a file to hold the output.
            using (StreamWriter output = new StreamWriter("output.txt"))
            {
                // Create and write a string containing the symbol for pi.
                string srcString = "Area = \u03A0r^2";
                output.WriteLine("Source Text : " + srcString);

                // Write the UTF-16 encoded bytes of the source string.
                byte[] utf16String = Encoding.Unicode.GetBytes(srcString);
                output.WriteLine("UTF-16 Bytes: {0}",
                    BitConverter.ToString(utf16String));
```

```
                // Convert the UTF-16 encoded source string to UTF-8 and ASCII.
                byte[] utf8String = Encoding.UTF8.GetBytes(srcString);
                byte[] asciiString = Encoding.ASCII.GetBytes(srcString);

                // Write the UTF-8 and ASCII encoded byte arrays.
                output.WriteLine("UTF-8  Bytes: {0}",
                    BitConverter.ToString(utf8String));
                output.WriteLine("ASCII  Bytes: {0}",
                    BitConverter.ToString(asciiString));

                // Convert UTF-8 and ASCII encoded bytes back to UTF-16 encoded
                // string and write.
                output.WriteLine("UTF-8  Text : {0}",
                    Encoding.UTF8.GetString(utf8String));
                output.WriteLine("ASCII  Text : {0}",
                    Encoding.ASCII.GetString(asciiString));
            }

            // Wait to continue.
            Console.WriteLine("\nMain method complete. Press Enter");
            Console.ReadLine();
        }
    }
}
```

Usage

Running the code will generate a file named `output.txt`. If you open this file in a text editor that supports Unicode, you will see the following content:

```
Source Text : Area = πr^2

UTF-16 Bytes: 41-00-72-00-65-00-61-00-20-00-3D-00-20-00-A0-03-72-00-5E-00-32-00

UTF-8  Bytes: 41-72-65-61-20-3D-20-CE-A0-72-5E-32

ASCII  Bytes: 41-72-65-61-20-3D-20-3F-72-5E-32

UTF-8  Text : Area = πr^2

ASCII  Text : Area = ?r^2
```

Notice that using UTF-16 encoding, each character occupies 2 bytes, but because most of the characters are standard characters, the high-order byte is 0. (The use of little-endian byte ordering means that the low-order byte appears first.) This means that most of the characters are encoded using the same numeric values across all three encoding schemes. However, the numeric value for the symbol pi (emphasized in bold in the preceding output) is different in each of the encodings. The value of pi requires more than 1 byte to represent. UTF-8 encoding uses 2 bytes, but ASCII has no direct equivalent and so replaces pi with the code 3F. As you can see in the ASCII text version of the string, 3F is the symbol for an English question mark (?).

■ **Caution** If you convert Unicode characters to ASCII or a specific code page–encoding scheme, you risk losing data. Any Unicode character with a character code that cannot be represented in the scheme will be ignored.

Notes

The Encoding class also provides the static method Convert to simplify the conversion of a byte array from one encoding scheme to another without the need to manually perform an interim conversion to UTF-16. For example, the following statement converts the ASCII-encoded bytes contained in the asciiString byte array directly from ASCII encoding to UTF-8 encoding:

```
byte[] utf8String = Encoding.Convert(Encoding.ASCII, Encoding.UTF8,asciiString);
```

2-3. Convert Basic Value Types to Byte Arrays

Problem

You need to convert basic value types to byte arrays.

Solution

The static methods of the System.BitConverter class provide a convenient mechanism for converting most basic value types to and from byte arrays. An exception is the decimal type. To convert a decimal type to or from a byte array, you need to use a System.IO.MemoryStream object.

How It Works

The static method GetBytes of the BitConverter class provides overloads that take most of the standard value types and return the value encoded as an array of bytes. Support is provided for the bool, char, double, short, int, long, float, ushort, uint, and ulong data types. BitConverter also provides a set of static methods that support the conversion of byte arrays to each of the standard value types. These are named ToBoolean, ToUInt32, ToDouble, and so on.

Unfortunately, the BitConverter class does not provide support for converting the decimal type. Instead, write the decimal type to a MemoryStream instance using a System.IO.BinaryWriter object, and then call the MemoryStream.ToArray method. To create a decimal type from a byte array, create a MemoryStream object from the byte array and read the decimal type from the MemoryStream object using a System.IO.BinaryReader instance.

The Code

The following example demonstrates the use of BitConverter to convert a bool type and an int type to and from a byte array. The second argument to each of the ToBoolean and ToInt32 methods is a zero-based offset into the byte array where the BitConverter should start taking the bytes to create the data value. The code also shows how to convert a decimal type to a byte array using a MemoryStream object and a BinaryWriter object, as well as how to convert a byte array to a decimal type using a BinaryReader object to read from the MemoryStream object.

```
using System;
using System.IO;

namespace Apress.VisualCSharpRecipes.Chapter02
{
    class Recipe02_03
    {
        // Create a byte array from a decimal.
        public static byte[] DecimalToByteArray (decimal src)
        {
            // Create a MemoryStream as a buffer to hold the binary data.
            using (MemoryStream stream = new MemoryStream())
            {
                // Create a BinaryWriter to write binary data to the stream.
                using (BinaryWriter writer = new BinaryWriter(stream))
                {
                    // Write the decimal to the BinaryWriter/MemoryStream.
                    writer.Write(src);

                    // Return the byte representation of the decimal.
                    return stream.ToArray();
                }
            }
        }

        // Create a decimal from a byte array.
        public static decimal ByteArrayToDecimal (byte[] src)
        {
            // Create a MemoryStream containing the byte array.
            using (MemoryStream stream = new MemoryStream(src))
            {
                // Create a BinaryReader to read the decimal from the stream.
                using (BinaryReader reader = new BinaryReader(stream))
                {
                    // Read and return the decimal from the
                    // BinaryReader/MemoryStream.
                    return reader.ReadDecimal();
                }
            }
        }

        public static void Main()
```

```
        {
            byte[] b = null;

            // Convert a bool to a byte array and display.
            b = BitConverter.GetBytes(true);
            Console.WriteLine(BitConverter.ToString(b));

            // Convert a byte array to a bool and display.
            Console.WriteLine(BitConverter.ToBoolean(b,0));

            // Convert an int to a byte array and display.
            b = BitConverter.GetBytes(3678);
            Console.WriteLine(BitConverter.ToString(b));

            // Convert a byte array to an int and display.
            Console.WriteLine(BitConverter.ToInt32(b,0));

            // Convert a decimal to a byte array and display.
            b = DecimalToByteArray(285998345545.563846696m);
            Console.WriteLine(BitConverter.ToString(b));

            // Convert a byte array to a decimal and display.
            Console.WriteLine(ByteArrayToDecimal(b));

            // Wait to continue.
            Console.WriteLine("Main method complete. Press Enter");
            Console.ReadLine();
        }
    }
}
```

■ **Tip** The `BitConverter.ToString` method provides a convenient mechanism for obtaining a `String` representation of a byte array. Calling `ToString` and passing a byte array as an argument will return a `String` object containing the hexadecimal value of each byte in the array separated by a hyphen—for example `"34-A7-2C"`. Unfortunately, there is no standard method for reversing this process to obtain a byte array from a string with this format.

2-4. Base64 Encode Binary Data

Problem

You need to convert binary data into a form that can be stored as part of an ASCII text file (such as an XML file) or sent as part of a text e-mail message.

Solution

Use the static methods `ToBase64CharArray` and `FromBase64CharArray` of the `System.Convert` class to convert your binary data to and from a Base64-encoded `char` array. If you need to work with the encoded data as a string value instead of a `char` array, you can use the `ToBase64String` and `FromBase64String` methods of the `Convert` class instead.

How It Works

Base64 is an encoding scheme that enables you to represent binary data as a series of ASCII characters so that it can be included in text files and e-mail messages in which raw binary data is unacceptable. Base64 encoding works by spreading the contents of 3 bytes of input data across 4 bytes and ensuring each byte uses only the 7 low-order bits to contain data. This means that each byte of Base64-encoded data is equivalent to an ASCII character and can be stored or transmitted anywhere ASCII characters are permitted.

The `ToBase64CharArray` and `FromBase64CharArray` methods of the `Convert` class make it straightforward to Base64 encode and decode data. However, before Base64 encoding, you must convert your data to a byte array. Similarly, when decoding you must convert the byte array back to the appropriate data type. See recipe 2-2 for details on converting string data to and from byte arrays and recipe 2-3 for details on converting basic value types. The `ToBase64String` and `FromBase64String` methods of the `Convert` class deal with string representations of Base64-encoded data.

The Code

The example shown here demonstrates how to Base64 encode and decode a byte array, a Unicode string, an `int` type, and a `decimal` type using the `Convert` class. The `DecimalToBase64` and `Base64ToDecimal` methods rely on the `ByteArrayToDecimal` and `DecimalToByteArray` methods listed in recipe 2-3.

```
using System;
using System.IO;
using System.Text;

namespace Apress.VisualCSharpRecipes.Chapter02
{
    class Recipe02_04
    {
        // Create a byte array from a decimal.
        public static byte[] DecimalToByteArray (decimal src)
        {
            // Create a MemoryStream as a buffer to hold the binary data.
            using (MemoryStream stream = new MemoryStream())
            {
                // Create a BinaryWriter to write binary data the stream.
                using (BinaryWriter writer = new BinaryWriter(stream))
                {
                    // Write the decimal to the BinaryWriter/MemoryStream.
                    writer.Write(src);
```

```
                // Return the byte representation of the decimal.
                return stream.ToArray();
            }
        }
    }

    // Create a decimal from a byte array.
    public static decimal ByteArrayToDecimal (byte[] src)
    {
        // Create a MemoryStream containing the byte array.
        using (MemoryStream stream = new MemoryStream(src))
        {
            // Create a BinaryReader to read the decimal from the stream.
            using (BinaryReader reader = new BinaryReader(stream))
            {
                // Read and return the decimal from the
                // BinaryReader/MemoryStream.
                return reader.ReadDecimal();
            }
        }
    }

    // Base64 encode a Unicode string.
    public static string StringToBase64 (string src)
    {
        // Get a byte representation of the source string.
        byte[] b = Encoding.Unicode.GetBytes(src);

        // Return the Base64-encoded string.
        return Convert.ToBase64String(b);
    }

    // Decode a Base64-encoded Unicode string.
    public static string Base64ToString (string src)
    {
        // Decode the Base64-encoded string to a byte array.
        byte[] b = Convert.FromBase64String(src);

        // Return the decoded Unicode string.
        return Encoding.Unicode.GetString(b);
    }

    // Base64 encode a decimal.
    public static string DecimalToBase64 (decimal src)
    {
        // Get a byte representation of the decimal.
        byte[] b = DecimalToByteArray(src);

        // Return the Base64-encoded decimal.
        return Convert.ToBase64String(b);
    }
```

```
// Decode a Base64-encoded decimal.
public static decimal Base64ToDecimal (string src)
{
    // Decode the Base64-encoded decimal to a byte array.
    byte[] b = Convert.FromBase64String(src);

    // Return the decoded decimal.
    return ByteArrayToDecimal(b);
}

// Base64 encode an int.
public static string IntToBase64 (int src)
{
    // Get a byte representation of the int.
    byte[] b = BitConverter.GetBytes(src);

    // Return the Base64-encoded int.
    return Convert.ToBase64String(b);
}

// Decode a Base64-encoded int.
public static int Base64ToInt (string src)
{
    // Decode the Base64-encoded int to a byte array.
    byte[] b = Convert.FromBase64String(src);

    // Return the decoded int.
    return BitConverter.ToInt32(b,0);
}

public static void Main()
{
    // Encode and decode a general byte array. Need to create a char[]
    // to hold the Base64-encoded data. The size of the char[] must
    // be at least 4/3 the size of the source byte[] and must be
    // divisible by 4.
    byte[] data = { 0x04, 0x43, 0x5F, 0xFF, 0x0, 0xF0, 0x2D, 0x62, 0x78,
        0x22, 0x15, 0x51, 0x5A, 0xD6, 0x0C, 0x59, 0x36, 0x63, 0xBD, 0xC2,
        0xD5, 0x0F, 0x8C, 0xF5, 0xCA, 0x0C};
```

```
            char[] base64data =
                new char[(int)(Math.Ceiling((double)data.Length / 3) * 4)];

            Console.WriteLine("\nByte array encoding/decoding");
            Convert.ToBase64CharArray(data, 0, data.Length, base64data, 0);
            Console.WriteLine(new String(base64data));
            Console.WriteLine(BitConverter.ToString(
                Convert.FromBase64CharArray(base64data, 0, base64data.Length)));

            // Encode and decode a string.
            Console.WriteLine(StringToBase64
                ("Welcome to Visual C# Recipes from Apress"));
            Console.WriteLine(Base64ToString("VwBlAGwAYwBvAGOAZQAgAHQAbwA" +
                "gAFYAaQBzAHUAYQBsACAAQwAjACAAUgBlAGMAaQBwAGUAcwAgAGYAcgB" +
                "vAGOAIABBAHAAcgBlAHMAcwA="));

            // Encode and decode a decimal.
            Console.WriteLine(DecimalToBase64(285998345545.563846696m));
            Console.WriteLine(Base64ToDecimal("KDjBUP07BoEPAAAAAAAJAA=="));

            // Encode and decode an int.
            Console.WriteLine(IntToBase64(35789));
            Console.WriteLine(Base64ToInt("zYsAAA=="));

            // Wait to continue.
            Console.WriteLine("\nMain method complete. Press Enter");
            Console.ReadLine();
        }
    }
}
```

■ **Caution** If you Base64 encode binary data for the purpose of including it as MIME data in an e-mail message, be aware that the maximum allowed line length in MIME for Base64-encoded data is 76 characters. Therefore, if your data is longer than 76 characters, you must insert a new line. For further information about the MIME standard, consult RFCs 2045 through 2049, which can be found at `www.ietf.org/rfc.html`.

2-5. Validate Input Using Regular Expressions

Problem

You need to validate that user input or data read from a file has the expected structure and content. For example, you want to ensure that a user enters a valid IP address, telephone number, or e-mail address.

Solution

Use regular expressions to ensure that the input data follows the correct structure and contains only valid characters for the expected type of information.

How It Works

When a user inputs data to your application or your application reads data from a file, it's good practice to assume that the data is bad until you have verified its accuracy. One common validation requirement is to ensure that data entries such as e-mail addresses, telephone numbers, and credit card numbers follow the pattern and content constraints expected of such data. Obviously, you cannot be sure the actual data entered is valid until you use it, and you cannot compare it against values that are known to be correct. However, ensuring the data has the correct structure and content is a good first step to determining whether the input is accurate. Regular expressions provide an excellent mechanism for evaluating strings for the presence of patterns, and you can use this to your advantage when validating input data.

The first thing you must do is figure out the regular expression syntax that will correctly match the structure and content of the data you are trying to validate. This is by far the most difficult aspect of using regular expressions. Many resources exist to help you with regular expressions, such as The Regulator (`http://osherove.com/tools`), and RegExDesigner.NET, by Chris Sells (`www.sellsbrothers.com/tools/#regexd`). The RegExLib.com web site (`www.regxlib.com`) also provides hundreds of useful prebuilt expressions.

Regular expressions are constructed from two types of elements: literals and metacharacters. *Literals* represent specific characters that appear in the pattern you want to match. *Metacharacters* provide support for wildcard matching, ranges, grouping, repetition, conditionals, and other control mechanisms. Table 2-2 describes some of the more commonly used regular expression metacharacter elements. (Consult the .NET SDK documentation for a full description of regular expressions. A good starting point is `http://msdn.microsoft.com/en-us/library/system.text.regularexpressions.regex.aspx`.)

Table 2-2. *Commonly Used Regular Expression Metacharacter Elements*

Element	Description
`.`	Specifies any character except a newline character (`\n`)
`\d`	Specifies any decimal digit
`\D`	Specifies any nondigit
`\s`	Specifies any whitespace character
`\S`	Specifies any non-whitespace character
`\w`	Specifies any word character
`\W`	Specifies any nonword character

<table>
<tr><th>Element</th><th>Description</th></tr>
<tr><td>^</td><td>Specifies the beginning of the string or line</td></tr>
<tr><td>\A</td><td>Specifies the beginning of the string</td></tr>
<tr><td>$</td><td>Specifies the end of the string or line</td></tr>
<tr><td>\z</td><td>Specifies the end of the string</td></tr>
<tr><td>|</td><td>Matches one of the expressions separated by the vertical bar (pipe symbol); for example, AAA|ABA|ABB will match one of AAA, ABA, or ABB (the expression is evaluated left to right)</td></tr>
<tr><td>[abc]</td><td>Specifies a match with one of the specified characters; for example, [AbC] will match A, b, or C, but no other characters</td></tr>
<tr><td>[^abc]</td><td>Specifies a match with any one character except those specified; for example, [^AbC] will not match A, b, or C, but will match B, F, and so on</td></tr>
<tr><td>[a-z]</td><td>Specifies a match with any one character in the specified range; for example, [A-C] will match A, B, or C</td></tr>
<tr><td>( )</td><td>Identifies a subexpression so that it's treated as a single element by the regular expression elements described in this table</td></tr>
<tr><td>?</td><td>Specifies one or zero occurrencesof the previous character or subexpression; for example, A?B matches B and AB, but not AAB</td></tr>
<tr><td>*</td><td>Specifies zero or more occurrences of the previous character or subexpression; for example, A*B matches B, AB, AAB, AAAB, and so on</td></tr>
<tr><td>+</td><td>Specifies one or more occurrences of the previous character or subexpression; for example, A+B matches AB, AAB, AAAB, and so on, but not B</td></tr>
<tr><td>{n}</td><td>Specifies exactly n occurrences of the preceding character or subexpression; for example, A{2} matches only AA</td></tr>
<tr><td>{n,}</td><td>Specifies a minimum of n occurrences of the preceding character or subexpression; for example, A{2,} matches AA, AAA, AAAA, and so on, but not A</td></tr>
<tr><td>{n, m}</td><td>Specifies a minimum of n and a maximum of m occurrences of the preceding character; for example, A{2,4} matches AA, AAA, and AAAA, but not A or AAAAA</td></tr>
</table>

The more complex the data you are trying to match, the more complex the regular expression syntax becomes. For example, ensuring that input contains only numbers or is of a minimum length is trivial, but ensuring a string contains a valid URL is extremely complex. Table 2-3 shows some examples of regular expressions that match against commonly required data types.

Table 2-3. Commonly Used Regular Expressions

Input Type	Description	Regular Expression
Numeric input	The input consists of one or more decimal digits; for example, 5 or 5683874674.	`^\d+$`
Personal identification number (PIN)	The input consists of four decimal digits; for example, 1234.	`^\d{4}$`
Simple password	The input consists of six to eight characters; for example, `ghtd6f` or `b8c7hogh`.	`^\w{6,8}$`
Credit card number	The input consists of data that matches the pattern of most major credit card numbers; for example, 4921835221552042 or 4921-8352-2155-2042.	`^\d{4}-?\d{4}-?\d{4}-?\d{4}$`
E-mail address	The input consists of an Internet e-mail address. The `[\w-]+` expression indicates that each address element must consist of one or more word characters or hyphens; for example, `somebody@adatum.com`.	`^[\w-]+@([\w-]+\.)+[\w-]+$`
HTTP or HTTPS URL	The input consists of an HTTP-based or HTTPS-based URL; for example, `http://www.apress.com`.	`^https?://([\w-]+\.)+ [\w-]+(/[\w-./?%=]*)?$`

Once you know the correct regular expression syntax, create a new `System.Text.RegularExpressions.Regex` object, passing a string containing the regular expression to the `Regex` constructor. Then call the `IsMatch` method of the `Regex` object and pass the string that you want to validate. `IsMatch` returns a `bool` value indicating whether the `Regex` object found a match in the string. The regular expression syntax determines whether the `Regex` object will match against only the full string or match against patterns contained within the string. (See the `^`, `\A`, `$`, and `\z` entries in Table 2-2.)

The Code

The `ValidateInput` method shown in the following example tests any input string to see if it matches a specified regular expression.

```
using System;
using System.Text.RegularExpressions;

namespace Apress.VisualCSharpRecipes.Chapter02
{
    class Recipe02_05
    {
```

```
        public static bool ValidateInput(string regex, string input)
        {
            // Create a new Regex based on the specified regular expression.
            Regex r = new Regex(regex);

            // Test if the specified input matches the regular expression.
            return r.IsMatch(input);
        }

        public static void Main(string[] args)
        {
            // Test the input from the command line. The first argument is the
            // regular expression, and the second is the input.
            Console.WriteLine("Regular Expression: {0}", args[0]);
            Console.WriteLine("Input: {0}", args[1]);
            Console.WriteLine("Valid = {0}", ValidateInput(args[0], args[1]));

            // Wait to continue.
            Console.WriteLine("\nMain method complete. Press Enter");
            Console.ReadLine();
        }
    }
}
```

Usage

To execute the example, run Recipe02-05.exe and pass the regular expression and data to test as command-line arguments. For example, to test for a correctly formed e-mail address, type the following:

```
Recipe02-05 ^[\w-]+@([\w-]+\.)+[\w-]+$ myname@mydomain.com
```

The result would be as follows:

```
Regular Expression: ^[\w-]+@([\w-]+\.)+[\w-]+$

Input: myname@mydomain.com

Valid = True
```

Notes

You can use a Regex object repeatedly to test multiple strings, but you cannot change the regular expression tested for by a Regex object. You must create a new Regex object to test for a different pattern. Because the ValidateInput method creates a new Regex instance each time it's called, you do not get the ability to reuse the Regex object. As such, a more suitable alternative in this case would be to use a static overload of the IsMatch method, as shown in the following variant of the ValidateInput method:

```
// Alternative version of the ValidateInput method that does not create
```

```
// Regex instances.
public static bool ValidateInput(string regex, string input)
{
    // Test if the specified input matches the regular expression.
    return Regex.IsMatch(input, regex);
}
```

2-6. Use Compiled Regular Expressions

Problem

You need to minimize the impact on application performance that arises from using complex regular expressions frequently.

Solution

When you instantiate the `System.Text.RegularExpressions.Regex` object that represents your regular expression, specify the `Compiled` option of the `System.Text.RegularExpressions.RegexOptions` enumeration to compile the regular expression to Microsoft Intermediate Language (MSIL).

How It Works

By default, when you create a `Regex` object, the regular expression pattern you specify in the constructor is compiled to an intermediate form (not MSIL). Each time you use the `Regex` object, the runtime interprets the pattern's intermediate form and applies it to the target string. With complex regular expressions that are used frequently, this repeated interpretation process can have a detrimental effect on the performance of your application.

By specifying the `RegexOptions.Compiled` option when you create a `Regex` object, you force the .NET runtime to compile the regular expression to MSIL instead of the interpreted intermediary form. This MSIL is just-in-time (JIT) compiled by the runtime to native machine code on first execution, just like regular assembly code. You use a compiled regular expression in the same way as you use any `Regex` object; compilation simply results in faster execution.

However, a couple downsides offset the performance benefits provided by compiling regular expressions. First, the JIT compiler needs to do more work, which will introduce delays during JIT compilation. This is most noticeable if you create your compiled regular expressions as your application starts up. Second, the runtime cannot unload a compiled regular expression once you have finished with it. Unlike as with a normal regular expression, the runtime's garbage collector will not reclaim the memory used by the compiled regular expression. The compiled regular expression will remain in memory until your program terminates or you unload the application domain in which the compiled regular expression is loaded.

As well as compiling regular expressions in memory, the static `Regex.CompileToAssembly` method allows you to create a compiled regular expression and write it to an external assembly. This means that you can create assemblies containing standard sets of regular expressions, which you can use from multiple applications. To compile a regular expression and persist it to an assembly, take the following steps:

1. Create a System.Text.RegularExpressions.RegexCompilationInfo array large enough to hold one RegexCompilationInfo object for each of the compiled regular expressions you want to create.
2. Create a RegexCompilationInfo object for each of the compiled regular expressions. Specify values for its properties as arguments to the object constructor. The following are the most commonly used properties:
    - IsPublic, a bool value that specifies whether the generated regular expression class has public visibility
    - Name, a String value that specifies the class name
    - Namespace, a String value that specifies the namespace of the class
    - Pattern, a String value that specifies the pattern that the regular expression will match (see recipe 2-5 for more details)
    - Options, a System.Text.RegularExpressions.RegexOptions value that specifies options for the regular expression
3. Create a System.Reflection.AssemblyName object. Configure it to represent the name of the assembly that the Regex.CompileToAssembly method will create.
4. Execute Regex.CompileToAssembly, passing the RegexCompilationInfo array and the AssemblyName object.

This process creates an assembly that contains one class declaration for each compiled regular expression—each class derives from Regex. To use the compiled regular expression contained in the assembly, instantiate the regular expression you want to use and call its method as if you had simply created it with the normal Regex constructor. (Remember to add a reference to the assembly when you compile the code that uses the compiled regular expression classes.)

The Code

This line of code shows how to create a Regex object that is compiled to MSIL instead of the usual intermediate form:

```
Regex reg = new Regex(@"[\w-]+@([\w-]+\.)+[\w-]+", RegexOptions.Compiled);
```

The following example shows how to create an assembly named MyRegEx.dll, which contains two regular expressions named PinRegex and CreditCardRegex:

```
using System;
using System.Reflection;
using System.Text.RegularExpressions;

namespace Apress.VisualCSharpRecipes.Chapter02
{
    class Recipe02_06
    {
```

```
        public static void Main()
        {
            // Create the array to hold the Regex info objects.
            RegexCompilationInfo[] regexInfo = new RegexCompilationInfo[2];

            // Create the RegexCompilationInfo for PinRegex.
            regexInfo[0] = new RegexCompilationInfo(@"^\d{4}$",
                RegexOptions.Compiled, "PinRegex", "", true);

            // Create the RegexCompilationInfo for CreditCardRegex.
            regexInfo[1] = new RegexCompilationInfo(
                @"^\d{4}-?\d{4}-?\d{4}-?\d{4}$",
                RegexOptions.Compiled, "CreditCardRegex", "", true);

            // Create the AssemblyName to define the target assembly.
            AssemblyName assembly = new AssemblyName();
            assembly.Name = "MyRegEx";

            // Create the compiled regular expression
            Regex.CompileToAssembly(regexInfo, assembly);
        }
    }
}
```

2-7. Create Dates and Times from Strings

Problem

You need to create a `System.DateTime` instance that represents the time and date specified in a string.

Solution

Use the `Parse` or `ParseExact` method of the `DateTime` class.

■ **Caution** Many subtle issues are associated with using the `DateTime` class to represent dates and times in your applications. Although the `Parse` and `ParseExact` methods create `DateTime` objects from strings as described in this recipe, you must be careful how you use the resulting `DateTime` objects within your program. See the article titled "Coding Best Practices Using DateTime in the .NET Framework," at `http://msdn.microsoft.com/netframework/default.aspx?pull=/library/en-us/dndotnet/html/datetimecode.asp`, for details about the problems you may encounter.

How It Works

Dates and times can be represented as text in many different ways. For example, 1st June 2005, 1/6/2005, 6/1/2005, and 1-Jun-2005 are all possible representations of the same date, and 16:43 and 4:43 p.m. can both be used to represent the same time. The static `DateTime.Parse` method provides a flexible mechanism for creating `DateTime` instances from a wide variety of string representations.

The `Parse` method goes to great lengths to generate a `DateTime` object from a given string. It will even attempt to generate a `DateTime` object from a string containing partial or erroneous information and will substitute defaults for any missing values. Missing date elements default to the current date, and missing time elements default to 12:00:00 a.m. After all efforts, if `Parse` cannot create a `DateTime` object, it throws a `System.FormatException` exception.

The `Parse` method is both flexible and forgiving. However, for many applications, this level of flexibility is unnecessary. Often, you will want to ensure that `DateTime` parses only strings that match a specific format. In these circumstances, use the `ParseExact` method instead of `Parse`. The simplest overload of the `ParseExact` method takes three arguments: the time and date string to parse, a format string that specifies the structure that the time and date string must have, and an `IFormatProvider` reference that provides culture-specific information to the `ParseExact` method. If the `IFormatProvider` value is `null`, the current thread's culture information is used.

The time and date must meet the requirements specified in the format string, or else `ParseExact` will throw a `System.FormatException` exception. You use the same format specifiers for the format string as you use to format a `DateTime` object for display as a string. This means that you can use both standard and custom format specifiers.

The Code

The following example demonstrates the flexibility of the `Parse` method and the use of the `ParseExact` method. Refer to the documentation for the `System.Globalization.DateTimeFormatInfo` class in the .NET Framework SDK document for complete details on all available format specifiers.

```
using System;

namespace Apress.VisualCSharpRecipes.Chapter02
{
    class Recipe02_07
    {
        public static void Main(string[] args)
        {
            string ds1 = "Sep 2005";
            string ds2 = "Monday 5 September 2005 14:15:33";
            string ds3 = "5,9,5";
            string ds4 = "5/9/2005 14:15:33";
            string ds5 = "2:15 PM";

            // 1st September 2005 00:00:00
            DateTime dt1 = DateTime.Parse(ds1);

            // 5th September 2005 14:15:33
            DateTime dt2 = DateTime.Parse(ds2);
```

```
            // 5th September 2005 00:00:00
            DateTime dt3 = DateTime.Parse(ds3);

            // 5th September 2005 14:15:33
            DateTime dt4 = DateTime.Parse(ds4);

            // Current Date 14:15:00
            DateTime dt5 = DateTime.Parse(ds5);

            // Display the converted DateTime objects.
            Console.WriteLine("String: {0} DateTime: {1}", ds1, dt1);
            Console.WriteLine("String: {0} DateTime: {1}", ds2, dt2);
            Console.WriteLine("String: {0} DateTime: {1}", ds3, dt3);
            Console.WriteLine("String: {0} DateTime: {1}", ds4, dt4);
            Console.WriteLine("String: {0} DateTime: {1}", ds5, dt5);

            // Parse only strings containing LongTimePattern.
            DateTime dt6 = DateTime.ParseExact("2:13:30 PM", "h:mm:ss tt", null);

            // Parse only strings containing RFC1123Pattern.
            DateTime dt7 = DateTime.ParseExact(
                "Mon, 05 Sep 2005 14:13:30 GMT", "ddd, dd MMM yyyy HH':'mm':'ss 'GMT'",
null);

            // Parse only strings containing MonthDayPattern.
            DateTime dt8 = DateTime.ParseExact("September 05", "MMMM dd", null);

            // Display the converted DateTime objects.
            Console.WriteLine(dt6);
            Console.WriteLine(dt7);
            Console.WriteLine(dt8);

            // Wait to continue.
            Console.WriteLine("\nMain method complete. Press Enter");
            Console.ReadLine();
        }
    }
}
```

2-8. Add, Subtract, and Compare Dates and Times

Problem

You need to perform basic arithmetic operations or comparisons using dates and times.

Solution

Use the DateTime and TimeSpan structures, which support standard arithmetic and comparison operators.

How It Works

A DateTime instance represents a specific time (such as 4:15 a.m. on September 5, 1970), whereas a TimeSpan instance represents a period of time (such as 2 hours, 35 minutes). You may want to add, subtract, and compare TimeSpan and DateTime instances.

Internally, both DateTime and TimeSpan use *ticks* to represent time. A tick is equal to 100 nanoseconds (ns). TimeSpan stores its time interval as the number of ticks equal to that interval, and DateTime stores time as the number of ticks since 12:00:00 midnight on January 1 in 0001 CE. (*CE* stands for *Common Era* and is equivalent to AD in the Gregorian calendar.) This approach and the use of operator overloading makes it easy for DateTime and TimeSpan to support basic arithmetic and comparison operations. Table 2-4 summarizes the operator support provided by the DateTime and TimeSpan structures.

Table 2-4. *Operators Supported by DateTime and TimeSpan*

Operator	TimeSpan	DateTime
Assignment (=)	Because TimeSpan is a structure, assignment returns a copy, not a reference	Because DateTime is a structure, assignment returns a copy, not a reference
Addition (+)	Adds two TimeSpan instances	Adds a TimeSpan instance to a DateTime instance
Subtraction (-)	Subtracts one TimeSpan instance from another TimeSpan instance	Subtracts a TimeSpan instance or a DateTime instance from a DateTime instance
Equality (==)	Compares two TimeSpan instances and returns true if they are equal	Compares two DateTime instances and returns true if they are equal
Inequality (!=)	Compares two TimeSpan instances and returns true if they are not equal	Compares two DateTime instances and returns true if they are not equal
Greater than (>)	Determines if one TimeSpan instance is greater than another TimeSpan instance	Determines if one DateTime instance is greater than another DateTime instance
Greater than or equal to (>=)	Determines if one TimeSpan instance is greater than or equal to another TimeSpan instance	Determines if one DateTime instance is greater than or equal to another DateTime instance

Operator	TimeSpan	DateTime
Less than (<)	Determines if one TimeSpan instance is less than another TimeSpan instance	Determines if one DateTime instance is less than another DateTime instance
Less than or equal to (<=)	Determines if one TimeSpan instance is less than or equal to another TimeSpan	Determines if one DateTime instance is less than or equal to another DateTime instance
Unary negation (-)	Returns a TimeSpan instance with a negated value of the specified TimeSpan instance	Not supported
Unary plus (+)	Returns the TimeSpan instance specified	Not supported

The DateTime structure also implements the AddTicks, AddMilliseconds, AddSeconds, AddMinutes, AddHours, AddDays, AddMonths, and AddYears methods. Each of these methods allows you to add (or subtract using negative values) the appropriate element of time to a DateTime instance. These methods and the operators listed in Table 2-4 do not modify the original DateTime; instead, they create a new instance with the modified value.

The Code

The following example demonstrates the use of operators to manipulate the DateTime and TimeSpan structures:

```
using System;

namespace Apress.VisualCSharpRecipes.Chapter02
{
    class Recipe02_08
    {
        public static void Main()
        {
            // Create a TimeSpan representing 2.5 days.
            TimeSpan timespan1 = new TimeSpan(2, 12, 0, 0);

            // Create a TimeSpan representing 4.5 days.
            TimeSpan timespan2 = new TimeSpan(4, 12, 0, 0);

            // Create a TimeSpan representing 3.2 days.
            // using the static convenience method
            TimeSpan timespan3 = TimeSpan.FromDays(3.2);

            // Create a TimeSpan representing 1 week.
            TimeSpan oneWeek = timespan1 + timespan2;
```

```
            // Create a DateTime with the current date and time.
            DateTime now = DateTime.Now;

            // Create a DateTime representing 1 week ago.
            DateTime past = now - oneWeek;

            // Create a DateTime representing 1 week in the future.
            DateTime future = now + oneWeek;

            // Display the DateTime instances.
            Console.WriteLine("Now   : {0}", now);
            Console.WriteLine("Past  : {0}", past);
            Console.WriteLine("Future: {0}", future);

            // Use the comparison operators.
            Console.WriteLine("Now is greater than past: {0}", now > past);
            Console.WriteLine("Now is equal to future: {0}", now == future);

            // Wait to continue.
            Console.WriteLine("\nMain method complete. Press Enter");
            Console.ReadLine();
        }
    }
}
```

2-9. Sort an Array or a Collection

Problem

You need to sort the elements contained in an array or a collection.

Solution

Use the static `System.Linq.Enumerable.OrderBy` method to sort generic collections and arrays. For other collections, use the `Cast` method to convert to a generic collection and then use `Enumerable.OrderBy`. Use `ArrayList.Sort` for `ArrayList` objects.

How It Works

The static `Enumerable.OrderBy` method takes an implementation of the `IEnumerable` interface and a function delegate (which can be a lambda expression). The generic collection classes all implement `IEnumerable` and they, as well as arrays, can be sorted. The function delegate allows you to specify which property or method will be used to sort the data—the parameter is a data element from the collection or array and the return value is what you wish to represent that value in the sort operation. So, for example, if you wish to sort a collection of `MyType` instances using the `myProperty` property for sorting, you would call

```
List<MyType> list = new List<MyType>();
Enumerable.OrderBy(list, x => x.myProperty);
```

`Enumerable.OrderBy` returns an instance of `IOrderedEnumerable`, which you can use to enumerate the sorted data (for example, in a `foreach` loop) or use to create a new sorted collection, by calling the `ToArray`, `ToDictionary`, or `ToList` method.

Nongeneric collections (those that are created without the `<type>` syntax) must be converted to generic collections using the `Cast<>` method. You must either ensure that all of the items in your collection are of the type specified or use `Cast<object>()` to obtain a collection that will work with any type that is contained.

The `ArrayList` collection is an exception in that it cannot be used with the generic syntax. For instances of `ArrayList`, use the `ArrayList.Sort()` method.

The Code

The following example demonstrates how to sort an array, a generic `List`, and an `ArrayList`:

```
using System;
using System.Collections;
using System.Collections.Generic;
using System.Linq;

namespace Apress.VisualCSharpRecipes.Chapter02
{
    class Recipe02_09
    {
        public static void Main()
        {
            // Create a new array and populate it.
            int[] array = { 4, 2, 9, 3 };

            // Created a new, sorted array
            array = Enumerable.OrderBy(array, e => e).ToArray<int>();

            // Display the contents of the sorted array.
            foreach (int i in array) {
                Console.WriteLine(i);
            }

            // Create a list and populate it.
            List<string> list = new List<string>();
            list.Add("Michael");
            list.Add("Kate");
            list.Add("Andrea");
            list.Add("Angus");
```

```
            // Enumerate the sorted contents of the list.
            Console.WriteLine("\nList sorted by content");
            foreach (string person in Enumerable.OrderBy(list, e => e))
            {
                Console.WriteLine(person);
            }

            // Sort and enumerate based on a property.
            Console.WriteLine("\nList sorted by length property");
            foreach (string person in Enumerable.OrderBy(list, e => e.Length))
            {
                Console.WriteLine(person);
            }

            // Create a new ArrayList and populate it.
            ArrayList arraylist = new ArrayList(4);
            arraylist.Add("Michael");
            arraylist.Add("Kate");
            arraylist.Add("Andrea");
            arraylist.Add("Angus");

            // Sort the ArrayList.
            arraylist.Sort();

            // Display the contents of the sorted ArrayList.
            Console.WriteLine("\nArraylist sorted by content");
            foreach (string s in list) {
                Console.WriteLine(s);
            }

            // Wait to continue.
            Console.WriteLine("\nMain method complete. Press Enter");
            Console.ReadLine();
        }
    }
}
```

2-10. Copy a Collection to an Array

Problem

You need to copy the contents of a collection to an array.

Solution

Use the `ICollection.CopyTo` method implemented by all collection classes, or use the `ToArray` method implemented by the `ArrayList`, `Stack`, and `Queue` collections.

How It Works

The ICollection.CopyTo method and the ToArray method perform roughly the same function: they perform a shallow copy of the elements contained in a collection to an array. The key difference is that CopyTo copies the collection's elements to an existing array, whereas ToArray creates a new array before copying the collection's elements into it.

The CopyTo method takes two arguments: an array and an index. The array is the target of the copy operation and must be of a type appropriate to handle the elements of the collection. If the types do not match, or no implicit conversion is possible from the collection element's type to the array element's type, a System.InvalidCastException exception is thrown. The index is the starting element of the array where the collection's elements will be copied. If the index is equal to or greater than the length of the array, or the number of collection elements exceeds the capacity of the array, a System.ArgumentException exception is thrown.

The ArrayList, Stack, and Queue classes and their generic versions also implement the ToArray method, which automatically creates an array of the correct size to accommodate a copy of all the elements of the collection. If you call ToArray with no arguments, it returns an object[] array, regardless of the type of objects contained in the collection. For convenience, the ArrayList.ToArray method has an overload to which you can pass a System.Type object that specifies the type of array that the ToArray method should create. (You must still cast the returned strongly typed array to the correct type.) The layout of the array's contents depends on which collection class you are using. For example, an array produced from a Stack object will be inverted compared to the array generated by an ArrayList object.

The Code

This example demonstrates how to copy the contents of an ArrayList structure to an array using the CopyTo method, and then shows how to use the ToArray method on the ArrayList object.

```
using System;
using System.Collections;

namespace Apress.VisualCSharpRecipes.Chapter02
{
    class Recipe02_10
    {
        public static void Main()
        {
            // Create a new ArrayList and populate it.
            ArrayList list = new ArrayList(5);
            list.Add("Brenda");
            list.Add("George");
            list.Add("Justin");
            list.Add("Shaun");
            list.Add("Meaghan");

            // Create a string array and use the ICollection.CopyTo method
            // to copy the contents of the ArrayList.
            string[] array1 = new string[list.Count];
            list.CopyTo(array1, 0);
```

```
            // Use ArrayList.ToArray to create an object array from the
            // contents of the collection.
            object[] array2 = list.ToArray();

            // Use ArrayList.ToArray to create a strongly typed string
            // array from the contents of the collection.
            string[] array3 = (string[])list.ToArray(typeof(String));

            // Display the contents of the three arrays.
            Console.WriteLine("Array 1:");
            foreach (string s in array1)
            {
                Console.WriteLine("\t{0}",s);
            }

            Console.WriteLine("Array 2:");
            foreach (string s in array2)
            {
                Console.WriteLine("\t{0}", s);
            }

            Console.WriteLine("Array 3:");
            foreach (string s in array3)
            {
                Console.WriteLine("\t{0}", s);
            }

            // Wait to continue.
            Console.WriteLine("\nMain method complete. Press Enter");
            Console.ReadLine();
        }
    }
}
```

2-11. Use a Strongly Typed Collection

Problem

You need a collection that works with elements of a specific type so that you do not need to work with `System.Object` references in your code.

Solution

Use the appropriate collection class from the `System.Collections.Generic` namespace. When you instantiate the collection, specify the type of object the collection should contain using the generics syntax.

How It Works

The generics functionality makes it easy to create type-safe collections and containers (see recipe 2-12). To meet the most common requirements for collection classes, the `System.Collections.Generic` namespace contains a number of predefined generic collections, including the following:

- `Dictionary`
- `LinkedList`
- `List`
- `Queue`
- `Stack`

When you instantiate one of these collections, you specify the type of object that the collection will contain by including the type name in angled brackets after the collection name; for example, `List<System.Reflection.AssemblyName>`. As a result, all members that add objects to the collection expect the objects to be of the specified type, and all members that return objects from the collection will return object references of the specified type. Using strongly typed collections and working directly with objects of the desired type simplifies development and reduces the errors that can occur when working with general `Object` references and casting them to the desired type.

The Code

The following example demonstrates the use of generic collections to create a variety of collections specifically for the management of `AssemblyName` objects. Notice that you never need to cast to or from the `Object` type.

```
using System;
using System.Reflection;
using System.Collections.Generic;

namespace Apress.VisualCSharpRecipes.Chapter02
{
    class Recipe02_11
    {
        public static void Main(string[] args)
        {
            // Create an AssemblyName object for use during the example.
            AssemblyName assembly1 = new AssemblyName("com.microsoft.crypto, " +
                "Culture=en, PublicKeyToken=a5d015c7d5a0b012, Version=1.0.0.0");

            // Create and use a Dictionary of AssemblyName objects.
            Dictionary<string,AssemblyName> assemblyDictionary =
                new Dictionary<string,AssemblyName>();

            assemblyDictionary.Add("Crypto", assembly1);

            AssemblyName a1 = assemblyDictionary["Crypto"];
```

```
            Console.WriteLine("Got AssemblyName from dictionary: {0}", a1);

            // Create and use a List of Assembly Name objects.
            List<AssemblyName> assemblyList = new List<AssemblyName>();

            assemblyList.Add(assembly1);

            AssemblyName a2 = assemblyList[0];

            Console.WriteLine("\nFound AssemblyName in list: {0}", a1);

            // Create and use a Stack of Assembly Name objects.
            Stack<AssemblyName> assemblyStack = new Stack<AssemblyName>();

            assemblyStack.Push(assembly1);

            AssemblyName a3 = assemblyStack.Pop();

            Console.WriteLine("\nPopped AssemblyName from stack: {0}", a1);

            // Wait to continue.
            Console.WriteLine("\nMain method complete. Press Enter");
            Console.ReadLine();
        }
    }
}
```

2-12. Create a Generic Type

Problem

You need to create a new general-purpose type such as a collection or container that supports strong typing of the elements it contains.

Solution

Define your class using the .NET Framework generics syntax.

How It Works

You can leverage the generics capabilities of the .NET Framework in any class you define. This allows you to create general-purpose classes that can be used as type-safe instances by other programmers. When you declare your type, you identify it as a generic type by following the type name with a pair of angled brackets that contain a list of identifiers for the types used in the class. Here is an example:

```
public class MyGenericType<T1, T2, T3>
```

This declaration specifies a new class named `MyGenericType`, which uses three generic types in its implementation (`T1`, `T2`, and `T3`). When implementing the type, you substitute the generic type names into the code instead of using specific type names. For example, one method might take an argument of type `T1` and return a result of type `T2`, as shown here:

```
public T2 MyGenericMethod(T1 arg)
```

When other people use your class and create an instance of it, they specify the actual types to use as part of the instantiation. Here is an example:

```
MyGenericType<string,Stream,string> obj = new MyGenericType<string,Stream,string>();
```

The types specified replace `T1`, `T2`, and `T3` throughout the implementation, so with this instance, `MyGenericMethod` would actually be interpreted as follows:

```
public Stream MyGenericMethod(string arg)
```

You can also include constraints as part of your generic type definition. This allows you to make specifications such as the following:

- Only value types or only reference types can be used with the generic type.
- Only types that implement a default (empty) constructor can be used with the generic type.
- Only types that implement a specific interface can be used with the generic type.
- Only types that inherit from a specific base class can be used with the generic type.
- One generic type must be the same as another generic type (for example, `T1` must be the same as `T3`).

For example, to specify that `T1` must implement the `System.IDisposable` interface and provide a default constructor, that `T2` must be or derive from the `System.IO.Stream` class, and that `T3` must be the same type as `T1`, change the definition of `MyGenericType` as follows:

```
public class MyGenericType<T1, T2, T3>
    where T1 : System.IDisposable, new()
    where T2 : System.IO.Stream
    where T3 : T1
{ \* ...Implementation... *\ }
```

The Code

The following example demonstrates a simplified bag implementation that returns those objects put into it at random. A *bag* is a data structure that can contain zero or more items, including duplicates of items, but does not guarantee any ordering of the items it contains.

```
using System;
using System.Collections.Generic;
```

```
namespace Apress.VisualCSharpRecipes.Chapter02
{
    public class Bag<T>
    {
        // A List to hold the bags's contents. The list must be
        // of the same type as the bag.
        private List<T> items = new List<T>();

        // A method to add an item to the bag.
        public void Add(T item)
        {
            items.Add(item);
        }

        // A method to get a random item from the bag.
        public T Remove()
        {
            T item = default(T);

            if (items.Count != 0)
            {
                // Determine which item to remove from the bag.
                Random r = new Random();
                int num = r.Next(0, items.Count);

                // Remove the item.
                item = items[num];
                items.RemoveAt(num);
            }
            return item;
        }

        // A method to provide an enumerator from the underlying list
        public IEnumerator<T> GetEnumerator()
        {
            return items.GetEnumerator();
        }

        // A method to remove all items from the bag and return them
        // as an array
        public T[] RemoveAll()
        {
            T[] i = items.ToArray();
            items.Clear();
            return i;
        }
    }
```

```
    public class Recipe02_12
    {
        public static void Main(string[] args)
        {
            // Create a new bag of strings.
            Bag<string> bag = new Bag<string>();

            // Add strings to the bag.
            bag.Add("Darryl");
            bag.Add("Bodders");
            bag.Add("Gary");
            bag.Add("Mike");
            bag.Add("Nigel");
            bag.Add("Ian");

            Console.WriteLine("Bag contents are:");
            foreach (string elem in bag)
            {
                Console.WriteLine("Element: {0}", elem);
            }

            // Take four strings from the bag and display.
            Console.WriteLine("\nRemoving individual elements");
            Console.WriteLine("Removing = {0}", bag.Remove());
            Console.WriteLine("Removing = {0}", bag.Remove());
            Console.WriteLine("Removing = {0}", bag.Remove());
            Console.WriteLine("Removing = {0}", bag.Remove());

            Console.WriteLine("\nBag contents are:");
            foreach (string elem in bag)
            {
                Console.WriteLine("Element: {0}", elem);
            }

            // Remove the remaining items from the bag.
            Console.WriteLine("\nRemoving all elements");
            string[] s = bag.RemoveAll();

            Console.WriteLine("\nBag contents are:");
            foreach (string elem in bag)
            {
                Console.WriteLine("Element: {0}", elem);
            }

            // Wait to continue.
            Console.WriteLine("\nMain method complete. Press Enter");
            Console.ReadLine();
        }
    }
}
```

2-13. Store a Serializable Object to a File

Problem

You need to store a serializable object and its state to a file, and then deserialize it later.

Solution

Use a *formatter* to serialize the object and write it to a `System.IO.FileStream` object. When you need to retrieve the object, use the same type of formatter to read the serialized data from the file and deserialize the object. The .NET Framework class library includes the following formatter implementations for serializing objects to binary or SOAP format:

- `System.Runtime.Serialization.Formatters.Binary.BinaryFormatter`
- `System.Runtime.Serialization.Formatters.Soap.SoapFormatter`

How It Works

Using the `BinaryFormatter` and `SoapFormatter` classes, you can serialize an instance of any serializable type. (See recipe 13-1 for details on how to make a type serializable.) The `BinaryFormatter` class produces a binary data stream representing the object and its state. The `SoapFormatter` class produces a SOAP document.

Both the `BinaryFormatter` and `SoapFormatter` classes implement the interface `System.Runtime.Serialization.IFormatter`, which defines two methods: `Serialize` and `Deserialize`. The `Serialize` method takes a `System.IO.Stream` reference and a `System.Object` reference as arguments, serializes the `Object`, and writes it to the `Stream`. The `Deserialize` method takes a `Stream` reference as an argument, reads the serialized object data from the `Stream`, and returns an `Object` reference to a deserialized object. You must cast the returned `Object` reference to the correct type.

■ **Note** You will need to reference the `System.Runtime.Serialization.Formatters.Soap` assembly in order to use `SoapFormatter`. The `BinaryFormatter` class is contained in the core assembly and requires no additional project references

---

The Code

The example shown here demonstrates the use of both `BinaryFormatter` and `SoapFormatter` to serialize a `System.Collections.ArrayList` object containing a list of people to a file. The `ArrayList` object is then deserialized from the files and the contents displayed to the console.

```
using System;
using System.IO;
using System.Collections;
using System.Runtime.Serialization.Formatters.Soap;
using System.Runtime.Serialization.Formatters.Binary;

namespace Apress.VisualCSharpRecipes.Chapter02
{
    class Recipe02_13
    {
        // Serialize an ArrayList object to a binary file.
        private static void BinarySerialize(ArrayList list)
        {
            using (FileStream str = File.Create("people.bin"))
            {
                BinaryFormatter bf = new BinaryFormatter();
                bf.Serialize(str, list);
            }
        }

        // Deserialize an ArrayList object from a binary file.
        private static ArrayList BinaryDeserialize()
        {
            ArrayList people = null;

            using (FileStream str = File.OpenRead("people.bin"))
            {
                BinaryFormatter bf = new BinaryFormatter();
                people = (ArrayList)bf.Deserialize(str);
            }
            return people;
        }

        // Serialize an ArrayList object to a SOAP file.
        private static void SoapSerialize(ArrayList list)
        {
            using (FileStream str = File.Create("people.soap"))
            {
                SoapFormatter sf = new SoapFormatter();
                sf.Serialize(str, list);
            }
        }

        // Deserialize an ArrayList object from a SOAP file.
        private static ArrayList SoapDeserialize()
        {
            ArrayList people = null;
```

```
            using (FileStream str = File.OpenRead("people.soap"))
            {
                SoapFormatter sf = new SoapFormatter();
                people = (ArrayList)sf.Deserialize(str);
            }
            return people;
        }

        public static void Main()
        {
            // Create and configure the ArrayList to serialize.
            ArrayList people = new ArrayList();
            people.Add("Graeme");
            people.Add("Lin");
            people.Add("Andy");

            // Serialize the list to a file in both binary and SOAP form.
            BinarySerialize(people);
            SoapSerialize(people);

            // Rebuild the lists of people from the binary and SOAP
            // serializations and display them to the console.
            ArrayList binaryPeople = BinaryDeserialize();
            ArrayList soapPeople = SoapDeserialize();

            Console.WriteLine("Binary people:");
            foreach (string s in binaryPeople)
            {
                Console.WriteLine("\t" + s);
            }

            Console.WriteLine("\nSOAP people:");
            foreach (string s in soapPeople)
            {
                Console.WriteLine("\t" + s);
            }

            // Wait to continue.
            Console.WriteLine("\nMain method complete. Press Enter");
            Console.ReadLine();
        }
    }
}
```

The SOAP file that the example produces is show following. The binary file is not human-readable.

```
<SOAP-ENV:Envelope xmlns:xsi="http://www.w3.org/2001/XMLSchema-instance"
xmlns:xsd="http://www.w3.org/2001/XMLSchema" xmlns:SOAP-
ENC="http://schemas.xmlsoap.org/soap/encoding/" xmlns:SOAP-
ENV="http://schemas.xmlsoap.org/soap/envelope/"
xmlns:clr="http://schemas.microsoft.com/soap/encoding/clr/1.0" SOAP-
ENV:encodingStyle="http://schemas.xmlsoap.org/soap/encoding/">
<SOAP-ENV:Body>
<a1:ArrayList id="ref-1" xmlns:a1="http://schemas.microsoft.com/clr/ns/System.Collections">
<_items href="#ref-2"/>
<_size>3</_size>
<_version>3</_version>
</a1:ArrayList>
<SOAP-ENC:Array id="ref-2" SOAP-ENC:arrayType="xsd:anyType[4]">
<item id="ref-3" xsi:type="SOAP-ENC:string">Graeme</item>
<item id="ref-4" xsi:type="SOAP-ENC:string">Lin</item>
<item id="ref-5" xsi:type="SOAP-ENC:string">Andy</item>
</SOAP-ENC:Array>
</SOAP-ENV:Body>
</SOAP-ENV:Envelope>
```


2-14. Serialize an Object Using JSON

Problem

You need to serialize an object to or from JavaScript Object Notation (JSON).

Solution

Create a Stream that either writes to the destination you wish to serialize to or is the source of the data you wish to deserialize from. Create an instance of DataContractJsonSerializer, using the type of the object that you wish to serialize or deserialize as the constructor argument. Call WriteObject (to serialize) or ReadObject (to deserialize) using the object you wish to process as a method argument.

How It Works

The DataContractJsonSerializer class is part of the wider .NET data contract support, which allows you to create a formal contract between a client and a service about the way in which data will be exchanged. For our purposes, we need only know that Microsoft has included data contract support for most .NET data types (including collections), allowing easy serialization to and from JSON.

■ **Note** You will need to reference the System.ServiceModel.Web and System.Runtime.Serialization assemblies in order to use DataContractJsonSerializer.

When creating an instance of DataContractJsonSerializer, you must supply the type of the object that you are going to serialize or deserialize as a constructor argument—you can obtain this by calling the GetType method on any object. To serialize an object, call the WriteObject method using the object you wish to serialize and the Stream you wish to serialize it to as method arguments. The WriteObject method will throw an exception if you try to serialize an object that does not match the type you used in the constructor.

To deserialize an object, call the ReadObject method using a Stream that contains the JSON data you wish to process—if you have received the JSON data as a string, you can use the MemoryStream class (see the code following for an illustration of this technique). The ReadObject method returns an object, and so you must cast to your target type.

To serialize a data type that you have created, use the [Serializable] annotation as follows:

```
[Serializable]
class MyJSONType
{
    public string myFirstProperty { get; set;}
    public string mySecondProperty { get; set; }
}
```

Using [Serializable] will serialize all of the members of your class. If you wish to be selective about which members are included in the JSON data, then use the [DataContract] annotation at the class level, and mark each member you wish to be included with the [DataMember] annotation, as follows:

```
[DataContract]
class MyJSONType
{
    [DataMember]
    public string myFirstProperty { get; set;}
    public string mySecondProperty { get; set; }
}
```

For the simple class shown, this will result in the `myFirstProperty` member being included in the JSON output and `mySecondProperty` excluded.

The Code

The following example serializes a `List` of strings using a `MemoryStream`, prints out the resulting JSON, and then deserializes the `List` in order to print out the contents.

```
using System;
using System.Collections.Generic;
using System.Runtime.Serialization.Json;
using System.IO;
using System.Text;

namespace Apress.VisualCSharpRecipes.Chapter02
{
    class Recipe02_14
    {
        public static void Main()
        {

            // Create a list of strings.
            List<string> myList = new List<string>()
            {
                "apple", "orange", "banana", "cherry"
            };

            // Create memory stream - we will use this
            // to get the JSON serialization as a string.
            MemoryStream memoryStream = new MemoryStream();

            // Create the JSON serializer.
            DataContractJsonSerializer jsonSerializer
                = new DataContractJsonSerializer(myList.GetType());

            // Serialize the list.
            jsonSerializer.WriteObject(memoryStream, myList);

            // Get the JSON string from the memory stream.
            string jsonString = Encoding.Default.GetString(memoryStream.ToArray());
```

```
            // Write the string to the console.
            Console.WriteLine(jsonString);

            // Create a new stream so we can read the JSON data.
            memoryStream = new MemoryStream(Encoding.Default.GetBytes(jsonString));

            // Deserialize the list.
            myList = jsonSerializer.ReadObject(memoryStream) as List<string>;

            // Enumerate the strings in the list.
            foreach (string strValue in myList)
            {
                Console.WriteLine(strValue);
            }

            // Wait to continue.
            Console.WriteLine("\nMain method complete. Press Enter");
            Console.ReadLine();
        }
    }
}
```

2-15. Read User Input from the Console

Problem

You want to read user input from the Windows console, either a line or character at a time.

Solution

Use the `Read` or `ReadLine` method of the `System.Console` class to read input when the user presses Enter. To read input without requiring the user to press Enter, use the `Console.ReadKey` method.

How It Works

The simplest way to read input from the console is to use the static `Read` or `ReadLine` methods of the `Console` class. These methods will both cause your application to block, waiting for the user to enter input and press Enter. In both instances, the user will see the input characters in the console. Once the user presses Enter, the `Read` method will return an `int` value representing the next character of input data, or `-1` if no more data is available. The `ReadLine` method will return a string containing all the data entered, or an empty string if no data was entered.

The .NET Framework includes the `Console.ReadKey` method, which provides a way to read input from the console without waiting for the user to press Enter. The `ReadKey` method waits for the user to press a key and returns a `System.ConsoleKeyInfo` object to the caller. By passing `true` as an argument to an overload of the `ReadKey` method, you can also prevent the key pressed by the user from being echoed to the console.

The returned ConsoleKeyInfo object contains details about the key pressed. The details are accessible through the properties of the ConsoleKeyInfo class (summarized in Table 2-5).

Table 2-5. *Properties of the ConsoleKeyInfo Class*

Property	Description
Key	Gets a value of the System.ConsoleKey enumeration representing the key pressed. The ConsoleKey enumeration contains values that represent all of the keys usually found on a keyboard. These include all the character and function keys; navigation and editing keys like Home, Insert, and Delete; and more modern specialized keys like the Windows key, media player control keys, browser activation keys, and browser navigation keys.
KeyChar	Gets a char value containing the Unicode character representation of the key pressed.
Modifiers	Gets a bitwise combination of values from the System.ConsoleModifiers enumeration that identifies one or more modifier keys pressed simultaneously with the console key. The members of the ConsoleModifiers enumeration are Alt, Control, and Shift.

The KeyAvailable method of the Console class returns a bool value indicating whether input is available in the input buffer without blocking your code.

The Code

The following example reads input from the console one character at a time using the ReadKey method. If the user presses F1, the program toggles in and out of "secret" mode, where input is masked by asterisks. When the user presses Esc, the console is cleared and the input the user has entered is displayed. If the user presses Alt+X or Alt+x, the example terminates.

```
using System;
using System.Collections.Generic;

namespace Apress.VisualCSharpRecipes.Chapter02
{
    class Recipe02_15
    {
        public static void Main()
        {
            // Local variable to hold the key entered by the user.
            ConsoleKeyInfo key;

            // Control whether character or asterisk is displayed.
            bool secret = false;

            // Character List for the user data entered.
            List<char> input = new List<char>();
```

```
string msg = "Enter characters and press Escape to see input." +
    "\nPress F1 to enter/exit Secret mode and Alt-X to exit.";

Console.WriteLine(msg);

// Process input until the user enters "Alt+X" or "Alt+x".
do
{
    // Read a key from the console. Intercept the key so that it is not
    // displayed to the console. What is displayed is determined later
    // depending on whether the program is in secret mode.
    key = Console.ReadKey(true);

    // Switch secret mode on and off.
    if (key.Key == ConsoleKey.F1)
    {
        if (secret)
        {
            // Switch secret mode off.
            secret = false;
        }
        else
        {
            // Switch secret mode on.
            secret = true;
        }
    }

    // Handle Backspace.
    if (key.Key == ConsoleKey.Backspace)
    {
        if (input.Count > 0)
        {
            // Backspace pressed, remove the last character.
            input.RemoveAt(input.Count - 1);

            Console.Write(key.KeyChar);
            Console.Write(" ");
            Console.Write(key.KeyChar);
        }
    }
    // Handle Escape.
    else if (key.Key == ConsoleKey.Escape)
    {
        Console.Clear();
        Console.WriteLine("Input: {0}\n\n",
            new String(input.ToArray()));
        Console.WriteLine(msg);
        input.Clear();
    }
    // Handle character input.
```

```
                else if (key.Key >= ConsoleKey.A && key.Key <= ConsoleKey.Z)
                {
                    input.Add(key.KeyChar);
                    if (secret)
                    {
                        Console.Write("*");
                    }
                    else
                    {
                        Console.Write(key.KeyChar);
                    }
                }
            } while (key.Key != ConsoleKey.X
                || key.Modifiers != ConsoleModifiers.Alt);

            // Wait to continue.
            Console.WriteLine("\n\nMain method complete. Press Enter");
            Console.ReadLine();
        }
    }
}
```

2-16. Using Large Integer Values

Problem

You need to work with an integer value that exceeds the size of the default numeric types.

Solution

Use the `System.Numerics.BigInteger` class.

How It Works

Numeric values in the .NET Framework have maximum and minimum values based on how much memory is allocated by the data type. The `System.Numerics.BigInteger` class has no such limits, and can be used to perform operations on very large integer values.

Instances of `BigInteger` are immutable, and you perform operations using the static methods of the `BigInteger` class, each of which will return a new instance of `BigInteger` as the result—see the code in this recipe for an example.

The Code

The following example creates a `BigInteger` with a value that is twice the maximum value of `Int64` and then adds another `Int64.MaxValue`.

```
using System;
using System.Collections.Generic;
using System.Linq;
using System.Text;
using System.Numerics;

namespace Apress.VisualCSharpRecipes.Chapter02
{
    class Recipe2_16
    {
        static void Main(string[] args)
        {
            // Create a new big integer.
            BigInteger myBigInt = BigInteger.Multiply(Int64.MaxValue, 2);
            // Add another value.
            myBigInt = BigInteger.Add(myBigInt, Int64.MaxValue);
            // Print out the value.
            Console.WriteLine("Big Integer Value: {0}", myBigInt);

            // Wait to continue.
            Console.WriteLine("\n\nMain method complete. Press Enter");
            Console.ReadLine();
        }
    }
}
```

2-17. Select Collection or Array Elements

Problem

You need to select elements from a collection or an array.

Solution

Use the basic features of Language-Integrated Query (LINQ).

How It Works

LINQ allows you to select elements from a collection based on characteristics of the elements contained within the collection. The basic sequence for querying a collection or array using LINQ is as follows:

1. Start a new LINQ query using the from keyword.
2. Identify the conditions to use in selecting elements with the where keyword.
3. Indicate what value will be added to the result set from each matching element using the select keyword.
4. Specify the way you want the results to be sorted using the orderby keyword.

The output of a LINQ query is an instance of IEnumerable containing the collection/array elements that meet your search criteria—you can use IEnumerable to walk through the matching elements using a foreach loop, or as the data source for further LINQ queries. The following is an example of a LINQ query against a string array—we select the first character of any entry longer than four characters and order the results based on length:

```
IEnumerable<char> linqResult
= from e in stringArray where e.Length > 4 orderby e.Length select e[0];
```

Queries can also be written using lambda expressions and the methods available on the collections classes and array types. The preceding query would be as follows with lambda expressions:

```
IEnumerable<char> linqResult
= stringArray.Where(e => e.Length > 4).OrderBy(e => e.Length).Select(e => e[0]);
```

For large collections and arrays, you can use Parallel LINQ (PLINQ), which will partition your query and use multiple threads to process the data in parallel. You enable PLINQ by using the AsParallel method on your collection or array—for example:

```
IEnumerable<char> linqResult
= from e in stringArray.AsParallel() where e.Length > 4 orderby e.Length select e[0];
```

LINQ is a rich and flexible feature and provides additional keywords to specify more complex queries—see Chapter 16 for further LINQ recipes.

The Code

The following example defines a class Fruit, which has properties for the name and color of a type of fruit. A List is created and populated with fruits, which are then used as the basis of a LINQ query—the query is performed using keywords and then repeated using lambda expressions.

```
using System;
using System.Collections.Generic;
using System.Linq;
using System.Text;

namespace Apress.VisualCSharpRecipes.Chapter02
{
    class Recipe02_17
    {
        static void Main(string[] args)
        {
```

```
            // Create a list of fruit.
            List<Fruit> myList = new List<Fruit>() {
                new Fruit("apple", "green"),
                new Fruit("orange", "orange"),
                new Fruit("banana", "yellow"),
                new Fruit("mango", "yellow"),
                new Fruit("cherry", "red"),
                new Fruit("fig", "brown"),
                new Fruit("cranberry", "red"),
                new Fruit("pear", "green")
            };

            // Select the names of fruit that isn't red and whose name
            // does not start with the letter "c."
            IEnumerable<string> myResult = from e in myList where e.Color
                != "red" && e.Name[0] != 'c' orderby e.Name select e.Name;
            // Write out the results.
            foreach (string result in myResult)
            {
                Console.WriteLine("Result: {0}", result);
            }

            // Perform the same query using lambda expressions.
            myResult = myList.Where(e => e.Color != "red" && e.Name[0]
                != 'c').OrderBy(e => e.Name).Select(e => e.Name);
            // Write out the results.
            foreach (string result in myResult)
            {
                Console.WriteLine("Lambda Result: {0}", result);
            }

            // Wait to continue.
            Console.WriteLine("\n\nMain method complete. Press Enter");
            Console.ReadLine();
        }
    }

    class Fruit
    {
        public Fruit(string nameVal, string colorVal)
        {
            Name = nameVal;
            Color = colorVal;
        }
        public string Name { get; set; }
        public string Color { get; set; }
    }
}
```

2-18. Remove Duplicate Items from an Array or Collection

Problem

You need to remove duplicate entries from an array or collection.

Solution

Use the `Distinct` method available in array and collection types.

How It Works

The `Distinct` method is part of the LINQ feature of the .NET Framework, which we used in the previous recipe to select items from a collection. The `Distinct` method returns an instance of `IEnumerable`, which can be converted into an array or collection with the `ToArray`, `ToList`, and `ToDictionary` methods. You can provide an instance of `IEqualityComparer` as an argument to the `Distinct` method in order to provide your rules for identifying duplicates.

The Code

The following example removes duplicates from a `List<Fruit>` using a custom implementation of `IEqualityComparer` passed to the `List.Distinct` method and prints out the unique items:

```
using System;
using System.Collections.Generic;
using System.Linq;
using System.Text;

namespace Apress.VisualCSharpRecipes.Chapter02
{
    class Recipe02_18
    {
        static void Main(string[] args)
        {

            // Create a list of fruit, including duplicates.
            List<Fruit> myList = new List<Fruit>() {
                new Fruit("apple", "green"),
                new Fruit("apple", "red"),
                new Fruit("orange", "orange"),
                new Fruit("orange", "orange"),
                new Fruit("banana", "yellow"),
                new Fruit("mango", "yellow"),
                new Fruit("cherry", "red"),
                new Fruit("fig", "brown"),
                new Fruit("fig", "brown"),
```

```
                new Fruit("fig", "brown"),
                new Fruit("cranberry", "red"),
                new Fruit("pear", "green")
            };

            // Use the Distinct method to remove duplicates
            // and print out the unique entries that remain.
            foreach (Fruit fruit in myList.Distinct(new FruitComparer()))
            {
                Console.WriteLine("Fruit: {0}:{1}", fruit.Name, fruit.Color);
            }

            // Wait to continue.
            Console.WriteLine("\n\nMain method complete. Press Enter");
            Console.ReadLine();
        }
    }

    class FruitComparer : IEqualityComparer<Fruit>
    {
        public bool Equals(Fruit first, Fruit second)
        {
            return first.Name == second.Name && first.Color == second.Color;
        }

        public int GetHashCode(Fruit fruit)
        {
            return fruit.Name.GetHashCode() + fruit.Name.GetHashCode();
        }
    }

    class Fruit
    {
        public Fruit(string nameVal, string colorVal)
        {
            Name = nameVal;
            Color = colorVal;
        }
        public string Name { get; set; }
        public string Color { get; set; }
    }
}
```

CHAPTER 3

■ ■ ■

Application Domains, Reflection, and Metadata

The power and flexibility of the Microsoft .NET Framework is enhanced by the ability to inspect and manipulate types and metadata at runtime. The recipes in this chapter describe how to use application domains, reflection, and metadata. Specifically, the recipes in this chapter describe how to do the following:

- Create application domains into which you can load assemblies that are isolated from the rest of your application (recipe 3-1)
- Create types that have the capability to cross application domain boundaries (recipe 3-2) and types that are guaranteed to be unable to cross application domain boundaries (recipe 3-4)
- Control the loading of assemblies and the instantiation of types in local and remote application domains (recipes 3-3, 3-5, 3-6, and 3-7)
- Pass simple configuration data between application domains (recipe 3-8)
- Unload application domains, which provides the only means through which you can unload assemblies at runtime (recipe 3-9)
- Inspect and test the type of an object using a variety of mechanisms built into the C# language and capabilities provided by the objects themselves (recipes 3-10 and 3-11)
- Dynamically instantiate an object and execute its methods at runtime using reflection (recipe 3-12)
- Create custom attributes (recipe 3-13), allowing you to associate metadata with your program elements and inspect the value of those custom attributes at runtime (recipe 3-14)
- Use reflection to discover type members and to invoke a member at runtime (recipes 3-15 and 3-16)

- Use dynamic types to simplify invoking a member using reflection (recipe 3-17)
- Create custom dynamic types (recipe 3-18)

3-1. Create an Application Domain

Problem

You need to create a new application domain.

Solution

Use the static method `CreateDomain` of the `System.AppDomain` class.

How It Works

The simplest overload of the `CreateDomain` method takes a single `string` argument specifying a human-readable name (friendly name) for the new application domain. Other overloads allow you to specify evidence and configuration settings for the new application domain. You specify evidence using a `System.Security.Policy.Evidence` object, and you specify configuration settings using a `System.AppDomainSetup` object.

The `AppDomainSetup` class is a container of configuration information for an application domain. Table 3-1 lists some of the properties of the `AppDomainSetup` class that you will use most often when creating application domains. These properties are accessible after creation through members of the `AppDomain` object. Some have different names, and some are modifiable at runtime; refer to the .NET Framework's software development kit (SDK) documentation on the `AppDomain` class for a comprehensive discussion.

Table 3-1. *Commonly Used AppDomainSetup Properties*

Property	Description
`ApplicationBase`	The directory where the CLR will look during probing to resolve private assemblies. (Recipe 3-5 discusses probing.) Effectively, `ApplicationBase` is the root directory for the executing application. By default, this is the directory containing the assembly. This is readable after creation using the `AppDomain.BaseDirectory` property.
`ConfigurationFile`	The name of the configuration file used by code loaded into the application domain. This is readable after creation using the `AppDomain.GetData` method with the key `APP_CONFIG_FILE`. By default, the configuration file is stored in the same folder as the application EXE file, but if you set `ApplicationBase`, it will be in that same folder.

Property	Description
DisallowPublisherPolicy	Controls whether the publisher policy section of the application configuration file is taken into consideration when determining which version of a strongly named assembly to bind to. Recipe 3-5 discusses publisher policy.
PrivateBinPath	A semicolon-separated list of directories that the runtime uses when probing for private assemblies. These directories are relative to the directory specified in ApplicationBase. This is readable after application domain creation using the AppDomain.RelativeSearchPath property.

The Code

The following code demonstrates the creation and initial configuration of an application domain:

```
using System;

namespace Apress.VisualCSharpRecipes.Chapter03
{
    class Recipe03_01
    {
        public static void Main()
        {
            // Instantiate an AppDomainSetup object.
            AppDomainSetup setupInfo = new AppDomainSetup();

            // Configure the application domain setup information.
            setupInfo.ApplicationBase = @"C:\MyRootDirectory";
            setupInfo.ConfigurationFile = "MyApp.config";
            setupInfo.PrivateBinPath = "bin;plugins;external";

            // Create a new application domain passing null as the evidence
            // argument. Remember to save a reference to the new AppDomain as
            // this cannot be retrieved any other way.
            AppDomain newDomain =
                AppDomain.CreateDomain("My New AppDomain",null, setupInfo);

            // Wait to continue.
            Console.WriteLine("\nMain method complete. Press Enter.");
            Console.ReadLine();
        }
    }
}
```

3-2. Create Types That Can Be Passed Across Application Domain Boundaries

Problem

You need to pass objects across application domain boundaries as arguments or return values.

Solution

Use marshal-by-value or marshal-by-reference objects.

How It Works

The .NET Remoting system (discussed in Chapter 10) makes passing objects across application domain boundaries straightforward. However, to those unfamiliar with .NET Remoting, the results can be very different from those expected. In fact, the most confusing aspect of using multiple application domains stems from the interaction with .NET Remoting and the way objects traverse application domain boundaries.

All types fall into one of three categories: nonremotable, marshal-by-value (MBV), or marshal-by-reference (MBR). Nonremotable types cannot cross application domain boundaries and cannot be used as arguments or return values in cross-application domain calls. Recipe 3-4 discusses nonremotable types.

MBV types are serializable types. When you pass an MBV object across an application domain boundary as an argument or a return value, the .NET Remoting system serializes the object's current state, passes it to the destination application domain, and creates a new copy of the object with the same state as the original. This results in a copy of the MBV object existing in both application domains. The content of the two instances are initially identical, but they are independent; changes made to one instance are not reflected in the other instance (this applies to static members as well). This often causes confusion as you try to update the remote object but are in fact updating the local copy. If you actually want to be able to call and change an object from a remote application domain, the object needs to be an MBR type.

MBR types are those classes that derive from `System.MarshalByRefObject`. When you pass an MBR object across an application domain boundary as an argument or a return value, the .NET Remoting system creates a *proxy* in the destination application domain that represents the remote MBR object. To any class in the destination application domain, the proxy looks and behaves like the remote MBR object that it represents. In reality, when a call is made against the proxy, the .NET Remoting system transparently passes the call and its arguments to the remote application domain and issues the call against the original object. Any results are passed back to the caller via the proxy. Figure 3-1 illustrates the relationship between an MBR object and the objects that access it across application domains via a proxy.

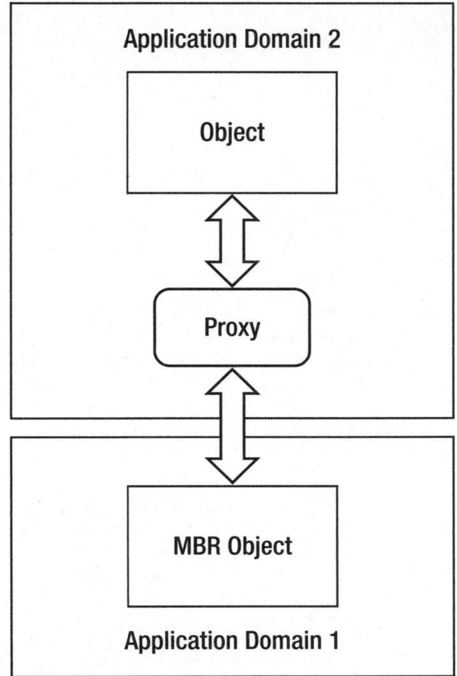

Figure 3-1. An MBR object is accessed across application domains via a proxy.

The Code

The following example highlights (in bold) the fundamental difference between creating classes that are passed by value (`Recipe03_02MBV`) and those passed by reference (`Recipe03_02MBR`). The code creates a new application domain and instantiates two remotable objects in it (discussed further in recipe 3-7). However, because the `Recipe03_02MBV` object is an MBV object, when it is created in the new application domain, it is serialized, passed across the application domain boundary, and deserialized as a new independent object in the caller's application domain. Therefore, when the code retrieves the name of the application domain hosting each object, `Recipe03_02MBV` returns the name of the main application domain, and `Recipe03_02MBR` returns the name of the new application domain in which it was created.

```
using System;

namespace Apress.VisualCSharpRecipes.Chapter03
{
    // Declare a class that is passed by value.
    [Serializable]
    public class Recipe03_02MBV
    {
```

```
        public string HomeAppDomain
        {
            get
            {
                return AppDomain.CurrentDomain.FriendlyName;
            }
        }
    }

    // Declare a class that is passed by reference.
    public class Recipe03_02MBR: MarshalByRefObject
    {
        public string HomeAppDomain
        {
            get
            {
                return AppDomain.CurrentDomain.FriendlyName;
            }
        }
    }

    public class Recipe03_02
    {
        public static void Main(string[] args)
        {
            // Create a new application domain.
            AppDomain newDomain =
                AppDomain.CreateDomain("My New AppDomain");

            // Instantiate an MBV object in the new application domain.
            Recipe03_02MBV mbvObject =
                (Recipe03_02MBV)newDomain.CreateInstanceFromAndUnwrap(
                    "Recipe03-02.exe",
                    "Apress.VisualCSharpRecipes.Chapter03.Recipe03_02MBV");

            // Instantiate an MBR object in the new application domain.
            Recipe03_02MBR mbrObject =
                (Recipe03_02MBR)newDomain.CreateInstanceFromAndUnwrap(
                    "Recipe03-02.exe",
                    "Apress.VisualCSharpRecipes.Chapter03.Recipe03_02MBR");

            // Display the name of the application domain in which each of
            // the objects is located.
            Console.WriteLine("Main AppDomain = {0}",
                AppDomain.CurrentDomain.FriendlyName);
            Console.WriteLine("AppDomain of MBV object = {0}",
                mbvObject.HomeAppDomain);
            Console.WriteLine("AppDomain of MBR object = {0}",
                mbrObject.HomeAppDomain);
```

```
            // Wait to continue.
            Console.WriteLine("\nMain method complete. Press Enter.");
            Console.ReadLine();
        }
    }
}
```

■ **Note** Recipe 13-1 provides more details on creating serializable types, and recipe 10-16 describes how to create remotable types.

3-3. Avoid Loading Unnecessary Assemblies into Application Domains

Problem

You need to pass an object reference across multiple application domain boundaries; however, to conserve memory and avoid impacting performance, you want to ensure that the Common Language Runtime (CLR) loads only the object's type metadata into the application domains where it is required (that is, where you will actually use the object).

Solution

Wrap the object reference in a `System.Runtime.Remoting.ObjectHandle`, and unwrap the object reference only when you need to access the object.

How It Works

When you pass an MBV object across application domain boundaries, the runtime creates a new instance of that object in the destination application domain. This means the runtime must load the assembly containing that type metadata into the application domain. Passing MBV references across intermediate application domains can result in the runtime loading unnecessary assemblies into application domains. Once loaded, these superfluous assemblies cannot be unloaded without unloading the containing application domain. (See recipe 3-9 for more information.)

The `ObjectHandle` class allows you to wrap an object reference so that you can pass it between application domains without the runtime loading additional assemblies. When the object reaches the destination application domain, you can unwrap the object reference, causing the runtime to load the required assembly and allowing you to access the object as usual.

The Code

The following code contains some simple methods that demonstrate how to wrap and unwrap a `System.Data.DataSet` using an `ObjectHandle`:

```
using System;
using System.Data;
using System.Runtime.Remoting;

namespace Apress.VisualCSharpRecipes.Chapter03
{
    class Recipe03_03
    {
        // A method to wrap a DataSet.
        public static ObjectHandle WrapDataSet(DataSet ds)
        {
            // Wrap the DataSet.
            ObjectHandle objHandle = new ObjectHandle(ds);

            // Return the wrapped DataSet.
            return objHandle;
        }

        // A method to unwrap a DataSet.
        public static DataSet UnwrapDataSet(ObjectHandle handle)
        {
            // Unwrap the DataSet.
            DataSet ds = (System.Data.DataSet)handle.Unwrap();

            // Return the wrapped DataSet.
            return ds;
        }

        public static void Main()
        {
            DataSet ds = new DataSet();
            Console.WriteLine(ds.ToString());

            ObjectHandle oh = WrapDataSet(ds);
            DataSet ds2 = UnwrapDataSet(oh);
            Console.WriteLine(ds2.ToString());

            // Wait to continue.
            Console.WriteLine("\nMain method complete. Press Enter.");
            Console.ReadLine();
        }
    }
}
```

3-4. Create a Type That Cannot Cross Application Domain Boundaries

Problem

You need to create a type so that instances of the type are inaccessible to code in other application domains.

Solution

Ensure the type is nonremotable by making sure it is not serializable and it does not derive from the `MarshalByRefObject` class.

How It Works

On occasion, you will want to ensure that instances of a type cannot transcend application domain boundaries. To create a nonremotable type, ensure that it isn't serializable and that it doesn't derive (directly or indirectly) from the `MarshalByRefObject` class. If you take these steps, you ensure that an object's state can never be accessed from outside the application domain in which the object was instantiated—such objects cannot be used as arguments or return values in cross–application domain method calls.

Ensuring that a type isn't serializable is easy because a class doesn't inherit the ability to be serialized from its parent class. To ensure that a type isn't serializable, make sure it does not have `System.SerializableAttribute` applied to the type declaration.

Ensuring that a class cannot be passed by reference requires a little more attention. Many classes in the .NET class library derive directly or indirectly from `MarshalByRefObject`; you must be careful you don't inadvertently derive your class from one of these. Commonly used base classes that derive from `MarshalByRefObject` include `System.ComponentModel.Component`, `System.IO.Stream`, `System.IO.TextReader`, `System.IO.TextWriter`, `System.NET.WebRequest`, and `System.Net.WebResponse`. (Check the .NET Framework SDK documentation on `MarshalByRefObject`. The inheritance hierarchy listed for the class provides a complete list of classes that derive from it.)

3-5. Load an Assembly into the Current Application Domain

Problem

You need to load an assembly at runtime into the current application domain.

Solution

Use the static `Load` method or the `LoadFrom` method of the `System.Reflection.Assembly` class.

How It Works

The CLR will only load the assemblies identified at build time as being referenced by your assembly when the metadata for their contained types is required. However, you can also explicitly instruct the runtime to load assemblies. The `Load` and `LoadFrom` methods both result in the runtime loading an assembly into the current application domain, and both return an `Assembly` instance that represents the newly loaded assembly. The differences between each method are the arguments you must provide to identify the assembly to load and the process that the runtime undertakes to locate the specified assembly.

The `Load` method provides overloads that allow you to specify the assembly to load using one of the following:

- A `string` containing the fully or partially qualified *display name* of the assembly
- A `System.Reflection.AssemblyName` containing details of the assembly
- A `byte` array containing the raw bytes that constitute the assembly

A fully qualified display name contains the assembly's text name, version, culture, and public key token, separated by commas (for example, `System.Data, Version=2.0.0.0, Culture=neutral, PublicKeyToken=b77a5c561934e089`). To specify an assembly that doesn't have a strong name, use `PublicKeyToken=null`. You can also specify a partial display name, but as a minimum, you must specify the assembly name (without the file extension).

In response to the `Load` call, the runtime undertakes an extensive process to locate and load the specified assembly. The following is a summary; consult the section "How the Runtime Locates Assemblies" in the .NET Framework SDK documentation for more details:

1. If you specify a strongly named assembly, the `Load` method will apply the version policy and publisher policy to enable requests for one version of an assembly to be satisfied by another version. You specify the version policy in your machine or application configuration file using `<bindingRedirect>` elements. You specify the publisher policy in special resource assemblies installed in the Global Assembly Cache (GAC).

2. Once the runtime has established the correct version of an assembly to use, it attempts to load strongly named assemblies from the GAC.

3. If the assembly is not strongly named or is not found in the GAC, the runtime looks for applicable `<codeBase>` elements in your machine and application configuration files. A `<codeBase>` element maps an assembly name to a file or a uniform resource locator (URL). If the assembly is strongly named, `<codeBase>` can refer to any location, including Internet-based URLs; otherwise, `<codeBase>` must refer to a directory relative to the application directory. If the assembly doesn't exist at the specified location, `Load` throws a `System.IO.FileNotFoundException`.

4. If no `<codeBase>` elements are relevant to the requested assembly, the runtime will locate the assembly using `probing`. Probing looks for the first file with the assembly's name (with either a `.dll` or an `.exe` extension) in the following locations:

- The application root directory
- Directories under the application root that match the assembly's name and culture
- Directories under the application root that are specified in the private `binpath`

The `Load` method is the easiest way to locate and load assemblies but can also be expensive in terms of processing if the runtime needs to start probing many directories for a weakly named assembly. The `LoadFrom` method allows you to load an assembly from a specific location. If the specified file isn't found, the runtime will throw a `FileNotFoundException`. The runtime won't attempt to locate the assembly in the same way as the `Load` method—`LoadFrom` provides no support for the GAC, policies, `<codebase>` elements, or probing.

The Code

The following code demonstrates various forms of the `Load` and `LoadFrom` methods. Notice that unlike the `Load` method, `LoadFrom` requires you to specify the extension of the assembly file.

```
using System;
using System.Reflection;
using System.Globalization;

namespace Apress.VisualCSharpRecipes.Chapter03
{
    class Recipe03_05
    {
        public static void ListAssemblies()
        {
            // Get an array of the assemblies loaded into the current
            // application domain.
            Assembly[] assemblies = AppDomain.CurrentDomain.GetAssemblies();

            foreach (Assembly a in assemblies)
            {
                Console.WriteLine(a.GetName());
            }
        }

        public static void Main()
        {
            // List the assemblies in the current application domain.
            Console.WriteLine("**** BEFORE ****");
            ListAssemblies();

            // Load the System.Data assembly using a fully qualified display name.
            string name1 = "System.Data,Version=2.0.0.0," +
                "Culture=neutral,PublicKeyToken=b77a5c561934e089";
            Assembly a1 = Assembly.Load(name1);
```

```
            // Load the System.Xml assembly using an AssemblyName.
            AssemblyName name2 = new AssemblyName();
            name2.Name = "System.Xml";
            name2.Version = new Version(2, 0, 0, 0);
            name2.CultureInfo = new CultureInfo("");    //Neutral culture.
            name2.SetPublicKeyToken(
                new byte[] {0xb7, 0x7a, 0x5c, 0x56, 0x19, 0x34, 0xe0, 0x89});
            Assembly a2 = Assembly.Load(name2);

            // Load the SomeAssembly assembly using a partial display name.
            Assembly a3 = Assembly.Load("SomeAssembly");

            // Load the assembly named c:\shared\MySharedAssembly.dll.
            Assembly a4 = Assembly.LoadFrom(@"c:\shared\MySharedAssembly.dll");

            // List the assemblies in the current application domain.
            Console.WriteLine("\n\n**** AFTER ****");
            ListAssemblies();

            // Wait to continue.
            Console.WriteLine("\nMain method complete. Press Enter.");
            Console.ReadLine();
        }
    }
}
```

3-6. Execute an Assembly in a Different Application Domain

Problem

You need to execute an assembly in an application domain other than the current one.

Solution

Call the `ExecuteAssembly` or `ExecuteAssemlyByName` method of the `AppDomain` object that represents the application domain, and specify the file name of an executable assembly.

How It Works

If you have an executable assembly that you want to load and run in an application domain, the `ExecuteAssembly` or `ExecuteAssemblyByName` methods provides the easiest solution. The `ExecuteAssembly` method provides several overloads. The simplest overload takes only a `string` containing the name of the executable assembly to run; you can specify a local file or a URL. Other overloads allow you to specify arguments to pass to the assembly's entry point (equivalent to command-line arguments).

The `ExecuteAssembly` method loads the specified assembly and executes the method defined in metadata as the assembly's entry point (usually the `Main` method). If the specified assembly isn't executable, ExecuteAssembly throws a System.MissingMethodException. The CLR doesn't start execution of the assembly in a new thread, so control won't return from the ExecuteAssembly method until the newly executed assembly exits. Because the ExecuteAssembly method loads an assembly using partial information (only the file name), the CLR won't use the GAC or probing to resolve the assembly. (See recipe 3-5 for more information.)

The ExecuteAssemblyByName method provides a similar set of overloads and takes the same argument types, but instead of taking just the file name of the executable assembly, it gets passed the display name of the assembly. This overcomes the limitations inherent in ExecuteAssembly as a result of supplying only partial names. Again, see recipe 3-5 for more information on the structure of assembly display names.

The Code

The following code demonstrates how to use the ExecuteAssembly method to load and run an assembly. The Recipe03-06 class creates an AppDomain and executes itself in that AppDomain using the ExecuteAssembly method. This results in two copies of the Recipe03-06 assembly loaded into two different application domains.

```
using System;

namespace Apress.VisualCSharpRecipes.Chapter03
{
    class Recipe03_06
    {
        public static void Main(string[] args)
        {
            // For the purpose of this example, if this assembly is executing
            // in an AppDomain with the friendly name "NewAppDomain", do not
            // create a new AppDomain. This avoids an infinite loop of
            // AppDomain creation.
            if (AppDomain.CurrentDomain.FriendlyName != "NewAppDomain")
            {
                // Create a new application domain.
                AppDomain domain = AppDomain.CreateDomain("NewAppDomain");

                // Execute this assembly in the new application domain and
                // pass the array of command-line arguments.
                domain.ExecuteAssembly("Recipe03-06.exe", args);
            }

            // Display the command-line arguments to the screen prefixed with
            // the friendly name of the AppDomain.
            foreach (string s in args)
            {
                Console.WriteLine(AppDomain.CurrentDomain.FriendlyName + " : " + s);
            }
```

```
            // Wait to continue.
            if (AppDomain.CurrentDomain.FriendlyName != "NewAppDomain")
            {
                Console.WriteLine("\nMain method complete. Press Enter.");
                Console.ReadLine();
            }
        }
    }
}
```

Usage

If you run Recipe03-06 using the following command:

```
Recipe03-06 Testing AppDomains
```

you will see that the command-line arguments are listed from both the existing and new application domains:

```
NewAppDomain : Testing

NewAppDomain : AppDomains

Recipe03-06.exe : Testing

Recipe03-06.exe : AppDomains
```

3-7. Instantiate a Type in a Different Application Domain

Problem

You need to instantiate a type in an application domain other than the current one.

Solution

Call the `CreateInstance` method or the `CreateInstanceFrom` method of the `AppDomain` object that represents the target application domain.

How It Works

The `ExecuteAssembly` method discussed in recipe 3-6 is straightforward to use, but when you are developing sophisticated applications that use application domains, you are likely to want more control over loading assemblies, instantiating types, and invoking object members within the application domain.

The `CreateInstance` and `CreateInstanceFrom` methods provide a variety of overloads that offer fine-grained control over the process of object instantiation. The simplest overloads assume the use of a type's default constructor, but both methods implement overloads that allow you to provide arguments to use any constructor.

The `CreateInstance` method loads a named assembly into the application domain using the process described for the `Assembly.Load` method in recipe 3-5. `CreateInstance` then instantiates a named type and returns a reference to the new object wrapped in an `ObjectHandle` (described in recipe 3-3). The `CreateInstanceFrom` method also instantiates a named type and returns an `ObjectHandle`-wrapped object reference; however, `CreateInstanceFrom` loads the specified assembly file into the application domain using the process described in recipe 3-5 for the `Assembly.LoadFrom` method.

`AppDomain` also provides two convenience methods named `CreateInstanceAndUnwrap` and `CreateInstanceFromAndUnwrap` that automatically extract the reference of the instantiated object from the returned `ObjectHandle` object; you must cast the returned `object` to the correct type.

■ **Caution** Be aware that if you use `CreateInstance` or `CreateInstanceFrom` to instantiate MBV types in another application domain, the object will be created, but the returned `object` reference won't refer to that object. Because of the way MBV objects cross application domain boundaries, the reference will refer to a copy of the object created automatically in the local application domain. Only if you create an MBR type will the returned reference refer to the object in the other application domain. (See recipe 3-2 for more details about MBV and MBR types.)

A common technique to simplify the management of application domains is to use a *controller class*. A controller class is a custom MBR type. You create an application domain and then instantiate your controller class in the application domain using `CreateInstance`. The controller class implements the functionality required by your application to manipulate the application domain and its contents. This could include loading assemblies, creating further application domains, cleaning up prior to deleting the application domain, or enumerating program elements (something you cannot normally do from outside an application domain). It is best to create your controller class in an assembly of its own to avoid loading unnecessary classes into each application domain. You should also be careful about what types you pass as return values from your controller to your main application domain to avoid loading additional assemblies.

The Code

The following code demonstrates how to use a simplified controller class named `PluginManager`. When instantiated in an application domain, `PluginManager` allows you to instantiate classes that implement the `IPlugin` interface, start and stop those plug-ins, and return a list of currently loaded plug-ins.

```
using System;
using System.Reflection;
using System.Collections;
```

```
using System.Collections.Generic;
using System.Collections.Specialized;

namespace Apress.VisualCSharpRecipes.Chapter03
{
    // A common interface that all plug-ins must implement.
    public interface IPlugin
    {
        void Start();
        void Stop();
    }

    // A simple IPlugin implementation to demonstrate the PluginManager
    // controller class.
    public class SimplePlugin : IPlugin
    {
        public void Start()
        {
            Console.WriteLine(AppDomain.CurrentDomain.FriendlyName +
                ": SimplePlugin starting...");
        }

        public void Stop()
        {
            Console.WriteLine(AppDomain.CurrentDomain.FriendlyName +
                ": SimplePlugin stopping...");
        }
    }

    // The controller class, which manages the loading and manipulation
    // of plug-ins in its application domain.
    public class PluginManager : MarshalByRefObject
    {
        // A Dictionary to hold keyed references to IPlugin instances.
        private Dictionary<string, IPlugin> plugins =
            new Dictionary<string, IPlugin> ();

        // Default constructor.
        public PluginManager() { }

        // Constructor that loads a set of specified plug-ins on creation.
        public PluginManager(NameValueCollection pluginList)
        {
            // Load each of the specified plug-ins.
            foreach (string plugin in pluginList.Keys)
            {
                this.LoadPlugin(pluginList[plugin], plugin);
            }
        }

        // Load the specified assembly and instantiate the specified
```

```
// IPlugin implementation from that assembly.
public bool LoadPlugin(string assemblyName, string pluginName)
{
    try
    {
        // Load the named private assembly.
        Assembly assembly = Assembly.Load(assemblyName);

        // Create the IPlugin instance, ignore case.
        IPlugin plugin = assembly.CreateInstance(pluginName, true)
            as IPlugin;

        if (plugin != null)
        {
            // Add new IPlugin to ListDictionary.
            plugins[pluginName] = plugin;

            return true;
        }
        else
        {
            return false;
        }
    }
    catch
    {
        // Return false on all exceptions for the purpose of
        // this example. Do not suppress exceptions like this
        // in production code.
        return false;
    }
}

public void StartPlugin(string plugin)
{
    try
    {
        // Extract the IPlugin from the Dictionary and call Start.
        plugins[plugin].Start();
    }
    catch
    {
        // Log or handle exceptions appropriately.
    }
}
```

```
        public void StopPlugin(string plugin)
        {
            try
            {
                // Extract the IPlugin from the Dictionary and call Stop.
                plugins[plugin].Stop();
            }
            catch
            {
                // Log or handle exceptions appropriately.
            }
        }

        public ArrayList GetPluginList()
        {
            // Return an enumerable list of plug-in names. Take the keys
            // and place them in an ArrayList, which supports marshal-by-value.
            return new ArrayList(plugins.Keys);
        }
    }

    class Recipe03_07
    {
        public static void Main()
        {
            // Create a new application domain.
            AppDomain domain1 = AppDomain.CreateDomain("NewAppDomain1");

            // Create a PluginManager in the new application domain using
            // the default constructor.
            PluginManager manager1 =
                (PluginManager)domain1.CreateInstanceAndUnwrap("Recipe03-07",
                "Apress.VisualCSharpRecipes.Chapter03.PluginManager");

            // Load a new plugin into NewAppDomain1.
            manager1.LoadPlugin("Recipe03-07",
                "Apress.VisualCSharpRecipes.Chapter03.SimplePlugin");

            // Start and stop the plug-in in NewAppDomain1.
            manager1.StartPlugin(
                "Apress.VisualCSharpRecipes.Chapter03.SimplePlugin");
            manager1.StopPlugin(
                "Apress.VisualCSharpRecipes.Chapter03.SimplePlugin");

            // Create a new application domain.
            AppDomain domain2 = AppDomain.CreateDomain("NewAppDomain2");

            // Create a ListDictionary containing a list of plug-ins to create.
            NameValueCollection pluginList = new NameValueCollection();
            pluginList["Apress.VisualCSharpRecipes.Chapter03.SimplePlugin"] =
                "Recipe03-07";
```

```
            // Create a PluginManager in the new application domain and
            // specify the default list of plug-ins to create.
            PluginManager manager2 = (PluginManager)domain1.CreateInstanceAndUnwrap(
                "Recipe03-07", "Apress.VisualCSharpRecipes.Chapter03.PluginManager",
                true, 0, null, new object[] { pluginList }, null, null);

            // Display the list of plug-ins loaded into NewAppDomain2.
            Console.WriteLine("\nPlugins in NewAppDomain2:");
            foreach (string s in manager2.GetPluginList())
            {
                Console.WriteLine(" - " + s);
            }

            // Wait to continue.
            Console.WriteLine("\nMain method complete. Press Enter.");
            Console.ReadLine();
        }
    }
}
```

3-8. Pass Data Between Application Domains

Problem

You need a simple mechanism to pass general configuration or state data between application domains.

Solution

Use the SetData and GetData methods of the AppDomain class.

How It Works

You can pass data between application domains as arguments and return values when you invoke the methods and properties of objects that exist in other application domains. However, at times it is useful to pass data between application domains in such a way that the data is easily accessible by all code within the application domain.

Every application domain maintains a data cache that contains a set of name/value pairs. Most of the cache content reflects configuration settings of the application domain, such as the values from the AppDomainSetup object provided during application domain creation. (See recipe 3-1 for more information.) You can also use this data cache as a mechanism to exchange data between application domains or as a simple state storage mechanism for code running within the application domain.

The SetData method allows you to associate a string key with an object and store it in the application domain's data cache. The GetData method allows you to retrieve an object from the data cache using the key. If code in one application domain calls the SetData method or the GetData method to access the data cache of another application domain, the data object must support MBV or MBR semantics, or a System.Runtime.Serialization.SerializationException will be thrown. (See recipe 3-3 for details on the characteristics required to allow objects to transcend application domain boundaries.)

When using the SetData or GetData methods to exchange data between application domains, you should avoid using the following keys, which are already used by the .NET Framework:

- APP_CONFIG_FILE
- APP_NAME
- APPBASE
- APP_CONFIG_BLOB
- BINPATH_PROBE_ONLY
- CACHE_BASE
- CODE_DOWNLOAD_DISABLED
- DEV_PATH
- DYNAMIC_BASE
- DISALLOW_APP
- DISALLOW_APP_REDIRECTS
- DISALLOW_APP_BASE_PROBING
- FORCE_CACHE_INSTALL
- LICENSE_FILE
- PRIVATE_BINPATH
- SHADOW_COPY_DIRS

The Code

The following example demonstrates how to use the SetData and GetData methods by passing a System.Collections.ArrayList between two application domains. After passing a list of pets to a second application domain for modification, the application displays both the original and modified lists. Notice that the code running in the second application domain does not modify the original list because ArrayList is a pass-by-value type, meaning that the second application domain only has a copy of the original list. (See recipe 3-2 for more details.)

```
using System;
using System.Reflection;
using System.Collections;

namespace Apress.VisualCSharpRecipes.Chapter03
{
    public class ListModifier
    {
```

```
        public ListModifier()
        {
            // Get the list from the data cache.
            ArrayList list = (ArrayList)AppDomain.CurrentDomain.GetData("Pets");

            // Modify the list.
            list.Add("turtle");
        }
    }

    class Recipe03_08
    {
        public static void Main()
        {
            // Create a new application domain.
            AppDomain domain = AppDomain.CreateDomain("Test");

            // Create an ArrayList and populate with information.
            ArrayList list = new ArrayList();
            list.Add("dog");
            list.Add("cat");
            list.Add("fish");

            // Place the list in the data cache of the new application domain.
            domain.SetData("Pets", list);

            // Instantiate a ListModifier in the new application domain.
            domain.CreateInstance("Recipe03-08",
                "Apress.VisualCSharpRecipes.Chapter03.ListModifier");

            // Display the contents of the original list.
            Console.WriteLine("Original list contents:");
            foreach (string s in list)
            {
                Console.WriteLine("  - " + s);
            }

            // Get the list and display its contents.
            Console.WriteLine("\nModified list contents:");
            foreach (string s in (ArrayList)domain.GetData("Pets"))
            {
                Console.WriteLine("  - " + s);
            }

            // Wait to continue.
            Console.WriteLine("\nMain method complete. Press Enter.");
            Console.ReadLine();
        }
    }
}
```

3-9. Unload Assemblies and Application Domains

Problem

You need to unload assemblies or application domains at runtime.

Solution

You have no way to unload individual assemblies from a `System.AppDomain`. You can unload an entire application domain using the static `AppDomain.Unload` method, which has the effect of unloading all assemblies loaded into the application domain.

How It Works

The only way to unload an assembly is to unload the application domain in which the assembly is loaded. Unfortunately, unloading an application domain will unload all the assemblies that have been loaded into it. This might seem like a heavy-handed and inflexible approach, but with appropriate planning of your application domain, the assembly loading structure, and the runtime dependency of your code on that application domain, it is not overly restrictive.

You unload an application domain using the static `AppDomain.Unload` method and passing it an `AppDomain` reference to the application domain you want to unload. You cannot unload the default application domain created by the CLR at startup.

The `Unload` method stops any new threads from entering the specified application domain and calls the `Thread.Abort` method on all threads currently active in the application domain. If the thread calling the `Unload` method is currently running in the specified application domain (making it the target of a `Thread.Abort` call), a new thread starts in order to carry out the unload operation. If a problem is encountered unloading an application domain, the thread performing the unload operation throws a `System.CannotUnloadAppDomainException`.

While an application domain is unloading, the CLR calls the finalization method of all objects in the application domain. Depending on the number of objects and nature of their finalization methods, this can take an variable amount of time. The `AppDomain.IsFinalizingForUnload` method returns `true` if the application domain is unloading and the CLR has started to finalize contained objects; otherwise, it returns `false`.

The Code

This code fragment demonstrates the syntax of the `Unload` method:

```
// Create a new application domain.
AppDomain newDomain = AppDomain.CreateDomain("New Domain");

// Load assemblies into the application domain.
...

// Unload the new application domain.
AppDomain.Unload(newDomain);
```

3-10. Retrieve Type Information

Problem

You need to obtain a `System.Type` object that represents a specific type.

Solution

Use one of the following:

- The `typeof` operator
- The static `GetType` method of the `System.Type` class
- The `GetType` method of an existing instance of the type
- The `GetNestedType` or `GetNestedTypes` method of the `Type` class
- The `GetType` or `GetTypes` method of the `Assembly` class
- The `GetType`, `GetTypes`, or `FindTypes` method of the `System.Reflection.Module` class

How It Works

The `Type` class provides a starting point for working with types using reflection. A `Type` object allows you to inspect the metadata of the type, obtain details of the type's members, and create instances of the type. Because of its importance, the .NET Framework provides a variety of mechanisms for obtaining references to `Type` objects.

One method of obtaining a `Type` object for a specific type is to use the `typeof` operator shown here:

```
System.Type t1 = typeof(System.Text.StringBuilder);
```

The type name is not enclosed in quotes and must be resolvable by the compiler (meaning you must reference the assembly using a compiler switch). Because the reference is resolved at compile time, the assembly containing the type becomes a static dependency of your assembly and will be listed as such in your assembly's manifest.

An alternative to the `typeof` operator is the static method `Type.GetType`, which takes a string containing the type name. Because you use a string to specify the type, you can vary it at runtime, which opens the door to a world of dynamic programming opportunities using reflection (see recipe 3-12). If you specify just the type name, the runtime must be able to locate the type in an already loaded assembly. Alternatively, you can specify an assembly-qualified type name. Refer to the .NET Framework SDK documentation for the `Type.GetType` method for a complete description of how to structure assembly-qualified type names. Table 3-2 summarizes some other methods that provide access to `Type` objects.

Table 3-2. Methods That Return Type Objects

Method	Description
`Type.GetNestedType`	Gets a specified type declared as a nested type within the existing `Type` object.
`Type.GetNestedTypes`	Gets an array of `Type` objects representing the nested types declared within the existing `Type` object.
`Assembly.GetType`	Gets a `Type` object for the specified type declared within the assembly.
`Assembly.GetTypes`	Gets an array of `Type` objects representing the types declared within the assembly.
`Module.GetType`	Gets a `Type` object for the specified type declared within the module. (See recipe 1-3 for a discussion of modules.)
`Module.GetTypes`	Gets an array of `Type` objects representing the types declared within the module.
`Module.FindTypes`	Gets a filtered array of `Type` objects representing the types declared within the module. The types are filtered using a delegate that determines whether each `Type` should appear in the final array.

The Code

The following example demonstrates how to use `typeof` and the `GetType` method to return a `Type` object for a named type and from existing objects:

```
using System;
using System.Text;

namespace Apress.VisualCSharpRecipes.Chapter03
{
    class Recipe03_10
    {
        public static void Main()
        {
            // Obtain type information using the typeof operator.
            Type t1 = typeof(StringBuilder);
            Console.WriteLine(t1.AssemblyQualifiedName);

            // Obtain type information using the Type.GetType method.
            // Case-sensitive, return null if not found.
            Type t2 = Type.GetType("System.String");
            Console.WriteLine(t2.AssemblyQualifiedName);
```

```
            // Case-sensitive, throw TypeLoadException if not found.
            Type t3 = Type.GetType("System.String", true);
            Console.WriteLine(t3.AssemblyQualifiedName);

            // Case-insensitive, throw TypeLoadException if not found.
            Type t4 = Type.GetType("system.string", true, true);
            Console.WriteLine(t4.AssemblyQualifiedName);

            // Assembly-qualifed type name.
            Type t5 = Type.GetType("System.Data.DataSet,System.Data," +
                "Version=2.0.0.0,Culture=neutral,PublicKeyToken=b77a5c561934e089");
            Console.WriteLine(t5.AssemblyQualifiedName);

            // Obtain type information using the Object.GetType method.
            StringBuilder sb = new StringBuilder();
            Type t6 = sb.GetType();
            Console.WriteLine(t6.AssemblyQualifiedName);

            // Wait to continue.
            Console.WriteLine("\nMain method complete. Press Enter.");
            Console.ReadLine();
        }
    }
}
```

3-11. Test an Object's Type

Problem

You need to test the type of an object.

Solution

Use the inherited `Object.GetType` method to obtain a `Type` for the object. You can also use the `is` and `as` operators to test an object's type.

How It Works

All types inherit the `GetType` method from the `Object` base class. As discussed in recipe 3-10, this method returns a `Type` reference representing the type of the object. The runtime maintains a single instance of `Type` for each type loaded, and all references for this type refer to this same object. This means you can compare two type references efficiently. For convenience, C# provides the `is` operator as a quick way to check whether an object is a specified type. In addition, `is` will return `true` if the tested object is derived from the specified class.

Both of these approaches require that the type used with the `typeof` and `is` operators be known and resolvable at compile time. A more flexible (but slower) alternative is to use the `Type.GetType` method to return a Type reference for a named type. The Type reference is not resolved until runtime, which causes the performance hit but allows you to change the type comparison at runtime based on the value of a string.

Finally, you can use the as operator to perform a safe cast of any object to a specified type. Unlike a standard cast, which triggers a System.InvalidCastException if the object cannot be cast to the specified type, the as operator returns null. This allows you to perform safe casts that are easy to verify, but the compared type must be resolvable at runtime.

■ **Note** The runtime will usually maintain more than one instance of each type depending on how assemblies are loaded into application domains. Usually, an assembly will be loaded into a specific application domain, meaning a Type instance will exist in each application domain in which the assembly is loaded. However, assemblies can also be loaded by a runtime host in a domain-neutral configuration, which means the assembly's type metadata (and Type instances) is shared across all application domains. By default, only the mscorlib assembly is loaded in a domain-neutral configuration.

The Code

The following example demonstrates the various type-testing alternatives described in this recipe:

```
using System;
using System.IO;

namespace Apress.VisualCSharpRecipes.Chapter03
{
    class Recipe03_11
    {
        // A method to test whether an object is an instance of a type
        // or a derived type.
        public static bool IsType(object obj, string type)
        {
            // Get the named type, use case-insensitive search, throw
            // an exception if the type is not found.
            Type t = Type.GetType(type, true, true);

            return t == obj.GetType() || obj.GetType().IsSubclassOf(t);
        }

        public static void Main()
        {
            // Create a new StringReader for testing.
            Object someObject = new StringReader("This is a StringReader");
```

```
            // Test if someObject is a StringReader by obtaining and
            // comparing a Type reference using the typeof operator.
            if (typeof(StringReader) == someObject.GetType())
            {
                Console.WriteLine("typeof: someObject is a StringReader");
            }

            // Test if someObject is, or is derived from, a TextReader
            // using the is operator.
            if (someObject is TextReader)
            {
                Console.WriteLine(
                    "is: someObject is a TextReader or a derived class");
            }

            // Test if someObject is, or is derived from, a TextReader using
            // the Type.GetType and Type.IsSubclassOf methods.
            if (IsType(someObject, "System.IO.TextReader"))
            {
                Console.WriteLine("GetType: someObject is a TextReader");
            }

            // Use the "as" operator to perform a safe cast.
            StringReader reader = someObject as StringReader;
            if (reader != null)
            {
                Console.WriteLine("as: someObject is a StringReader");
            }

            // Wait to continue.
            Console.WriteLine("\nMain method complete. Press Enter.");
            Console.ReadLine();
        }
    }
}
```

■ **Tip** The static method `GetUnderlyingType` of the `System.Enum` class allows you to retrieve the underlying type of an enumeration.

3-12. Instantiate an Object Using Reflection

Problem

You need to instantiate an object at runtime using reflection.

Solution

Obtain a Type object representing the type of object you want to instantiate, call its GetConstructor method to obtain a System.Reflection.ConstructorInfo object representing the constructor you want to use, and execute the ConstructorInfo.Invoke method.

How It Works

The first step in creating an object using reflection is to obtain a Type object that represents the type you want to instantiate. (See recipe 3-10 for details.) Once you have a Type instance, call its GetConstructor method to obtain a ConstructorInfo representing one of the type's constructors. The most commonly used overload of the GetConstructor method takes a Type array argument and returns a ConstructorInfo representing the constructor that takes the number, order, and type of arguments specified in the Type array. To obtain a ConstructorInfo representing a parameterless (default) constructor, pass an empty Type array (use the static field Type.EmptyTypes or new Type[0]); don't use null, or else GetConstructor will throw a System.ArgumentNullException. If GetConstructor cannot find a constructor with a signature that matches the specified arguments, it will return null.

Once you have the desired ConstructorInfo, call its Invoke method. You must provide an object array containing the arguments you want to pass to the constructor. Invoke instantiates the new object and returns an object reference to it, which you must cast to the appropriate type.

Reflection functionality is commonly used to implement factories in which you use reflection to instantiate concrete classes that either extend a common base class or implement a common interface. Often, both an interface and a common base class are used. The abstract base class implements the interface and any common functionality, and then each concrete implementation extends the base class.

No mechanism exists to formally declare that each concrete class must implement constructors with specific signatures. If you intend third parties to implement concrete classes, your documentation must specify the constructor signature called by your factory. A common approach to avoiding this problem is to use a default (empty) constructor and configure the object after instantiation using properties and methods.

The Code

The following code fragment demonstrates how to instantiate a System.Text.StringBuilder object using reflection and how to specify the initial content for the StringBuilder (a string) and its capacity (an int):

```
using System;
using System.Text;
using System.Reflection;

namespace Apress.VisualCSharpRecipes.Chapter03
{
    class Recipe03_12
    {
        public static StringBuilder CreateStringBuilder()
        {
```

```
            // Obtain the Type for the StringBuilder class.
            Type type = typeof(StringBuilder);

            // Create a Type[] containing Type instances for each
            // of the constructor arguments - a string and an int.
            Type[] argTypes = new Type[] { typeof(System.String),
              typeof(System.Int32) };

            // Obtain the ConstructorInfo object.
            ConstructorInfo cInfo = type.GetConstructor(argTypes);

            // Create an object[] containing the constructor arguments.
            object[] argVals = new object[] { "Some string", 30 };

            // Create the object and cast it to StringBuilder.
            StringBuilder sb = (StringBuilder)cInfo.Invoke(argVals);

            return sb;
        }
    }
}
```

The following code demonstrates a factory to instantiate objects that implement the **IPlugin** interface (first used in recipe 3-7):

```
using System;
using System.Reflection;

namespace Apress.VisualCSharpRecipes.Chapter03
{
    // A common interface that all plug-ins must implement.
    public interface IPlugin
    {
        string Description { get; set; }
        void Start();
        void Stop();
    }

    // An abstract base class from which all plug-ins must derive.
    public abstract class AbstractPlugin : IPlugin
    {
        // Hold a description for the plug-in instance.
        private string description = "";

        // Sealed property to get the plug-in description.
        public string Description
        {
            get { return description; }
            set { description = value; }
        }
```

```
        // Declare the members of the IPlugin interface as abstract.
        public abstract void Start();
        public abstract void Stop();
    }

    // A simple IPlugin implementation to demonstrate the PluginFactory class.
    public class SimplePlugin : AbstractPlugin
    {
        // Implement Start method.
        public override void Start()
        {
            Console.WriteLine(Description + ": Starting...");
        }

        // Implement Stop method.
        public override void Stop()
        {
            Console.WriteLine(Description + ": Stopping...");
        }
    }

    // A factory to instantiate instances of IPlugin.
    public sealed class PluginFactory
    {
        public static IPlugin CreatePlugin(string assembly,
            string pluginName, string description)
        {
            // Obtain the Type for the specified plug-in.
            Type type = Type.GetType(pluginName + ", " + assembly);

            // Obtain the ConstructorInfo object.
            ConstructorInfo cInfo = type.GetConstructor(Type.EmptyTypes);

            // Create the object and cast it to StringBuilder.
            IPlugin plugin = cInfo.Invoke(null) as IPlugin;

            // Configure the new IPlugin.
            plugin.Description = description;

            return plugin;
        }

        public static void Main(string[] args)
        {
            // Instantiate a new IPlugin using the PluginFactory.
            IPlugin plugin = PluginFactory.CreatePlugin(
                "Recipe03-12",  // Private assembly name
                "Apress.VisualCSharpRecipes.Chapter03.SimplePlugin",
                  // Plug-in class name.
                "A Simple Plugin"       // Plug-in instance description
            );
```

```
            // Start and stop the new plug-in.
            plugin.Start();
            plugin.Stop();

            // Wait to continue.
            Console.WriteLine("\nMain method complete. Press Enter.");
            Console.ReadLine();
        }
    }
}
```

■ **Tip** The `System.Activator` class provides two static methods named `CreateInstance` and `CreateInstanceFrom` that instantiate objects based on `Type` objects or strings containing type names. The key difference between using `GetConstructor` and `Activator` is that the constructor used by `Activator` is implied by the constructor arguments you pass to `CreateInstance` or `CreateInstanceFrom`. Using `GetConstructor`, you can determine exactly which constructor you want to use to instantiate the object. See the description of the `Activator` class in the .NET Framework SDK documentation for more details.

3-13. Create a Custom Attribute

Problem

You need to create a custom attribute.

Solution

Create a class that derives from the abstract base class `System.Attribute`. Implement constructors, fields, and properties to allow users to configure the attribute. Use `System.AttributeUsageAttribute` to define the following:

- Which program elements are valid targets of the attribute
- Whether you can apply more than one instance of the attribute to a program element
- Whether the attribute is inherited by derived types

How It Works

Attributes provide a mechanism for associating declarative information (metadata) with program elements. This metadata is contained in the compiled assembly, allowing programs to retrieve it through reflection at runtime without creating an instance of the type. (See recipe 3-14 for more details.) Other programs, particularly the CLR, use this information to determine how to interact with and manage program elements.

To create a custom attribute, derive a class from the abstract base class `System.Attribute`. Custom attribute classes by convention should have a name ending in `Attribute` (but this is not essential). A custom attribute must have at least one public constructor—the automatically generated default constructor is sufficient. The constructor parameters become the attribute's mandatory (or positional) parameters. When you use the attribute, you must provide values for these parameters in the order they appear in the constructor. As with any other class, you can declare more than one constructor, giving users of the attribute the option of using different sets of positional parameters when applying the attribute. Any public nonconstant writable fields and properties declared by an attribute are automatically exposed as named parameters. Named parameters are optional and are specified in the format of name/value pairs where the name is the property or field name. The following example will clarify how to specify positional and named parameters.

To control how and where a user can apply your attribute, apply the attribute `AttributeUsageAttribute` to your custom attribute. `AttributeUsageAttribute` supports the one positional and two named parameters described in Table 3-3. The default values specify the value that is applied to your custom attribute if you do not apply `AttributeUsageAttribute` or do not specify a value for that particular parameter.

Table 3-3. *Members of the AttributeUsage Type*

Parameter	Type	Description	Default
`ValidOn`	Positional	A member of the `System.AttributeTargets` enumeration that identifies the program elements on which the attribute is valid	`AttributeTargets.All`
`AllowMultiple`	Named	Whether the attribute can be specified more than once for a single element	`False`
`Inherited`	Named	Whether the attribute is inherited by derived classes or overridden members	`True`

The Code

The following example shows a custom attribute named `AuthorAttribute`, which you can use to identify the name and company of the person who created an assembly or a class. `AuthorAttribute` declares a single public constructor that takes a `string` containing the author's name. This means users of `AuthorAttribute` must always provide a positional `string` parameter containing the author's name. The `Company` property is public, making it an optional named parameter, but the `Name` property is read-only—no `set` accessor is declared—meaning that it isn't exposed as a named parameter.

```
using System;

namespace Apress.VisualCSharpRecipes.Chapter03
{
    [AttributeUsage(AttributeTargets.Class | AttributeTargets.Assembly,
        AllowMultiple = true, Inherited = false)]
```

```
    public class AuthorAttribute : System.Attribute
    {
        private string company; // Creator's company
        private string name;    // Creator's name

        // Declare a public constructor.
        public AuthorAttribute(string name)
        {
            this.name = name;
            company = "";
        }

        // Declare a property to get/set the company field.
        public string Company
        {
            get { return company; }
            set { company = value; }
        }

        // Declare a property to get the internal field.
        public string Name
        {
            get { return name; }
        }
    }
}
```

Usage

The following example demonstrates how to decorate types with **AuthorAttribute**:

```
using System;

// Declare Allen as the assembly author. Assembly attributes
// must be declared after using statements but before any other.
// Author name is a positional parameter.
// Company name is a named parameter.
[assembly: Apress.VisualCSharpRecipes.Chapter03.Author("Allen",
    Company = "Apress")]

namespace Apress.VisualCSharpRecipes.Chapter03
{
    // Declare a class authored by Allen.
    [Author("Allen", Company = "Apress")]
    public class SomeClass
    {
        // Class implementation.
    }
```

```
    // Declare a class authored by Lena.
    [Author("Lena")]
    public class SomeOtherClass
    {
        // Class implementation.
    }
}
```

3-14. Inspect the Attributes of a Program Element Using Reflection

Problem

You need to use reflection to inspect the custom attributes applied to a program element.

Solution

All program elements implement the `System.Reflection.ICustomAttributeProvider` interface. Call the `IsDefined` method of the `ICustomAttributeProvider` interface to determine whether an attribute is applied to a program element, or call the `GetCustomAttributes` method of the `ICustomAttributeProvider` interface to obtain objects representing the attributes applied to the program element.

How It Works

All the classes that represent program elements implement the `ICustomAttributeProvider` interface. This includes `Assembly`, `Module`, `Type`, `EventInfo`, `FieldInfo`, `PropertyInfo`, and `MethodBase`. `MethodBase` has two further subclasses: `ConstructorInfo` and `MethodInfo`. If you obtain instances of any of these classes, you can call the method `GetCustomAttributes`, which will return an `object` array containing the custom attributes applied to the program element. The `object` array contains only custom attributes, not those contained in the .NET Framework base class library.

The `GetCustomAttributes` method provides two overloads. The first takes a `bool` that controls whether `GetCustomAttributes` should return attributes inherited from parent classes. The second `GetCustomAttributes` overload takes an additional `Type` argument that acts as a filter, resulting in `GetCustomAttributes` returning only attributes of the specified type.

Alternatively, you can call the `IsDefined` method. `IsDefined` provides a single overload that takes two arguments. The first argument is a `System.Type` object representing the type of attribute you are interested in, and the second is a `bool` that indicates whether `IsDefined` should look for inherited attributes of the specified type. `IsDefined` returns a `bool` indicating whether the specified attribute is applied to the program element, and is less expensive than calling the `GetCustomAttributes` method, which actually instantiates the attribute objects.

The Code

The following example uses the custom AuthorAttribute declared in recipe 3-13 and applies it to the Recipe03-14 class. The Main method calls the GetCustomAttributes method, filtering the attributes so that the method returns only AuthorAttribute instances. You can safely cast this set of attributes to AuthorAttribute references and access their members without needing to use reflection.

```
using System;

namespace Apress.VisualCSharpRecipes.Chapter03
{
    [Author("Lena")]
    [Author("Allen", Company = "Apress")]
    class Recipe03_15
    {
        public static void Main()
        {
            // Get a Type object for this class.
            Type type = typeof(Recipe03_15);

            // Get the attributes for the type. Apply a filter so that only
            // instances of AuthorAttribute are returned.
            object[] attrs =
                type.GetCustomAttributes(typeof(AuthorAttribute), true);

            // Enumerate the attributes and display their details.
            foreach (AuthorAttribute a in attrs) {
                Console.WriteLine(a.Name + ", " + a.Company);
            }

            // Wait to continue.
            Console.WriteLine("\nMain method complete. Press Enter.");
            Console.ReadLine();
        }
    }
}
```

3-15. Programmatically Discover the Members of a Type

Problem

You need to determine the members of a type at runtime.

Solution

Obtain the System.Type for the type you need to reflect on, and call the GetMembers method to get information about all of the members of the type, or call the GetConstructors, GetMethods, and GetProperties methods to get information about specific categories of a member.

How It Works

You can get details of the members of a given type through the System.Type class. You can get an instance of Type by calling the GetType method on any object or by using the typeof keyword. Once you have a Type instance, the GetMembers method returns information about all members, while the GetConstructors, GetMethods, and GetProperties methods return just constructors, methods, and properties, respectively. The Type class also contains methods to get less commonly used member types (such as events) and interfaces that the type implements.

The GetMembers method returns an array of System.Reflection.MemberInfo instances, one for each member in the type you are reflecting on. You can differentiate between different categories of member using the MemberInfo.MemberType property, as shown by the following fragment:

```
MemberInfo[] members = myType.GetMembers();
foreach (MemberInfo member in members)
{
    switch (member.MemberType)
    {
        case MemberTypes.Constructor:
            // Do something.
            break;
        case MemberTypes.Method:
            // Do something.
            break;
    }
}
```

The other System.Type methods return arrays of classes from the System.Reflection namespace specific to the member category—for example, GetConstructors returns an array of System.Reflection.ConstructorInfo and GetMethods returns an array of System.Reflection.MethodInfo.

The Code

The following example uses reflection on its own type to enumerate the constructors, methods and properties.

```
using System;
using System.Collections.Generic;
using System.Linq;
using System.Text;
using System.Reflection;
```

```
namespace Apress.VisualCSharpRecipes.Chapter03
{
    class Recipe03_15
    {
        static void Main(string[] args)
        {

            // Get the type we are interested in.
            Type myType = typeof(Recipe03_15);

            // Get the constructor details.
            Console.WriteLine("\nConstructors...");
            foreach (ConstructorInfo constr in myType.GetConstructors())
            {
                Console.Write("Constructor: ");
                // Get the paramters for this constructor.
                foreach (ParameterInfo param in constr.GetParameters())
                {
                    Console.Write("{0} ({1}), ", param.Name, param.ParameterType);
                }
                Console.WriteLine();
            }

            // Get the method details.
            Console.WriteLine("\nMethods...");
            foreach (MethodInfo method in myType.GetMethods())
            {
                Console.Write(method.Name);
                // Get the paramters for this constructor.
                foreach (ParameterInfo param in method.GetParameters())
                {
                    Console.Write("{0} ({1}), ", param.Name, param.ParameterType);
                }
                Console.WriteLine();
            }

            // Get the property details.
            Console.WriteLine("\nProperty...");
            foreach (PropertyInfo property in myType.GetProperties())
            {
                Console.Write("{0} ", property.Name);
                // Get the paramters for this constructor.
                foreach (MethodInfo accessor in property.GetAccessors())
                {
                    Console.Write("{0}, ", accessor.Name);
                }
                Console.WriteLine();
            }
```

```
            // Wait to continue.
            Console.WriteLine("\nMain method complete. Press Enter.");
            Console.ReadLine();
        }

        public string MyProperty
        {
            get;
            set;
        }

        public Recipe03_15(string param1, int param2, char param3)
        {

        }
    }
}
```

3-16. Invoke a Type Member Using Reflection

Problem

You need to invoke a method on a type.

Solution

Use the `InvokeMember` method of `System.Type` or the `Invoke` method on the `MemberInfo` class or its derived types (`MethodInfo`, `PropertyInfo`, etc.).

How It Works

You can call a member directly on a `Type`, using the `InvokeMember` method, to which you must supply the name of the method you wish to call, the instance of the type you wish to call against, and an array of objects containing the parameters you wish to pass to the member. You must also provide a value from the `BindingFlags` enumeration that specifies what kind of call should be made—values exist for invoking a method (`BindingFlags.InvokeMethod`), getting and setting properties (`BindingFlags.GetProperty` and `BindingFlags.SetProperty`), and so on.

You can obtain an instance of `MemberInfo` or one of its derived types (such as `MethodInfo` for methods, `PropertyInfo` for properties, etc.) and call the `Invoke` method. See the code for this recipe for an example of both approaches.

The Code

The following example calls a method using the `InvokeMember` method of `System.Type` and calls it again through the `MemberInfo` class:

```
using System;
using System.Reflection;

namespace Apress.VisualCSharpRecipes.Chapter03
{
    class Recipe03_16
    {
        static void Main(string[] args)
        {

            // Create an instance of this type.
            object myInstance = new Recipe03_16();

            // Get the type we are interested in.
            Type myType = typeof(Recipe03_16);

            // Get the method information.
            MethodInfo methodInfo = myType.GetMethod("printMessage",
                new Type[] { typeof(string), typeof(int), typeof(char) });

            // Invoke the method using the instance we created.
            myType.InvokeMember("printMessage", BindingFlags.InvokeMethod,
                null, myInstance, new object[] { "hello", 37, 'c' });

            methodInfo.Invoke(null, BindingFlags.InvokeMethod, null,
                new object[] { "hello", 37, 'c' }, null);

            // Wait to continue.
            Console.WriteLine("\nMain method complete. Press Enter.");
            Console.ReadLine();
        }

        public static void printMessage(string param1, int param2, char param3)
        {
            Console.WriteLine("PrintMessage {0} {1} {2}", param1, param2, param3);
        }
    }
}
```

Running the program gives the following results:

```
PrintMessage hello 37 c

PrintMessage hello 37 c

PrintMessage hello 37 c


Main method complete. Press Enter.
```

3-17. Dynamically Invoke a Type Member

Problem

You want to invoke a member dynamically.

Solution

Declare your object using the special type `dynamic`.

How It Works

Recipe 3-16 illustrated how to use reflection to invoke a member on a type. An alternative approach to the same problem is to use the dynamic runtime support introduced in .NET 4.0. The net results are the same—you are responsible for ensuring that the member you want to call exists and that your parameters are of the right type—but the source code required to invoke the member is much simpler.

Simply declare your object as the special type `dynamic` and then invoke the members directly—the C# compiler will not check to see that the member you have called exists or that you have supplied the correct parameters. See the code for this recipe for an illustration.

The Code

The following example calls the same method as in the previous recipe, but does so dynamically:

```
using System;
using System.Collections.Generic;
using System.Linq;
using System.Text;
using System.Reflection;
```

```
namespace Apress.VisualCSharpRecipes.Chapter03
{
    class Recipe03_17
    {
        static void Main(string[] args)
        {
            // Create an instance of this type.
            dynamic myInstance = new Recipe03_17();

            // Call the method dynamically.
            myInstance.printMessage("hello", 37, 'c');

            // Wait to continue.
            Console.WriteLine("\nMain method complete. Press Enter.");
            Console.ReadLine();
        }

        public void printMessage(string param1, int param2, char param3)
        {
            Console.WriteLine("PrintMessage {0} {1} {2}", param1, param2, param3);
        }
    }
}
```

3-18. Create a Custom Dynamic Type

Problem

You need to create a type with custom behavior when dynamic member invocations are performed.

Solution

Extend the `System.Dynamic.DynamicObject` class and override one or more of the instance methods in that class that begin with `Try`, such as `TrySetMember` and `TryGetMember`.

How It Works

The previous recipe showed how to invoke a method dynamically. The `System.Dynamic.DynamicObject` class puts you on the other side of that equation and allows you to create a dynamic type with custom behavior.

When deriving a type from `DynamicObject`, you can implement members as you would usually and override one or more of the `Try`*`XXX`* methods, such as `TrySetMember` and `TryGetMember`. When you instantiate and call a member of your type, the runtime will look for a member you have implemented, and if it cannot find one, it will call the appropriate `Try`*`XXX`* method. Table 3-4 lists the `Try`*`XXX`* methods.

Table 3-4. Useful Methods from the System.Dynamic.DynamicObject Class

Method	Description
TryBinaryOperation	Called for binary operations such as addition and multiplication
TryConvert	Called for operations that convert from one type to another
TryCreateInstance	Called when the type is instantiated
TryGetIndex	Called when a value is requested via an array-style index
TryGetMember	Called when a value is requested via a property
TryInvokeMember	Called when a method is invoked
TrySetIndex	Called when a value is set via an array-style index
TrySetMember	Called when a property value is set

Each of the Try*XXX* methods defines arguments that allow you to determine what member the caller has called and the arguments or values that have been passed to you. For example, to implement custom behavior for getting a property value, we would implement the TryGetMember method, which is declared as follows:

```
public override bool TryGetMember(GetMemberBinder binder, out object result)
```

The GetMemberBinder class provides us with information about the property that the caller has requested—the most useful member being Name, which returns the name of the property that the caller wants—remember that dynamic types allow the caller to request any property, not just the ones we have implemented. You set the value of the result parameter to whatever you want to return to the caller and use the bool returned from the method to indicate whether you are willing to support the property that has been requested. For example, the following fragment uses the GetMemberBinder parameter to determine which property the caller has asked for, and will only return a value for those properties that begin with the letter *a*:

```
public override bool TryGetMember(GetMemberBinder binder, out object result)
{
    if (binder.Name.StartsWith("A"))
    {
       result = "Hello";
        return true;
    } else {
        result = null;
        return false;
    }
}
```

Returning `false` from a `TryXXX` method will cause a runtime exception to be thrown to the caller—see the example code for this recipe for an example of this. Note that you must assign a value to the `result` parameter even if you are returning `false` from the method.

You must declare an instance of your type using the `dynamic` keyword—if you do not, the compiler will perform static checking, and you will only be able to access the members you have defined and the `TryXXX` members of the `DynamicObject` class.

The Code

The following example extends the `DynamicObject` class to create a wrapper around a dictionary such that calls to `get` and `set` properties on the `dynamic` type are mapped to the key/value pairs contained in the dictionary:

```
using System;
using System.Collections.Generic;
using System.Linq;
using System.Text;
using System.Reflection;
using System.Dynamic;

namespace Apress.VisualCSharpRecipes.Chapter03
{
    class Recipe03_18
    {
        static void Main(string[] args)
        {

            dynamic dynamicDict = new MyDynamicDictionary();
            // Set some properties.
            Console.WriteLine("Setting property values");
            dynamicDict.FirstName = "Adam";
            dynamicDict.LastName = "Freeman";

            // Get some properties.
            Console.WriteLine("\nGetting property values");
            Console.WriteLine("Firstname {0}", dynamicDict.FirstName);
            Console.WriteLine("Lastname {0}", dynamicDict.LastName);

            // Call an implemented member.
            Console.WriteLine("\nGetting a static property");
            Console.WriteLine("Count {0}", dynamicDict.Count);

            Console.WriteLine("\nGetting a non-existent property");
            try
            {
                Console.WriteLine("City {0}", dynamicDict.City);
            }
```

```
            catch (Microsoft.CSharp.RuntimeBinder.RuntimeBinderException e)
            {
                Console.WriteLine("Caught exception");
            }

            // Wait to continue.
            Console.WriteLine("\nMain method complete. Press Enter.");
            Console.ReadLine();
        }
    }
    class MyDynamicDictionary : DynamicObject
    {
        private IDictionary<string, object> dict = new Dictionary<string, object>();

        public int Count
        {
            get
            {
                Console.WriteLine("Get request for Count property");
                return dict.Count;
            }
        }

        public override bool TryGetMember(GetMemberBinder binder, out object result)
        {
            Console.WriteLine("Get request for {0}", binder.Name);
            return dict.TryGetValue(binder.Name, out result);
        }

        public override bool TrySetMember(SetMemberBinder binder, object value)
        {
            Console.WriteLine("Set request for {0}, value {1}", binder.Name, value);
            dict[binder.Name] = value;
            return true;
        }

    }
}
```

Running the example gives the following results:

```
Setting property values
Set request for FirstName, value Adam
Set request for LastName, value Freeman

Getting property values
Get request for FirstName
Firstname Adam
Get request for LastName
Lastname Freeman

Getting a static property
Get request for Count property
Count 2

Getting a non-existent property
Get request for City
Caught exception

Main method complete. Press Enter.
```

CHAPTER 4

■ ■ ■

Threads, Processes, and Synchronization

One of the strengths of the Microsoft Windows operating system is that it allows many programs (processes) to run concurrently and allows each process to perform many tasks concurrently (using multiple threads). When you run an executable application, a new process is created. The process isolates your application from other programs running on the computer. The process provides the application with its own virtual memory and its own copies of any libraries it needs to run, allowing your application to execute as if it were the only application running on the machine.

Along with the process, an initial thread is created that runs your `Main` method. In single-threaded applications, this one thread steps through your code and sequentially performs each instruction. If an operation takes time to complete, such as reading a file from the Internet or doing a complex calculation, the application will be unresponsive (will *block*) until the operation is finished, at which point the thread will continue with the next operation in your program.

To avoid blocking, the main thread can create additional threads and specify which code each should start running. As a result, many threads may be running in your application's process, each running (potentially) different code and performing different operations seemingly simultaneously. In reality, unless you have multiple processors (or a single multicore processor) in your computer, the threads are not really running simultaneously. Instead, the operating system coordinates and schedules the execution of all threads across all processes; each thread is given a tiny portion (or `time slice`) of the processor's time, which gives the impression they are executing at the same time.

The difficulty of having multiple threads executing within your application arises when those threads need to access shared data and resources. If multiple threads are changing an object's state or writing to a file at the same time, your data will quickly become corrupt. To avoid problems, you must synchronize the threads to make sure they each get a chance to access the resource, but only one at a time. Synchronization is also important when waiting for a number of threads to reach a certain point of execution before proceeding with a different task, and for controlling the number of threads that are at any given time actively performing a task—perhaps processing requests from client applications.

.NET 4.0 includes two mechanisms for creating multithreaded applications. The "classic" approach is the one that has been included in .NET since version 1.0, in which the programmer takes responsibility for creating and managing threads directly. The Task Parallel Library is newly added and manages threads automatically but reduces the developer's control over the application.

For information about the Task Parallel Library, please see Chapter 15. This chapter describes how to control processes and threads using the classic techniques, which are more complex, but offer a greater degree of control. Specifically, the recipes in this chapter describe how to do the following:

- Execute code in independent threads using features including the thread pool, asynchronous method invocation, and timers (recipes 4-1 through 4-6)
- Synchronize the execution of multiple threads using a host of synchronization techniques including monitors, events, mutexes, and semaphores (recipes 4-7 and 4-11)
- Terminate threads and know when threads have terminated (recipes 4-12 and 4-13)
- Create thread-safe instances of the .NET collection classes (recipe 4-14)
- Start and stop applications running in new processes (recipes 4-15 and 4-16)
- Ensure that only one instance of an application is able to run at any given time (recipe 4-17)

As you will see in this chapter, delegates are used extensively in multithreaded programs to wrap the method that a thread should execute or that should act as a callback when an asynchronous operation is complete. Prior to C# 2.0, it was necessary to

1. Declare a method that matches the signature of the required delegate
2. Create a delegate instance of the required type by passing it the name of the method
3. Pass the delegate instance to the new thread or asynchronous operation

C# 2.0 added two important new features that simplify the code you must write when using delegates:

- First, you no longer need to create a delegate instance to wrap the method you want to execute. You can pass a method name where a delegate is expected, and as long as the method signature is correct, the compiler infers the need for the delegate and creates it automatically. This is a compiler enhancement only—the intermediate language (IL) generated is as if the appropriate delegate had been instantiated. Recipes 4-1 and 4-2 (along with many others) demonstrate how to use this capability.
- Second, you no longer need to explicitly declare a method for use with the delegate. Instead, you can provide an anonymous method wherever a delegate is required. In effect, you actually write the method code at the point where you would usually pass the method name (or delegate instance). The only difference is that you use the keyword `delegate` instead of giving the method a name. This approach can reduce the need to implement methods solely for use as callbacks and event handlers, which reduces code clutter, but it can quickly become confusing if the anonymous method is longer than a couple of lines of code. Recipes 4-3 and 4-4 demonstrate how to use anonymous methods.

4-1. Execute a Method Using the Thread Pool

Problem

You need to execute a task using a thread from the runtime's thread pool.

Solution

Declare a method containing the code you want to execute. The method's signature must match that defined by the `System.Threading.WaitCallback` delegate; that is, it must return `void` and take a single `object` argument. Call the static method `QueueUserWorkItem` of the `System.Threading.ThreadPool` class, passing it your method name. The runtime will queue your method and execute it when a thread-pool thread becomes available.

How It Works

Applications that use many short-lived threads or maintain large numbers of concurrent threads can suffer performance degradation because of the overhead associated with the creation, operation, and destruction of threads. In addition, it is common in multithreaded systems for threads to sit idle a large portion of the time while they wait for the appropriate conditions to trigger their execution. Using a thread pool provides a common solution to improve the scalability, efficiency, and performance of multithreaded systems.

The .NET Framework provides a simple thread-pool implementation accessible through the members of the `ThreadPool` static class. The `QueueUserWorkItem` method allows you to execute a method using a thread-pool thread by placing a work item on a queue. As a thread from the thread pool becomes available, it takes the next work item from the queue and executes it. The thread performs the work assigned to it, and when it is finished, instead of terminating, the thread returns to the thread pool and takes the next work item from the work queue.

■ **Tip** If you need to execute a method with a signature that does not match the `WaitCallback` delegate, then you must use one of the other techniques described in this chapter. See recipe 4-2 or 4-6.

The Code

The following example demonstrates how to use the `ThreadPool` class to execute a method named `DisplayMessage`. The example passes `DisplayMessage` to the thread pool twice, first with no arguments and then with a `MessageInfo` object, which allows you to control which message the new thread will display:

```
using System;
using System.Threading;

namespace Apress.VisualCSharpRecipes.Chapter04
{
    class Recipe04_01
    {
        // A private class used to pass data to the DisplayMessage method when it is
        // executed using the thread pool.
        private class MessageInfo
        {
            private int iterations;
            private string message;

            // A constructor that takes configuration settings for the thread.
            public MessageInfo(int iterations, string message)
            {
                this.iterations = iterations;
                this.message = message;
            }

            // Properties to retrieve configuration settings.
            public int Iterations { get { return iterations; } }
            public string Message { get { return message; } }
        }

        // A method that conforms to the System.Threading.WaitCallback delegate
        // signature. Displays a message to the console.
        public static void DisplayMessage(object state)
        {
            // Safely cast the state argument to a MessageInfo object.
            MessageInfo config = state as MessageInfo;

            // If the config argument is null, no arguments were passed to
            // the ThreadPool.QueueUserWorkItem method; use default values.
            if (config == null)
            {
                // Display a fixed message to the console three times.
                for (int count = 0; count < 3; count++)
                {
                    Console.WriteLine("A thread pool example.");

                    // Sleep for the purpose of demonstration. Avoid sleeping
                    // on thread-pool threads in real applications.
                    Thread.Sleep(1000);
                }

            }
            else
            {
```

```
                // Display the specified message the specified number of times.
                for (int count = 0; count < config.Iterations; count++)
                {
                    Console.WriteLine(config.Message);

                    // Sleep for the purpose of demonstration. Avoid sleeping
                    // on thread-pool threads in real applications.
                    Thread.Sleep(1000);
                }
            }
        }

        public static void Main()
        {
            // Execute DisplayMessage using the thread pool and no arguments.
            ThreadPool.QueueUserWorkItem(DisplayMessage);

            // Create a MessageInfo object to pass to the DisplayMessage method.
            MessageInfo info = new MessageInfo(5,
                "A thread pool example with arguments.");

            // Set the max number of threads.
            ThreadPool.SetMaxThreads(2, 2);

            // Execute DisplayMessage using the thread pool and providing an
            // argument.
            ThreadPool.QueueUserWorkItem(DisplayMessage, info);

            // Wait to continue.
            Console.WriteLine("Main method complete. Press Enter.");
            Console.ReadLine();
        }
    }
}
```

Notes

Using the runtime's thread pool simplifies multithreaded programming dramatically; however, be aware that the implementation is a simple, general-purpose thread pool. Before deciding to use the thread pool, consider the following points:

- Each process has one thread pool, which supports by default a maximum of 25 concurrent threads per processor. You can change the maximum number of threads using the method `ThreadPool.SetMaxThreads`, but some runtime hosts (Internet Information Services [IIS] and SQL Server, for example) will limit the maximum number of threads and may not allow the default value to be changed at all.

- As well as allowing you to use the thread pool to execute code directly, the runtime uses the thread pool for other purposes internally. This includes the asynchronous execution of methods (see recipe 4-2), execution of timer events (see recipes 4-3 and 4-4), and execution of wait-based methods (see recipe 4-5). All of these uses can lead to heavy contention for the thread-pool threads, meaning that the work queue can become very long. Although the work queue's maximum length is limited only by the amount of memory available to the runtime's process, an excessively long queue will result in long delays before queued work items are executed. The `ThreadPool.GetAvailableThreads` method returns the number of threads currently available in the thread pool. This can be useful in determining whether your application is placing too much load on the thread pool, indicating that you should increase the number of available threads using the `ThreadPool.SetMaxThreads` method.
- Where possible, avoid using the thread pool to execute long-running processes. The limited number of threads in the thread pool means that a handful of threads tied up with long-running processes can significantly affect the overall performance of the thread pool. Specifically, you should avoid putting thread-pool threads to sleep for any length of time.
- Thread-pool threads are background threads. You can configure threads as either foreground threads or background threads. Foreground and background threads are identical except that a background thread will not keep an application process alive. Therefore, your application will terminate automatically when the last foreground thread of your application terminates.
- You have no control over the scheduling of thread-pool threads, and you cannot prioritize work items. The thread pool handles each work item in the sequence in which you add it to the work queue.
- Once a work item is queued, it cannot be canceled or stopped.
- Do not try to use thread-pool threads to directly update or manipulate Windows Forms controls, because they can be updated only by the thread that created them. Instead, use the controls' `Dispatcher` property—see the .NET Framework documentation for details.

4-2. Execute a Method Asynchronously

Problem

You need to start execution of a method and continue with other tasks while the method runs on a separate thread. After the method completes, you need to retrieve the method's return value.

Solution

Declare a delegate with the same signature as the method you want to execute. Create an instance of the delegate that references the method. Call the `BeginInvoke` method of the delegate instance to start executing your method. Use the EndInvoke method to determine the method's status as well as obtain the method's return value if complete.

How It Works

Typically, when you invoke a method, you do so synchronously, meaning that the calling code blocks until the method is complete. Most of the time, this is the expected, desired behavior because your code requires the operation to complete before it can continue. However, sometimes it is useful to execute a method asynchronously, meaning that you start the method in a separate thread and then continue with other operations.

The .NET Framework implements an asynchronous execution pattern that allows you to call any method asynchronously using a delegate. When you declare and compile a delegate, the compiler automatically generates two methods that support asynchronous execution: BeginInvoke and EndInvoke. When you call BeginInvoke on a delegate instance, the method referenced by the delegate is queued for asynchronous execution. Control returns to the caller immediately, and the referenced method executes in the context of the first available thread-pool thread.

The signature of the BeginInvoke method includes the same arguments as those specified by the delegate signature, followed by two additional arguments to support asynchronous completion. These additional arguments are as follows:

- A System.AsyncCallback delegate instance that references a method that the runtime will call when the asynchronous method completes. The method will be executed by a thread-pool thread. Passing null means no method is called and means you must use another mechanism (discussed later in this recipe) to determine when the asynchronous method is complete.
- A reference to an object that the runtime associates with the asynchronous operation for you. The asynchronous method does not use or have access to this object, but it is available to your code when the method completes, allowing you to associate useful state information with an asynchronous operation. For example, this object allows you to map results against initiated operations in situations where you initiate many asynchronous operations that use a common callback method to perform completion.

The EndInvoke method allows you to retrieve the return value of a method that was executed asynchronously, but you must first determine when it has finished. If your asynchronous method threw an exception, it will be rethrown so that you can handle it when you call EndInvoke. Here are the four techniques for determining whether an asynchronous method has finished:

- *Blocking* stops the execution of the current thread until the asynchronous method completes execution. In effect, this is much the same as synchronous execution. However, you have the flexibility to decide exactly when your code enters the blocked state, giving you the opportunity to perform some additional processing before blocking.

- *Polling* involves repeatedly testing the state of an asynchronous method to determine whether it is complete. This is a simple technique and is not particularly efficient from a processing perspective. You should avoid tight loops that consume processor time; it is best to put the polling thread to sleep for a period using `Thread.Sleep` between completion tests. Because polling involves maintaining a loop, the actions of the waiting thread are limited, but you can easily update some kind of progress indicator.
- *Waiting* depends on the `AsyncWaitHandle` property of the `IAsyncResult` returned by `BeginInvoke`. This object derives from the `System.Threading.WaitHandle` class signals when the asynchronous method completes. Waiting is a more efficient version of polling, and in addition allows you to wait for multiple asynchronous methods to complete. You can also specify timeout values to allow your waiting thread to notify a failure if the asynchronous method takes too long or if you want to periodically update a status indicator.
- A *callback* is a method that the runtime calls when an asynchronous operation completes. The calling code does not have to take any steps to determine when the asynchronous method is complete and is free to continue with other processing. Callbacks provide the greatest flexibility but also introduce the greatest complexity, especially if you have many asynchronous operations active concurrently that all use the same callback. In such cases, you must use appropriate state objects as the last parameter of `BeginInvoke` to match the completed methods against those you initiated.

■ **Caution** Even if you do not want to handle the return value of your asynchronous method, you should call `EndInvoke`; otherwise, you risk leaking memory each time you initiate an asynchronous call using `BeginInvoke`.

The Code

The following code demonstrates how to use the asynchronous execution pattern. It uses a delegate named `AsyncExampleDelegate` to execute a method named `LongRunningMethod` asynchronously. `LongRunningMethod` simulates a long-running method using a configurable delay (produced using `Thread.Sleep`). The example contains the following five methods, which demonstrate the various approaches to handling asynchronous method completion:

- The `BlockingExample` method executes `LongRunningMethod` asynchronously and continues with a limited set of processing. Once this processing is complete, `BlockingExample` blocks until `LongRunningMethod` completes. To block, `BlockingExample` calls the `EndInvoke` method of the `AsyncExampleDelegate` delegate instance. If `LongRunningMethod` has already finished, `EndInvoke` returns immediately; otherwise, `BlockingExample` blocks until `LongRunningMethod` completes.

- The `PollingExample` method executes `LongRunningMethod` asynchronously and then enters a polling loop until `LongRunningMethod` completes. `PollingExample` tests the `IsCompleted` property of the `IAsyncResult` instance returned by `BeginInvoke` to determine whether `LongRunningMethod` is complete; otherwise, `PollingExample` calls `Thread.Sleep`.
- The `WaitingExample` method executes `LongRunningMethod` asynchronously and then waits until `LongRunningMethod` completes. `WaitingExample` uses the `AsyncWaitHandle` property of the `IAsyncResult` instance returned by `BeginInvoke` to obtain a `WaitHandle` and then calls its `WaitOne` method. Using a timeout allows `WaitingExample` to break out of waiting in order to perform other processing or to fail completely if the asynchronous method is taking too long.
- The `WaitAllExample` method executes `LongRunningMethod` asynchronously multiple times and then uses an array of `WaitHandle` objects to wait efficiently until all the methods are complete.
- The `CallbackExample` method executes `LongRunningMethod` asynchronously and passes an `AsyncCallback` delegate instance (that references the `CallbackHandler` method) to the `BeginInvoke` method. The referenced `CallbackHandler` method is called automatically when the asynchronous `LongRunningMethod` completes, leaving the `CallbackExample` method free to continue processing.

■ **Note** For the purpose of demonstrating the various synchronization techniques, the example performs several tasks that should be avoided when using the thread pool, including putting thread-pool threads to sleep and calling long-running methods. See recipe 4-1 for more suggestions on using the thread pool appropriately.

```
using System;
using System.Threading;
using System.Collections;

namespace Apress.VisualCSharpRecipes.Chapter04
{
    class Recipe04_02
    {
        // A utility method for displaying useful trace information to the
        // console along with details of the current thread.
        private static void TraceMsg(DateTime time, string msg)
        {
            Console.WriteLine("[{0,3}/{1}] - {2} : {3}",
                Thread.CurrentThread.ManagedThreadId,
                Thread.CurrentThread.IsThreadPoolThread ? "pool" : "fore",
                time.ToString("HH:mm:ss.ffff"), msg);
        }

        // A delegate that allows you to perform asynchronous execution of
        // LongRunningMethod.
```

```
public delegate DateTime AsyncExampleDelegate(int delay, string name);

// A simulated long-running method.
public static DateTime LongRunningMethod(int delay, string name)
{
    TraceMsg(DateTime.Now, name + " example - thread starting.");

    // Simulate time-consuming processing.
    Thread.Sleep(delay);

    TraceMsg(DateTime.Now, name + " example - thread stopping.");

    // Return the method's completion time.
    return DateTime.Now;
}

// This method executes LongRunningMethod asynchronously and continues
// with other processing. Once the processing is complete, the method
// blocks until LongRunningMethod completes.
public static void BlockingExample()
{
    Console.WriteLine(Environment.NewLine +
        "*** Running Blocking Example ***");

    // Invoke LongRunningMethod asynchronously. Pass null for both the
    // callback delegate and the asynchronous state object.
    AsyncExampleDelegate longRunningMethod = LongRunningMethod;

    IAsyncResult asyncResult = longRunningMethod.BeginInvoke(2000,
        "Blocking", null, null);

    // Perform other processing until ready to block.
    for (int count = 0; count < 3; count++)
    {
        TraceMsg(DateTime.Now,
            "Continue processing until ready to block...");

        Thread.Sleep(200);
    }

    // Block until the asynchronous method completes.
    TraceMsg(DateTime.Now,
        "Blocking until method is complete...");

    // Obtain the completion data for the asynchronous method.
    DateTime completion = DateTime.MinValue;

    try
    {
        completion = longRunningMethod.EndInvoke(asyncResult);
    }
```

```
    catch
    {
        // Catch and handle those exceptions you would if calling
        // LongRunningMethod directly.
    }

    // Display completion information.
    TraceMsg(completion,"Blocking example complete.");
}

// This method executes LongRunningMethod asynchronously and then
// enters a polling loop until LongRunningMethod completes.
public static void PollingExample()
{
    Console.WriteLine(Environment.NewLine +
        "*** Running Polling Example ***");

    // Invoke LongRunningMethod asynchronously. Pass null for both the
    // callback delegate and the asynchronous state object.
    AsyncExampleDelegate longRunningMethod = LongRunningMethod;

    IAsyncResult asyncResult = longRunningMethod.BeginInvoke(2000,
        "Polling", null, null);

    // Poll the asynchronous method to test for completion. If not
    // complete, sleep for 300 ms before polling again.
    TraceMsg(DateTime.Now, "Poll repeatedly until method is complete.");

    while (!asyncResult.IsCompleted)
    {
        TraceMsg(DateTime.Now, "Polling...");
        Thread.Sleep(300);
    }

    // Obtain the completion data for the asynchronous method.
    DateTime completion = DateTime.MinValue;

    try
    {
        completion = longRunningMethod.EndInvoke(asyncResult);
    }
    catch
    {
        // Catch and handle those exceptions you would if calling
        // LongRunningMethod directly.
    }

    // Display completion information.
    TraceMsg(completion, "Polling example complete.");
}
```

```
// This method executes LongRunningMethod asynchronously and then
// uses a WaitHandle to wait efficiently until LongRunningMethod
// completes. Use of a timeout allows the method to break out of
// waiting in order to update the user interface or fail if the
// asynchronous method is taking too long.
public static void WaitingExample()
{
    Console.WriteLine(Environment.NewLine +
        "*** Running Waiting Example ***");

    // Invoke LongRunningMethod asynchronously. Pass null for both the
    // callback delegate and the asynchronous state object.
    AsyncExampleDelegate longRunningMethod = LongRunningMethod;

    IAsyncResult asyncResult = longRunningMethod.BeginInvoke(2000,
        "Waiting", null, null);

    // Wait for the asynchronous method to complete. Time out after
    // 300 ms and display status to the console before continuing to
    // wait.
    TraceMsg(DateTime.Now, "Waiting until method is complete...");

    while (!asyncResult.AsyncWaitHandle.WaitOne(300, false))
    {
        TraceMsg(DateTime.Now, "Wait timeout...");
    }

    // Obtain the completion data for the asynchronous method.
    DateTime completion = DateTime.MinValue;

    try
    {
        completion = longRunningMethod.EndInvoke(asyncResult);
    }
    catch
    {
        // Catch and handle those exceptions you would if calling
        // LongRunningMethod directly.
    }

    // Display completion information.
    TraceMsg(completion, "Waiting example complete.");
}

// This method executes LongRunningMethod asynchronously multiple
// times and then uses an array of WaitHandle objects to wait
// efficiently until all of the methods are complete. Use of
// a timeout allows the method to break out of waiting in order
// to update the user interface or fail if the asynchronous
// method is taking too long.
```

```
public static void WaitAllExample()
{
    Console.WriteLine(Environment.NewLine +
        "*** Running WaitAll Example ***");

    // An ArrayList to hold the IAsyncResult instances for each of the
    // asynchronous methods started.
    ArrayList asyncResults = new ArrayList(3);

    // Invoke three LongRunningMethods asynchronously. Pass null for
    // both the callback delegate and the asynchronous state object.
    // Add the IAsyncResult instance for each method to the ArrayList.
    AsyncExampleDelegate longRunningMethod = LongRunningMethod;

    asyncResults.Add(longRunningMethod.BeginInvoke(3000,
        "WaitAll 1", null, null));

    asyncResults.Add(longRunningMethod.BeginInvoke(2500,
        "WaitAll 2", null, null));

    asyncResults.Add(longRunningMethod.BeginInvoke(1500,
        "WaitAll 3", null, null));

    // Create an array of WaitHandle objects that will be used to wait
    // for the completion of all the asynchronous methods.
    WaitHandle[] waitHandles = new WaitHandle[3];

    for (int count = 0; count < 3; count++)
    {
        waitHandles[count] =
            ((IAsyncResult)asyncResults[count]).AsyncWaitHandle;
    }

    // Wait for all three asynchronous method to complete. Time out
    // after 300 ms and display status to the console before continuing
    // to wait.
    TraceMsg(DateTime.Now, "Waiting until all 3 methods are complete...");

    while (!WaitHandle.WaitAll(waitHandles, 300, false))
    {
        TraceMsg(DateTime.Now, "WaitAll timeout...");
    }

    // Inspect the completion data for each method, and determine the
    // time at which the final method completed.
    DateTime completion = DateTime.MinValue;
```

```
        foreach (IAsyncResult result in asyncResults)
        {
            try
            {
                DateTime time = longRunningMethod.EndInvoke(result);
                if (time > completion) completion = time;
            }
            catch
            {
                // Catch and handle those exceptions you would if calling
                // LongRunningMethod directly.
            }
        }

        // Display completion information.
        TraceMsg(completion, "WaitAll example complete.");
    }

    // This method executes LongRunningMethod asynchronously and passes
    // an AsyncCallback delegate instance. The referenced CallbackHandler
    // method is called automatically when the asynchronous method
    // completes, leaving this method free to continue processing.
    public static void CallbackExample()
    {
        Console.WriteLine(Environment.NewLine +
            "*** Running Callback Example ***");

        // Invoke LongRunningMethod asynchronously. Pass an AsyncCallback
        // delegate instance referencing the CallbackHandler method that
        // will be called automatically when the asynchronous method
        // completes. Pass a reference to the AsyncExampleDelegate delegate
        // instance as asynchronous state; otherwise, the callback method
        // has no access to the delegate instance in order to call
        // EndInvoke.
        AsyncExampleDelegate longRunningMethod = LongRunningMethod;

        IAsyncResult asyncResult = longRunningMethod.BeginInvoke(2000,
            "Callback", CallbackHandler, longRunningMethod);

        // Continue with other processing.
        for (int count = 0; count < 15; count++)
        {
            TraceMsg(DateTime.Now, "Continue processing...");
            Thread.Sleep(200);
        }
    }

    // A method to handle asynchronous completion using callbacks.
    public static void CallbackHandler(IAsyncResult result)
    {
```

```
            // Extract the reference to the AsyncExampleDelegate instance
            // from the IAsyncResult instance. This allows you to obtain the
            // completion data.
            AsyncExampleDelegate longRunningMethod =
                (AsyncExampleDelegate)result.AsyncState;

            // Obtain the completion data for the asynchronous method.
            DateTime completion = DateTime.MinValue;

            try
            {
                completion = longRunningMethod.EndInvoke(result);
            }
            catch
            {
                // Catch and handle those exceptions you would if calling
                // LongRunningMethod directly.
            }

            // Display completion information.
            TraceMsg(completion, "Callback example complete.");
        }

        public static void Main()
        {
            // Demonstrate the various approaches to asynchronous method completion.
            BlockingExample();
            PollingExample();
            WaitingExample();
            WaitAllExample();
            CallbackExample();

            // Wait to continue.
            Console.WriteLine(Environment.NewLine);
            Console.WriteLine("Main method complete. Press Enter.");
            Console.ReadLine();
        }
    }
}
```

4-3. Execute a Method Periodically

Problem

You need to execute a method in a separate thread periodically.

Solution

Declare a method containing the code you want to execute periodically. The method's signature must match that defined by the `System.Threading.TimerCallback` delegate; in other words, it must return `void` and take a single `object` argument. Create a `System.Threading.Timer` object and pass it the method you want to execute along with a state `object` that the timer will pass to your method when the timer expires. The runtime will wait until the timer expires and then call your method using a thread from the thread pool.

■ **Tip** If you are implementing a timer in a Windows Forms application, you should consider using the `System.Windows.Forms.Timer`, which also provides additional support in Visual Studio that allows you to drag the timer from your toolbox onto your application. For server-based applications where you want to signal multiple listeners each time the timer fires, consider using the `System.Timers.Timer` class, which notifies listeners using events.

How It Works

It is often useful to execute a method at regular intervals. For example, you might need to clean a data cache every 20 minutes. The `Timer` class makes the periodic execution of methods straightforward, allowing you to execute a method referenced by a `TimerCallback` delegate at specified intervals. The referenced method executes in the context of a thread from the thread pool. (See recipe 4-1 for notes on the appropriate use of thread-pool threads.)

When you create a `Timer` object, you specify two time intervals. The first value specifies the millisecond delay until the `Timer` first executes your method. Specify 0 to execute the method immediately, and specify `System.Threading.Timeout.Infinite` to create the `Timer` in an unstarted state. The second value specifies the interval in milliseconds; then the `Timer` will repeatedly call your method following the initial execution. If you specify a value of 0 or `Timeout.Infinite`, the `Timer` will execute the method only once (as long as the initial delay is not `Timeout.Infinite`). You can specify the time intervals as `int`, `long`, `uint`, or `System.TimeSpan` values.

Once you have created a `Timer` object, you can modify the intervals used by the timer using the `Change` method, but you cannot change the method that is called. When you have finished with a `Timer` object, you should call its `Dispose` method to free system resources held by the timer. Disposing of the `Timer` object cancels any method that is scheduled for execution.

The Code

The `TimerExample` class shown next demonstrates how to use a `Timer` object to call a method named `TimerHandler`. Initially, the `Timer` object is configured to call `TimerHandler` after 2 seconds and then at 1-second intervals. The example allows you to enter a new millisecond interval in the console, which is applied using the `Timer.Change` method.

```
using System;
using System.Threading;

namespace Apress.VisualCSharpRecipes.Chapter04
{
    class Recipe04_03
    {
        public static void Main()
        {
            // Create the state object that is passed to the TimerHandler
            // method when it is triggered. In this case, a message to display.
            string state = "Timer expired.";

            Console.WriteLine("{0} : Creating Timer.",
                DateTime.Now.ToString("HH:mm:ss.ffff"));

            // Create a timer that fires first after 2 seconds and then every
            // second. Use an anonymous method for the timer expiry handler.
            using (Timer timer =
                new Timer(delegate(object s)
                            {Console.WriteLine("{0} : {1}",
                             DateTime.Now.ToString("HH:mm:ss.ffff"),s);
                            }
                , state, 2000, 1000))
            {
                int period;

                // Read the new timer interval from the console until the
                // user enters 0 (zero). Invalid values use a default value
                // of 0, which will stop the example.
                do
                {
                    try
                    {
                        period = Int32.Parse(Console.ReadLine());
                    }
                    catch (FormatException)
                    {
                        period = 0;
                    }

                    // Change the timer to fire using the new interval starting
                    // immediately.
                    if (period > 0) timer.Change(0, period);
                } while (period > 0);
            }
```

```
            // Wait to continue.
            Console.WriteLine("Main method complete. Press Enter.");
            Console.ReadLine();
        }
    }
}
```

4-4. Execute a Method at a Specific Time

Problem

You need to execute a method in a separate thread at a specific time.

Solution

Declare a method containing the code you want to execute. The method's signature must match that defined by the `System.Threading.TimerCallback` delegate; that is, it must return `void` and take a single `object` argument. Create a `System.Threading.Timer` object, and pass it the method you want to execute along with a state `object` that the timer will pass to your method when the timer expires. Calculate the time difference between the current time and the desired execution time, and configure the `Timer` object to fire once after this period of time.

How It Works

Executing a method at a particular time is often useful. For example, you might need to back up data at 1 a.m. daily. Although primarily used for calling methods at regular intervals, the `Timer` object also provides the flexibility to call a method at a specific time.

When you create a `Timer` object, you specify two time intervals. The first value specifies the millisecond delay until the `Timer` first executes your method. To execute the method at a specific time, you should set this value to the difference between the current time (`System.DateTime.Now`) and the desired execution time. The second value specifies the interval after which the `Timer` will repeatedly call your method following the initial execution. If you specify a value of 0, `System.Threading.Timeout.Infinite`, or `TimeSpan(-1)`, the `Timer` object will execute the method only once. If you need the method to execute at a specific time every day, you can easily set this figure using `TimeSpan.FromDays(1)`, which represents the number of milliseconds in 24 hours.

The Code

The following code demonstrates how to use a `Timer` object to execute a method at a specified time:

```
using System;
using System.Threading;
using System.Globalization;
```

```
namespace Apress.VisualCSharpRecipes.Chapter04
{
    class Recipe04_04
    {
        public static void Main(string[] args)
        {
            // Create a 30-second timespan.
            TimeSpan waitTime = new TimeSpan(0, 0, 30);

            // Create a Timer that fires once at the specified time. Specify
            // an interval of -1 to stop the timer executing the method
            // repeatedly. Use an anonymouse method for the timer expiry handler.
            new Timer(delegate(object s)
            {
                Console.WriteLine("Timer fired at {0}",
                DateTime.Now.ToString("HH:mm:ss.ffff"));
            }
                    , null, waitTime, new TimeSpan(-1));

            Console.WriteLine("Waiting for timer. Press Enter to terminate.");
            Console.ReadLine();
        }
    }
}
```

4-5. Execute a Method by Signaling a WaitHandle Object

Problem

You need to execute one or more methods automatically when an object derived from `System.Threading.WaitHandle` is signaled.

Solution

Declare a method containing the code you want to execute. The method's signature must match that defined by the `System.Threading.WaitOrTimerCallback` delegate. Using the static `ThreadPool.RegisterWaitForSingleObject` method, register the method to execute and the `WaitHandle` object that will trigger execution when signaled.

How It Works

You can use classes derived from the `WaitHandle` class to trigger the execution of a method. Using the `RegisterWaitForSingleObject` method of the `ThreadPool` class, you can register a `WaitOrTimerCallback` delegate instance for execution by a thread-pool thread when a specified `WaitHandle`-derived object enters a signaled state. You can configure the thread pool to execute the method only once or to automatically reregister the method for execution each time the `WaitHandle` is signaled. If the `WaitHandle` is already signaled when you call RegisterWaitForSingleObject, the method will execute immediately. The Unregister method of the System.Threading.RegisteredWaitHandle object returned by the RegisterWaitForSingleObject method is used to cancel a registered wait operation.

The class most commonly used as a trigger is AutoResetEvent, which automatically returns to an unsignaled state after it is signaled. However, you can also use the ManualResetEvent, Mutex, and Semaphore classes, which require you to change the signaled state manually.

The Code

The following example demonstrates how to use an AutoResetEvent to trigger the execution of a method named EventHandler. (The AutoResetEvent class is discussed further in recipe 4-8.)

```
using System;
using System.Threading;

namespace Apress.VisualCSharpRecipes.Chapter04
{
    class Recipe04_05
    {
        // A method that is executed when the AutoResetEvent is signaled
        // or the wait operation times out.
        private static void EventHandler(object state, bool timedout)
        {
            // Display appropriate message to the console based on whether
            // the wait timed out or the AutoResetEvent was signaled.
            if (timedout)
            {
                Console.WriteLine("{0} : Wait timed out.",
                    DateTime.Now.ToString("HH:mm:ss.ffff"));
            }
            else
            {
                Console.WriteLine("{0} : {1}",
                    DateTime.Now.ToString("HH:mm:ss.ffff"), state);
            }
        }

        public static void Main()
        {
            // Create the new AutoResetEvent in an unsignaled state.
            AutoResetEvent autoEvent = new AutoResetEvent(false);

            // Create the state object that is passed to the event handler
            // method when it is triggered. In this case, a message to display.
            string state = "AutoResetEvent signaled.";

            // Register the EventHandler method to wait for the AutoResetEvent to
            // be signaled. Set a timeout of 10 seconds, and configure the wait
            // operation to reset after activation (last argument).
```

```
            RegisteredWaitHandle handle = ThreadPool.RegisterWaitForSingleObject(
                autoEvent, EventHandler, state, 10000, false);

            Console.WriteLine("Press ENTER to signal the AutoResetEvent" +
                " or enter \"Cancel\" to unregister the wait operation.");

            while (Console.ReadLine().ToUpper() != "CANCEL")
            {
                // If "Cancel" has not been entered into the console, signal
                // the AutoResetEvent, which will cause the EventHandler
                // method to execute. The AutoResetEvent will automatically
                // revert to an unsignaled state.
                autoEvent.Set();
            }

            // Unregister the wait operation.
            Console.WriteLine("Unregistering wait operation.");
            handle.Unregister(null);

            // Wait to continue.
            Console.WriteLine("Main method complete. Press Enter.");
            Console.ReadLine();
        }
    }
}
```

4-6. Execute a Method Using a New Thread

Problem

You need to execute code in its own thread, and you want complete control over the thread's state and operation.

Solution

Declare a method containing the code you want to execute. The method's signature must match that defined by the `System.Threading.ThreadStart` or `System.Threading.ParameterizedThreadStart` delegate. Create a new `System.Threading.Thread` object and pass the method as an argument to its constructor. Call the `Thread.Start` method to start the execution of your method.

How It Works

For maximum control and flexibility when creating multithreaded applications, you need to take a direct role in creating and managing threads. This is the most complex approach to multithreaded programming, but it is the only way to overcome the restrictions and limitations inherent in the approaches using thread-pool threads, as discussed in the preceding recipes. The `Thread` class provides the mechanism through which you create and control threads. To create and start a new thread, follow this process:

1. Define a method that matches the `ThreadStart` or `ParameterizedThreadStart` delegate. The `ThreadStart` delegate takes no arguments and returns `void`. This means you cannot easily pass data to your new thread. The `ParameterizedThreadStart` delegate also returns `void` but takes a single `object` as an argument, allowing you to pass data to the method you want to run. (The `ParameterizedThreadStart` delegate is a welcome addition to .NET 2.0.) The method you want to execute can be static or an instance method.
2. Create a new `Thread` object and pass your method as an argument to the `Thread` constructor. The new thread has an initial state of `Unstarted` (a member of the `System.Threading.ThreadState` enumeration) and is a foreground thread by default. If you want to configure it to be a background thread, you need to set its `IsBackground` property to `true`.
3. Call `Start` on the `Thread` object, which changes its state to `ThreadState.Running` and begins execution of your method. If you need to pass data to your method, include it as an argument to the `Start` call. If you call `Start` more than once, it will throw a `System.Threading.ThreadStateException`.

The Code

The following code demonstrates how to execute a method in a new thread and shows you how to pass data to the new thread:

```
using System;
using System.Threading;

namespace Apress.VisualCSharpRecipes.Chapter04
{
    class Recipe04_06
    {

        // A utility method for displaying useful trace information to the
        // console along with details of the current thread.
        private static void TraceMsg(string msg)
        {
            Console.WriteLine("[{0,3}] - {1} : {2}",
                Thread.CurrentThread.ManagedThreadId,
                DateTime.Now.ToString("HH:mm:ss.ffff"), msg);
        }

        // A private class used to pass initialization data to a new thread.
        private class ThreadStartData
        {
            public ThreadStartData(int iterations, string message, int delay)
            {
                this.iterations = iterations;
```

```
            this.message = message;
            this.delay = delay;
        }

        // Member variables hold initialization data for a new thread.
        private readonly int iterations;
        private readonly string message;
        private readonly int delay;

        // Properties provide read-only access to initialization data.
        public int Iterations { get { return iterations; } }
        public string Message { get { return message; } }
        public int Delay { get { return delay; } }
    }

    // Declare the method that will be executed in its own thread. The
    // method displays a message to the console a specified number of
    // times, sleeping between each message for a specified duration.
    private static void DisplayMessage(object config)
    {
        ThreadStartData data = config as ThreadStartData;

        if (data != null)
        {
            for (int count = 0; count < data.Iterations; count++)
            {
                TraceMsg(data.Message);

                // Sleep for the specified period.
                Thread.Sleep(data.Delay);
            }
        }
        else
        {
            TraceMsg("Invalid thread configuration.");
        }
    }

    public static void Main()
    {
        // Create a new Thread object specifying DisplayMessage
        // as the method it will execute.
        Thread thread = new Thread(DisplayMessage);
        // Make this a foreground thread - this is the
        // default - call used for example purposes.
        thread.IsBackground = false;

        // Create a new ThreadStartData object to configure the thread.
        ThreadStartData config =
            new ThreadStartData(5, "A thread example.", 500);
        TraceMsg("Starting new thread.");
```

```
            // Start the new thread and pass the ThreadStartData object
            // containing the initialization data.
            thread.Start(config);

            // Continue with other processing.
            for (int count = 0; count < 13; count++)
            {
                TraceMsg("Main thread continuing processing...");
                Thread.Sleep(200);
            }

            // Wait to continue.
            Console.WriteLine(Environment.NewLine);
            Console.WriteLine("Main method complete. Press Enter.");
            Console.ReadLine();
        }
    }
}
```

4-7. Synchronize the Execution of Multiple Threads Using a Monitor

Problem

You need to coordinate the activities of multiple threads within a single process to ensure the efficient use of shared resources or to ensure that several threads are not updating the same shared resource at the same time. (See recipe 4-9 for details of coordination between processes.)

Solution

Identify an appropriate object to use as a mechanism to control access to the shared resource/data. Use the static method `Monitor.Enter` to acquire a lock on the object, and use the static method `Monitor.Exit` to release the lock so another thread may acquire it.

How It Works

The greatest challenge in writing a multithreaded application is ensuring that the threads work in concert. This is commonly referred to as *thread synchronization*, and includes the following:

- Ensuring that threads access shared objects and data correctly so that they do not cause corruption
- Ensuring that threads execute only when they are meant to and cause minimum overhead when they are idle

The most commonly used synchronization mechanism is the `System.Threading.Monitor` class. The `Monitor` class allows a single thread to obtain an exclusive lock on an object by calling the static method `Monitor.Enter`. By acquiring an exclusive lock prior to accessing a shared resource or shared data, you ensure that only one thread can access the resource concurrently. Once the thread has finished with the resource, release the lock to allow another thread to access it. A block of code that enforces this behavior is often referred to as a *critical section.*

■ **Note** Monitors are managed-code synchronization mechanisms that do not rely on any specific operating system primitives. This ensures that your code is portable should you want to run it on a non-Windows platform. This is in contrast to the synchronization mechanisms discussed in recipes 4-8, 4-9, and 4-10, which rely on Win32 operating system–based synchronization objects.

You can use any object to act as the lock; it is common to use the keyword `this` to obtain a lock on the current object, but it is better to use a separate object dedicated to the purpose of synchronization. The key point is that all threads attempting to access a shared resource must try to acquire the *same* lock. Other threads that attempt to acquire a lock using `Monitor.Enter` on the same object will block (enter a `WaitSleepJoin` state), and will be added to the lock's *ready queue* until the thread that owns the lock releases it by calling the *static* method `Monitor.Exit`. When the owning thread calls `Exit`, one of the threads from the ready queue acquires the lock. If the owner of a lock does not release it by calling `Exit`, all other threads will block indefinitely. Therefore, it is important to place the `Exit` call within a `finally` block to ensure that it is called even if an exception occurs. To ensure that threads do not wait indefinitely, you can specify a timeout value when you call `Monitor.Enter`.

■ **Tip** Because `Monitor` is used so frequently in multithreaded applications, C# provides language-level support through the `lock` statement, which the compiler translates to the use of the `Monitor` class. A block of code encapsulated in a `lock` statement is equivalent to calling `Monitor.Enter` when entering the block and `Monitor.Exit` when exiting the block. In addition, the compiler automatically places the `Monitor.Exit` call in a `finally` block to ensure that the lock is released if an exception is thrown.

Using `Monitor.Enter` and `Monitor.Exit` is often all you will need to correctly synchronize access to a shared resource in a multithreaded application. However, when you are trying to coordinate the activation of a pool of threads to handle work items from a shared queue, `Monitor.Enter` and `Monitor.Exit` will not be sufficient. In this situation, you want a potentially large number of threads to wait efficiently until a work item becomes available without putting unnecessary load on the central processing unit (CPU). This is where you need the fine-grained synchronization control provided by the `Monitor.Wait`, `Monitor.Pulse`, and `Monitor.PulseAll` methods.

The thread that currently owns the lock can call `Monitor.Wait`, which will release the lock and place the calling thread on the lock's *wait queue.* Threads in a wait queue also have a state of `WaitSleepJoin`, and will continue to block until a thread that owns the lock calls either the `Monitor.Pulse` method or the `Monitor.PulseAll` method. `Monitor.Pulse` moves one of the waiting threads from the wait queue to the ready queue, and `Monitor.PulseAll` moves all threads. Once a thread has moved from the wait queue to the ready queue, it can acquire the lock the next time the lock is released. It is important to understand that threads on a lock's wait queue *will not* acquire a released lock; they will wait indefinitely until you call `Monitor.Pulse` or `Monitor.PulseAll` to move them to the ready queue.

So, in practice, when your pool threads are inactive, they sit on the wait queue. As a new work item arrives, a dispatcher obtains the lock and calls `Monitor.Pulse`, moving one worker thread to the ready queue where it will obtain the lock as soon as the dispatcher releases it. The worker thread takes the work item, releases the lock, and processes the work item. Once the worker thread has finished with the work item, it again obtains the lock in order to take the next work item, but if there is no work item to process, the thread calls `Monitor.Wait` and goes back to the wait queue.

The Code

The following example demonstrates how to synchronize access to a shared resource (the console) and the activation of waiting threads using the `Monitor.Wait`, `Monitor.Pulse`, and `Monitor.PulseAll` methods. The example starts three worker threads that take work items from a queue and processes them. When the user presses Enter the first two times, work items (`strings` in the example) are added to the work queue, and `Monitor.Pulse` is called to release one waiting thread for each work item. The third time the user presses Enter, `Monitor.PulseAll` is called, releasing all waiting threads and allowing them to terminate.

```
using System;
using System.Threading;
using System.Collections.Generic;

namespace Apress.VisualCSharpRecipes.Chapter04
{
    class Recipe04_07
    {
        // Declare an object for synchronization of access to the console.
        // A static object is used because you are using it in static methods.
        private static object consoleGate = new Object();

        // Declare a Queue to represent the work queue.
        private static Queue<string> workQueue = new Queue<string>();

        // Declare a flag to indicate to activated threads that they should
        // terminate and not process more work items.
        private static bool processWorkItems = true;

        // A utility method for displaying useful trace information to the
        // console along with details of the current thread.
        private static void TraceMsg(string msg)
        {
            lock (consoleGate)
            {
```

```
            Console.WriteLine("[{0,3}/{1}] - {2} : {3}",
                Thread.CurrentThread.ManagedThreadId,
                Thread.CurrentThread.IsThreadPoolThread ? "pool" : "fore",
                DateTime.Now.ToString("HH:mm:ss.ffff"), msg);
        }
    }

    // Declare the method that will be executed by each thread to process
    // items from the work queue.
    private static void ProcessWorkItems()
    {
        // A local variable to hold the work item taken from the work queue.
        string workItem = null;

        TraceMsg("Thread started, processing items from queue...");

        // Process items from the work queue until termination is signaled.
        while (processWorkItems)
        {
            // Obtain the lock on the work queue.
            Monitor.Enter(workQueue);

            try
            {
                // Pop the next work item and process it, or wait if none
                // is available.
                if (workQueue.Count == 0)
                {
                    TraceMsg("No work items, waiting...");

                    // Wait until Pulse is called on the workQueue object.
                    Monitor.Wait(workQueue);
                }
                else
                {
                    // Obtain the next work item.
                    workItem = workQueue.Dequeue();
                }
            }
            finally
            {
                // Always release the lock.
                Monitor.Exit(workQueue);
            }

            // Process the work item if one was obtained.
            if (workItem != null)
            {
```

```
                // Obtain a lock on the console and display a series
                // of messages.
                lock (consoleGate)
                {
                    for (int i = 0; i < 5; i++)
                    {
                        TraceMsg("Processing " + workItem);
                        Thread.Sleep(200);
                    }
                }

                // Reset the status of the local variable.
                workItem = null;
            }
        }

        // This will be reached only if processWorkItems is false.
        TraceMsg("Terminating.");
    }

    public static void Main()
    {
        TraceMsg("Starting worker threads.");

        // Add an initial work item to the work queue.
        lock (workQueue)
        {
            workQueue.Enqueue("Work Item 1");
        }

        // Create and start three new worker threads running the
        // ProcessWorkItems method.
        for (int count = 0; count < 3; count++)
        {
            (new Thread(ProcessWorkItems)).Start();
        }

        Thread.Sleep(1500);

        // The first time the user presses Enter, add a work item and
        // activate a single thread to process it.
        TraceMsg("Press Enter to pulse one waiting thread.");
        Console.ReadLine();

        // Acquire a lock on the workQueue object.
        lock (workQueue)
        {
            // Add a work item.
            workQueue.Enqueue("Work Item 2.");
```

```
                // Pulse one waiting thread.
                Monitor.Pulse(workQueue);
            }

            Thread.Sleep(2000);

            // The second time the user presses Enter, add three work items and
            // activate three threads to process them.
            TraceMsg("Press Enter to pulse three waiting threads.");
            Console.ReadLine();

            // Acquire a lock on the workQueue object.
            lock (workQueue)
            {
                // Add work items to the work queue, and activate worker threads.
                workQueue.Enqueue("Work Item 3.");
                Monitor.Pulse(workQueue);
                workQueue.Enqueue("Work Item 4.");
                Monitor.Pulse(workQueue);
                workQueue.Enqueue("Work Item 5.");
                Monitor.Pulse(workQueue);
            }

            Thread.Sleep(3500);

            // The third time the user presses Enter, signal the worker threads
            // to terminate and activate them all.
            TraceMsg("Press Enter to pulse all waiting threads.");
            Console.ReadLine();

            // Acquire a lock on the workQueue object.
            lock (workQueue)
            {
                // Signal that threads should terminate.
                processWorkItems = false;

                // Pulse all waiting threads.
                Monitor.PulseAll(workQueue);
            }

            Thread.Sleep(1000);

            // Wait to continue.
            TraceMsg("Main method complete. Press Enter.");
            Console.ReadLine();
        }
    }
}
```

4-8. Synchronize the Execution of Multiple Threads Using an Event

Problem

You need a mechanism to synchronize the execution of multiple threads in order to coordinate their activities or access to shared resources.

Solution

Use the `EventWaitHandle`, `AutoResetEvent`, and `ManualResetEvent` classes from the `System.Threading` namespace.

How It Works

The `EventWaitHandle`, `AutoResetEvent`, and `ManualResetEvent` classes provide similar functionality. `EventWaitHandle` is the base class from which the `AutoResetEvent` and `ManualResetEvent` classes are derived. (`EventWaitHandle` inherits from `System.Threading.WaitHandle` and allows you to create named events.) All three event classes allow you to synchronize multiple threads by manipulating the state of the event between two possible values: `signaled` and `unsignaled`.

Threads requiring synchronization call static or inherited methods of the `WaitHandle` abstract base class (summarized in Table 4-1) to test the state of one or more event objects. If the events are signaled when tested, the thread continues to operate unhindered. If the events are unsignaled, the thread enters a `WaitSleepJoin` state, blocking until one or more of the events become signaled or when a given timeout expires.

Table 4-1. *WaitHandle Methods for Synchronizing Thread Execution*

Method	Description
`WaitOne`	Causes the calling thread to enter a `WaitSleepJoin` state and wait for a specific `WaitHandle`-derived object to be signaled. You can also specify a timeout value. The `WaitingExample` method in recipe 4-2 demonstrates how to use the `WaitOne` method.
`WaitAny`	A static method that causes the calling thread to enter a `WaitSleepJoin` state and wait for any one of the objects in a `WaitHandle` array to be signaled. You can also specify a timeout value.
`WaitAll`	A static method that causes the calling thread to enter a `WaitSleepJoin` state and wait for all the `WaitHandle` objects in a `WaitHandle` array to be signaled. You can also specify a timeout value. The `WaitAllExample` method in recipe 4-2 demonstrates how to use the `WaitAll` method.

Method	Description
SignalAndWait	A static method that causes the calling thread to signal a specified event object and then wait on a specified event object. The signal and wait operations are carried out as an atomic operation. You can also specify a timeout value. SignalAndWait is new to .NET 2.0.

The key differences between the three event classes are how they transition from a signaled to an unsignaled state, and their visibility. Both the AutoResetEvent and ManualResetEvent classes are local to the process in which they are declared. To signal an AutoResetEvent class, call its Set method, which will release only one thread that is waiting on the event. The AutoResetEvent class will then automatically return to an unsignaled state. The code in recipe 4-4 demonstrates how to use an AutoResetEvent class.

The ManualResetEvent class must be manually switched back and forth between signaled and unsignaled states using its Set and Reset methods. Calling Set on a ManualResetEvent class will set it to a signaled state, releasing all threads that are waiting on the event. Only by calling Reset does the ManualResetEvent class become unsignaled.

You can configure the EventWaitHandle class to operate in a manual or automatic reset mode, making it possible to act like either the AutoResetEvent class or the ManualResetEvent class. When you create the EventWaitHandle, you pass a value of the System.Threading.EventResetMode enumeration to configure the mode in which the EventWaitHandle will function; the two possible values are AutoReset and ManualReset. The unique benefit of the EventWaitHandle class is that it is not constrained to the local process. When you create an EventWaitHandle class, you can associate a name with it that makes it accessible to other processes, including unmanaged Win32 code. This allows you to synchronize the activities of threads across process and application domain boundaries and synchronize access to resources that are shared by multiple processes. To obtain a reference to an existing named EventWaitHandle, call the static method EventWaitHandle.OpenExisting and specify the name of the event.

The Code

The following example demonstrates how to use a named EventWaitHandle in manual mode that is initially signaled. A thread is spawned that waits on the event and then displays a message to the console—repeating the process every 2 seconds. When you press Enter, you toggle the event between a signaled and a unsignaled state. This example uses the Thread.Join instance method, which we describe in recipe 4-12.

```
using System;
using System.Threading;

namespace Apress.VisualCSharpRecipes.Chapter04
{
    class Recipe04_08
    {
        // Boolean to signal that the second thread should terminate.
        static bool terminate = false;

        // A utility method for displaying useful trace information to the
        // console along with details of the current thread.
```

```
        private static void TraceMsg(string msg)
        {
            Console.WriteLine("[{0,3}] - {1} : {2}",
                Thread.CurrentThread.ManagedThreadId,
                DateTime.Now.ToString("HH:mm:ss.ffff"), msg);
        }

        // Declare the method that will be executed on the separate thread.
        // The method waits on the EventWaitHandle before displaying a message
        // to the console and then waits two seconds and loops.
        private static void DisplayMessage()
        {
            // Obtain a handle to the EventWaitHandle with the name "EventExample".
            EventWaitHandle eventHandle =
                EventWaitHandle.OpenExisting("EventExample");

            TraceMsg("DisplayMessage Started.");

            while (!terminate)
            {
                // Wait on the EventWaitHandle, time out after 2 seconds. WaitOne
                // returns true if the event is signaled; otherwise, false. The
                // first time through, the message will be displayed immediately
                // because the EventWaitHandle was created in a signaled state.
                if (eventHandle.WaitOne(2000, true))
                {
                    TraceMsg("EventWaitHandle In Signaled State.");
                }
                else
                {
                    TraceMsg("WaitOne Timed Out -- " +
                        "EventWaitHandle In Unsignaled State.");
                }
                Thread.Sleep(2000);
            }

            TraceMsg("Thread Terminating.");
        }

        public static void Main()
        {
            // Create a new EventWaitHandle with an initial signaled state, in
            // manual mode, with the name "EventExample".
            using (EventWaitHandle eventWaitHandle =
                new EventWaitHandle(true, EventResetMode.ManualReset,
                "EventExample"))
            {
```

```
            // Create and start a new thread running the DisplayMesssage
            // method.
            TraceMsg("Starting DisplayMessageThread.");
            Thread trd = new Thread(DisplayMessage);
            trd.Start();

            // Allow the EventWaitHandle to be toggled between a signaled and
            // unsignaled state up to three times before ending.
            for (int count = 0; count < 3; count++)
            {
                // Wait for Enter to be pressed.
                Console.ReadLine();

                // You need to toggle the event. The only way to know the
                // current state is to wait on it with a 0 (zero) timeout
                // and test the result.
                if (eventWaitHandle.WaitOne(0, true))
                {
                    TraceMsg("Switching Event To UnSignaled State.");

                    // Event is signaled, so unsignal it.
                    eventWaitHandle.Reset();
                }
                else
                {
                    TraceMsg("Switching Event To Signaled State.");

                    // Event is unsignaled, so signal it.
                    eventWaitHandle.Set();
                }
            }

            // Terminate the DisplayMessage thread, and wait for it to
            // complete before disposing of the EventWaitHandle.
            terminate = true;
            eventWaitHandle.Set();
            trd.Join(5000);
        }

        // Wait to continue.
        Console.WriteLine(Environment.NewLine);
        Console.WriteLine("Main method complete. Press Enter.");
        Console.ReadLine();
    }
  }
}
```

4-9. Synchronize the Execution of Multiple Threads Using a Mutex

Problem

You need to coordinate the activities of multiple threads (possibly across process boundaries) to ensure the efficient use of shared resources or to ensure that several threads are not updating the same shared resource at the same time.

Solution

Use the `System.Threading.Mutex` class.

How It Works

The `Mutex` has a similar purpose to the `Monitor` discussed in recipe 4-7—it provides a means to ensure that only a single thread has access to a shared resource or section of code at any given time. However, unlike the `Monitor`, which is implemented fully within managed code, the `Mutex` is a wrapper around an operating system synchronization object. This, and because `Mutex`es can be given names, means you can use a `Mutex` to synchronize the activities of threads across process boundaries, even with threads running in unmanaged Win32 code.

Like the `EventWaitHandle`, `AutoResetEvent`, and `ManualResetEvent` classes discussed in recipe 4-8, the `Mutex` is derived from `System.Threading.WaitHandle` and enables thread synchronization in a similar fashion. A `Mutex` is in either a signaled state or an unsignaled state. A thread acquires ownership of the `Mutex` at construction or by using one of the methods listed in Table 4-1. If a thread has ownership of the `Mutex`, the `Mutex` is unsignaled, meaning other threads will block if they try to acquire ownership. Ownership of the `Mutex` is released by the owning thread calling the `Mutex.ReleaseMutex` method, which signals the `Mutex` and allows another thread to acquire ownership. A thread may acquire ownership of a `Mutex` any number of times without problems, but it must release the `Mutex` an equal number of times to free it and make it available for another thread to acquire. If the thread with ownership of a `Mutex` terminates normally, the `Mutex` becomes signaled, allowing another thread to acquire ownership.

The Code

The following example demonstrates how to use a named `Mutex` to limit access to a shared resource (the console) to a single thread at any given time:

```
using System;
using System.Threading;

namespace Apress.VisualCSharpRecipes.Chapter04
{
    class Recipe04_09
    {
```

```
// Boolean to signal that the second thread should terminate.
static bool terminate = false;

// A utility method for displaying useful trace information to the
// console along with details of the current thread.
private static void TraceMsg(string msg)
{
    Console.WriteLine("[{0,3}] - {1} : {2}",
        Thread.CurrentThread.ManagedThreadId,
        DateTime.Now.ToString("HH:mm:ss.ffff"), msg);
}

// Declare the method that will be executed on the separate thread.
// In a loop the method waits to obtain a Mutex before displaying a
// message to the console and then waits 1 second before releasing the
// Mutex.
private static void DisplayMessage()
{
    // Obtain a handle to the Mutex with the name "MutexExample".
    // Do not attempt to take ownership immediately.
    using (Mutex mutex = new Mutex(false, "MutexExample"))
    {
        TraceMsg("Thread started.");

        while (!terminate)
        {
            // Wait on the Mutex.
            mutex.WaitOne();

            TraceMsg("Thread owns the Mutex.");

            Thread.Sleep(1000);

            TraceMsg("Thread releasing the Mutex.");

            // Release the Mutex.
            mutex.ReleaseMutex();

            // Sleep a little to give another thread a good chance of
            // acquiring the Mutex.
            Thread.Sleep(100);
        }

        TraceMsg("Thread terminating.");
    }
}
```

```
        public static void Main()
        {
            // Create a new Mutex with the name "MutexExample".
            using (Mutex mutex = new Mutex(false, "MutexExample"))
            {
                TraceMsg("Starting threads -- press Enter to terminate.");

                // Create and start three new threads running the
                // DisplayMesssage method.
                Thread trd1 = new Thread(DisplayMessage);
                Thread trd2 = new Thread(DisplayMessage);
                Thread trd3 = new Thread(DisplayMessage);
                trd1.Start();
                trd2.Start();
                trd3.Start();

                // Wait for Enter to be pressed.
                Console.ReadLine();

                // Terminate the DisplayMessage threads, and wait for them to
                // complete before disposing of the Mutex.
                terminate = true;
                trd1.Join(5000);
                trd2.Join(5000);
                trd3.Join(5000);
            }

            // Wait to continue.
            Console.WriteLine(Environment.NewLine);
            Console.WriteLine("Main method complete. Press Enter.");
            Console.ReadLine();
        }
    }
}
```

■ **Note** Recipe 4-17 demonstrates how to use a named `Mutex` as a means to ensure that only a single instance of an application can be started at any given time.

4-10. Synchronize the Execution of Multiple Threads Using a Semaphore

Problem

You need to control the number of threads that can access a shared resource or section of code concurrently.

Solution

Use the System.Threading.Semaphore class.

How It Works

The Semaphore is another synchronization class derived from the System.Threading.WaitHandle class and will be familiar to those with Win32 programming experience. The purpose of the Semaphore is to allow a specified maximum number of threads to access a shared resource or section of code concurrently.

As with the other synchronization classes derived from WaitHandle (discussed in recipe 4-8 and recipe 4-9), a Semaphore is either in a signaled state or an unsignaled state. Threads wait for the Semaphore to become signaled using the methods described in Table 4-1. The Semaphore maintains a count of the active threads it has allowed through and automatically switches to an unsignaled state once the maximum number of threads is reached. To release the Semaphore and allow other waiting threads the opportunity to act, a thread calls the Release method on the Semaphore object. A thread may acquire ownership of the Semaphore more than once, reducing the maximum number of threads that can be active concurrently, and must call Release the same number of times to fully release it.

The Code

The following example demonstrates how to use a named Semaphore to limit access to a shared resource (the console) to two threads at any given time. The code is similar to that used in recipe 4-9 but substitutes a Semaphore for the Mutex.

```
using System;
using System.Threading;

namespace Apress.VisualCSharpRecipes.Chapter04
{
    class Recipe04_10
    {
        // Boolean to signal that the second thread should terminate.
        static bool terminate = false;
```

```
        // A utility method for displaying useful trace information to the
        // console along with details of the current thread.
        private static void TraceMsg(string msg)
        {
            Console.WriteLine("[{0,3}] - {1} : {2}",
                Thread.CurrentThread.ManagedThreadId,
                DateTime.Now.ToString("HH:mm:ss.ffff"), msg);
        }

        // Declare the method that will be executed on the separate thread.
        // In a loop the method waits to obtain a Semaphore before displaying a
        // message to the console and then waits 1 second before releasing the
        // Semaphore.
        private static void DisplayMessage()
        {
            // Obtain a handle to the Semaphore with the name "SemaphoreExample".
            using (Semaphore sem = Semaphore.OpenExisting("SemaphoreExample"))
            {
                TraceMsg("Thread started.");

                while (!terminate)
                {
                    // Wait on the Semaphore.
                    sem.WaitOne();

                    TraceMsg("Thread owns the Semaphore.");

                    Thread.Sleep(1000);

                    TraceMsg("Thread releasing the Semaphore.");

                    // Release the Semaphore.
                    sem.Release();

                    // Sleep a little to give another thread a good chance of
                    // acquiring the Semaphore.
                    Thread.Sleep(100);
                }

                TraceMsg("Thread terminating.");
            }
        }

        public static void Main()
        {
            // Create a new Semaphore with the name "SemaphoreExample". The
            // Semaphore can be owned by up to two threads at the same time.
            using (Semaphore sem = new Semaphore(2,2,"SemaphoreExample"))
            {
                TraceMsg("Starting threads -- press Enter to terminate.");
```

```
                // Create and start three new threads running the
                // DisplayMesssage method.
                Thread trd1 = new Thread(DisplayMessage);
                Thread trd2 = new Thread(DisplayMessage);
                Thread trd3 = new Thread(DisplayMessage);
                trd1.Start();
                trd2.Start();
                trd3.Start();

                // Wait for Enter to be pressed.
                Console.ReadLine();

                // Terminate the DisplayMessage threads and wait for them to
                // complete before disposing of the Semaphore.
                terminate = true;
                trd1.Join(5000);
                trd2.Join(5000);
                trd3.Join(5000);
            }

            // Wait to continue.
            Console.WriteLine(Environment.NewLine);
            Console.WriteLine("Main method complete. Press Enter.");
            Console.ReadLine();
        }
    }
}
```

4-11. Synchronize Access to a Shared Data Value

Problem

You need to ensure operations on a numeric data value are executed atomically so that multiple threads accessing the value do not cause errors or corruption.

Solution

Use the static members of the `System.Threading.Interlocked` class.

How It Works

The `Interlocked` class contains several static methods that perform some simple arithmetic and comparison operations on a variety of data types and ensure the operations are carried out atomically. Table 4-2 summarizes the methods and the data types on which they can be used. Note that the methods use the `ref` keyword on their arguments to allow the method to update the value of the actual value type variable passed in. If the operations you want to perform are not supported by the

Interlocked class, you will need to implement your own synchronization using the other approaches described in this chapter.

■ **Caution** The atomicity of 64-bit interlocked operations on 32-bit platforms are guaranteed only when the data value is accessed through the Interlocked class—i.e., that the variable is not accessed directly.

Table 4-2. *Interlocked Methods for Synchronizing Data Access*

Method	Description
Add	Adds two int or long values and sets the value of the first argument to the sum of the two values.
CompareExchange	Compares two values; if they are the same, sets the first argument to a specified value. This method has overloads to support the comparison and exchange of int, long, float, double, object, and System.IntPtr.
Decrement	Decrements an int or long value.
Exchange	Sets the value of a variable to a specified value. This method has overloads to support the exchange of int, long, float, double, object, and System.IntPtr.
Increment	Increments an int or a long value.

The Code

The following simple example demonstrates how to use the methods of the Interlocked class. The example does not demonstrate Interlocked in the context of a multithreaded program and is provided only to clarify the syntax and effect of the various methods.

```
using System;
using System.Threading;

namespace Apress.VisualCSharpRecipes.Chapter04
{
    class Recipe04_11
    {
        public static void Main()
        {
            int firstInt = 2500;
            int secondInt = 8000;
```

```
            Console.WriteLine("firstInt initial value = {0}", firstInt);
            Console.WriteLine("secondInt initial value = {0}", secondInt);

            // Decrement firstInt in a thread-safe manner.
            // The thread-safe equivalent of firstInt = firstInt - 1.
            Interlocked.Decrement(ref firstInt);

            Console.WriteLine(Environment.NewLine);
            Console.WriteLine("firstInt after decrement = {0}", firstInt);

            // Increment secondInt in a thread-safe manner.
            // The thread-safe equivalent of secondInt = secondInt + 1.
            Interlocked.Increment(ref secondInt);

            Console.WriteLine("secondInt after increment = {0}", secondInt);

            // Add the firstInt and secondInt values, and store the result in
            // firstInt.
            // The thread-safe equivalent of firstInt = firstInt + secondInt.
            Interlocked.Add(ref firstInt, secondInt);

            Console.WriteLine(Environment.NewLine);
            Console.WriteLine("firstInt after Add = {0}", firstInt);
            Console.WriteLine("secondInt after Add = {0}", secondInt);

            // Exchange the value of firstInt with secondInt.
            // The thread-safe equivalenet of secondInt = firstInt.
            Interlocked.Exchange(ref secondInt, firstInt);

            Console.WriteLine(Environment.NewLine);
            Console.WriteLine("firstInt after Exchange = {0}", firstInt);
            Console.WriteLine("secondInt after Exchange = {0}", secondInt);

            // Compare firstInt with secondInt, and if they are equal, set
            // firstInt to 5000.
            // The thread-safe equivalenet of:
            //     if (firstInt == secondInt) firstInt = 5000.
            Interlocked.CompareExchange(ref firstInt, 5000, secondInt);

            Console.WriteLine(Environment.NewLine);
            Console.WriteLine("firstInt after CompareExchange = {0}", firstInt);
            Console.WriteLine("secondInt after CompareExchange = {0}", secondInt);

            // Wait to continue.
            Console.WriteLine(Environment.NewLine);
            Console.WriteLine("Main method complete. Press Enter.");
            Console.ReadLine();
        }
    }
}
```

4-12. Know When a Thread Finishes

Problem

You need to know when a thread has finished.

Solution

Use the IsAlive property or the Join method of the Thread class.

How It Works

The easiest way to test whether a thread has finished executing is to test the Thread.IsAlive property. The IsAlive property returns true if the thread has been started but has not terminated or been aborted. The IsAlive property provides a simple test to see whether a thread has finished executing, but commonly you will need one thread to wait for another thread to complete its processing. Instead of testing IsAlive in a loop, which is inefficient, you can use the Thread.Join method.

Join causes the calling thread to block until the referenced thread terminates, at which point the calling thread will continue. You can optionally specify an int or a TimeSpan value that specifies the time, after which the Join operation will time out and execution of the calling thread will resume. If you specify a timeout value, Join returns true if the thread terminated and false if Join timed out.

The Code

The following example executes a second thread and then calls Join (with a timeout of 2 seconds) to wait for the second thread to terminate. Because the second thread takes about 5 seconds to execute, the Join method will always time out, and the example will display a message to the console. The example then calls Join again without a timeout and blocks until the second thread terminates.

```
using System;
using System.Threading;

namespace Apress.VisualCSharpRecipes.Chapter04
{
    class Recipe04_12
    {
        private static void DisplayMessage()
        {
            // Display a message to the console five times.
            for (int count = 0; count < 5; count++)
            {
                Console.WriteLine("{0} : DisplayMessage thread",
                    DateTime.Now.ToString("HH:mm:ss.ffff"));
```

```
                // Sleep for 1 second.
                Thread.Sleep(1000);
            }
        }

        public static void Main()
        {
            // Create a new Thread to run the DisplayMessage method.
            Thread thread = new Thread(DisplayMessage);

            Console.WriteLine("{0} : Starting DisplayMessage thread.",
                DateTime.Now.ToString("HH:mm:ss.ffff"));

            // Start the DisplayMessage thread.
            thread.Start();

            // Block until the DisplayMessage thread finishes, or time out after
            // 2 seconds.
            if (!thread.Join(2000))
            {
                Console.WriteLine("{0} : Join timed out !!",
                    DateTime.Now.ToString("HH:mm:ss.ffff"));
            }

            // Print out the thread status.
            Console.WriteLine("Thread alive: {0}", thread.IsAlive);

            // Block again until the DisplayMessage thread finishes with no timeout.
            thread.Join();

            // Print out the thread status.
            Console.WriteLine("Thread alive: {0}", thread.IsAlive);

            // Wait to continue.
            Console.WriteLine("Main method complete. Press Enter.");
            Console.ReadLine();
        }
    }
}
```

4-13. Terminate the Execution of a Thread

Problem

You need to terminate an executing thread without waiting for it to finish on its own.

Solution

Call the `Abort` method of the `Thread` object you want to terminate.

How It Works

It is better to write your code so that you can signal to a thread that it should shut down and allow it to terminate naturally. Recipes 4-7, 4-8, and 4-9 demonstrate this technique (using a Boolean flag). However, sometimes you will want a more direct method of terminating an active thread.

Calling `Abort` on an active `Thread` object terminates the thread by throwing a `System.Threading.ThreadAbortException` in the code that the thread is running. You can pass an object as an argument to the `Abort` method, which is accessible to the aborted thread through the `ExceptionState` property of the `ThreadAbortException`. When called, `Abort` returns immediately, but the runtime determines exactly when the exception is thrown, so you cannot assume the thread has terminated by the `Abort` returns. You should use the techniques described in recipe 4-12 if you need to determine when the aborted thread is actually done.

The aborted thread's code can catch the `ThreadAbortException` to perform cleanup, but the runtime will automatically throw the exception again when exiting the `catch` block to ensure that the thread terminates. So, you should not write code after the `catch` block: it will never execute. However, calling the static `Thread.ResetAbort` in the `catch` block will cancel the abort request and allow the thread to continue executing. Once you abort a thread, you cannot restart it by calling `Thread.Start`.

The Code

The following example creates a new thread that continues to display messages to the console until you press Enter, at which point the thread is terminated by a call to `Thread.Abort`:

```
using System;
using System.Threading;

namespace Apress.VisualCSharpRecipes.Chapter04
{
    class Recipe04_13
    {
        private static void DisplayMessage()
        {
            try
            {
                while (true)
                {
                    // Display a message to the console.
                    Console.WriteLine("{0} : DisplayMessage thread active",
                        DateTime.Now.ToString("HH:mm:ss.ffff"));

                    // Sleep for 1 second.
                    Thread.Sleep(1000);
                }
            }
```

```
        catch (ThreadAbortException ex)
        {
            // Display a message to the console.
            Console.WriteLine("{0} : DisplayMessage thread terminating - {1}",
                DateTime.Now.ToString("HH:mm:ss.ffff"),
                (string)ex.ExceptionState);

            // Call Thread.ResetAbort here to cancel the abort request.
        }

        // This code is never executed unless Thread.ResetAbort
        // is called in the previous catch block.
        Console.WriteLine("{0} : nothing is called after the catch block",
            DateTime.Now.ToString("HH:mm:ss.ffff"));
    }

    public static void Main()
    {
        // Create a new Thread to run the DisplayMessage method.
        Thread thread = new Thread(DisplayMessage);

        Console.WriteLine("{0} : Starting DisplayMessage thread" +
            " - press Enter to terminate.",
            DateTime.Now.ToString("HH:mm:ss.ffff"));

        // Start the DisplayMessage thread.
        thread.Start();

        // Wait until Enter is pressed and terminate the thread.
        Console.ReadLine();

        thread.Abort("User pressed Enter");

        // Block again until the DisplayMessage thread finishes.
        thread.Join();

        // Wait to continue.
        Console.WriteLine("Main method complete. Press Enter.");
        Console.ReadLine();
    }
  }
}
```

4-14. Create a Thread-Safe Collection Instance

Problem

You need multiple threads to be able to safely access the contents of a collection concurrently.

Solution

Use `lock` statements in your code to synchronize thread access to the collection, or to access the collection through a thread-safe wrapper.

How It Works

By default, the standard collection classes from the `System.Collections`, `System.Collections.Specialized`, and `System.Collections.Generic` namespaces will support multiple threads reading the collection's content concurrently. However, if more than one of these threads tries to modify the collection, you will almost certainly encounter problems. This is because the operating system can interrupt the actions of the thread while modifications to the collection have been only partially applied. This leaves the collection in an indeterminate state, which will almost certainly cause another thread accessing the collection to fail, return incorrect data, or corrupt the collection.

■ **Note**.NET 4.0 introduces a set of efficient thread-safe collections in the `System.Collections.Concurrent` namespace that can be used. See Chapter 15 and the .NET Framework documentation for details.

The most commonly used collections from the `System.Collections` namespace implement a static method named `Synchronized`; this includes only the `ArrayList`, `Hashtable`, `Queue`, `SortedList`, and `Stack` classes. The `Synchronized` method takes a collection object of the appropriate type as an argument and returns an object that provides a synchronized wrapper around the specified collection object. The wrapper object is returned as the same type as the original collection, but all the methods and properties that read and write the collection ensure that only a single thread has access to the initial collection content concurrently. You can test whether a collection is thread-safe using the `IsSynchronized` property. One final note: Once you get the wrapper, you should neither access the initial collection nor create a new wrapper. In both cases, you will lose thread safety.

Collection classes such as `HybridDictionary`, `ListDictionary`, and `StringCollection` from the `System.Collections.Specialized` namespace do not implement a `Synchronized` method. To provide thread-safe access to instances of these classes, you must implement manual synchronization using the `object` returned by their `SyncRoot` property. This property and `IsSynchronized` are both defined by the `ICollection` interface that is implemented by all collection classes from `System.Collections` and `System.Collections.Specialized` (except `BitVector32`); you can therefore synchronize all your collections in a fine-grained way.

However, the new 2.0 classes in the `System.Collections.Generic` namespace provide no built-in synchronization mechanisms, leaving it to you to implement thread synchronization manually using the techniques discussed in this chapter.

■ **Caution** Often you will have multiple collections and data elements that are related and need to be updated atomically. In these instances, you should not use the synchronization mechanisms provided by the individual collection classes. This approach will introduce synchronization problems into your code such as deadlocks and race conditions. You must decide what collections and other data elements need to be managed atomically and use the techniques described in this chapter to synchronize access to these elements as a unit.

The Code

The following code snippet shows how to create a thread-safe `Hashtable` instance:

```
// Create a standard Hashtable.
Hashtable hUnsync = new Hashtable();

// Create a synchronized wrapper.
Hashtable hSync = Hashtable.Synchronized(hUnsync);
```

The following code snippet shows how to create a thread-safe `NameValueCollection`. Notice that the `NameValueCollection` class derives from the `NameObjectCollectionBase` class, which uses an explicit interface implementation to implement the `ICollection.SyncRoot` property. As shown, you must cast the `NameValueCollection` to an `ICollection` instance before you can access the `SyncRoot` property. Casting is not necessary with other specialized collection classes such as `HybridDictionary`, `ListDictionary`, and `StringCollection`, which do not use explicit interface implementations to implement `SyncRoot`.

```
// Create a NameValueCollection.
NameValueCollection nvCollection = new NameValueCollection();

// Obtain a lock on the NameValueCollection before modification.
lock (((ICollection)nvCollection).SyncRoot) {

    // Modify the NameValueCollection...
}
```

4-15. Start a New Process

Problem

You need to execute an application in a new process.

Solution

Call one of the static Start method overloads of the System.Diagnostics.Process class. Specify the configuration details of the process you want to start as individual arguments to the Start method or in a System.Diagnostics.ProcessStartInfo object that you pass to the Start method.

How It Works

The Process class provides a managed representation of an operating system process and provides a simple mechanism through which you can execute both managed and unmanaged applications. The Process class implements five static overloads of the Start method, which you use to start a new process. All these methods return a Process object that represents the newly started process. Two of these overloads are methods that allow you to specify only the name and arguments to pass to the new process. For example, the following statements both execute Notepad in a new process:

```
// Execute notepad.exe with no command-line arguments.
Process.Start("notepad.exe");

// Execute notepad.exe passing the name of the file to open as a
// command-line argument.
Process.Start("notepad.exe", "SomeFile.txt");
```

Another two overloads extend these and allow you to specify the name of a Windows user who the process should run as. You must specify the username, password, and Windows domain. The password is specified as a System.Security.SecureString for added security. (See recipe 11-18 for more information about the SecureString class.) Here is an example:

```
System.Security.SecureString mySecureString = new System.Security.SecureString();

// Obtain a password and place in SecureString (see Recipe 11-18).

// Execute notepad.exe with no command-line arguments.
Process.Start("notepad.exe", "allen", mySecureString, "MyDomain");

// Execute notepad.exe passing the name of the file to open as a
// command-line argument.
Process.Start("notepad.exe", "SomeFile.txt", "allen", mySecureString, "MyDomain");
```

The remaining static overload requires you to create a ProcessStartInfo object configured with the details of the process you want to run; using the ProcessStartInfo object provides greater control over the behavior and configuration of the new process. Table 4-3 summarizes some of the commonly used properties of the ProcessStartInfo class.

Table 4-3. Properties of the ProcessStartInfo Class

Property	Description
`Arguments`	The command-line arguments to pass to the new process.
`Domain`	A `string` containing the Windows domain name to which the user belongs.
`ErrorDialog`	If `Process.Start` cannot start the specified process, it will throw a `System.ComponentModel.Win32Exception`. If `ErrorDialog` is true, `Start` displays an error dialog box to the user before throwing the exception.
`FileName`	The name of the application to start. You can also specify any type of file for which you have configured an application association. For example, you could specify a file with a `.doc` or an `.xls` extension, which would cause Microsoft Word or Microsoft Excel to run.
`LoadUserProfile`	A `bool` indicating whether the user's profile should be loaded from the registry when the new process is started.
`Password`	A `SecureString` containing the password of the user.
`UserName`	A `string` containing the name of the user to use when starting the process.
`WindowStyle`	A member of the `System.Diagnostics.ProcessWindowStyle` enumeration, which controls how the window is displayed. Valid values include `Hidden`, `Maximized`, `Minimized`, and `Normal`.
`WorkingDirectory`	The fully qualified name of the initial directory for the new process.

When finished with a `Process` object, you should dispose of it in order to release system resources—call `Close`, call `Dispose`, or create the `Process` object within the scope of a `using` statement.

■ **Note** Disposing of a `Process` object does not affect the underlying system process, which will continue to run.

The Code

The following example uses `Process` to execute Notepad in a maximized window and open a file named `C:\Temp\file.txt`. After creation, the example calls the `Process.WaitForExit` method, which blocks the calling thread until a process terminates or a specified timeout expires. This method returns `true` if the process ends before the timeout and returns `false` otherwise.

```
using System;
using System.Diagnostics;

namespace Apress.VisualCSharpRecipes.Chapter04
{
    class Recipe04_15
    {
        public static void Main()
        {
            // Create a ProcessStartInfo object and configure it with the
            // information required to run the new process.
            ProcessStartInfo startInfo = new ProcessStartInfo();

            startInfo.FileName = "notepad.exe";
            startInfo.Arguments = "file.txt";
            startInfo.WorkingDirectory = @"C:\Temp";
            startInfo.WindowStyle = ProcessWindowStyle.Maximized;
            startInfo.ErrorDialog = true;

            // Declare a new Process object.
            Process process;

            try
            {
                // Start the new process.
                process = Process.Start(startInfo);

                // Wait for the new process to terminate before exiting.
                Console.WriteLine("Waiting 30 seconds for process to finish.");

                if (process.WaitForExit(30000))
                {
                    Console.WriteLine("Process terminated.");
                }
                else
                {
                    Console.WriteLine("Timed out waiting for process to end.");
                }
            }
            catch (Exception ex)
            {
                Console.WriteLine("Could not start process.");
                Console.WriteLine(ex);
            }
```

```
            // Wait to continue.
            Console.WriteLine(Environment.NewLine);
            Console.WriteLine("Main method complete. Press Enter.");
            Console.ReadLine();
        }
    }
}
```

4-16. Terminate a Process

Problem

You need to terminate a process such as an application or a service.

Solution

Obtain a `Process` object representing the operating system process you want to terminate. For Windows-based applications, call `Process.CloseMainWindow` to send a close message to the application's main window. For Windows-based applications that ignore `CloseMainWindow`, or for non-Windows-based applications, call the `Process.Kill` method.

How It Works

If you start a new process from managed code using the `Process` class (discussed in recipe 4-15), you can terminate the process using the `Process` object that represents the new process. You can also obtain `Process` objects that refer to other currently running processes using the static methods of the `Process` class summarized in Table 4-4.

Table 4-4. *Methods for Obtaining Process References*

Method	Description
`GetCurrentProcess`	Returns a `Process` object representing the currently active process.
`GetProcessById`	Returns a `Process` object representing the process with the specified ID. This is the process ID (PID) you can get using Windows Task Manager.
`GetProcesses`	Returns an array of `Process` objects representing all currently active processes.
`GetProcessesByName`	Returns an array of `Process` objects representing all currently active processes with a specified friendly name. The friendly name is the name of the executable excluding file extension or path; for example, a friendly name could be `notepad` or `calc`.

Once you have a Process object representing the process you want to terminate, you need to call either the CloseMainWindow method or the Kill method. The CloseMainWindow method posts a WM_CLOSE message to a Windows-based application's main window. This method has the same effect as if the user had closed the main window using the system menu, and it gives the application the opportunity to perform its normal shutdown routine. CloseMainWindow will not terminate applications that do not have a main window or applications with a disabled main window—possibly because a modal dialog box is currently displayed. Under such circumstances, CloseMainWindow will return false.

CloseMainWindow returns true if the close message was successfully sent, but this does not guarantee that the process is actually terminated. For example, applications used to edit data will usually give the user the opportunity to save unsaved data if a close message is received. The user usually has the chance to cancel the close operation under such circumstances. This means CloseMainWindow will return true, but the application will still be running once the user cancels. You can use the Process.WaitForExit method to signal process termination and the Process.HasExited property to test whether a process has terminated. Alternatively, you can use the Kill method.

The Kill method simply terminates a process immediately; the user has no chance to stop the termination, and all unsaved data is lost. Kill is the only option for terminating Windows-based applications that do not respond to CloseMainWindow and for terminating non-Windows-based applications.

The Code

The following example starts a new instance of Notepad, waits 5 seconds, and then terminates the Notepad process. The example first tries to terminate the process using CloseMainWindow. If CloseMainWindow returns false, or the Notepad process is still running after CloseMainWindow is called, the example calls Kill and forces the Notepad process to terminate; you can force CloseMainWindow to return false by leaving the File Open dialog box open.

```
using System;
using System.Threading;
using System.Diagnostics;

namespace Apress.VisualCSharpRecipes.Chapter04
{
    class Recipe04_16
    {
        public static void Main()
        {
            // Create a new Process and run notepad.exe.
            using (Process process =
                Process.Start("notepad.exe",@"c:\SomeFile.txt"))
            {
                // Wait for 5 seconds and terminate the notepad process.
                Console.WriteLine(
                    "Waiting 5 seconds before terminating notepad.exe.");
                Thread.Sleep(5000);

                // Terminate notepad process.
                Console.WriteLine("Terminating Notepad with CloseMainWindow.");
```

```
                // Try to send a close message to the main window.
                if (!process.CloseMainWindow())
                {
                    // Close message did not get sent - Kill Notepad.
                    Console.WriteLine("CloseMainWindow returned false - " +
                        " terminating Notepad with Kill.");
                    process.Kill();
                }
                else
                {
                    // Close message sent successfully; wait for 2 seconds
                    // for termination confirmation before resorting to Kill.
                    if (!process.WaitForExit(2000))
                    {
                        Console.WriteLine("CloseMainWindow failed to" +
                            " terminate - terminating Notepad with Kill.");
                        process.Kill();
                    }
                }
            }

            // Wait to continue.
            Console.WriteLine("Main method complete. Press Enter.");
            Console.ReadLine();
        }
    }
}
```

4-17. Ensure That Only One Instance of an Application Can Execute Concurrently

Problem

You need to ensure that a user can have only one instance of an application running concurrently.

Solution

Create a named `System.Threading.Mutex` object, and have your application try to acquire ownership of it at startup.

How It Works

The `Mutex` provides a mechanism for synchronizing the execution of threads across process boundaries and in addition provides a convenient mechanism through which to ensure that only a single instance of an application is running concurrently. By trying to acquire ownership of a named `Mutex` at startup and exiting if the Mutex cannot be acquired, you can ensure that only one instance of your application is running.

The Code

This example uses a Mutex named MutexExample to ensure that only a single instance of the example can execute:

```
using System;
using System.Threading;

namespace Apress.VisualCSharpRecipes.Chapter04
{
    class Recipe04_17
    {
        public static void Main()
        {
            // A Boolean that indicates whether this application has
            // initial ownership of the Mutex.
            bool ownsMutex;

            // Attempt to create and take ownership of a Mutex named
            // MutexExample.
            using (Mutex mutex =
                        new Mutex(true, "MutexExample", out ownsMutex))
            {
                // If the application owns the Mutex it can continue to execute;
                // otherwise, the application should exit.
                if (ownsMutex)
                {
                    Console.WriteLine("This application currently owns the" +
                        " mutex named MutexExample. Additional instances of" +
                        " this application will not run until you release" +
                        " the mutex by pressing Enter.");

                    Console.ReadLine();

                    // Release the mutex.
                    mutex.ReleaseMutex();
                }
                else
                {
                    Console.WriteLine("Another instance of this application " +
                        " already owns the mutex named MutexExample. This" +
                        " instance of the application will terminate.");
                }
            }
```

```
            // Wait to continue.
            Console.WriteLine("Main method complete. Press Enter.");
            Console.ReadLine();
        }
    }
}
```

■ **Note** If you do not construct the `Mutex` in a `using` statement and encapsulate the body of your application in the body of the `using` block as shown in this example, in long-running applications the garbage collector may dispose of the `Mutex` if it is not referenced after initial creation. This will result in releasing the `Mutex` and allow additional instances of the application to execute concurrently. In these circumstances, you should include the statement `System.GC.KeepAlive(mutex)` to ensure the `Mutex` is not garbage collected. Thanks to Michael A. Covington for highlighting this possibility.

CHAPTER 5

■ ■ ■

Files, Directories, and I/O

The Microsoft .NET Framework I/O classes fall into two basic categories. First are the classes that retrieve information from the file system and allow you to perform file system operations such as copying files and moving directories. Two examples include the `FileInfo` and the `DirectoryInfo` classes. The second and possibly more important category includes a broad range of classes that allow you to read and write data from all types of streams. Streams can correspond to binary or text files, a file in an isolated store, a network connection, or even a memory buffer. In all cases, the way you interact with a stream is the same. This chapter describes how to use the file system classes and a wide range of stream-based classes.

The recipes in this chapter describe how to do the following:

- Retrieve or modify information about a file, directory, or a drive (recipes 5-1, 5-2, 5-4, 5-5, and 5-16)
- Copy, move, and delete files and directories (recipe 5-3)
- Show a directory tree in a Microsoft Windows-based application use the common file dialog boxes and monitor the file system for changes (recipes 5-6, 5-17, and 5-19)
- Create, read, and write text and binary files; create temporary files; and use isolated storage (recipes 5-7, 5-8, 5-9, 5-15, 5-18, and 5-21)
- Search for specific files and test files for equality and work with strings that contain path information (recipes 5-10, 5-11, 5-12, 5-13, and 5-14)
- Write to a COM port (recipe 5-20)
- Retrieve or modify the access control lists (ACLs) of a file or directory (recipe 5-22)
- Compress and decompress data (recipe 5-23)
- Log data to a file and process a log file (recipes 5-24 and 5-25)
- Communicate between processes (recipes 5-26)

5-1. Retrieve Information About a File, Directory, or Drive

Problem

You need to retrieve information about a file, directory, or drive.

Solution

Create a new `System.IO.FileInfo`, `System.IO.DirectoryInfo`, or `System.IO.DriveInfo` object, depending on the type of resource about which you need to retrieve information. Supply the path of the resource to the constructor, and then you will be able to retrieve information through the properties of the class.

How It Works

To create a `FileInfo`, `DirectoryInfo`, or `DriveInfo` object, you supply a relative or fully qualified path in the constructor. You can retrieve information through the corresponding object properties. Table 5-1 lists some of the key members that are found in these objects.

Table 5-1. *Key Members for Files, Directories, and Drives*

Member	Applies To	Description
`Exists`	`FileInfo` and `DirectoryInfo`	Returns `true` or `false`, depending on whether a file or a directory exists at the specified location.
`Attributes`	`FileInfo` and `DirectoryInfo`	Returns one or more values from the `System.IO.FileAttributes` enumeration, which represents the attributes of the file or the directory.
`CreationTime`, `LastAccessTime`,	`FileInfo` and `DirectoryInfo`	Return `System.DateTime` and `LastWriteTime` instances that describe when a file or a directory was created, last accessed, and last updated, respectively.
`FullName`, `Name`, and `Extension`	`FileInfo` and `DirectoryInfo`	Return a string that represents the fully qualified name, the directory, or the file name (with extension), and the extension on its own.
`IsReadOnly`	`FileInfo`	Returns `true` or `false`, depending on whether a file is read-only.
`Length`	`FileInfo`	Returns the file size as a number of bytes.

Member	Applies To	Description
DirectoryName and Directory	FileInfo	DirectoryName returns the name of the parent directory as a string. Directory returns a full DirectoryInfo object that represents the parent directory and allows you to retrieve more information about it.
Parent and Root	DirectoryInfo	Return a DirectoryInfo object that represents the parent or root directory.
CreateSubdirectory	DirectoryInfo	Creates a directory with the specified name in the directory represented by the DirectoryInfo object. It also returns a new DirectoryInfo object that represents the subdirectory.
GetDirectories	DirectoryInfo	Returns an array of DirectoryInfo objects, with one element for each subdirectory contained in this directory.
GetFiles	DirectoryInfo	Returns an array of FileInfo objects, with one element for each file contained in this directory.
EnumerateFiles	DirectoryInfo	Returns an IEnumerable of FileInfo objects, with one element for each file contained in this directory
EnumerateDirectories	DirectoryInfo	Returns an IEnumerable of DirectoryInfo objects, with one element for each subdirectory.
DriveType	DriveInfo	Returns a DriveType enumeration value that represents the type of the specified drive; for example, Fixed or CD Rom.
AvailableFreeSpace	DriveInfo	Returns a long that represents the free space available in the drive.
GetDrives	DriveInfo	Returns an array of DriveInfo objects that represents the logical drives in the computer.

The following are a few points to note while working with these objects:

- FileInfo and DirectoryInfo classes derive from the abstract FileSystemInfo class, which defines common methods like CreationTime, Exists, and so on. The DriveInfo class does not inherit from this base class, so it does not provide some of the common members available in the other two classes.

- The full set of properties that `FileInfo` and `DirectoryInfo` objects expose is read the first time you interrogate any property. If the file or directory changes after this point, you must call the `Refresh` method to update the properties. However, this is not the case for `DriveInfo`; each property access asks the file system for an up-to-date value.
- You will not encounter an error if you specify a path that does not correspond to an existing file, directory, or drive. Instead, you will receive an object that represents an entity that does not exist—its `Exists` (or `IsReady` property for `DriveInfo`) property will be `false`. You can use this object to manipulate the entity. However, if you attempt to read most other properties, exceptions like `FileNotFoundException`, `DirectoryNotFoundException`, and so on will be thrown.

The Code

The following console application takes a file path from a command-line argument, and then displays information about the file, the containing directory, and the drive.

```
using System;
using System.IO;

namespace Apress.VisualCSharpRecipes.Chapter05
{
    static class Recipe05_01
    {
        static void Main(string[] args)
        {
            if (args.Length == 0)
            {
                Console.WriteLine("Please supply a filename.");
                return;
            }

            // Display file information.
            FileInfo file = new FileInfo(args[0]);

            Console.WriteLine("Checking file: " + file.Name);
            Console.WriteLine("File exists: " + file.Exists.ToString());

            if (file.Exists)
            {
                Console.Write("File created: ");
                Console.WriteLine(file.CreationTime.ToString());
                Console.Write("File last updated: ");
                Console.WriteLine(file.LastWriteTime.ToString());
                Console.Write("File last accessed: ");
                Console.WriteLine(file.LastAccessTime.ToString());
                Console.Write("File size (bytes): ");
                Console.WriteLine(file.Length.ToString());
```

```
                Console.Write("File attribute list: ");
                Console.WriteLine(file.Attributes.ToString());
            }
            Console.WriteLine();

            // Display directory information.
            DirectoryInfo dir = file.Directory;

            Console.WriteLine("Checking directory: " + dir.Name);
            Console.WriteLine("In directory: " + dir.Parent.Name);
            Console.Write("Directory exists: ");
            Console.WriteLine(dir.Exists.ToString());

            if (dir.Exists)
            {
                Console.Write("Directory created: ");
                Console.WriteLine(dir.CreationTime.ToString());
                Console.Write("Directory last updated: ");
                Console.WriteLine(dir.LastWriteTime.ToString());
                Console.Write("Directory last accessed: ");
                Console.WriteLine(dir.LastAccessTime.ToString());
                Console.Write("Directory attribute list: ");
                Console.WriteLine(dir.Attributes.ToString());
                Console.WriteLine("Directory contains: " +
                  dir.GetFiles().Length.ToString() + " files");
            }
            Console.WriteLine();

            // Display drive information.
            DriveInfo drv = new DriveInfo(file.FullName);

            Console.Write("Drive: ");
            Console.WriteLine(drv.Name);

            if (drv.IsReady)
            {
                Console.Write("Drive type: ");
                Console.WriteLine(drv.DriveType.ToString());
                Console.Write("Drive format: ");
                Console.WriteLine(drv.DriveFormat.ToString());
                Console.Write("Drive free space: ");
                Console.WriteLine(drv.AvailableFreeSpace.ToString());
            }

            // Wait to continue.
            Console.WriteLine(Environment.NewLine);
            Console.WriteLine("Main method complete. Press Enter.");
            Console.ReadLine();
        }
    }
}
```

Usage

If you execute the command `Recipe05-01.exe c:\windows\win.ini`, you might expect the following output:

```
Checking file: win.ini

File exists: True

File created: 31.Mar.2003 5:30:00 PM

File last updated: 24.Sep.2005 11:11:13 PM

File last accessed: 10.Nov.2005 9:41:05 PM

File size (bytes): 658

File attribute list: Archive


Checking directory: windows

In directory: c:\

Directory exists: True

Directory created: 04.Jun.2005 4:47:56 PM

Directory last updated: 01.Nov.2005 10:09:45 AM

Directory last accessed: 11.Nov.2005 6:24:59 AM

Directory attribute list: Directory

Directory contains: 134 files
```

```
Drive: c:\

Drive type: Fixed

Drive format: NTFS

Drive free space: 14045097984
```

5-2. Set File and Directory Attributes

Problem

You need to test or modify file or directory attributes.

Solution

Create a `System.IO.FileInfo` object for a file or a `System.IO.DirectoryInfo` object for a directory and use the bitwise AND (&) and OR (|) arithmetic operators to modify the value of the `Attributes` property.

How It Works

The `FileInfo.Attributes` and `DirectoryInfo.Attributes` properties represent file attributes such as archive, system, hidden, read-only, compressed, and encrypted. Because a file can possess any combination of attributes, the `Attributes` property accepts a combination of enumerated values. To individually test for a single attribute or change a single attribute, you need to use bitwise arithmetic. `FileInfo.Attributes` and `DirectoryInfo.Attributes` both return values from the `FileAttributes` enumeration, whose most commonly used values are

- `ReadOnly` (the file is read-only)
- `Hidden` (the file is hidden from ordinary directory listings)
- `System` (the file part of the operating system)
- `Directory` (the file is a directory)
- `Archive` (used by backup applications)
- `Temporary` (this is a temporary file and will be deleted when no longer required)
- `Compressed` (the contents of the file are compressed)
- `Encrypted` (the contents of the file are encrypted)

The Code

The following example takes a read-only test file and checks for the read-only attribute:

```
using System;
using System.IO;

namespace Apress.VisualCSharpRecipes.Chapter05
{
    static class Recipe05_02
    {
        static void Main()
        {
            // This file has the archive and read-only attributes.
            FileInfo file = new FileInfo(@"C:\Windows\win.ini");

            // This displays the attributes.
            Console.WriteLine(file.Attributes.ToString());

            // This test fails because other attributes are set.
            if (file.Attributes == FileAttributes.ReadOnly)
            {
                Console.WriteLine("File is read-only (faulty test).");
            }

            // This test succeeds because it filters out just the
            // read-only attribute.
            if ((file.Attributes & FileAttributes.ReadOnly) ==
              FileAttributes.ReadOnly)
            {
                Console.WriteLine("File is read-only (correct test).");
            }

            // Wait to continue.
            Console.WriteLine(Environment.NewLine);
            Console.WriteLine("Main method complete. Press Enter.");
            Console.ReadLine();
        }
    }
}
```

When setting an attribute, you must also use bitwise arithmetic, as demonstrated in the following example. In this case, it's needed to ensure that you don't inadvertently clear the other attributes.

```
// This adds just the read-only attribute.
file.Attributes = file.Attributes | FileAttributes.ReadOnly;

// This removes just the read-only attribute.
file.Attributes = file.Attributes & ~FileAttributes.ReadOnly;
```

5-3. Copy, Move, or Delete a File or Directory

Problem

You need to copy, move, or delete a file or directory.

Solution

Create a `System.IO.FileInfo` object for a file or a `System.IO.DirectoryInfo` object for a directory, supplying the path in the constructor. You can then use the object's methods to copy, move, and delete the file or directory.

How It Works

The `FileInfo` and `DirectoryInfo` classes include a host of valuable methods for manipulating files and directories. Table 5-2 shows methods for the `FileInfo` class, and Table 5-3 shows methods for the `DirectoryInfo` class.

Table 5-2. *Key Methods for Manipulating a FileInfo Object*

Method	Description
`CopyTo`	Copies a file to the new path and file name specified as a parameter. It also returns a new `FileInfo` object that represents the new (copied) file. You can supply an optional additional parameter of `true` to allow overwriting.
`Create` and `CreateText`	`Create` creates the specified file and returns a `FileStream` object that you can use to write to it. `CreateText` performs the same task, but returns a `StreamWriter` object that wraps the stream. For more information about writing files, see recipes 5-7 and 5-8.
`Open`, `OpenRead`, `OpenText`, and `OpenWrite`	Open a file (provided it exists). `OpenRead` and `OpenText` open a file in read-only mode, returning a `FileStream` or `StreamReader` object. `OpenWrite` opens a file in write-only mode, returning a `FileStream` object. For more information about reading files, see recipes 5-7 and 5-8.
`Delete`	Removes the file, if it exists.
`Encrypt` and `Decrypt`	Encrypt/decrypt a file using the current account. This applies to NTFS file systems only.

Method	Description
MoveTo	Moves the file to the new path and file name specified as a parameter. MoveTo can also be used to rename a file without changing its location.
Replace	Replaces contents of a file by the current FileInfo object. This method could also take a backup copy of the replaced file.

Table 5-3. Key Methods for Manipulating a DirectoryInfo Object

Method	Description
Create	Creates the specified directory. If the path specifies multiple directories that do not exist, they will all be created at once.
CreateSubdirectory	Creates a directory with the specified name in the directory represented by the DirectoryInfo object. It also returns a new DirectoryInfo object that represents the subdirectory.
Delete	Removes the directory, if it exists. If you want to delete a directory that contains other directories, you must use the overloaded Delete method that accepts a parameter named recursive and set it to true.
MoveTo	Moves the directory (contents and all) to a new path on the same drive. MoveTo can also be used to rename a directory without changing its location.

The Code

One useful feature that is missing from the DirectoryInfo class is a copy method. Fortunately, you can write this logic easily enough by relying on recursive logic and the FileInfo object.

The following example contains a helper function that can copy any directory, and its contents.

```
using System;
using System.IO;

namespace Apress.VisualCSharpRecipes.Chapter05
{
    static class Recipe05_03
    {
        static void Main(string[] args)
        {
            if (args.Length != 2)
            {
```

```
            Console.WriteLine("USAGE:  " +
              "Recipe05_03 [sourcePath] [destinationPath]");
              Console.ReadLine();
              return;
        }

        DirectoryInfo sourceDir = new DirectoryInfo(args[0]);
        DirectoryInfo destinationDir = new DirectoryInfo(args[1]);

        CopyDirectory(sourceDir, destinationDir);

        // Wait to continue.
        Console.WriteLine(Environment.NewLine);
        Console.WriteLine("Main method complete. Press Enter.");
        Console.ReadLine();
    }

    static void CopyDirectory(DirectoryInfo source,
        DirectoryInfo destination)
    {
        if (!destination.Exists)
        {
            destination.Create();
        }

        // Copy all files.
        foreach (FileInfo file in source.EnumerateFiles())
        {
            file.CopyTo(Path.Combine(destination.FullName,
                file.Name));
        }

        // Process subdirectories.
        foreach (DirectoryInfo dir in source.EnumerateDirectories())
        {
            // Get destination directory.
            string destinationDir = Path.Combine(destination.FullName,
                dir.Name);

            // Call CopyDirectory() recursively.
            CopyDirectory(dir, new DirectoryInfo(destinationDir));
        }
    }
  }
}
```

5-4. Calculate the Size of a Directory

Problem

You need to calculate the size of all files contained in a directory (and optionally, its subdirectories).

Solution

Examine all the files in a directory and add together their `FileInfo.Length` properties. Use recursive logic to include the size of files in contained subdirectories.

How It Works

The `DirectoryInfo` class does not provide any property that returns size information. However, you can easily calculate the size of all files contained in a directory using the `FileInfo.Length` property.

The Code

The following example calculates the size of a directory and optionally examines contained directories recursively.

```
using System;
using System.IO;

namespace Apress.VisualCSharpRecipes.Chapter05
{
    static class Recipe05_04
    {
        static void Main(string[] args)
        {
            if (args.Length == 0)
            {
                Console.WriteLine("Please supply a directory path.");
                return;
            }

            DirectoryInfo dir = new DirectoryInfo(args[0]);
            Console.WriteLine("Total size: " +
              CalculateDirectorySize(dir, true).ToString() +
              " bytes.");

            // Wait to continue.
            Console.WriteLine(Environment.NewLine);
            Console.WriteLine("Main method complete. Press Enter.");
            Console.ReadLine();
        }
```

```
        static long CalculateDirectorySize(DirectoryInfo directory,
      bool includeSubdirectories)
        {
            long totalSize = 0;

            // Examine all contained files.
            foreach (FileInfo file in directory.EnumerateFiles())
            {
                totalSize += file.Length;
            }

            // Examine all contained directories.
            if (includeSubdirectories)
            {
                foreach (DirectoryInfo dir in directory.EnumerateDirectories())
                {
                    totalSize += CalculateDirectorySize(dir, true);
                }
            }

            return totalSize;
        }
    }
}
```

5-5. Retrieve Version Information for a File

Problem

You want to retrieve file version information, such as the publisher of a file, its revision number, associated comments, and so on.

Solution

Use the static `GetVersionInfo` method of the `System.Diagnostics.FileVersionInfo` class.

How It Works

The .NET Framework allows you to retrieve file information without resorting to the Windows API. Instead, you simply need to use the `FileVersionInfo` class and call the `GetVersionInfo` method with the file name as a parameter. You can then retrieve extensive information through the `FileVersionInfo` properties.

The Code

The FileVersionInfo properties are too numerous to list here, but the following code snippet shows an example of what you might retrieve:

```
using System;
using System.Diagnostics;

namespace Apress.VisualCSharpRecipes.Chapter05
{
    static class Recipe05_05
    {
        static void Main(string[] args)
        {
            if (args.Length == 0)
            {
                Console.WriteLine("Please supply a filename.");
                return;
            }

            FileVersionInfo info = FileVersionInfo.GetVersionInfo(args[0]);

            // Display version information.
            Console.WriteLine("Checking File: " + info.FileName);
            Console.WriteLine("Product Name: " + info.ProductName);
            Console.WriteLine("Product Version: " + info.ProductVersion);
            Console.WriteLine("Company Name: " + info.CompanyName);
            Console.WriteLine("File Version: " + info.FileVersion);
            Console.WriteLine("File Description: " + info.FileDescription);
            Console.WriteLine("Original Filename: " + info.OriginalFilename);
            Console.WriteLine("Legal Copyright: " + info.LegalCopyright);
            Console.WriteLine("InternalName: " + info.InternalName);
            Console.WriteLine("IsDebug: " + info.IsDebug);
            Console.WriteLine("IsPatched: " + info.IsPatched);
            Console.WriteLine("IsPreRelease: " + info.IsPreRelease);
            Console.WriteLine("IsPrivateBuild: " + info.IsPrivateBuild);
            Console.WriteLine("IsSpecialBuild: " + info.IsSpecialBuild);

            // Wait to continue.
            Console.WriteLine(Environment.NewLine);
            Console.WriteLine("Main method complete. Press Enter.");
            Console.ReadLine();
        }
    }
}
```

Usage

If you run the command Recipe05_05 c:\windows\explorer.exe, the example produces the following output:

```
Checking File: c:\windows\explorer.exe
Product Name: Microsoftr Windowsr Operating System
Product Version: 6.00.2900.2180
Company Name: Microsoft Corporation
File Version: 6.00.2900.2180 (xpsp_sp2_rtm.040803-2158)
File Description: Windows Explorer
Original Filename: EXPLORER.EXE
Legal Copyright: c Microsoft Corporation. All rights reserved.
InternalName: explorer
IsDebug: False
IsPatched: False
IsPreRelease: False
IsPrivateBuild: False
IsSpecialBuild: False
```

5-6. Show a Just-in-Time Directory Tree in the TreeView Control

Problem

You need to display a directory tree in a `TreeView` control. However, filling the directory tree structure at startup is too time-consuming.

Solution

Fill the first level of directories in the `TreeView` control and add a hidden dummy node to each directory branch. React to the `TreeView.BeforeExpand` event to fill in subdirectories in a branch just before it's displayed.

How It Works

You can use recursion to build an entire directory tree. However, scanning the file system in this way can be slow, particularly for large drives. For this reason, professional file management software programs (including Windows Explorer) use a different technique. They query the necessary directory information when the user requests it.

The `TreeView` control is particularly well suited to this approach because it provides a `BeforeExpand` event that fires before a new level of nodes is displayed. You can use a placeholder (such as an asterisk or empty `TreeNode`) in all the directory branches that are not filled in. This allows you to fill in parts of the directory tree as they are displayed.

To use this type of solution, you need the following three ingredients:

- A `Fill` method that adds a single level of directory nodes based on a single directory. You will use this method to fill directory levels as they are expanded.
- A basic `Form.Load` event handler that uses the `Fill` method to add the first level of directories for the drive.
- A `TreeView.BeforeExpand` event handler that reacts when the user expands a node and calls the `Fill` method if this directory information has not yet been added.

The Code

The following shows the code element of a Windows Forms application that demonstrates this recipe. Download the source code that accompanies this book for the full Visual Studio project.

```
using System;
using System.Windows.Forms;
using System.IO;

namespace Apress.VisualCSharpRecipes.Chapter05
{
    public partial class DirectoryTree : Form
    {
        public DirectoryTree()
        {
            InitializeComponent();
        }

        private void DirectoryTree_Load(object sender, EventArgs e)
        {
            // Set the first node.
            TreeNode rootNode = new TreeNode(@"C:\");
            treeDirectory.Nodes.Add(rootNode);
```

```
            // Fill the first level and expand it.
            Fill(rootNode);
            treeDirectory.Nodes[0].Expand();
        }

        private void treeDirectory_BeforeExpand(object sender,
            TreeViewCancelEventArgs e)
        {
            // If a dummy node is found, remove it and read the
            // real directory list.
            if (e.Node.Nodes[0].Text == "*")
            {
                e.Node.Nodes.Clear();
                Fill(e.Node);
            }
        }

        private void Fill(TreeNode dirNode)
        {
            DirectoryInfo dir = new DirectoryInfo(dirNode.FullPath);

            // An exception could be thrown in this code if you don't
            // have sufficient security permissions for a file or directory.
            // You can catch and then ignore this exception.
            foreach (DirectoryInfo dirItem in dir.GetDirectories())
            {
                // Add node for the directory.
                TreeNode newNode = new TreeNode(dirItem.Name);
                dirNode.Nodes.Add(newNode);
                newNode.Nodes.Add("*");
            }
        }
    }
}
```

Figure 5-1 shows the directory tree in action.

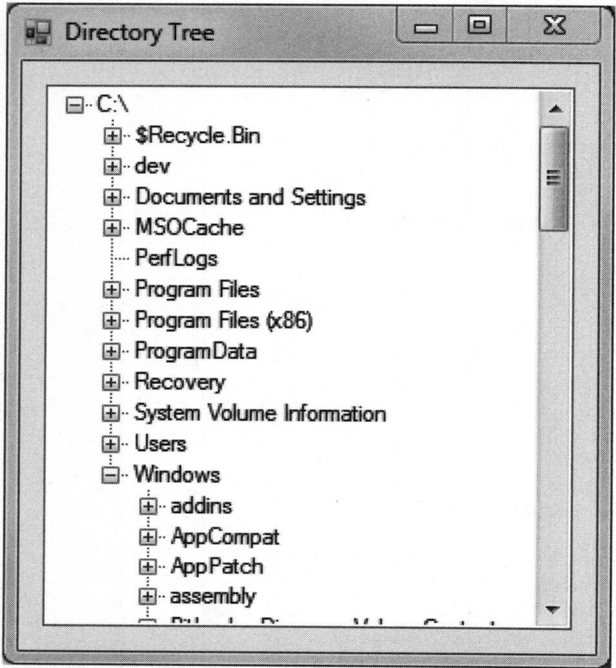

Figure 5-1. A directory tree with the TreeView

5-7. Read and Write a Text File

Problem

You need to write data to a sequential text file using ASCII, Unicode, or UTF-8 encoding.

Solution

Create a new `System.IO.FileStream` object that references the file. To write the file, wrap the `FileStream` in a `System.IO.StreamWriter` and use the overloaded `Write` method. To read the file, wrap the `FileStream` in a `System.IO.StreamReader` and use the `Read` or `ReadLine` method.

How It Works

The .NET Framework allows you to write or read text with any stream by using the `StreamWriter` and `StreamReader` classes. When writing data with the `StreamWriter`, you use the `StreamWriter.Write` method. This method is overloaded to support all the common C# .NET data types, including strings, chars, integers, floating-point numbers, decimals, and so on. However, the `Write` method always converts the supplied data to text. If you want to be able to convert the text back to its original data type, you should use the `WriteLine` method to make sure each value is placed on a separate line.

The way a string is represented depends on the encoding you use. The most common encodings include the following:

- ASCII, which encodes each character in a string using 7 bits. ASCII-encoded data cannot contain extended Unicode characters. When using ASCII encoding in .NET, the bits will be padded and the resulting byte array will have 1 byte for each character.
- Full Unicode (or UTF-16), which represents each character in a string using 16 bits. The resulting byte array will have 2 bytes for each character.
- UTF-7 Unicode, which uses 7 bits for ordinary ASCII characters and multiple 7-bit pairs for extended characters. This encoding is primarily for use with 7-bit protocols such as mail, and it is not regularly used.
- UTF-8 Unicode, which uses 8 bits for ordinary ASCII characters and multiple 8-bit pairs for extended characters. The resulting byte array will have 1 byte for each character (provided there are no extended characters).

The .NET Framework provides a class for each type of encoding in the `System.Text` namespace. When using `StreamReader` and `StreamWriter`, you can specify the encoding you want to use or simply use the default UTF-8 encoding.

When reading information, you use the `Read` or `ReadLine` method of `StreamReader`. The `Read` method reads a single character, or the number of characters you specify, and returns the data as a `char` or `char` array. The `ReadLine` method returns a string with the content of an entire line. The `ReadToEnd` method will return a string with the content starting from the current position to the end of the stream.

The Code

The following console application writes and then reads a text file:

```
using System;
using System.IO;
using System.Text;

namespace Apress.VisualCSharpRecipes.Chapter05
{
    static class Recipe05_07
    {
        static void Main()
        {
            // Create a new file.
            using (FileStream fs = new FileStream("test.txt", FileMode.Create))
            {
                // Create a writer and specify the encoding.
                // The default (UTF-8) supports special Unicode characters,
                // but encodes all standard characters in the same way as
                // ASCII encoding.
```

```
                using (StreamWriter w = new StreamWriter(fs, Encoding.UTF8))
                {
                    // Write a decimal, string, and char.
                    w.WriteLine(124.23M);
                    w.WriteLine("Test string");
                    w.WriteLine('!');
                }
            }
            Console.WriteLine("Press Enter to read the information.");
            Console.ReadLine();

            // Open the file in read-only mode.
            using (FileStream fs = new FileStream("test.txt", FileMode.Open))
            {
                using (StreamReader r = new StreamReader(fs, Encoding.UTF8))
                {
                    // Read the data and convert it to the appropriate data type.
                    Console.WriteLine(Decimal.Parse(r.ReadLine()));
                    Console.WriteLine(r.ReadLine());
                    Console.WriteLine(Char.Parse(r.ReadLine()));
                }
            }

            // Wait to continue.
            Console.WriteLine(Environment.NewLine);
            Console.WriteLine("Main method complete. Press Enter.");
            Console.ReadLine();
        }
    }
}
```

Running the program creates a file that contains the following content:

```
124.23

Test string

!
```

5-8. Read and Write a Binary File

Problem

You need to write data to a binary file with strong data typing.

Solution

Create a new `System.IO.FileStream` object that references the file. To write the file, wrap the `FileStream` in a `System.IO.BinaryWriter` and use the overloaded `Write` method. To read the file, wrap the `FileStream` in a `System.IO.BinaryReader` and use the `Read` method that corresponds to the expected data type.

How It Works

The .NET Framework allows you to write or read binary data with any stream by using the `BinaryWriter` and `BinaryReader` classes. When writing data with the `BinaryWriter`, you use the `BinaryWriter.Write` method. This method is overloaded to support all the common C# .NET data types, including strings, chars, integers, floating-point numbers, decimals, and so on. The information will then be encoded as a series of bytes and written to the file. You can configure the encoding used for strings by using an overloaded constructor that accepts a `System.Text.Encoding` object, as described in recipe 5-7.

You must be particularly fastidious with data types when using binary files. This is because when you retrieve the information, you must use one of the strongly typed `Read` methods from the `BinaryReader`. For example, to retrieve decimal data, you use `ReadDecimal`. To read a string, you use `ReadString`. (The `BinaryWriter` always records the length of a string when it writes it to a binary file to prevent any possibility of error.)

The Code

The following console application writes and then reads a binary file:

```
using System;
using System.IO;

namespace Apress.VisualCSharpRecipes.Chapter05
{
    static class Recipe05_08
    {
        static void Main()
        {
            // Create a new file and writer.
            using (FileStream fs = new FileStream("test.bin", FileMode.Create))
            {
                using (BinaryWriter w = new BinaryWriter(fs))
                {
                    // Write a decimal, two strings, and a char.
                    w.Write(124.23M);
                    w.Write("Test string");
                    w.Write("Test string 2");
                    w.Write('!');
                }
            }
            Console.WriteLine("Press Enter to read the information.");
            Console.ReadLine();
```

```
            // Open the file in read-only mode.
            using (FileStream fs = new FileStream("test.bin", FileMode.Open))
            {
                // Display the raw information in the file.
                using (StreamReader sr = new StreamReader(fs))
                {
                    Console.WriteLine(sr.ReadToEnd());
                    Console.WriteLine();

                    // Read the data and convert it to the appropriate data type.
                    fs.Position = 0;
                    using (BinaryReader br = new BinaryReader(fs))
                    {
                        Console.WriteLine(br.ReadDecimal());
                        Console.WriteLine(br.ReadString());
                        Console.WriteLine(br.ReadString());
                        Console.WriteLine(br.ReadChar());
                    }
                }
            }

            // Wait to continue.
            Console.WriteLine(Environment.NewLine);
            Console.WriteLine("Main method complete. Press Enter.");
            Console.ReadLine();
        }
    }
}
```

5-9. Read a File Asynchronously

Problem

You need to read data from a file without blocking the execution of your code. This technique is commonly used if the file is stored on a slow backing store (such as a networked drive in a wide area network).

Solution

Create a separate class that will read the file asynchronously. Start reading a block of data using the `FileStream.BeginRead` method and supply a callback method. When the callback is triggered, retrieve the data by calling `FileStream.EndRead`, process it, and read the next block asynchronously with `BeginRead`.

How It Works

The FileStream includes basic support for asynchronous use through the BeginRead and EndRead methods. Using these methods, you can read a block of data on one of the threads provided by the .NET Framework thread pool, without needing to directly use the threading classes in the System.Threading namespace.

When reading a file asynchronously, you choose the amount of data that you want to read at a time. Depending on the situation, you might want to read a very small amount of data at a time (for example, if you are copying it block by block to another file) or a relatively large amount of data (for example, if you need a certain amount of information before your processing logic can start). You specify the block size when calling BeginRead, and you pass a buffer where the data will be placed. Because the BeginRead and EndRead methods need to be able to access many of the same pieces of information, such as the FileStream, the buffer, the block size, and so on, it's usually easiest to encapsulate your asynchronous file reading code in a single class.

The Code

The following example demonstrates reading a file asynchronously. The AsyncProcessor class provides a public StartProcess method, which starts an asynchronous read. Every time the read operation finishes, the OnCompletedRead callback is triggered and the block of data is processed. If there is more data in the file, a new asynchronous read operation is started. AsyncProcessor reads 2 kilobytes (2048 bytes) at a time.

```
using System;
using System.IO;
using System.Threading;

namespace Apress.VisualCSharpRecipes.Chapter05
{
    public class AsyncProcessor
    {
        private Stream inputStream;

        // The amount that will be read in one block (2KB).
        private int bufferSize = 2048;

        public int BufferSize
        {
            get { return bufferSize; }
            set { bufferSize = value; }
        }

        // The buffer that will hold the retrieved data.
        private byte[] buffer;

        public AsyncProcessor(string fileName)
        {
            buffer = new byte[bufferSize];
```

```
            // Open the file, specifying true for asynchronous support.
            inputStream = new FileStream(fileName, FileMode.Open,
              FileAccess.Read, FileShare.Read, bufferSize, true);
        }

        public void StartProcess()
        {

            // Start the asynchronous read, which will fill the buffer.
            inputStream.BeginRead(buffer, 0, buffer.Length,
              OnCompletedRead, null);
        }

        private void OnCompletedRead(IAsyncResult asyncResult)
        {
            // One block has been read asynchronously.
            // Retrieve the data.
            int bytesRead = inputStream.EndRead(asyncResult);

            // If no bytes are read, the stream is at the end of the file.
            if (bytesRead > 0)
            {
                // Pause to simulate processing this block of data.
                Console.WriteLine("\t[ASYNC READER]: Read one block.");
                Thread.Sleep(TimeSpan.FromMilliseconds(20));

                // Begin to read the next block asynchronously.
                inputStream.BeginRead(
                buffer, 0, buffer.Length, OnCompletedRead,
                  null);
            }
            else
            {
                // End the operation.
                Console.WriteLine("\t[ASYNC READER]: Complete.");
                inputStream.Close();
            }
        }
    }
}
```

Usage

The following example shows a console application that uses `AsyncProcessor` to read a 2MB file:

```
using System;
using System.IO;
using System.Threading;
```

```
namespace Apress.VisualCSharpRecipes.Chapter05
{
    static class Recipe05_09
    {
        static void Main(string[] args)
        {
            // Create a test file.
            using (FileStream fs = new FileStream("test.txt", FileMode.Create))
            {
                fs.SetLength(100000);
            }

            // Start the asynchronous file processor on another thread.
            AsyncProcessor asyncIO = new AsyncProcessor("test.txt");
            asyncIO.StartProcess();

            // At the same time, do some other work.
            // In this example, we simply loop for 10 seconds.
            DateTime startTime = DateTime.Now;
            while (DateTime.Now.Subtract(startTime).TotalSeconds < 2)
            {
                Console.WriteLine("[MAIN THREAD]: Doing some work.");

                // Pause to simulate a time-consuming operation.
                Thread.Sleep(TimeSpan.FromMilliseconds(100));
            }

            Console.WriteLine("[MAIN THREAD]: Complete.");
            Console.ReadLine();

            // Remove the test file.
            File.Delete("test.txt");
        }
    }
}
```

The following is an example of the output you will see when you run this test:

```
[MAIN THREAD]: Doing some work.

        [ASYNC READER]: Read one block.

        [ASYNC READER]: Read one block.

[MAIN THREAD]: Doing some work.

        [ASYNC READER]: Read one block.

        [ASYNC READER]: Read one block.
```

```
        [ASYNC READER]: Read one block.
        [ASYNC READER]: Read one block.
[MAIN THREAD]: Doing some work.
        [ASYNC READER]: Read one block.
        [ASYNC READER]: Read one block.
        [ASYNC READER]: Read one block.
        . . .
```

5-10. Find Files That Match a Wildcard Expression

Problem

You need to process multiple files based on a filter expression (such as `*.dll or mysheet20??.xls`).

Solution

Use the overloaded versions of the `System.IO.DirectoryInfo.GetFiles` or `System.IO.DirectoryInfo.EnumerateFiles` methods that accept a filter expression and return an array of `FileInfo` objects. For searching recursively across all subdirectories, use the overloaded version that accepts the `SearchOption` enumeration.

How It Works

The `DirectoryInfo` and `Directory` objects both provide a way to search the directories for files that match a specific filter expression. These search expressions can use the standard `?` and `*` wildcards. You can use a similar technique to retrieve directories that match a specified search pattern by using the overloaded `DirectoryInfo.GetDirectories` or `DirectoryInfo.EnumerateDirectories` methods. You can also use the overload of `GetFiles` for searching recursively using the `SearchOption.AllDirectories` enumeration constant.

The Code

The following example retrieves the names of all the files in a specified directory that match a specified filter string. The directory and filter expression are submitted as command-line arguments. The code then iterates through the retrieved `FileInfo` collection of matching files and displays the name and size of each one:

```
using System;
using System.IO;

namespace Apress.VisualCSharpRecipes.Chapter05
{
    static class Recipe05_10
    {
        static void Main(string[] args)
        {
            if (args.Length != 2)
            {
                Console.WriteLine(
                  "USAGE:  Recipe05_10 [directory] [filterExpression]");
                return;
            }

            DirectoryInfo dir = new DirectoryInfo(args[0]);
            FileInfo[] files = dir.GetFiles(args[1]);

            // Display the name of all the files.
            foreach (FileInfo file in files)
            {
                Console.Write("Name: " + file.Name + "  ");
                Console.WriteLine("Size: " + file.Length.ToString());
            }

            // Wait to continue.
            Console.WriteLine(Environment.NewLine);
            Console.WriteLine("Main method complete. Press Enter.");
            Console.ReadLine();
        }
    }
}
```

5-11. Test Two Files for Equality

Problem

You need to quickly compare the content of two files and determine if it matches exactly.

Solution

Calculate the hash code of each file using the `System.Security.Cryptography.HashAlgorithm` class, and then compare the hash codes.

How It Works

You might compare file contents in a number of ways. For example, you could examine a portion of the file for similar data, or you could read through each file byte by byte, comparing each byte as you go. Both of these approaches are valid, but in some cases it's more convenient to use a *hash code* algorithm.

A hash code algorithm generates a small (typically about 20 bytes) binary fingerprint for a file. While it's *possible* for different files to generate the same hash codes, that is statistically unlikely to occur. In fact, even a minor change (for example, modifying a single bit in the source file) has an approximately 50 percent chance of independently changing each bit in the hash code. For this reason, hash codes are often used in security code to detect data tampering. (Hash codes are discussed in more detail in recipes 11-14, 11-15, and 11-16.)

To create a hash code, you must first create a `HashAlgorithm` object, typically by calling the static `HashAlgorithm.Create` method. You can then call `HashAlgorithm.ComputeHash`, which returns a byte array with the hash data.

The Code

The following example demonstrates a simple console application that reads two file names that are supplied as arguments and uses hash codes to test the files for equality. The hashes are compared by converting them into strings. Alternatively, you could compare them by iterating over the byte array and comparing each value. This approach would be slightly faster, but because the overhead of converting 20 bytes into a string is minimal, it's not required.

```
using System;
using System.IO;
using System.Security.Cryptography;

namespace Apress.VisualCSharpRecipes.Chapter05
{
    static class Recipe05_11
    {
        static void Main(string[] args)
        {
            if (args.Length != 2)
            {
                Console.WriteLine("USAGE:  Recipe05_11 [fileName] [fileName]");
                return;
            }

            Console.WriteLine("Comparing " + args[0] + " and " + args[1]);

            // Create the hashing object.
            using (HashAlgorithm hashAlg = HashAlgorithm.Create())
            {
                using (FileStream fsA = new FileStream(args[0], FileMode.Open),
                    fsB = new FileStream(args[1], FileMode.Open))
                {
                    // Calculate the hash for the files.
                    byte[] hashBytesA = hashAlg.ComputeHash(fsA);
                    byte[] hashBytesB = hashAlg.ComputeHash(fsB);
```

```
                // Compare the hashes.
                if (BitConverter.ToString(hashBytesA) ==
                    BitConverter.ToString(hashBytesB))
                {
                    Console.WriteLine("Files match.");
                }
                else
                {
                    Console.WriteLine("No match.");
                }
            }
        }

        // Wait to continue.
        Console.WriteLine(Environment.NewLine);
        Console.WriteLine("Main method complete. Press Enter.");
        Console.ReadLine();
    }
  }
}
```

5-12. Manipulate Strings Representing File Names

Problem

You want to retrieve a portion of a path or verify that a file path is in a normal (standardized) form.

Solution

Process the path using the `System.IO.Path` class. You can use `Path.GetFileName` to retrieve a file name from a path, `Path.ChangeExtension` to modify the extension portion of a path string, and `Path.Combine` to create a fully qualified path without worrying about whether your directory includes a trailing directory separation character(\).

How It Works

File paths are often difficult to work with in code because of the many different ways to represent the same directory. For example, you might use an absolute path (`C:\Temp`), a UNC path (`\\MyServer\\MyShare\temp`), or one of many possible relative paths (`C:\Temp\MyFiles\..\` or `C:\Temp\MyFiles\..\..\temp`).

The easiest way to handle file system paths is to use the static methods of the `Path` class to make sure you have the information you expect. For example, here is how you take a file name that might include a qualified path and extract just the file name:

```
string filename = @"..\System\MyFile.txt";
filename = Path.GetFileName(filename);

// Now filename = "MyFile.txt"
```

And here is how you might append the file name to a directory path using the `Path.Combine` method:

```
string filename = @"..\..\myfile.txt";
string fullPath = @"c:\Temp";

string filename = Path.GetFileName(filename);
string fullPath = Path.Combine(fullPath, filename);

// (fullPath is now "c:\Temp\myfile.txt")
```

The advantage of this approach is that a trailing backslash (\) is automatically added to the path name if required. The `Path` class also provides the following useful methods for manipulating path information:

- `ChangeExtension` modifies the current extension of the file in a string. If no extension is specified, the current extension will be removed.
- `GetDirectoryName` returns all the directory information, which is the text between the first and last directory separators (\).
- `GetFileNameWithoutExtension` is similar to `GetFileName`, but it omits the extension.
- `GetFullPath` has no effect on an absolute path, and it changes a relative path into an absolute path using the current directory. For example, if `C:\Temp\` is the current directory, calling `GetFullPath` on a file name such as `test.txt` returns `C:\Temp\test.txt`.
- `GetPathRoot` retrieves a string with the root (for example, "`C:\`"), provided that information is in the string. For a relative path, it returns a `null` reference.
- `HasExtension` returns `true` if the path ends with an extension.
- `IsPathRooted` returns `true` if the path is an absolute path and `false` if it's a relative path.

■ **Note** In most cases, an exception will be thrown if you try to supply an invalid path to one of these methods (for example, paths that include illegal characters). However, path names that are invalid because they contain a wildcard character (* or ?) will not cause the methods to throw an exception. You could use the `Path.GetInvalidPathChars` method to obtain an array of characters that are illegal in path names.

5-13. Determine If a Path Is a Directory or a File

Problem

You have a path (in the form of a string), and you want to determine whether it corresponds to a directory or a file.

Solution

Test the path with the `Directory.Exists` and the `File.Exists` methods.

How It Works

The `System.IO.Directory` and `System.IO.File` classes both provide an `Exists` method. The `Directory.Exists` method returns `true` if a supplied relative or absolute path corresponds to an existing directory, even a shared folder with an UNC name. `File.Exists` returns `true` if the path corresponds to an existing file.

The Code

The following example demonstrates how you can quickly determine if a path corresponds to a file or directory:

```
using System;
using System.IO;

namespace Apress.VisualCSharpRecipes.Chapter05
{
    static class Recipe05_13
    {
        static void Main(string[] args)
        {
            foreach (string arg in args)
            {
                Console.Write(arg);

                if (Directory.Exists(arg))
                {
                    Console.WriteLine(" is a directory");
                }
                else if (File.Exists(arg))
                {
                    Console.WriteLine(" is a file");
                }
```

```
                else
                {
                    Console.WriteLine(" does not exist");
                }
            }

            // Wait to continue.
            Console.WriteLine(Environment.NewLine);
            Console.WriteLine("Main method complete. Press Enter.");
            Console.ReadLine();
        }
    }
}
```

5-14. Work with Relative Paths

Problem

You want to set the current working directory so that you can use relative paths in your code.

Solution

Use the static `GetCurrentDirectory` and `SetCurrentDirectory` methods of the `System.IO.Directory` class.

How It Works

Relative paths are automatically interpreted in relation to the current working directory. You can retrieve the current working directory by calling `Directory.GetCurrentDirectory` or change it using `Directory.SetCurrentDirectory`. In addition, you can use the static `GetFullPath` method of the `System.IO.Path` class to convert a relative path into an absolute path using the current working directory.

The Code

The following is a simple example that demonstrates working with relative paths:

```
using System;
using System.IO;

namespace Apress.VisualCSharpRecipes.Chapter05
{
    static class Recipe05_14
    {
        static void Main()
        {
```

```
            Console.WriteLine("Using: " + Directory.GetCurrentDirectory());
            Console.WriteLine("The relative path 'file.txt' " +
              "will automatically become: '" +
              Path.GetFullPath("file.txt") + "'");

            Console.WriteLine();

            Console.WriteLine("Changing current directory to c:\\");
            Directory.SetCurrentDirectory(@"c:\");

            Console.WriteLine("Now the relative path 'file.txt' " +
              "will automatically become '" +
              Path.GetFullPath("file.txt") + "'");

            // Wait to continue.
            Console.WriteLine(Environment.NewLine);
            Console.WriteLine("Main method complete. Press Enter.");
            Console.ReadLine();
        }
    }
}
```

Usage

The output for this example might be the following (if you run the application in the directory `C:\temp`):

```
Using: c:\temp

The relative path 'file.txt' will automatically become 'c:\temp\file.txt'



Changing current directory to c:\

The relative path 'file.txt' will automatically become 'c:\file.txt'
```

■ **Caution** If you use relative paths, it's recommended that you set the working path at the start of each file interaction. Otherwise, you could introduce unnoticed security vulnerabilities that could allow a malicious user to force your application into accessing or overwriting system files by tricking it into using a different working directory.

5-15. Create a Temporary File

Problem

You need to create a file that will be placed in the user-specific temporary directory and will have a unique name, so that it will not conflict with temporary files generated by other programs.

Solution

Use the static `GetTempFileName` method of the `System.IO.Path` class, which returns a path made up of the user's temporary directory and a randomly generated file name.

How It Works

You can use a number of approaches to generate temporary files. In simple cases, you might just create a file in the application directory, possibly using a GUID or a timestamp in conjunction with a random value as the file name. However, the `Path` class provides a helper method that can save you some work. It creates a file with a unique file name in the current user's temporary directory that is stored in a folder like `C:\Documents and Settings\[username]\Local Settings\temp`.

The Code

The following example demonstrates creating a temporary file:

```
using System;
using System.IO;

namespace Apress.VisualCSharpRecipes.Chapter05
{
    static class Recipe05_15
    {
        static void Main()
        {
            string tempFile = Path.GetTempFileName();

            Console.WriteLine("Using " + tempFile);

            using (FileStream fs = new FileStream(tempFile, FileMode.Open))
            {
                // (Write some data.)
            }

            // Now delete the file.
            File.Delete(tempFile);
```

```
            // Wait to continue.
            Console.WriteLine(Environment.NewLine);
            Console.WriteLine("Main method complete. Press Enter.");
            Console.ReadLine();
        }
    }
}
```

5-16. Get the Total Free Space on a Drive

Problem

You need to examine a drive and determine how many bytes of free space are available.

Solution

Use the `DriveInfo.AvailableFreeSpace` property.

How It Works

The `DriveInfo` class provides members that let you find out the drive type, free space, and many other details of a drive. In order to create a new `DriveInfo` object, you need to pass the drive letter or the drive root string to the constructor, such as `'C'` or `"C:\"` for creating a `DriveInfo` instance representing the C drive of the computer. You could also retrieve the list of logical drives available by using the static `Directory.GetLogicalDrives` method, which returns an array of strings, each containing the root of the drive, such as `"C:\"`. For more details on each drive, you create a `DriveInfo` instance, passing either the root or the letter corresponding to the logical drive. If you need a detailed description of each logical drive, call the `DriveInfo.GetDrives` method, which returns an array of `DriveInfo` objects, instead of using `Directory.GetLogicalDrives`.

■ **Note** A `System.IO.IOException` is thrown if you try to access an unavailable network drive.

The Code

The following console application shows the available free space using the `DriveInfo` class for the given drive or for all logical drives if no argument is passed to the application:

```
using System;
using System.IO;

namespace Apress.VisualCSharpRecipes.Chapter05
{
    static class Recipe05_16
    {
        static void Main(string[] args)
        {
            if (args.Length == 1)
            {
                DriveInfo drive = new DriveInfo(args[0]);

                Console.Write("Free space in {0}-drive (in kilobytes): ", args[0]);
                Console.WriteLine(drive.AvailableFreeSpace / 1024);
                Console.ReadLine();
                return;
            }

            foreach (DriveInfo drive in DriveInfo.GetDrives())
            {
                try
                {
                    Console.WriteLine(
                        "{0} - {1} KB",
                        drive.RootDirectory,
                        drive.AvailableFreeSpace / 1024
                        );
                }
                catch (IOException) // network drives may not be available
                {
                    Console.WriteLine(drive);
                }
            }

            // Wait to continue.
            Console.WriteLine(Environment.NewLine);
            Console.WriteLine("Main method complete. Press Enter.");
            Console.ReadLine();
        }
    }
}
```

■ **Note** In addition to the `AvailableFreeSpace` property, `DriveInfo` also defines a `TotalFreeSpace` property. The difference between these two properties is that `AvailableFreeSpace` takes into account disk quotas.

5-17. Show the Common File Dialog Boxes

Problem

You need to show the standard Windows dialog boxes for opening and saving files and for selecting a folder.

Solution

Use the `OpenFileDialog`, `SaveFileDialog`, and `FolderBrowserDialog` classes in the `System.Windows.Forms` namespace. Call the `ShowDialog` method to display the dialog box, examine the return value to determine whether the user clicked OK or Cancel, and retrieve the selection from the `FileName` or `SelectedPath` property.

How It Works

The .NET Framework provides objects that wrap many of the standard Windows dialog boxes, including those used for saving and selecting files and directories. These classes all inherit from `System.Windows.Forms.CommonDialog` and include the following:

- `OpenFileDialog`, which allows the user to select a file, as shown in Figure 5-2. The file name and path are provided to your code through the `FileName` property (or the `FileNames` collection, if you have enabled multiple-file select by setting `Multiselect` to `true`). Additionally, you can use the `Filter` property to set the file format choices and set `CheckFileExists` to enforce validation.
- `SaveFileDialog`, which allows the user to specify a new file. The file name and path are provided to your code through the `FileName` property. You can also use the `Filter` property to set the file format choices, and set the `CreatePrompt` and `OverwritePrompt` Boolean properties to instruct .NET to display a confirmation if the user selects a new file or an existing file, respectively.
- `FolderBrowserDialog`, which allows the user to select (and optionally create) a directory. The selected path is provided through the `SelectedPath` property, and you can specify whether or not a Create New button should appear.

When using `OpenFileDialog` or `SaveFileDialog`, you need to set the filter string, which specifies the allowed file extensions. The filter string is separated with the pipe character (`|`) in this format:

```
[Text label] | [Extension list separated by semicolons] | [Text label]
| [Extension list separated by semicolons] |  . . .
```

You can also set the `Title` (form caption) and the `InitialDirectory`.

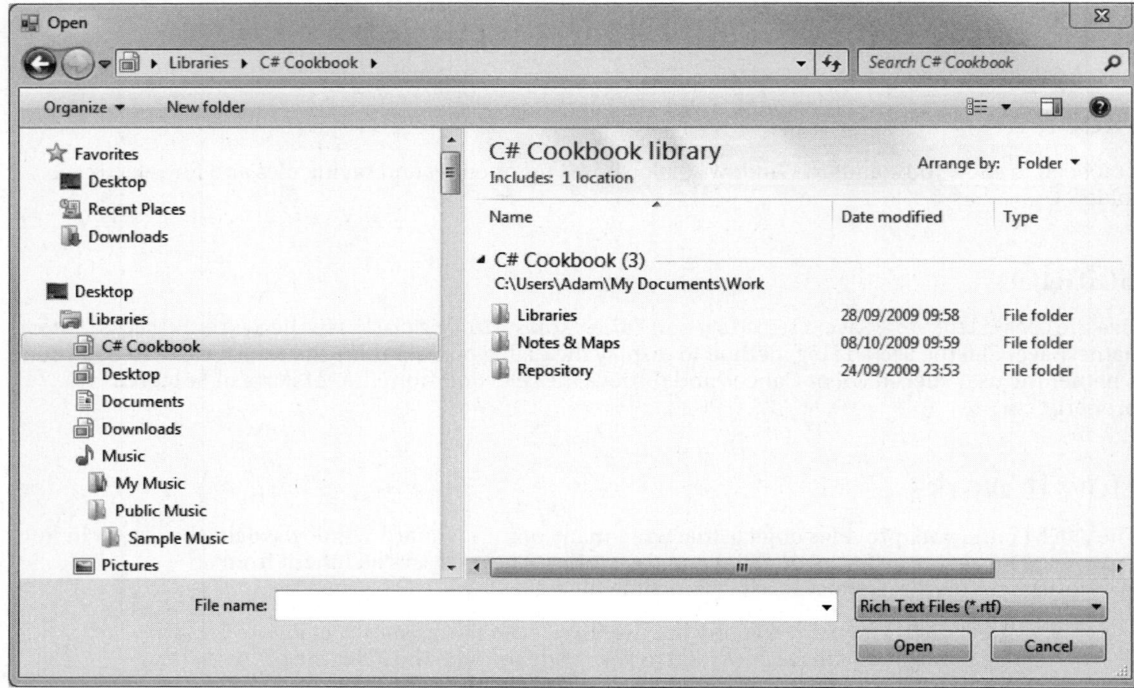

Figure 5-2. *OpenFileDialog shows the Open dialog box.*

The Code

The following code shows the code part of a Windows Forms application that allows the user to load documents into a `RichTextBox`, edit the content, and then save the modified document. When opening and saving a document, the `OpenFileDialog` and `SaveFileDialog` classes are used. Download the source code that accompanies this book from `www.apress.com/book/sourcecode` to see the full Visual Studio project.

```
using System;
using System.Windows.Forms;

namespace Apress.VisualCSharpRecipes.Chapter05
{
    public partial class MainForm : Form
    {
        public MainForm()
        {
            InitializeComponent();
        }
```

```
        private void mnuOpen_Click(object sender, EventArgs e)
        {
            OpenFileDialog dlg = new OpenFileDialog();
            dlg.Filter = "Rich Text Files (*.rtf)|*.RTF|" +
              "All files (*.*)|*.*";
            dlg.CheckFileExists = true;
            dlg.InitialDirectory = Application.StartupPath;

            if (dlg.ShowDialog() == DialogResult.OK)
            {
                rtDoc.LoadFile(dlg.FileName);
                rtDoc.Enabled = true;
            }
        }

        private void mnuSave_Click(object sender, EventArgs e)
        {
            SaveFileDialog dlg = new SaveFileDialog();
            dlg.Filter = "RichText Files (*.rtf)|*.RTF|Text Files (*.txt)|*.TXT" +
              "|All files (*.*)|*.*";
            dlg.CheckFileExists = true;
            dlg.InitialDirectory = Application.StartupPath;

            if (dlg.ShowDialog() == DialogResult.OK)
            {
                rtDoc.SaveFile(dlg.FileName);
            }
        }

        private void mnuExit_Click(object sender, EventArgs e)
        {
            this.Close();
        }
    }
}
```

5-18. Use an Isolated Store

Problem

You need to store data in a file, but your application does not have the required `FileIOPermission` for the local hard drive.

Solution

Use the IsolatedStorageFile and IsolatedStorageFileStream classes from the System.IO.IsolatedStorage namespace. These classes allow your application to write data to a file in a user-specific directory without needing permission to access the local hard drive directly.

How It Works

The .NET Framework includes support for isolated storage, which allows you to read and write to a user-specific virtual file system that the Common Language Runtime (CLR) manages. When you create isolated storage files, the data is automatically serialized to a unique location in the user profile path (typically a path like C:\Documents and Settings\[username]\Local Settings\Application Data\isolated storage\[guid_identifier]).

One reason you might use isolated storage is to give a partially trusted application limited ability to store data. For example, the default CLR security policy gives local code unrestricted FileIOPermission, which allows it to open or write to any file. Code that you run from a remote server on the local intranet is automatically assigned fewer permissions. It lacks the FileIOPermission, but it has the IsolatedStoragePermission, giving it the ability to use isolated stores. (The security policy also limits the maximum amount of space that can be used in an isolated store.) Another reason you might use an isolated store is to better secure data. For example, data in one user's isolated store will be restricted from another nonadministrative user.

By default, each isolated store is segregated by user and assembly. That means that when the same user runs the same application, the application will access the data in the same isolated store. However, you can choose to segregate it further by application domain so that multiple AppDomain instances running in the same application receive different isolated stores.

The files are stored as part of a user's profile, so users can access their isolated storage files on any workstation they log onto if roaming profiles are configured on your local area network. (In this case, the store must be specifically designated as a roaming store by applying the IsolatedStorageFile.Roaming flag when it's created.) By letting the .NET Framework and the CLR provide these levels of isolation, you can relinquish responsibility for maintaining the separation between files, and you do not need to worry that programming oversights or misunderstandings will cause loss of critical data.

The Code

The following example shows how you can access isolated storage:

```
using System;
using System.IO;
using System.IO.IsolatedStorage;

namespace Apress.VisualCSharpRecipes.Chapter05
{
    static class Recipe05_18
    {
        static void Main(string[] args)
        {
            // Create the store for the current user.
            using (IsolatedStorageFile store =
```

```
                IsolatedStorageFile.GetUserStoreForAssembly())
            {
                // Create a folder in the root of the isolated store.
                store.CreateDirectory("MyFolder");

                // Create a file in the isolated store.
                using (Stream fs = new IsolatedStorageFileStream(
                  "MyFile.txt", FileMode.Create, store))
                {
                    StreamWriter w = new StreamWriter(fs);

                    // You can now write to the file as normal.
                    w.WriteLine("Test");
                    w.Flush();
                }

                Console.WriteLine("Current size: " +
                    store.UsedSize.ToString());
                Console.WriteLine("Scope: " + store.Scope.ToString());

                Console.WriteLine("Contained files include:");
                string[] files = store.GetFileNames("*.*");
                foreach (string file in files)
                {
                    Console.WriteLine(file);
                }
            }

            // Wait to continue.
            Console.WriteLine(Environment.NewLine);
            Console.WriteLine("Main method complete. Press Enter.");
            Console.ReadLine();
        }
    }
}
```

The following demonstrates using multiple AppDomain instances running in the same application to receive different isolated stores:

```
// Access isolated storage for the current user and assembly
// (which is equivalent to the first example).
store = IsolatedStorageFile.GetStore(IsolatedStorageScope.User |
  IsolatedStorageScope.Assembly, null, null);

// Access isolated storage for the current user, assembly,
// and application domain. In other words, this data is
// accessible only by the current AppDomain instance.
store = IsolatedStorageFile.GetStore(IsolatedStorageScope.User |
  IsolatedStorageScope.Assembly | IsolatedStorageScope.Domain,
  null, null);
```

5-19. Monitor the File System for Changes

Problem

You need to react when a file system change is detected in a specific path (such as a file modification or creation).

Solution

Use the `System.IO.FileSystemWatcher` component, specify the path or file you want to monitor, and handle the `Created`, `Deleted`, `Renamed`, and `Changed` events.

How It Works

When linking together multiple applications and business processes, it's often necessary to create a program that waits idly and becomes active only when a new file is received or changed. You can create this type of program by scanning a directory periodically, but you face a key trade-off. The more often you scan, the more system resources you waste. The less often you scan, the longer it will take to detect a change. The solution is to use the `FileSystemWatcher` class to react directly to Windows file events.

To use `FileSystemWatcher`, you must create an instance and set the following properties:

- `Path` indicates the directory you want to monitor.
- `Filter` indicates the types of files you are monitoring.
- `NotifyFilter` indicates the type of changes you are monitoring.

`FileSystemWatcher` raises four key events: `Created`, `Deleted`, `Renamed`, and `Changed`. All of these events provide information through their `FileSystemEventArgs` parameter, including the name of the file (`Name`), the full path (`FullPath`), and the type of change (`ChangeType`). The `Renamed` event provides a `RenamedEventArgs` instance, which derives from `FileSystemEventArgs`, and adds information about the original file name (`OldName` and `OldFullPath`). If you need to, you can disable these events by setting the `FileSystemWatcher.EnableRaisingEvents` property to `false`. The `Created`, `Deleted`, and `Renamed` events are easy to handle. However, if you want to use the `Changed` event, you need to use the `NotifyFilter` property to indicate the types of changes you want to watch. Otherwise, your program might be swamped by an unceasing series of events as files are modified.

The `NotifyFilter` property can be set using any combination of the following values from the `System.IO.NotifyFilters` enumeration:

- `Attributes`
- `CreationTime`
- `DirectoryName`
- `FileName`
- `LastAccess`

- LastWrite
- Security
- Size

The Code

The following example shows a console application that handles Created and Deleted events, and tests these events by creating a test file:

```
using System;
using System.IO;
using System.Windows.Forms;

namespace Apress.VisualCSharpRecipes.Chapter05
{
    static class Recipe05_19
    {
        static void Main()
        {
            // Configure the FileSystemWatcher.
            using (FileSystemWatcher watch = new FileSystemWatcher())
            {
                watch.Path = Application.StartupPath;
                watch.Filter = "*.*";
                watch.IncludeSubdirectories = true;

                // Attach the event handler.
                watch.Created += new FileSystemEventHandler(OnCreatedOrDeleted);
                watch.Deleted += new FileSystemEventHandler(OnCreatedOrDeleted);
                watch.EnableRaisingEvents = true;

                Console.WriteLine("Press Enter to create a file.");
                Console.ReadLine();

                if (File.Exists("test.bin"))
                {
                    File.Delete("test.bin");
                }

                // Create test.bin.
                using (FileStream fs = new FileStream("test.bin", FileMode.Create))
                {
                    // Do something.
                }

                Console.WriteLine("Press Enter to terminate the application.");
                Console.ReadLine();
            }
```

```
            // Wait to continue.
            Console.WriteLine(Environment.NewLine);
            Console.WriteLine("Main method complete. Press Enter.");
            Console.ReadLine();
        }

        // Fires when a new file is created in the directory being monitored.
        private static void OnCreatedOrDeleted(object sender,
          FileSystemEventArgs e)
        {
            // Display the notification information.
            Console.WriteLine("\tNOTIFICATION: " + e.FullPath +
              "' was " + e.ChangeType.ToString());
            Console.WriteLine();
        }
    }
}
```

5-20. Access a COM Port

Problem

You need to send data directly to a serial port.

Solution

Use the `System.IO.Ports.SerialPort` class. This class represents a serial port resource and defines methods that enable communication through it.

How It Works

The .NET Framework defines a `System.IO.Ports` namespace that contains several classes. The central class is `SerialPort`. The `SerialPort` class also exposes properties that let you specify the port, baud rate, parity, and other information.

The Code

The following example demonstrates a simple console application that writes a string into the COM1 port:

```
using System;
using System.IO.Ports;

namespace Apress.VisualCSharpRecipes.Chapter05
{
```

```
    static class Recipe05_20
    {
        static void Main(string[] args)
        {
            using (SerialPort port = new SerialPort("COM1"))
            {
                // Set the properties.
                port.BaudRate = 9600;
                port.Parity = Parity.None;
                port.ReadTimeout = 10;
                port.StopBits = StopBits.One;

                // Write a message into the port.
                port.Open();
                port.Write("Hello world!");

                Console.WriteLine("Wrote to the port.");
            }

            // Wait to continue.
            Console.WriteLine(Environment.NewLine);
            Console.WriteLine("Main method complete. Press Enter.");
            Console.ReadLine();
        }
    }
}
```

5-21. Get a Random File Name

Problem

You need to get a random name for creating a folder or a file.

Solution

Use the `Path.GetRandomFileName` method, which returns a random name.

How It Works

The `System.IO.Path` class includes a new `GetRandomFileName` method, which generates a random string. You could use this string for creating a new file or folder.

The difference between `GetRandomFileName` and `GetTempFileName` (discussed in recipe 5-15) of the `Path` class is that `GetRandomFileName` just returns a random string and does not create a file, whereas `GetTempFileName` creates a new zero-byte temporary file and returns the path to the file.

The Code

The following example demonstrates using a random file name. Note that this example differs from that in recipe 5-15 in that we have to ensure that the file exists before opening it—we do this be using the `FileMode.OpenOrCreate` enumeration value as an argument to the constructor of `FileStream`.

```
using System;
using System.IO;

namespace Apress.VisualCSharpRecipes.Chapter05
{
    static class Recipe05_21
    {
        static void Main()
        {
            string tempFile = Path.GetRandomFileName();

            Console.WriteLine("Using " + tempFile);

            using (FileStream fs = new FileStream(tempFile, FileMode.OpenOrCreate))
            {
                // (Write some data.)
            }

            // Now delete the file.
            File.Delete(tempFile);

            // Wait to continue.
            Console.WriteLine(Environment.NewLine);
            Console.WriteLine("Main method complete. Press Enter.");
            Console.ReadLine();
        }
    }
}
```

5-22. Manipulate the Access Control List of a File or Directory

Problem

You want to modify the access control list (ACL) of a file or directory in the computer.

Solution

Use the `GetAccessControl` and `SetAccessControl` methods of the `File` or `Directory` class.

How It Works

The .NET Framework includes support for ACLs for resources like I/O, registry, and threading classes. You can retrieve and apply the ACL for a resource by using the `GetAccessControl` and `SetAccessControl` methods defined in the corresponding resource classes. For example, the `File` and `Directory` classes define both these methods, which let you manipulate the ACLs for a file or directory.

To add or remove an ACL-associated right of a file or directory, you need to first retrieve the `FileSecurity` or `DirectorySecurity` object currently applied to the resource using the `GetAccessControl` method. Once you retrieve this object, you need to perform the required modification of the rights, and then apply the ACL back to the resource using the `SetAccessControl` method. Access rights are updated using any of the add and remove methods provided in the security class.

The Code

The following example demonstrates the effect of denying Everyone Read access to a temporary file, using a console application. An attempt to read the file after a change in the ACL triggers a security exception.

```
using System;
using System.IO;
using System.Security.AccessControl;

namespace Apress.VisualCSharpRecipes.Chapter05
{
    static class Recipe05_22
    {
        static void Main(string[] args)
        {
            FileStream stream;
            string fileName;

            // Create a new file and assign full control to 'Everyone'.
            Console.WriteLine("Press any key to write a new file...");
            Console.ReadKey(true);

            fileName = Path.GetRandomFileName();
            using (stream = new FileStream(fileName, FileMode.Create))
            {
                // Do something.
            }
            Console.WriteLine("Created a new file " + fileName + ".");
            Console.WriteLine();


            // Deny 'Everyone' access to the file
            Console.WriteLine("Press any key to deny 'Everyone' " +
                "access to the file...");
            Console.ReadKey(true);
            SetRule(fileName, "Everyone",
                FileSystemRights.Read, AccessControlType.Deny);
```

```
        Console.WriteLine("Removed access rights of 'Everyone'.");
        Console.WriteLine();

        // Attempt to access file.
        Console.WriteLine("Press any key to attempt " +
            "access to the file...");
        Console.ReadKey(true);

        try
        {
            stream = new FileStream(fileName, FileMode.Create);
        }
        catch (Exception ex)
        {
            Console.WriteLine("Exception thrown: ");
            Console.WriteLine(ex.ToString());
        }
        finally
        {
            stream.Close();
            stream.Dispose();
        }

        // Wait to continue.
        Console.WriteLine(Environment.NewLine);
        Console.WriteLine("Main method complete. Press Enter.");
        Console.ReadLine();
    }

    static void AddRule(string filePath, string account,
        FileSystemRights rights, AccessControlType controlType)
    {
        // Get a FileSecurity object that represents the
        // current security settings.
        FileSecurity fSecurity = File.GetAccessControl(filePath);

        // Add the FileSystemAccessRule to the security settings.
        fSecurity.AddAccessRule(new FileSystemAccessRule(account,
            rights, controlType));

        // Set the new access settings.
        File.SetAccessControl(filePath, fSecurity);
    }

    static void SetRule(string filePath, string account,
        FileSystemRights rights, AccessControlType controlType)
    {
        // Get a FileSecurity object that represents the
        // current security settings.
        FileSecurity fSecurity = File.GetAccessControl(filePath);
```

```
            // Add the FileSystemAccessRule to the security settings.
            fSecurity.ResetAccessRule(new FileSystemAccessRule(account,
                rights, controlType));

            // Set the new access settings.
            File.SetAccessControl(filePath, fSecurity);
        }
    }
}
```

5-23. Compress Data

Problem

You need to read or write compressed data.

Solution

Use the `System.IO.Compression.GZipStream` or `System.IO.Compression.DeflateStream` to compress or decompress data.

How It Works

The `GZipStream` and `DeflateStream` classes allow you to use the popular ZIP and Deflate compression algorithms to compress or decompress data. The constructors for both classes accept a `System.IO.Stream` instance (which is where data should be written to or read from) and a value from the `CompressionMode` enumeration, which allows you to specify that you wish to compress or decompress data. Both of these classes only read and write bytes and byte arrays—it is often convenient to combine these classes with streams that are able to read and write other data types, such as in the example for this recipe.

The Code

The following sample creates a new file and uses the `GZipStream` class to write compressed data to it from a `StreamWriter` instance. The file is closed and then opened in read mode so that the compressed data can be decompressed and written to the console:

```
using System;
using System.IO;
using System.IO.Compression;
```

```
namespace Recipe05_23
{
    class Recipe05_23
    {
        static void Main(string[] args)
        {
            // Create the compression stream.
            GZipStream zipout = new GZipStream(
                File.OpenWrite("compressed_data.gzip"),
                CompressionMode.Compress);
            // wrap the gzip stream in a stream writer
            StreamWriter writer = new StreamWriter(zipout);

            // Write the data to the file.
            writer.WriteLine("the quick brown fox");
            // Close the streams.
            writer.Close();

            // Open the same file so we can read the
            // data and decompress it.
            GZipStream zipin = new GZipStream(
                File.OpenRead("compressed_data.gzip"),
                CompressionMode.Decompress);
            // Wrap the gzip stream in a stream reader.
            StreamReader reader = new StreamReader(zipin);

            // Read a line from the stream and print it out.
            Console.WriteLine(reader.ReadLine());

            // Wait to continue.
            Console.WriteLine(Environment.NewLine);
            Console.WriteLine("Main method complete. Press Enter.");
            Console.ReadLine();
        }
    }
}
```

5-24. Log Data to a File

Problem

You need to write data from a collection or an array to a log file.

Solution

Use the static `System.IO.File.WriteAllLines` method.

How It Works

The `File.WriteAllLines` method takes a file name and a collection or array of strings as parameters, and writes each entry on a separate line in the file specified. You can select which entries in the collection or array are written by applying a LINQ expression before calling the `WriteAllLinesMethod`.

The Code

The following example creates a `List` that contains a number of strings, representing two kinds of logging data. All of the entries are written to one file, and LINQ is used to query the collection so that only certain entries are written to a second file. See Chapter 2 for recipes that use LINQ to query collections.

```
using System;
using System.Collections.Generic;
using System.Linq;
using System.Text;
using System.IO;

namespace Recipe05_24
{
    class Recipe05_24
    {
        static void Main(string[] args)
        {
            // Create a list and populate it.
            List<string> myList = new List<string>();
            myList.Add("Log entry 1");
            myList.Add("Log entry 2");
            myList.Add("Log entry 3");
            myList.Add("Error entry 1");
            myList.Add("Error entry 2");
            myList.Add("Error entry 3");

            // Write all of the entries to a file.
            File.WriteAllLines("all_entries.log", myList);

            // Only write out the errors.
            File.WriteAllLines("only_errors.log",
                myList.Where(e => e.StartsWith("Error")));
        }
    }
}
```

5-25. Process a Log File

Problem

You need to easily obtain specific entries from a log file.

Solution

Use the static `System.IO.File.ReadLines` method to read lines from the file. Apply a LINQ expression to select specific lines.

How It Works

The `File.ReadLines` method reads the contents of a file, returning a string array containing one entry for each line in the file. You can filter the contents by using LINQ with the results—for example, using the `Where` method to select which lines are included in the results, or the `Select` method to include only part of each string.

The Code

The following example reads lines from one of the files created in the previous recipe. In order to demonstrate how to read entries and be selective with LINQ, the program reads all of the entries, just the entries that begin with "Error" and the first character of entries that do not begin with "Error."

```
using System;
using System.Collections.Generic;
using System.Linq;
using System.Text;
using System.IO;

namespace Recipe05_25
{
    class Program
    {
        static void Main(string[] args)
        {
            // Read all of the entries from the file.
            IEnumerable<string> alldata = File.ReadAllLines("all_entries.log");
            foreach (string entry in alldata)
            {
                Console.WriteLine("Entry: {0}", entry);
            }

            // Read the entries and select only some of them.
            IEnumerable<string> somedata
                = File.ReadLines("all_entries.log").Where(e => e.StartsWith("Error"));
```

```
            foreach (string entry in somedata)
            {
                Console.WriteLine("Error entry: {0}", entry);
            }

            // Read selected lines and write only the first character.
            IEnumerable<char> chardata = File.ReadLines("all_entries.log").Where(e
                => !e.StartsWith("Error")).Select(e => e[0]);
            foreach (char entry in chardata)
            {
                Console.WriteLine("Character entry: {0}", entry);
            }
        }
    }
}
```

5-26. Communicate Between Processes

Problem

You need to send and receive data from one process to another.

Solution

Use named pipes. You create an instance of `System.IO.Pipes.NamedPipeServerStream` and call the `WaitForConnection` method in one of your processes. In the other process, create an instance of `System.IO.Pipes.NamedPipeClientStream` and call the `Connect` method. This creates a two-way data stream between your processes that you can use to read and write data.

How It Works

Named pipes are an interprocess communication mechanism that allows processes to exchange data. Each pipe is created by a server and can accept multiple client connections—once the connection is established (using the `WaitForConnection` and `Connect` methods described previously), the server and client can communicate using the normal .NET Framework streams mechanism—see the other recipes in this chapter to learn more about streams. You must use the same name for both the server and client pipes.

The Code

The following example contains both a pipe server and a pipe client in one class—if the executable is started with the command-line argument `client`, then the pipe client will operate; otherwise, the pipe server will run. The server creates a named pipe and waits for a client to connect. When the client connects, the server writes ten messages to the client, and then reads ten responses.

■ **Note** Named pipes can be used to communicate between processes running on different computers. See the .NET Framework documentation for details.

```
using System;
using System.Collections.Generic;
using System.Linq;
using System.Text;
using System.IO;
using System.IO.Pipes;

namespace Recipe05_26
{
    class Recipe05_26
    {
        static void Main(string[] args)
        {
            if (args.Length > 0 && args[0] == "client")
            {
                pipeClient();
            }
            else
            {
                pipeServer();
            }
        }

        static void pipeServer()
        {
            // Create the server pipe.
            NamedPipeServerStream pipestream = new
NamedPipeServerStream("recipe_05_26_pipe");
            // Wait for a client to connect.
            Console.WriteLine("Waiting for a client connection");
            pipestream.WaitForConnection();

            Console.WriteLine("Received a client connection");
            // Wrap a stream writer and stream reader around the pipe.
            StreamReader reader = new StreamReader(pipestream);
            StreamWriter writer = new StreamWriter(pipestream);

            // Write some data to the pipe.
            for (int i = 0; i < 10; i++)
            {
                Console.WriteLine("Writing message ", i);
                writer.WriteLine("Message {0}", i);
                writer.Flush();
            }
```

```
            // Read data from the pipe.
            for (int i = 0; i < 10; i++)
            {
                Console.WriteLine("Received: {0}", reader.ReadLine()); ;
            }
            // Close the pipe.
            pipestream.Close();
        }

        static void pipeClient()
        {
            // Create the client pipe.
            NamedPipeClientStream pipestream = new
NamedPipeClientStream("recipe_05_26_pipe");
            // connect to the pipe server
            pipestream.Connect();

            // Wrap a reader around the stream.
            StreamReader reader = new StreamReader(pipestream);
            StreamWriter writer = new StreamWriter(pipestream);

            // Read the data.
            for (int i = 0; i < 10; i++)
            {
                Console.WriteLine("Received: {0}", reader.ReadLine());
            }

            // Write data to the pipe.
            for (int i = 0; i < 10; i++)
            {
                Console.WriteLine("Writing response ", i);
                writer.WriteLine("Response {0}", i);
                writer.Flush();
            }
            // Close the pipe.
            pipestream.Close();
        }
    }
}
```

CHAPTER 6

XML Processing

One of the most remarkable aspects of the Microsoft .NET Framework is its deep integration with XML. In many .NET applications, you won't even be aware you're using XML technologies—they'll just be used behind the scenes when you serialize a Microsoft ADO.NET `DataSet`, call a web service, or read application settings from a `Web.config` configuration file. In other cases, you'll want to work directly with the `System.Xml` namespaces to manipulate Extensible Markup Language (XML) data. Common XML tasks don't just include parsing an XML file, but also include validating it against a schema, applying an Extensible Stylesheet Language (XSL) transform to create a new document or Hypertext Markup Language (HTML) page, and searching intelligently with XPath.

In .NET 3.5, Microsoft added *LINQ to XML*, which integrates XML handling into the LINQ model for querying data sources. You can use the same keywords and syntax to query XML as you would a collection or a database.

The recipes in this chapter describe how to do the following:

- Read, parse, and manipulate XML data (recipes 6-1, 6-2, 6-3, and 6-7)
- Search an XML document for specific nodes, either by name (recipe 6-4), by namespace (recipe 6-5), or by using XPath (recipe 6-6)
- Validate an XML document with an XML schema (recipe 6-8)
- Serialize an object to XML (recipe 6-9), create an XML schema for a class (recipe 6-10), and generate the source code for a class based on an XML schema (recipe 6-11)
- Transform an XML document to another document using an XSL Transformations (XSLT) stylesheet (recipe 6-12)
- Use LINQ to XML to load, create, query and modify XML trees (recipes 6-13, 6-14, 6-15, and 6-16).

6-1. Show the Structure of an XML Document in a TreeView

Problem

You need to display the structure and content of an XML document in a Windows-based application.

Solution

Load the XML document using the `System.Xml.XmlDocument` class. Create a reentrant method that converts a single `XmlNode` into a `System.Windows.Forms.TreeNode`, and call it recursively to walk through the entire document.

How It Works

The .NET Framework provides several different ways to process XML documents. The one you use depends in part upon your programming task. One of the most fully featured classes is `XmlDocument`, which provides an in-memory representation of an XML document that conforms to the W3C Document Object Model (DOM). The `XmlDocument` class allows you to browse through the nodes in any direction, insert and remove nodes, and change the structure on the fly. For details of the DOM specification, go to `www.w3c.org`.

■ **Note** The `XmlDocument` class is not scalable for very large XML documents, because it holds the entire XML content in memory at once. If you want a more memory-efficient alternative, and you can afford to read and process the XML piece by piece, consider the `XmlReader` and `XmlWriter` classes described in recipe 6-7.

To use the `XmlDocument` class, simply create a new instance of the class and call the `Load` method with a file name, a `Stream`, a `TextReader`, or an `XmlReader` object. It is also possible to read the XML from a simple `string` with the `LoadXML` method. You can even supply a `string` with a URL that points to an XML document on the Web using the `Load` method. The `XmlDocument` instance will be populated with the tree of elements, or *nodes*, from the source document. The entry point for accessing these nodes is the root element, which is provided through the `XmlDocument.DocumentElement` property. `DocumentElement` is an `XmlElement` object that can contain one or more nested `XmlNode` objects, which in turn can contain more `XmlNode` objects, and so on. An `XmlNode` is the basic ingredient of an XML file. Common XML nodes include elements, attributes, comments, and contained text.

When dealing with an `XmlNode` or a class that derives from it (such as `XmlElement` or `XmlAttribute`), you can use the following basic properties:

- `ChildNodes` is an `XmlNodeList` collection that contains the first level of nested nodes.
- `Name` is the name of the node.
- `NodeType` returns a member of the `System.Xml.XmlNodeType` enumeration that indicates the type of the node (element, attribute, text, and so on).
- `Value` is the content of the node, if it's a text or CDATA node.
- `Attributes` provides a collection of node objects representing the attributes applied to the element.
- `InnerText` retrieves a string with the concatenated value of the node and all nested nodes.

- InnerXml retrieves a string with the concatenated XML markup for all nested nodes.
- OuterXml retrieves a string with the concatenated XML markup for the current node and all nested nodes.

The Code

The following example walks through every element of an XmlDocument using the ChildNodes property and a recursive method. Each node is displayed in a TreeView control, with descriptive text that either identifies it or shows its content.

```
using System;
using System.Windows.Forms;
using System.Xml;
using System.IO;

namespace Apress.VisualCSharpRecipes.Chapter06
{
    public partial class Recipe06_01 : System.Windows.Forms.Form
    {
        public Recipe06_01()
        {
            InitializeComponent();
        }

        // Default the file name to the sample document.
        private void Recipe06_01_Load(object sender, EventArgs e)
        {
            txtXmlFile.Text = Path.Combine(Application.StartupPath,
               @"..\..\ProductCatalog.xml");
        }

        private void cmdLoad_Click(object sender, System.EventArgs e)
        {
            // Clear the tree.
            treeXml.Nodes.Clear();

            // Load the XML document.
            XmlDocument doc = new XmlDocument();
            try
            {
                doc.Load(txtXmlFile.Text);
            }
            catch (Exception err)
            {
                MessageBox.Show(err.Message);
                return;
            }
```

```
        // Populate the TreeView.
        ConvertXmlNodeToTreeNode(doc, treeXml.Nodes);

        // Expand all nodes.
        treeXml.Nodes[0].ExpandAll();
    }

    private void ConvertXmlNodeToTreeNode(XmlNode xmlNode,
      TreeNodeCollection treeNodes)
    {
        // Add a TreeNode node that represents this XmlNode.
        TreeNode newTreeNode = treeNodes.Add(xmlNode.Name);

        // Customize the TreeNode text based on the XmlNode
        // type and content.
        switch (xmlNode.NodeType)
        {
            case XmlNodeType.ProcessingInstruction:
            case XmlNodeType.XmlDeclaration:
                newTreeNode.Text = "<?" + xmlNode.Name + " " +
                  xmlNode.Value + "?>";
                break;
            case XmlNodeType.Element:
                newTreeNode.Text = "<" + xmlNode.Name + ">";
                break;
            case XmlNodeType.Attribute:
                newTreeNode.Text = "ATTRIBUTE: " + xmlNode.Name;
                break;
            case XmlNodeType.Text:
            case XmlNodeType.CDATA:
                newTreeNode.Text = xmlNode.Value;
                break;
            case XmlNodeType.Comment:
                newTreeNode.Text = "<!--" + xmlNode.Value + "-->";
                break;
        }

        // Call this routine recursively for each attribute.
        // (XmlAttribute is a subclass of XmlNode.)
        if (xmlNode.Attributes != null)
        {
            foreach (XmlAttribute attribute in xmlNode.Attributes)
            {
                ConvertXmlNodeToTreeNode(attribute, newTreeNode.Nodes);
            }
        }
```

```
            // Call this routine recursively for each child node.
            // Typically, this child node represents a nested element
            // or element content.
            foreach (XmlNode childNode in xmlNode.ChildNodes)
            {
                ConvertXmlNodeToTreeNode(childNode, newTreeNode.Nodes);
            }
        }
    }
}
```

Usage

As an example, consider the following simple XML file (which is included with the sample code as the ProductCatalog.xml file):

```
<?xml version="1.0" ?>
<!--This document is a sample catalog for demonstration purposes-->
<productCatalog>
    <catalogName>Freeman and Freeman Unique Catalog 2010</catalogName>
    <expiryDate>2012-01-01</expiryDate>

    <products>
        <product id="1001">
            <productName>Gourmet Coffee</productName>
            <description>Beans from rare Chillean plantations.</description>
            <productPrice>0.99</productPrice>
            <inStock>true</inStock>
        </product>
        <product id="1002">
            <productName>Blue China Tea Pot</productName>
            <description>A trendy update for tea drinkers.</description>
            <productPrice>102.99</productPrice>
            <inStock>true</inStock>
        </product>
    </products>
</productCatalog>
```

Figure 6-1 shows how this file will be rendered in the Recipe06_01 form.

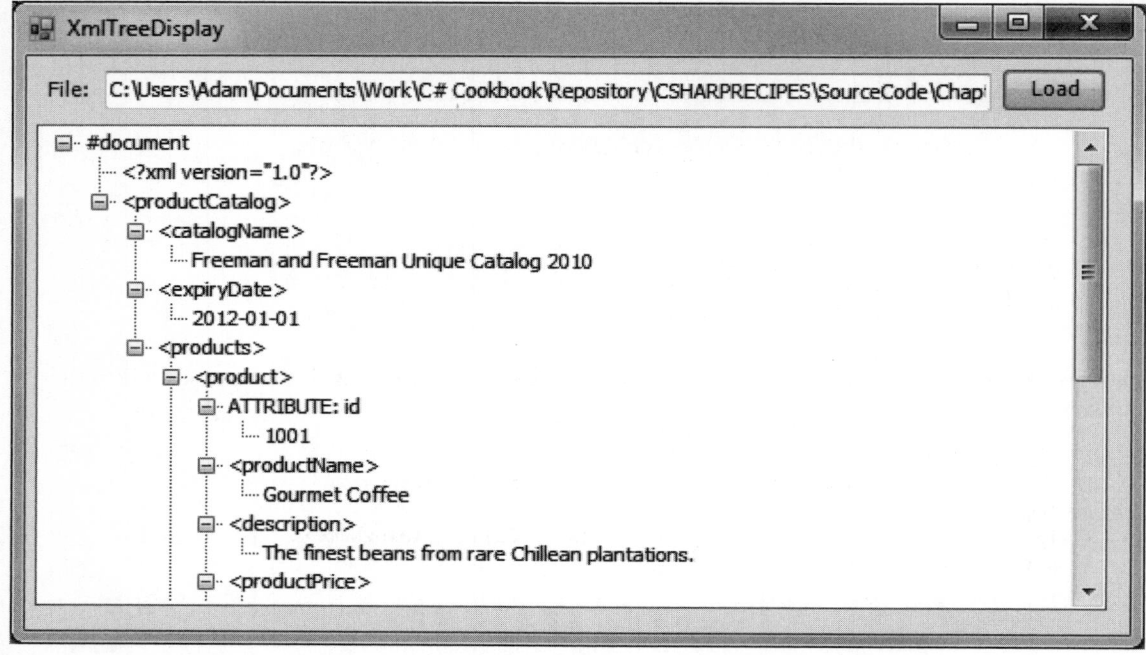

Figure 6-1. *The displayed structure of an XML document*

6-2. Insert Nodes in an XML Document

Problem

You need to modify an XML document by inserting new data, or you want to create an entirely new XML document in memory.

Solution

Create the node using the appropriate `XmlDocument` method (such as `CreateElement`, `CreateAttribute`, `CreateNode`, and so on). Then insert it using the appropriate `XmlNode` method (such as `InsertAfter`, `InsertBefore`, or `AppendChild`).

How It Works

Inserting a node into the `XmlDocument` class is a two-step process. You must first create the node, and then you insert it at the appropriate location. You can then call `XmlDocument.Save` to persist changes.

To create a node, you use one of the XmlDocument methods starting with the word Create, depending on the type of node. This ensures that the node will have the same namespace as the rest of the document. (Alternatively, you can supply a namespace as an additional string argument.) Next, you must find a suitable related node and use one of its insertion methods to add the new node to the tree.

The Code

The following example demonstrates this technique by programmatically creating a new XML document:

```
using System;
using System.Xml;

namespace Apress.VisualCSharpRecipes.Chapter06
{
    public class Recipe06_02
    {
        private static void Main()
        {
            // Create a new, empty document.
            XmlDocument doc = new XmlDocument();
            XmlNode docNode = doc.CreateXmlDeclaration("1.0", "UTF-8", null);
            doc.AppendChild(docNode);

            // Create and insert a new element.
            XmlNode productsNode = doc.CreateElement("products");
            doc.AppendChild(productsNode);

            // Create a nested element (with an attribute).
            XmlNode productNode = doc.CreateElement("product");
            XmlAttribute productAttribute = doc.CreateAttribute("id");
            productAttribute.Value = "1001";
            productNode.Attributes.Append(productAttribute);
            productsNode.AppendChild(productNode);

            // Create and add the subelements for this product node
            // (with contained text data).
            XmlNode nameNode = doc.CreateElement("productName");
            nameNode.AppendChild(doc.CreateTextNode("Gourmet Coffee"));
            productNode.AppendChild(nameNode);
            XmlNode priceNode = doc.CreateElement("productPrice");
            priceNode.AppendChild(doc.CreateTextNode("0.99"));
            productNode.AppendChild(priceNode);

            // Create and add another product node.
            productNode = doc.CreateElement("product");
            productAttribute = doc.CreateAttribute("id");
            productAttribute.Value = "1002";
            productNode.Attributes.Append(productAttribute);
            productsNode.AppendChild(productNode);
```

```
            nameNode = doc.CreateElement("productName");
            nameNode.AppendChild(doc.CreateTextNode("Blue China Tea Pot"));
            productNode.AppendChild(nameNode);
            priceNode = doc.CreateElement("productPrice");
            priceNode.AppendChild(doc.CreateTextNode("102.99"));
            productNode.AppendChild(priceNode);

            // Save the document (to the console window rather than a file).
            doc.Save(Console.Out);
            Console.ReadLine();
        }
    }
}
```

When you run this code, the generated XML document looks like this:

```
<?xml version="1.0"?>

<products>

  <product id="1001">

    <productName>Gourmet Coffee</productName>

    <productPrice>0.99</productPrice>

  </product>

  <product id="1002">

    <productName>Blue China Tea Pot</productName>

    <productPrice>102.99</productPrice>

  </product>

</products>
```

6-3. Quickly Append Nodes in an XML Document

Problem

You need to add nodes to an XML document without requiring lengthy, verbose code.

Solution

Create a helper function that accepts a tag name and content, and can generate the entire element at once. Alternatively, use the `XmlDocument.CloneNode` method to copy branches of an `XmlDocument`.

How It Works

Inserting a single element into an `XmlDocument` requires several lines of code. You can shorten this code in several ways. One approach is to create a dedicated helper class with higher-level methods for adding elements and attributes. For example, you could create an `AddElement` method that generates a new element, inserts it, and adds any contained text—the three operations needed to insert most elements.

The Code

Here's an example of one such helper class:

```
using System;
using System.Xml;

namespace Apress.VisualCSharpRecipes.Chapter06
{
    public class XmlHelper
    {
        public static XmlNode AddElement(string tagName,
          string textContent, XmlNode parent)
        {
            XmlNode node = parent.OwnerDocument.CreateElement(tagName);
            parent.AppendChild(node);

            if (textContent != null)
            {
                XmlNode content;
                content = parent.OwnerDocument.CreateTextNode(textContent);
                node.AppendChild(content);
            }
            return node;
        }

        public static XmlNode AddAttribute(string attributeName,
          string textContent, XmlNode parent)
        {
            XmlAttribute attribute;
            attribute = parent.OwnerDocument.CreateAttribute(attributeName);
            attribute.Value = textContent;
            parent.Attributes.Append(attribute);
```

```
            return attribute;
        }
    }
}
```

You can now condense the XML-generating code from recipe 6-2 with the simpler syntax shown here:

```
public class Recipe06_03
{
    private static void Main()
    {
        // Create the basic document.
        XmlDocument doc = new XmlDocument();
        XmlNode docNode = doc.CreateXmlDeclaration("1.0", "UTF-8", null);
        doc.AppendChild(docNode);
        XmlNode products = doc.CreateElement("products");
        doc.AppendChild(products);

        // Add two products.
        XmlNode product = XmlHelper.AddElement("product", null, products);
        XmlHelper.AddAttribute("id", "1001", product);
        XmlHelper.AddElement("productName", "Gourmet Coffee", product);
        XmlHelper.AddElement("productPrice", "0.99", product);

        product = XmlHelper.AddElement("product", null, products);
        XmlHelper.AddAttribute("id", "1002", product);
        XmlHelper.AddElement("productName", "Blue China Tea Pot", product);
        XmlHelper.AddElement("productPrice", "102.99", product);

        // Save the document (to the console window rather than a file).
        doc.Save(Console.Out);
        Console.ReadLine();
    }
}
```

Alternatively, you might want to take the helper methods such as `AddAttribute` and `AddElement` and make them instance methods in a custom class you derive from `XmlDocument`.

Another approach to simplifying writing XML is to duplicate nodes using the `XmlNode.CloneNode` method. `CloneNode` accepts a Boolean `deep` parameter. If you supply `true`, `CloneNode` will duplicate the entire branch, with all nested nodes.

Here is an example that creates a new product node by copying the first node:

```
// (Add first product node.)

// Create a new element based on an existing product.
product = product.CloneNode(true);
```

```
// Modify the node data.
product.Attributes[0].Value = "1002";
product.ChildNodes[0].ChildNodes[0].Value = "Blue China Tea Pot";
product.ChildNodes[1].ChildNodes[0].Value = "102.99";

// Add the new element.
products.AppendChild(product);
```

Notice that in this case, certain assumptions are being made about the existing nodes (for example, that the first child in the item node is always the name, and the second child is always the price). If this assumption is not guaranteed to be true, you might need to examine the node name programmatically.

6-4. Find Specific Elements by Name

Problem

You need to retrieve a specific node from an `XmlDocument`, and you know its name but not its position.

Solution

Use the `XmlDocument.GetElementsByTagName` method, which searches an entire document and returns a `System.Xml.XmlNodeList` containing any matches.

How It Works

The `XmlDocument` class provides a convenient `GetElementsByTagName` method that searches an entire document for nodes that have the indicated element name. It returns the results as a collection of `XmlNode` objects.

The Code

The following code demonstrates how you could use `GetElementsByTagName` to calculate the total price of items in a catalog by retrieving all elements with the name `productPrice`:

```
using System;
using System.Xml;

namespace Apress.VisualCSharpRecipes.Chapter06
{
    public class Recipe06_04
    {
        private static void Main()
        {
```

```
            // Load the document.
            XmlDocument doc = new XmlDocument();
            doc.Load(@"..\..\ProductCatalog.xml");

            // Retrieve all prices.
            XmlNodeList prices = doc.GetElementsByTagName("productPrice");

            decimal totalPrice = 0;
            foreach (XmlNode price in prices)
            {
                // Get the inner text of each matching element.
                totalPrice += Decimal.Parse(price.ChildNodes[0].Value);
            }

            Console.WriteLine("Total catalog value: " + totalPrice.ToString());
            Console.ReadLine();
        }
    }
}
```

Notes

You can also search portions of an XML document by using the `XmlElement.GetElementsByTagName` method. It searches all the descendant nodes looking for matches. To use this method, first retrieve an `XmlNode` that corresponds to an element. Then cast this object to an `XmlElement`. The following example demonstrates how to find the `price` node under the first `product` element:

```
// Retrieve a reference to the first product.
XmlNode product = doc.GetElementsByTagName("products")[0];

// Find the price under this product.
XmlNode productPrice
    = ((XmlElement)product).GetElementsByTagName("productPrice")[0];
Console.WriteLine("Price is " + productPrice.InnerText);
```

If your elements include an attribute of type `ID`, you can also use a method called `GetElementById` to retrieve an element that has a matching `ID` value.

6-5. Get XML Nodes in a Specific XML Namespace

Problem

You need to retrieve nodes from a specific namespace using an `XmlDocument`.

Solution

Use the overload of the `XmlDocument.GetElementsByTagName` method that requires a namespace name as a `string` argument. Additionally, supply an asterisk (*) for the element name if you want to match all tags.

How It Works

Many XML documents contain nodes from more than one namespace. For example, an XML document that represents a scientific article might use a separate type of markup for denoting math equations and vector diagrams, or an XML document with information about a purchase order might aggregate client and order information with a shipping record. Similarly, an XML document that represents a business-to-business transaction might include portions from both companies, written in separate markup languages.

A common task in XML programming is to retrieve the elements found in a specific namespace. You can perform this task with the overloaded version of the `XmlDocument.GetElementsByTagName` method that requires a namespace name. You can use this method to find tags by name or to find all the tags in the specified namespace if you supply an asterisk for the tag `name` parameter.

The Code

As an example, consider the following compound XML document, which includes order and client information, in two different namespaces (`http://mycompany/OrderML` and `http://mycompany/ClientML`):

```
<?xml version="1.0" ?>
<ord:order xmlns:ord="http://mycompany/OrderML"
 xmlns:cli="http://mycompany/ClientML">

  <cli:client>
    <cli:firstName>Sally</cli:firstName>
    <cli:lastName>Sergeyeva</cli:lastName>
  </cli:client>

  <ord:orderItem itemNumber="3211"/>
  <ord:orderItem itemNumber="1155"/>

</ord:order>
```

Here is a simple console application that selects all the tags in the `http://mycompany/OrderML` namespace:

```
using System;
using System.Xml;

namespace Apress.VisualCSharpRecipes.Chapter06
{
    public class Recipe06_05
    {
        private static void Main()
```

```
        {
            // Load the document.
            XmlDocument doc = new XmlDocument();
            doc.Load(@"..\..\Order.xml");

            // Retrieve all order tags.
            XmlNodeList matches = doc.GetElementsByTagName("*",
              "http://mycompany/OrderML");

            // Display all the information.
            Console.WriteLine("Element \tAttributes");
            Console.WriteLine("******* \t**********");

            foreach (XmlNode node in matches)
            {
                Console.Write(node.Name + "\t");
                foreach (XmlAttribute attribute in node.Attributes)
                {
                    Console.Write(attribute.Value + "  ");
                }
                Console.WriteLine();
            }
            Console.ReadLine();
        }
    }
}
```

The output of this program is as follows:

```
Element         Attributes

*******         **********

ord:order       http://mycompany/OrderML  http://mycompany/ClientML

ord:orderItem   3211

ord:orderItem   1155
```

6-6. Find Elements with an XPath Search

Problem

You need to search an XML document for nodes using advanced search criteria. For example, you might want to search a particular branch of an XML document for nodes that have certain attributes or contain a specific number of nested child nodes.

Solution

Execute an XPath expression using the `SelectNodes` or `SelectSingleNode` method of the `XmlDocument` class.

How It Works

The `XmlNode` class defines two methods that perform `XPath` searches: `SelectNodes` and `SelectSingleNode`. These methods operate on all contained child nodes. Because the `XmlDocument` inherits from `XmlNode`, you can call `XmlDocument.SelectNodes` to search an entire document.

The Code

For example, consider the following XML document, which represents an order for two items. This document includes text and numeric data, nested elements, and attributes, and so is a good way to test simple XPath expressions.

```
<?xml version="1.0"?>
<Order id="2004-01-30.195496">
  <Client id="ROS-930252034">
    <Name>Remarkable Office Supplies</Name>
  </Client>

  <Items>
    <Item id="1001">
      <Name>Electronic Protractor</Name>
      <Price>42.99</Price>
    </Item>
    <Item id="1002">
      <Name>Invisible Ink</Name>
      <Price>200.25</Price>
    </Item>
  </Items>
</Order>
```

Basic XPath syntax uses a pathlike notation. For example, the path `/Order/Items/Item` indicates an `<Item>` element that is nested inside an `<Items>` element, which in turn is nested in a root `<Order>` element. This is an absolute path. The following example uses an XPath absolute path to find the name of every item in an order:

```
using System;
using System.Xml;

namespace Apress.VisualCSharpRecipes.Chapter06
{
    public class Recipe06_06
    {
        private static void Main()
        {
```

```
            // Load the document.
            XmlDocument doc = new XmlDocument();
            doc.Load(@"..\..\orders.xml");

            // Retrieve the name of every item.
            // This could not be accomplished as easily with the
            // GetElementsByTagName method, because Name elements are
            // used in Item elements and Client elements, and so
            // both types would be returned.
            XmlNodeList nodes = doc.SelectNodes("/Order/Items/Item/Name");

            foreach (XmlNode node in nodes)
            {
                Console.WriteLine(node.InnerText);
            }
            Console.ReadLine();
        }
    }
}
```

The output of this program is as follows:

```
Electronic Protractor

Invisible Ink
```

Notes

XPath provides a rich and powerful search syntax, and it is impossible to explain all the variations you can use in a short recipe. However, Table 6-1 outlines some of the key ingredients in more advanced XPath expressions and includes examples that show how they would work with the order document. For a more detailed reference, refer to the W3C XPath recommendation, at `www.w3.org/TR/xpath`.

Table 6-1. XPath Expression Syntax

Expression	Description	Example
/	Starts an absolute path that selects from the root node.	`/Order/Items/Item` selects all `Item` elements that are children of an `Items` element, which is itself a child of the root `Order` element.
//	Starts a relative path that selects nodes anywhere.	`//Item/Name` selects all the `Name` elements that are children of an `Item` element, regardless of where they appear in the document.

Expression	Description	Example
@	Selects an attribute of a node.	/Order/@id selects the attribute named id from the root Order element.
*	Selects any element in the path.	/Order/* selects both Items and Client nodes because both are contained by a root Order element.
|	Combines multiple paths.	/Order/Items/Item/Name|Order/Client/Name selects the Name nodes used to describe a Client and the Name nodes used to describe an Item.
.	Indicates the current (default) node.	If the current node is an Order, the expression ./Items refers to the related items for that order.
..	Indicates the parent node.	//Name/.. selects any element that is parent to a Name, which includes the Client and Item elements.
[ ]	Defines selection criteria that can test a contained node or an attribute value.	/Order[@id="2004-01-30.195496"] selects the Order elements with the indicated attribute value. /Order/Items/Item[Price > 50] selects products higher than $50 in price. /Order/Items/Item[Price > 50 and Name="Laser Printer"] selects products that match two criteria.
starts-with	Retrieves elements based on what text a contained element starts with.	/Order/Items/Item[starts-with(Name, "C")] finds all Item elements that have a Name element that starts with the letter C.
position	Retrieves elements based on position.	/Order/Items/Item[position ()=2] selects the second Item element.
count	Counts elements. You specify the name of the child element to count or an asterisk (*) for all children.	/Order/Items/Item[count(Price) = 1] retrieves Item elements that have exactly one nested Price element.

■ **Note** XPath expressions and all element and attribute names you use inside them are always case-sensitive, because XML itself is case-sensitive.

6-7. Read and Write XML Without Loading an Entire Document into Memory

Problem

You need to read XML from a stream or write it to a stream. However, you want to process the information one node at a time, rather than loading it all into memory with an `XmlDocument`.

Solution

To write XML, create an `XmlWriter` that wraps a stream and use `Write` methods (such as `WriteStartElement` and `WriteEndElement`). To read XML, create an `XmlReader` that wraps a stream, and call `Read` to move from node to node.

How It Works

The `XmlWriter` and `XmlReader` classes read or write XML directly from a stream one node at a time. These classes do not provide the same features for navigating and manipulating your XML as `XmlDocument`, but they do provide higher performance and a smaller memory footprint, particularly if you need to deal with large XML documents.

Both `XmlWriter` and `XmlReader` are abstract classes, which means you cannot create an instance of them directly. Instead, you should call the `Create` method of `XmlWriter` or `XmlReader` and supply a file or stream. The `Create` method will return the right derived class based on the options you specify. This allows for a more flexible model. Because your code uses the base classes, it can work seamlessly with any derived class. For example, you could switch to a validating reader (as shown in the next recipe) without needing to modify your code.

To write XML to any stream, you can use the streamlined `XmlWriter`. It provides `Write` methods that write one node at a time. These include the following:

- `WriteStartDocument`, which writes the document prologue, and `WriteEndDocument`, which closes any open elements at the end of the document.
- `WriteStartElement`, which writes an opening tag for the element you specify. You can then add more elements nested inside this element, or you can call `WriteEndElement` to write the closing tag.
- `WriteElementString`, which writes an entire element, with an opening tag, a closing tag, and text content.
- `WriteAttributeString`, which writes an entire attribute for the nearest open element, with a name and value.

Using these methods usually requires less code than creating an `XmlDocument` by hand, as demonstrated in recipes 6-2 and 6-3.

To read the XML, you use the `Read` method of the `XmlReader`. This method advances the reader to the next node and returns `true`. If no more nodes can be found, it returns `false`. You can retrieve information about the current node through `XmlReader` properties, including its `Name`, `Value`, and `NodeType`.

To find out whether an element has attributes, you must explicitly test the `HasAttributes` property and then use the `GetAttribute` method to retrieve the attributes by name or index number. The `XmlTextReader` class can access only one node at a time, and it cannot move backward or jump to an arbitrary node, which gives much less flexibility than the `XmlDocument` class.

The Code

The following console application writes and reads a simple XML document using the `XmlWriter` and `XmlReader` classes. This is the same XML document created in recipes 6-2 and 6-3 using the `XmlDocument` class.

```
using System;
using System.Xml;
using System.IO;
using System.Text;

namespace Apress.VisualCSharpRecipes.Chapter06
{
    public class Recipe06_07
    {
        private static void Main()
        {
            // Create the file and writer.
            FileStream fs = new FileStream("products.xml", FileMode.Create);

            // If you want to configure additional details (like indenting,
            // encoding, and new line handling), use the overload of the Create
            // method that accepts an XmlWriterSettings object instead.
            XmlWriter w = XmlWriter.Create(fs);

            // Start the document.
            w.WriteStartDocument();
            w.WriteStartElement("products");

            // Write a product.
            w.WriteStartElement("product");
            w.WriteAttributeString("id", "1001");
            w.WriteElementString("productName", "Gourmet Coffee");
            w.WriteElementString("productPrice", "0.99");
            w.WriteEndElement();

            // Write another product.
            w.WriteStartElement("product");
            w.WriteAttributeString("id", "1002");
            w.WriteElementString("productName", "Blue China Tea Pot");
            w.WriteElementString("productPrice", "102.99");
            w.WriteEndElement();
```

```
            // End the document.
            w.WriteEndElement();
            w.WriteEndDocument();
            w.Flush();
            fs.Close();

            Console.WriteLine("Document created. " +
             "Press Enter to read the document.");
            Console.ReadLine();

            fs = new FileStream("products.xml", FileMode.Open);

            // If you want to configure additional details (like comments,
            // whitespace handling, or validation), use the overload of the Create
            // method that accepts an XmlReaderSettings object instead.
            XmlReader r = XmlReader.Create(fs);

            // Read all nodes.
            while (r.Read())
            {
                if (r.NodeType == XmlNodeType.Element)
                {
                    Console.WriteLine();
                    Console.WriteLine("<" + r.Name + ">");

                    if (r.HasAttributes)
                    {
                        for (int i = 0; i < r.AttributeCount; i++)
                        {
                            Console.WriteLine("\tATTRIBUTE: " +
                              r.GetAttribute(i));
                        }
                    }
                }
                else if (r.NodeType == XmlNodeType.Text)
                {
                    Console.WriteLine("\tVALUE: " + r.Value);
                }
            }
            Console.ReadLine();
        }
    }
}
```

Often, when using the `XmlReader`, you are searching for specific nodes rather than processing every element, as in this example. The approach used in this example does not work as well in this situation. It forces you to read element tags, text content, and CDATA sections separately, which means you need to explicitly keep track of where you are in the document. A better approach is to read the entire node and text content at once (for simple text-only nodes) by using the `ReadElementString` method. You can also use methods such as `ReadToDescendant`, `ReadToFollowing`, and `ReadToNextSibling`, all of which allow you to skip some nodes.

For example, you can use ReadToFollowing("Price"); to skip straight to the next Price element, without worrying about whitespace, comments, or other elements before it. (If a Price element cannot be found, the XmlReader moves to the end of the document, and the ReadToFollowing method returns false.)

6-8. Validate an XML Document Against a Schema

Problem

You need to validate the content of an XML document by ensuring that it conforms to an XML schema.

Solution

When you call XmlReader.Create, supply an XmlReaderSettings object that indicates you want to perform validation. Then move through the document one node at a time by calling XmlReader.Read, catching any validation exceptions. To find all the errors in a document without catching exceptions, handle the ValidationEventHandler event on the XmlReaderSettings object given as parameter to XmlReader.

How It Works

An XML schema defines the rules that a given type of XML document must follow. The schema includes rules that define the following:

- The elements and attributes that can appear in a document
- The data types for elements and attributes
- The structure of a document, including what elements are children of other elements
- The order and number of child elements that appear in a document
- Whether elements are empty, can include text, or require fixed values

XML schema documents are beyond the scope of this chapter, but you can learn much from a simple example. This recipe uses the product catalog first presented in recipe 6-1.

At its most basic level, XML Schema Definition (XSD) defines the elements that can occur in an XML document. XSD documents are themselves written in XML, and you use a separate predefined element (named <element>) in the XSD document to indicate each element that is required in the target document. The type attribute indicates the data type. Here is an example for a product name:

```
<xsd:element name="productName" type="xsd:string" />
```

And here is an example for the product price:

```
<xsd:element name="productPrice" type="xsd:decimal" />
```

The basic schema data types are defined at www.w3.org/TR/xmlschema-2. They map closely to .NET data types and include string, int, long, decimal, float, dateTime, boolean, and base64Binary—to name a few of the most frequently used types.

Both productName and productPrice are *simple types* because they contain only character data. Elements that contain nested elements are called *complex types*. You can nest them together using a

<sequence> tag, if order is important, or an <all> tag if it is not. Here is how you might model the <product> element in the product catalog. Notice that attributes are always declared after elements, and they are not grouped with a <sequence> or <all> tag because order is never important:

```
<xsd:complexType name="product">
  <xsd:sequence>
    <xsd:element name="productName" type="xsd:string"/>
    <xsd:element name="productPrice" type="xsd:decimal"/>
    <xsd:element name="inStock" type="xsd:boolean"/>
  </xsd:sequence>
  <xsd:attribute name="id" type="xsd:integer"/>
</xsd:complexType>
```

By default, a listed element can occur exactly one time in a document. You can configure this behavior by specifying the maxOccurs and minOccurs attributes. Here is an example that allows an unlimited number of products in the catalog:

```
<xsd:element name="product" type="product" maxOccurs="unbounded" />
```

Here is the complete schema for the product catalog XML:

```
<?xml version="1.0"?>
<xsd:schema xmlns:xsd="http://www.w3.org/2001/XMLSchema">

   <!-- Define the complex type product. -->
   <xsd:complexType name="product">
      <xsd:sequence>
         <xsd:element name="productName" type="xsd:string"/>
         <xsd:element name="description" type="xsd:string"/>
         <xsd:element name="productPrice" type="xsd:decimal"/>
         <xsd:element name="inStock" type="xsd:boolean"/>
      </xsd:sequence>
      <xsd:attribute name="id" type="xsd:integer"/>
   </xsd:complexType>

   <!-- This is the structure the document must match.
        It begins with a productCatalog element that nests other elements. -->
   <xsd:element name="productCatalog">
      <xsd:complexType>
         <xsd:sequence>
            <xsd:element name="catalogName" type="xsd:string"/>
            <xsd:element name="expiryDate" type="xsd:date"/>

            <xsd:element name="products">
               <xsd:complexType>
                  <xsd:sequence>
                     <xsd:element name="product" type="product"
                      maxOccurs="unbounded" />
                  </xsd:sequence>
               </xsd:complexType>
            </xsd:element>
```

```
        </xsd:sequence>
      </xsd:complexType>
   </xsd:element>

</xsd:schema>
```

The XmlReader class can enforce these schema rules, providing you explicitly request a validating reader when you use the XmlReader.Create method. (Even if you do not use a validating reader, an exception will be thrown if the reader discovers XML that is not well formed, such as an illegal character, improperly nested tags, and so on.)

Once you have created your validating reader, the validation occurs automatically as you read through the document. As soon as an error is found, the XmlReader raises a ValidationEventHandler event with information about the error on the XmlReaderSettings object given at creation time. If you want, you can handle this event and continue processing the document to find more errors. If you do not handle this event, an XmlException will be raised when the first error is encountered, and processing will be aborted.

The Code

The next example shows a utility class that displays all errors in an XML document when the ValidateXml method is called. Errors are displayed in a console window, and a final Boolean variable is returned to indicate the success or failure of the entire validation operation.

```
using System;
using System.Xml;
using System.Xml.Schema;

namespace Apress.VisualCSharpRecipes.Chapter06
{
    public class ConsoleValidator
    {
        // Set to true if at least one error exists.
        private bool failed;

        public bool Failed
        {
            get {return failed;}
        }

        public bool ValidateXml(string xmlFilename, string schemaFilename)
        {
            // Set the type of validation.
            XmlReaderSettings settings = new XmlReaderSettings();
            settings.ValidationType = ValidationType.Schema;

            // Load the schema file.
            XmlSchemaSet schemas = new XmlSchemaSet();
            settings.Schemas = schemas;
            // When loading the schema, specify the namespace it validates
            // and the location of the file. Use null to use
```

```
            // the targetNamespace value from the schema.
            schemas.Add(null, schemaFilename);

            // Specify an event handler for validation errors.
            settings.ValidationEventHandler += ValidationEventHandler;

            // Create the validating reader.
            XmlReader validator = XmlReader.Create(xmlFilename, settings);

            failed = false;
            try
            {
                // Read all XML data.
                while (validator.Read()) {}
            }
            catch (XmlException err)
            {
                // This happens if the XML document includes illegal characters
                // or tags that aren't properly nested or closed.
                Console.WriteLine("A critical XML error has occurred.");
                Console.WriteLine(err.Message);
                failed = true;
            }
            finally
            {
                validator.Close();
            }

            return !failed;
        }

        private void ValidationEventHandler(object sender,
          ValidationEventArgs args)
         {
            failed = true;

            // Display the validation error.
            Console.WriteLine("Validation error: " + args.Message);
            Console.WriteLine();
        }
    }
}
```

Here is how you would use the class to validate the product catalog:

```
public class Recipe06_08
{
    private static void Main()
    {
        ConsoleValidator consoleValidator = new ConsoleValidator();
        Console.WriteLine("Validating ProductCatalog.xml.");
```

```
        bool success = consoleValidator.ValidateXml(@"..\..\ProductCatalog.xml",
           @"..\..\ProductCatalog.xsd");
        if (!success)
            Console.WriteLine("Validation failed.");
        else
            Console.WriteLine("Validation succeeded.");

        Console.ReadLine();
    }
}
```

If the document is valid, no messages will appear, and the success variable will be set to true. But consider what happens if you use a document that breaks schema rules, such as the ProductCatalog_Invalid.xml file shown here:

```
<?xml version="1.0" ?>
<productCatalog>
    <catalogName>Acme Fall 2003 Catalog</catalogName>
    <expiryDate>Jan 1, 2004</expiryDate>

    <products>
        <product id="1001">
            <productName>Magic Ring</productName>
            <productPrice>$342.10</productPrice>
            <inStock>true</inStock>
        </product>
        <product id="1002">
            <productName>Flying Carpet</productName>
            <productPrice>982.99</productPrice>
            <inStock>Yes</inStock>
        </product>
    </products>
</productCatalog>
```

If you attempt to validate this document, the success variable will be set to false, and the output will indicate each error:

```
Validating ProductCatalog_Invalid.xml.

Validation error: The 'expiryDate' element has an invalid value according to
 its data type. [path information truncated]

Validation error: The 'productPrice' element has an invalid value according to
```

```
 its data type. [path information truncated]


Validation error: The 'inStock' element has an invalid value according to its

 data type. [path information truncated]


Validation failed.
```

Finally, if you want to validate an XML document and load it into an in-memory `XmlDocument`, you need to take a slightly different approach. The `XmlDocument` provides its own `Schemas` property, along with a `Validate` method that checks the entire document in one step. When you call `Validate`, you supply a delegate that points to your validation event handler.

Here is how it works:

```
XmlDocument doc = new XmlDocument();
doc.Load(@"..\..\Product_Catalog.xml");

// Specify the schema information.
XmlSchemaSet schemas = new XmlSchemaSet();
schemas.Add(null, @"..\..\ProductCatalog.xsd");
doc.Schemas = schemas;

// Validate the document.
doc.Validate(new ValidationEventHandler(ValidationEventHandler));
```

6-9. Use XML Serialization with Custom Objects

Problem

You need to use XML as a serialization format. However, you don't want to process the XML directly in your code—instead, you want to interact with the data using custom objects.

Solution

Use the `System.Xml.Serialization.XmlSerializer` class to transfer data from your object to XML, and vice versa. You can also mark up your class code with attributes to customize its XML representation.

How It Works

The `XmlSerializer` class allows you to convert objects to XML data, and vice versa. This process is used natively by web services and provides a customizable serialization mechanism that does not require a single line of custom code. The `XmlSerializer` class is even intelligent enough to correctly create arrays when it finds nested elements.

The only requirements for using `XmlSerializer` are as follows:

- The `XmlSerializer` serializes only properties and public variables.
- The classes you want to serialize must include a default zero-argument constructor. The `XmlSerializer` uses this constructor when creating the new object during deserialization.
- All class properties must be readable *and* writable. This is because `XmlSerializer` uses the property `get` accessor to retrieve information and the property `set` accessor to restore the data after deserialization.

■ **Note** You can also store your objects in an XML-based format using .NET serialization and `System.Runtime.Serialization.Formatters.Soap.SoapFormatter`. In this case, you simply need to make your class serializable—you do not need to provide a default constructor or ensure all properties are writable. However, this gives you no control over the format of the serialized XML.

To use XML serialization, you must first mark up your data objects with attributes that indicate the desired XML mapping. You can find these attributes in the `System.Xml.Serialization` namespace and include the following:

- `XmlRoot` specifies the name of the root element of the XML file. By default, `XmlSerializer` will use the name of the class. You can apply this attribute to the class declaration.
- `XmlElement` indicates the element name to use for a property or public variable. By default, `XmlSerializer` will use the name of the property or public variable.
- `XmlAttribute` indicates that a property or public variable should be serialized as an attribute, not an element, and specifies the attribute name.
- `XmlEnum` configures the text that should be used when serializing enumerated values. If you don't use `XmlEnum`, the name of the enumerated constant will be used.
- `XmlIgnore` indicates that a property or public variable should not be serialized.

The Code

For example, consider the product catalog first shown in recipe 6-1. You can represent this XML document using ProductCatalog and Product objects. Here's the class code that you might use:

```
using System;
using System.Xml.Serialization;

namespace Apress.VisualCSharpRecipes.Chapter06
{
    [XmlRoot("productCatalog")]
    public class ProductCatalog
    {
        [XmlElement("catalogName")]
        public string CatalogName;

        // Use the date data type (and ignore the time portion in the
        // serialized XML).
        [XmlElement(ElementName="expiryDate", DataType="date")]
        public DateTime ExpiryDate;

        // Configure the name of the tag that holds all products
        // and the name of the product tag itself.
        [XmlArray("products")]
        [XmlArrayItem("product")]
        public Product[] Products;

        public ProductCatalog()
        {
            // Default constructor for deserialization.
        }

        public ProductCatalog(string catalogName, DateTime expiryDate)
        {
            this.CatalogName = catalogName;
            this.ExpiryDate = expiryDate;
        }
    }

    public class Product
    {
        [XmlElement("productName")]
        public string ProductName;

        [XmlElement("productPrice")]
        public decimal ProductPrice;

        [XmlElement("inStock")]
        public bool InStock;

        [XmlAttributeAttribute(AttributeName="id", DataType="integer")]
```

```
        public string Id;

        public Product()
        {
            // Default constructor for serialization.
        }

        public Product(string productName, decimal productPrice)
        {
            this.ProductName = productName;
            this.ProductPrice = productPrice;
        }
    }
}
```

Notice that these classes use the XML serialization attributes to rename element names (using Pascal casing in the class member names and camel casing in the XML tag names), indicate data types that are not obvious, and specify how `<product>` elements will be nested in the `<productCatalog>`.

Using these custom classes and the `XmlSerializer` object, you can translate XML into objects, and vice versa. The following is the code you would need to create a new `ProductCatalog` object, serialize the results to an XML document, deserialize the document back to an object, and then display the XML document:

```
using System;
using System.Xml;
using System.Xml.Serialization;
using System.IO;

namespace Apress.VisualCSharpRecipes.Chapter06
{
    public class Recipe06_09
    {
        private static void Main()
        {
            // Create the product catalog.
            ProductCatalog catalog = new ProductCatalog("New Catalog",
              DateTime.Now.AddYears(1));
            Product[] products = new Product[2];
            products[0] = new Product("Product 1", 42.99m);
            products[1] = new Product("Product 2", 202.99m);
            catalog.Products = products;

            // Serialize the order to a file.
            XmlSerializer serializer = new XmlSerializer(typeof(ProductCatalog));
            FileStream fs = new FileStream("ProductCatalog.xml", FileMode.Create);
            serializer.Serialize(fs, catalog);
            fs.Close();

            catalog = null;

            // Deserialize the order from the file.
            fs = new FileStream("ProductCatalog.xml", FileMode.Open);
```

```
            catalog = (ProductCatalog)serializer.Deserialize(fs);

            // Serialize the order to the console window.
            serializer.Serialize(Console.Out, catalog);
            Console.ReadLine();
        }
    }
}
```

6-10. Create a Schema for a .NET Class

Problem

You need to create an XML schema based on one or more C# classes. This will allow you to validate XML documents before deserializing them with the `XmlSerializer`.

Solution

Use the XML Schema Definition Tool (`xsd.exe`) command-line utility included with the .NET Framework. Specify the name of your assembly as a command-line argument, and add the `/t:[TypeName]` parameter to indicate the types you want to convert.

How It Works

Recipe 6-9 demonstrated how to use the `XmlSerializer` to serialize .NET objects to XML and deserialize XML into .NET objects. But if you want to use XML as a way to interact with other applications, business processes, or non–.NET Framework applications, you'll need an easy way to validate the XML before you attempt to deserialize it. You will also need to define an XML schema document that defines the structure and data types used in your XML format so that other applications can work with it. One quick solution is to generate an XML schema using the `xsd.exe` command-line utility.

The `xsd.exe` utility is included with the .NET Framework. If you have installed Microsoft Visual Studio .NET, you will find it in a directory like `C:\Program Files\Microsoft Visual Studio .NET\FrameworkSDK\Bin`. The `xsd.exe` utility can generate schema documents from compiled assemblies. You simply need to supply the file name and indicate the class that represents the XML document with the `/ t:[TypeName]` parameter.

Usage

For example, consider the `ProductCatalog` and `Product` classes shown in recipe 6-9. You could create the XML schema for a product catalog with the following command line:

```
xsd Recipe06-09.exe /t:ProductCatalog
```

You need to specify only the `ProductCatalog` class on the command line because this class represents the actual XML document. The generated schema in this example will represent a complete product catalog, with contained product items. It will be given the default file name `schema0.xsd`. You can now use the validation technique shown in recipe 6-8 to test whether the XML document can be successfully validated with the schema.

6-11. Generate a Class from a Schema

Problem

You need to create one or more C# classes based on an XML schema. You can then create an XML document in the appropriate format using these objects and the `XmlSerializer`.

Solution

Use the `xsd.exe` command-line utility included with the .NET Framework. Specify the name of your schema file as a command-line argument, and add the `/c` parameter to indicate you want to generate class code.

How It Works

Recipe 6-10 introduced the `xsd.exe` command-line utility, which you can use to generate schemas based on class definitions. The reverse operation—generating C# source code based on an XML schema document—is also possible. This is primarily useful if you want to write a certain format of XML document but you do not want to manually create the document by writing individual nodes with the `XmlDocument` class or the `XmlWriter` class. Instead, by using `xsd.exe`, you can generate a set of full .NET objects. You can then serialize these objects to the required XML representation using the `XmlSerializer`, as described in recipe 6-9.

To generate source code from a schema, you simply need to supply the file name of the schema document and add the `/c` parameter to indicate you want to generate the required classes.

Usage

For example, consider the schema shown in recipe 6-8. You can generate C# code for this schema with the following command line:

```
xsd ProductCatalog.xsd /c
```

This will generate one file (`ProductCatalog.cs`) with two classes: `Product` and `ProductCalalog`. These classes are similar to the ones created in recipe 6-9, except that the class member names match the XML document exactly. Optionally, you can add the `/f` parameter. If you do, the generated classes will be composed of public fields. If you do not, the generated classes will use public properties instead (which simply wrap private fields).

6-12. Perform an XSL Transform

Problem

You need to transform an XML document into another document using an XSLT stylesheet.

Solution

Use the `System.Xml.Xsl.XslCompiledTransform` class. Load the XSLT stylesheet using the `XslCompiledTransform.Load` method, and generate the output document by using the `Transform` method and supplying a source document.

How It Works

XSLT is an XML-based language designed to transform one XML document into another document. You can use XSLT to create a new XML document with the same data but arranged in a different structure, or to select a subset of the data in a document. You can also use it to create a different type of structured document. XSLT is commonly used in this manner to format an XML document into an HTML page.

The Code

XSLT is a rich language, and creating XSL transforms is beyond the scope of this book. However, you can learn how to create simple XSLT documents by looking at a basic example. This recipe transforms the `orders.xml` document shown in recipe 6-6 into an HTML document with a table, and then displays the results. To perform this transformation, you'll need the following XSLT stylesheet:

```
<?xml version="1.0" encoding="UTF-8" ?>
<xsl:stylesheet xmlns:xsl="http://www.w3.org/1999/XSL/Transform"
    version="1.0" >

  <xsl:template match="Order">
    <html><body><p>
    Order <b><xsl:value-of select="Client/@id"/></b>
    for <xsl:value-of select="Client/Name"/></p>
    <table border="1">
    <td>ID</td><td>Name</td><td>Price</td>
    <xsl:apply-templates select="Items/Item"/>
    </table></body></html>
  </xsl:template>
```

```
  <xsl:template match="Items/Item">
    <tr>
    <td><xsl:value-of select="@id"/></td>
    <td><xsl:value-of select="Name"/></td>
    <td><xsl:value-of select="Price"/></td>
    </tr>
  </xsl:template>

</xsl:stylesheet>
```

Essentially, every XSLT stylesheet consists of a set of templates. Each template matches some set of elements in the source document and then describes the contribution that the matched element will make to the resulting document. To match the template, the XSLT document uses XPath expressions, as described in recipe 6-6.

The orders.xslt stylesheet contains two template elements (as children of the root stylesheet element). The first template matches the root Order element. When the XSLT processor finds an Order element, it outputs the tags necessary to start an HTML table with appropriate column headings and inserts some data about the client using the value-of command, which outputs the text result of an XPath expression. In this case, the XPath expressions (Client/@id and Client/Name) match the id attribute and the Name element.

Next, the apply-templates command branches off and performs processing of any contained Item elements. This is required because there might be multiple Item elements. Each Item element is matched using the XPath expression Items/Item. The root Order node is not specified because Order is the current node. Finally, the initial template writes the tags necessary to end the HTML document.

If you execute this transform on the sample orders.xml file shown in recipe 6-6, you will end up with the following HTML document:

```
<html>
  <body>
    <p>
    Order <b>ROS-930252034</b>
    for Remarkable Office Supplies</p>
    <table border="1">
      <td>ID</td>
      <td>Name</td>
      <td>Price</td>
      <tr>
        <td>1001</td>
        <td>Electronic Protractor</td>
        <td>42.99</td>
      </tr>
      <tr>
        <td>1002</td>
        <td>Invisible Ink</td>
        <td>200.25</td>
      </tr>
    </table>
  </body>
</html>
```

To apply an XSLT stylesheet in .NET, you use the `XslCompiledTransform` class. The following code shows a Windows-based application that programmatically applies the transformation and then displays the transformed file in a window using the `WebBrowser` control:

```
using System;
using System.Collections.Generic;
using System.ComponentModel;
using System.Data;
using System.Drawing;
using System.Text;
using System.Windows.Forms;
using System.Xml.Xsl;
using System.Xml;

namespace Apress.VisualCSharpRecipes.Chapter06
{
    public partial class TransformXml : Form
    {
        public TransformXml()
        {
            InitializeComponent();
        }

        private void TransformXml_Load(object sender, EventArgs e)
        {
            XslCompiledTransform transform = new XslCompiledTransform();

            // Load the XSTL stylesheet.
            transform.Load(@"..\..\orders.xslt");

            // Transform orders.xml into orders.html using orders.xslt.
            transform.Transform(@"..\..\orders.xml", @"..\..\orders.html");

            webBrowser1.Navigate(Application.StartupPath + @"\..\..\orders.html");
        }
    }
}
```

Figure 6-2 shows the application.

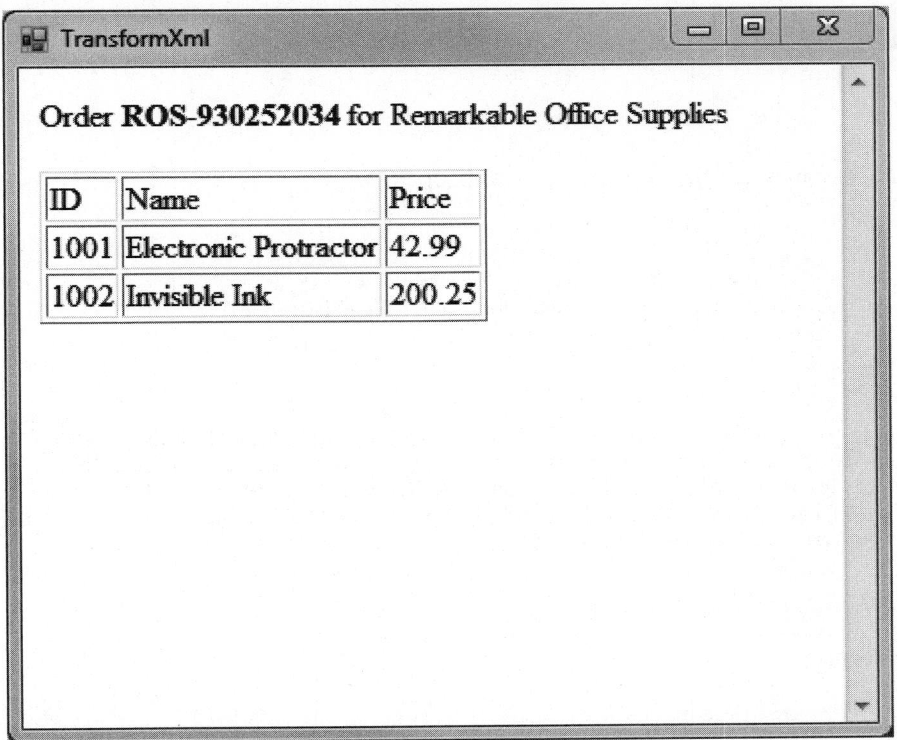

Figure 6-2. *The stylesheet output for orders.xml*

In this example, the code uses the overloaded version of the `Transform` method that saves the result document directly to disk, although you could receive it as a stream and process it inside your application instead. The following code shows an alternate approach that keeps the document content in memory at all times (with no external results file). The `XslCompiledTransform` writes the results to an `XmlWriter` that wraps a `StringBuilder`. The content is then copied from the `StringBuilder` into the `WebBrowser` through the handy `WebBrowser.DocumentText` property. The results are identical.

```
StringBuilder htmlContent = new StringBuilder();
XmlWriter results = XmlWriter.Create(htmlContent);
transform.Transform(@"..\..\orders.xml", results);
webBrowser1.DocumentText = htmlContent.ToString();
```

6-13. Load XML with LINQ

Problem

You need to load an XML tree in order to perform LINQ to XML operations.

Solution

Use the static methods of the `System.Xml.Linq.XElement` class to handle existing XML.

How It Works

The `System.Xml.Linq.XElement` class represents an XML element. LINQ represents XML as a tree of `XElements`, such that one class is used for every element from the root nodes to the terminating child nodes. The static `XElement.Load` method will load and parse an XML document from a number of sources, returning an instance of `XElement` representing the root node. The `Load` method is overloaded to support a range of data sources, as shown in Table 6-2.

Table 6-2. Overloads of the XElement.Load Method

Method	Description
`Load(Stream)`	Loads the XML data from a stream
`Load(String)`	Loads the XML from a file, the name of which is obtained from the string
`Load(TextReader)`	Loads the XML from a `System.IO.TextReader`
`Load(XMLReader)`	Loads the XML from a `System.Xml.XmlReader` (see recipe 6-7)

You can control some of the load options by using the `System.Xml.Linq.LoadOptions` enumeration as an additional argument to the `Load` method—see the .NET Framework documentation for details.

The Code

The following example demonstrates using the four different data sources accepted by the `XElement.Load` method:

```
using System;
using System.IO;
using System.Xml;
using System.Xml.Linq;
```

```
namespace Recipe06_13
{
    class Recipe06_13
    {
        static void Main(string[] args)
        {
            // Define the path to the sample file.
            string filename = @"..\..\ProductCatalog.xml";

            // Load the XML using the file name.
            Console.WriteLine("Loading using file name");
            XElement root = XElement.Load(filename);
            // Write out the XML.
            Console.WriteLine(root);
            Console.WriteLine("Press enter to continue");
            Console.ReadLine();

            // Load via a stream to the file.
            Console.WriteLine("Loading using a stream");
            FileStream filestream = File.OpenRead(filename);
            root = XElement.Load(filestream);
            // Write out the XML.
            Console.WriteLine(root);
            Console.WriteLine("Press enter to continue");
            Console.ReadLine();

            // Load via a textreader.
            Console.WriteLine("Loading using a TextReader");
            TextReader reader = new StreamReader(filename);
            root = XElement.Load(reader);
            // Write out the XML.
            Console.WriteLine(root);
            Console.WriteLine("Press enter to continue");
            Console.ReadLine();

            // Load via an xmlreader.
            Console.WriteLine("Loading using an XmlReader");
            XmlReader xmlreader = new XmlTextReader(new StreamReader(filename));
            root = XElement.Load(xmlreader);
            // Write out the XML.
            Console.WriteLine(root);
            Console.WriteLine("Press enter to continue");
            Console.ReadLine();

        }
    }
}
```

6-14. Create a New XML Tree with LINQ

Problem

You need to create a new XML tree for use with LINQ.

Solution

Create a new instance of `System.Xml.Linq.XElement` for the root element. Child nodes and attributes can be added by passing instances of `XElement` or `XAttribute` as constructor arguments or by calling the `Add` instance method.

How It Works

There are two ways to create an XML tree using LINQ to XML. The first is to create an instance of `XElement` and pass in instances of `XElement` for child nodes and `XAttribute` for attributes of the root node as constructor arguments. A simple example follows:

```
XElement root = new XElement("myrootnode",
    new XAttribute("first_attribute", "first_attribute_value"),
    new XAttribute("second_attribute", "second_attribute_value"),
    new XElement("first_element", "first_element"),
    new XElement("second_element", "second_element",
        new XAttribute("nested_attribute", "nested_attribute_value"))
);
```

This approach looks confusing, but starts to make sense once you start to write code yourself. You can supply any number of constructor arguments, and each `XElement` you create to represent a child node will accept constructor arguments itself to represent its own children and attributes. The preceding example is equivalent to the following XML:

```
<myrootnode

  first_attribute="first_attribute_value" second_attribute="second_attribute_value">

<first_element>first_element</first_element>

<second_element

  nested_attribute="nested_attribute_value">second_element</second_element>

</myrootnode>
```

The second approach to create an XML tree with XML to LINQ is to create individual instances of XElement and XAttribute and add them to their parent node using the XElement.Add instance method. See the example in this recipe for a demonstration.

In addition to XElement and XAttribute, the System.Xml.Linq namespace includes classes that represent other XML types—including XComment, XDeclaration, and XCData. The .NET Framework contains a full description of each type available, but of particular interest are XDocument and XDeclaration—these classes allow you to create the standard XML declaration at the start of your data.

The Code

The following example creates one element using the constructor arguments and adds another using the XElement.Add method. The root element is then added to an instance of XDocument along with an XDeclaration. The XDocument is written out to the console via an XMLTextWriter, which ensures that the XML header is included (it is omitted if the XDocument instance is passed to Console.WriteLine).

```
using System;
using System.Xml.Linq;
using System.Xml;

namespace Recipe06_14
{
    class Recipe06_14
    {
        static void Main(string[] args)
        {

            XElement root = new XElement("products",
                new XElement("product",
                    new XAttribute("id", 1001),
                    new XElement("productName", "Gourmet Coffee"),
                    new XElement("description",
                        "The finest beans from rare Chillean plantations."),
                    new XElement("productPrice", 0.99),
                    new XElement("inStock", true)
                ));

            XElement teapot = new XElement("product");
            teapot.Add(new XAttribute("id", 1002));
            teapot.Add(new XElement("productName", "Blue China Tea Pot"));
            teapot.Add(new XElement("description",
                "A trendy update for tea drinkers."));
            teapot.Add(new XElement("productPrice", 102.99));
            teapot.Add(new XElement("inStock", true));
            root.Add(teapot);

            XDocument doc = new XDocument(
                new XDeclaration("1.0", "", ""),
                root);
```

```
            doc.Save(Console.Out);          }
    }
}
```

The output of the example is as follows (formatted for easier reading):

```
<?xml version="1.0" encoding="ibm850"?>

<products>

<product id="1001">

<productName>Gourmet Coffee</productName>

<description>The finest beans from rare Chillean plantations.</description>

<productPrice>0.99</productPrice>

<inStock>true</inStock>

</product>

<product id="1002">

<productName>Blue China Tea Pot</productName>

<description>A trendy update for tea drinkers.</description>

<productPrice>102.99</productPrice>

<inStock>true</inStock>

</product>

</products>

Press any key to continue . . .
```

6-15. Query XML with LINQ

Problem

You need to query an XML tree to find elements with a given name, attribute, or other characteristic.

Solution

Use the XML tree as the data source for a LINQ query.

How It Works

The `System.Xml.Linq.XElement` class is a valid data source for LINQ queries. The basic sequence for querying an XML tree is the same as the one we used in Chapter 2 when querying a collection:

1. Start a new LINQ query using the `from` keyword, providing a variable name that you will use to make selections (for example, `from element in root.Elements()`).
2. Identify the conditions to use in selecting elements with the `where` keyword.
3. Indicate what value will be added to the result set from each matching element using the `select` keyword.
4. Specify the way in which you wish the results to be sorted using the `orderby` keyword.

When using `XElement` as the LINQ source, the result is an `IEnumerable` of `XElements`, containing those elements from your XML tree that match your search criteria. LINQ queries can be written using the keywords that have been added to C# (`from`, `where`, `select`, etc.), or by using instance methods that fulfill the same purpose—in the case of `XElement`, you should call the `Elements` instance method to obtain an `IEnumerable<XElement>` to use as the basis for your queries.

To select an element, you use the properties and methods of the `XElement` class. For example, to find all elements in an XML tree that have an attribute `color` with value `blue`, you would call

```
from element in root.Elements() where (string)element.Attribute("color")

    == "blue" select element;
```

To achieve the same result using instance methods, you would call

```
root.Elements().Where(e => (string)e.Attribute("color") == "blue").Select(e => e);
```

The result type from a LINQ query depends on what kind of element you retrieve with the `select` keyword, but will always return an instance of `IEnumerable`, which you can use in a `foreach` loop to run through the matched elements, or as the basis for further LINQ queries. The preceding example calls (which are functionally equivalent) return an `IEnumerable<XElement>`. If you use the `select` keyword to obtain a value representing a characteristic of an element, such as an attribute value, then the generic type of `IEnumerable` will be different.

The Code

The following example loads an XML tree from the file `store.xml`, which is included in the sample code. Elements that are named `Products` and that have a value of `16` for the child element `CategoryID` are selected, and the value of the `ModelName` child element is printed out. The query is performed once using the LINQ keywords and again using the instance methods and lambda expressions—it is a matter of preference as to which technique you adopt.

```
using System;
using System.Collections.Generic;
using System.Linq;
using System.Text;
using System.Xml.Linq;


namespace Recipe06_15
{
    class Recipe06_15
    {
        static void Main(string[] args)
        {
            // Load the XML tree from the sample file.
            XElement rootElement = XElement.Load(@"..\..\store.xml");

            // Select the name of elements who have a category ID of 16.
            IEnumerable<string> catEnum = from elem in rootElement.Elements()
                                          where (elem.Name == "Products" &&
                                            ((string)elem.Element("CategoryID"))
                                                == "16")
                                          select ((string)elem.Element("ModelName"));

            foreach (string stringVal in catEnum)
            {
                Console.WriteLine("Category 16 item: {0}", stringVal);
            }

            Console.WriteLine("Press enter to proceed");
            Console.ReadLine();

            // Perform the select again using instance methods.
            IEnumerable<string> catEnum2 = rootElement.Elements().Where(e
                => e.Name == "Products"
                && (string)e.Element("CategoryID") == "16").Select(
                        e => (string)e.Element("ModelName"));

            foreach (string stringVal in catEnum2)
            {
                Console.WriteLine("Category 16 item: {0}", stringVal);
            }
        }
    }
}
```

6-16. Modify an XML Tree with LINQ

The Problem

You need to add, remove, or modify elements in an XML tree.

The Solution

Use the **Add**, **Replace***, and **Remove*** methods of the `XElement` class.

How It Works

The first step to add, remove, or modify an XML tree is to select the element you wish to change. You can do this by using a LINQ query, or through the `Attribute` and `Element` methods of `XElement`.

To add a new element, call the **Add** method of the `XElement` you wish to use as the parent.

To modify elements, perform a LINQ query to select the elements of interest and enumerate the results, calling the `ReplaceAttributes` or `ReplaceNodes` methods to modify the `XElement` you have selected, or the `ReplaceWith` method to replace the selected element with a new element.

To remove an element, call the **Remove** method on the `XElement` instance that you no longer require.

The Code

The following example loads an XML file called `ProductCatalog.xml`, which is included with the source code for this chapter. After printing out the XML that has been loaded, the following tasks are performed:

1. Find all elements called `product` and modify the value of the attribute `id`.
2. Remove all elements that contain the word *tea* in a child node called `description`.
3. Create a new element and add it to a suitable parent.

```
using System;
using System.Collections.Generic;
using System.Linq;
using System.Xml.Linq;

namespace Recipe06_16
{
    class Recipe06_16
    {
        static void Main(string[] args)
        {
            // Load the XML tree from the file.
            XElement rootElem = XElement.Load(@"..\..\ProductCatalog.xml");
```

```
// Write out the XML.
Console.WriteLine(rootElem);

Console.WriteLine("Press enter to continue");
Console.ReadLine();

// Select all of the product elements.
IEnumerable<XElement> prodElements
    = from elem in rootElem.Element("products").Elements()
        where (elem.Name == "product")
        select elem;

// Run through the elements and change the ID attribute.
foreach(XElement elem in prodElements)
{
    // Get the current product ID.
    int current_id = Int32.Parse((string)elem.Attribute("id"));
    // Perform the replace operation on the attribute.
    elem.ReplaceAttributes(new XAttribute("id", current_id + 500));
}

Console.WriteLine(rootElem);
Console.WriteLine("Press enter to continue");
Console.ReadLine();

// Remove all elements that contain the word "tea" in the description.
IEnumerable<XElement> teaElements = from elem in
            rootElem.Element("products").Elements()
        where (((string)elem.Element("description")).Contains("tea"))
        select elem;

foreach (XElement elem in teaElements)
{
    elem.Remove();
}

Console.WriteLine(rootElem);
Console.WriteLine("Press enter to continue");
Console.ReadLine();

// Define and add a new element.
XElement newElement = new XElement("product",
    new XAttribute("id", 3000),
    new XElement("productName", "Chrome French Press"),
    new XElement("description",
        "A simple and elegant way of making great coffee"),
    new XElement("productPrice", 25.00),
    new XElement("inStock", true));
```

```
            rootElem.Element("products").Add(newElement);

            Console.WriteLine(rootElem);
        }
    }
}
```

CHAPTER 7

■ ■ ■

Windows Forms

The Microsoft .NET Framework includes a rich set of classes for creating traditional Windows-based applications in the `System.Windows.Forms` namespace. These range from basic controls such as the `TextBox`, `Button`, and `MainMenu` classes to specialized controls such as `TreeView`, `LinkLabel`, and `NotifyIcon`. In addition, you will find all the tools you need to manage multiple document interface (MDI) applications, integrate context-sensitive help, and even create multilingual user interfaces—all without needing to resort to the complexities of the Win32 API.

Most C# developers quickly find themselves at home with the Windows Forms programming model, and despite the arrival of Windows Presentation Foundation (discussed in Chapter 17) as an alternative thick-client development technology, Windows Forms is still the best choice for many types of applications.

■ **Note** Most of the recipes in this chapter use control classes, which are defined in the `System.Windows.Forms` namespace. When introducing these classes, the full namespace name is not indicated, and `System.Windows.Forms` is assumed.

The recipes in this chapter describe how to do the following:

- Add controls to a form programmatically at runtime so that you can build forms dynamically instead of only building static forms in the Visual Studio forms designer (recipe 7-1)
- Link arbitrary data objects to controls to provide an easy way to associate data with a control without the need to maintain additional data structures (recipe 7-2)
- Process all the controls on a form in a generic way (recipe 7-3)
- Track all the forms and MDI forms in an application (recipes 7-4 and 7-5)
- Save user-based and computer-based configuration information for Windows Forms applications using the mechanisms built into the .NET Framework and Windows (recipe 7-6)

- Force a list box to always display the most recently added item, so that users do not need to scroll up and down to find it (recipe 7-7)
- Assist input validation by restricting what data a user can enter into a text box, and implement a component-based mechanism for validating user input and reporting errors (recipes 7-8 and 7-17)
- Implement a custom autocomplete combo box so that you can make suggestions for completing words as users type data (recipe 7-9)
- Allow users to sort a list view based on the values in any column (recipe 7-10)
- Avoid the need to explicitly lay out controls on a form by using the Windows Forms layout controls (recipe 7-11)
- Use part of a main menu in a context menu (recipe 7-12)
- Provide multilingual support in your Windows Forms application (recipe 7-13)
- Create forms that cannot be moved and create borderless forms that can be moved (recipes 7-14 and 7-15)
- Create an animated system tray icon for your application (recipe 7-16)
- Support drag-and-drop functionality in your Windows Forms application (recipe 7-18)
- Correctly update the user interface in a multithreaded application (recipe 7-19)
- Display web-based information within your Windows application and allow users to browse the Web from within your application (recipe 7-20)
- Display WPF windows in a Windows Forms application (recipe 7-21)
- Display WPF controls in a Windows Forms application (recipe 7-22)

■ **Note** Visual Studio, with its advanced design and editing capabilities, provides the easiest and most productive way to develop Windows Forms applications. Therefore, the sample code projects for the recipes in this chapter—unlike those in most other chapters—rely heavily on the use of Visual Studio. Instead of focusing on the library classes that provide the required functionality, or looking at the code generated by Visual Studio, these recipes focus on how to achieve the recipe's goal using the Visual Studio user interface and the code that you must write manually to complete the required functionality. The separation of generated and manual code is particularly elegant in Visual Studio 2005 and later versions due to the extensive use of partial types.

7-1. Add a Control Programmatically

Problem

You need to add a control to a form at runtime, not design time.

Solution

Create an instance of the appropriate control class. Then add the control object to a form or a container control by calling `Controls.Add` on the container. (The container's `Controls` property returns a `ControlCollection` instance.)

How It Works

In a .NET form-based application, there is really no difference between creating a control at design time and creating it at runtime. When you create controls at design time, Visual Studio generates code to instantiate the desired control and places the code in a special method named `InitializeComponent`, which is called from your form's constructor. Visual Studio makes use of the partial class functionality of C# to keep the bulk of the code it generates in a separate file with the extension `Designer.cs`.

If you want to create a control at runtime, just follow these steps:

1. Create an instance of the appropriate control class.
2. Configure the control properties accordingly (particularly the size and position coordinates).
3. Add the control to the form or another container. Every control implements a read-only `Controls` property that references a `ControlCollection` containing references to all of its child controls. To add a child control, invoke the `ControlCollection.Add` method.
4. If you need to handle the events for the new control, you can wire them up to existing methods.

If you need to add multiple controls to a form or container, you should call `SuspendLayout` on the parent control before dynamically adding the new controls, and then call `ResumeLayout` once you have finished. This temporarily disables the layout logic used to position controls and will allow you to avoid significant performance overheads and weird flickering if you are adding many controls at once.

The Code

The following example demonstrates the dynamic creation of a list of check boxes. One check box is added for each item in a `string` array. All the check boxes are added to a panel that has its `AutoScroll` property set to `true`, which gives basic scrolling support to the check box list (see Figure 7-1).

```
using System;
using System.Windows.Forms;

namespace Apress.VisualCSharpRecipes.Chapter07
{
    public partial class Recipe07_01 : Form
    {
        public Recipe07_01()
        {
            // Initialization code is designer generated and contained
            // in a separate file named Recipe07-01.Designer.cs.
            InitializeComponent();
        }

        protected override void OnLoad(EventArgs e)
        {
            // Call the OnLoad method of the base class to ensure the Load
            // event is raised correctly.
            base.OnLoad(e);

            // Create an array of strings to use as the labels for
            // the dynamic check boxes.
            string[] foods = {"Grain", "Bread", "Beans", "Eggs",
                              "Chicken", "Milk", "Fruit", "Vegetables",
                              "Pasta", "Rice", "Fish", "Beef"};

            // Suspend the form's layout logic while multiple controls
            // are added.
            this.SuspendLayout();

            // Specify the Y coordinate of the topmost check box in the list.
            int topPosition = 10;

            // Create one new check box for each name in the list of
            // food types.
            foreach (string food in foods)
            {
                // Create a new check box.
                CheckBox checkBox = new CheckBox();

                // Configure the new check box.
                checkBox.Top = topPosition;
                checkBox.Left = 10;
                checkBox.Text = food;

                // Set the Y coordinate of the next check box.
                topPosition += 30;

                // Add the check box to the panel contained by the form.
                panel1.Controls.Add(checkBox);
            }
```

```
            // Resume the form's layout logic now that all controls
            // have been added.
            this.ResumeLayout();
        }

        [STAThread]
        public static void Main(string[] args)
        {
            Application.Run(new Recipe07_01());
        }
    }
}
```

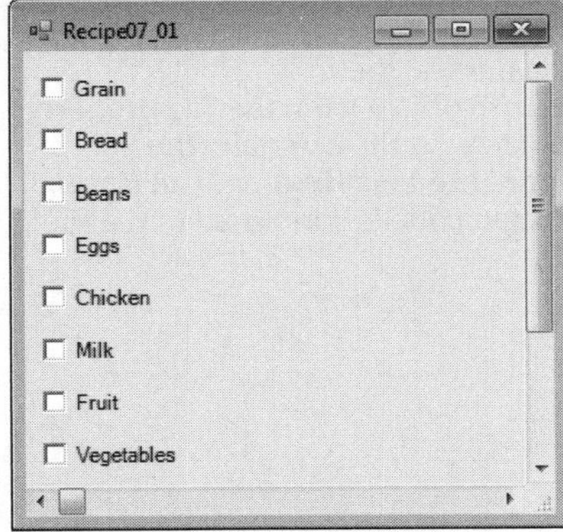

Figure 7-1. A dynamically generated check box list

7-2. Store Data with a Control

Problem

You need a simple way to store data associated with a control (perhaps to store some arbitrary information that relates to a given display item).

Solution

Store a reference to the data object in the `Tag` property of the control.

How It Works

Every class that derives from Control inherits a Tag property. The Tag property is not used by the control or the .NET Framework. Instead, it's reserved as a convenient storage place for application-specific data. In addition, some other classes not derived from Control also provide a Tag property. Useful examples include the ListViewItem, TreeNode, and MenuItem classes.

Because the Tag property is defined as an Object type, you can use it to store any value type or reference type, from a simple number or string to a custom object you have defined. When retrieving data from the Tag property, you must cast the Object to the correct type before use.

The Code

The following example, shown in Figure 7-2, adds a list of file names (as ListViewItem objects) to a ListView control. The corresponding System.IO.FileInfo object for each file is stored in the Tag property of its respective ListViewItem. When a user double-clicks one of the file names, the listView1_ItemActive event handler is called, which retrieves the FileInfo object from the Tag property and displays the file name and size using the MessageBox static method Show. In the example, the listView1_ItemActive event handler is wired to the ItemActivate event of the listView1 control through the listView1 control's properties in Visual Studio, meaning the generated code is contained in the file Recipe07-02.Designer.cs.

```
using System;
using System.IO;
using System.Windows.Forms;

namespace Apress.VisualCSharpRecipes.Chapter07
{
    public partial class Recipe07_02 : Form
    {
        public Recipe07_02()
        {
            // Initialization code is designer generated and contained
            // in a separate file named Recipe07-02.Designer.cs.
            InitializeComponent();
        }

        protected override void OnLoad(EventArgs e)
        {
            // Call the OnLoad method of the base class to ensure the Load
            // event is raised correctly.
            base.OnLoad(e);

            // Get all the files in the root directory.
            DirectoryInfo directory = new DirectoryInfo(@"C:\");
            FileInfo[] files = directory.GetFiles();

            // Display the name of each file in the ListView.
            foreach (FileInfo file in files)
            {
```

```
                ListViewItem item = listView1.Items.Add(file.Name);
                item.ImageIndex = 0;

                // Associate each FileInfo object with its ListViewItem.
                item.Tag = file;
            }
        }

        private void listView1_ItemActivate(object sender, EventArgs e)
        {
            // Get information from the linked FileInfo object and display
            // it using MessageBox.
            ListViewItem item = ((ListView)sender).SelectedItems[0];
            FileInfo file = (FileInfo)item.Tag;
            string info = file.FullName + " is " + file.Length + " bytes.";

            MessageBox.Show(info, "File Information");
        }

        [STAThread]
        public static void Main(string[] args)
        {
            Application.Run(new Recipe07_02());
        }
    }
}
```

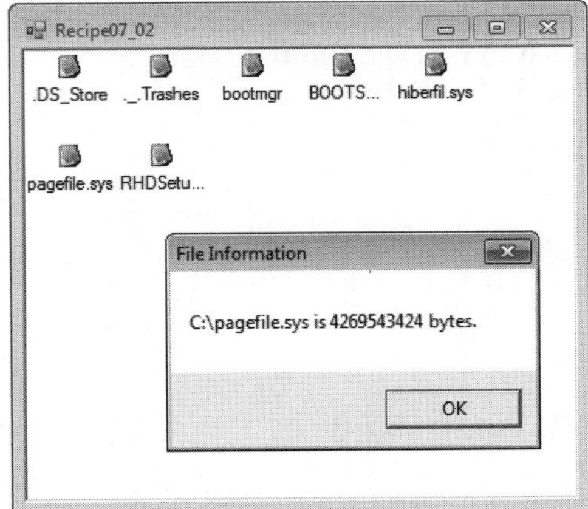

Figure 7-2. *Storing data in the Tag property*

7-3. Process All the Controls on a Form

Problem

You need to perform a generic task with all the controls on the form. For example, you may need to retrieve or clear their Text property, change their color, or resize them.

Solution

Iterate recursively through the collection of controls. Interact with each control using the properties and methods of the base Control class.

How It Works

You can iterate through the controls on a form using the Control.ControlCollection object obtained from the Form.Controls property. The ControlCollection includes all the controls that are placed directly on the form surface. However, if any of these controls are container controls (such as GroupBox, Panel, or TabPage), they might contain more controls. Thus, it's necessary to use recursive logic that searches the Controls collection of every control on the form.

The Code

The following example demonstrates the use of recursive logic to find every TextBox on a form and clears the text they contain. The example form contains a number of TextBox controls contained within nested GroupBox containers. When a button is clicked, the code tests each control in the form's ControlCollection to determine whether it is a TextBox by using the is operator.

```
using System;
using System.Windows.Forms;

namespace Apress.VisualCSharpRecipes.Chapter07
{
    public partial class Recipe07_03 : Form
    {
        public Recipe07_03()
        {
            // Initialization code is designer generated and contained
            // in a separate file named Recipe07-03.Designer.cs.
            InitializeComponent();
        }

        // The event handler for the button click event.
        private void cmdProcessAll_Click(object sender, System.EventArgs e)
        {
            ProcessControls(this);
        }
```

```
        private void ProcessControls(Control ctrl)
        {
            // Ignore the control unless it's a text box.
            if (ctrl is TextBox)
            {
                ctrl.Text = "";
            }

            // Process controls recursively.
            // This is required if controls contain other controls
            // (for example, if you use panels, group boxes, or other
            // container controls).
            foreach (Control ctrlChild in ctrl.Controls)
            {
                ProcessControls(ctrlChild);
            }
        }

        [STAThread]
        public static void Main(string[] args)
        {
            Application.Run(new Recipe07_03());
        }
    }
}
```

7-4. Track the Visible Forms in an Application

Problem

You need access to all of the open forms that are currently owned by an application.

Solution

Iterate through the `FormCollection` object that you get from the static property `OpenForms` of the `Application` object.

How It Works

Windows Forms applications automatically keep track of the open forms that they own. This information is accessed through the `Application.OpenForms` property, which returns a `FormCollection` object containing a `Form` object for each form the application owns. You can iterate through the `FormCollection` to access all `Form` objects or obtain a single `Form` object using its name (`Form.Name`) or its position in the `FormCollection` as an index.

The Code

The following example demonstrates the use of the Application.OpenForms property and the FormCollection it contains to manage the active forms in an application. The example allows you to create new forms with specified names. A list of active forms is displayed when you click the Refresh List button. When you click the name of a form in the list, it is made the active form.

Because of the way the FormCollection works, more than one form may have the same name. If duplicate forms have the same name, the first one found will be activated. If you try to retrieve a Form using a name that does not exist, null is returned. The following is the code for the application's main form:

```
using System;
using System.Windows.Forms;

namespace Apress.VisualCSharpRecipes.Chapter07
{
    public partial class Recipe07_04 : Form
    {
        public Recipe07_04()
        {
            // Initialization code is designer generated and contained
            // in a separate file named Recipe07-04.Designer.cs.
            InitializeComponent ();
        }

        // Override the OnLoad method to show the initial list of forms.
        protected override void OnLoad(EventArgs e)
        {
            // Call the OnLoad method of the base class to ensure the Load
            // event is raised correctly.
            base.OnLoad(e);

            // Refresh the list to display the initial set of forms.
            this.RefreshForms();
        }

        // A button click event handler to create a new child form.
        private void btnNewForm_Click(object sender, EventArgs e)
        {
            // Create a new child form and set its name as specified.
            // If no name is specified, use a default name.
            Recipe07_04Child child = new Recipe07_04Child();

            if (this.txtFormName.Text == String.Empty)
            {
                child.Name = "Child Form";
            }
            else
            {
                child.Name = this.txtFormName.Text;
            }
```

```
        // Show the new child form.
        child.Show();
    }

    // List selection event handler to activate the selected form based on
    // its name.
    private void listForms_SelectedIndexChanged(object sender, EventArgs e)
    {
        // Activate the selected form using its name as the index into the
        // collection of active forms. If there are duplicate forms with the
        // same name, the first one found will be activated.
        Form form = Application.OpenForms[this.listForms.Text];

        // If the form has been closed, using its name as an index into the
        // FormCollection will return null. In this instance, update the
        // list of forms.
        if (form != null)
        {
            // Activate the selected form.
            form.Activate();
        }
        else
        {
            // Display a message and refresh the form list.
            MessageBox.Show("Form closed; refreshing list...",
                "Form Closed");
            this.RefreshForms();
        }
    }

    // A button click event handler to initiate a refresh of the list of
    // active forms.
    private void btnRefresh_Click(object sender, EventArgs e)
    {
        RefreshForms();
    }

    // A method to perform a refresh of the list of active forms.
    private void RefreshForms()
    {
        // Clear the list and repopulate from the Application.OpenForms
        // property.
        this.listForms.Items.Clear();

        foreach (Form f in Application.OpenForms)
        {
            this.listForms.Items.Add(f.Name);
        }
    }
```

```
        [STAThread]
        public static void Main(string[] args)
        {
            Application.Run(new Recipe07_04());
        }
    }
}
```

The following is the code for the child forms you create by clicking the New Form button:

```
using System;
using System.Windows.Forms;

namespace Apress.VisualCSharpRecipes.Chapter07
{
    public partial class Recipe07_04Child : Form
    {
        public Recipe07_04Child()
        {
            // Initialization code is designer generated and contained
            // in a separate file named Recipe07-04Child.Designer.cs.
            InitializeComponent();
        }

        // Override the OnPaint method to correctly display the name of the
        // form.
        protected override void OnPaint(PaintEventArgs e)
        {
            // Call the OnPaint method of the base class to ensure the Paint
            // event is raised correctly.
            base.OnPaint(e);

            // Display the name of the form.
            this.lblFormName.Text = this.Name;
        }

        // A button click event handler to close the child form.
        private void btnClose_Click(object sender, EventArgs e)
        {
            this.Close();
        }
    }
}
```

Notes

Versions 1.0 and 1.1 of the .NET Framework do not provide any way of determining which forms are currently owned by an application. (The one exception is MDI applications, as described in recipe 7-5.) If you want to determine which forms exist or which forms are displayed, or you want one form to call the methods or set the properties of another form, you will need to keep track of form instances on your own.

For tracking small numbers of forms, one useful approach is to create a static class consisting of static members. Each static member holds a reference to a specific `Form`. If you have many forms you need to track, such as in a document-based application where the user can create multiple instances of the same form, one per document, a generic collection such as a `System.Collections.Generic.Dictionary<string,Form>` is very useful. This lets you map a `Form` object to a name.

Whichever approach you take, each `Form` object should register itself with the tracker class when it is first created. A logical place to put this code is in the `Form.OnLoad` method. Conversely, when the `Form` object is closed, it should deregister itself with the tracker class. Deregistration should occur in the `OnClosing` or `OnClosed` method of the `Form` class.

Using either of these approaches, any code that requires access to a `Form` object can obtain a reference to it from the members of the tracker class, and even invoke operations on the `Form` instance directly through the tracker class if you are sure the `Form` object exists.

7-5. Find All MDI Child Forms

Problem

You need to find all the forms that are currently being displayed in an MDI application.

Solution

Iterate through the forms returned by the `MdiChildren` collection property of the MDI parent.

How It Works

The .NET Framework includes two convenient shortcuts for managing the forms open in MDI applications: the `MdiChildren` and the `MdiParent` properties of the `Form` class. The `MdiParent` property of any MDI child returns a `Form` representing the containing parent window. The `MdiChildren` property returns an array containing all of the MDI child forms.

The Code

The following example presents an MDI parent window that allows you to create new MDI children by clicking the New item on the File menu. As shown in Figure 7-3, each child window contains a label, which displays the date and time when the MDI child was created, and a button. When the button is clicked, the event handler walks through all the MDI child windows and displays the label text that each one contains. Notice that when the example enumerates the collection of MDI child forms, it converts the generic `Form` reference to the derived `Recipe07-05Child` form class so that it can use the `LabelText` property. The following is the `Recipe07-05Parent` class:

```
using System;
using System.Windows.Forms;

namespace Apress.VisualCSharpRecipes.Chapter07
{
    // An MDI parent form.
    public partial class Recipe07_05Parent : Form
    {
        public Recipe07_05Parent()
        {
            // Initialization code is designer generated and contained
            // in a separate file named Recipe07-05Parent.Designer.cs.
            InitializeComponent();
        }

        // When the New menu item is clicked, create a new MDI child.
        private void mnuNew_Click(object sender, EventArgs e)
        {
            Recipe07_05Child frm = new Recipe07_05Child();
            frm.MdiParent = this;
            frm.Show();
        }

        [STAThread]
        public static void Main(string[] args)
        {
            Application.Run(new Recipe07_05Parent());
        }
    }
}
```

The following is the Recipe07-05Child class:

```
using System;
using System.Windows.Forms;

namespace Apress.VisualCSharpRecipes.Chapter07
{
    // An MDI child form.
    public partial class Recipe07_05Child : Form
    {
        public Recipe07_05Child()
        {
            // Initialization code is designer generated and contained
            // in a separate file named Recipe07-05Child.Designer.cs.
            InitializeComponent();
        }
```

```
        // When a button on any of the MDI child forms is clicked, display the
        // contents of each form by enumerating the MdiChildren collection.
        private void cmdShowAllWindows_Click(object sender, EventArgs e)
        {
            foreach (Form frm in this.MdiParent.MdiChildren)
            {
                // Cast the generic Form to the Recipe07_05Child derived class
                // type.
                Recipe07_05Child child = (Recipe07_05Child)frm;
                MessageBox.Show(child.LabelText, frm.Text);
            }
        }

        // On load, set the MDI child form's label to the current date/time.
        protected override void OnLoad(EventArgs e)
        {
            // Call the OnLoad method of the base class to ensure the Load
            // event is raised correctly.
            base.OnLoad(e);

            label.Text = DateTime.Now.ToString();
        }

        // A property to provide easy access to the label data.
        public string LabelText
        {
            get { return label.Text; }
        }
    }
}
```

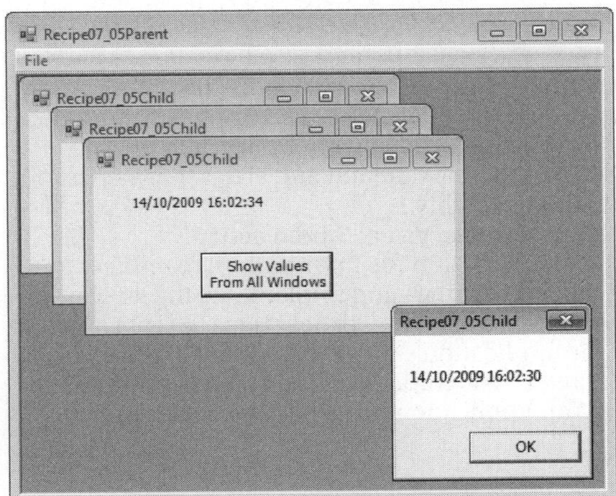

Figure 7-3. Getting information from multiple MDI child windows

7-6. Save Configuration Settings for a Form

Problem

You need to store configuration settings for a form so that they are remembered the next time that the form is shown.

Solution

Use the .NET Framework Application Settings functionality, which is configurable at design time in Visual Studio.

How It Works

The Application Settings functionality included in the .NET Framework provides an easy-to-use mechanism through which you can save application and user settings used to customize the appearance and operation of a Windows Forms application. You configure Application Settings through the Properties panel of each Windows control (including the main Windows `Form`) in your application (see Figure 7-4 for an example). By expanding the `ApplicationSettings` property (item 1 in Figure 7-4) and clicking the ellipsis (three dots) to the right of `(PropertyBinding)`, you can review application settings for each property of the active control (item 2 in Figure 7-4). When you configure a new application setting for a control's property, you must assign it a name, a default value, and a scope (item 3).

- The name allows you to both access the setting programmatically and reuse the application setting across multiple controls.
- The default value is used if the application cannot obtain a value from a configuration file at runtime.
- The scope is either User or Application.

Settings with an Application scope are stored in the application's configuration file (usually located in the same folder as the application assembly) and are read-only. The benefit of an Application scope is that you can change configuration settings by editing the configuration file without needing to recompile the application. Settings with a User scope are read-write by default and are stored as part of the user's Windows profile in a file named after the executing assembly.

When you configure your application to use application settings, Visual Studio actually autogenerates a wrapper class that provides access to the configuration file information, regardless of whether it is scoped as Application or User. The class is named `Settings` and implements the singleton pattern (discussed in recipe 13-10); the singleton instance is accessed through `Settings.Default`. This class contains properties with names matching each of the application setting names you configured for your controls' properties. The controls will automatically read their configuration at startup, but you should store configuration changes prior to terminating your application by calling the `Settings.Default.Save` method.

The Code

The following example, shown in Figure 7-4, displays a simple Form containing a TextBox. Using Visual Studio, the application is configured to store the location of the Form and the background color of the TextBox. The sample also programmatically records the size of the Form.

```
using System;
using System.ComponentModel;
using System.Windows.Forms;
using Apress.VisualCSharpRecipes.Chapter07.Properties;

namespace Apress.VisualCSharpRecipes.Chapter07
{
    public partial class Recipe07_06 : Form
    {
        public Recipe07_06()
        {
            // Initialization code is designer generated and contained
            // in a separate file named Recipe07-06.Designer.cs.
            InitializeComponent();
        }

        private void Button_Click(object sender, EventArgs e)
        {
            // Change the color of the text box depending on which button
            // was pressed.
            Button btn = sender as Button;

            if (btn != null)
            {
                // Set the background color of the text box.
                textBox1.BackColor = btn.ForeColor;

                // Update the application settings with the new value.
                Settings.Default.Color = textBox1.BackColor;
            }
        }

        protected override void OnClosing(CancelEventArgs e)
        {
            // Call the OnClosing method of the base class to ensure the
            // FormClosing event is raised correctly.
            base.OnClosing(e);

            // Update the application settings for Form.
            Settings.Default.Size = this.Size;

            // Store all application settings.
            Settings.Default.Save();
        }
```

```
        [STAThread]
        public static void Main(string[] args)
        {
            Application.Run(new Recipe07_06());
        }
    }
}
```

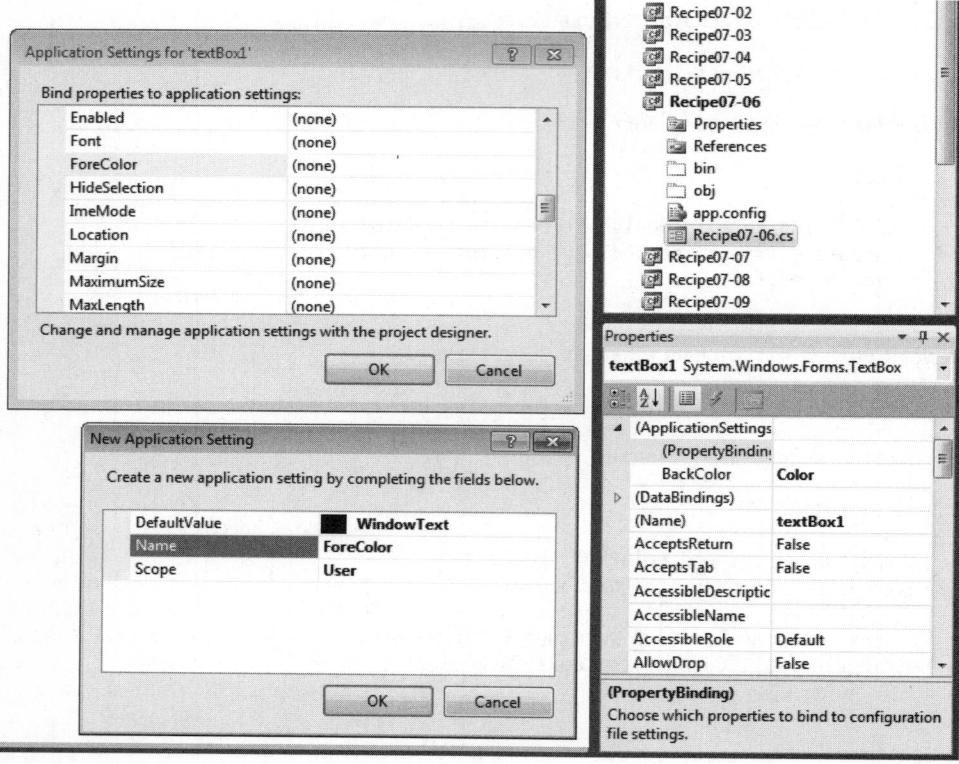

Figure 7-4. Configuring Application Settings in Visual Studio

7-7. Force a List Box to Scroll to the Most Recently Added Item

Problem

You need to scroll a list box programmatically so that the most recently added items are visible.

Solution

Set the `ListBox.TopIndex` property, which sets the first visible list item.

How It Works

In some cases, you might have a list box that stores a significant amount of information or one that you add information to periodically. Often, the most recent information, which is added at the end of the list, is more important than the information at the top of the list. One solution is to scroll the list box so that recently added items are visible. The `ListBox.TopIndex` property enables you to do this by allowing you to specify which item is visible at the top of the list.

The Code

The following sample form includes a list box and a button. Each time the button is clicked, 20 items are added to the list box. Each time new items are added, the code sets the `ListBox.TopIndex` property and forces the list box to display the most recently added items. To provide better feedback, the same line is also selected.

The example uses an unsorted `ListBox`, which means that new items are added to the end of the `ListBox`. If you set `ListBox.Sorted` to `true`, the `ListBox` will sort the items it contains alphabetically. In this case, new items added to the `ListBox` will be inserted at the appropriate point in the list and the `ListBox.Add` method returns an `int` containing the zero-based index of where the new item was inserted. You can assign this value to the `ListBox.TopIndex` property and force a sorted list box to display the most recently added item.

```
using System;
using System.Windows.Forms;

namespace Apress.VisualCSharpRecipes.Chapter07
{
    public partial class Recipe07_07 : Form
    {
        // A counter to keep track of the number of items added
        // to the ListBox.
        private int counter = 0;
```

```
        public Recipe07_07()
        {
            // Initialization code is designer generated and contained
            // in a separate file named Recipe07-07.Designer.cs.
            InitializeComponent();
        }

        // Button click event handler adds 20 new items to the ListBox.
        private void cmdTest_Click(object sender, EventArgs e)
        {
            // Add 20 items.
            for (int i = 0; i < 20; i++)
            {
                counter++;
                listBox1.Items.Add("Item " + counter.ToString());
            }

            // Set the TopIndex property of the ListBox to ensure the
            // most recently added items are visible.
            listBox1.TopIndex = listBox1.Items.Count - 1;
            listBox1.SelectedIndex = listBox1.Items.Count - 1;
        }

        [STAThread]
        public static void Main(string[] args)
        {
            Application.Run(new Recipe07_07());
        }
    }
}
```

7-8. Restrict a Text Box to Accept Only Specific Input

Problem

You need to create a text box that will reject all nonnumeric keystrokes.

Solution

Use the `MaskedTextBox` control and set the `Mask` property to configure the input that is acceptable.

How It Works

One way to ensure user input is valid is to prevent invalid data from being entered in the first place. The `MaskedTextBox` control facilitates this approach. The `MaskedTextBox.Mask` property takes a string that specifies the input mask for the control. This mask determines what type of input a user can enter at each point in the control's text area. If the user enters an incorrect character, the control will beep if the BeepOnError property is true, and the MaskInputRejected event will be raised so that you can customize the handling of incorrect input.

■ **Note** The MaskedTextBox control will not solve all your user input validation problems. While it does make some types of validation easy to implement, without customization it will not ensure some common validation requirements are met. For example, you can specify that only numeric digits can be input, but you cannot specify that they must be less than a specific value, nor can you control the overall characteristics of the input value. Recipe 2-5 discusses regular expressions which provide a great deal of flexibility when testing whether text meets complex formatting requirements.

The Code

The following example demonstrates the use of the MaskedTextBox control. A series of buttons allows you to change the active mask on the MaskedTextBox control and experiment with the various masks. Notice that the control tries to accommodate existing content with the new mask when the mask is changed. If the content is not allowed with the new mask, the control is cleared.

```
using System;
using System.Threading;
using System.Windows.Forms;

namespace Apress.VisualCSharpRecipes.Chapter07
{
    public partial class Recipe07_08 : Form
    {

        public Recipe07_08()
        {
            // Initialization code is designer generated and contained
            // in a separate file named Recipe07-08.Designer.cs.
            InitializeComponent();
        }

        private void btnTime_Click(object sender, EventArgs e)
        {
            // Set the input mask to that of a short time.
            this.mskTextBox.UseSystemPasswordChar = false;
            this.mskTextBox.Mask = "00:00";
            this.lblActiveMask.Text = this.mskTextBox.Mask;
            this.mskTextBox.Focus();
        }
```

```
private void btnUSZip_Click(object sender, EventArgs e)
{
    // Set the input mask to that of a US ZIP code.
    this.mskTextBox.UseSystemPasswordChar = false;
    this.mskTextBox.Mask = "00000-9999";
    this.lblActiveMask.Text = this.mskTextBox.Mask;
    this.mskTextBox.Focus();
}

private void btnUKPost_Click(object sender, EventArgs e)
{
    // Set the input mask to that of a UK postcode.
    this.mskTextBox.UseSystemPasswordChar = false;
    this.mskTextBox.Mask = ">LCCC 9LL";
    this.lblActiveMask.Text = this.mskTextBox.Mask;
    this.mskTextBox.Focus();
}

private void btnCurrency_Click(object sender, EventArgs e)
{
    // Set the input mask to that of a currency.
    this.mskTextBox.UseSystemPasswordChar = false;
    this.mskTextBox.Mask = "$999,999.00";
    this.lblActiveMask.Text = this.mskTextBox.Mask;
    this.mskTextBox.Focus();
}

private void btnDate_Click(object sender, EventArgs e)
{
    // Set the input mask to that of a short date.
    this.mskTextBox.UseSystemPasswordChar = false;
    this.mskTextBox.Mask = "00/00/0000";
    this.lblActiveMask.Text = this.mskTextBox.Mask;
    this.mskTextBox.Focus();
}

private void btnSecret_Click(object sender, EventArgs e)
{
    // Set the input mask to that of a secret PIN.
    this.mskTextBox.UseSystemPasswordChar = true;
    this.mskTextBox.Mask = "0000";
    this.lblActiveMask.Text = this.mskTextBox.Mask;
    this.mskTextBox.Focus();
}
```

```
        [STAThread]
        public static void Main(string[] args)
        {
            Application.Run(new Recipe07_08());
        }
    }
}
```

Notes

The MaskedTextBox used in this recipe was introduced in the .NET Framework 2.0. In previous versions of the .NET Framework, one approach was to use a standard TextBox control and handle the KeyPress events it raises. The KeyPress event is raised after each keystroke has been received but before it is displayed. You can use the KeyPressEventArgs event parameter to effectively cancel an invalid keystroke by setting its Handled property to true.

For example, to allow only numeric input, you must allow a keystroke only if it corresponds to a number (0 through 9) or a special control key (such as Delete or the arrow keys). The keystroke character is provided to the KeyPress event through the KeyPressEventArgs.KeyChar property. You can use two static methods of the System.Char class—IsDigit and IsControl—to quickly test the character.

7-9. Use an Autocomplete Combo Box or Text Box

Problem

You want to display a combo box or text box that automatically completes what the user is typing based on a list of predefined items.

Solution

Configure the autocomplete features of the standard .NET ComboBox or TextBox control. The AutoCompleteMode property controls the autocompletion behavior, and the AutoCompleteSource property allows you to specify the source of the autocomplete data.

■ **Note** Prior to the addition of the autocomplete functionality to the ComboBox and TextBox controls in the .NET Framework 2.0, to implement autocomplete functionality it was necessary to create a custom control that inherited from ComboBox or TextBox and overrode the inherited OnKeyPress and OnTextChanged methods.

How It Works

Autocomplete functionality is common and comes in many different variations. For example, a control may fill in values based on a list of recent selections (as Microsoft Excel does when you are entering cell values), or the control might display a drop-down list of near matches (as Microsoft Internet Explorer does when you are typing a URL). The AutoCompleteMode takes one of the following values, which define how the control's autocomplete behavior works:

- None: Autocomplete is disabled. This is the default behavior for ComboBox and TextBox.
- Suggest: This displays suggestions as a drop-down list.
- Append: This appends the remainder of the most likely suggestion to the end of the text as the user enters it.
- SuggestAppend: This combines the functionality of both Suggest and Append.

The AutoCompleteSource property defines where the ComboBox or TextBox control sources the autocomplete suggestions it presents to the user. It is possible to make use of various system-level data sources like the file system or URL histories. The most commonly used values for the AutoCompleteSource property are ListItems, where the ComboBox uses its current content and CustomSource. If you specify CustomSource, you must populate the AutoCompleteCustomSource property of the ComboBox or TextBox with the set of strings you want to use as autocomplete suggestions.

The Code

The following example enables autocomplete on a ComboBox and populates it with a list of values using a custom source. Figure 7-5 shows how the control offers suggestions to the user when AutoCompleteMode is set to the value SuggestAppend.

```
using System;
using System.IO;
using System.Drawing;
using System.Windows.Forms;

namespace Apress.VisualCSharpRecipes.Chapter07
{
    public partial class Recipe07_09 : Form
    {
        public Recipe07_09()
        {
            // Initialization code is designer generated and contained
            // in a separate file named Recipe07-09.Designer.cs.
            InitializeComponent();

            // Configure ComboBox1 to make its autocomplete
            // suggestions from a custom source.
            this.comboBox1.AutoCompleteCustomSource.AddRange(
                new string[] { "Man", "Mark", "Money", "Motley",
                    "Mostly", "Mint", "Minion", "Milk", "Mist",
                    "Mush", "More", "Map", "Moon", "Monkey"});
```

```
            this.comboBox1.AutoCompleteMode
                = AutoCompleteMode.SuggestAppend;
            this.comboBox1.AutoCompleteSource
                = AutoCompleteSource.CustomSource;

            // Configure ComboBox2 to make its autocomplete
            // suggestions from its current contents.
            this.comboBox2.Items.AddRange(
                new string[] { "Man", "Mark", "Money", "Motley",
                    "Mostly", "Mint", "Minion", "Milk", "Mist",
                    "Mush", "More", "Map", "Moon", "Monkey"});

            this.comboBox2.AutoCompleteMode
                = AutoCompleteMode.SuggestAppend;
            this.comboBox2.AutoCompleteSource
                = AutoCompleteSource.ListItems;

            // Configure ComboBox3 to make its autocomplete
            // suggestions from the system's URL history.
            this.comboBox3.AutoCompleteMode
                = AutoCompleteMode.SuggestAppend;
            this.comboBox3.AutoCompleteSource
                = AutoCompleteSource.AllUrl;
        }

        [STAThread]
        public static void Main(string[] args)
        {
            Application.Run(new Recipe07_09());
        }
    }
}
```

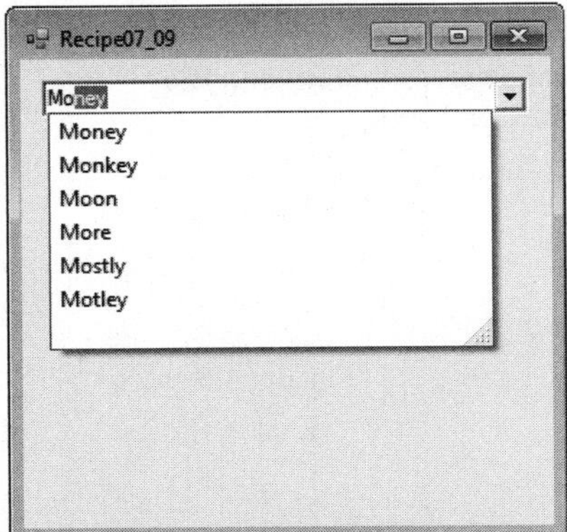

Figure 7-5. An autocomplete combo box

7-10. Sort a List View by Any Column

Problem

You need to sort a list view, but the built-in `ListView.Sort` method sorts based on only the first column.

Solution

Create a type that implements the `System.Collections.IComparer` interface and can sort `ListViewItem` objects. The `IComparer` type can sort based on any `ListViewItem` criteria you specify. Set the `ListView.ListViewItemSorter` property with an instance of the `IComparer` type before calling the `ListView.Sort` method.

How It Works

The `ListView` control provides a `Sort` method that orders items alphabetically based on the text in the first column. If you want to sort based on other column values or order items numerically, you need to create a custom implementation of the `IComparer` interface that can perform the work. The `IComparer` interface defines a single method named `Compare`, which takes two `object` arguments and determines which one should be ordered first. Full details of how to implement the `IComparer` interface are available in recipe 13-3.

The Code

The following example demonstrates the creation of an `IComparer` implementation named `ListViewItemComparer`. The `ListViewItemComparer` class also implements two additional properties: `Column` and `Numeric`. The `Column` property identifies the column that should be used for sorting. The `Numeric` property is a Boolean flag that can be set to `true` if you want to perform number-based comparisons instead of alphabetic comparisons.

When the user clicks a column heading, the example creates a `ListViewItemComparer` instance, configures the column to use for sorting, and assigns the `ListViewItemComparer` instance to the `ListView.ListViewItemSorter` property before calling the `ListView.Sort` method.

```
using System;
using System.Collections;
using System.Windows.Forms;

namespace Apress.VisualCSharpRecipes.Chapter07
{
    public partial class Recipe07_10 : Form
    {
        public Recipe07_10()
        {
```

```
        // Initialization code is designer generated and contained
        // in a separate file named Recipe07-10.Designer.cs.
        InitializeComponent();
    }

    // Event handler to handle user clicks on column headings.
    private void listView1_ColumnClick(object sender, ColumnClickEventArgs e)
    {
        // Create and/or configure the ListViewItemComparer to sort based on
        // the column that was clicked.
        ListViewItemComparer sorter =
            listView1.ListViewItemSorter as ListViewItemComparer;

        if (sorter == null)
        {
            // Create a new ListViewItemComparer.
            sorter = new ListViewItemComparer(e.Column);
            listView1.ListViewItemSorter = sorter;
        }
        else
        {
            // Configure the existing ListViewItemComparer.
            sorter.Column = e.Column;
        }

        // Sort the ListView.
        listView1.Sort();
    }

    [STAThread]
    public static void Main(string[] args)
    {
        Application.Run(new Recipe07_10());
    }
}

public class ListViewItemComparer : IComparer
{
    // Property to get/set the column to use for comparison.
    public int Column { get; set; }

    // Property to get/set whether numeric comparison is required
    // as opposed to the standard alphabetic comparison.
    public bool Numeric { get; set; }


    public ListViewItemComparer(int columnIndex)
    {
        Column = columnIndex;
    }
```

```
        public int Compare(object x, object y)
        {
            // Convert the arguments to ListViewItem objects.
            ListViewItem itemX = x as ListViewItem;
            ListViewItem itemY = y as ListViewItem;

            // Handle logic for null reference as dictated by the
            // IComparer interface; null is considered less than
            // any other value.
            if (itemX == null && itemY == null) return 0;
            else if (itemX == null) return -1;
            else if (itemY == null) return 1;

            // Short-circuit condition where the items are references
            // to the same object.
            if (itemX == itemY) return 0;

            // Determine if numeric comparison is required.
            if (Numeric)
            {
                // Convert column text to numbers before comparing.
                // If the conversion fails, just use the value 0.
                decimal itemXVal, itemYVal;

                if (!Decimal.TryParse(itemX.SubItems[Column].Text, out itemXVal))
                {
                    itemXVal = 0;
                }
                if (!Decimal.TryParse(itemY.SubItems[Column].Text, out itemYVal))
                {
                    itemYVal = 0;
                }

                return Decimal.Compare(itemXVal, itemYVal);
            }
            else
            {
                // Keep the column text in its native string format
                // and perform an alphabetic comparison.
                string itemXText = itemX.SubItems[Column].Text;
                string itemYText = itemY.SubItems[Column].Text;

                return String.Compare(itemXText, itemYText);
            }
        }
    }
}
```

7-11. Lay Out Controls Automatically

Problem

You have a large set of controls on a form and you want them arranged automatically.

Solution

Use the `FlowLayoutPanel` container to dynamically arrange the controls using a horizontal or vertical flow, or use the `TableLayoutPanel` container to dynamically arrange the controls in a grid.

How It Works

The `FlowLayoutPanel` and `TableLayoutPanel` containers simplify the design-time and runtime layout of the controls they contain. At both design time and runtime, as you add controls to one of these panels, the panel's logic determines where the control should be positioned, so you do not need to determine the exact location.

With the `FlowLayoutPanel` container, the `FlowDirection` and `WrapContents` properties determine where controls are positioned. `FlowDirection` controls the order and location of controls, and it can be set to `LeftToRight`, `TopDown`, `RightToLeft`, or `BottomUp`. The `WrapContents` property controls whether controls run off the edge of the panel or wrap around to form a new line of controls.

With the `TableLayoutPanel` container, the `RowCount` and `ColumnCount` properties control how many rows and columns are currently in the panel's grid. The `GrowStyle` property determines how the grid grows to accommodate more controls once it is full, and it can be set to `AddRows`, `AddColumns`, or `FixedSize` (which means the grid cannot grow).

Figure 7-6 shows the design-time appearance of both a `TableLayoutPanel` container and a `FlowLayoutPanel` container. The `TableLayoutPanel` panel is configured with three rows and three columns. The `FlowLayoutPanel` panel is configured to wrap contents and use left-to-right flow direction.

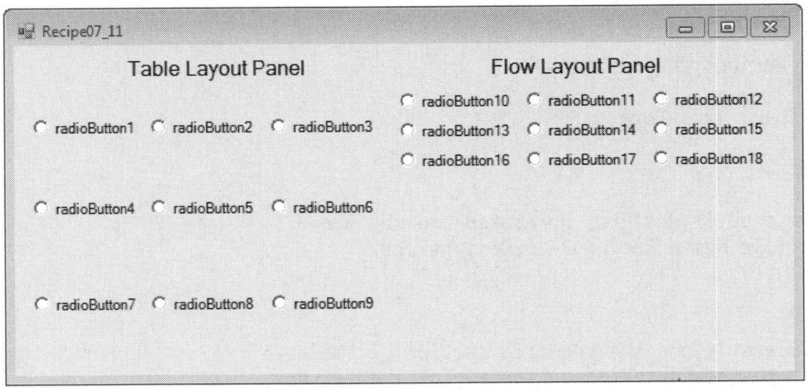

Figure 7-6. *Using a FlowLayoutPanel panel and a TableLayoutPanel panel*

7-12. Use Part of a Main Menu for a Context Menu

Problem

You need to create a context menu that shows the same menu items as those displayed as part of an application's main menu.

Solution

Use the `CloneMenu` method of the `MenuItem` class to duplicate the required portion of the main menu.

How It Works

In many applications, a control's context-sensitive menu duplicates a portion of the main menu. However, .NET does not allow you to create a `MenuItem` instance that is contained in more than one menu at a time.

The solution is to make a duplicate copy of a portion of the menu using the `CloneMenu` method. The `CloneMenu` method not only copies the appropriate `MenuItem` items (and any contained submenus), but also registers each `MenuItem` object with the same event handlers. Thus, when a user clicks a cloned menu item in a context menu, the event handler will be triggered as if the user had clicked the duplicate menu item in the main menu.

The Code

The following example uses the `CloneMenu` method to configure the context menu for a `TextBox` to be a duplicate of the File menu. Figure 7-7 shows how the example will look when run.

```
using System;
using System.Drawing;
using System.Windows.Forms;

namespace Apress.VisualCSharpRecipes.Chapter07
{
    public partial class Recipe07_12 : Form
    {
        public Recipe07_12()
        {
            // Initialization code is designer generated and contained
            // in a separate file named Recipe07-12.Designer.cs.
            InitializeComponent();
        }

        // As the main form loads, clone the required section of the main
        // menu and assign it to the ContextMenu property of the TextBox.
        protected override void OnLoad(EventArgs e)
        {
```

```
        // Call the OnLoad method of the base class to ensure the Load
        // event is raised correctly.
        base.OnLoad(e);

        ContextMenu mnuContext = new ContextMenu();

        // Copy the menu items from the File menu into a context menu.
        foreach (MenuItem mnuItem in mnuFile.MenuItems)
        {
            mnuContext.MenuItems.Add(mnuItem.CloneMenu());
        }

        // Attach the cloned menu to the TextBox.
        TextBox1.ContextMenu = mnuContext;
    }

    // Event handler to display the ContextMenu for the ListBox.
    private void TextBox1_MouseDown(object sender, MouseEventArgs e)
    {
        if (e.Button == MouseButtons.Right)
        {
            TextBox1.ContextMenu.Show(TextBox1, new Point(e.X, e.Y));
        }
    }

    // Event handler to process clicks on File/Open menu item.
    // For the purpose of the example, simply show a message box.
    private void mnuOpen_Click(object sender, EventArgs e)
    {
        MessageBox.Show("This is the event handler for Open.","Recipe07-12");
    }

    // Event handler to process clicks on File/Save menu item.
    // For the purpose of the example, simply show a message box.
    private void mnuSave_Click(object sender, EventArgs e)
    {
        MessageBox.Show("This is the event handler for Save.","Recipe07-12");
    }

    // Event handler to process clicks on File/Exit menu item.
    // For the purpose of the example, simply show a message box.
    private void mnuExit_Click(object sender, EventArgs e)
    {
        MessageBox.Show("This is the event handler for Exit.","Recipe07-12");
    }
```

```
        public static void Main(string[] args)
        {
            Application.Run(new Recipe07_12());
        }
    }
}
```

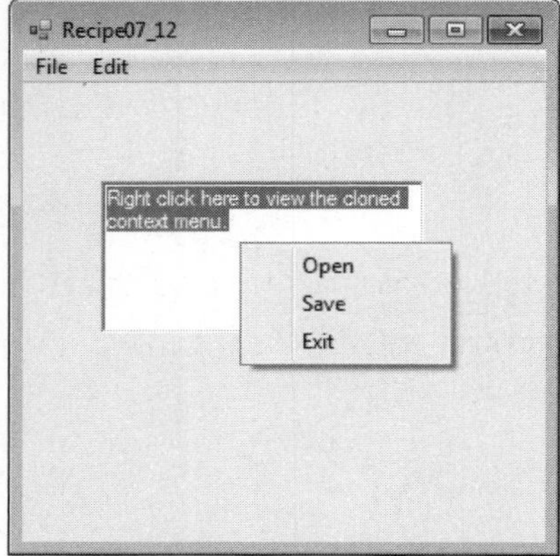

Figure 7-7. Copying part of a main menu to a context menu

7-13. Make a Multilingual Form

Problem

You need to create a localizable form that can be deployed in more than one language.

Solution

Store all locale-specific information in resource files, which are compiled into satellite assemblies.

How It Works

The .NET Framework includes built-in support for localization through its use of resource files. The basic idea is to store information that is locale-specific (for example, button text) in a resource file. You can create resource files for each culture you need to support and compile them into satellite assemblies. When you run the application, .NET will automatically use the correct satellite assembly based on the locale settings of the current user/computer.

You can read to and write from resource files manually; they are XML files. However, Visual Studio also includes extensive design-time support for localized forms. It works like this:

1. Set the `Localizable` property of a `Form` to `true` using the Properties window.
2. Set the `Language` property of the form to the locale for which you would like to enter information (see Figure 7-8). Then configure the localizable properties of all the controls on the form. Instead of storing your changes in the designer-generated code for the form, Visual Studio will actually create a new resource file to hold your data.
3. Repeat step 2 for each language that you want to support. Each time you enter a new locale for the form's `Language` property, a new resource file will be generated. If you change the `Language` property to a locale you have already configured, your previous settings will reappear, and you will be able to modify them.

You can now compile and test your application on differently localized systems. Visual Studio will create a separate directory and satellite assembly for each resource file in the project. You can select Project/Show All Files from the Visual Studio menu to see how these files are arranged, as shown in Figure 7-9.

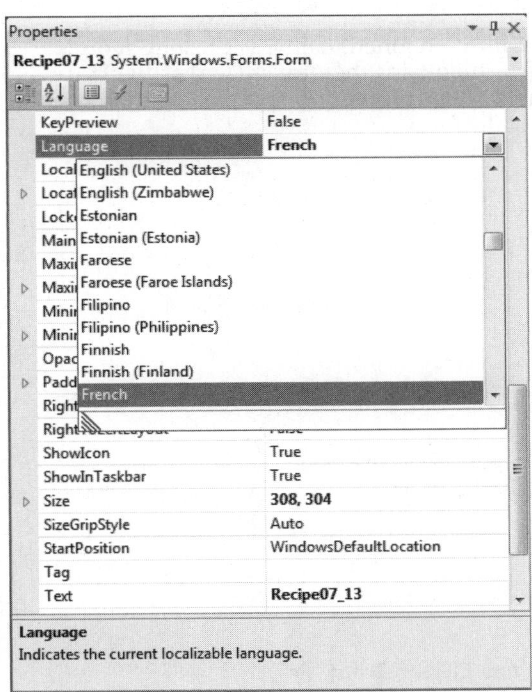

Figure 7-8. Selecting a language for localizing a form

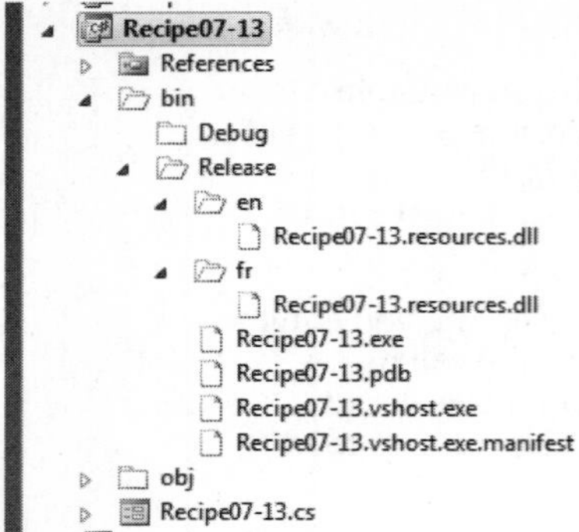

Figure 7-9. *Satellite assembly structure*

The Code

Although you do not need to manually code any of the localization functionality, as a testing shortcut you can force your application to adopt a specific culture by modifying the `Thread.CurrentUICulture` property of the application thread. However, you must modify this property before the form has loaded. Figure 7-10 shows both the English and French versions of the form.

```
using System;
using System.Threading;
using System.Globalization;
using System.Windows.Forms;

namespace Apress.VisualCSharpRecipes.Chapter07
{
    public partial class Recipe07_13 : Form
    {
        public Recipe07_13()
        {
            // Initialization code is designer generated and contained
            // in a separate file named Recipe07-13.Designer.cs.
            InitializeComponent();
        }

        [STAThread]
        public static void Main(string[] args)
        {
            Thread.CurrentThread.CurrentUICulture = new CultureInfo("fr");
            Application.Run(new Recipe07_13());
        }
    }
}
```

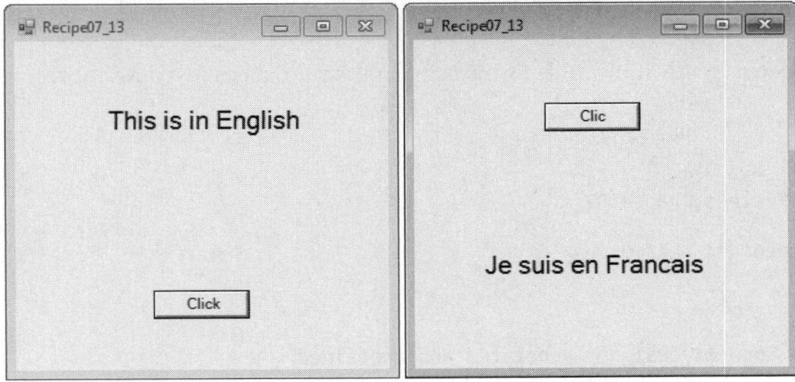

Figure 7-10. English and French localizations of Recipe07-13

7-14. Create a Form That Cannot Be Moved

Problem

You want to create a form that occupies a fixed location on the screen and cannot be moved.

Solution

Make a borderless form by setting the `FormBorderStyle` property of the `Form` class to the value `FormBorderStyle.None`.

How It Works

You can create a borderless form by setting the `FormBorderStyle` property of a `Form` to `None`. Borderless forms cannot be moved. However, as their name implies, they also lack any kind of border. If you want the customary blue border, you will need to add it yourself, either with manual drawing code or by using a background image.

One other approach to creating an immovable form does provide a basic control-style border. First, set the `ControlBox`, `MinimizeBox`, and `MaximizeBox` properties of the form to `false`. Then set the `Text` property to an empty string. To ensure the user cannot resize the form, set the `FormBorderStyle` property to the value `FixedSingle`.

The Code

The following example shows how to create immovable forms using both approaches just described:

```
using System;
using System.Windows.Forms;

namespace Apress.VisualCSharpRecipes.Chapter07
{
    public partial class Recipe07_14 : Form
    {
        public Recipe07_14()
        {
            // Initialization code is designer generated and contained
            // in a separate file named Recipe07-14.cs.
            InitializeComponent();
        }

        private void button1_Click(object sender, EventArgs e)
        {
            Form form = new Form();
            form.FormBorderStyle = FormBorderStyle.None;
            form.Show();
        }

        private void button2_Click(object sender, EventArgs e)
        {
            Form form = new Form();
            form.ControlBox = false;
            form.MinimizeBox = false;
            form.MaximizeBox = false;
            form.FormBorderStyle = FormBorderStyle.FixedSingle;
            form.Text = String.Empty;
            form.Show();
        }

        private void button3_Click(object sender, EventArgs e)
        {
            Application.Exit();
        }

        [STAThread]
        public static void Main(string[] args)
        {
            Application.Run(new Recipe07_14());
        }
    }
}
```

7-15. Make a Borderless Form Movable

Problem

You need to create a borderless form that can be moved. This might be the case if you are creating a custom window that has a unique look (e.g., for a visually rich application such as a game or a media player).

Solution

Create another control that responds to the `MouseDown`, `MouseUp`, and `MouseMove` events and programmatically moves the form.

How It Works

Borderless forms omit a title bar, which makes it impossible for a user to move them. You can compensate for this shortcoming by adding a control to the form that serves the same purpose.

For example, Figure 7-11 shows a form that includes a label to support dragging. The user can click this label and then drag the form to a new location on the screen while holding down the mouse button. As the user moves the mouse, the form moves correspondingly, as though it were "attached" to the mouse pointer.

To implement this solution, take the following steps:

1. Create a form-level Boolean variable that tracks whether or not the form is currently being dragged.
2. When the label is clicked, the code sets the flag to indicate that the form is in drag mode. At the same time, the current mouse position is recorded. You add this logic to the event handler for the `Label.MouseDown` event.
3. When the user moves the mouse over the label, the form is moved correspondingly, so that the position of the mouse over the label is unchanged. You add this logic to the event handler for the `Label.MouseMove` event.
4. When the user releases the mouse button, the dragging mode is switched off. You add this logic to the event handler for the `Label.MouseUp` event.

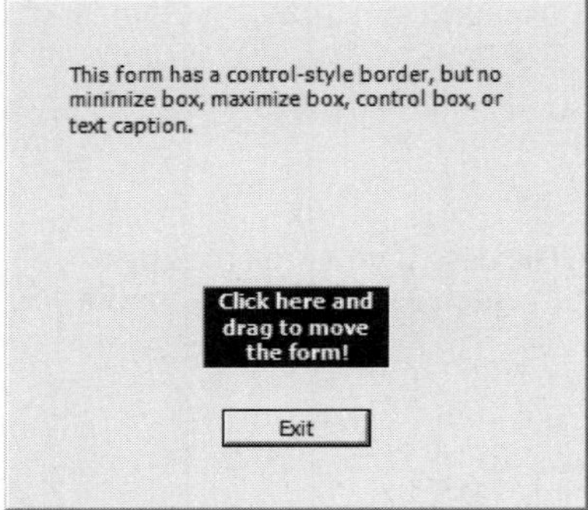

Figure 7-11. A movable borderless form

The Code

The following example creates a borderless form that a user can move by clicking a form control and dragging the form:

```
using System;
using System.Drawing;
using System.Windows.Forms;

namespace Apress.VisualCSharpRecipes.Chapter07
{
    public partial class Recipe07_15 : Form
    {
        // Boolean member tracks whether the form is in drag mode. If it is,
        // mouse movements over the label will be translated into form movements.
        private bool dragging;

        // Stores the offset where the label is clicked.
        private Point pointClicked;

        public Recipe07_15()
        {
            // Initialization code is designer generated and contained
            // in a separate file named Recipe07-15.Designer.cs.
            InitializeComponent();
        }

        // MouseDown event handler for the label initiates the dragging process.
        private void lblDrag_MouseDown(object sender, MouseEventArgs e)
        {
```

```
            if (e.Button == MouseButtons.Left)
            {
                // Turn drag mode on and store the point clicked.
                dragging = true;
                pointClicked = new Point(e.X, e.Y);
            }
            else
            {
                dragging = false;
            }
        }

        // MouseMove event handler for the label processes dragging movements if
        // the form is in drag mode.
        private void lblDrag_MouseMove(object sender, MouseEventArgs e)
        {
            if (dragging)
            {
                Point pointMoveTo;

                // Find the current mouse position in screen coordinates.
                pointMoveTo = this.PointToScreen(new Point(e.X, e.Y));

                // Compensate for the position the control was clicked.
                pointMoveTo.Offset(-pointClicked.X, -pointClicked.Y);

                // Move the form.
                this.Location = pointMoveTo;
            }
        }

        // MouseUp event handler for the label switches off drag mode.
        private void lblDrag_MouseUp(object sender, MouseEventArgs e)
        {
            dragging = false;
        }

        private void cmdClose_Click(object sender, EventArgs e)
        {
            this.Close();
        }

        [STAThread]
        public static void Main(string[] args)
        {
            Application.Run(new Recipe07_15());
        }
    }
}
```

7-16. Create an Animated System Tray Icon

Problem

You need to create an animated system tray icon (perhaps to indicate the status of a long-running task).

Solution

Create and show a NotifyIcon control. Use a timer that fires periodically (every second or so) and updates the NotifyIcon.Icon property.

How It Works

The .NET Framework makes it easy to show a system tray icon with the NotifyIcon component. You simply need to add this component to a form and supply an icon by setting the Icon property. You can animate a system tray icon by swapping the icon periodically. Optionally, you can add a linked context menu to the NotifyIcon through the ContextMenuStrip property. The NotifyIcon component automatically displays its context menu when it's right-clicked.

The Code

The following example uses eight icons, each of which shows a moon graphic in a different stage of fullness. By moving from one image to another, the illusion of animation is created.

```
using System;
using System.Drawing;
using System.Windows.Forms;

namespace Apress.VisualCSharpRecipes.Chapter07
{
    public partial class Recipe07_16 : Form
    {
        // An array to hold the set of icons used to create the
        // animation effect.
        private Icon[] images = new Icon[8];

        // An integer to identify the current icon to display.
        int offset = 0;

        public Recipe07_16()
        {
            // Initialization code is designer generated and contained
            // in a separate file named Recipe07-16.Designer.cs.
            InitializeComponent();
```

```
            // Declare a ContextMenuStrip for use by the NotifyIcon.
            ContextMenuStrip contextMenuStrip = new ContextMenuStrip();
            contextMenuStrip.Items.Add(new ToolStripMenuItem("About..."));
            contextMenuStrip.Items.Add(new ToolStripSeparator());
            contextMenuStrip.Items.Add(new ToolStripMenuItem("Exit"));

            // Assign the ContextMenuStrip to the NotifyIcon.
            notifyIcon.ContextMenuStrip = contextMenuStrip;
        }

        protected override void OnLoad(EventArgs e)
        {
            // Call the OnLoad method of the base class to ensure the Load
            // event is raised correctly.
            base.OnLoad(e);

            // Load the basic set of eight icons.
            images[0] = new Icon("moon01.ico");
            images[1] = new Icon("moon02.ico");
            images[2] = new Icon("moon03.ico");
            images[3] = new Icon("moon04.ico");
            images[4] = new Icon("moon05.ico");
            images[5] = new Icon("moon06.ico");
            images[6] = new Icon("moon07.ico");
            images[7] = new Icon("moon08.ico");
        }

        private void timer_Elapsed(object sender, System.Timers.ElapsedEventArgs e)
        {
            // Change the icon. This event handler fires once every second
            // (1000 ms).
            notifyIcon.Icon = images[offset];
            offset++;
            if (offset > 7) offset = 0;
        }

        [STAThread]
        public static void Main(string[] args)
        {
            Application.Run(new Recipe07_16());
        }
    }
}
```

7-17. Validate an Input Control

Problem

You need to alert the user of invalid input in a control, such as a TextBox.

Solution

Use the `ErrorProvider` component to display an error icon next to the offending control. Check for errors before allowing the user to continue.

How It Works

You can perform validation in a Windows-based application in a number of ways. One approach is to refuse any invalid character as the user presses a key, by using a `MaskedTextBox` control, as shown in recipe 7-8. Another approach is to respond to control validation events and prevent users from changing focus from one control to another if an error exists. A less invasive approach is to simply flag the offending control in some way so that the user can review all the errors at once. You can use this approach by adding the `ErrorProvider` component to your form.

The `ErrorProvider` is a special property extender component that displays error icons next to invalid controls. You show the error icon next to a control by using the `ErrorProvider.SetError` method and specifying the appropriate control and a string error message. The `ErrorProvider` will then show a warning icon to the right of the control. When the user hovers the mouse above the warning icon, the detailed message appears.

You need to add only one `ErrorProvider` component to your form, and you can use it to display an error icon next to any control. To add the `ErrorProvider`, drag it on the form or into the component tray or create it manually in code.

The Code

The following example checks the value that a user has entered into a text box whenever the text box loses focus. The code validates this text box using a regular expression that checks to see if the value corresponds to the format of a valid e-mail address (see recipe 2-5 for more details on regular expressions). If validation fails, the `ErrorProvider` is used to display an error message. If the text is valid, any existing error message is cleared from the `ErrorProvider`.

Finally, the `Click` event handler for the OK button steps through all the controls on the form and verifies that none of them have errors before allowing the example to continue. In this example, an empty text box is allowed, although it would be a simple matter to perform additional checks when the OK button is pressed for situations where empty text boxes are not acceptable. Figure 7-12 shows how the `ErrorProvider` control indicates an input error for the `TextBox` control when Recipe07-17 is run.

```
using System;
using System.Windows.Forms;
using System.Text.RegularExpressions;

namespace Apress.VisualCSharpRecipes.Chapter07
{
    public partial class Recipe07_17 : Form
    {
        public Recipe07_17()
        {
            // Initialization code is designer generated and contained
            // in a separate file named Recipe07-17.Designer.cs.
            InitializeComponent();
        }

        // Button click event handler ensures the ErrorProvider is not
        // reporting any error for each control before proceeding.
        private void Button1_Click(object sender, EventArgs e)
        {
            string errorText = "";
            bool invalidInput = false;

            foreach (Control ctrl in this.Controls)
            {
                if (errProvider.GetError(ctrl) != "")
                {
                    errorText += "   * " + errProvider.GetError(ctrl) + "\n";
                    invalidInput = true;
                }
            }

            if (invalidInput)
            {
                MessageBox.Show(
                    "The form contains the following unresolved errors:\n\n" +
                    errorText, "Invalid Input", MessageBoxButtons.OK,
                    MessageBoxIcon.Warning);
            }
            else
            {
                this.Close();
            }
        }

        // When the TextBox loses focus, check that the contents are a valid
        // e-mail address.
        private void txtEmail_Leave(object sender, EventArgs e)
        {
            // Create a regular expression to check for valid e-mail addresses.
            Regex regex = new Regex(@"^[\w-]+@([\w-]+\.)+[\w-]+$");
```

```
            // Validate the text from the control that raised the event.
            Control ctrl = (Control)sender;
            if (String. IsNullOrEmpty(ctrl.Text) || regex.IsMatch(ctrl.Text))
            {
                errProvider.SetError(ctrl, "");
            }
            else
            {
                errProvider.SetError(ctrl, "This is not a valid email address.");
            }
        }

        [STAThread]
        public static void Main(string[] args)
        {
            Application.Run(new Recipe07_17());
        }
    }
}
```

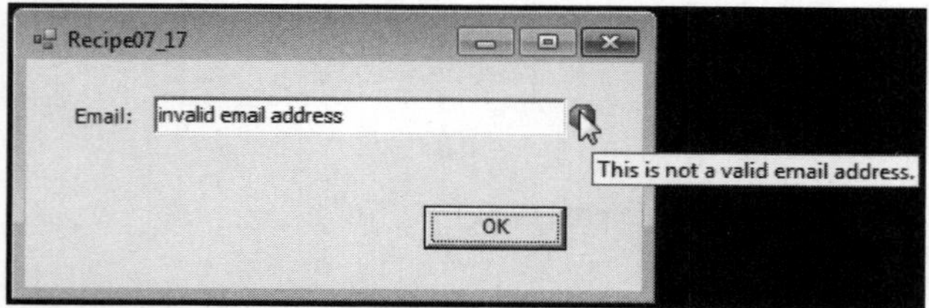

Figure 7-12. A validated form with the ErrorProvider

7-18. Use a Drag-and-Drop Operation

Problem

You need to use the drag-and-drop feature to exchange information between two controls (possibly in separate windows or separate applications).

Solution

Start a drag-and-drop operation using the `DoDragDrop` method of the `Control` class, and then respond to the `DragEnter` and `DragDrop` events in the target control.

How It Works

A drag-and-drop operation allows the user to transfer information from one place to another by clicking an item and dragging it to another location. A drag-and-drop operation consists of the following three basic steps:

1. The user clicks a control, holds down the mouse button, and begins dragging. If the control supports the drag-and-drop feature, it sets aside some information.
2. The user drags the mouse over another control. If this control accepts the dragged type of content, the mouse cursor changes to the special drag-and-drop icon (arrow and page). Otherwise, the mouse cursor becomes a circle with a line drawn through it.
3. When the user releases the mouse button, the data is sent to the control, which can then process it appropriately.

To support drag-and-drop functionality, you must handle the `DragEnter`, `DragDrop`, and (typically) `MouseDown` events. To start a drag-and-drop operation, you call the source control's `DoDragDrop` method. At this point, you submit the data and specify the type of operations that will be supported (copying, moving, and so on). Controls that can receive dragged data must have the `AllowDrop` property set to `true`. These controls will receive a `DragEnter` event when the mouse drags the data over them. At this point, you can examine the data that is being dragged, decide whether the control can accept the drop, and set the `DragEventArgs.Effect` property accordingly. The final step is to respond to the `DragDrop` event, which occurs when the user releases the mouse button.

■ **Note** It is very important that the `Main` method of your Windows application be annotated with the `STAThread` attribute if your application will provide drag-and-drop functionality.

The Code

The following example allows you to drag content between a `RichTextBox` and a standard `TextBox` control. Using the standard `TextBox`, it is not possible to drag only the currently selected text because as soon as you click the selected text to initiate a drag operation, the selection is cleared. Even handling the `MouseDown` event will not allow you to work around this because the selected text is already cleared by the event is raised.

However, the `RichTextBox` leaves the selection in place, avoiding the problem. Unfortunately, the `RichTextBox` has quirks of its own. To drop successfully onto a `RichTextBox`, you must be holding down the Ctrl key when you let go of the mouse button. You can also use the example with other applications that support text drag-and-drop operations.

```
using System;
using System.Drawing;
using System.Windows.Forms;

namespace Apress.VisualCSharpRecipes.Chapter07
{
    public partial class Recipe07_18 : Form
    {
        public Recipe07_18()
        {
            // Initialization code is designer generated and contained
            // in a separate file named Recipe07-18.Designer.cs.
            InitializeComponent();

            this.richTextBox1.AllowDrop = true;
            this.richTextBox1.EnableAutoDragDrop = false;
            this.richTextBox1.DragDrop
                += new System.Windows.Forms.DragEventHandler
                    (this.RichTextBox_DragDrop);
            this.richTextBox1.DragEnter
                += new System.Windows.Forms.DragEventHandler
                    (this.RichTextBox_DragEnter);
        }

        private void RichTextBox_DragDrop(object sender, DragEventArgs e)
        {
            RichTextBox txt = sender as RichTextBox;

            if (txt != null)
            {
                // Insert the dragged text.
                int pos = txt.SelectionStart;

                string newText = txt.Text.Substring(0, pos)
                    + e.Data.GetData(DataFormats.Text).ToString()
                    + txt.Text.Substring(pos);

                txt.Text = newText;
            }
        }

        private void RichTextBox_DragEnter(object sender, DragEventArgs e)
        {
            if (e.Data.GetDataPresent(DataFormats.Text))
            {
                e.Effect = DragDropEffects.Copy;
            }
```

```
        else
        {
            e.Effect = DragDropEffects.None;
        }
    }

    private void RichTextBox_MouseDown(object sender, MouseEventArgs e)
    {
        RichTextBox txt = sender as RichTextBox;

        // If the left mouse button is pressed and text is selected,
        // this is a possible drag event.
        if (sender != null && txt.SelectionLength > 0
            && Form.MouseButtons == MouseButtons.Left)
        {
            // Only initiate a drag if the cursor is currently inside
            // the region of selected text.
            int pos = txt.GetCharIndexFromPosition(e.Location);

            if (pos >= txt.SelectionStart
                && pos <= (txt.SelectionStart + txt.SelectionLength))
            {
                txt.DoDragDrop(txt.SelectedText, DragDropEffects.Copy);
            }
        }
    }

    private void TextBox_DragDrop(object sender, DragEventArgs e)
    {
        TextBox txt = sender as TextBox;

        if (txt != null)
        {
            txt.Text = (string)e.Data.GetData(DataFormats.Text);
        }
    }

    private void TextBox_DragEnter(object sender, DragEventArgs e)
    {
        if (e.Data.GetDataPresent(DataFormats.Text))
        {
            e.Effect = DragDropEffects.Copy;
        }
        else
        {
            e.Effect = DragDropEffects.None;
        }
    }
```

```
        private void TextBox_MouseDown(object sender, MouseEventArgs e)
        {
            TextBox txt = sender as TextBox;

            if (txt != null && Form.MouseButtons == MouseButtons.Left)
            {
                txt.SelectAll();
                txt.DoDragDrop(txt.Text, DragDropEffects.Copy);
            }
        }

        [STAThread]
        public static void Main(string[] args)
        {
            Application.Run(new Recipe07_18());
        }
    }
}
```

7-19. Update the User Interface in a Multithreaded Application

Problem

You need to ensure a Windows Forms user interface is updated correctly in a multithreaded application.

Solution

Ensure all interaction with a control is performed on the thread that initially created the control. When calling operations on controls from a thread that did not create the control, make the call using the control's `Invoke` or `BeginInvoke` methods and pass in a delegate to the code you want executed.

How It Works

Windows Forms is not inherently thread safe, meaning you are not free to interact with controls from just any thread. Instead, you must marshal all calls to a control onto the thread that owns the message queue for that control (i.e., the thread that created the control).

You can determine if the executing thread can call a control directly by testing the control's `InvokeRequired` property. If the value is `false`, then the currently executing thread can interact with the control directly; otherwise, you must marshal any interaction back onto the correct thread. This potentially difficult task is made trivial through the use of the `Invoke` and `BeginInvoke` methods implemented by the `Control` base class.

Both methods take a delegate (or an equivalent anonymous method or lambda expression) and invoke the specified method on the control using the correct thread. `Invoke` executes the delegate synchronously and BeginInvoke executes the delegate asynchronously. To complete an asynchronous operation initiated using BeginInvoke, you call the Control.EndInvoke method. The BeginInvoke and EndInvoke methods make up a common asynchronous execution pattern known as the Classic Async pattern. The details of this pattern and the options you have available for handling method completion are discussed in recipe 4-2.

The Code

The following example shows how to update a Windows Forms control from multiple threads. The example uses two timers that fire at differing intervals to change the color of a Button control between red and green. The code shows how to use both an anonymous method and a lambda expression with the Invoke call. Both approaches use System.Action, a delegate type that can encapsulate any method that returns void and takes no arguments.

```
using System;
using System.Collections.Generic;
using System.ComponentModel;
using System.Data;
using System.Drawing;
using System.Text;
using System.Windows.Forms;

namespace Apress.VisualCSharpRecipes.Chapter07
{
    public partial class Recipe07_19 : Form
    {
        // Declare timers that change the button color.
        System.Timers.Timer greenTimer;
        System.Timers.Timer redTimer;

        public Recipe07_19()
        {
            // Initialization code is designer generated and contained
            // in a separate file named Recipe07-19.Designer.cs.
            InitializeComponent();

            // Create autoreset timers that fire at varying intervals
            // to change the color of the button on the form.
            greenTimer = new System.Timers.Timer(3000);
            greenTimer.Elapsed +=
                new System.Timers.ElapsedEventHandler(greenTimer_Elapsed);
            greenTimer.Start();

            redTimer = new System.Timers.Timer(5000);
            redTimer.Elapsed +=
                new System.Timers.ElapsedEventHandler(redTimer_Elapsed);
            redTimer.Start();
        }
```

```
        void redTimer_Elapsed(object sender, System.Timers.ElapsedEventArgs e)
        {
            // Use an anonymous method to set the button color to red.
            button1.Invoke((Action)delegate {button1.BackColor = Color.Red;});
        }

        void greenTimer_Elapsed(object sender, System.Timers.ElapsedEventArgs e)
        {
            // Use a lambda expression to set the button color to green.
            button1.Invoke(new Action(() => button1.BackColor = Color.Green));
        }

        private void button1_Click(object sender, EventArgs e)
        {
            Application.Exit();
        }

        [STAThread]
        public static void Main(string[] args)
        {
            Application.Run(new Recipe07_19());
        }
    }
}
```

7-20. Display a Web Page in a Windows-Based Application

Problem

You want to display a web page and provide web-navigation capabilities within your Windows Forms application.

Solution

Use the `WebBrowser` control to display the web page and other standard controls like buttons and text boxes to allow the user to control the operation of the `WebBrowser`.

■ **Caution** The `WebBrowser` control is a managed wrapper around the `WebBrowser` ActiveX control. This means that you must ensure you annotate the `Main` method of your Windows application with the `STAThread` attribute and that you dispose of the `WebBrowser` control (by calling the `WebBrowser.Dispose` method) when it is no longer required.

How It Works

The WebBrowser control makes it a trivial task to embed highly functional web browser capabilities into your Windows applications. The WebBrowser control is responsible for the display of web pages and maintaining page history, but it does not provide any controls for user interaction. Instead, the WebBrowser control exposes properties and events that you can manipulate programmatically to control the operation of the WebBrowser. This approach makes the WebBrowser control highly flexible and adaptable to most common browsing requirements. Table 7-1 summarizes some of the WebBrowser members related to web navigation that you will find particularly useful.

Table 7-1. *Commonly Used Members of the WebBrowser Control*

Member	Description
Property	
AllowNavigation	Controls whether the WebBrowser can navigate to another page after its initial page has been loaded
CanGoBack	Indicates whether the WebBrowser currently holds back page history, which would allow the GoBack method to succeed
CanGoForward	Indicates whether the WebBrowser currently holds forward page history, which would allow the GoForward method to succeed
IsBusy	Indicates whether the WebBrowser is currently busy downloading a page
Url	Holds the URL of the currently displayed/downloading page
Method	
GoBack	Displays the previous page in the page history
GoForward	Displays the next page in the page history
GoHome	Displays the home page of the current user as configured in Windows
Navigate	Displays the web page at the specified URL
Stop	Stops the current WebBrowser activity
Event	
DocumentCompleted	Signals that the active download has completed and the document is displayed in the WebBrowser

You can also use the WebBrowser.DocumentText property to set (or get) the currently displayed HTML contents of the WebBrowser. To manipulate the contents using the Document Object Model (DOM), get an HtmlDocument instance via the Document property.

The Code

The following example uses the WebBrowser control to allow users to navigate to a web page whose address is entered into a TextBox. Buttons also allow users to move forward and backward through page history and navigate directly to their personal home page.

```
using System;
using System.Windows.Forms;

namespace Apress.VisualCSharpRecipes.Chapter07
{
    public partial class Recipe07_20 : Form
    {
        public Recipe07_20()
        {
            // Initialization code is designer generated and contained
            // in a separate file named Recipe07-20.Designer.cs.
            InitializeComponent();
        }

        private void goButton_Click(object sender, EventArgs e)
        {
            // Navigate to the URL specified in the text box.
            webBrowser1.Navigate(textURL.Text);
        }

        private void homeButton_Click(object sender, EventArgs e)
        {
            // Navigate to the current user's home page.
            webBrowser1.GoHome();
        }

        protected override void OnLoad(EventArgs e)
        {
            // Call the OnLoad method of the base class to ensure the Load
            // event is raised correctly.
            base.OnLoad(e);

            // Navigate to the Apress home page when the application first
            // loads.
            webBrowser1.Navigate("http://www.apress.com");
        }
```

```
        private void backButton_Click(object sender, EventArgs e)
        {
            // Go to the previous page in the WebBrowser history.
            webBrowser1.GoBack();
        }

        private void forwarButton_Click(object sender, EventArgs e)
        {
            // Go to the next page in the WebBrowser history.
            webBrowser1.GoForward();
        }

        // Event handler to perform general interface maintenance once a document
        // has been loaded into the WebBrowser.
        private void webBrowser1_DocumentCompleted(object sender,
            WebBrowserDocumentCompletedEventArgs e)
        {
            // Update the content of the TextBox to reflect the current URL.
            textURL.Text = webBrowser1.Url.ToString();

            // Enable or disable the Back button depending on whether the
            // WebBrowser has back history.
            if (webBrowser1.CanGoBack)
            {
                backButton.Enabled = true;
            }
            else
            {
                backButton.Enabled = false;
            }

            // Enable or disable the Forward button depending on whether the
            // WebBrowser has forward history.
            if (webBrowser1.CanGoForward)
            {
                forwarButton.Enabled = true;
            }
            else
            {
                forwarButton.Enabled = false;
            }
        }

        [STAThread]
        public static void Main(string[] args)
        {
            Application.Run(new Recipe07_20());
        }
    }
}
```

7-21. Display WPF Windows in a Windows Forms Application

Problem

You need to display a WPF window in a Windows Forms application.

Solution

Create an instance of the WPF window (`System.Windows.Window`) you want to display in your Windows Forms code. Call `Window.ShowDialog` to display a modal window, or call `Window.Show` to display a modeless window.

How It Works

The trickiest thing about displaying a WPF window in a Windows Forms application is actually integrating the WPF source code into your project correctly if you are using Visual Studio. There is no option in your Windows Forms project to add a WPF `Window` when you select Add New Item in Solution Explorer.

The easiest way around this is to import an existing WPF `Window` using the Add Existing option in Solution Explorer. This will set everything up appropriately (adding the necessary assembly references), and you can then edit the WPF `Window` as you would when creating a WPF application. Alternatively, Visual Studio will allow you to add a new WPF user control to your Windows Forms application. You can use that option and then change the XAML and code-behind as required.

Once you have a WPF `Window` declared, you can reference and instantiate the class the same as you would any other class. Calling `Window.ShowDialog` will display the window modally, meaning that the user can interact with only that window and must close it before they can interact again with the rest of the application. Calling `Window.Show` will display a modeless window, allowing the user to interact with the new window as well as the rest of the application.

The Code

The following example (shown running in Figure 7-13) displays a Windows `Form` with two buttons. The left button opens and closes a modeless WPF window, and the right button opens a modal window. When the example creates the modeless window, it subscribes an event handler to the `Window.Closing` event so that the application can update the button state should the user choose to close the window directly instead of using the button. The following code is the code-behind for the main Windows `Form`:

```
using System;
using System.ComponentModel;
using System.Windows.Forms;

namespace Apress.VisualCSharpRecipes.Chapter07
{
    public partial class Recipe07_21 : Form
    {
        private Window1 modelessWindow;
```

```
private CancelEventHandler modelessWindowCloseHandler;

public Recipe07_21()
{
    // Initialization code is designer generated and contained
    // in a separate file named Recipe07-21.Designer.cs.
    InitializeComponent();
    modelessWindowCloseHandler = new CancelEventHandler(Window_Closing);
}

// Handles the button click event to open and close the modeless
// WPF window.
private void OpenModeless_Click(object sender, EventArgs e)
{
    if (modelessWindow == null)
    {
        modelessWindow = new Window1();

        // Add an event handler to get notification when the window
        // is closing.
        modelessWindow.Closing += modelessWindowCloseHandler;

        // Change the button text.
        btnOpenModeless.Text = "Close Modeless Window";

        // Show the Windows Form.
        modelessWindow.Show();
    }
    else
    {
        modelessWindow.Close();
    }
}

// Handles the button click event to open the modal WPF Window.
private void OpenModal_Click(object sender, EventArgs e)
{
    // Create and display the modal window.
    Window1 window = new Window1();
    window.ShowDialog();
}

// Handles the WPF Window's Closing event for the modeless window.
private void Window_Closing(object sender, CancelEventArgs e)
{
    // Remove the event handler reference.
    modelessWindow.Closing -= modelessWindowCloseHandler;
    modelessWindow = null;
```

```
            // Change the button text.
            btnOpenModeless.Text = "Open Modeless Window";
        }
    }
}
```

The following XAML provides the declaration of the WPF `Window` that is opened when the user clicks either of the buttons on the Windows Forms application:

```
<Window x:Class="Apress.VisualCSharpRecipes.Chapter07.Window1"
    xmlns="http://schemas.microsoft.com/winfx/2006/xaml/presentation"
    xmlns:x="http://schemas.microsoft.com/winfx/2006/xaml"
    Title="Recipe07_21" Height="200" Width="300">
    <StackPanel Margin="20">
        <TextBlock FontSize="20" Text="A WPF Window" TextAlignment="Center"/>
        <Button Click="btnClose_Click" Content="Close" Margin="50"
                MaxWidth="50" Name="btnClose" />
    </StackPanel>
</Window>
```

The following is the code-behind for the WPF `Window` that allows the user to close the window by clicking the Close button:

```
using System.Windows;
using System.Windows.Forms;

namespace Apress.VisualCSharpRecipes.Chapter07
{
    /// <summary>
    /// Interaction logic for Window1.xaml
    /// </summary>
    public partial class Window1 : Window
    {
        public Window1()
        {
            InitializeComponent();
        }

        private void btnClose_Click(object sender, RoutedEventArgs e)
        {
            this.Close();
        }
    }
}
```

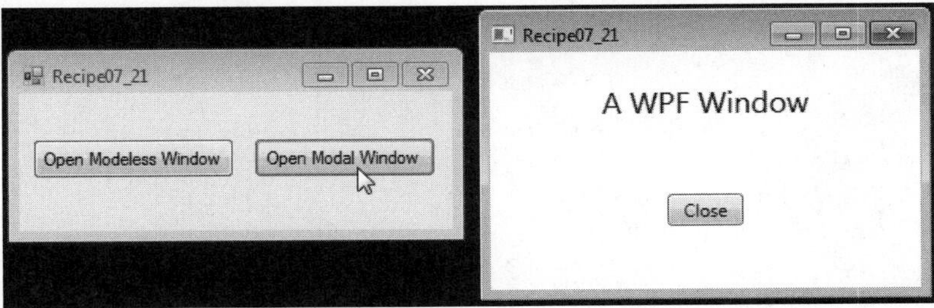

Figure 7-13. Displaying a WPF window from a Windows Forms application

7-22. Display WPF Controls in Windows Forms

Problem

You need to display WPF user interface elements alongside Windows Forms controls in a Windows `Form`.

Solution

Use a `System.Windows.Forms.Integration.ElementHost` control on your Windows `Form`, and host the WPF control inside it.

How It Works

The `ElementHost` control is a Windows Forms control that allows you to host WPF controls in Windows Forms. The `ElementHost` control makes integrating WPF controls into your Windows Forms application relatively simple and even provides some limited visual design-time support.

The `ElementHost` can contain a single WPF element that inherits from `System.Windows.UIElement`. The element can be one of the layout containers discussed in Chapter 17, which allows you to create rich, structured WPF content within the `ElementHost` control. Often, the WPF element you place in the `ElementHost` control will be a WPF user control (see Chapter 17), but can also be any common WPF control.

To use the `ElementHost` control in Visual Studio's graphical design environment, open the toolbox and browse to the WPF Interoperability category. Drag the `ElementHost` control and drop it on the Windows `Form` as you would with any other control. Using the ElementHost Tasks window, you can then select any WPF user control currently in your project to place in the `ElementHost` control (see Figure 7-14).

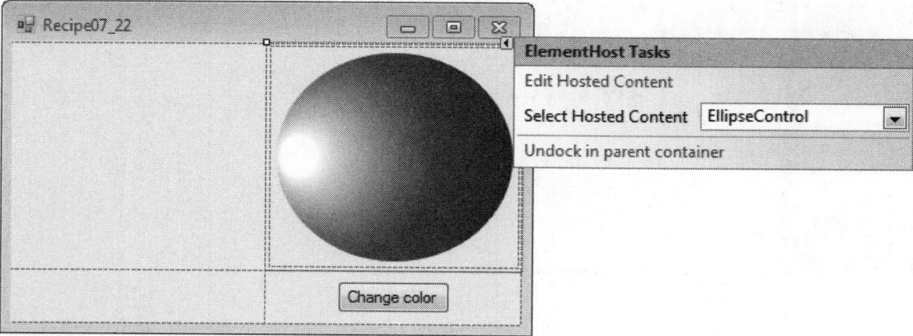

Figure 7-14. *Using ElementHost in Visual Studio*

If you do not want to use a user control, then you will need to populate the `ElementHost` control programmatically by assigning the desired WPF element to the `Child` property of the `ElementHost` control.

The Code

The following example demonstrates how to integrate WPF controls into a Windows Forms application. The example (shown in Figure 7-15) uses a simple WPF user control consisting of a `System.Windows.Shapes.Ellipse` that can change between red and blue color gradients. This `EllipseControl` is assigned to one `ElementHost` using the Visual Studio form builder. Another `ElementHost` is populated programmatically with a `System.Windows.Controls.TextBox`. A standard Windows Forms button triggers the `EllipseControl` to change color, and then writes a log entry to the `TextBox`. Here is the XAML for the WPF user control:

```
<UserControl x:Class="Apress.VisualCSharpRecipes.Chapter07.EllipseControl"
    xmlns="http://schemas.microsoft.com/winfx/2006/xaml/presentation"
    xmlns:x="http://schemas.microsoft.com/winfx/2006/xaml"
    Height="300" Width="300">
    <Grid x:Name="Grid1">
        <Grid.Resources>
            <RadialGradientBrush x:Key="RedBrush" RadiusX=".8" RadiusY="1"
                                 Center="0.5,0.5" GradientOrigin="0.05,0.5">
                <GradientStop Color="#ffffff" Offset="0.1" />
                <GradientStop Color="#ff0000" Offset="0.5" />
                <GradientStop Color="#880000" Offset="0.8" />
            </RadialGradientBrush>
            <RadialGradientBrush x:Key="BlueBrush" RadiusX=".8" RadiusY="1"
                                 Center="0.5,0.5" GradientOrigin="0.05,0.5">
                <GradientStop Color="#ffffff" Offset="0.1" />
                <GradientStop Color="#0000ff" Offset="0.5" />
                <GradientStop Color="#000088" Offset="0.8" />
            </RadialGradientBrush>
        </Grid.Resources>
```

```
        <Ellipse Margin="5" Name="Ellipse1" ToolTip="A WPF Ellipse."
                 Fill="{StaticResource RedBrush}">
        </Ellipse>
    </Grid>
</UserControl>
```

Here is the code-behind for the `EllipseControl`, which is used to control and query its current color gradient:

```
using System.Windows.Controls;
using System.Windows.Media;

namespace Apress.VisualCSharpRecipes.Chapter07
{
    /// <summary>
    /// Interaction logic for EllipseControl.xaml
    /// </summary>
    public partial class EllipseControl : UserControl
    {
        public EllipseControl()
        {
            // Initialization code is designer generated and contained
            // in a separate file named Recipe07-22.Designer.cs.
            InitializeComponent();
        }

        // Gets the name of the current color.
        public string Color
        {
            get
            {
                if (Ellipse1.Fill == (Brush)Grid1.Resources["RedBrush"])
                {
                    return "Red";
                }
                else
                {
                    return "Blue";
                }
            }
        }

        // Switch the fill to the red gradient.
        public void ChangeColor()
        {
            // Check the current fill of the ellipse.
            if (Ellipse1.Fill == (Brush)Grid1.Resources["RedBrush"])
            {
                // Ellipse is red, change to blue.
                Ellipse1.Fill = (Brush)Grid1.Resources["BlueBrush"];
            }
```

```
                else
                {
                    // Ellipse is blue, change to red.
                    Ellipse1.Fill = (Brush)Grid1.Resources["RedBrush"];
                }
            }
        }
    }
```

The following is the code-behind for the main Windows Forms form. The `form` constructor demonstrates the programmatic creation and configuration of an `ElementHost` control to display a standard WPF `TextBox` control. The `button1_Click` method is invoked when the user clicks the button, and it changes the color of the ellipse and appends a message to the content of the `TextBox`. The rest of the application code generated by Visual Studio is not shown here, but is provided in the sample code (available on the book's page on the Apress web site, `www.apress.com`).

```
using System;
using System.Windows;
using System.Windows.Forms;
using WPFControls=System.Windows.Controls;
using System.Windows.Forms.Integration;

namespace Apress.VisualCSharpRecipes.Chapter07
{
    public partial class Recipe07_22: Form
    {
        WPFControls.TextBox textBox;

        public Recipe07_22 ()
        {
            InitializeComponent();

            // Create a new WPF TextBox control.
            textBox = new WPFControls.TextBox();
            textBox.Text = "A WPF TextBox\n\r\n\r";
            textBox.TextAlignment = TextAlignment.Center;
            textBox.VerticalAlignment = VerticalAlignment.Center;
            textBox.VerticalScrollBarVisibility =
                WPFControls.ScrollBarVisibility.Auto;
            textBox.IsReadOnly = true;

            // Create a new ElementHost to host the WPF TextBox.
            ElementHost elementHost2 = new ElementHost();
            elementHost2.Name = "elementHost2";
            elementHost2.Dock = DockStyle.Fill;
            elementHost2.Child = textBox;
            elementHost2.Size = new System.Drawing.Size(156, 253);
            elementHost2.RightToLeft = RightToLeft.No;
```

```
            // Place the new ElementHost in the bottom-left table cell.
            tableLayoutPanel1.Controls.Add(elementHost2, 1, 0);
        }

        private void button1_Click(object sender, EventArgs e)
        {
            // Change the ellipse color.
            ellipseControl1.ChangeColor();

            // Get the current ellipse color and append to TextBox.
            textBox.Text +=
                String.Format("Ellipse color changed to {0}\n\r",
                ellipseControl1.Color);

            textBox.ScrollToEnd();
        }
    }
}
```

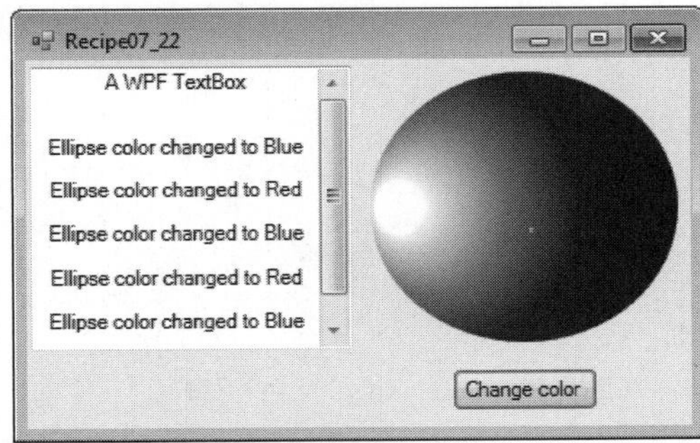

Figure 7-15. *Using WPF controls in a Windows Forms form*

CHAPTER 8

Graphics, Multimedia, and Printing

Graphics, video, sound, and printing are the hallmarks of a traditional rich client on the Microsoft Windows operating system. When it comes to multimedia, the Microsoft .NET Framework delivers a compromise, providing support for some of these features while ignoring others. For example, you will find a sophisticated set of tools for two-dimensional drawing and event-based printing with GDI+ and the types in the `System.Drawing` namespaces. These classes wrap `GDI32.dll` and `USER32.dll`, which provide the native graphics device interface (GDI) functions in the Windows application programming interface (API), and they make it much easier to draw complex shapes, work with coordinates and transforms, and process images. On the other hand, if you want to show a video file or get information about the current print jobs, you will need to look beyond the .NET Framework.

This chapter presents recipes that show you how to use built-in .NET features and, where necessary, native Win32 libraries via P/Invoke or COM Interop. The recipes in this chapter describe how to do the following:

- Find the fonts installed in your system (recipe 8-1)
- Perform hit testing with shapes (recipe 8-2)
- Create an irregularly shaped form or control (recipe 8-3)
- Create a sprite that can be moved around (recipe 8-4)
- Display an image that could be made to scroll (recipe 8-5), learn how to capture the image of the desktop (recipe 8-6), and create a thumbnail for an existing image (recipe 8-8)
- Enable double buffering to increase performance while redrawing (recipe 8-7)
- Play a beep or a system-defined sound (recipe 8-9), play a WAV file (recipe 8-10), play a non-WAV file such as an MP3 file (recipe 8-11), and play an animation with DirectShow (recipe 8-12)
- Retrieve information about the printers installed on the machine (recipe 8-13), print a simple document (recipe 8-14), print a document that has multiple pages (recipe 8-15), print wrapped text (recipe 8-16), show a print preview (recipe 8-17), and manage print jobs (recipe 8-18)

- Perform text-to-speech (TTS) (recipe 8-19)
- Perform optical character recognition (OCR) to find words in an image (recipe 8-20).

8-1. Find All Installed Fonts

Problem

You need to retrieve a list of all the fonts installed on the current computer.

Solution

Create a new instance of the `System.Drawing.Text.InstalledFontCollection` class, which contains a collection of `FontFamily` objects representing all the installed fonts.

How It Works

The `InstalledFontCollection` class allows you to retrieve information about currently installed fonts. It derives from the `FontCollection` class, which allows you to get a list of font families as a collection in the `Families` property.

The Code

The following code shows a form that iterates through the font collection when it is first created. Every time it finds a font, it creates a new `Label` control that will display the font name in the given font face (at a size of 14 points). The `Label` is added to a `Panel` control named `pnlFonts` with `AutoScroll` set to `true`, allowing the user to scroll through the list of available fonts.

```
using System;
using System.Drawing;
using System.Windows.Forms;
using System.Drawing.Text;

namespace Apress.VisualCSharpRecipes.Chapter08
{
    public partial class Recipe08_01: Form
    {
        public Recipe08_01()
        {
            InitializeComponent();
        }

        private void Recipe08_01_Load(object sender, EventArgs e)
        {
```

```
            // Create the font collection.
            using (InstalledFontCollection fontFamilies =
                new InstalledFontCollection())
            {
                // Iterate through all font families.
                int offset = 10;
                foreach (FontFamily family in fontFamilies.Families)
                {
                    try
                    {
                        // Create a label that will display text in this font.
                        Label fontLabel = new Label();
                        fontLabel.Text = family.Name;
                        fontLabel.Font = new Font(family, 14);
                        fontLabel.Left = 10;
                        fontLabel.Width = pnlFonts.Width;
                        fontLabel.Top = offset;

                        // Add the label to a scrollable Panel.
                        pnlFonts.Controls.Add(fontLabel);
                        offset += 30;
                    }
                    catch
                    {
                        // An error will occur if the selected font does
                        // not support normal style (the default used when
                        // creating a Font object). This problem can be
                        // harmlessly ignored.
                    }
                }
            }
        }
    }
}
```

Figure 8-1 shows this simple test application.

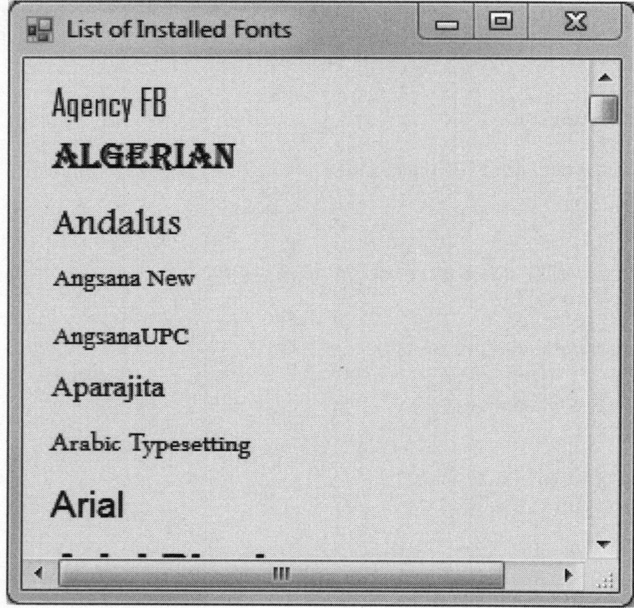

Figure 8-1. A list of installed fonts

8-2. Perform Hit Testing with Shapes

Problem

You need to detect whether a user clicks inside a shape.

Solution

Test the point where the user clicked with methods such as `Rectangle.Contains` and `Region.IsVisible` (in the `System.Drawing` namespace) or `GraphicsPath.IsVisible` (in the `System.Drawing.Drawing2D` namespace), depending on the type of shape.

How It Works

Often, if you use GDI+ to draw shapes on a form, you need to be able to determine when a user clicks inside a given shape. The .NET Framework provides three methods to help with this task:

- The `Rectangle.Contains` method takes a point and returns `true` if the point is inside a given rectangle. In many cases, you can retrieve a rectangle for another type of shape. For example, you can use `Image.GetBounds` to retrieve the invisible rectangle that represents the image boundaries. The `Rectangle` structure is a member of the `System.Drawing` namespace.
- The `GraphicsPath.IsVisible` method takes a point and returns `true` if the point is inside the area defined by a closed `GraphicsPath`. Because a `GraphicsPath` can contain multiple lines, shapes, and figures, this approach is useful if you want to test whether a point is contained inside a nonrectangular region. The `GraphicsPath` class is a member of the `System.Drawing.Drawing2D` namespace.
- The `Region.IsVisible` method takes a point and returns `true` if the point is inside the area defined by a `Region`. A `Region`, like the `GraphicsPath`, can represent a complex nonrectangular shape. `Region` is a member of the `System.Drawing` namespace.

The Code

The following example shows a form that creates a `Rectangle` and a `GraphicsPath`. By default, these two shapes are given light-blue backgrounds. However, an event handler responds to the `Form.MouseMove` event, checks to see whether the mouse pointer is in one of these shapes, and updates the background to bright pink if the pointer is there.

Note that the highlighting operation takes place directly inside the `MouseMove` event handler. The painting is performed only if the current selection has changed. For simpler code, you could invalidate the entire form every time the mouse pointer moves in or out of a region and handle all the drawing in the `Form.Paint` event handler, but this would lead to more drawing and generate additional flicker as the entire form is repainted.

```
using System;
using System.Drawing;
using System.Windows.Forms;
using System.Drawing.Drawing2D;

namespace Apress.VisualCSharpRecipes.Chapter08
{
    public partial class Recipe08_02 : Form
    {
        // Define the shapes used on this form.
        private GraphicsPath path;
        private Rectangle rectangle;

        // Define the flags that track where the mouse pointer is.
        private bool inPath = false;
        private bool inRectangle = false;
```

```
// Define the brushes used for painting the shapes.
Brush highlightBrush = Brushes.HotPink;
Brush defaultBrush = Brushes.LightBlue;

public Recipe08_02()
{
    InitializeComponent();
}

private void Recipe08_02_Load(object sender, EventArgs e)
{
    // Create the shapes that will be displayed.
    path = new GraphicsPath();
    path.AddEllipse(10, 10, 100, 60);
    path.AddCurve(new Point[] {new Point(50, 50),
              new Point(10,33), new Point(80,43)});
    path.AddLine(50, 120, 250, 80);
    path.AddLine(120, 40, 110, 50);
    path.CloseFigure();

    rectangle = new Rectangle(100, 170, 220, 120);
}

private void Recipe08_02_Paint(object sender, PaintEventArgs e)
{
    Graphics g = e.Graphics;

    // Paint the shapes according to the current selection.
    if (inPath)
    {
        g.FillPath(highlightBrush, path);
        g.FillRectangle(defaultBrush, rectangle);
    }
    else if (inRectangle)
    {
        g.FillRectangle(highlightBrush, rectangle);
        g.FillPath(defaultBrush, path);
    }
    else
    {
        g.FillPath(defaultBrush, path);
        g.FillRectangle(defaultBrush, rectangle);
    }
    g.DrawPath(Pens.Black, path);
    g.DrawRectangle(Pens.Black, rectangle);
}
```

```
        private void Recipe08_02_MouseMove(object sender, MouseEventArgs e)
        {
            using (Graphics g = this.CreateGraphics())
            {
                // Perform hit testing with rectangle.
                if (rectangle.Contains(e.X, e.Y))
                {
                    if (!inRectangle)
                    {
                        inRectangle = true;

                        // Highlight the rectangle.
                        g.FillRectangle(highlightBrush, rectangle);
                        g.DrawRectangle(Pens.Black, rectangle);
                    }
                }
                else if (inRectangle)
                {
                    inRectangle = false;

                    // Restore the unhighlighted rectangle.
                    g.FillRectangle(defaultBrush, rectangle);
                    g.DrawRectangle(Pens.Black, rectangle);
                }

                // Perform hit testing with path.
                if (path.IsVisible(e.X, e.Y))
                {
                    if (!inPath)
                    {
                        inPath = true;

                        // Highlight the path.
                        g.FillPath(highlightBrush, path);
                        g.DrawPath(Pens.Black, path);
                    }
                }
                else if (inPath)
                {
                    inPath = false;

                    // Restore the unhighlighted path.
                    g.FillPath(defaultBrush, path);
                    g.DrawPath(Pens.Black, path);
                }
            }
        }
    }
}
```

Figure 8-2 shows the application in action.

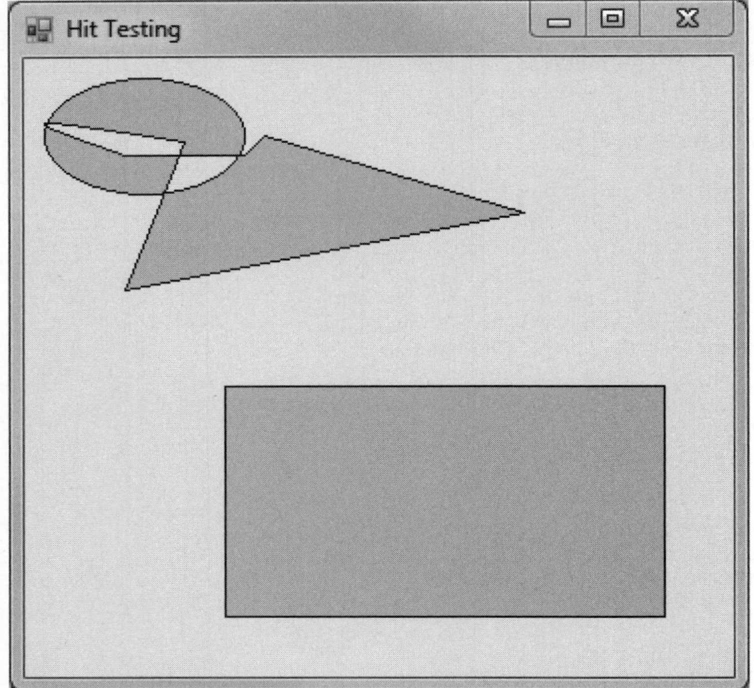

Figure 8-2. Hit testing with a Rectangle and a GraphicsPath object

8-3. Create an Irregularly Shaped Control

Problem

You need to create a nonrectangular form or control.

Solution

Create a new `System.Drawing.Region` object that has the shape you want for the form, and assign it to the `Form.Region` or `Control.Region` property.

How It Works

To create a nonrectangular form or control, you first need to define the shape you want. The easiest approach is to use the `System.Drawing.Drawing2D.GraphicsPath` object, which can accommodate any combination of ellipses, rectangles, closed curves, and even strings. You can add shapes to a

GraphicsPath instance using methods such as AddEllipse, AddRectangle, AddClosedCurve, and AddString. Once you are finished defining the shape you want, you can create a Region object from this GraphicsPath—just submit the GraphicsPath in the Region class constructor. Finally, you can assign the Region to the Form.Region property or the Control.Region property.

The Code

The following example creates an irregularly shaped form (shown in Figure 8-3) using two curves made of multiple points, which are converted into a closed figure using the GraphicsPath.CloseAllFigures method.

```
using System;
using System.Drawing;
using System.Windows.Forms;
using System.Drawing.Drawing2D;

namespace Apress.VisualCSharpRecipes.Chapter08
{
    public partial class Recipe08_03 : Form
    {
        public Recipe08_03()
        {
            InitializeComponent();
        }

        private void Recipe08_03_Load(object sender, EventArgs e)
        {
            GraphicsPath path = new GraphicsPath();

            Point[] pointsA = new Point[]
                {
                    new Point(0, 0),
                    new Point(40, 60),
                    new Point(this.Width - 100, 10)
                };
            path.AddCurve(pointsA);

            Point[] pointsB = new Point[]
                {
                    new Point(this.Width - 40, this.Height - 60),
                    new Point(this.Width, this.Height),
                    new Point(10, this.Height)
                };
            path.AddCurve(pointsB);

            path.CloseAllFigures();

            this.Region = new Region(path);
        }
```

```
        private void cmdClose_Click(object sender, EventArgs e)
        {
            this.Close();
        }
    }
}
```

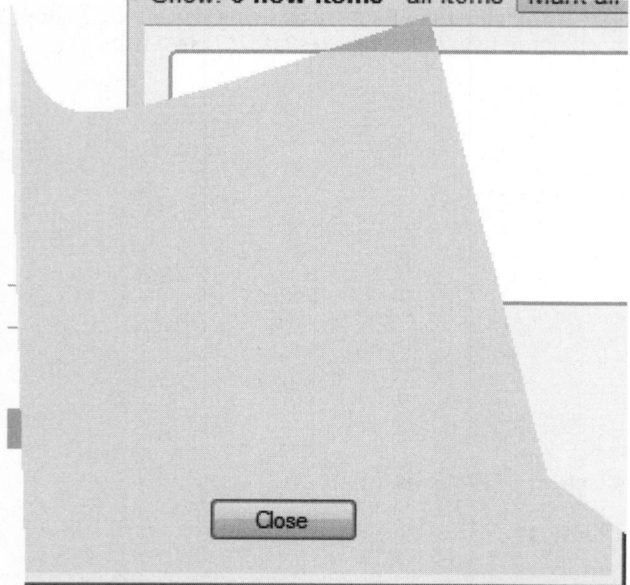

Figure 8-3. A nonrectangular form

■ **Note** Another method for creating nonrectangular forms (not controls) is using the `BackgroundImage` and `TransparentKey` properties available in the `Form` class. However, this method could cause display problems when monitors are set to a color depth greater than 24-bit. For more information about this topic, refer to the Microsoft Developer Network (MSDN) documentation.

For an example that demonstrates a nonrectangular control, refer to recipe 8-4.

8-4. Create a Movable Sprite

Problem

You need to create a shape the user can manipulate on a form, perhaps by dragging it, resizing it, or otherwise interacting with it.

Solution

Create a custom control, and override the painting logic to draw a shape. Assign your shape to the `Control.Region` property. You can then use this `Region` to perform hit testing.

How It Works

If you need to create a complex user interface that incorporates many custom-drawn elements, you need a way to track these elements and allow the user to interact with them. The easiest approach in .NET is to create a dedicated control by deriving a class from `System.Windows.Forms.Control`. You can then customize the way this control is painted in the way its basic set of events is raised.

The Code

The following example shows a control that represents a simple ellipse shape on a form. All controls are associated with a rectangular region on a form, so the `EllipseShape` control generates an ellipse that fills these boundaries (provided through the `Control.ClientRectangle` property). Once the shape has been generated, the `Control.Region` property is set according to the bounds on the ellipse. This ensures that events such as `MouseMove`, `MouseDown`, `Click`, and so on, will occur only if the mouse is over the ellipse, not the entire client rectangle.

The following code shows the full `EllipseShape` code:

```
using System;
using System.Drawing;
using System.Windows.Forms;
using System.Drawing.Drawing2D;

namespace Apress.VisualCSharpRecipes.Chapter08
{
    public partial class EllipseShape : Control
    {
        public EllipseShape()
        {
            InitializeComponent();
        }

        private GraphicsPath path = null;
```

```
        private void RefreshPath()
        {
            // Create the GraphicsPath for the shape (in this case
            // an ellipse that fits inside the full control area)
            // and apply it to the control by setting
            // the Region property.
            path = new GraphicsPath();
            path.AddEllipse(this.ClientRectangle);
            this.Region = new Region(path);
        }

        protected override void OnPaint(PaintEventArgs e)
        {
            base.OnPaint(e);
            if (path != null)
            {
                e.Graphics.SmoothingMode = SmoothingMode.AntiAlias;
                e.Graphics.FillPath(new SolidBrush(this.BackColor), path);
                e.Graphics.DrawPath(new Pen(this.ForeColor, 4), path);
            }
        }

        protected override void OnResize(System.EventArgs e)
        {
            base.OnResize(e);
            RefreshPath();
            this.Invalidate();
        }
    }
}
```

You could define the `EllipseShape` control in a separate class library assembly so that you could add it to the Microsoft Visual Studio .NET toolbox and use it at design time. However, even without taking this step, it is easy to create a simple test application. The following Windows Forms application creates two ellipses and allows the user to drag both of them around the form, simply by holding the mouse down and moving the pointer:

```
using System;
using System.Drawing;
using System.Windows.Forms;

namespace Apress.VisualCSharpRecipes.Chapter08
{
    public partial class Recipe08_04 : Form
    {
        public Recipe08_04()
        {
            InitializeComponent();
        }
```

```
// Tracks when drag mode is on.
private bool isDraggingA = false;
private bool isDraggingB = false;

// The ellipse shape controls.
private EllipseShape ellipseA, ellipseB;

private void Recipe08_04_Load(object sender, EventArgs e)
{
    // Create and configure both ellipses.
    ellipseA = new EllipseShape();
    ellipseA.Width = ellipseA.Height = 100;
    ellipseA.Top = ellipseA.Left = 30;
    ellipseA.BackColor = Color.Red;
    this.Controls.Add(ellipseA);

    ellipseB = new EllipseShape();
    ellipseB.Width = ellipseB.Height = 100;
    ellipseB.Top = ellipseB.Left = 130;
    ellipseB.BackColor = Color.Azure;
    this.Controls.Add(ellipseB);

    // Attach both ellipses to the same set of event handlers.
    ellipseA.MouseDown += Ellipse_MouseDown;
    ellipseA.MouseUp += Ellipse_MouseUp;
    ellipseA.MouseMove += Ellipse_MouseMove;

    ellipseB.MouseDown += Ellipse_MouseDown;
    ellipseB.MouseUp += Ellipse_MouseUp;
    ellipseB.MouseMove += Ellipse_MouseMove;
}

private void Ellipse_MouseDown(object sender, MouseEventArgs e)
{
    // Get the ellipse that triggered this event.
    Control control = (Control)sender;

    if (e.Button == MouseButtons.Left)
    {
        control.Tag = new Point(e.X, e.Y);
        if (control == ellipseA)
        {
            isDraggingA = true;
        }
        else
        {
            isDraggingB = true;
        }
    }
}
```

```
        private void Ellipse_MouseUp(object sender, MouseEventArgs e)
        {
            isDraggingA = false;
            isDraggingB = false;
        }

        private void Ellipse_MouseMove(object sender, MouseEventArgs e)
        {
            // Get the ellipse that triggered this event.
            Control control = (Control)sender;

            if ((isDraggingA && control == ellipseA) ||
             (isDraggingB && control == ellipseB))
            {
                // Get the offset.
                Point point = (Point)control.Tag;

                // Move the control.
                control.Left = e.X + control.Left - point.X;
                control.Top = e.Y + control.Top - point.Y;
            }
        }
    }
}
```

Figure 8-4 shows the user about to drag an ellipse.

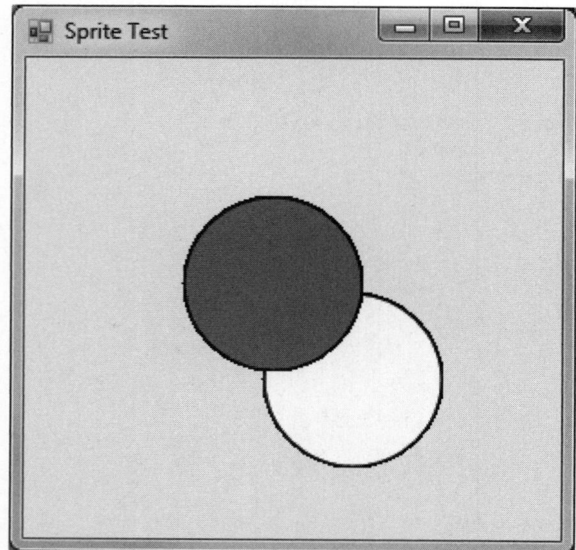

Figure 8-4. *Dragging custom shape controls on a form*

8-5. Create a Scrollable Image

Problem

You need to create a scrollable picture with dynamic content.

Solution

Leverage the automatic scroll capabilities of the `System.Windows.Forms.Panel` control by setting `Panel.AutoScroll` to `true` and placing a `System.Windows.Forms.PictureBox` control with the image content inside the `Panel`.

How It Works

The `Panel` control has built-in scrolling support, as shown in recipe 8-1. If you place any controls in it that extend beyond its bounds and you set `Panel.AutoScroll` to `true`, the panel will show scroll bars that allow the user to move through the content. This works particularly well with large images. You can load or create the image in memory, assign it to a picture box (which has no intrinsic support for scrolling), and then show the picture box inside the panel. The only consideration you need to remember is to make sure you set the picture box dimensions equal to the full size of the image you want to show.

The Code

The following example creates an image that represents a document. The image is generated as an in-memory bitmap, and several lines of text are added using the `Graphics.DrawString` method. The image is then bound to a picture box, which is shown in a scrollable panel, as shown in Figure 8-5.

```
using System;
using System.Drawing;
using System.Windows.Forms;

namespace Apress.VisualCSharpRecipes.Chapter08
{
    public partial class Recipe08_05 : Form
    {
        public Recipe08_05()
        {
            InitializeComponent();
        }

        private void Recipe08_05_Load(object sender, EventArgs e)
        {
            string text = "The quick brown fox jumps over the lazy dog.";
            using (Font font = new Font("Tahoma", 20))
            {
```

```
                // Create an in-memory bitmap.
                Bitmap b = new Bitmap(600, 600);
                using (Graphics g = Graphics.FromImage(b))
                {
                    g.FillRectangle(Brushes.White, new Rectangle(0, 0,
                        b.Width, b.Height));

                    // Draw several lines of text on the bitmap.
                    for (int i = 0; i < 10; i++)
                    {
                        g.DrawString(text, font, Brushes.Black,
                            50, 50 + i * 60);
                    }
                }

                // Display the bitmap in the picture box.
                pictureBox1.BackgroundImage = b;
                pictureBox1.Size = b.Size;
            }
        }
    }
}
```

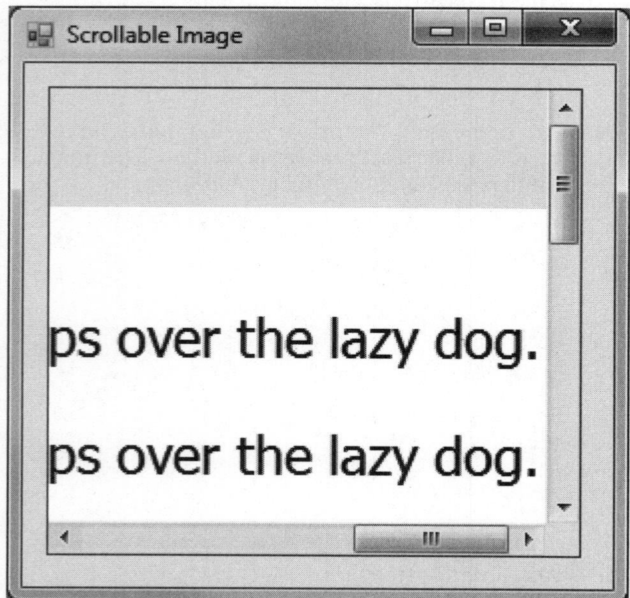

Figure 8-5. Adding scrolling support to custom content

8-6. Perform a Screen Capture

Problem

You need to take a snapshot of the current desktop.

Solution

Use the CopyFromScreen method of the Graphics class to copy screen contents.

How It Works

The Graphics class includes CopyFromScreen methods that copy color data from the screen onto the drawing surface represented by a Graphics object. This method requires you to pass the source and destination points and the size of the image to be copied.

The Code

The following example captures the screen and displays it in a picture box. It first creates a new Bitmap object and then invokes CopyFromScreen to draw onto the Bitmap. After drawing, the image is assigned to the picture box, as shown in Figure 8-6.

```
using System;
using System.Drawing;
using System.Windows.Forms;

namespace Apress.VisualCSharpRecipes.Chapter08
{
    public partial class Recipe08_06 : Form
    {
        public Recipe08_06()
        {
            InitializeComponent();
        }

        private void cmdCapture_Click(object sender, EventArgs e)
        {
            Bitmap screen = new Bitmap(Screen.PrimaryScreen.Bounds.Width,
                Screen.PrimaryScreen.Bounds.Height);

            using (Graphics g = Graphics.FromImage(screen))
            {
                g.CopyFromScreen(0, 0, 0, 0, screen.Size);
            }
```

```
            pictureBox1.Image = screen;
        }
    }
}
```

Figure 8-6. Capturing the screen contents

8-7. Use Double Buffering to Increase Redraw Speed

Problem

You need to optimize drawing for a form or an authored control that is frequently refreshed, and you want to reduce flicker.

Solution

Set the `DoubleBuffered` property of the form to `true`.

How It Works

In some applications you need to repaint a form or control frequently. This is commonly the case when creating animations. For example, you might use a timer to invalidate your form every second. Your painting code could then redraw an image at a new location, creating the illusion of motion. The problem with this approach is that every time you invalidate the form, Windows repaints the window background (clearing the form) and then runs your painting code, which draws the graphic element by element. This can cause substantial onscreen flicker.

Double buffering is a technique you can implement to reduce this flicker. With double buffering, your drawing logic writes to an in-memory bitmap, which is copied to the form at the end of the drawing operation in a single, seamless repaint operation. Flickering is reduced dramatically.

The .NET Framework provides a default double buffering mechanism for forms and controls. You can enable this by setting the `DoubleBuffered` property of your form or control to `true` or by using the `SetStyle` method.

The Code

The following example sets the `DoubleBuffered` property of the form to `true` and shows an animation of an image alternately growing and shrinking on the page. The drawing logic takes place in the `Form.Paint` event handler, and a timer invalidates the form in a preset interval so that the image can be redrawn. The user can choose whether to enable double buffering through a check box on the form. Without double buffering, the form flickers noticeably. When double buffering is enabled, however, the image grows and shrinks with smooth, flicker-free animation.

```
using System;
using System.Drawing;
using System.Windows.Forms;
using System.Drawing.Drawing2D;

namespace Apress.VisualCSharpRecipes.Chapter08
{
   public partial class Recipe08_07 : Form
   {
       public Recipe08_07()
       {
           InitializeComponent();
       }

       // Track the image size and the type of animation
       // (expanding or shrinking).
       private bool isShrinking = false;
       private int imageSize = 0;

       // Store the logo that will be painted on the form.
       private Image image;
```

```
private void Recipe08_07_Load(object sender, EventArgs e)
{
   // Load the logo image from the file.
   image = Image.FromFile("test.jpg");

    // Start the timer that invalidates the form.
    tmrRefresh.Start();
}

private void tmrRefresh_Tick(object sender, EventArgs e)
{
    // Change the desired image size according to the animation mode.
    if (isShrinking)
    {
        imageSize--;
    }
    else
    {
        imageSize++;
    }

    // Change the sizing direction if it nears the form border.
    if (imageSize > (this.Width - 150))
    {
        isShrinking = true;
    }
    else if (imageSize < 1)
    {
        isShrinking = false;
    }

    // Repaint the form.
    this.Invalidate();
}

private void Recipe08_07_Paint(object sender, PaintEventArgs e)
{
    Graphics g;

    g = e.Graphics;

    g.SmoothingMode = SmoothingMode.HighQuality;

    // Draw the background.
    g.FillRectangle(Brushes.Yellow, new Rectangle(new Point(0, 0),
    this.ClientSize));

    // Draw the logo image.
    g.DrawImage(image, 50, 50, 50 + imageSize, 50 + imageSize);
}
```

```
        private void chkUseDoubleBuffering_CheckedChanged(object sender, EventArgs e)
        {
            this.DoubleBuffered = chkUseDoubleBuffering.Checked;
        }
    }
}
```

8-8. Show a Thumbnail for an Image

Problem

You need to show thumbnails (small representations of pictures) for the images in a directory.

Solution

Read the image from the file using the static `FromFile` method of the `System.Drawing.Image` class. You can then retrieve a thumbnail using the `Image.GetThumbnailImage` method.

How It Works

The `Image` class provides the functionality for generating thumbnails through the `GetThumbnailImage` method. You simply need to pass the width and height of the thumbnail you want (in pixels), and the `Image` class will create a new `Image` object that fits these criteria. Anti-aliasing is used when reducing the image to ensure the best possible image quality, although some blurriness and loss of detail are inevitable. (*Anti-aliasing* is the process of removing jagged edges, often in resized graphics, by adding shading with an intermediate color.) In addition, you can supply a notification callback, allowing you to create thumbnails asynchronously.

When generating a thumbnail, it is important to ensure that the aspect ratio remains constant. For example, if you reduce a 200×100 picture to a 50×50 thumbnail, the width will be compressed to one quarter and the height will be compressed to one half, distorting the image. To ensure that the aspect ratio remains constant, you can change either the width or the height to a fixed size and then adjust the other dimension proportionately.

The Code

The following example reads a bitmap file and generates a thumbnail that is not greater than 200×200 pixels while preserving the original aspect ratio:

```
using System;
using System.Drawing;
using System.Windows.Forms;
```

```
namespace Apress.VisualCSharpRecipes.Chapter08
{
    public partial class Recipe08_08 : Form
    {
        public Recipe08_08()
        {
            InitializeComponent();
        }

        Image thumbnail;

        private void Recipe08_08_Load(object sender, EventArgs e)
        {
            using (Image img = Image.FromFile("test.jpg"))
            {
                int thumbnailWidth = 0, thumbnailHeight = 0;

                // Adjust the largest dimension to 200 pixels.
                // This ensures that a thumbnail will not be larger than
                // 200x200 pixels.
                // If you are showing multiple thumbnails, you would reserve a
                // 200x200-pixel square for each one.
                if (img.Width > img.Height)
                {
                    thumbnailWidth = 200;
                    thumbnailHeight = Convert.ToInt32(((200F / img.Width) *
                      img.Height));
                }
                else
                {
                    thumbnailHeight = 200;
                    thumbnailWidth = Convert.ToInt32(((200F / img.Height) *
                      img.Width));
                }

                thumbnail = img.GetThumbnailImage(thumbnailWidth, thumbnailHeight,
                  null, IntPtr.Zero);
            }
        }

        private void Recipe08_08_Paint(object sender, PaintEventArgs e)
        {
            e.Graphics.DrawImage(thumbnail, 10, 10);
        }
    }
}
```

8-9. Play a Simple Beep or System Sound

Problem

You need to play a simple system-defined beep or sound.

Solution

Use the `Beep` method of the `Console` class or the `Play` method of the `SystemSound` class.

How It Works

The .NET Framework has provides the `Beep` method in the `Console` class and the `System.Media` namespace, which provides classes for playing sound files.

Overloads of the `Console.Beep` method let you play a beep with the default frequency and duration or with a frequency and duration you specify. Frequency is represented in hertz (and must range from 37 to 32,767), and the duration is represented in milliseconds. Internally, these methods invoke the `Beep` Win32 function and use the computer's internal speaker. Thus, if the computer does not have an internal speaker, no sound will be produced.

The `System.Media` namespace contains the `SystemSound`, `SystemSounds`, and `SoundPlayer` classes. The `SystemSound` class represents a Windows sound event, such as an asterisk, beep, question, and so on. It also defines a `Play` method, which lets you play the sound associated with it.

The `SystemSounds` class defines properties that let you obtain the `SystemSound` instance of a specific Windows sound event. For example, it defines an `Asterisk` property that returns a `SystemSound` instance associated with the asterisk Windows sound event.

The `SoundPlayer` class lets you play WAV files. For more information on how to play a WAV file using this class, refer to recipe 8-10.

The Code

The following example plays two different beeps and the asterisk sound in succession, using the `Console` and `SystemSound` classes:

```
using System;
using System.Windows.Forms;
using System.Media;
using System.Threading;

namespace Apress.VisualCSharpRecipes.Chapter08
{
    public partial class Recipe08_09 : Form
    {
        public Recipe08_09()
        {
            InitializeComponent();
        }
```

```
        private void Recipe08_09_Load(object sender, EventArgs e)
        {
            // Play a beep with default frequency
            // and duration (800 and 200, respectively).
            Console.Beep();
            Thread.Sleep(500);

            // Play a beep with frequency as 200 and duration as 300.
            Console.Beep(200, 300);
            Thread.Sleep(500);

            // Play the sound associated with the Asterisk event.
            SystemSounds.Asterisk.Play();
        }
    }
}
```

8-10. Play a WAV File

Problem

You need to play a WAV file.

Solution

Create a new instance of the `System.Media.SoundPlayer` class, pass the location or stream of the WAV file, and invoke the `Play` method.

How It Works

The .NET Framework includes the `System.Media` namespace, which contains a `SoundPlayer` class. `SoundPlayer` contains constructors that let you specify the location of a WAV file or its stream. Once you have created an instance, you just invoke the `Play` method to play the file. The `Play` method creates a new thread to play the sound and is thus asynchronous (unless a stream is used). For playing the sound synchronously, use the `PlaySync` method. Note that `SoundPlayer` supports only the WAV format.

Before a file is played, it is loaded into memory. You can load a file in advance by invoking the `Load` or `LoadSync` method depending upon whether you want the operation to be asynchronous or synchronous.

The Code

The following example shows a simple form that allows users to open any WAV file and play it:

```
using System;
using System.Windows.Forms;
using System.Media;

namespace Apress.VisualCSharpRecipes.Chapter08
{
    public partial class Recipe08_10 : Form
    {
        public Recipe08_10()
        {
            InitializeComponent();
        }

        private void cmdOpen_Click(object sender, EventArgs e)
        {
            // Allow the user to choose a file.
            OpenFileDialog openDialog = new OpenFileDialog();
            openDialog.InitialDirectory = "C:\\Windows\\Media";
            openDialog.Filter = "WAV Files|*.wav|All Files|*.*";

            if (DialogResult.OK == openDialog.ShowDialog())
            {
                SoundPlayer player = new SoundPlayer(openDialog.FileName);

                try
                {
                    player.Play();
                }
                catch (Exception)
                {
                    MessageBox.Show("An error occurred while playing media.");
                }
                finally
                {
                    player.Dispose();
                }
            }
        }
    }
}
```

8-11. Play a Sound File

Problem

You need to play a non-WAV format audio file such as an MP3 file.

Solution

Use the ActiveMovie COM component included with Windows Media Player, which supports WAV and MP3 audio.

How It Works

The ActiveMovie Quartz library provides a COM component that can play various types of audio files, including the WAV and MP3 formats. The Quartz type library is provided through `quartz.dll` and is included as a part of Microsoft DirectX with Media Player and the Windows operating system.

The first step for using the library is to generate an Interop class that can manage the interaction between your .NET application and the unmanaged Quartz library. You can generate a C# class with this Interop code using the Type Library Importer utility (`Tlbimp.exe`) and the following command line, where `[WindowsDir]` is the path for your installation of Windows:

```
tlbimp [WindowsDir]\system32\quartz.dll /out:QuartzTypeLib.dll
```

Alternatively, you can generate the Interop class using Visual Studio .NET by adding a reference. Simply right-click your project in Solution Explorer, and choose Add Reference from the context menu. Then select the COM tab and scroll down to select ActiveMovie Control Type Library.

Once the Interop class is generated, you can work with the `IMediaControl` interface. You can specify the file you want to play using `RenderFile`, and you can control playback using methods such as `Run`, `Stop`, and `Pause`. The actual playback takes place on a separate thread, so it will not block your code.

The Code

The following example shows a simple form that allows you to open any audio file and play it.

You can also use the Quartz library to show movie files, as demonstrated in recipe 8-12.

```
using System;
using System.Windows.Forms;
using QuartzTypeLib;

namespace Apress.VisualCSharpRecipes.Chapter08
{
    public partial class Recipe08_11 : Form
    {
        public Recipe08_11()
        {
            InitializeComponent();
        }

        private void cmdOpen_Click(object sender, EventArgs e)
        {
            // Allow the user to choose a file.
            OpenFileDialog openFileDialog = new OpenFileDialog();
            openFileDialog.Filter =
                "Media Files|*.wav;*.mp3;*.mp2;*.wma|All Files|*.*";

            if (DialogResult.OK == openFileDialog.ShowDialog())
            {
```

```
                // Access the IMediaControl interface.
                QuartzTypeLib.FilgraphManager graphManager =
                  new QuartzTypeLib.FilgraphManager();
                QuartzTypeLib.IMediaControl mc =
                  (QuartzTypeLib.IMediaControl)graphManager;

                // Specify the file.
                mc.RenderFile(openFileDialog.FileName);

                // Start playing the audio asynchronously.
                mc.Run();
            }
        }
    }
}
```

8-12. Play a Video

Problem

You need to play a video file (such as an MPEG, AVI, or WMV file) in a Windows Forms application.

Solution

Use the ActiveMovie COM component included with Windows Media Player. Bind the video output to a picture box on your form by setting the `IVideoWindow.Owner` property to the `PictureBox.Handle` property.

How It Works

Although the .NET Framework does not include any managed classes for interacting with video files, you can leverage the functionality of DirectShow using the COM-based Quartz library included with Windows Media Player and the Windows operating system. For information about creating an Interop assembly for the Quartz type library, refer to the instructions in recipe 8-11.

Once you have created the Interop assembly, you can use the `IMediaControl` interface to load and play a movie. This is essentially the same technique demonstrated in recipe 8-11 with audio files. However, if you want to show the video window inside your application interface (rather than in a separate stand-alone window), you must also use the `IVideoWindow` interface. The core `FilgraphManager` object can be cast to both the `IMediaControl` interface and the `IVideoWindow` interface—and several other interfaces are also supported, such as `IBasicAudio` (which allows you to configure balance and volume settings). With the `IVideoWindow` interface, you can bind the video output to a control on your form, such as a `Panel` or a `PictureBox`. To do so, set the `IVideoWindow.Owner` property to the handle for the control, which you can retrieve using the `Control.Handle` property. Then call `IVideoWindow.SetWindowPosition` to set the window size and location. You can call this method to change the video size during playback (for example, if the form is resized).

The Code

The following example shows a simple form that allows users to access a video file and play it back in the provided picture box. The picture box is anchored to all sides of the form, so it changes size as the form resizes. The code responds to the `PictureBox.SizeChanged` event to change the size of the corresponding video window.

```
using System;
using System.Windows.Forms;
using QuartzTypeLib;

namespace Apress.VisualCSharpRecipes.Chapter08
{
    public partial class Recipe08_12 : Form
    {
        public Recipe08_12()
        {
            InitializeComponent();
        }

        // Define constants used for specifying the window style.
        private const int WS_CHILD = 0x40000000;
        private const int WS_CLIPCHILDREN = 0x2000000;

        // Hold a form-level reference to the media control interface,
        // so the code can control playback of the currently loaded
        // movie.
        private IMediaControl mc = null;

        // Hold a form-level reference to the video window in case it
        // needs to be resized.
        private IVideoWindow videoWindow = null;

        private void cmdOpen_Click(object sender, EventArgs e)
        {
            // Allow the user to choose a file.
            OpenFileDialog openFileDialog = new OpenFileDialog();
            openFileDialog.Filter =
            "Media Files|*.mpg;*.avi;*.wma;*.mov;*.wav;*.mp2;*.mp3|" +
            "All Files|*.*";

            if (DialogResult.OK == openFileDialog.ShowDialog())
            {
                // Stop the playback for the current movie, if it exists.
                if (mc != null) mc.Stop();

                // Load the movie file.
                FilgraphManager graphManager = new FilgraphManager();
                graphManager.RenderFile(openFileDialog.FileName);
```

```
            // Attach the view to a picture box on the form.
            try
            {
                videoWindow = (IVideoWindow)graphManager;
                videoWindow.Owner = (int)pictureBox1.Handle;
                videoWindow.WindowStyle = WS_CHILD | WS_CLIPCHILDREN;
                videoWindow.SetWindowPosition(
                  pictureBox1.ClientRectangle.Left,
                  pictureBox1.ClientRectangle.Top,
                  pictureBox1.ClientRectangle.Width,
                  pictureBox1.ClientRectangle.Height);
            }
            catch
            {
                // An error can occur if the file does not have a video
                // source (for example, an MP3 file).
                // You can ignore this error and still allow playback to
                // continue (without any visualization).
            }

            // Start the playback (asynchronously).
            mc = (IMediaControl)graphManager;
            mc.Run();
        }
    }

    private void pictureBox1_SizeChanged(object sender, EventArgs e)
    {
        if (videoWindow != null)
        {
            try
            {
                videoWindow.SetWindowPosition(
                    pictureBox1.ClientRectangle.Left,
                    pictureBox1.ClientRectangle.Top,
                    pictureBox1.ClientRectangle.Width,
                    pictureBox1.ClientRectangle.Height);
            }
            catch
            {
                // Ignore the exception thrown when resizing the form
                // when the file does not have a video source.
            }
        }
    }
  }
}
```

Figure 8-7 shows an example of the output you will see.

Figure 8-7. Playing a video file

8-13. Retrieve Information About Installed Printers

Problem

You need to retrieve a list of available printers.

Solution

Read the names in the `InstalledPrinters` collection of the `System.Drawing.Printing.PrinterSettings` class.

How It Works

The `PrinterSettings` class encapsulates the settings for a printer and information about the printer. For example, you can use the `PrinterSettings` class to determine supported paper sizes, paper sources, and resolutions, and check for the ability to print color or double-sided (duplexed) pages. In addition, you can retrieve default page settings for margins, page orientation, and so on.

The `PrinterSettings` class provides a static `InstalledPrinters` string collection, which includes the name of every printer installed on the computer. If you want to find out more information about the settings for a specific printer, you simply need to create a `PrinterSettings` instance and set the `PrinterName` property accordingly.

The Code

The following code shows a console application that finds all the printers installed on a computer and displays information about the paper sizes and the resolutions supported by each one.

You do not need to take this approach when creating an application that provides printing features. As you will see in recipe 8-14, you can use the `PrintDialog` class to prompt the user to choose a printer and its settings. The `PrintDialog` class can automatically apply its settings to the appropriate `PrintDocument` without any additional code.

```
using System;
using System.Drawing.Printing;

namespace Apress.VisualCSharpRecipes.Chapter08
{
    class Recipe08_13
    {
        static void Main(string[] args)
        {
            foreach (string printerName in PrinterSettings.InstalledPrinters)
            {
                // Display the printer name.
                Console.WriteLine("Printer: {0}", printerName);

                // Retrieve the printer settings.
                PrinterSettings printer = new PrinterSettings();
                printer.PrinterName = printerName;

                // Check that this is a valid printer.
                // (This step might be required if you read the printer name
                // from a user-supplied value or a registry or configuration file
                // setting.)
                if (printer.IsValid)
                {
                    // Display the list of valid resolutions.
                    Console.WriteLine("Supported Resolutions:");

                    foreach (PrinterResolution resolution in
                      printer.PrinterResolutions)
                    {
                        Console.WriteLine("  {0}", resolution);
                    }
                    Console.WriteLine();
```

```
                    // Display the list of valid paper sizes.
                    Console.WriteLine("Supported Paper Sizes:");

                    foreach (PaperSize size in printer.PaperSizes)
                    {
                        if (Enum.IsDefined(size.Kind.GetType(), size.Kind))
                        {
                            Console.WriteLine("  {0}", size);
                        }
                    }
                    Console.WriteLine();
                }
            }
            Console.ReadLine();
        }
    }
}
```

Usage

Here is the type of output this utility displays:

```
Printer: HP LaserJet 5L

Supported Resolutions:

  [PrinterResolution High]

  [PrinterResolution Medium]

  [PrinterResolution Low]

  [PrinterResolution Draft]

  [PrinterResolution X=600 Y=600]

  [PrinterResolution X=300 Y=300]


Supported Paper Sizes:

  [PaperSize Letter Kind=Letter Height=1100 Width=850]

  [PaperSize Legal Kind=Legal Height=1400 Width=850]

  [PaperSize Executive Kind=Executive Height=1050 Width=725]
```

```
  [PaperSize A4 Kind=A4 Height=1169 Width=827]

  [PaperSize Envelope #10 Kind=Number10Envelope Height=950 Width=412]

  [PaperSize Envelope DL Kind=DLEnvelope Height=866 Width=433]

  [PaperSize Envelope C5 Kind=C5Envelope Height=902 Width=638]

  [PaperSize Envelope B5 Kind=B5Envelope Height=984 Width=693]

  [PaperSize Envelope Monarch Kind=MonarchEnvelope Height=750 Width=387]


Printer: Generic PostScript Printer

. . .
```

■ **Note** You can print a document in almost any type of application. However, your application must include a reference to the `System.Drawing.dll` assembly. If you are using a project type in Visual Studio .NET that would not normally have this reference (such as a console application), you must add it.

8-14. Print a Simple Document

Problem

You need to print text or images.

Solution

Create a `PrintDocument` and write a handler for the `PrintDocument.PrintPage` event that uses the `DrawString` and `DrawImage` methods of the `Graphics` class to print data to the page.

How It Works

.NET uses an asynchronous event-based printing model. To print a document, you create a `System.Drawing.Printing.PrintDocument` instance, configure its properties, and then call its `Print` method, which schedules the print job. The Common Language Runtime (CLR) will then fire the `BeginPrint`, `PrintPage`, and `EndPrint` events of the `PrintDocument` class on a new thread. You handle these events and use the provided `System.Drawing.Graphics` object to output data to the page. Graphics and text are written to a page in the same way as you draw to a window using GDI+. However, you might need to track your position on a page, because every `Graphics` class method requires explicit coordinates that indicate where to draw.

You configure printer settings through the `PrintDocument.PrinterSettings` and `PrintDocument.DefaultPageSettings` properties. The `PrinterSettings` property returns a full `PrinterSettings` object (as described in recipe 8-11), which identifies the printer that will be used. The `DefaultPageSettings` property provides a full `PageSettings` object that specifies printer resolution, margins, orientation, and so on. You can configure these properties in code, or you can use the `System.Windows.Forms.PrintDialog` class to let the user make the changes using the standard Windows Print dialog box (shown in Figure 8-8). In the Print dialog box, the user can select a printer and choose the number of copies. The user can also click the Properties button to configure advanced settings such as page layout and printer resolution. Finally, the user can either accept or cancel the print operation by clicking OK or Cancel.

Before using the `PrintDialog` class, you must explicitly attach it to a `PrintDocument` object by setting the `PrintDialog.Document` property. Then, any changes the user makes in the Print dialog box will be automatically applied to the `PrintDocument` object.

■ **Note** The `PrintDialog` class may not work on 64-bit systems unless the `UseEXDialog` property is set to `true`. This displays a Windows XP–style dialog box, but is the only reliable way to display the dialog in a 64-bit installation of Windows. Alternatively, set the platform target for your application to be `x86` instead of `Any CPU` in Visual Studio.

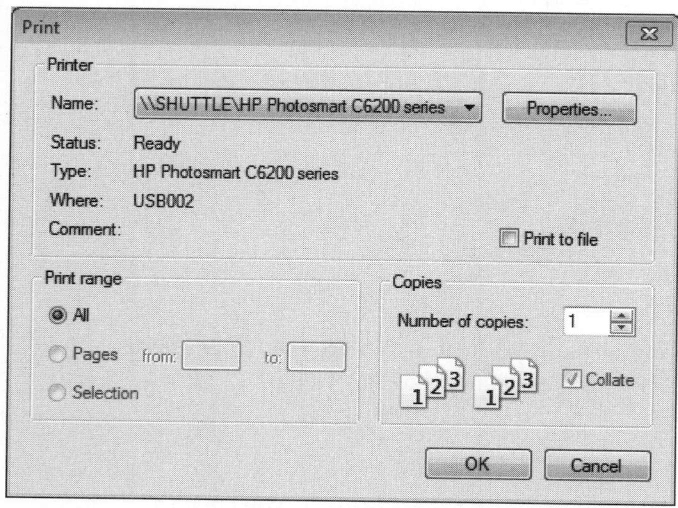

Figure 8-8. *Using the PrintDialog class*

The Code

The following example provides a form with a single button. When the user clicks the button, the application creates a new `PrintDocument`, allows the user to configure print settings, and then starts an asynchronous print operation (provided the user clicks OK). An event handler responds to the `PrintPage` event and writes several lines of text and an image.

This example has one limitation: it can print only a single page. To print more complex documents and span multiple pages, you will want to create a specialized class that encapsulates the document information, the current page, and so on. Recipe 8-15 demonstrates this technique.

```
using System;
using System.Drawing;
using System.Windows.Forms;
using System.Drawing.Printing;
using System.IO;

namespace Apress.VisualCSharpRecipes.Chapter08
{
    public partial class Recipe08_14 : Form
    {
        public Recipe08_14()
        {
            InitializeComponent();
        }

        private void cmdPrint_Click(object sender, EventArgs e)
        {
            // Create the document and attach an event handler.
            PrintDocument doc = new PrintDocument();
            doc.PrintPage += this.Doc_PrintPage;

            // Allow the user to choose a printer and specify other settings.
            PrintDialog dlgSettings = new PrintDialog();
            dlgSettings.Document = doc;

            // If the user clicked OK, print the document.
            if (dlgSettings.ShowDialog() == DialogResult.OK)
            {

                // This method returns immediately, before the print job starts.
                // The PrintPage event will fire asynchronously.
                doc.Print();
            }
        }

        private void Doc_PrintPage(object sender, PrintPageEventArgs e)
        {
            // Define the font.
            using (Font font = new Font("Arial", 30))
            {
```

```
                // Determine the position on the page.
                // In this case, we read the margin settings
                // (although there is nothing that prevents your code
                // from going outside the margin bounds).
                float x = e.MarginBounds.Left;
                float y = e.MarginBounds.Top;

                // Determine the height of a line (based on the font used).
                float lineHeight = font.GetHeight(e.Graphics);

                // Print five lines of text.
                for (int i = 0; i < 5; i++)
                {

                    // Draw the text with a black brush,
                    // using the font and coordinates we have determined.
                    e.Graphics.DrawString("This is line " + i.ToString(),
                      font, Brushes.Black, x, y);

                    // Move down the equivalent spacing of one line.
                    y += lineHeight;
                }
                y += lineHeight;

                // Draw an image.
                e.Graphics.DrawImage(
                   Image.FromFile(
                       Path.Combine(Application.StartupPath,"test.jpg")
                       ),
                   x, y);
            }
        }
    }
}
```

8-15. Print a Multipage Document

Problem

You need to print complex documents with multiple pages and possibly print several different documents at once.

Solution

Place the information you want to print into a custom class that derives from `PrintDocument`, and in the `PrintPage` event handler, set the `PrintPageEventArgs.HasMorePages` property to `true` as long as pages are remaining.

How It Works

The PrintDocument.PrintPage event is triggered to let you to print only a single page. If you need to print more pages, you need to set the PrintPageEventArgs.HasMorePages property to true in the PrintPage event handler. As long as HasMorePages is set to true, the PrintDocument class will continue firing PrintPage events. However, it is up to you to track which page you are on, what data should be placed on each page, and what is the last page for which HasMorePage is not set to true. To facilitate this tracking, it is a good idea to create a custom class.

The Code

The following example shows a class called TextDocument. This class inherits from PrintDocument and adds three properties. Text stores an array of text lines, PageNumber reflects the last printed page, and Offset indicates the last line that was printed from the Text array.

```
public class TextDocument : PrintDocument {

    private string[] text;
    private int pageNumber;
    private int offset;

    public string[] Text {
        get {return text;}
        set {text = value;}
    }

    public int PageNumber {
        get {return pageNumber;}
        set {pageNumber = value;}
    }

    public int Offset {
        get {return offset;}
        set {offset = value;}
    }

    public TextDocument(string[] text) {
        this.Text = text;
    }
}
```

Depending on the type of material you are printing, you might want to modify this class. For example, you could store an array of image data, some content that should be used as a header or footer on each page, font information, or even the name of a file from which you want to read the information. Encapsulating the information in a single class makes it easier to print more than one document at the same time. This is especially important because the printing process runs in a new dedicated thread. As a consequence, the user is able to keep working in the application and therefore update your data while the pages are printing. So, this dedicated class should contain a copy of the data to print to avoid any concurrency problems.

The code that initiates printing is the same as in recipe 8-14, only now it creates a TextDocument instance instead of a PrintDocument instance. The PrintPage event handler keeps track of the current line and checks whether the page has space before attempting to print the next line. If a new page is needed, the HasMorePages property is set to true and the PrintPage event fires again for the next page. If not, the print operation is deemed complete. This simple code sample does not take into account whether a line fits into the width of the page; refer to recipe 8-16 for a solution to this problem.

The full form code is as follows:

```
using System;
using System.Drawing;
using System.Windows.Forms;
using System.Drawing.Printing;

namespace Apress.VisualCSharpRecipes.Chapter08
{
    public partial class Recipe08_15 : Form
    {
        public Recipe08_15()
        {
            InitializeComponent();
        }

        private void cmdPrint_Click(object sender, EventArgs e)
        {
            // Create a document with 100 lines.
            string[] printText = new string[101];
            for (int i = 0; i < 101; i++)
            {
                printText[i] = i.ToString();
                printText[i] +=
                    ": The quick brown fox jumps over the lazy dog.";
            }

            PrintDocument doc = new TextDocument(printText);
            doc.PrintPage += this.Doc_PrintPage;

            PrintDialog dlgSettings = new PrintDialog();
            dlgSettings.Document = doc;

            // If the user clicked OK, print the document.
            if (dlgSettings.ShowDialog() == DialogResult.OK)
            {
                doc.Print();
            }
        }
```

```
        private void Doc_PrintPage(object sender, PrintPageEventArgs e)
        {
            // Retrieve the document that sent this event.
            TextDocument doc = (TextDocument)sender;

            // Define the font and determine the line height.
            using (Font font = new Font("Arial", 10))
            {
                float lineHeight = font.GetHeight(e.Graphics);

                // Create variables to hold position on page.
                float x = e.MarginBounds.Left;
                float y = e.MarginBounds.Top;

                // Increment the page counter (to reflect the page that
                // is about to be printed).
                doc.PageNumber += 1;

                // Print all the information that can fit on the page.
                // This loop ends when the next line would go over the
                // margin bounds, or there are no more lines to print.

                while ((y + lineHeight) < e.MarginBounds.Bottom &&
                  doc.Offset <= doc.Text.GetUpperBound(0))
                {
                    e.Graphics.DrawString(doc.Text[doc.Offset], font,
                      Brushes.Black, x, y);

                    // Move to the next line of data.
                    doc.Offset += 1;

                    // Move the equivalent of one line down the page.
                    y += lineHeight;
                }

                if (doc.Offset < doc.Text.GetUpperBound(0))
                {
                    // There is still at least one more page.
                    // Signal this event to fire again.
                    e.HasMorePages = true;
                }
                else
                {
                    // Printing is complete.
                    doc.Offset = 0;
                }
            }
        }
    }
}
```

8-16. Print Wrapped Text

Problem

You need to parse a large block of text into distinct lines that fit on one page.

Solution

Use the Graphics.DrawString method overload that accepts a bounding rectangle.

How It Works

Often, you will need to break a large block of text into separate lines that can be printed individually on a page. The .NET Framework can perform this task automatically, provided you use a version of the Graphics.DrawString method that accepts a bounding rectangle. You specify a rectangle that represents where you want the text to be displayed. The text is then wrapped automatically to fit within those confines.

The Code

The following code demonstrates this approach, using the bounding rectangle that represents the printable portion of the page. It prints a large block of text from a text box on the form.

```
using System;
using System.Drawing;
using System.Windows.Forms;
using System.Drawing.Printing;

namespace Apress.VisualCSharpRecipes.Chapter08
{
    public partial class Recipe08_16 : Form
    {
        public Recipe08_16()
        {
            InitializeComponent();
        }

        private void cmdPrint_Click(object sender, EventArgs e)
        {
            // Create the document and attach an event handler.
            string text = "Windows Server 2003 builds on the core strengths " +
              "of the Windows family of operating systems--security, " +
              "manageability, reliability, availability, and scalability. " +
              "Windows Server 2003 provides an application environment to " +
              "build, deploy, manage, and run XML Web services. " +
```

```
                "Additionally, advances in Windows Server 2003 provide many " +
                "benefits for developing applications.";
            PrintDocument doc = new ParagraphDocument(text);
            doc.PrintPage += this.Doc_PrintPage;

            // Allow the user to choose a printer and specify other settings.
            PrintDialog dlgSettings = new PrintDialog();
            dlgSettings.Document = doc;

            // If the user clicked OK, print the document.
            if (dlgSettings.ShowDialog() == DialogResult.OK)
            {
                doc.Print();
            }
        }

        private void Doc_PrintPage(object sender, PrintPageEventArgs e)
        {
            // Retrieve the document that sent this event.
            ParagraphDocument doc = (ParagraphDocument)sender;

            // Define the font and text.
            using (Font font = new Font("Arial", 15))
            {
                e.Graphics.DrawString(doc.Text, font, Brushes.Black,
                   e.MarginBounds, StringFormat.GenericDefault);
            }
        }
    }

    public class ParagraphDocument : PrintDocument
    {
        private string text;
        public string Text
        {
            get { return text; }
            set { text = value; }
        }

        public ParagraphDocument(string text)
        {
            this.Text = text;
        }
    }
}
```

Figure 8-9 shows the wrapped text.

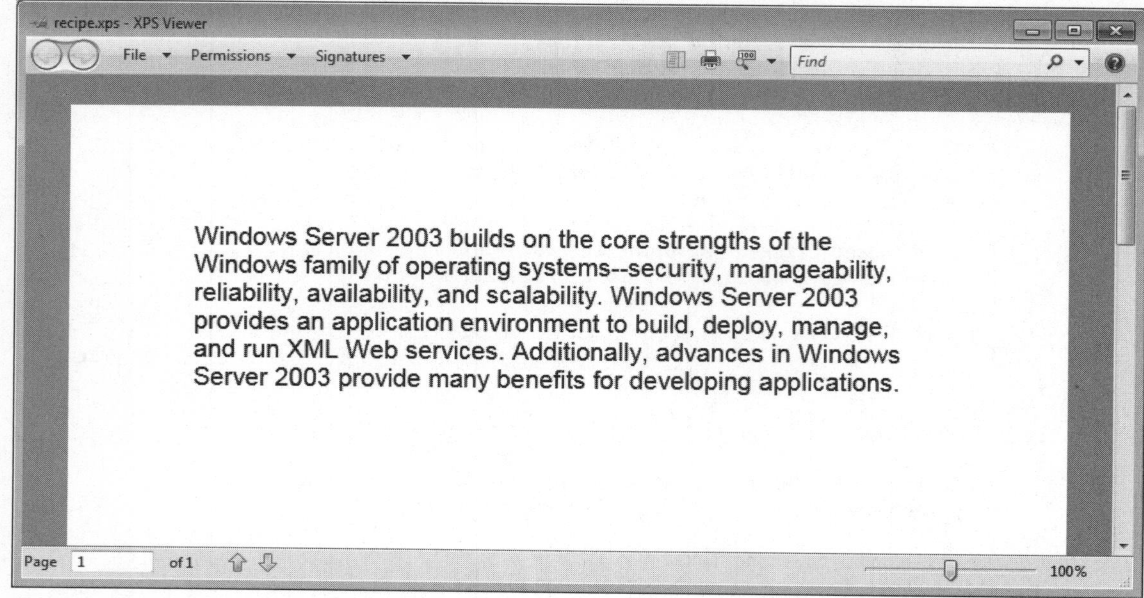

Figure 8-9. *The printed document with wrapping*

8-17. Show a Dynamic Print Preview

Problem

You need to use an onscreen preview that shows how a printed document will look.

Solution

Use `PrintPreviewDialog` or `PrintPreviewControl` (both of which are found in the `System.Windows.Forms` namespace).

How It Works

.NET provides two elements of user interface that can take a `PrintDocument` instance, run your printing code, and use it to generate a graphical onscreen preview:

- The `PrintPreviewDialog`, which shows a preview in a stand-alone form
- The `PrintPreviewControl`, which shows a preview in a control that can be embedded in one of your own custom forms

To use a stand-alone print preview form, you simply create a PrintPreviewDialog object, assign its Document property, and call the Show method:

```
PrintPreviewDialog dlgPreview = new PrintPreviewDialog();
dlgPreview.Document = doc;
dlgPreview.Show();
```

The Print Preview window provides all the controls the user needs to move from page to page, zoom in, and so on. The window even provides a print button that allows the user to send the document directly to the printer. You can tailor the window to some extent by modifying the PrintPreviewDialog properties.

You can also add a PrintPreviewControl control to any of your forms to show a preview alongside other information. In this case, you do not need to call the Show method. As soon as you set the PrintPreviewControl.Document property, the preview is generated. To clear the preview, set the Document property to null, and to refresh the preview, simply reassign the Document property. PrintPreviewControl shows only the preview pages, not any additional controls. However, you can add your own controls for zooming, tiling multiple pages, and so on. You simply need to adjust the PrintPreviewControl properties accordingly.

The Code

The following example is the complete for code that incorporates a PrintPreviewControl and allows the user to select a zoom setting:

```
using System;
using System.Drawing;
using System.Windows.Forms;
using System.Drawing.Printing;

namespace Apress.VisualCSharpRecipes.Chapter08
{
    public partial class Recipe08_17 : Form
    {
        public Recipe08_17()
        {
            InitializeComponent();
        }

        private PrintDocument doc;
        // (PrintDocument.PrintPage event handler code omitted.
        // See code in recipe 8-15.)

        private void Recipe08_17_Load(object sender, EventArgs e)
        {
            // Set the allowed zoom settings.
            for (int i = 1; i <= 10; i++)
            {
                lstZoom.Items.Add((i * 10).ToString());
            }
```

```
            // Create a document with 100 lines.
            string[] printText = new string[100];
            for (int i = 0; i < 100; i++)
            {
                printText[i] = i.ToString();
                printText[i] += ": The quick brown fox jumps over the lazy dog.";
            }

            doc = new TextDocument(printText);
            doc.PrintPage += this.Doc_PrintPage;

            lstZoom.Text = "100";
            printPreviewControl.Zoom = 1;
            printPreviewControl.Document = doc;
            printPreviewControl.Rows = 2;
        }

        private void cmdPrint_Click(object sender, EventArgs e)
        {
            // Set the zoom.
            printPreviewControl.Zoom = Single.Parse(lstZoom.Text) / 100;

            // Show the full two pages, one above the other.
            printPreviewControl.Rows = 2;

            // Rebind the PrintDocument to refresh the preview.
            printPreviewControl.Document = doc;
        }
    }

    // (TextDocument class code omitted. See recipe 8-15.)
}
```

8-18. Manage Print Jobs

Problem

You need to pause or resume a print job or a print queue.

Solution

Use Windows Management Instrumentation (WMI). You can retrieve information from the print queue using a query with the `Win32_PrintJob` class, and you can use the `Pause` and `Resume` methods of the WMI `Win32_PrintJob` and `Win32_Printer` classes to manage the queue.

How It Works

WMI allows you to retrieve a vast amount of system information using a query-like syntax. One of the tasks you can perform with WMI is to retrieve a list of outstanding print jobs, along with information about each one. You can also perform operations such as printing and resuming a job or all the jobs for a printer. To use WMI, you need to add a reference to the `System.Management.dll` assembly.

The Code

The following code shows a Windows application that interacts with the print queue. It performs a WMI query to get a list of all the outstanding jobs on the computer and displays the job ID for each one in a list box. When the user selects the item, a more complete WMI query is performed, and additional details about the print job are displayed in a text box. Finally, the user can click the Pause and Resume buttons after selecting a job to change its status.

Remember that Windows permissions might prevent you from pausing or removing a print job created by another user. In fact, permissions might even prevent you from retrieving status information and could cause a security exception to be thrown.

```
using System;
using System.Drawing;
using System.Windows.Forms;
using System.Management;
using System.Collections;
using System.Text;

namespace Apress.VisualCSharpRecipes.Chapter08
{
    public partial class Recipe08_18 : Form
    {
        public PrintQueueTest()
        {
            InitializeComponent();
        }

        private void cmdRefresh_Click(object sender, EventArgs e)
        {
            // Select all the outstanding print jobs.
            string query = "SELECT * FROM Win32_PrintJob";
            using (ManagementObjectSearcher jobQuery =
              new ManagementObjectSearcher(query))
            {
                using (ManagementObjectCollection jobs = jobQuery.Get())
                {
                    // Add the jobs in the queue to the list box.
                    lstJobs.Items.Clear();
                    txtJobInfo.Text = "";
```

```
                foreach (ManagementObject job in jobs)
                {
                    lstJobs.Items.Add(job["JobID"]);
                }
            }
        }
    }

    private void Recipe08_18_Load(object sender, EventArgs e)
    {
        cmdRefresh_Click(null, null);
    }

    // This helper method performs a WMI query and returns the
    // WMI job for the currently selected list box item.
    private ManagementObject GetSelectedJob()
    {
        try
        {
            // Select the matching print job.
            string query = "SELECT * FROM Win32_PrintJob " +
              "WHERE JobID='" + lstJobs.Text + "'";
            ManagementObject job = null;
            using (ManagementObjectSearcher jobQuery =
              new ManagementObjectSearcher(query))
            {
                ManagementObjectCollection jobs = jobQuery.Get();
                IEnumerator enumerator = jobs.GetEnumerator();
                enumerator.MoveNext();
                job = (ManagementObject)enumerator.Current;
            }
            return job;
        }
        catch (InvalidOperationException)
        {
            // The Current property of the enumerator is invalid.
            return null;
        }
    }

    private void lstJobs_SelectedIndexChanged(object sender, EventArgs e)
    {
      ManagementObject job = GetSelectedJob();
      if (job == null)
      {
          txtJobInfo.Text = "";
          return;
      }
```

```
    // Display job information.
    StringBuilder jobInfo = new StringBuilder();
    jobInfo.AppendFormat("Document: {0}", job["Document"].ToString());
    jobInfo.Append(Environment.NewLine);
    jobInfo.AppendFormat("DriverName: {0}", job["DriverName"].ToString());
    jobInfo.Append(Environment.NewLine);
    jobInfo.AppendFormat("Status: {0}", job["Status"].ToString());
    jobInfo.Append(Environment.NewLine);
    jobInfo.AppendFormat("Owner: {0}", job["Owner"].ToString());
    jobInfo.Append(Environment.NewLine);

    jobInfo.AppendFormat("PagesPrinted: {0}", job["PagesPrinted"].ToString());
    jobInfo.Append(Environment.NewLine);
    jobInfo.AppendFormat("TotalPages: {0}", job["TotalPages"].ToString());

    if (job["JobStatus"] != null)
    {
        txtJobInfo.Text += Environment.NewLine;
        txtJobInfo.Text += "JobStatus: " + job["JobStatus"].ToString();
    }
    if (job["StartTime"] != null)
    {
        jobInfo.Append(Environment.NewLine);
        jobInfo.AppendFormat("StartTime: {0}", job["StartTime"].ToString());
    }

    txtJobInfo.Text = jobInfo.ToString();
}

private void cmdPause_Click(object sender, EventArgs e)
{
    if (lstJobs.SelectedIndex == -1) return;
    ManagementObject job = GetSelectedJob();
    if (job == null) return;

    // Attempt to pause the job.
    int returnValue = Int32.Parse(
      job.InvokeMethod("Pause", null).ToString());

    // Display information about the return value.
    if (returnValue == 0)
    {
        MessageBox.Show("Successfully paused job.");
    }
    else
    {
        MessageBox.Show("Unrecognized return value when pausing job.");
    }
}
```

```
        private void cmdResume_Click(object sender, EventArgs e)
        {
            if (lstJobs.SelectedIndex == -1) return;
            ManagementObject job = GetSelectedJob();
            if (job == null) return;

            if ((Int32.Parse(job["StatusMask"].ToString()) & 1) == 1)
            {
                // Attempt to resume the job.
                int returnValue = Int32.Parse(
                  job.InvokeMethod("Resume", null).ToString());

                // Display information about the return value.
                if (returnValue == 0)
                {
                    MessageBox.Show("Successfully resumed job.");
                }
                else if (returnValue == 5)
                {
                    MessageBox.Show("Access denied.");
                }
                else
                {
                    MessageBox.Show(
                      "Unrecognized return value when resuming job.");
                }
            }
        }
    }
}
```

Figure 8-10 shows the window for this application.

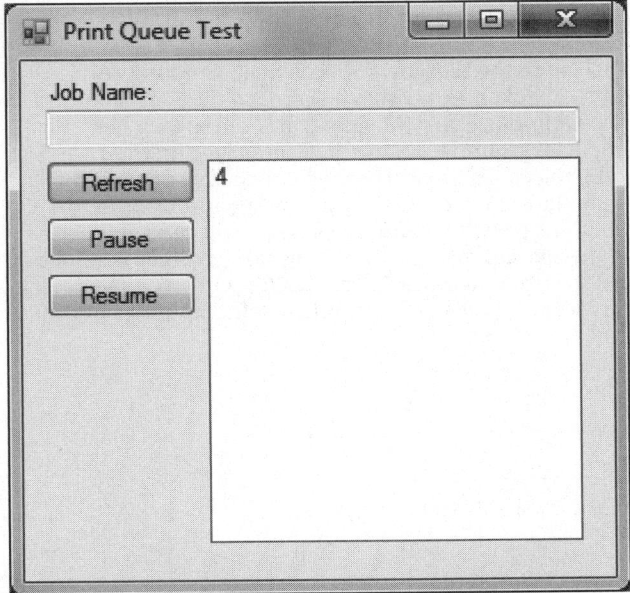

Figure 8-10. Retrieving information from the print queue

■ **Note** Other WMI methods you might use in a printing scenario include `AddPrinterConnection`, `SetDefaultPrinter`, `CancelAllJobs`, and `PrintTestPage`, all of which work with the `Win32_Printer` class. For more information about using WMI to retrieve information about Windows hardware, refer to the MSDN documentation.

8-19. Perform Text-to-Speech

Problem

You need to read a piece of text aloud.

Solution

Create an instance of `System.Speech.Synthesis.SpeechSynthesizer`, contained in the `System.Speech` assembly, and call the `Speak` instance method, passing in the `string` that you wish to be spoken.

How It Works

The SpeechSynthesizer class provides managed access to the Windows Speech SDK. Creating an instance of SpeechSynthesizer allows you to have text spoken by passing a string to the Speak method. The Speak method is synchronous, meaning that your application will pause until the speech has completed—you can have text spoken aloud in the background by using the SpeakAsync method.

Windows provides support for having different voices read text. The voices available on your machine will depend on the version of Windows you have installed and which other applications are available—some Microsoft and third-party applications provide additional voices. You can get information about the voices available by calling the SpeechSynthesizer.GetInstalledVoices instance method, which returns an enumeration of System.Speech.Synthesis.InstalledVoice. You can select the voice to use for speech with the SpeechSyntheizer.SelectVoice method. Other useful members of the SpeechSynthesizer class are listed in Table 8-1.

Table 8-1. *Useful Members of SpeechSynthesizer*

Member	Description
GetInstalledVoices	Returns an enumeration of InstalledVoice
Pause	Pauses the synthesizer
Resume	Resumes the synthesizer playback
SelectVoice	Selects an installed synthesizer voice
SetOutputToWaveFile	Saves the synthesized speed to a sound file
Speak	Synchronously speaks a string
SpeakAsync	Asynchronously speaks a string
Rate	Returns the speed at which speech is performed
Volume	Returns the volume of the speech output

The Code

The following example displays information about each speech synthesis voice installed on the local machine, and then enters a loop where lines of text read from the console are passed to the Speak method of a SpeechSynthesizer instance.

■ **Note** You will need to add the `System.Speech` assembly as a reference to your Visual Studio project in order to use the `System.Speech.Synthesis` namespace.

```
using System;
using System.Collections.Generic;
using System.Linq;
using System.Text;
using System.Speech.Synthesis;

namespace Apress.VisualCSharpRecipes.Chapter08
{
    class Recipe08_19
    {
        static void Main(string[] args)
        {
            // Create a new synthesizer.
            SpeechSynthesizer mySynth = new SpeechSynthesizer();

            Console.WriteLine("--- Start of voices list ---");
            foreach (InstalledVoice voice in mySynth.GetInstalledVoices())
            {
                Console.WriteLine("Voice: {0}", voice.VoiceInfo.Name);
                Console.WriteLine("Gender: {0}", voice.VoiceInfo.Gender);
                Console.WriteLine("Age: {0}", voice.VoiceInfo.Age);
                Console.WriteLine("Culture: {0}", voice.VoiceInfo.Culture);
                Console.WriteLine("Description: {0}", voice.VoiceInfo.Description);
            }
            Console.WriteLine("--- End of voices list ---");

            while (true)
            {
                Console.WriteLine("Enter string to speak");
                mySynth.Speak(Console.ReadLine());
                Console.WriteLine("Completed");
            }
        }
    }
}
```

8-20. Recognize Characters in an Image (OCR)

Problem

You need to perform optical character recognition (OCR) to recognize words in an image.

Solution

Use COM Interop to access the features of Microsoft Office Document Imaging.

■ **Note** This recipe requires Microsoft Office 2007.

How It Works

The first step is to install the Microsoft Office Document Imaging (MODI), which is not installed by default by the Microsoft Office installation. Run the Office installer, and select Microsoft Office Document Imaging from the Office Tools section, as shown in Figure 8-11.

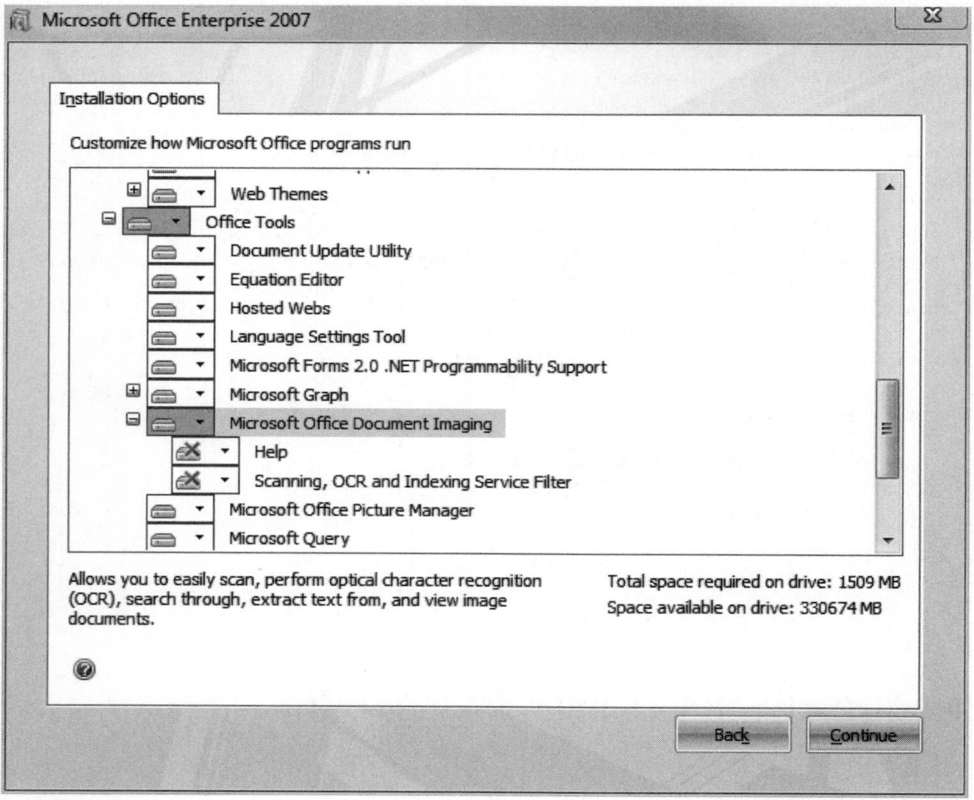

Figure 8-11. Installing MODI

Once the Office feature has been installed, you can add a reference to your project for the Microsoft Office Document Imaging 12.0 Type Library entry, available under the COM tab and import the `MODI` namespace into your class file. Because we are accessing MODI through COM, the API calls we have to make are a little awkward. The sequence for performing OCR follows:

- Create a new instance of `Document` by calling `new Document()`.
- Load the image that you wish to process by calling the `Create` method on the `Document` instance from the previous step, passing in a `string` that contains the name of the image file. OCR can be performed on PNG, JPG, GIF, and TIFF files.
- Call the OCR method on the `Document` instance.
- Obtain the first element of the `Images` array property from the `Document` instance, and from that `Image` instance, get the `Layout` by calling the `Image.Layout` property.

The `Layout` class is what we are trying to obtain—it represents the scanned content, and its members allow us to get information about the OCR results and access the words that have been scanned. The most important member of `Layout` is `Words`, which is a collection of `Word` instances, each of which represents a word scanned from the source image and that you can enumerate through to create the processed result. The `Word` class has two useful members—the most important is `Text`, which returns the `string` value of the scanned word. The second useful member is `RecognitionConfidence`, which returns a value indicating how confident the OCR process was in recognizing the word correctly, on a scale of 0 to 999.

The Code

The following example loads an image called `ocr.GIF` (which we have included in the sample code for this chapter) and performs OCR on it. Each word found is printed out, along with the

`RecognitionConfidence` value.

```
using System;
using System.Collections.Generic;
using System.Linq;
using System.Text;
using MODI;

namespace Apress.VisualCSharpRecipes.Chapter08
{
    class Recipe08_20
    {
        static void Main(string[] args)
        {
            // Create the new document instance.
            Document myOCRDoc = new Document();
            // Load the sample file.
            myOCRDoc.Create(@"..\..\ocr.GIF");

            // Perform the OCR.
            myOCRDoc.OCR();
```

```
            // Get the processed document.
            Image image = (Image)myOCRDoc.Images[0];
            Layout layout = image.Layout;

            // Print out each word that has been found.
            foreach (Word word in layout.Words)
            {
                Console.WriteLine("Word: {0} Confidence: {1}",
                        word.Text, word.RecognitionConfidence);
            }
        }
    }
}
```

CHAPTER 9

Database Access

In the Microsoft .NET Framework, access to a wide variety of data sources is enabled through a group of classes collectively named Microsoft ADO.NET. Each type of data source is supported through the provision of a data provider. Each data provider contains a set of classes that not only implement a standard set of interfaces (defined in the `System.Data` namespace), but also provide functionality unique to the data source they support. These classes include representations of connections, commands, properties, data adapters, and data readers through which you interact with a data source.

Table 9-1 lists the data providers included as standard with the .NET Framework.

Table 9-1. *.NET Framework Data Provider Implementations*

Data Provider	Description
.NET Framework Data Provider for ODBC	Provides connectivity (via COM Interop) to any data source that implements an ODBC interface. This includes Microsoft SQL Server, Oracle, and Microsoft Access databases. Data provider classes are contained in the `System.Data.Odbc` namespace and have the prefix `Odbc`.
.NET Framework Data Provider for OLE DB	Provides connectivity (via COM Interop) to any data source that implements an OLE DB interface. This includes Microsoft SQL Server, MSDE, Oracle, and Jet databases. Data provider classes are contained in the `System.Data.OleDb` namespace and have the prefix `OleDb`.
.NET Framework Data Provider for Oracle	Provides optimized connectivity to Oracle databases via Oracle client software version 8.1.7 or later. Data provider classes are contained in the `System.Data.OracleClient` namespace and have the prefix `Oracle`.
.NET Framework Data Provider for SQL Server	Provides optimized connectivity to Microsoft SQL Server version 7 and later (including MSDE) by communicating directly with the SQL Server data source, without the need to use ODBC or OLE DB. Data provider classes are contained in the `System.Data.SqlClient` namespace and have the prefix `Sql`.
.NET Compact Framework Data Provider	Provides connectivity to Microsoft SQL Server CE. Data provider classes are contained in the `System.Data.SqlServerCe` namespace and have the prefix `SqlCe`.

■ **Tip** Where possible, the recipes in this chapter are programmed against the interfaces defined in the `System.Data` namespace. This approach makes it easier to apply the solutions to any database. Adopting this approach in your own code will make it more portable. However, the data provider classes that implement these interfaces often implement additional functionality specific to their own database. Generally, you must trade off portability against access to proprietary functionality when it comes to database code. Recipe 9-10 describes how you can use the `System.Data.Common.DbProviderFactory` and associated classes to write code not tied to a specific database implementation.

This chapter describes some of the most commonly used aspects of ADO.NET. The recipes in this chapter describe how to do the following:

- Create, configure, open, and close database connections (recipe 9-1)
- Employ connection pooling to improve the performance and scalability of applications that use database connections (recipe 9-2)
- Create and securely store database connection strings (recipes 9-3 and 9-4)
- Execute SQL commands and stored procedures, and use parameters to improve their flexibility (recipes 9-5 and 9-6)
- Process the results returned by database queries as either a set of rows or as XML (recipes 9-7 and 9-8)
- Execute database operations asynchronously, allowing your main code to continue with other tasks while the database operation executes in the background (recipe 9-9)
- Write generic ADO.NET code that can be configured to work against any relational database for which a data provider is available (recipe 9-10)
- Discover all instances of SQL Server 2000 and SQL Server 2005 available on a network (recipe 9-11)
- Create an in-memory cache and programmatically create a `DataSet` (recipes 9-12 and 9-13)
- Perform LINQ database queries using a `DataSet`, and use entity types (recipes 9-14 and 9-15)
- Compare the results of LINQ queries (recipe 9-16)

■ **Note** Unless otherwise stated, the recipes in this chapter have been written to use SQL Server 2008 Express Edition running on the local machine and the `Northwind` sample database provided by Microsoft. To run the examples against your own database, ensure the `Northwind` sample is installed and update the recipe's connection string to contain the name of your server instead of `.\sqlexpress`. You can obtain the script to set up the `Northwind` database from the Microsoft web site. On that site, search for the file named `SQL2000SampleDb.msi` to find links to where the file is available for download. The download includes a Readme file with instructions on how to run the installation script.

9-1. Connect to a Database

Problem

You need to open a connection to a database.

Solution

Create a connection object appropriate to the type of database to which you need to connect. All connection objects implement the `System.Data.IDbConnection` interface. Configure the connection object by setting its `ConnectionString` property. Open the connection by calling the connection object's `Open` method.

How It Works

The first step in database access is to open a connection to the database. The `IDbConnection` interface represents a database connection, and each data provider includes a unique implementation. Here is the list of `IDbConnection` implementations for the five standard data providers:

- `System.Data.Odbc.OdbcConnection`
- `System.Data.OleDb.OleDbConnection`
- `System.Data.OracleClient.OracleConnection`
- `System.Data.SqlServerCe.SqlCeConnection`
- `System.Data.SqlClient.SqlConnection`

You configure a connection object using a *connection string*. A connection string is a set of semicolon-separated name/value pairs. You can supply a connection string either as a constructor argument or by setting a connection object's `ConnectionString` property before opening the connection. Each connection class implementation requires that you provide different information in the connection string. Refer to the `ConnectionString` property documentation for each implementation to see the values you can specify. Possible settings include the following:

- The name of the target database server
- The name of the database to open initially
- Connection timeout values
- Connection-pooling behavior (see recipe 9-2)
- Authentication mechanisms to use when connecting to secured databases, including provision of a username and password if needed

Once configured, call the connection object's `Open` method to open the connection to the database. You can then use the connection object to execute commands against the data source (discussed in recipe 9-3). The properties of a connection object also allow you to retrieve information about the state of a connection and the settings used to open the connection. When you're finished with a connection, you should always call its `Close` method to free the underlying database connection and system resources. `IDbConnection` extends `System.IDisposable`, meaning that each connection class implements the `Dispose` method. `Dispose` automatically calls `Close`, making the `using` statement a very clean and efficient way of using connection objects in your code.

The Code

The following example demonstrates how to use both the `SqlConnection` and `OleDbConnection` classes to open a connection to a Microsoft SQL Server Express database running on the local machine that uses integrated Windows security:

```
using System;
using System.Data;
using System.Data.SqlClient;
using System.Data.OleDb;

namespace Apress.VisualCSharpRecipes.Chapter09
{
    class Recipe09_01
    {
        public static void SqlConnectionExample()
        {
            // Create an empty SqlConnection object.
            using (SqlConnection con = new SqlConnection())
            {
                // Configure the SqlConnection object's connection string.
                con.ConnectionString =
                    @"Data Source=.\sqlexpress;" + // local SQL Server instance
                    "Database=Northwind;" +        // the sample Northwind DB
                    "Integrated Security=SSPI";    // integrated Windows security

                // Open the database connection.
                con.Open();
```

```
            // Display information about the connection.
            if (con.State == ConnectionState.Open)
            {
                Console.WriteLine("SqlConnection Information:");
                Console.WriteLine("  Connection State = " + con.State);
                Console.WriteLine("  Connection String = " +
                    con.ConnectionString);
                Console.WriteLine("  Database Source = " + con.DataSource);
                Console.WriteLine("  Database = " + con.Database);
                Console.WriteLine("  Server Version = " + con.ServerVersion);
                Console.WriteLine("  Workstation Id = " + con.WorkstationId);
                Console.WriteLine("  Timeout = " + con.ConnectionTimeout);
                Console.WriteLine("  Packet Size = " + con.PacketSize);
            }
            else
            {
                Console.WriteLine("SqlConnection failed to open.");
                Console.WriteLine("  Connection State = " + con.State);
            }
            // At the end of the using block Dispose() calls Close().
        }
    }

    public static void OleDbConnectionExample()
    {

        // Create an empty OleDbConnection object.
        using (OleDbConnection con = new OleDbConnection())
        {
            // Configure the OleDbConnection object's connection string.
            con.ConnectionString =
                "Provider=SQLOLEDB;" +          // OLE DB Provider for SQL Server
                @"Data Source=.\sqlexpress;" + // local SQL Server instance
                "Initial Catalog=Northwind;" + // the sample Northwind DB
                "Integrated Security=SSPI";      // integrated Windows security

            // Open the database connection.
            con.Open();

            // Display information about the connection.
            if (con.State == ConnectionState.Open)
            {
                Console.WriteLine("OleDbConnection Information:");
                Console.WriteLine("  Connection State = " + con.State);
                Console.WriteLine("  Connection String = " +
                    con.ConnectionString);
                Console.WriteLine("  Database Source = " + con.DataSource);
                Console.WriteLine("  Database = " + con.Database);
                Console.WriteLine("  Server Version = " + con.ServerVersion);
                Console.WriteLine("  Timeout = " + con.ConnectionTimeout);
            }
```

```
                else
                {
                    Console.WriteLine("OleDbConnection failed to open.");
                    Console.WriteLine("  Connection State = " + con.State);
                }
                // At the end of the using block Dispose() calls Close().
            }
        }

        public static void Main()
        {
            // Open connection using SqlConnection.
            SqlConnectionExample();
            Console.WriteLine(Environment.NewLine);

            // Open connection using OleDbConnection.
            OleDbConnectionExample();

            // Wait to continue.
            Console.WriteLine(Environment.NewLine);
            Console.WriteLine("Main method complete. Press Enter.");
            Console.ReadLine();
        }
    }
}
```

9-2. Use Connection Pooling

Problem

You need to use a pool of database connections to improve application performance and scalability.

Solution

Configure the connection pool using settings in the connection string of a connection object.

How It Works

Connection pooling reduces the overhead associated with creating and destroying database connections. Connection pooling also improves the scalability of solutions by reducing the number of concurrent connections a database must maintain. Many of these connections sit idle for a significant portion of their lifetimes. With connection pooling, instead of creating and opening a new connection object whenever you need one, you take an already open connection from the connection pool. When you have finished using the connection, instead of closing it, you return it to the pool and allow other code to use it.

The SQL Server and Oracle data providers encapsulate connection-pooling functionality, which is enabled by default. One connection pool is created for each unique connection string you specify when you open a new connection. Each time you open a new connection with a connection string that you used previously, the connection is taken from the existing pool. Only if you specify a different connection string will the data provider create a new connection pool. You can control some characteristics of your pool using the connection string settings described in Table 9-2.

■ **Note** Once created, a pool exists until your process terminates.

Table 9-2. Connection String Settings That Control Connection Pooling

Setting	Description
`Connection Lifetime`	Specifies the maximum time in seconds that a connection is allowed to live in the pool before it's closed. The age of a connection is tested only when the connection is returned to the pool. This setting is useful for minimizing pool size if the pool is not heavily used, and also ensures optimal load balancing is achieved in clustered database environments. The default value is `0`, which means connections exist for the life of the current process.
`Connection Reset`	Supported only by the SQL Server data provider. Specifies whether connections are reset as they are taken from the pool. A value of `True` (the default) ensures that a connection's state is reset, but requires additional communication with the database.
`Max Pool Size`	Specifies the maximum number of connections that should be in the pool. Connections are created and added to the pool as required until this value is reached. If a request for a connection is made but there are no free connections, the caller will block until a connection becomes available. The default value is `100`.
`Min Pool Size`	Specifies the minimum number of connections that should be in the pool. On pool creation, this number of connections is created and added to the pool. During periodic maintenance, or when a connection is requested, connections are added to the pool to ensure that the minimum number of connections are available. The default value is `0`.
`Pooling`	Set to `False` to obtain a nonpooled connection. The default value is `True`.

The Code

The following example demonstrates the configuration of a connection pool that contains a minimum of 5 and a maximum of 15 connections. Connections expire after 10 minutes (600 seconds) and are reset each time a connection is obtained from the pool. The example also demonstrates how to use the `Pooling` setting to obtain a connection object that is not from a pool. This is useful if your application uses a single long-lived connection to a database.

```
using System;
using System.Data.SqlClient;

namespace Apress.VisualCSharpRecipes.Chapter09
{
    class Recipe09_02
    {
        public static void Main()
        {
            // Obtain a pooled connection.
            using (SqlConnection con = new SqlConnection())
            {
                // Configure the SqlConnection object's connection string.
                con.ConnectionString =
                    @"Data Source = .\sqlexpress;" +// local SQL Server instance
                    "Database = Northwind;" +       // the sample Northwind DB
                    "Integrated Security = SSPI;" + // integrated Windows security
                    "Min Pool Size = 5;" +          // configure minimum pool size
                    "Max Pool Size = 15;" +         // configure maximum pool size
                    "Connection Reset = True;" +    // reset connections each use
                    "Connection Lifetime = 600";    // set max connection lifetime

                // Open the database connection.
                con.Open();

                // Access the database . . .

                // At the end of the using block, the Dispose calls Close, which
                // returns the connection to the pool for reuse.
            }

            // Obtain a nonpooled connection.
            using (SqlConnection con = new SqlConnection())
            {
                // Configure the SqlConnection object's connection string.
                con.ConnectionString =
                    @"Data Source = .\sqlexpress;" +//local SQL Server instance
                    "Database = Northwind;" +       //the sample Northwind DB
                    "Integrated Security = SSPI;" + //integrated Windows security
                    "Pooling = False";              //specify nonpooled connection

                // Open the database connection.
                con.Open();

                // Access the database . . .

                // At the end of the using block, the Dispose calls Close, which
                // closes the nonpooled connection.
            }
```

```
            // Wait to continue.
            Console.WriteLine(Environment.NewLine);
            Console.WriteLine("Main method complete. Press Enter.");
            Console.ReadLine();
        }
    }
}
```

Notes

The ODBC and OLE DB data providers also support connection pooling, but they do not implement connection pooling within managed .NET classes, and you do not configure the pool in the same way as you do for the SQL Server or Oracle data providers. ODBC connection pooling is managed by the ODBC Driver Manager and configured using the ODBC Data Source Administrator tool in the Control Panel. OLE DB connection pooling is managed by the native OLE DB implementation. The most you can do is disable pooling by including the setting `OLE DB Services=-4;` in your connection string.

The SQL Server CE data provider does not support connection pooling, because SQL Server CE supports only a single concurrent connection.

9-3. Create a Database Connection String Programmatically

Problem

You need to programmatically create or modify a syntactically correct connection string by working with its component parts or parsing a given connection string.

Solution

Use the `System.Data.Common.DbConnectionStringBuilder` class or one of its strongly typed subclasses that form part of an ADO.NET data provider.

How It Works

Connection strings are `String` objects that contain a set of configuration parameters in the form of name/value pairs separated by semicolons. These configuration parameters instruct the ADO.NET infrastructure how to open a connection to the data source you want to access and how to handle the life cycle of connections to that data source. As a developer, you will often simply define your connection string by hand and store it in a configuration file (see recipe 9-4). However, you may want to build a connection string from component elements entered by a user, or you may want to parse an existing connection string into its component parts so that you can manipulate it programmatically. The `DbConnectionStringBuilder` class and the classes derived from it provide both these capabilities.

`DbConnectionStringBuilder` is a class used to create connection strings from name/value pairs or to parse connection strings, but it does not enforce any logic on which configuration parameters are valid. Instead, each data provider (except the SQL Server CE data provider) includes a unique implementation derived from `DbConnectionStringBuilder` that accurately enforces the configuration rules for a connection string of that type. Here is the list of available DbConnectionStringBuilder implementations for standard data providers:

- System.Data.Odbc.OdbcConnectionStringBuilder
- System.Data.OleDb.OleDbConnectionStringBuilder
- System.Data.OracleClient.OracleConnectionStringBuilder
- System.Data.SqlClient.SqlConnectionStringBuilder

Each of these classes exposes properties for getting and setting the possible parameters for a connection string of that type. To parse an existing connection string, pass it as an argument when creating the DbConnectionStringBuilder-derived class, or set the ConnectionString property. If this string contains a keyword not supported by the type of connection, an ArgumentException will be thrown.

The Code

The following example demonstrates the use of the SqlConnectionStringBuilder class to parse and construct SQL Server connection strings:

```
using System;
using System.Data.SqlClient;

namespace Apress.VisualCSharpRecipes.Chapter09
{
    class Recipe09_03
    {
        public static void Main(string[] args)
        {
            string conString = @"Data Source=.\sqlexpress;" +
                "Database=Northwind;Integrated Security=SSPI;" +
                "Min Pool Size=5;Max Pool Size=15;Connection Reset=True;" +
                "Connection Lifetime=600;";

            // Parse the SQL Server connection string and display the component
            // configuration parameters.
            SqlConnectionStringBuilder sb1 =
                new SqlConnectionStringBuilder(conString);

            Console.WriteLine("Parsed SQL Connection String Parameters:");
            Console.WriteLine("  Database Source = " + sb1.DataSource);
            Console.WriteLine("  Database = " + sb1.InitialCatalog);
            Console.WriteLine("  Use Integrated Security = "
                + sb1.IntegratedSecurity);
            Console.WriteLine("  Min Pool Size = " + sb1.MinPoolSize);
            Console.WriteLine("  Max Pool Size = " + sb1.MaxPoolSize);
            Console.WriteLine("  Lifetime = " + sb1.LoadBalanceTimeout);
```

```
            // Build a connection string from component parameters and display it.
            SqlConnectionStringBuilder sb2 =
                new SqlConnectionStringBuilder(conString);

            sb2.DataSource = @".\sqlexpress";
            sb2.InitialCatalog = "Northwind";
            sb2.IntegratedSecurity = true;
            sb2.MinPoolSize = 5;
            sb2.MaxPoolSize = 15;
            sb2.LoadBalanceTimeout = 600;

            Console.WriteLine(Environment.NewLine);
            Console.WriteLine("Constructed connection string:");
            Console.WriteLine("  " + sb2.ConnectionString);

            // Wait to continue.
            Console.WriteLine(Environment.NewLine);
            Console.WriteLine("Main method complete. Press Enter.");
            Console.ReadLine();
        }
    }
}
```

9-4. Store a Database Connection String Securely

Problem

You need to store a database connection string securely.

Solution

Store the connection string in an encrypted section of the application's configuration file.

■ **Note** Protected configuration—the .NET Framework feature that lets you encrypt configuration information—relies on the key storage facilities of the Data Protection API (DPAPI) to store the secret key used to encrypt the configuration file. This solves the very difficult problem of code-based secret key management.

How It Works

Database connection strings often contain secret information, or at the very least information that would be valuable to someone trying to attack your system. As such, you should not store connection strings in plain text, nor should you hard-code them into the application code. Strings embedded in an assembly can easily be retrieved using a disassembler. The .NET Framework includes a number of classes and capabilities that make storing and retrieving encrypted connection strings in your application's configuration trivial.

Unencrypted connection strings are stored in the machine or application configuration file in the `<connectionStrings>` section in the format shown here:

```
<configuration>
    <connectionStrings>
        <add name="ConnectionString1" connectionString="Data Source=.\sqlexpress
;Database=Northwind;Integrated Security=SSPI;Min Pool Size=5;Max Pool Size=15;Co
nnection Reset=True;Connection Lifetime=600;"
            providerName="System.Data.SqlClient" />
    </connectionStrings>
</configuration>
```

The easiest way to read this connection string is to use the indexed `ConnectionStrings` property of the `System.Configuration.ConfigurationManager` class. Specifying the name of the connection string you want as the property index will return a `System.Configuration.ConnectionStringSettings` object. The `ConnectionStringSettings.ConnectionString` property gets the connection string, and the `ConnectionStringSettings.ProviderName` property gets the provider name that you can use to create a data provider factory (see recipe 9-10). This process will work regardless of whether the connection string has been encrypted or written in plain text.

To write a connection string to the application's configuration file, you must first obtain a `System.Configuration.Configuration` object, which represents the application's configuration file. The easiest way to do this is by calling the `System.Configuration.ConfigurationManager.OpenExeConfiguration` method. You should then create and configure a new `System.Configuration.ConnectionStringSettings` object to represent the stored connection string. You should provide a name, connection string, and data provider name for storage. Add the `ConnectionStringSettings` object to `Configuration`'s `ConnectionStringsSection` collection, available through the `Configuration.ConnectionStrings` property. Finally, save the updated file by calling the `Configuration.Save` method.

To encrypt the connection strings section of the configuration file, before saving the file, you must configure the `ConnectionStringsSection` collection. To do this, call the `ConnectionStringsSection.SectionInformation.ProtectSection` method and pass it a string containing the name of the protected configuration provider to use: either `RsaProtectedConfigurationProvider` or `DPAPIProtectedConfigurationProvider`. To disable encryption, call the `SectionInformation.Unprotect` method.

■ **Note** To use the classes from the `System.Configuration` namespace discussed in this recipe, you must add a reference to the `System.Configuration.dll` assembly when you build your application.

The Code

The following example demonstrates the writing of an encrypted connection string to the application's configuration file and the subsequent reading and use of that connection string.

■ **Note** The configuration file will be created alongside the compiled program in the `bin/Release` or `bin/Debug` directory of the Visual Studio project folder. If you have downloaded the source code that accompanies this book, the configuration tile will be called `Recipe09-04.exe.Config`.

```
using System;
using System.Configuration;
using System.Data.SqlClient;

namespace Apress.VisualCSharpRecipes.Chapter09
{
    class Recipe09_04
    {
        private static void WriteEncryptedConnectionStringSection(
            string name, string constring, string provider)
        {
            // Get the configuration file for the current application. Specify
            // the ConfigurationUserLevel.None argument so that we get the
            // configuration settings that apply to all users.
            Configuration config = ConfigurationManager.OpenExeConfiguration(
                ConfigurationUserLevel.None);

            // Get the connectionStrings section from the configuration file.
            ConnectionStringsSection section = config.ConnectionStrings;

            // If the connectionString section does not exist, create it.
            if (section == null)
            {
                section = new ConnectionStringsSection();
                config.Sections.Add("connectionSettings", section);
            }

            // If it is not already encrypted, configure the connectionStrings
            // section to be encrypted using the standard RSA Proected
            // Configuration Provider.
            if (!section.SectionInformation.IsProtected)
            {
                // Remove this statement to write the connection string in clear
                // text for the purpose of testing.
                section.SectionInformation.ProtectSection(
                    "RsaProtectedConfigurationProvider");
            }

            // Create a new connection string element and add it to the
            // connection string configuration section.
            ConnectionStringSettings cs =
                new ConnectionStringSettings(name, constring, provider);
            section.ConnectionStrings.Add(cs);
```

```
            // Force the connection string section to be saved.
            section.SectionInformation.ForceSave = true;

            // Save the updated configuration file.
            config.Save(ConfigurationSaveMode.Full);
        }

        public static void Main(string[] args)
        {
            // The connection string information to be written to the
            // configuration file.
            string conName = "ConnectionString1";
            string conString = @"Data Source=.\sqlexpress;" +
                "Database=Northwind;Integrated Security=SSPI;" +
                "Min Pool Size=5;Max Pool Size=15;Connection Reset=True;" +
                "Connection Lifetime=600;";
            string providerName = "System.Data.SqlClient";

            // Write the new connection string to the application's
            // configuration file.
            WriteEncryptedConnectionStringSection(conName, conString, providerName);

            // Read the encrypted connection string settings from the
            // application's configuration file.
            ConnectionStringSettings cs2 =
                ConfigurationManager.ConnectionStrings["ConnectionString1"];

            // Use the connection string to create a new SQL Server connection.
            using (SqlConnection con = new SqlConnection(cs2.ConnectionString))
            {
                // Issue database commands/queries . . .

            }

            // Wait to continue.
            Console.WriteLine(Environment.NewLine);
            Console.WriteLine("Main method complete. Press Enter.");
            Console.ReadLine();
        }
    }
}
```

9-5. Execute a SQL Command or Stored Procedure

Problem

You need to execute a SQL command or stored procedure on a database.

Solution

Create a command object appropriate to the type of database you intend to use. All command objects implement the `System.Data.IDbCommand` interface. Configure the command object by setting its `CommandType` and `CommandText` properties. Execute the command using the `ExecuteNonQuery`, `ExecuteReader`, or `ExecuteScalar` method, depending on the type of command and its expected results.

How It Works

The `IDbCommand` interface represents a database command, and each data provider includes a unique implementation. Here is the list of `IDbCommand` implementations for the five standard data providers:

- `System.Data.Odbc.OdbcCommand`
- `System.Data.OleDb.OleDbCommand`
- `System.Data.OracleClient.OracleCommand`
- `System.Data.SqlServerCe.SqlCeCommand`
- `System.Data.SqlClient.SqlCommand`

To execute a command against a database, you must have an open connection (discussed in recipe 9-1) and a properly configured command object appropriate to the type of database you are accessing. You can create command objects directly using a constructor, but a simpler approach is to use the `CreateCommand` factory method of a connection object. The `CreateCommand` method returns a command object of the correct type for the data provider and configures it with basic information obtained from the connection you used to create the command. Before executing the command, you must configure the properties described in Table 9-3, which are common to all command implementations.

Table 9-3. *Common Command Object Properties*

Property	Description
`CommandText`	A `string` containing the text of the SQL command to execute or the name of a stored procedure. The content of the `CommandText` property must be compatible with the value you specify in the `CommandType` property.
`CommandTimeout`	An `int` that specifies the number of seconds to wait for the command to return before timing out and raising an exception. Defaults to 30 seconds.
`CommandType`	A value of the `System.Data.CommandType` enumeration that specifies the type of command represented by the command object. For most data providers, valid values are `StoredProcedure`, when you want to execute a stored procedure; and `Text`, when you want to execute a SQL text command. If you are using the OLE DB data provider, you can specify `TableDirect` when you want to return the entire contents of one or more tables; refer to the .NET Framework SDK documentation for more details. Defaults to `Text`.

Property	Description
Connection	An IDbConnection instance that provides the connection to the database on which you will execute the command. If you create the command using the IDbConnection.CreateCommand method, this property will be automatically set to the IDbConnection instance from which you created the command.
Parameters	A System.Data.IDataParameterCollection instance containing the set of parameters to substitute into the command. (See recipe 9-6 for details on how to use parameters.)
Transaction	A System.Data.IDbTransaction instance representing the transaction into which to enlist the command. (See the .NET Framework SDK documentation for details about transactions.)

Once you have configured your command object, you can execute it in a number of ways, depending on the nature of the command, the type of data returned by the command, and the format in which you want to process the data.

- To execute a command that does not return database data (such as INSERT, DELETE, or CREATE TABLE), call ExecuteNonQuery. For the UPDATE, INSERT, and DELETE commands, the ExecuteNonQuery method returns an int that specifies the number of rows affected by the command. For other commands, such as CREATE TABLE, ExecuteNonQuery returns the value -1.
- To execute a command that returns a result set, such as a SELECT statement or stored procedure, use the ExecuteReader method. ExecuteReader returns an IDataReader instance (discussed in recipe 9-7) through which you have access to the result data. Most data providers also allow you to execute multiple SQL commands in a single call to the ExecuteReader method, as demonstrated in the example in recipe 9-7, which also shows how to access each result set.
- If you want to execute a query but only need the value from the first column of the first row of result data, use the ExecuteScalar method. The value is returned as an object reference that you must cast to the correct type.

■ **Note** The IDbCommand implementations included in the Oracle and SQL data providers implement additional command execution methods. Recipe 9-8 describes how to use the ExecuteXmlReader method provided by the SqlCommand class. Refer to the .NET Framework's SDK documentation for details on the additional ExecuteOracleNonQuery and ExecuteOracleScalar methods provided by the OracleCommand class.

The Code

The following example demonstrates the use of command objects to update a database record, run a stored procedure, and obtain a scalar value:

```
using System;
using System.Data;
using System.Data.SqlClient;

namespace Apress.VisualCSharpRecipes.Chapter09
{
    class Recipe09_05
    {
        public static void ExecuteNonQueryExample(IDbConnection con)
        {
            // Create and configure a new command.
            IDbCommand com = con.CreateCommand();
            com.CommandType = CommandType.Text;
            com.CommandText = "UPDATE Employees SET Title = 'Sales Director'" +
                " WHERE EmployeeId = '5'";

            // Execute the command and process the result.
            int result = com.ExecuteNonQuery();

            if (result == 1)
            {
                Console.WriteLine("Employee title updated.");
            }
            else
            {
                Console.WriteLine("Employee title not updated.");
            }
        }

        public static void ExecuteReaderExample(IDbConnection con)
        {
            // Create and configure a new command.
            IDbCommand com = con.CreateCommand();
            com.CommandType = CommandType.StoredProcedure;
            com.CommandText = "Ten Most Expensive Products";

            // Execute the command and process the results.
            using (IDataReader reader = com.ExecuteReader())
            {
                Console.WriteLine("Price of the Ten Most Expensive Products.");

                while (reader.Read())
                {
                    // Display the product details.
                    Console.WriteLine("  {0} = {1}",
                        reader["TenMostExpensiveProducts"],
                        reader["UnitPrice"]);
                }
            }
        }
```

```
        public static void ExecuteScalarExample(IDbConnection con)
        {
            // Create and configure a new command.
            IDbCommand com = con.CreateCommand();
            com.CommandType = CommandType.Text;
            com.CommandText = "SELECT COUNT(*) FROM Employees";

            // Execute the command and cast the result.
            int result = (int)com.ExecuteScalar();

            Console.WriteLine("Employee count = " + result);
        }

        public static void Main()
        {
            // Create a new SqlConnection object.
            using (SqlConnection con = new SqlConnection())
            {
                // Configure the SqlConnection object's connection string.
                con.ConnectionString = @"Data Source = .\sqlexpress;" +
                    "Database = Northwind; Integrated Security=SSPI";

                // Open the database connection and execute the example
                // commands through the connection.
                con.Open();

                ExecuteNonQueryExample(con);
                Console.WriteLine(Environment.NewLine);

                ExecuteReaderExample(con);
                Console.WriteLine(Environment.NewLine);

                ExecuteScalarExample(con);
            }

            // Wait to continue.
            Console.WriteLine(Environment.NewLine);
            Console.WriteLine("Main method complete. Press Enter.");
            Console.ReadLine();
        }
    }
}
```

9-6. Use Parameters in a SQL Command or Stored Procedure

Problem

You need to set the arguments of a stored procedure or use parameters in a SQL command to improve flexibility.

Solution

Create parameter objects appropriate to the type of command object you intend to execute. All parameter objects implement the `System.Data.IDataParameter` interface. Configure the parameter objects' data types, values, and directions, and add them to the command object's parameter collection using the `IDbCommand.Parameters.Add` method.

How It Works

All command objects support the use of parameters, so you can do the following:

- Set the arguments of stored procedures.
- Receive stored procedure return values.
- Substitute values into text commands at runtime.

The `IDataParameter` interface represents a parameter, and each data provider includes a unique implementation. Here is the list of `IDataParameter` implementations for the five standard data providers:

- `System.Data.Odbc.OdbcParameter`
- `System.Data.OleDb.OleDbParameter`
- `System.Data.OracleClient.OracleParameter`
- `System.Data.SqlServerCe.SqlCeParameter`
- `System.Data.SqlClient.SqlParameter`

To use parameters with a text command, you must identify where to substitute the parameter's value within the command. The ODBC, OLE DB, and SQL Server CE data providers support positional parameters; the location of each argument is identified by a question mark (`?`). For example, the following command identifies two locations to be substituted with parameter values:

```
UPDATE Employees SET Title = ? WHERE EmployeeId = ?
```

The SQL Server and Oracle data providers support named parameters, which allow you to identify each parameter location using a name preceded by the at symbol (`@`). Here is the equivalent command using named parameters:

```
UPDATE Employees SET Title = @title WHERE EmployeeId = @id
```

To specify the parameter values to substitute into a command, you must create parameter objects of the correct type and add them to the command object's parameter collection accessible through the `Parameters` property. You can add named parameters in any order, but you must add positional parameters in the same order they appear in the text command. When you execute your command, the value of each parameter is substituted into the command string before the command is executed against the data source. You can create parameter objects in the following ways:

- Use the `IDbCommand.CreateParameter` method.
- Use the `IDbCommand.Parameters.Add` method.
- Use `System.Data.Common.DbProviderFactory`.
- Directly create parameter objects using constructors and configure them using constructor arguments or through setting their properties. (This approach ties you to a specific database provider.)

A parameter object's properties describe everything about a parameter that the command object needs to use the parameter object when executing a command against a data source. Table 9-4 describes the properties that you will use most frequently when configuring parameters.

Table 9-4. *Commonly Used Parameter Properties*

Property	Description
`DbType`	A value of the `System.Data.DbType` enumeration that specifies the type of data contained in the parameter. Commonly used values include `String`, `Int32`, `DateTime`, and `Currency`.
`Direction`	A value from the `System.Data.ParameterDirection` enumeration that indicates the direction in which the parameter is used to pass data. Valid values are `Input`, `InputOutput`, `Output`, and `ReturnValue`.
`IsNullable`	A `bool` that indicates whether the parameter accepts `null` values.
`ParameterName`	A `string` containing the name of the parameter.
`Value`	An `object` containing the value of the parameter.

When using parameters to execute stored procedures, you must provide parameter objects to satisfy each argument required by the stored procedure, including both input and output arguments. You must set the `Direction` property of each parameter as described in Table 9-4; parameters are `Input` by default. If a stored procedure has a return value, the parameter to hold the return value (with a `Direction` property equal to `ReturnValue`) must be the first parameter added to the parameter collection.

The Code

The following example demonstrates the use of parameters in SQL commands. The `ParameterizedCommandExample` method demonstrates the use of parameters in a SQL Server `UPDATE` statement. The `ParameterizedCommandExample` method's arguments include an open `SqlConnection` and two strings. The values of the two strings are substituted into the `UPDATE` command using parameters. The `StoredProcedureExample` method demonstrates the use of parameters to call a stored procedure.

```
using System;
using System.Data;
using System.Data.SqlClient;

namespace Apress.VisualCSharpRecipes.Chapter09
{
    class Recipe09_06
    {
        public static void ParameterizedCommandExample(SqlConnection con,
            string employeeID, string title)
        {
            // Create and configure a new command containing two named parameters.
            using (SqlCommand com = con.CreateCommand())
            {
                com.CommandType = CommandType.Text;
                com.CommandText = "UPDATE Employees SET Title = @title" +
                    " WHERE EmployeeId = @id";

                // Create a SqlParameter object for the title parameter.
                SqlParameter p1 = com.CreateParameter();
                p1.ParameterName = "@title";
                p1.SqlDbType = SqlDbType.VarChar;
                p1.Value = title;
                com.Parameters.Add(p1);

                // Use a shorthand syntax to add the id parameter.
                com.Parameters.Add("@id", SqlDbType.Int).Value = employeeID;

                // Execute the command and process the result.
                int result = com.ExecuteNonQuery();

                if (result == 1)
                {
                    Console.WriteLine("Employee {0} title updated to {1}.",
                        employeeID, title);
                }
                else
                {
                    Console.WriteLine("Employee {0} title not updated.",
                        employeeID);
                }
            }
        }

        public static void StoredProcedureExample(SqlConnection con,
            string category, string year)
        {
```

```
        // Create and configure a new command.
        using (SqlCommand com = con.CreateCommand())
        {
            com.CommandType = CommandType.StoredProcedure;
            com.CommandText = "SalesByCategory";

            // Create a SqlParameter object for the category parameter.
            com.Parameters.Add("@CategoryName", SqlDbType.NVarChar).Value =
                category;

            // Create a SqlParameter object for the year parameter.
            com.Parameters.Add("@OrdYear", SqlDbType.NVarChar).Value = year;

            // Execute the command and process the results.
            using (IDataReader reader = com.ExecuteReader())
            {
                Console.WriteLine("Sales By Category ({0}).", year);

                while (reader.Read())
                {
                    // Display the product details.
                    Console.WriteLine("  {0} = {1}",
                        reader["ProductName"],
                        reader["TotalPurchase"]);
                }
            }
        }
    }

    public static void Main()
    {
        // Create a new SqlConnection object.
        using (SqlConnection con = new SqlConnection())
        {
            // Configure the SqlConnection object's connection string.
            con.ConnectionString = @"Data Source = .\sqlexpress;" +
                "Database = Northwind; Integrated Security=SSPI";

            // Open the database connection and execute the example
            // commands through the connection.
            con.Open();

            ParameterizedCommandExample(con, "5", "Cleaner");
            Console.WriteLine(Environment.NewLine);

            StoredProcedureExample(con, "Seafood", "1999");
            Console.WriteLine(Environment.NewLine);
        }
```

```
            // Wait to continue.
            Console.WriteLine(Environment.NewLine);
            Console.WriteLine("Main method complete. Press Enter.");
            Console.ReadLine();
        }
    }
}
```

9-7. Process the Results of a SQL Query Using a Data Reader

Problem

You need to process the data contained in a `System.Data.IDataReader` instance returned when you execute the `IDbCommand.ExecuteReader` method (discussed in recipe 9-5).

Solution

Use the members of the `IDataReader` instance to move through the rows in the result set sequentially and access the individual data items contained in each row.

How It Works

The `IDataReader` interface represents a data reader, which is a forward-only, read-only mechanism for accessing the results of a SQL query. Each data provider includes a unique `IDataReader` implementation. Here is the list of `IDataReader` implementations for the five standard data providers:

- `System.Data.Odbc.OdbcDataReader`
- `System.Data.OleDb.OleDbDataReader`
- `System.Data.OracleClient.OracleDataReader`
- `System.Data.SqlServerCe.SqlCeDataReader`
- `System.Data.SqlClient.SqlDataReader`

The `IDataReader` interface extends the `System.Data.IDataRecord` interface. Together, these interfaces declare the functionality that provides access to both the data and the structure of the data contained in the result set. Table 9-5 describes some of the commonly used members of the `IDataReader` and `IDataRecord` interfaces.

Table 9-5. Commonly Used Members of Data Reader Classes

Member	Description
Property	
FieldCount	Gets the number of columns in the current row.
IsClosed	Returns true if IDataReader is closed, and false if it's currently open.
Item	Returns an object representing the value of the specified column in the current row. Columns can be specified using a zero-based integer index or a string containing the column name. You must cast the returned value to the appropriate type. This is the indexer for data record and reader classes.
Method	
GetDataTypeName	Gets the name of the data source data type for a specified column.
GetFieldType	Gets a System.Type instance representing the data type of the value contained in the column specified using a zero-based integer index.
GetName	Gets the name of the column specified by using a zero-based integer index.
GetOrdinal	Gets the zero-based column ordinal for the column with the specified name.
GetSchemaTable	Returns a System.Data.DataTable instance that contains metadata describing the columns contained in IDataReader.
IsDBNull	Returns true if the value in the specified column contains a data source null value; otherwise, it returns false.
NextResult	Moves to the next set of results if IDataReader includes multiple result sets because multiple statements were executed. By default, IDataReader is positioned on the first result set.
Read	Advances the reader to the next record. The reader always starts prior to the first record.

In addition to those members listed in Table 9-5, the data reader provides a set of methods for retrieving typed data from the current row. Each of the following methods takes an integer argument that identifies the zero-based index of the column from which the data should be returned: GetBoolean, GetByte, GetBytes, GetChar, GetChars, GetDateTime, GetDecimal, GetDouble, GetFloat, GetGuid, GetInt16, GetInt32, GetInt64, GetString, GetValue, and GetValues.

The SQL Server and Oracle data readers also include methods for retrieving data as data source–specific data types. For example, SqlDataReader includes methods such as GetSqlByte, GetSqlDecimal, and GetSqlMoney; and OracleDataReader includes methods such as GetOracleLob, GetOracleNumber, and GetOracleMonthSpan. Refer to the .NET Framework SDK documentation for more details.

When you have finished with a data reader, you should always call its Close method so that you can use the database connection again. IDataReader extends System.IDisposable, meaning that each data reader class implements the Dispose method. Dispose automatically calls Close, making the using statement a very clean and efficient way of using data readers.

The Code

The following example demonstrates the use of a data reader to process the contents of two result sets returned by executing a batch query containing two SELECT queries. The first result set is enumerated and displayed to the console. The second result set is inspected for metadata information, which is then displayed.

```
using System;
using System.Data;
using System.Data.SqlClient;

namespace Apress.VisualCSharpRecipes.Chapter09
{
    class Recipe09_07
    {
        public static void Main()
        {
            // Create a new SqlConnection object.
            using (SqlConnection con = new SqlConnection())
            {
                // Configure the SqlConnection object's connection string.
                con.ConnectionString = @"Data Source = .\sqlexpress;" +
                    "Database = Northwind; Integrated Security=SSPI";

                // Create and configure a new command.
                using (SqlCommand com = con.CreateCommand())
                {
                    com.CommandType = CommandType.Text;
                    com.CommandText = "SELECT BirthDate,FirstName,LastName FROM "+
                        "Employees ORDER BY BirthDate;SELECT * FROM Employees";

                    // Open the database connection and execute the example.
                    // commands through the connection.
                    con.Open();

                    // Execute the command and obtain a SqlReader.
                    using (SqlDataReader reader = com.ExecuteReader())
                    {
                        // Process the first set of results and display the
                        // content of the result set.
                        Console.WriteLine("Employee Birthdays (By Age).");
```

```
                        while (reader.Read())
                        {
                            Console.WriteLine("  {0,18:D} - {1} {2}",
                                reader.GetDateTime(0),  // Retrieve typed data
                                reader["FirstName"],    // Use string index
                                reader[2]);             // Use ordinal index
                        }
                        Console.WriteLine(Environment.NewLine);

                        // Process the second set of results and display details
                        // about the columns and data types in the result set.
                        reader.NextResult();
                        Console.WriteLine("Employee Table Metadata.");
                        for (int field = 0; field < reader.FieldCount; field++)
                        {
                            Console.WriteLine("  Column Name:{0}  Type:{1}",
                                reader.GetName(field),
                                reader.GetDataTypeName(field));
                        }
                    }
                }
            }

            // Wait to continue.
            Console.WriteLine(Environment.NewLine);
            Console.WriteLine("Main method complete. Press Enter.");
            Console.ReadLine();
        }
    }
}
```

9-8. Obtain an XML Document from a SQL Server Query

Problem

You need to execute a query against a SQL Server database and retrieve the results as XML.

Solution

Specify the `FOR XML` clause in your SQL query to return the results as XML. Execute the command using the `ExecuteXmlReader` method of the `System.Data.SqlClient.SqlCommand` class, which returns a `System.Xml.XmlReader` object through which you can access the returned XML data.

How It Works

SQL Server 2000 (and later versions) provides direct support for XML. You simply need to add the clause `FOR XML AUTO` to the end of a SQL query to indicate that the results should be returned as XML. By default, the XML representation is not a full XML document. Instead, it simply returns the result of each record in a separate element, with all the fields as attributes. For example, the query

```
SELECT CustomerID, CompanyName FROM Customers FOR XML AUTO
```

returns XML with the following structure:

```
<Customers CustomerID="ALFKI" CompanyName="Alfreds Futterkiste"/>
<Customers CustomerID="ANTON" CompanyName="Antonio Moreno Taquería"/>
<Customers CustomerID="GOURL" CompanyName="Gourmet Lanchonetes"/>
```

Alternatively, you can add the `ELEMENTS` keyword to the end of a query to structure the results using nested elements rather than attributes. For example, the query

```
SELECT CustomerID, CompanyName FROM Customers FOR XML AUTO, ELEMENTS
```

returns XML with the following structure:

```
<Customers>
  <CustomerID>ALFKI</CustomerID>
  <CompanyName>Alfreds Futterkiste</CompanyName>
</Customers>
<Customers>
  <CustomerID>ANTON</CustomerID>
  <CompanyName>Antonio Moreno Taquería</CompanyName>
</Customers>
<Customers>
  <CustomerID>GOURL</CustomerID>
  <CompanyName>Gourmet Lanchonetes</CompanyName>
</Customers>
```

■ **Tip** You can also fine-tune the format in more detail using the `FOR XML EXPLICIT` syntax. For example, this allows you to convert some fields to attributes and others to elements. Refer to SQL Server Books Online for more information.

When the `ExecuteXmlReader` command returns, the connection cannot be used for any other commands while `XmlReader` is open. You should process the results as quickly as possible, and you must always close `XmlReader`. Instead of working with `XmlReader` and accessing the data sequentially, you can read the XML data into a `System.Xml.XmlDocument`. This way, all the data is retrieved into memory, and the database connection can be closed. You can then continue to interact with the XML document. (Chapter 6 contains numerous examples of how to use the `XmlReader` and `XmlDocument` classes.)

The Code

The following example demonstrates how to retrieve results as XML using the `FOR XML` clause and the `ExecuteXmlReader` method:

```
using System;
using System.Xml;
using System.Data;
using System.Data.SqlClient;

namespace Apress.VisualCSharpRecipes.Chapter09
{
    class Recipe09_08
    {
        public static void ConnectedExample()
        {
            // Create a new SqlConnection object.
            using (SqlConnection con = new SqlConnection())
            {
                // Configure the SqlConnection object's connection string.
                con.ConnectionString = @"Data Source = .\sqlexpress;" +
                    "Database = Northwind; Integrated Security=SSPI";

                // Create and configure a new command that includes the
                // FOR XML AUTO clause.
                using (SqlCommand com = con.CreateCommand())
                {
                    com.CommandType = CommandType.Text;
                    com.CommandText = "SELECT CustomerID, CompanyName" +
                        " FROM Customers FOR XML AUTO";

                    // Open the database connection.
                    con.Open();

                    // Execute the command and retrieve an XmlReader to access
                    // the results.
                    using (XmlReader reader = com.ExecuteXmlReader())
                    {
                        while (reader.Read())
                        {
                            Console.Write("Element: " + reader.Name);
                            if (reader.HasAttributes)
                            {
                                for (int i = 0; i < reader.AttributeCount; i++)
                                {
                                    reader.MoveToAttribute(i);
                                    Console.Write("  {0}: {1}",
                                        reader.Name, reader.Value);
                                }
```

```
                        // Move the XmlReader back to the element node.
                        reader.MoveToElement();
                        Console.WriteLine(Environment.NewLine);
                    }
                }
            }
        }
    }
}

public static void DisconnectedExample()
{
    XmlDocument doc = new XmlDocument();

    // Create a new SqlConnection object.
    using (SqlConnection con = new SqlConnection())
    {
        // Configure the SqlConnection object's connection string.
        con.ConnectionString = @"Data Source = .\sqlexpress;" +
            "Database = Northwind; Integrated Security=SSPI";

        // Create and configure a new command that includes the
        // FOR XML AUTO clause.
        SqlCommand com = con.CreateCommand();
        com.CommandType = CommandType.Text;
        com.CommandText =
            "SELECT CustomerID, CompanyName FROM Customers FOR XML AUTO";

        // Open the database connection.
        con.Open();

        // Load the XML data into the XmlDocument. Must first create a
        // root element into which to place each result row element.
        XmlReader reader = com.ExecuteXmlReader();
        doc.LoadXml("<results></results>");

        // Create an XmlNode from the next XML element read from the
        // reader.
        XmlNode newNode = doc.ReadNode(reader);

        while (newNode != null)
        {
            doc.DocumentElement.AppendChild(newNode);
            newNode = doc.ReadNode(reader);
        }
    }

    // Process the disconnected XmlDocument.
    Console.WriteLine(doc.OuterXml);
}
```

```
        public static void Main(string[] args)
        {
            ConnectedExample();
            Console.WriteLine(Environment.NewLine);

            DisconnectedExample();
            Console.WriteLine(Environment.NewLine);

            // Wait to continue.
            Console.WriteLine(Environment.NewLine);
            Console.WriteLine("Main method complete. Press Enter.");
            Console.ReadLine();
        }
    }
}
```

9-9. Perform Asynchronous Database Operations Against SQL Server

Problem

You need to execute a query or command against a SQL Server database as a background task while your application continues with other processing.

Solution

Use the `BeginExecuteNonQuery`, `BeginExecuteReader`, or `BeginExecuteXmlReader` method of the `System.Data.SqlClient.SqlCommand` class to start the database operation as a background task. These methods all return a `System.IAsyncResult` object that you can use to determine the operation's status or use thread synchronization to wait for completion. Use the `IAsyncResult` object and the corresponding `EndExecuteNonQuery`, `EndExecuteReader`, or `EndExecuteXmlReader` method to obtain the result of the operation.

■ **Note** Only the `SqlCommand` class supports the asynchronous operations described in this recipe. The equivalent command classes for the Oracle, SQL Server CE, ODBC, and OLE DB data providers do not provide this functionality.

How It Works

You will usually execute operations against databases synchronously, meaning that the calling code blocks until the operation is complete. Synchronous calls are most common because your code will usually require the result of the operation before it can continue. However, sometimes it's useful to execute a database operation asynchronously, meaning that you start the method in a separate thread and then continue with other operations.

■ **Note** To execute asynchronous operations over a `System.Data.SqlClient.SqlConnection` connection, you must specify the value `Asynchronous Processing=true` in its connection string.

The `SqlCommand` class implements the asynchronous execution pattern similar to that discussed in recipe 4-2. As with the general asynchronous execution pattern described in recipe 4-2, the arguments of the asynchronous execution methods (`BeginExecuteNonQuery`, `BeginExecuteReader`, and `BeginExecuteXmlReader`) are the same as those of the synchronous variants (`ExecuteNonQuery`, `ExecuteReader`, and `ExecuteXmlReader`), but they take the following two additional arguments to support asynchronous completion:

- A `System.AsyncCallback` delegate instance that references a method that the runtime will call when the asynchronous operation completes. The method is executed in the context of a thread-pool thread. Passing `null` means that no method is called and you must use another completion mechanism (discussed later in this recipe) to determine when the asynchronous operation is complete.
- An `object` reference that the runtime associates with the asynchronous operation. The asynchronous operation does not use nor have access to this object, but it's available to your code when the operation completes, allowing you to associate useful state information with an asynchronous operation. For example, this object allows you to map results against initiated operations in situations where you initiate many asynchronous operations that use a common callback method to perform completion.

The `EndExecuteNonQuery`, `EndExecuteReader`, and `EndExecuteXmlReader` methods allow you to retrieve the return value of an operation that was executed asynchronously, but you must first determine when it has finished. Here are the four techniques for determining if an asynchronous method has finished:

- `Blocking`: This method stops the execution of the current thread until the asynchronous operation completes execution. In effect, this is much the same as synchronous execution. However, in this case, you have the flexibility to decide exactly when your code enters the blocked state, giving you the opportunity to carry out some additional processing before blocking.
- `Polling`: This method involves repeatedly testing the state of an asynchronous operation to determine whether it's complete. This is a very simple technique and is not particularly efficient from a processing perspective. You should avoid tight loops that consume processor time. It's best to put the polling thread to sleep for a period using `Thread.Sleep` between completion tests. Because polling involves maintaining a loop, the actions of the waiting thread are limited, but you can easily update some kind of progress indicator.

- `Waiting`: This method uses an object derived from the `System.Threading.WaitHandle` class to signal when the asynchronous method completes. Waiting is a more efficient version of polling and in addition allows you to wait for multiple asynchronous operations to complete. You can also specify timeout values to allow your waiting thread to fail if the asynchronous operation takes too long, or if you want to periodically update a status indicator.
- `Callback`: This a method that the runtime calls when an asynchronous operation completes. The calling code does not need to take any steps to determine when the asynchronous operation is complete and is free to continue with other processing. Callbacks provide the greatest flexibility, but also introduce the greatest complexity, especially if you have many concurrently active asynchronous operations that all use the same callback. In such cases, you must use appropriate state objects to match completed methods against those you initiated.

■ **Caution** When using the asynchronous capabilities of the SQL Server data provider, you must ensure that your code does not inadvertently dispose of objects that are still being used by other threads. Pay particular attention to `SqlConnection` and `SqlCommand` objects.

The Code

Recipe 4-2 provides examples of all of the completion techniques summarized in the preceding list. The following example demonstrates the use of an asynchronous call to execute a stored procedure on a SQL Server database. The code uses a callback to process the returned result set.

```
using System;
using System.Data;
using System.Threading;
using System.Data.SqlClient;

namespace Apress.VisualCSharpRecipes.Chapter09
{
    class Recipe09_09
    {
        // A method to handle asynchronous completion using callbacks.
        public static void CallbackHandler(IAsyncResult result)
        {
            // Obtain a reference to the SqlCommand used to initiate the
            // asynchronous operation.
            using (SqlCommand cmd = result.AsyncState as SqlCommand)
            {
                // Obtain the result of the stored procedure.
                using (SqlDataReader reader = cmd.EndExecuteReader(result))
                {
```

```
                // Display the results of the stored procedure to the console.
                lock (Console.Out)
                {
                    Console.WriteLine(
                        "Price of the Ten Most Expensive Products:");

                    while (reader.Read())
                    {
                        // Display the product details.
                        Console.WriteLine("  {0} = {1}",
                            reader["TenMostExpensiveProducts"],
                            reader["UnitPrice"]);
                    }
                }
            }
        }
    }

    public static void Main()
    {
        // Create a new SqlConnection object.
        using (SqlConnection con = new SqlConnection())
        {
            // Configure the SqlConnection object's connection string.
            // You must specify Asynchronous Processing=true to support
            // asynchronous operations over the connection.
            con.ConnectionString = @"Data Source = .\sqlexpress;" +
                "Database = Northwind; Integrated Security=SSPI;" +
                "Asynchronous Processing=true";

            // Create and configure a new command to run a stored procedure.
            // Do not wrap it in a using statement because the asynchronous
            // completion handler will dispose of the SqlCommand object.
            SqlCommand cmd = con.CreateCommand();
            cmd.CommandType = CommandType.StoredProcedure;
            cmd.CommandText = "Ten Most Expensive Products";

            // Open the database connection and execute the command
            // asynchronously. Pass the reference to the SqlCommand
            // used to initiate the asynchronous operation.
            con.Open();
            cmd.BeginExecuteReader(CallbackHandler, cmd);
```

```
                // Continue with other processing.
                for (int count = 0; count < 10; count++)
                {
                    lock (Console.Out)
                    {
                        Console.WriteLine("{0} : Continue processing...",
                            DateTime.Now.ToString("HH:mm:ss.ffff"));
                    }
                    Thread.Sleep(500);
                }
            }

            // Wait to continue.
            Console.WriteLine(Environment.NewLine);
            Console.WriteLine("Main method complete. Press Enter.");
            Console.ReadLine();
        }
    }
}
```

9-10. Write Database-Independent Code

Problem

You need to write code that can be configured to work against any relational database supported by an ADO.NET data provider.

Solution

Program to the ADO.NET data provider interfaces in the `System.Data` namespace, as opposed to the concrete implementations, and do not rely on features and data types that are unique to specific database implementations. Use factory classes and methods to instantiate the data provider objects you need to use.

How It Works

Using a specific data provider implementation (the SQL Server data provider, for example) simplifies your code, and may be appropriate if you need to support only a single type of database or require access to specific features provided by that data provider, such as the asynchronous execution for SQL Server detailed in recipe 9-9. However, if you program your application against a specific data provider implementation, you will need to rewrite and test those sections of your code if you want to use a different data provider at some point in the future.

Table 9-6 contains a summary of the main interfaces you must program against when writing generic ADO.NET code that will work with any relational database's data provider. The table also explains how to create objects of the appropriate type that implement the interface. Many of the recipes in this chapter demonstrate the use of ADO.NET data provider interfaces over specific implementation, as highlighted in the table.

Table 9-6. Data Provider Interfaces

Interface	Description	Demonstrated In
`IDbConnection`	Represents a connection to a relational database. You must program the logic to create a connection object of the appropriate type based on your application's configuration information, or use the `DbProviderFactory.CreateConnection` factory method (discussed in this recipe).	Recipe 9-1
`IDbCommand`	Represents a SQL command that is issued to a relational database. You can create `IDbCommand` objects of the appropriate type using the `IDbConnection.CreateCommand` or `DbProviderFactory.CreateCommand` factory method.	Recipe 9-5
`IDataParameter`	Represents a parameter to an `IDbCommand` object. You can create `IDataParameter` objects of the correct type using the `IDbCommand.CreateParameter`, `IDbCommand.Parameters.Add`, or `DbProviderFactory.CreateParameter` factory method.	Recipe 9-6
`IDataReader`	Represents the result set of a database query and provides access to the contained rows and columns. An object of the correct type will be returned when you call the `IDbCommand.ExecuteReader` method.	Recipes 9-5 and 9-6
`IDbDataAdapter`	Represents the set of commands used to fill a `System.Data.DataSet` from a relational database and to update the database based on changes to the `DataSet`. You must program the logic to create a data adapter object of the appropriate type based on your application's configuration information, or use the `DbProviderFactory.CreateAdapter` factory method (discussed in this recipe).	

The `System.Data.Common.DbProviderFactory` class provides a set of factory methods for creating all types of data provider objects, making it very useful for implementing generic database code. Most important, `DbProviderFactory` provides a mechanism for obtaining an initial `IDbConnection` instance, which is the critical starting point for writing generic ADO.NET code. Each of the standard data provider implementations (except the SQL Server CE data provider) includes a unique factory class derived from `DbProviderFactory`. Here is the list of `DbProviderFactory` subclasses:

- System.Data.Odbc.OdbcFactory
- System.Data.OleDb.OleDbFactory
- System.Data.OracleClient.OracleClientFactory
- System.Data.SqlClient.SqlClientFactory

You can obtain an instance of the appropriate DbProviderFactory subclass using the DbProviderFactories class, which is effectively a factory of factories. Each data provider factory is described by configuration information in the machine.config file, similar to that shown here for the SQL Server data adapter. This can be changed or overridden by application-specific configuration information if required.

```
<configuration>
 <system.data>
    <DbProviderFactories>
      <add name="SqlClient Data Provider" invariant="System.Data.SqlClient" ~CCC
description=".Net Framework Data Provider for SqlServer" type=  ~CCC
"System.Data.SqlClient.SqlClientFactory, System.Data, Version=2.0.0.0, ~CCC
Culture=neutral, PublicKeyToken=b77a5c561934e089" />
      <add name="Odbc Data Provider" ... />
      <add name="OleDb Data Provider" ... />
      <add name="OracleClient Data Provider" ... />
      <add name="SQL Server CE Data ... />
    </DbProviderFactories>
  </system.data>
</configuration>
```

You can enumerate the available data provider factories by calling DbProviderFactories.GetFactoryClasses, which returns a System.Data.DataTable containing the following columns:

- Name, which contains a human-readable name for the provider factory. Taken from the name attribute in the configuration information.
- Description, which contains a human-readable description for the provider factory. Taken from the description attribute of the configuration information.
- InvariantName, which contains the unique name used to refer to the data provider factory programmatically. Taken from the invariant attribute of the configuration information.
- AssemblyQualifiedName, which contains the fully qualified name of the DbProviderFactory class for the data provider. Taken from the type attribute of the configuration information.

Normally, you would allow the provider to be selected at install time or the first time the application is run, and then store the settings as user or application configuration data. The most important piece of information is the InvariantName, which you pass to the DbProviderFactories.GetFactory method to obtain the DbProviderFactory implementation you will use to create your IDbConnection instances.

The Code

The following example demonstrates the enumeration of all data providers configured for the local machine and application. It then uses the `DbProviderFactories` class to instantiate a `DbProviderFactory` object (actually a `SqlClientFactory`) from which it creates the appropriate `IDbConnection`. It then uses the factory methods of the data provider interfaces to create other required objects, resulting in code that is completely generic.

```
using System;
using System.Data;
using System.Data.Common;

namespace Apress.VisualCSharpRecipes.Chapter09
{
    class Recipe09_10
    {
        public static void Main(string[] args)
        {
            // Obtain the list of ADO.NET data providers registered in the
            // machine and application configuration files.
            using (DataTable providers = DbProviderFactories.GetFactoryClasses())
            {
                // Enumerate the set of data providers and display details.
                Console.WriteLine("Available ADO.NET Data Providers:");
                foreach (DataRow prov in providers.Rows)
                {
                    Console.WriteLine(" Name:{0}", prov["Name"]);
                    Console.WriteLine("   Description:{0}",
                        prov["Description"]);
                    Console.WriteLine("   Invariant Name:{0}",
                        prov["InvariantName"]);
                }
            }

            // Obtain the DbProviderFactory for SQL Server. The provider to use
            // could be selected by the user or read from a configuration file.
            // In this case, we simply pass the invariant name.
            DbProviderFactory factory =
                DbProviderFactories.GetFactory("System.Data.SqlClient");

            // Use the DbProviderFactory to create the initial IDbConnection, and
            // then the data provider interface factory methods for other objects.
            using (IDbConnection con = factory.CreateConnection())
            {
                // Normally, read the connection string from secure storage.
                // See recipe 9-3. In this case, use a default value.
                con.ConnectionString = @"Data Source = .\sqlexpress;" +
                    "Database = Northwind; Integrated Security=SSPI";
```

```
                // Create and configure a new command.
                using (IDbCommand com = con.CreateCommand())
                {
                    com.CommandType = CommandType.StoredProcedure;
                    com.CommandText = "Ten Most Expensive Products";

                    // Open the connection.
                    con.Open();

                    // Execute the command and process the results.
                    using (IDataReader reader = com.ExecuteReader())
                    {
                        Console.WriteLine(Environment.NewLine);
                        Console.WriteLine("Price of the Ten Most" +
                            " Expensive Products.");

                        while (reader.Read())
                        {
                            // Display the product details.
                            Console.WriteLine("  {0} = {1}",
                                reader["TenMostExpensiveProducts"],
                                reader["UnitPrice"]);
                        }
                    }
                }
            }

            // Wait to continue.
            Console.WriteLine(Environment.NewLine);
            Console.WriteLine("Main method complete. Press Enter.");
            Console.ReadLine();
        }
    }
}
```

9-11. Discover All Instances of SQL Server on Your Network

Problem

You need to obtain a list of all instances of SQL Server that are accessible on the network.

Solution

Use the `GetDataSources` method of the `System.Data.Sql.SqlDataSourceEnumerator` class.

How It Works

The SqlDataSourceEnumerator class makes it easy to enumerate the SQL Server instances accessible on the network. You simply obtain the singleton SqlDataSourceEnumerator instance via the static property SqlDataSourceEnumerator.Instance and call its GetDataSources method. The GetDataSources method returns a System.Data.DataTable that contains a set of System.Data.DataRow objects. Each DataRow represents a single SQL Server instance and contains the following columns:

- ServerName, which contains the name of the server where the SQL Server instance is hosted
- InstanceName, which contains the name of the SQL Server instance or the empty string if the SQL Server is the default instance
- IsClustered, which indicates whether the SQL Server instance is part of a cluster
- Version, which contains the version of the SQL Server instance

The Code

The following example demonstrates the use of the SqlDataSourceEnumerator class to discover and display details of all SQL Server instances accessible (and visible) on the network. The IsClustered and Version columns may be blank for some versions of SQL Server.

```
using System;
using System.Data;
using System.Data.Sql;

namespace Apress.VisualCSharpRecipes.Chapter09
{
    class Recipe09_11
    {
        public static void Main(string[] args)
        {
            // Obtain the DataTable of SQL Server instances.
            using (DataTable SqlSources =
                SqlDataSourceEnumerator.Instance.GetDataSources())
            {
                // Enumerate the set of SQL Servers and display details.
                Console.WriteLine("Discover SQL Server Instances:");
                foreach (DataRow source in SqlSources.Rows)
                {
                    Console.WriteLine(" Server Name:{0}", source["ServerName"]);
                    Console.WriteLine("   Instance Name:{0}",
                        source["InstanceName"]);
                    Console.WriteLine("   Is Clustered:{0}",
                        source["IsClustered"]);
                    Console.WriteLine("   Version:{0}", source["Version"]);
                }
            }
```

```
            // Wait to continue.
            Console.WriteLine(Environment.NewLine);
            Console.WriteLine("Main method complete. Press Enter.");
            Console.ReadLine();
        }
    }
}
```

9-12. Create an In-Memory Cache

Problem

You need to create an in-memory cache of part of the database.

Solution

Use `System.Data.DataSet` to represent the data and `System.Data.SqlClient.SqlDataAdapter` to read and sync data with the database.

How It Works

The `System.Data.DataSet` class contains one or more instances of `System.Data.DataTable`, each of which contains instances of `System.Data.DataRow`, representing data rows from the database. The `SqlDataAdapter` class acts as the bridge between the database and the `DataSet`, allowing you to populate the `DataSet` with data and write back any changes to the database when you are done. The sequence for using a `DataSet` is as follows:

1. Create a `SqlConnection` to your database as normal (see recipe 9-1).
2. Create a new instance of `DataSet` using the default constructor.
3. Create a new instance of `SqlDataAdapter`, passing in a query string for the data you require and the `SqlConnection` you created in step 1 as constructor arguments.
4. Create an instance of `SqlCommandBuilder`, passing in the `SqlDataAdapter` you created.
5. Call the `SqlDataAdapter.Fill` instance method, passing the `DataSet` you created in step 2 as a method argument.
6. Use the `DataSet` to access the `DataTables` contained within—read and modify data as required.
7. Call the `SqlDataAdapter.Update` method to write any changes back to the database.

To create a new row in a table, call the `DataTable.NewRow` instance method to obtain an instance of `DataRow` that has the same schema as the `DataTable`. The new row is not automatically added to the table when you call NewRow—call DataTable.Rows.Add once you have set the values for the row. Changes that you make to the data in the DataSet are not written back to the database until you call the SqpDataAdapter.Update method.

The Code

The following example creates a DataSet and fills it with the contents of the Region table of the Northwind sample database. The DataSet contains one DataTable, whose schema and contents are printed out. A new record is added and an existing one modified before the changes are written back to the database.

```
using System;
using System.Data;
using System.Data.SqlClient;

namespace Apress.VisualCSharpRecipes.Chapter09
{
    class Recipe09_12
    {
        static void Main(string[] args)
        {

            // Create a new SqlConnection object.
            using (SqlConnection con = new SqlConnection())
            {
                // Configure the SqlConnection object's connection string.
                con.ConnectionString = @"Data Source = .\sqlexpress;" +
                    "Database = Northwind; Integrated Security=SSPI";

                // Open the database connection.
                con.Open();

                // Create the query string.
                string query = "SELECT * from Region";

                // Create the data set.
                DataSet dataset = new DataSet();

                // Create the SQL data adapter.
                SqlDataAdapter adapter = new SqlDataAdapter(query, con);
                // Create the command builder so we can do modifications.
                SqlCommandBuilder commbuilder = new SqlCommandBuilder(adapter);

                // Populate the data set from the database.
                adapter.Fill(dataset);
```

```
                // Print details of the schema.
                Console.WriteLine("\nSchema for table");
                DataTable table = dataset.Tables[0];
                foreach (DataColumn col in table.Columns)
                {
                    Console.WriteLine("Column: {0} Type: {1}",
                       col.ColumnName, col.DataType);
                }

                // Enumerate the data we have received.
                Console.WriteLine("\nData in table");
                foreach (DataRow row in table.Rows)
                {
                    Console.WriteLine("Data {0} {1}", row[0], row[1]);
                }

                // Create a new row.
                DataRow newrow = table.NewRow();
                newrow["RegionID"] = 5;
                newrow["RegionDescription"] = "Central";
                table.Rows.Add(newrow);

                // Modify an existing row.
                table.Rows[0]["RegionDescription"] = "North Eastern";

                // Enumerate the cached data again.
                // Enumerate the data we have received.
                Console.WriteLine("\nData in (modified) table");
                foreach (DataRow row in table.Rows)
                {
                    Console.WriteLine("Data {0} {1}", row[0], row[1]);
                }

                // Write the data back to the database.
                adapter.Update(dataset);
            }

            // Wait to continue.
            Console.WriteLine(Environment.NewLine);
            Console.WriteLine("Main method complete. Press Enter.");
            Console.ReadLine();
        }
    }
}
```

Running the example produces the following results:

```
Schema for table

Column: RegionID Type: System.Int32

Column: RegionDescription Type: System.String


Data in table

Data 1 Eastern

Data 2 Western

Data 3 Northern

Data 4 Southern


Data in (modified) table

Data 1 North Eastern

Data 2 Western

Data 3 Northern

Data 4 Southern

Data 5 Central



Main method complete. Press Enter.
```

9-13. Create a DataSet Programmatically

Problem

You need to work with in-memory data without a database.

Solution

Create an instance of `System.Sql.DataSet` and manually populate it with instances of `System.Data.Datatable`. Create a schema for each table and create rows to represent data elements.

How It Works

In the previous recipe, we demonstrated how to use the `DataSet` and `DataTable` classes as part of a memory cache, in order to achieve disconnected data manipulation. However, you can create instances of these classes to represent data programmatically by calling constructors for the classes directly. The example code for this recipe illustrates how to do this in order to create the same kind of `DataSet` and `DataTable` that we used previously.

The Code

The following code creates a `DataSet` that contains a single `DataTable` and populates it with instances of `DataRow`. Once populated, the same queries, modifications, and additions are performed upon it as in the previous recipe.

```
using System;
sing System.Data;

namespace Apress.VisualCSharpRecipes.Chapter09
{
    class Recipe09_13
    {
        static void Main(string[] args)
        {
            // Create the data set.
            DataSet dataset = new DataSet();

            // Create the table and add it to the data set.
            DataTable table = new DataTable("Regions");
            dataset.Tables.Add(table);

            // Create the colums for the table.
            table.Columns.Add("RegionID", typeof(int));
            table.Columns.Add("RegionDescription", typeof(string));
```

```
            // Populate the table.
            string[] regions = { "Eastern", "Western", "Northern", "Southern" };
            for (int i = 0; i < regions.Length; i++)
            {
                DataRow row = table.NewRow();
                row["RegionID"] = i + 1;
                row["RegionDescription"] = regions[i];
                table.Rows.Add(row);
            }

            // Print details of the schema.
            Console.WriteLine("\nSchema for table");
            foreach (DataColumn col in table.Columns)
            {
                Console.WriteLine("Column: {0} Type: {1}",
                    col.ColumnName, col.DataType);
            }

            // Enumerate the data we have received.
            Console.WriteLine("\nData in table");
            foreach (DataRow row in table.Rows)
            {
                Console.WriteLine("Data {0} {1}", row[0], row[1]);
            }

            // Create a new row.
            DataRow newrow = table.NewRow();
            newrow["RegionID"] = 5;
            newrow["RegionDescription"] = "Central";
            table.Rows.Add(newrow);

            // Modify an existing row.
            table.Rows[0]["RegionDescription"] = "North Eastern";

            // Enumerate the cached data again.
            // Enumerate the data we have received.
            Console.WriteLine("\nData in (modified) table");
            foreach (DataRow row in table.Rows)
            {
                Console.WriteLine("Data {0} {1}", row[0], row[1]);
            }

            // Wait to continue.
            Console.WriteLine(Environment.NewLine);
            Console.WriteLine("Main method complete. Press Enter.");
            Console.ReadLine();
        }
    }
}
```

The program produces the following output:

```
Schema for table
Column: RegionID Type: System.Int32
Column: RegionDescription Type: System.String


Data in table
Data 1 Eastern
Data 2 Western
Data 3 Northern
Data 4 Southern


Data in (modified) table
Data 1 North Eastern
Data 2 Western
Data 3 Northern
Data 4 Southern
Data 5 Central



Main method complete. Press Enter.
```

9-14. Perform a LINQ Query

Problem

You need to use LINQ to query a database.

Solution

Create or obtain an instance of DataTable (see recipes 9-12 and 9-13) and call the AsEnumerable instance method to obtain an IEnumerable<DataRow>, which can be used as a data source for LINQ queries.

How It Works

LINQ performs queries on the IEnumerable<> type, which you can obtain from instances of DataTable using the AsEnumerable instance method. When using SQLDataAdapter to populate instances of DataTable with data (see recipe 9-12), remember that you are working with cached data that will not reflect changes made to the database. See Chapter 16 for recipes that demonstrate LINQ features.

The Code

The following example creates a DataSet that contains a DataTable with all of the rows of the Northwind Region table, and then performs a LINQ query using the DataTable as the data source:

```
using System;
using System.Collections.Generic;
using System.Linq;
using System.Text;
using System.Data;
using System.Data.SqlClient;

namespace Apress.VisualCSharpRecipes.Chapter09
{
    class Recipe09_14
    {
        static void Main(string[] args)
        {

            // Create a new SqlConnection object.
            using (SqlConnection con = new SqlConnection())
            {
                // Configure the SqlConnection object's connection string.
                con.ConnectionString = @"Data Source = .\sqlexpress;" +
                    "Database = Northwind; Integrated Security=SSPI";

                // Open the database connection.
                con.Open();

                // Create the query string.
                string query = "SELECT * from Region";

                // Create the data set.
                DataSet dataset = new DataSet();
```

```
                // Create the SQL data adapter.
                SqlDataAdapter adapter = new SqlDataAdapter(query, con);
                // Create the command builder so we can do modifications.
                SqlCommandBuilder commbuilder = new SqlCommandBuilder(adapter);

                // Populate the data set from the database.
                adapter.Fill(dataset);

                // Obtain the data table.
                DataTable table = dataset.Tables[0];

                // Perform the LINQ query.
                IEnumerable<string> result = from e in table.AsEnumerable()
                                             where e.Field<int>(0) < 3
                                             select e.Field<string>(1);

                // Enumerate the results of the LINQ query.
                foreach (string str in result)
                {
                    Console.WriteLine("Result: {0}", str);
                }
            }

            // Wait to continue.
            Console.WriteLine(Environment.NewLine);
            Console.WriteLine("Main method complete. Press Enter.");
            Console.ReadLine();
        }
    }
}
```

Running the program gives the following results:

```
Result: Eastern

Result: Western




Main method complete. Press Enter.
```

9-15. Perform a LINQ Query with Entity Types

Problem

You need to work with types when using LINQ.

Solution

Define and annotate types with the `Table` and `Column` annotations and use `System.Data.Linq.DataContext` to access the data in your database.

How It Works

LINQ includes support for entity classes, which map the schema from your database into .NET types. You create an entity type by defining a partial class with members representing columns in a given database table and apply annotations from the `System.Data.Linq.Mapping` namespace to give the .NET Framework details of how to map from the table to instances of your entity type.

■ **Tip** Visual Studio can automatically create types for you. Select the Add a New Item option for your project, and then select LINQ to SQL Classes to start a wizard that will generate the source files you require.

The first annotation to apply is `Table`, which creates the relationship between the partial class you have defined and the table in the database—this annotation takes one argument, which is, not surprisingly, the name of the table in question. You must then define one member for each column in the table (ensuring that the member type matches the schema type for the database table), and apply the `Column` annotation. For the `Region` table in the `Northwind` database, we would create a class like this:

```
[Table(Name = "Region")]
public partial class Region
{
    [Column]
    public int RegionID;
    [Column]
    public string RegionDescription;
}
```

To use the entity type, create an instance of `System.Data.Linq.DataContext`, passing in a `SqlConnection` to your database as the constructor argument. You then call the `DataContext.GetTable<>` instance method using your entity class as the type annotation—for example:

```
Table<Region> regionstable = context.GetTable<Region>();
```

The result from the `GetTable` method is a strongly typed instance of `System.Data.Linq.Table`, which you can use as the data source for a LINQ query. In the clauses of the query, you can refer to the members of your entity type to perform filters and select results—see the code for this recipe for a demonstration.

■ **Tip** LINQ entity types have a lot of features beyond what we have demonstrated here—see the .NET documentation for further details. The LINQ to SQL home page is a good starting point: `http://msdn.microsoft.com/en-us/library/bb386976(VS.100).aspx`.

The Code

The following example defines the type `Region` to represent rows in the `Northwind Region` table. A `DataContext` is created to access the data, and the `Region` table is used as the basis for a LINQ query, returning an `IEnumeration<Region>` as the result.

■ **Note** You must add the `System.Data.Linq.dll` assembly to your project in order to use the `System.Data.Linq` and `System.Data.Linq.Mapping` namespaces.

```
using System;
using System.Collections.Generic;
using System.Linq;
using System.Text;
using System.Data;
using System.Data.SqlClient;
using System.Data.Linq;
using System.Data.Linq.Mapping;

namespace Apress.VisualCSharpRecipes.Chapter09
{
    [Table(Name = "Region")]
    public partial class Region
    {
        [Column]
        public int RegionID;
        [Column]
        public string RegionDescription;
    }
    class Recipe09_15
    {
        static void Main(string[] args)
        {
```

```
            // Create a new SqlConnection object.
            using (SqlConnection con = new SqlConnection())
            {
                // Configure the SqlConnection object's connection string.
                con.ConnectionString = @"Data Source = .\sqlexpress;" +
                    "Database = Northwind; Integrated Security=SSPI";

                // Open the database connection.
                con.Open();

                // Create the data context.
                DataContext context = new DataContext(con);

                // Get the table we are interested in.
                Table<Region> regionstable = context.GetTable<Region>();

                IEnumerable<Region> result = from e in regionstable
                                             where e.RegionID < 3
                                             select e;
                foreach (Region res in result)
                {
                    Console.WriteLine("RegionID {0} Descr: {1}",
                                res.RegionID, res.RegionDescription);
                }
            }

            // Wait to continue.
            Console.WriteLine(Environment.NewLine);
            Console.WriteLine("Main method complete. Press Enter.");
            Console.ReadLine();
        }
    }
}
```

9-16. Compare LINQ DataSet Results

Problem

You need to compare the results of a LINQ query.

Solution

Use the `Union`, `Intersect`, or `Except` extension method to compare the results of two LINQ queries.

How It Works

The default result of a LINQ query on a DataSet is an IEnumerable<DataRow>, and LINQ provides extension methods that operate on this result type to allow you to compare results.

■ **Tip** See Chapter 16 for more information about LINQ extension methods, recipes for using them, and creating custom extension methods that you can apply to your own data types.

The three extension methods are Union, Intersect, and Except. In all three cases, you call the extension method on one result and supply another as the method argument—for example:

```
IEnumerable<DataRow> result1 = ...LINQ query on a DataSet...
IEnumerable<DataRow> result2 = ...LINQ query on a DataSet...
IEnumerable<DataRow> union = result1.Union(result2)
```

The Union method combines the contents of the two IEnumerable<DataRow> instances. The Intersect method returns just those rows that exist in both enumerations. The Except method returns all of the rows in the first enumeration except those that also exist in the second enumeration.

The result of these methods is another IEnumerable<DataRow>, meaning that you can use the result to enumerate the data rows or as the basis for a further LINQ query, and you can use the same extension methods to compare the result against another IEnumerable<DataRow>.

The Code

The following program performs two queries against the same table and then uses the Union, Intersect, and Except methods to compare the results:

```
using System;
using System.Collections.Generic;
using System.Linq;
using System.Text;
using System.Data;
using System.Data.SqlClient;

namespace Apress.VisualCSharpRecipes.Chapter09
{
    class Recipe09_16
    {
        static void Main(string[] args)
        {

            // Create a new SqlConnection object.
            using (SqlConnection con = new SqlConnection())
            {
```

```
// Configure the SqlConnection object's connection string.
con.ConnectionString = @"Data Source = .\sqlexpress;" +
    "Database = Northwind; Integrated Security=SSPI";

// Open the database connection.
con.Open();

// Create the query string.
string query = "SELECT * from Region";

// Create the data set.
DataSet dataset = new DataSet();

// Create the SQL data adapter.
SqlDataAdapter adapter = new SqlDataAdapter(query, con);
// Create the command builder so we can do modifications.
SqlCommandBuilder commbuilder = new SqlCommandBuilder(adapter);

// Populate the data set from the database.
adapter.Fill(dataset);

// Obtain the data table.
DataTable table = dataset.Tables[0];

// Perform the first LINQ query.
IEnumerable<DataRow> result1 = from e in table.AsEnumerable()
                               where e.Field<int>(0) < 3
                               select e;

// Enumerate the results of the first LINQ query.
Console.WriteLine("Results from first LINQ query");
foreach (DataRow row in result1)
{
    Console.WriteLine("ID: {0} Name: {1}",
        row.Field<int>(0), row.Field<string>(1));
}

// Perform the first LINQ query.
IEnumerable<DataRow> result2 = from e in table.AsEnumerable()
                               let name = e.Field<string>(1)
                               where name.StartsWith("North")
                                 || name.StartsWith("East")
                               select e;
```

```
                // Enumerate the results of the first LINQ query.
                Console.WriteLine("\nResults from second LINQ query");
                foreach (DataRow row in result2)
                {
                    Console.WriteLine("ID: {0} Name: {1}",
                        row.Field<int>(0), row.Field<string>(1));
                }
                IEnumerable<DataRow> union = result1.Union(result2);
                // Enumerate the results.
                Console.WriteLine("\nResults from union");
                foreach (DataRow row in union)
                {
                    Console.WriteLine("ID: {0} Name: {1}",
                        row.Field<int>(0), row.Field<string>(1));
                }


                IEnumerable<DataRow> intersect = result1.Intersect(result2);
                // Enumerate the results.
                Console.WriteLine("\nResults from intersect");
                foreach (DataRow row in intersect)
                {
                    Console.WriteLine("ID: {0} Name: {1}",
                        row.Field<int>(0), row.Field<string>(1));
                }

                IEnumerable<DataRow> except = result1.Except(result2);
                // Enumerate the results.
                Console.WriteLine("\nResults from except");
                foreach (DataRow row in except)
                {
                    Console.WriteLine("ID: {0} Name: {1}",
                        row.Field<int>(0), row.Field<string>(1));
                }

            }

            // Wait to continue.
            Console.WriteLine(Environment.NewLine);
            Console.WriteLine("Main method complete. Press Enter.");
            Console.ReadLine();
        }
    }
}
```

Running the sample program gives the following results:

```
Results from first LINQ query

ID: 1 Name: Eastern

ID: 2 Name: Western


Results from second LINQ query

ID: 1 Name: Eastern

ID: 3 Name: Northern


Results from union

ID: 1 Name: Eastern

ID: 2 Name: Western

ID: 3 Name: Northern


Results from intersect

ID: 1 Name: Eastern


Results from except

ID: 2 Name: Western



Main method complete. Press Enter.
```

CHAPTER 10

■ ■ ■

Networking

The Microsoft .NET Framework includes a full set of classes for network programming. These classes support low-level network programming tasks like querying the state of network interfaces and socket-based programming with Transmission Control Protocol/Internet Protocol (TCP/IP) to higher-level tasks like downloading files and HTML pages from the Web over Hypertext Transfer Protocol (HTTP). You can even build fully distributed applications using distributed objects or service-oriented approaches.

Included in the release of .NET Framework 3.0 was Windows Communication Foundation (WCF), a unified programming model for building service-oriented applications. Although earlier technologies are still available, WCF is generally seen as a replacement for technologies like .NET Remoting and ASP.NET Web Services, and also provides a flexible unified interface through which to access many other types of distributed communications, like message queues.

The recipes in this chapter describe how to do the following:

- Obtain configuration and network statistic information about the network interfaces on a computer as well as detect when network configuration changes occur (recipes 10-1 and 10-2)
- Download files from File Transfer Protocol (FTP) and HTTP servers (recipes 10-3, 10-4, and 10-6)
- Respond to HTTP requests from within your application (recipe 10-5)
- Send e-mail messages with attachments using Simple Mail Transfer Protocol (SMTP) (recipe 10-7)
- Use the Domain Name System (DNS) to resolve a host name into an Internet Protocol (IP) address (recipe 10-8)
- Ping an IP address to determine whether it is accessible and calculate round-trip communication speeds by sending it an Internet Control Message Protocol (ICMP) `Echo` request (recipe 10-9)
- Communicate between programs through the direct use of TCP in both synchronous and asynchronous communication models (recipes 10-10 and 10-11)
- Communicate using User Datagram Protocol (UDP) datagrams where connection-oriented and reliable TCP represents unnecessary overhead (recipe 10-12)

- Create a SOAP-based web service (recipe 10-13)
- Generate a WCF service proxy dynamically (recipe 10-14)
- Parse the contents of an Atom or RSS feed (recipe 10-15)
- Manipulate uniform resource locators (URIs) (recipe 10-16)

■ **Tip** A number of the recipes in this chapter include a client and a server component that must both be running for the recipe to work correctly. Where this is the case, the client and server code are contained in separate projects. To run these recipes from within Visual Studio, set the server project as the startup project and run it normally. Once the server is running, right-click the client project in Solution Explorer, click Debug on the context menu, and then click "Start new instance."

10-1. Obtain Information About the Local Network Interface

Problem

You need to obtain information about the network adapters and network configuration of the local machine.

Solution

Call the static method `GetAllNetworkInterfaces` of the `System.Net.NetworkInformation.NetworkInterface` class to get an array of objects derived from the abstract class `NetworkInterface`. Each object represents a network interface available on the local machine. Use the members of each `NetworkInterface` object to retrieve configuration information and network statistics for that interface.

How It Works

The `System.Net.NetworkInformation` namespace provides easy access to information about network configuration and statistics. The primary means of retrieving network information are the properties and methods of the `NetworkInterface` class. You do not instantiate `NetworkInterface` objects directly. Instead, you call the static method `NetworkInterface.GetAllNetworkInterfaces`, which returns an array of `NetworkInterface` objects. Each object represents a single network interface on the local machine. You can then obtain network information and statistics about the interface using the `NetworkInterface` members described in Table 10-1.

■ **Tip** The `System.Net.NetworkInformation.IPGlobalProperties` class also provides access to useful information about the network configuration of the local computer.

Table 10-1. Members of the NetworkInterface Class

Member	Description
Properties	
`Description`	Gets a `string` that provides a general description of the interface.
`Id`	Gets a `string` that contains the identifier of the interface.
`IsReceiveOnly`	Gets a `bool` indicating whether the interface can only receive or can both send and receive data.
`Name`	Gets a `string` containing the name of the interface.
`NetworkInterfaceType`	Gets a value from the `System.Net.NetworkInformation.NetworkInterfaceType` enumeration that identifies the type of interface. Common values include `Ethernet`, `FastEthernetT`, and `Loopback`.
`OperationalStatus`	Gets a value from the `System.Net.NetworkInformation.OperationalStatus` enumeration that identifies the status of the interface. Common values include `Down` and `Up`.
`Speed`	Gets a `long` that identifies the speed (in bits per second) of the interface as reported by the adapter, not based on dynamic calculation.
`SupportsMulticast`	Gets a `bool` indicating whether the interface is enabled to receive multicast packets.
Methods	
`GetIPProperties`	Returns a `System.Net.NetworkInformation.IPInterfaceProperties` object that provides access to the TCP/IP configuration information for the interface. Properties of the `IPInterfaceProperties` object provide access to WINS, DNS, gateway, and IP address configuration.

Member	Description
GetIPv4Statistics	Returns a System.Net.NetworkInformation.IPv4InterfaceStatistics object that provides access to the TCP/IP v4 statistics for the interface. The properties of the IPv4InterfaceStatistics object provide access to information about bytes sent and received, packets sent and received, discarded packets, and packets with errors.
GetPhysicalAddress	Returns a System.Net.NetworkInformation.PhysicalAddress object that provides access to the physical address of the interface. You can obtain the physical address as a byte array using the method PhysicalAddress.GetAddressBytes or as a string using PhysicalAddress.ToString.
Supports	Returns a bool indicating whether the interface supports a specified protocol. You specify the protocol using a value from the System.Net.NetworkInformation.NetworkInterfaceComponent enumeration. Possible values include IPv4 and IPv6.

The NetworkInterface class also provides two other static members that you will find useful:

- The static property LoopbackInterfaceIndex returns an int identifying the index of the loopback interface within the NetworkInterface array returned by GetAllNetworkInterfaces.
- The static method GetIsNetworkAvailable returns a bool indicating whether any network connection is available—that is, has an OperationalStatus value of Up.

The Code

The following example uses the members of the NetworkInterface class to display information about all the network interfaces on the local machine:

```
using System;
using System.Net.NetworkInformation;

namespace Apress.VisualCSharpRecipes.Chapter10
{
    class Recipe10_01
    {
        static void Main()
        {
            // Only proceed if there is a network available.
            if (NetworkInterface.GetIsNetworkAvailable())
            {
                // Get the set of all NetworkInterface objects for the local
                // machine.
                NetworkInterface[] interfaces =
                    NetworkInterface.GetAllNetworkInterfaces();
```

```
                // Iterate through the interfaces and display information.
                foreach (NetworkInterface ni in interfaces)
                {
                    // Report basic interface information.
                    Console.WriteLine("Interface Name: {0}", ni.Name);
                    Console.WriteLine("    Description: {0}", ni.Description);
                    Console.WriteLine("    ID: {0}", ni.Id);
                    Console.WriteLine("    Type: {0}", ni.NetworkInterfaceType);
                    Console.WriteLine("    Speed: {0}", ni.Speed);
                    Console.WriteLine("    Status: {0}", ni.OperationalStatus);

                    // Report physical address.
                    Console.WriteLine("    Physical Address: {0}",
                        ni.GetPhysicalAddress().ToString());

                    // Report network statistics for the interface.
                    Console.WriteLine("    Bytes Sent: {0}",
                        ni.GetIPv4Statistics().BytesSent);
                    Console.WriteLine("    Bytes Received: {0}",
                        ni.GetIPv4Statistics().BytesReceived);

                    // Report IP configuration.
                    Console.WriteLine("    IP Addresses:");
                    foreach (UnicastIPAddressInformation addr
                        in ni.GetIPProperties().UnicastAddresses)
                    {
                        Console.WriteLine("        - {0} (lease expires {1})",
                            addr.Address,
                            DateTime.Now +
                            new TimeSpan(0, 0, (int)addr.DhcpLeaseLifetime));
                    }

                    Console.WriteLine(Environment.NewLine);
                }
            }
            else
            {
                Console.WriteLine("No network available.");
            }

            // Wait to continue.
            Console.WriteLine(Environment.NewLine);
            Console.WriteLine("Main method complete. Press Enter");
            Console.ReadLine();
        }
    }
}
```

10-2. Detect Changes in Network Connectivity

Problem

You need a mechanism to check whether changes to the network occur during the life of your application.

Solution

Add handlers to the static `NetworkAddressChanged` and `NetworkAvailabilityChanged` events implemented by the `System.Net.NetworkInformation.NetworkChange` class.

How It Works

The `NetworkChange` class provides an easy-to-use mechanism that allows applications to be aware of changes to network addresses and general network availability. This allows your applications to adapt dynamically to the availability and configuration of the network.

The `NetworkAvailabilityChanged` event fires when a change occurs to general network availability. An instance of the `NetworkAvailabilityChangedEventHandler` delegate is needed to handle this event and is passed a `NetworkAvailabilityEventArgs` object when the event fires. The `NetworkAvailabilityEventArgs.IsAvailable` property returns a `bool` indicating whether the network is available or unavailable following the change.

The `NetworkAddressChanged` event fires when the IP address of a network interface changes. An instance of the `NetworkAddressChangedEventHandler` delegate is required to handle these events. No event-specific arguments are passed to the event handler, which must call `NetworkInterface.GetAllNetworkInterfaces` (discussed in recipe 10-1) to determine what has changed and to take appropriate action.

■ **Note** The `NetworkAddressChanged` and `NetworkAvailabilityChanged` events work on Windows 2000 and later operating systems.

The Code

The following example demonstrates how to use handlers that catch `NetworkAddressChanged` and `NetworkAvailabilityChanged` events and then display status information to the console. To observe how the code handles changing network conditions, unplug your network cable while the example is running, wait a few seconds, and then plug the cable back in.

```
using System;
using System.Net.NetworkInformation;

namespace Apress.VisualCSharpRecipes.Chapter10
{
    class Recipe10_02
    {
        // Declare a method to handle NetworkAvailabilityChanged events.
        private static void NetworkAvailabilityChanged(
            object sender, NetworkAvailabilityEventArgs e)
        {
            // Report whether the network is now available or unavailable.
            if (e.IsAvailable)
            {
                Console.WriteLine("Network Available");
            }
            else
            {
                Console.WriteLine("Network Unavailable");
            }
        }

        // Declare a method to handle NetworkAdressChanged events.
        private static void NetworkAddressChanged(object sender, EventArgs e)
        {
            Console.WriteLine("Current IP Addresses:");

            // Iterate through the interfaces and display information.
            foreach (NetworkInterface ni in
                NetworkInterface.GetAllNetworkInterfaces())
            {
                foreach (UnicastIPAddressInformation addr
                    in ni.GetIPProperties().UnicastAddresses)
                {
                    Console.WriteLine("    - {0} (lease expires {1})",
                        addr.Address, DateTime.Now +
                        new TimeSpan(0, 0, (int)addr.DhcpLeaseLifetime));
                }
            }
        }

        static void Main(string[] args)
        {
            // Add the handlers to the NetworkChange events.
            NetworkChange.NetworkAvailabilityChanged +=
                NetworkAvailabilityChanged;
            NetworkChange.NetworkAddressChanged +=
                NetworkAddressChanged;
```

```
            // Wait to continue.
            Console.WriteLine(Environment.NewLine);
            Console.WriteLine("Press Enter to stop waiting for network events");
            Console.ReadLine();
        }
    }
}
```

10-3. Download Data over HTTP or FTP

Problem

You need a quick, simple way to download data from the Internet using HTTP or FTP.

Solution

Use the methods of the `System.Net.WebClient` class.

How It Works

The .NET Framework provides several mechanisms for transferring data over the Internet. One of the easiest approaches is to use the `System.Net.WebClient` class. `WebClient` provides many high-level methods that simplify the transfer of data by specifying the source as a URI; Table 10-2 summarizes them. The URI can specify that a file (`file://`), FTP (`ftp://`), or HTTP (`http://` or `https://`) scheme be used to download the resource.

Table 10-2. *Data Download Methods of the WebClient Class*

Method	Description
`OpenRead`	Returns a `System.IO.Stream` that provides access to the data from a specified URI.
`OpenReadAsync`	Same as `OpenRead`, but performs the data transfer using a thread-pool thread so that the calling thread does not block. Add an event handler to the `OpenReadCompleted` event to receive notification that the operation has completed.
`DownloadData`	Returns a `byte` array that contains the data from a specified URI.
`DownloadDataAsync`	Same as `DownloadData`, but performs the data transfer using a thread-pool thread so that the calling thread does not block. Add an event handler to the `DownloadDataCompleted` event to receive notification that the operation has completed.

`DownloadFile`	Downloads data from a specified URI and saves it to a specified local file.
`DownloadFileAsync`	Same as `DownloadFile`, but performs the data transfer using a thread-pool thread so that the calling thread does not block. Add an event handler to the `DownloadFileCompleted` event to receive notification that the operation has completed.
`DownloadString`	Returns a `string` that contains the data from a specified URI.
`DownloadStringAsync`	Same as `DownloadString`, but performs the data transfer using a thread-pool thread so that the calling thread does not block. Add an event handler to the `DownloadStringCompleted` event to receive notification that the operation has completed.

The asynchronous download allows you to download data as a background task using a thread from the thread pool (discussed in recipe 4-1). When the download is finished or fails, the thread calls the appropriate `OnXXX` virtual methods that raise the corresponding event on the `WebClient` object, which you can handle using a method that matches the signature of the `System.ComponentModel.AsyncCompletedEventHandler` delegate if you don't want to derive a type from `WebClient` and override the virtual method. However, the `WebClient` object can handle only a single concurrent asynchronous download, making a `WebClient` object suitable for the background download of large single sets of data but not for the download of many files concurrently. (You could, of course, create multiple `WebClient` objects to handle multiple downloads.) You can cancel the outstanding asynchronous download using the method `CancelAsync`.

■ **Tip** The `WebClient` class derives from `System.ComponentModel.Component`, so you can add it to the Visual Studio Form Designer Toolbox in order to allow you to easily set the properties or define the event handlers in a Windows Forms–based application.

The Code

The following example downloads a specified resource from a URI as a string and, since it is an HTML page, parses it for any fully qualified URLs that refer to GIF files. It then downloads each of these files to the local hard drive.

```
using System;
using System.IO;
using System.Net;
using System.Text.RegularExpressions;

namespace Apress.VisualCSharpRecipes.Chapter10
{
    class Recipe10_03
    {
```

```
private static void Main()
{
    // Specify the URI of the resource to parse.
    string srcUriString = "http://www.apress.com";
    Uri srcUri = new Uri(srcUriString);

    // Create a WebClient to perform the download.
    WebClient client = new WebClient();

    Console.WriteLine("Downloading {0}", srcUri);

    // Perform the download getting the resource as a string.
    string str = client.DownloadString(srcUri);

    // Use a regular expression to extract all HTML <img>
    // elements and extract the path to any that reference
    // files with a gif, jpg, or jpeg extension.
    MatchCollection matches = Regex.Matches(str,
        "<img.*?src\\s*=\\s*[\"'](?<url>.*?\\.(gif|jpg|jpeg)).*?>",
        RegexOptions.Singleline | RegexOptions.IgnoreCase);

    // Try to download each referenced image file.
    foreach(Match match in matches)
    {
        var urlGrp = match.Groups["url"];

        if (urlGrp != null && urlGrp.Success)
        {
            Uri imgUri = null;

            // Determine the source URI.
            if (urlGrp.Value.StartsWith("http"))
            {
                // Absolute
                imgUri = new Uri(urlGrp.Value);
            }
            else if (urlGrp.Value.StartsWith("/"))
            {
                // Relative
                imgUri = new Uri(srcUri, urlGrp.Value);
            }
            else
            {
                // Skip it.
                Console.WriteLine("Skipping image {0}", urlGrp.Value);
            }
```

```
                    if (imgUri != null)
                    {
                        // Determine the local file name to use.
                        string fileName =
                            urlGrp.Value.Substring(urlGrp.Value.LastIndexOf('/')+1);

                        try
                        {
                            // Download and store the file.
                            Console.WriteLine("Downloading {0} to {1}",
                                imgUri.AbsoluteUri, fileName);

                            client.DownloadFile(imgUri, fileName);
                        }
                        catch
                        {
                            Console.WriteLine("Failed to download {0}",
                                imgUri.AbsoluteUri);
                        }
                    }
                }
            }

            // Wait to continue.
            Console.WriteLine(Environment.NewLine);
            Console.WriteLine("Main method complete. Press Enter");
            Console.ReadLine();
        }
    }
}
```

■ **Note** The regular expression used in the example is simple and is not designed to cater to all possible URL structures. Recipes 2-5 and 2-6 discuss regular expressions.

Notes

You may also want to upload data to resources specified as a URI, although this technique is not as commonly used. The `WebClient` class also provides methods for performing uploads that are equivalent to the download methods discussed previously:

- `OpenWrite`
- `OpenWriteAsync`
- `UploadData`
- `UploadDataAsync`

- `UploadFile`
- `UploadFileAsync`
- `UploadString`
- `UploadStringAsync`

10-4. Download a File and Process It Using a Stream

Problem

You need to retrieve a file from a web site, but you do not want or do not have permission to save it directly to the hard drive. Instead, you want to process the data in your application directly in memory.

Solution

Use the `System.Net.WebRequest` class to create your request, the `System.Net.WebResponse` class to retrieve the response from the web server, and some form of reader (typically a `System.IO.StreamReader` for HTML or text data or a `System.IO.BinaryReader` for a binary file) to parse the response data.

■ **Tip** You could also use the `OpenRead` method of the `System.Net.WebClient` class to open a stream. However, the additional capabilities of the `WebRequest` and `WebResponse` classes give you more control over the operation of the network request.

How It Works

Opening and downloading a stream of data from the Web using the `WebRequest` and `WebResponse` classes takes the following four basic steps:

1. Use the static method `Create` of the `WebRequest` class to specify the page you want. This method returns a `WebRequest`-derived object, depending on the type of URI you specify. For example, if you use an HTTP URI (with the scheme `http://` or `https://`), you will create an `HttpWebRequest` instance. If you use a file system URI (with the scheme `file://`), you will create a `FileWebRequest` instance. In the .NET Framework 2.0 and later, you can also use an FTP URL (with the scheme `ftp://`), which will create an `FtpWebRequest`.
2. Use the `GetResponse` method of the `WebRequest` object to return a `WebResponse` object for the page. If the request times out, a `System.Net.WebException` will be thrown. You can configure the timeout for the network request through the `WebRequest.Timeout` property in milliseconds (the default value is 100000).

3. Create a StreamReader or a BinaryReader that wraps the stream returned by the WebResponse.GetResponseStream method.
4. Perform any steps you need to with the stream contents.

The Code

The following example retrieves and displays a graphic and the HTML content of a web page. Figure 10-1 shows the output.

```
using System;
using System.Net;
using System.IO;
using System.Drawing;
using System.Windows.Forms;

namespace Apress.VisualCSharpRecipes.Chapter10
{
    public partial class Recipe10_04 : Form
    {
        public Recipe10_04()
        {
            InitializeComponent();
        }

        protected override void OnLoad(EventArgs e)
        {
            base.OnLoad(e);

            string picUri = "http://www.apress.com/img/img05/Hex_RGB4.jpg";
            string htmlUri = "http://www.apress.com";

            // Create the requests.
            WebRequest requestPic = WebRequest.Create(picUri);
            WebRequest requestHtml = WebRequest.Create(htmlUri);

            // Get the responses.
            // This takes the most significant amount of time, particularly
            // if the file is large, because the whole response is retrieved.
            WebResponse responsePic = requestPic.GetResponse();
            WebResponse responseHtml = requestHtml.GetResponse();

            // Read the image from the response stream.
            pictureBox1.Image = Image.FromStream(responsePic.GetResponseStream());
```

```
            // Read the text from the response stream.
            using (StreamReader r =
                new StreamReader(responseHtml.GetResponseStream()))
            {
                textBox1.Text = r.ReadToEnd();
            }
        }

        [STAThread]
        public static void Main(string[] args)
        {
            Application.Run(new Recipe10_04());
        }
    }
}
```

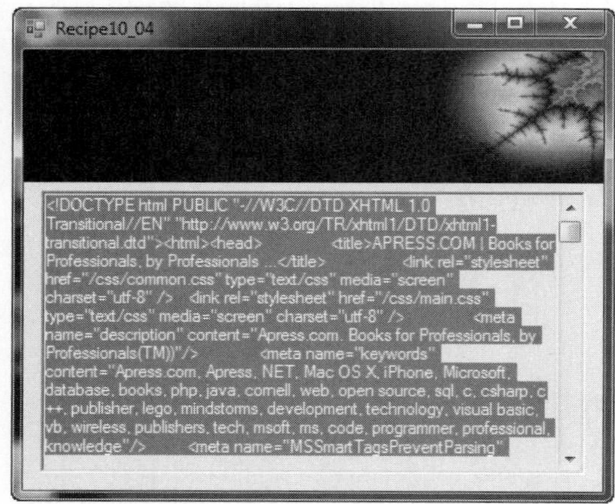

Figure 10-1. *Downloading content from the Web using a stream*

10-5. Respond to HTTP Requests from Within Your Application

Problem

You want your application to be able to respond to HTTP requests programmatically.

Solution

Use the new `System.Net.HttpListener` class.

■ **Note** Your application must be running on Windows XP Service Pack 2 (or later) or Windows 2003 to use the `HttpListener` class; otherwise, a `System.PlatformNotSupportedException` will be thrown when you try to instantiate it. You should check the `bool` returned by the static property `HttpListener.IsSupported` to check whether support is available.

How It Works

The `HttpListener` class provides an easy-to-use mechanism through which your programs can accept and respond to HTTP requests. To use the `HttpListener` class, follow these steps:

1. Instantiate an `HttpListener` object.
2. Configure the URI prefixes that the `HttpListener` object will handle using the `Prefixes` property. The `Prefixes` property returns a `System.Net.HttpListenerPrefixCollection` collection to which you can add URI prefixes (as `strings`) using the `Add` method. Each prefix must end with a forward slash (`/`), or else a `System.ArgumentException` will be thrown. If you specify a URL prefix that is already being handled, a `System.Net.HttpListenerException` will be thrown. When a client makes a request, the request will be handled by the listener configured with the prefix that most closely matches the client's requested URL.
3. Start the `HttpListener` object by calling its `Start` method. You must call `Start` before the `HttpListener` object can accept and process HTTP requests.
4. Accept client requests using the `GetContext` method of the `HttpListener` object. The `GetContext` method will block the calling thread until a request is received and then returns a `System.Net.HttpListenerContext` object. Alternatively, you can use the `BeginGetContext` and `EndGetContext` methods to listen for requests on a thread-pool thread. When a request is received, the `System.AsyncCallback` delegate specified as the argument to the `BeginGetContext` method will be called and passed the `HttpListenerContext` object. Regardless of how it is obtained, the `HttpListenerContext` object implements three read-only properties critical to the handling of a client request:
    - The `Request` property returns a `System.Net.HttpListenerRequest` through which you can access details of the client's request.
    - The `Response` property returns a `System.Net.HttpListenerResponse` through which you can configure the response to send to the client.

- The `User` property returns an instance of a type implementing `System.Security.Principal.IPrincipal`, which you can use to obtain identity, authentication, and authorization information about the user associated with the request.

5. Configure the HTTP response through the members of the `HttpListenerResponse` object accessible through the `HttpListenerContext.Response` property.
6. Send the response by calling the `Close` method of the `HttpListenerResponse` object.
7. Once you have finished processing HTTP requests, call `Stop` on the `HttpListener` object to stop accepting more requests. Call `Close` to shut down the `HttpListener` object, which will wait until all outstanding requests have been processed, or call `Abort` to terminate the `HttpListener` object without waiting for requests to complete.

The Code

The following example demonstrates how to use the `HttpListener` class to process HTTP requests. The example starts listening for five requests concurrently using the asynchronous `BeginGetContext` method and handles the response to each request by calling the `RequestHandler` method. Each time a request is handled, a new call is made to `BeginGetContext` so that you always have the capacity to handle up to five requests.

To open a connection to the example from your browser, enter the URL `http://localhost:19080/VisualCSharpRecipes/` or `http://localhost:20000/Recipe10-05/`, and you will see the response from the appropriate request handler.

```
using System;
using System.IO;
using System.Net;
using System.Text;
using System.Threading;

namespace Apress.VisualCSharpRecipes.Chapter10
{
    class Recipe10_05
    {
        // Configure the maximum number of request that can be
        // handled concurrently.
        private static int maxRequestHandlers = 5;

        // An integer used to assign each HTTP request handler a unique
        // identifier.
        private static int requestHandlerID = 0;

        // The HttpListener is the class that provides all the capabilities
        // to receive and process HTTP requests.
        private static HttpListener listener;
```

```
// A method to asynchronously process individual requests and send
// responses.
private static void RequestHandler(IAsyncResult result)
{
    Console.WriteLine("{0}: Activated.", result.AsyncState);

    try
    {
        // Obtain the HttpListenerContext for the new request.
        HttpListenerContext context = listener.EndGetContext(result);

        Console.WriteLine("{0}: Processing HTTP Request from {1} ({2}).",
            result.AsyncState,
            context.Request.UserHostName,
            context.Request.RemoteEndPoint);

        // Build the response using a StreamWriter feeding the
        // Response.OutputStream.
        StreamWriter sw =
           new StreamWriter(context.Response.OutputStream, Encoding.UTF8);

        sw.WriteLine("<html>");
        sw.WriteLine("<head>");
        sw.WriteLine("<title>Visual C# Recipes</title>");
        sw.WriteLine("</head>");
        sw.WriteLine("<body>");
        sw.WriteLine("Recipe 10-5: " + result.AsyncState);
        sw.WriteLine("</body>");
        sw.WriteLine("</html>");
        sw.Flush();

        // Configure the Response.
        context.Response.ContentType = "text/html";
        context.Response.ContentEncoding = Encoding.UTF8;

        // Close the Response to send it to the client.
        context.Response.Close();

        Console.WriteLine("{0}: Sent HTTP response.", result.AsyncState);
    }
    catch (ObjectDisposedException)
    {
        Console.WriteLine("{0}: HttpListener disposed--shutting down.",
            result.AsyncState);
    }
    finally
    {
```

```
                // Start another handler if unless the HttpListener is closing.
                if (listener.IsListening)
                {
                    Console.WriteLine("{0}: Creating new request handler.",
                        result.AsyncState);

                    listener.BeginGetContext(RequestHandler, "RequestHandler_" +
                        Interlocked.Increment(ref requestHandlerID));
                }
            }
        }

        public static void Main(string[] args)
        {
            // Quit gracefully if this feature is not supported.
            if (!HttpListener.IsSupported)
            {
                Console.WriteLine(
                    "You must be running this example on Windows XP SP2, ",
                    "Windows Server 2003, or higher to create ",
                    "an HttpListener.");
                return;
            }

            // Create the HttpListener.
            using (listener = new HttpListener())
            {
                // Configure the URI prefixes that will map to the HttpListener.
                listener.Prefixes.Add(
                    "http://localhost:19080/VisualCSharpRecipes/");
                listener.Prefixes.Add(
                    "http://localhost:20000/Recipe10-05/");

                // Start the HttpListener before listening for incoming requests.
                Console.WriteLine("Starting HTTP Server");
                listener.Start();
                Console.WriteLine("HTTP Server started");
                Console.WriteLine(Environment.NewLine);

                // Create a number of asynchronous request handlers up to
                // the configurable maximum. Give each a unique identifier.
                for (int count = 0; count < maxRequestHandlers; count++)
                {
                    listener.BeginGetContext(RequestHandler, "RequestHandler_" +
                        Interlocked.Increment(ref requestHandlerID));
                }

                // Wait for the user to stop the HttpListener.
                Console.WriteLine("Press Enter to stop the HTTP Server");
                Console.ReadLine();
```

```
                // Stop accepting new requests.
                listener.Stop();

                // Terminate the HttpListener without processing current requests.
                listener.Abort();
            }

            // Wait to continue.
            Console.WriteLine(Environment.NewLine);
            Console.WriteLine("Main method complete. Press Enter");
            Console.ReadLine();
        }
    }
}
```

10-6. Get an HTML Page from a Site That Requires Authentication

Problem

You need to retrieve a file from a web site, but the web site requires that you provide credentials for the purpose of authentication.

Solution

Use the `System.Net.WebRequest` and `System.Net.WebResponse` classes as described in recipe 10-4. Before making the request, configure the `WebRequest.Credentials` and `WebRequest.Certificates` properties with the necessary authentication information.

■ **Tip** You could also use the `System.Net.WebClient` class (discussed in recipe 10-3), which also has `Credentials` and `Certificates` properties that allow you to associate user credentials with a web request.

How It Works

Some web sites require user authentication information. When connecting through a browser, this information might be submitted transparently (for example, on a local intranet site that uses Windows integrated authentication), or the browser might request this information with a login dialog box. When accessing a web page programmatically, your code needs to submit this information. The approach you use depends on the type of authentication implemented by the web site:

- If the web site is using basic or digest authentication, you can transmit a username and password combination by manually creating a new System.Net.NetworkCredential object and assigning it to the WebRequest.Credentials property. With digest authentication, you may also supply a domain name.
- If the web site is using Windows integrated authentication, you can take the same approach and manually create a new System.Net.NetworkCredential object. Alternatively, you can retrieve the current user login information from the System.Net.CredentialCache object using the DefaultCredentials property.
- If the web site requires a client certificate, you can load the certificate from a file using the System.Security.Cryptography.X509Certificates.X509Certificate2 class and add that to the HttpWebRequest.ClientCertificates collection.
- You can load an X.509 certificate from a certificate store using the class System.Security.Cryptography.X509Certificates.X509Store defined in the System.Security.dll assembly. You can either find a certificate in the store programmatically using the X509Store.Certificates.Find method or present the user with a Windows dialog box and allow them to select the certificate. To present a dialog box, pass a collection of X.509 certificates contained in an X509Certificate2Collection object to the SelectFromCollection method of the System.Security.Cryptography.X509Certificates.X509Certificate2UI class.

The Code

The following example demonstrates all four of the basic approaches described previously. Note that you need to add a reference to the System.Security.dll assembly.

```
using System;
using System.Net;
using System.Security.Cryptography.X509Certificates;

namespace Apress.VisualCSharpRecipes.Chapter10
{
    class Recipe10_06
    {
        public static void Main()
        {
            // Create a WebRequest that authenticates the user with a
            // username and password combination over basic authentication.
            WebRequest requestA = WebRequest.Create("http://www.somesite.com");
            requestA.Credentials = new NetworkCredential("userName", "password");
            requestA.PreAuthenticate = true;

            // Create a WebRequest that authenticates the current user
            // with Windows integrated authentication.
            WebRequest requestB = WebRequest.Create("http://www.somesite.com");
            requestB.Credentials = CredentialCache.DefaultCredentials;
            requestB.PreAuthenticate = true;
```

```
            // Create a WebRequest that authenticates the user with a client
            // certificate loaded from a file.
            HttpWebRequest requestC =
                (HttpWebRequest)WebRequest.Create("http://www.somesite.com");
            X509Certificate cert1 =
                X509Certificate.CreateFromCertFile(@"..\..\TestCertificate.cer");
            requestC.ClientCertificates.Add(cert1);

            // Create a WebRequest that authenticates the user with a client
            // certificate loaded from a certificate store. Try to find a
            // certificate with a specific subject, but if it is not found,
            // present the user with a dialog so they can select the certificate
            // to use from their personal store.
            HttpWebRequest requestD =
                (HttpWebRequest)WebRequest.Create("http://www.somesite.com");
            X509Store store = new X509Store();
            X509Certificate2Collection certs =
                store.Certificates.Find(X509FindType.FindBySubjectName,
                "Allen Jones", false);

            if (certs.Count == 1)
            {
                requestD.ClientCertificates.Add(certs[0]);
            }
            else
            {
                certs = X509Certificate2UI.SelectFromCollection(
                    store.Certificates,
                    "Select Certificate",
                    "Select the certificate to use for authentication.",
                    X509SelectionFlag.SingleSelection);

                if (certs.Count != 0)
                {
                    requestD.ClientCertificates.Add(certs[0]);
                }
            }

            // Now issue the request and process the responses...
        }
    }
}
```

10-7. Send E-mail Using SMTP

Problem

You need to send e-mail using an SMTP server.

Solution

Use the `SmtpClient` and `MailMessage` classes in the `System.Net.Mail` namespace.

■ **Note** In versions 1.0 and 1.1 of the .NET Framework, you would send SMTP mail using the `SmtpMail` and `MailMessage` classes in the `System.Web.Mail` namespace from the `System.Web.dll` assembly. The `SmtpClient` and `MailMessage` classes discussed in this recipe were added to the `System.dll` assembly in the .NET Framework 2.0, and both simplify and extend the functionality provided by earlier versions.

How It Works

An instance of the `SmtpClient` class provides the mechanism through which you communicate with the SMTP server. You configure the `SmtpClient` using the properties described in Table 10-3.

Table 10-3. *Properties of the SmtpClient Class*

Property	Description
`ClientCertificates`	Gets a `System.Security.Cryptography.X509Certificates.X509CertificatesCollection` to which you add the certificates to use for communicating with the SMTP server (if required).
`Credentials`	Gets or sets an implementation of the `System.Net.ICredentialsByHost` interface that represents the credentials to use to gain access to the SMTP server. The `CredentialCache` and `NetworkCredential` classes implement the `ICredentialsByHost` interface. Use `NetworkCredential` if you want to specify a single set of credentials and `CredentialCache` if you want to specify more than one.
`EnableSsl`	Gets or sets a `bool` value that indicates whether the `SmtpClient` should use Secure Sockets Layer (SSL) to communicate with the SMTP server.
`Host`	Gets or sets a `string` containing the host name or IP address of the SMTP server to use to send e-mail.
`Port`	Gets or sets an `int` value containing the port number to connect to on the SMTP server. The default value is 25.
`Timeout`	Gets or sets an `int` value containing the timeout in milliseconds when attempting to send e-mail. The default is 100 seconds.

Property	Description
UseDefaultCredentials	Gets or sets a bool value indicating whether the default user credentials are used when communicating with the SMTP server. If true, the credentials passed to the SMTP server are automatically obtained from the static property CredentialCache.DefaultCredentials.

■ **Tip** You can specify default settings for the SmtpClient in the <mailSettings> section of your machine or application configuration files. Configurable default values include the host, port, username, and password.

Mail messages are represented by MailMessage objects, which you instantiate and then configure using the members summarized in Table 10-4.

■ **Tip** For simple mail messages, the MailMessage class provides a constructor that allows you to specify the from, to, subject, and body information for the mail message as string arguments—allowing you to create a complete mail message in a single call.

Table 10-4. *Properties of the MailMessage Class*

Property	Description
Attachments	Gets or sets a System.Net.Mail.AttachmentCollection containing the set of attachments for the e-mail message. A System.Net.Mail.Attachment object represents each attachment. You can create Attachment objects from files or streams, and you can configure the encoding and content type for each attachment.
Bcc	Gets or sets a System.Net.Mail.MailAddressCollection containing the blind carbon copy addresses for the e-mail message. The MailAddressCollection contains one or more MailAddress objects.
Body	Gets or sets a string value that contains the body text of the e-mail message.
BodyEncoding	Gets or sets a System.Text.Encoding object that specifies the encoding for the body of the e-mail message. The default value is null, resulting in a default encoding of US-ASCII, which is equivalent to the Encoding object returned by the static property Encoding.ASCII.

Property	Description
`CC`	Gets or sets a `System.Net.Mail.MailAddressCollection` containing the carbon copy addresses for the e-mail message. The `MailAddressCollection` contains one or more `MailAddress` objects.
`From`	Gets or sets a `System.Net.Mail.MailAddress` containing the from address for the e-mail message.
`IsBodyHtml`	Gets or sets a `bool` value identifying whether the body of the e-mail message contains HTML.
`ReplyTo`	Gets or sets a `System.Net.Mail.MailAddress` containing the reply address for the e-mail message.
`Subject`	Gets or sets a `string` containing the subject for the e-mail message.
`SubjectEncoding`	Gets or sets a `System.Text.Encoding` object that specifies the encoding used to encode the body of the e-mail subject. The default value is `null`, resulting in a default encoding of US-ASCII, which is equivalent to the `Encoding` object returned by the static property `Encoding.ASCII`.
`To`	Gets or sets a `System.Net.Mail.MailAddressCollection` containing the destination addresses for the e-mail message. The `MailAddressCollection` contains one or more `MailAddress` objects.

Once you have configured the `SmtpClient`, you can send your `MailMessage` objects using the `SmtpClient.Send` method, which will cause your code to block until the send operation is completed or fails. Alternatively, you can send mail using a thread from the thread pool by calling the `SendAsync` method. When you call `SendAsync`, your code will be free to continue other processing while the e-mail is sent. Add an event handler to the `SendCompleted` event to receive notification that the asynchronous send has completed.

■ **Note** Remember that you can't use SMTP to retrieve e-mail. For this task, you need the Post Office Protocol 3 (POP3) or the Internet Message Access Protocol (IMAP), neither of which is exposed natively in the .NET Framework.

The Code

The following example demonstrates how to use the `SmtpClient` class to send an e-mail message with multiple attachments to a set of recipients whose e-mail addresses are specified as command-line arguments:

```
using System;
using System.Net;
using System.Net.Mail;

namespace Apress.VisualCSharpRecipes.Chapter10
{
    class Recipe10_07
    {
        public static void Main(string[] args)
        {
            // Create and configure the SmtpClient that will send the mail.
            // Specify the host name of the SMTP server and the port used
            // to send mail.
            SmtpClient client = new SmtpClient("mail.somecompany.com", 25);

            // Configure the SmtpClient with the credentials used to connect
            // to the SMTP server.
            client.Credentials =
                new NetworkCredential("user@somecompany.com", "password");

            // Create the MailMessage to represent the e-mail being sent.
            using (MailMessage msg = new MailMessage())
            {
                // Configure the e-mail sender and subject.
                msg.From = new MailAddress("author@visual-csharp-recipes.com");
                msg.Subject = "Greetings from Visual C# Recipes";

                // Configure the e-mail body.
                msg.Body = "This is a message from Recipe 10-07 of" +
                    " Visual C# Recipes. Attached is the source file " +
                    " and the binary for the recipe.";

                // Attach the files to the e-mail message and set their MIME type.
                msg.Attachments.Add(
                    new Attachment(@"..\..\Recipe10-07.cs","text/plain"));
                msg.Attachments.Add(
                    new Attachment(@".\Recipe10-07.exe",
                    "application/octet-stream"));

                // Iterate through the set of recipients specified on the
                // command line. Add all addresses with the correct structure as
                //  recipients.
                foreach (string str in args)
                {
```

```
                // Create a MailAddress from each value on the command line
                // and add it to the set of recipients.
                try
                {
                    msg.To.Add(new MailAddress(str));
                }
                catch (FormatException ex)
                {
                    // Proceed to the next specified recipient.
                    Console.WriteLine("{0}: Error -- {1}", str, ex.Message);
                    continue;
                }
            }

            // Send the message.
            client.Send(msg);
        }

        // Wait to continue.
        Console.WriteLine(Environment.NewLine);
        Console.WriteLine("Main method complete. Press Enter");
        Console.ReadLine();
    }
  }
}
```

10-8. Resolve a Host Name to an IP Address

Problem

You want to determine the IP address for a computer based on its fully qualified domain name by performing a DNS query.

Solution

Use the method `GetHostEntry` of the `System.Net.Dns` class, and pass the computer's fully qualified domain name as a string parameter.

■ **Note** In versions 1.0 and 1.1 of the .NET Framework, you should use the method `GetHostByName` of the `Dns` class, but it is marked as obsolete as of version 2.0.

How It Works

On the Internet, the human-readable names that refer to computers are mapped to IP addresses, which is what TCP/IP requires in order to communicate between computers. For example, the name `www.apress.com` might be mapped to the IP address 66.211.109.45. It is not unusual for the IP address of computers to change while their name remains constant, meaning that it is usually better to reference computers with their name, not their IP address. To determine the current IP address for a given name, the computer contacts a DNS server. The name or IP address of the DNS server contacted is configured as part of a computer's network configuration.

The entire process of name resolution is transparent if you use the `System.Net.Dns` class, which allows you to retrieve the IP address for a host name by calling `GetHostEntry`.

■ **Tip** The `Dns` class also provides the `BeginGetHostEntry` and `EndGetHostEntry` methods, which allow you to resolve IP addresses asynchronously. Also, the static method `GetHostName` returns the computer name of the local machine.

The Code

The following example retrieves the IP addresses of all computers whose fully qualified domain names are specified as command-line arguments:

```
using System;
using System.Net;

namespace Apress.VisualCSharpRecipes.Chapter10
{
    class Recipe10_08
    {
        public static void Main(string[] args)
        {
            foreach (string comp in args)
            {
                try
                {
                    // Retrieve the DNS entry for the specified computer.
                    IPAddress[] addresses = Dns.GetHostEntry(comp).AddressList;

                    // The DNS entry may contain more than one IP address. Iterate
                    // through them and display each one along with the type of
                    // address (AddressFamily).
                    foreach (IPAddress address in addresses)
                    {
```

```
                        Console.WriteLine("{0} = {1} ({2})",
                            comp, address, address.AddressFamily);
                    }
                }
                catch (Exception ex)
                {
                    Console.WriteLine("{0} = Error ({1})", comp, ex.Message);
                }
            }

            // Wait to continue.
            Console.WriteLine(Environment.NewLine);
            Console.WriteLine("Main method complete. Press Enter");
            Console.ReadLine();
        }
    }
}
```

Usage

Running the example with the following command line:
`recipe10-08 www.apress.com www.microsoft.com localhost somejunk`
will produce output similar to the following. Notice that multiple IP addresses can be returned for some host names.

```
www.apress.com = 65.19.150.100 (InterNetwork)

www.microsoft.com = 207.46.198.30 (InterNetwork)

www.microsoft.com = 207.46.20.30 (InterNetwork)

www.microsoft.com = 207.46.20.60 (InterNetwork)

www.microsoft.com = 207.46.18.30 (InterNetwork)

www.microsoft.com = 207.46.19.30 (InterNetwork)

www.microsoft.com = 207.46.19.60 (InterNetwork)

www.microsoft.com = 207.46.199.30 (InterNetwork)

www.microsoft.com = 207.46.198.60 (InterNetwork)

localhost = 127.0.0.1 (InterNetwork)

somejunk = Error (No such host is known)
```

10-9. Ping an IP Address

Problem

You want to check whether a computer is online and accessible and gauge its response time.

Solution

Send a ping message. This message is sent using the ICMP, accessible through the `Send` method of the `System.Net.NetworkInformation.Ping` class.

■ **Note** The `Ping` class was introduced in the .NET Framework 2.0. To send a ping message in earlier versions of the .NET Framework, you had to undertake significant effort to manually create an ICMP request message using raw sockets and lengthy code.

How It Works

A ping message contacts a device at a specific IP address, passing it a test packet, and requests that the remote device respond by echoing back the packet. To gauge the connection latency between two computers, you can measure the time taken for a ping response to be received.

■ **Caution** Many commercial web sites do not respond to ping requests because they represent an unnecessary processing overhead and are often used in denial-of-service attacks. The firewall that protects the site will usually filter them out before they reach the specified destination. This will cause your ping request to time out.

The `Ping` class allows you to send ping messages using the `Send` method. The `Send` method provides a number of overloads, which allow you to specify some or all of the following:

- The IP address or host name of the target computer. You can specify this as a `string` or a `System.Net.IPAddress` object.
- The number of milliseconds to wait for a response before the request times out (specified as an `int`) with the default set to 5,000.
- A `byte` array of up to 65,500 data bytes that is sent with the ping request and that should be returned in the response.
- A `System.Net.NetworkInformation.PingOptions` object that specifies time-to-live and fragmentation options for the transmission of the ping message.

The Send method will return a System.Net.NetworkInformation.PingReply object. The Status property of the PingReply will contain a value from the System.Net.NetworkInformation.IPStatus enumeration from which you can determine the result of the ping request. The most common values will be Success and TimedOut. If the host name you pass to the Send method cannot be resolved, Send will throw an exception, but you must look at the InnerException to determine the cause of the problem.

The Ping class also provides a SendAsync method that performs the ping request using a thread-pool thread so that the calling thread does not block. When the ping is finished or fails because of a timeout, the thread raises the PingCompleted event on the Ping object, which you can handle using a method that matches the signature of the System.Net.NetworkInformation.PingCompletedEventHandler delegate. However, the Ping object can handle only a single concurrent request; otherwise, it will throw a System.InvalidOperationException.

■ **Tip** The Ping class derives from System.ComponentModel.Component, so you can add it to the Visual Studio Form Designer Toolbox in order to allow you to easily set the properties or define the event handlers in a Windows Forms–based application.

The Code

The following example pings the computers whose domain names or IP addresses are specified as command-line arguments:

```
using System;
using System.Net.NetworkInformation;

namespace Apress.VisualCSharpRecipes.Chapter10
{
    class Recipe10_09
    {
        public static void Main(string[] args)
        {
            // Create an instance of the Ping class.
            using (Ping ping = new Ping())
            {
                Console.WriteLine("Pinging:");

                foreach (string comp in args)
                {
                    try
                    {
                        Console.Write("    {0}...", comp);

                        // Ping the specified computer with a timeout of 100 ms.
                        PingReply reply = ping.Send(comp, 100);
```

```
                if (reply.Status == IPStatus.Success)
                {
                  Console.WriteLine("Success - IP Address:{0} Time:{1}ms",
                      reply.Address, reply.RoundtripTime);
                }
                else
                {
                    Console.WriteLine(reply.Status);
                }
            }
            catch (Exception ex)
            {
                Console.WriteLine("Error ({0})",
                    ex.InnerException.Message);
            }
        }
    }

    // Wait to continue.
    Console.WriteLine(Environment.NewLine);
    Console.WriteLine("Main method complete. Press Enter");
    Console.ReadLine();
        }
    }
}
```

Usage

Running the example with the following command line:

```
recipe10-09 www.apress.com www.google.com localhost somejunk
```

will produce output similar to the following:

```
Pinging:

    www.apress.com...TimedOut

    www.google.com...Success - IP Address:216.239.59.104 Time:42ms

    localhost...Success - IP Address:127.0.0.1 Time:0ms

    somejunk...Error (No such host is known)
```

10-10. Communicate Using TCP

Problem

You need to send data between two computers on a network using a TCP/IP connection.

Solution

One computer (the server) must begin listening using the `System.Net.Sockets.TcpListener` class. Another computer (the client) connects to it using the `System.Net.Sockets.TcpClient` class. Once a connection is established, both computers can communicate using the `System.Net.Sockets.NetworkStream` class.

How It Works

TCP is a reliable, connection-oriented protocol that allows two computers to communicate over a network. It provides built-in flow control, sequencing, and error handling, which makes it reliable and easy to program.

To create a TCP connection, one computer must act as the server and start listening on a specific endpoint. (An *endpoint* is a combination of an IP address and a port number.) The other computer must act as a client and send a connection request to the endpoint on which the first computer is listening. Once the connection is established, the two computers can take turns exchanging messages. .NET makes this process easy through its stream abstraction. Both computers simply write to and read from a `System.Net.Sockets.NetworkStream` to transmit data.

■ **Note** Even though a TCP connection always requires a server and a client, an individual application could be both. For example, in a peer-to-peer application, one thread is dedicated to listening for incoming requests (acting as a server), and another thread is dedicated to initiating outgoing connections (acting as a client). In the examples provided with this chapter, the client and server are provided as separate applications and are placed in separate subdirectories.

Once a TCP connection is established, the two computers can send any type of data by writing it to the `NetworkStream`. However, it's a good idea to begin designing a networked application by defining the application-level protocol that clients and servers will use to communicate. This protocol includes constants that represent the allowable commands, ensuring that your application code doesn't include hard-coded communication strings.

The Code

In this example, the defined protocol is basic. You would add more constants depending on the type of application. For example, in a file transfer application, you might include a client message for requesting a file. The server might then respond with an acknowledgment and return file details such as the file size. These constants should be compiled into a separate class library assembly, which must be referenced by both the client and server. Here is the code for the shared protocol:

```
namespace Apress.VisualCSharpRecipes.Chapter10
{
    public class Recipe10_10Shared
    {
        public const string AcknowledgeOK = "OK";
        public const string AcknowledgeCancel = "Cancel";
        public const string Disconnect = "Bye";
        public const string RequestConnect = "Hello";
    }
}
```

The following code is a template for a basic TCP server. It listens on a fixed port, accepts the first incoming connection, and then waits for the client to request a disconnect. At this point, the server could call the `TcpListener.AcceptTcpClient` method again to wait for the next client, but instead it simply shuts down.

```
using System;
using System.IO;
using System.Net;
using System.Net.Sockets;

namespace Apress.VisualCSharpRecipes.Chapter10
{
    public class Recipe10_10Server
    {
        public static void Main()
        {
            // Create a new listener on port 8000.
            TcpListener listener =
                new TcpListener(IPAddress.Parse("127.0.0.1"), 8000);

            Console.WriteLine("About to initialize port.");
            listener.Start();
            Console.WriteLine("Listening for a connection...");

            try
            {
                // Wait for a connection request, and return a TcpClient
                // initialized for communication.
                using (TcpClient client = listener.AcceptTcpClient())
                {
                    Console.WriteLine("Connection accepted.");
```

```
                    // Retrieve the network stream.
                    NetworkStream stream = client.GetStream();

                    // Create a BinaryWriter for writing to the stream.
                    using (BinaryWriter w = new BinaryWriter(stream))
                    {
                        // Create a BinaryReader for reading from the stream.
                        using (BinaryReader r = new BinaryReader(stream))
                        {
                            if (r.ReadString() ==
                                Recipe10_10Shared.RequestConnect)
                            {
                                w.Write(Recipe10_10Shared.AcknowledgeOK);
                                Console.WriteLine("Connection completed.");

                                while (r.ReadString() !=
                                    Recipe10_10Shared.Disconnect) { }

                                Console.WriteLine(Environment.NewLine);
                                Console.WriteLine("Disconnect request received.");
                            }
                            else
                            {
                                Console.WriteLine("Can't complete connection.");
                            }
                        }
                    }
                }

                Console.WriteLine("Connection closed.");
            }
            catch (Exception ex)
            {
                Console.WriteLine(ex.ToString());
            }
            finally
            {
                // Close the underlying socket (stop listening for new requests).
                listener.Stop();
                Console.WriteLine("Listener stopped.");
            }

            // Wait to continue.
            Console.WriteLine(Environment.NewLine);
            Console.WriteLine("Main method complete. Press Enter");
            Console.ReadLine();
        }
    }
}
```

The following code is a template for a basic TCP client. It contacts the server at the specified IP address and port. In this example, the loopback address (127.0.0.1) is used, which always points to the local computer. Keep in mind that a TCP connection requires two ports: one at the server end and one at the client end. However, only the server port to connect to needs to be specified. The outgoing client port can be chosen dynamically at runtime from the available ports, which is what the `TcpClient` class will do by default.

```
using System;
using System.IO;
using System.Net;
using System.Net.Sockets;

namespace Apress.VisualCSharpRecipes.Chapter10
{
    public class Recipe10_10Client
    {
        public static void Main()
        {
            TcpClient client = new TcpClient();

            try
            {
                Console.WriteLine("Attempting to connect to the server ",
                    "on port 8000.");
                client.Connect(IPAddress.Parse("127.0.0.1"), 8000);
                Console.WriteLine("Connection established.");

                // Retrieve the network stream.
                NetworkStream stream = client.GetStream();

                // Create a BinaryWriter for writing to the stream.
                using (BinaryWriter w = new BinaryWriter(stream))
                {
                    // Create a BinaryReader for reading from the stream.
                    using (BinaryReader r = new BinaryReader(stream))
                    {
                        // Start a dialog.
                        w.Write(Recipe10_10Shared.RequestConnect);

                        if (r.ReadString() == Recipe10_10Shared.AcknowledgeOK)
                        {
                            Console.WriteLine("Connected.");
                            Console.WriteLine("Press Enter to disconnect.");
                            Console.ReadLine();
                            Console.WriteLine("Disconnecting...");
                            w.Write(Recipe10_10Shared.Disconnect);
                        }
```

```
                        else
                        {
                            Console.WriteLine("Connection not completed.");
                        }
                    }
                }
            }
            catch (Exception err)
            {
                Console.WriteLine(err.ToString());
            }
            finally
            {
                // Close the connection socket.
                client.Close();
                Console.WriteLine("Port closed.");
            }

            // Wait to continue.
            Console.WriteLine(Environment.NewLine);
            Console.WriteLine("Main method complete. Press Enter");
            Console.ReadLine();
        }
    }
}
```

Usage

Here's a sample connection transcript on the server side:

```
About to initialize port.
Listening for a connection...
Connection accepted.
Connection completed.

Disconnect request received.
Connection closed.
Listener stopped.
```

And here's a sample connection transcript on the client side:

```
Attempting to connect to the server on port 8000.
Connection established.
Connected.
Press Enter to disconnect.

Disconnecting...
Port closed.
```

10-11. Create a Multithreaded TCP Server That Supports Asynchronous Communications

Problem

You need to handle multiple network requests concurrently or perform a network data transfer as a background task while your program continues with other processing.

Solution

Use the method `AcceptTcpClient` of the `System.Net.Sockets.TcpListener` class to accept connections. Every time a new client connects, start a new thread to handle the connection. Alternatively, use the `TcpListener.BeginAcceptTcpClient` to accept a new client connection on a thread-pool thread using the asynchronous execution pattern (discussed in recipe 4-2).

To start a background task to handle the asynchronous sending of data, you can use the `BeginWrite` method of the `System.Net.Sockets.NetworkStream` class and supply a callback method—each time the callback is triggered, send more data.

How It Works

A single TCP endpoint (IP address and port) can serve multiple connections. In fact, the operating system takes care of most of the work for you. All you need to do is create a worker object on the server that will handle each connection on a separate thread. The `TcpListener.AcceptTcpClient` method returns a `TcpClient` when a connection is established. This should be passed off to a threaded worker object so that the worker can communicate with the remote client.

Alternatively, call the `TcpListener.BeginAcceptTcpClient` method to start an asynchronous operation using a thread-pool thread that waits in the background for a client to connect. `BeginAcceptTcpClient` follows the asynchronous execution pattern, allowing you to wait for the operation to complete or specify a callback that the .NET runtime will call when a client connects. (See recipe 4-2 for details on the options available.) Whichever mechanism you use, once `BeginAcceptTcpClient` has completed, call `EndAcceptTcpClient` to obtain the newly created `TcpClient` object.

To exchange network data asynchronously, you can use the `NetworkStream` class, which includes basic support for asynchronous communication through the `BeginRead` and `BeginWrite` methods. Using these methods, you can send or receive a block of data on one of the threads provided by the thread pool, without blocking your code. When sending data asynchronously, you must send raw binary data (an array of bytes). It's up to you to choose the amount you want to send or receive at a time.

One advantage of this approach when sending files is that the entire content of the file does not have to be held in memory at once. Instead, it is retrieved just before a new block is sent. Another advantage is that the server can abort the transfer operation easily at any time.

The Code

The following example demonstrates various techniques for handling network connections and communications asynchronously. The server (`Recipe10-11Server`) starts a thread-pool thread listening for new connections using the `TcpListener.BeginAcceptTcpClient` method and specifying a callback method to handle the new connections. Every time a client connects to the server, the callback method obtains the new `TcpClient` object and passes it to a new threaded `ClientHandler` object to handle client communications.

The `ClientHandler` object waits for the client to request data and then sends a large amount of data (read from a file) to the client. This data is sent asynchronously, which means `ClientHandler` could continue to perform other tasks. In this example, it simply monitors the network stream for messages sent from the client. The client reads only a third of the data before sending a disconnect message to the server, which terminates the remainder of the file transfer and drops the client connection.

Here is the code for the shared protocol:

```
namespace Apress.VisualCSharpRecipes.Chapter10
{
    public class Recipe10_11Shared
    {
        public const string AcknowledgeOK = "OK";
        public const string AcknowledgeCancel = "Cancel";
        public const string Disconnect = "Bye";
        public const string RequestConnect = "Hello";
        public const string RequestData = "Data";
    }
}
```

Here is the server code:

```
using System;
using System.IO;
using System.Net;
using System.Threading;
using System.Net.Sockets;

namespace Apress.VisualCSharpRecipes.Chapter10
{
    public class Recipe10_11Server
    {
        // A flag used to indicate whether the server is shutting down.
        private static bool terminate;
        public static bool Terminate { get { return terminate; } }

        // A variable to track the identity of each client connection.
        private static int ClientNumber = 0;

        // A single TcpListener will accept all incoming client connections.
        private static TcpListener listener;

        public static void Main()
        {
```

```
    // Create a 100KB test file for use in the example. This file will be
    // sent to clients that connect.
    using (FileStream fs = new FileStream("test.bin", FileMode.Create))
    {
        fs.SetLength(100000);
    }

    try
    {
        // Create a TcpListener that will accept incoming client
        // connections on port 8000 of the local machine.
        listener = new TcpListener(IPAddress.Parse("127.0.0.1"), 8000);

        Console.WriteLine("Starting TcpListener...");

        // Start the TcpListener accepting connections.
        terminate = false;
        listener.Start();

        // Begin asynchronously listening for client connections. When a
        // new connection is established, call the ConnectionHandler
        // method to process the new connection.
        listener.BeginAcceptTcpClient(ConnectionHandler, null);

        // Keep the server active until the user presses Enter.
        Console.WriteLine("Server awaiting connections. " +
            "Press Enter to stop server.");
        Console.ReadLine();
    }
    finally
    {
        // Shut down the TcpListener. This will cause any outstanding
        // asynchronous requests to stop and throw an exception in
        // the ConnectionHandler when EndAcceptTcpClient is called.
        // More robust termination synchronization may be desired here,
        // but for the purpose of this example ClientHandler threads are
        // all background threads and will terminate automatically when
        // the main thread terminates. This is suitable for our needs.
        Console.WriteLine("Server stopping...");
        terminate = true;
        if (listener != null) listener.Stop();
    }

    // Wait to continue.
    Console.WriteLine(Environment.NewLine);
    Console.WriteLine("Server stopped. Press Enter");
    Console.ReadLine();
}

// A method to handle the callback when a connection is established
// from a client. This is a simple way to implement a dispatcher
```

```
    // but lacks the control and scalability required when implementing
    // full-blown asynchronous server applications.
    private static void ConnectionHandler(IAsyncResult result)
    {
        TcpClient client = null;

        // Always end the asynchronous operation to avoid leaks.
        try
        {
            // Get the TcpClient that represents the new client connection.
            client = listener.EndAcceptTcpClient(result);
        }
        catch (ObjectDisposedException)
        {
            // Server is shutting down and the outstanding asynchronous
            // request calls the completion method with this exception.
            // The exception is thrown when EndAcceptTcpClient is called.
            // Do nothing and return.
            return;
        }

        Console.WriteLine("Dispatcher: New connection accepted.");

        // Begin asynchronously listening for the next client
        // connection.
        listener.BeginAcceptTcpClient(ConnectionHandler, null);

        if (client != null)
        {
            // Determine the identifier for the new client connection.
            Interlocked.Increment(ref ClientNumber);
            string clientName = "Client " + ClientNumber.ToString();

            Console.WriteLine("Dispatcher: Creating client handler ({0})."
                , clientName);

            // Create a new ClientHandler to handle this connection.
            new ClientHandler(client, clientName);
        }
    }
}

// A class that encapsulates the logic to handle a client connection.
public class ClientHandler
{
    // The TcpClient that represents the connection to the client.
    private TcpClient client;

    // An ID that uniquely identifies this ClientHandler.
    private string ID;
```

```
// The amount of data that will be written in one block (2KB).
private int bufferSize = 2048;

// The buffer that holds the data to write.
private byte[] buffer;

// Used to read data from the local file.
private FileStream fileStream;

// A signal to stop sending data to the client.
private bool stopDataTransfer;

internal ClientHandler(TcpClient client, string ID)
{
    this.buffer = new byte[bufferSize];
    this.client = client;
    this.ID = ID;

    // Create a new background thread to handle the client connection
    // so that we do not consume a thread-pool thread for a long time
    // and also so that it will be terminated when the main thread ends.
    Thread thread = new Thread(ProcessConnection);
    thread.IsBackground = true;
    thread.Start();
}

private void ProcessConnection()
{
    using (client)
    {
        // Create a BinaryReader to receive messages from the client. At
        // the end of the using block, it will close both the BinaryReader
        // and the underlying NetworkStream.
        using (BinaryReader reader = new BinaryReader(client.GetStream()))
        {
            if (reader.ReadString() == Recipe10_11Shared.RequestConnect)
            {
                // Create a BinaryWriter to send messages to the client.
                // At the end of the using block, it will close both the
                // BinaryWriter and the underlying NetworkStream.
                using (BinaryWriter writer =
                    new BinaryWriter(client.GetStream()))
                {
                    writer.Write(Recipe10_11Shared.AcknowledgeOK);
                    Console.WriteLine(ID + ": Connection established.");

                    string message = "";
```

```
                while (message != Recipe10_11Shared.Disconnect)
                {
                    try
                    {
                        // Read the message from the client.
                        message = reader.ReadString();
                    }
                    catch
                    {
                        // For the purpose of the example, any
                        // exception should be taken as a
                        // client disconnect.
                        message = Recipe10_11Shared.Disconnect;
                    }

                    if (message == Recipe10_11Shared.RequestData)
                    {
                        Console.WriteLine(ID + ": Requested data. ",
                            "Sending...");

                        // The filename could be supplied by the
                        // client, but in this example a test file
                        // is hard-coded.
                        fileStream = new FileStream("test.bin",
                            FileMode.Open, FileAccess.Read);

                        // Send the file size--this is how the client
                        // knows how much to read.
                        writer.Write(fileStream.Length.ToString());

                        // Start an asynchronous send operation.
                        stopDataTransfer = false;
                        StreamData(null);
                    }
                    else if (message == Recipe10_11Shared.Disconnect)
                    {
                        Console.WriteLine(ID +
                            ": Client disconnecting...");
                        stopDataTransfer = true;
                    }
                    else
                    {
                        Console.WriteLine(ID + ": Unknown command.");
                    }
                }
            }
        }
```

```
            else
            {
                Console.WriteLine(ID +
                    ": Could not establish connection.");
            }
        }
    }

    Console.WriteLine(ID + ": Client connection closed.");
}

private void StreamData(IAsyncResult asyncResult)
{
    // Always complete outstanding asynchronous operations to avoid leaks.
    if (asyncResult != null)
    {
        try
        {
            client.GetStream().EndWrite(asyncResult);
        }
        catch
        {
            // For the purpose of the example, any exception obtaining
            // or writing to the network should just terminate the
            // download.
            fileStream.Close();
            return;
        }
    }

    if (!stopDataTransfer && !Recipe10_11Server.Terminate)
    {
        // Read the next block from the file.
        int bytesRead = fileStream.Read(buffer, 0, buffer.Length);

        // If no bytes are read, the stream is at the end of the file.
        if (bytesRead > 0)
        {
            Console.WriteLine(ID + ": Streaming next block.");

            // Write the next block to the network stream.
            client.GetStream().BeginWrite(buffer, 0, buffer.Length,
                StreamData, null);
        }
        else
        {
            // End the operation.
            Console.WriteLine(ID + ": File streaming complete.");
            fileStream.Close();
        }
    }
```

```
            else
            {
                // Client disconnected.
                Console.WriteLine(ID + ": Client disconnected.");
                fileStream.Close();
            }
        }
    }
}
```

And here is the client code:

```
using System;
using System.Net;
using System.Net.Sockets;
using System.IO;

namespace Apress.VisualCSharpRecipes.Chapter10
{
    public class Recipe10_11Client
    {
        private static void Main()
        {
            using (TcpClient client = new TcpClient())
            {
                Console.WriteLine("Attempting to connect to the server ",
                    "on port 8000.");

                // Connect to the server.
                client.Connect(IPAddress.Parse("127.0.0.1"), 8000);

                // Retrieve the network stream from the TcpClient.
                using (NetworkStream networkStream = client.GetStream())
                {
                    // Create a BinaryWriter for writing to the stream.
                    using (BinaryWriter writer = new BinaryWriter(networkStream))
                    {
                        // Start a dialog.
                        writer.Write(Recipe10_11Shared.RequestConnect);

                        // Create a BinaryReader for reading from the stream.
                        using (BinaryReader reader =
                            new BinaryReader(networkStream))
                        {
                            if (reader.ReadString() ==
                                Recipe10_11Shared.AcknowledgeOK)
                            {
                                Console.WriteLine("Connection established." +
                                    "Press Enter to download data.");

                                Console.ReadLine();
```

```
                    // Send message requesting data to server.
                    writer.Write(Recipe10_11Shared.RequestData);

                    // The server should respond with the size of
                    // the data it will send. Assume it does.
                    int fileSize = int.Parse(reader.ReadString());

                    // Only get part of the data, then carry out a
                    // premature disconnect.
                    for (int i = 0; i < fileSize / 3; i++)
                    {
                        Console.Write(networkStream.ReadByte());
                    }

                    Console.WriteLine(Environment.NewLine);
                    Console.WriteLine("Press Enter to disconnect.");
                    Console.ReadLine();
                    Console.WriteLine("Disconnecting...");
                    writer.Write(Recipe10_11Shared.Disconnect);
                }
                else
                {
                    Console.WriteLine("Connection not established.");
                }
            }
        }
    }
}

            // Wait to continue.
            Console.WriteLine(Environment.NewLine);
            Console.WriteLine("Connection closed. Press Enter");
            Console.ReadLine();
        }
    }
}
```

10-12. Communicate Using UDP

Problem

You need to send data between two computers on a network using a UDP stream.

Solution

Use the `System.Net.Sockets.UdpClient` class and use two threads: one to send data and the other to receive it.

How It Works

UDP is a connectionless protocol that doesn't include any flow control or error checking. Unlike TCP, UDP shouldn't be used where reliable communication is required. However, because of its lower overhead, UDP is often used for "chatty" applications where it is acceptable to lose some messages. For example, imagine you want to create a network in which individual clients send information about the current temperature at their locations to a server every few seconds. You might use UDP in this case because the communication frequency is high and the damage caused by losing a packet is trivial (because the server can just continue to use the last received temperature reading).

The Code

The application shown in the following code uses two threads: one to receive messages and one to send them. The application stops when the user presses the Enter key without any text to send. Notice that UDP applications cannot use the `NetworkStream` abstraction that TCP applications can. Instead, they must convert all data to a stream of bytes using an encoding class, as described in recipe 2-2.

```
using System;
using System.Text;
using System.Net;
using System.Net.Sockets;
using System.Threading;

namespace Apress.VisualCSharpRecipes.Chapter10
{
    class Recipe10_12
    {
        private static int localPort;

        private static void Main()
        {
            // Define endpoint where messages are sent.
            Console.Write("Connect to IP: ");
            string IP = Console.ReadLine();
            Console.Write("Connect to port: ");
            int port = Int32.Parse(Console.ReadLine());

            IPEndPoint remoteEndPoint =
                new IPEndPoint(IPAddress.Parse(IP), port);

            // Define local endpoint (where messages are received).
            Console.Write("Local port for listening: ");
            localPort = Int32.Parse(Console.ReadLine());

            // Create a new thread for receiving incoming messages.
            Thread receiveThread = new Thread(ReceiveData);
            receiveThread.IsBackground = true;
            receiveThread.Start();
```

```
    UdpClient client = new UdpClient();

    Console.WriteLine("Type message and press Enter to send:");

    try
    {
        string text;

        do
        {
            text = Console.ReadLine();

            // Send the text to the remote client.
            if (text.Length != 0)
            {
                // Encode the data to binary using UTF8 encoding.
                byte[] data = Encoding.UTF8.GetBytes(text);

                // Send the text to the remote client.
                client.Send(data, data.Length, remoteEndPoint);
            }
        } while (text.Length != 0);
    }
    catch (Exception err)
    {
        Console.WriteLine(err.ToString());
    }
    finally
    {
        client.Close();
    }

    // Wait to continue.
    Console.WriteLine(Environment.NewLine);
    Console.WriteLine("Main method complete. Press Enter");
    Console.ReadLine();
}

private static void ReceiveData()
{
    UdpClient client = new UdpClient(localPort);

    while (true)
    {
        try
        {
            // Receive bytes.
            IPEndPoint anyIP = new IPEndPoint(IPAddress.Any, 0);
            byte[] data = client.Receive(ref anyIP);
```

```
                    // Convert bytes to text using UTF8 encoding.
                    string text = Encoding.UTF8.GetString(data);

                    // Display the retrieved text.
                    Console.WriteLine(">> " + text);
                }
                catch (Exception err)
                {
                    Console.WriteLine(err.ToString());
                }
            }
        }
    }
}
```

To test this application, load two instances at the same time. On computer A, specify the IP address for computer B. On computer B, specify the address for computer A. You can then send text messages back and forth at will. You can test this application with clients on the local computer using the loopback alias 127.0.0.1, provided you use different listening ports. For example, imagine a situation with two UDP clients, client A and client B. Here's a sample transcript for client A:

```
Connect to IP: 127.0.0.1
Connect to port: 8001
Local port for listening: 8080

Hi there!
```

And here's the corresponding transcript for client B (with the received message):

```
Connect to IP: 127.0.0.1
Connect to port: 8080
Local port for listening: 8001

>> Hi there!
```

10-13. Create a SOAP-Based Web Service

Problem

You need to expose functionality as a SOAP-based web service so that it can be accessed across the Internet.

Solution

Declare an `interface` that contains the methods you want your web service to expose. Identify this interface as a Windows Communication Foundation (WCF) service contract by applying the `ServiceContractAttribute` attribute to the interface and the `OperationContractAttribute` attribute to each of the methods you want exposed by the web service. The `ServiceContractAttribute` and `OperationContractAttribute` classes are members of the `System.ServiceModel` namespace.

Define any complex data types passed to and from the service and identify them as WCF data contracts by applying the `DataContractAttribute` attribute to the class and the `DataMemberAttribute` attribute to the members that need to be passed across the network. The `DataContractAttribute` and `DataMemberAttribute` classes are members of the `System.Runtime.Serialization` namespace.

Implement the service contract functionality by implementing the `interface` on a class, configure the configuration settings that control the behavior and protocols used by the service, and host an instance of the service class in a service host.

How It Works

WCF allows you to quickly create web services that are accessible across the Internet and that offer many choices in terms of protocols, security, and communication models. To create a simple SOAP-based WCF web service, you need the following key ingredients:

- *A service contract*: This defines the functionality exposed by the web service and is usually in the form of a C# interface, where the interface is annotated with the `ServiceContractAttribute` attribute and the web service methods are annotated with the `OperationContractAttribute` attribute.
- *A service implementation*: This object implements the service contract interface and defines what each of the web service methods does when called by a client.
- *A service host*: The service host is a process that controls the life cycle of the web service. This can be a custom program that loads your service (called *self-hosting*), Internet Information Server (IIS), or Windows Activation Services (WAS).

There is potentially a lot of configuration information associated with a WCF web service, including things like network addresses, protocol selection, and security settings. But the beauty of WCF is that you really only need to worry about those bits of functionality that you are actively using and ignore the rest. You can also choose whether to manage your configuration in code or through the application config files. However, unless you need to make configuration decisions at runtime, it is usually best to use declarative configuration so that you can change settings without having to change your code.

Once you have created a SOAP-based web service, the easiest way to consume it is to automatically generate a proxy class using Visual Studio, or use the ServiceModel Metadata Utility Tool (`svcutil.exe`), which is part of the Windows SDK. In some circumstances, you can also generate proxy classes dynamically (see recipe 10-14 for details).

The Code

The following example demonstrates the creation of a simple SOAP-based web service that allows you to create, update, find, and delete employee records. The example is self-hosted, but could be moved to IIS or WAS without changes to the service code. The `IEmployeeService` interface defines the service contract.

```
using System;
using System.ServiceModel;

namespace Apress.VisualCSharpRecipes.Chapter10
{
```

```
    [ServiceContract(Namespace = "Apress.VisualCSharpRecipes.Chapter10")]
    public interface IEmployeeService
    {
        [OperationContract]
        Employee CreateEmployee(Employee newEmployee);

        [OperationContract]
        bool DeleteEmployee(int employeeId);

        [OperationContract(Name="GetEmployeeById")]
        Employee GetEmployee(int employeeId);

        [OperationContract(Name = "GetEmployeeByName")]
        Employee GetEmployee(string employeeName);

        [OperationContract]
        Employee UpdateEmployee(Employee updatedEmployee);
    }
}
```

Here is the class that declares the `Employee` data contract representing the data that is passed between the client and the service:

```
using System;
using System.Runtime.Serialization;

namespace Apress.VisualCSharpRecipes.Chapter10
{
    [DataContract]
    public class Employee
    {
        [DataMember]
        public DateTime DateOfBirth { get; set; }

        [DataMember]
        public int Id { get; set; }

        [DataMember]
        public string Name { get; set; }
    }
}
```

The `EmployeeService` class implements the `IEmployeeService` interface and provides the actual logic of the web service.

```
using System;
using System.Collections.Generic;
using System.Linq;

namespace Apress.VisualCSharpRecipes.Chapter10
{
```

```
public class EmployeeService : IEmployeeService
{
    private Dictionary<int, Employee> employees;

    public EmployeeService()
    {
        employees = new Dictionary<int, Employee>();
    }

    // Create an Employee based on the contents of a provided
    // Employee object. Return the new Employee object.
    public Employee CreateEmployee(Employee newEmployee)
    {
        // NOTE: Should validate new employee data.
        newEmployee.Id = employees.Count + 1;

        lock (employees)
        {
            employees[newEmployee.Id] = newEmployee;
        }

        return newEmployee;
    }

    // Delete an employee by the specified Id and return true
    // or false depending on if an Employee was deleted.
    public bool DeleteEmployee(int employeeId)
    {
        lock(employees)
        {
            return employees.Remove(employeeId);
        }
    }

    // Get an employee by the specified Id and return null if
    // the employee does not exist.
    public Employee GetEmployee(int employeeId)
    {
        Employee employee = null;

        lock (employees)
        {
            employees.TryGetValue(employeeId, out employee);
        }

        return employee;
    }
```

```
        // Get an employee by the specified Name and return null if
        // the employee does not exist.
        public Employee GetEmployee(string employeeName)
        {
            Employee employee = null;

            lock (employees)
            {
                employee = employees.Values.FirstOrDefault
                    (e => e.Name.ToLower() == employeeName.ToLower());
            }

            return employee;
        }

        // Update an employee based on the contents of a provided
        // Employee object. Return the updated Employee object.
        public Employee UpdateEmployee(Employee updatedEmployee)
        {
            Employee employee = GetEmployee(updatedEmployee.Id);

            // NOTE: Should validate new employee data.
            if (employee != null)
            {
                lock (employees)
                {
                    employees[employee.Id] = updatedEmployee;
                }
            }

            return updatedEmployee;
        }
    }
}
```

The following code shows the simple service host created to run the service:

```
using System;
using System.ServiceModel;

namespace Apress.VisualCSharpRecipes.Chapter10
{
    public static class Recipe10_13Service
    {
        static void Main(string[] args)
        {
            ServiceHost host = new ServiceHost(typeof(EmployeeService));
            host.Open();
```

```
            // Wait to continue.
            Console.WriteLine("Service host running. Press Enter to terminate.");
            Console.ReadLine();
        }
    }
}
```

The following shows the configuration information used by the service host:

```
<?xml version="1.0" encoding="utf-8" ?>
<configuration>
  <system.serviceModel>
    <behaviors>
      <serviceBehaviors>
        <behavior name="EmployeeServiceBehavior" >
          <serviceMetadata httpGetEnabled="true" />
        </behavior>
      </serviceBehaviors>
    </behaviors>
    <services>
      <service name="Apress.VisualCSharpRecipes.Chapter10.EmployeeService"
               behaviorConfiguration="EmployeeServiceBehavior">
        <endpoint address="http://localhost:8000/EmployeeService"
                  binding="wsHttpBinding"
                  contract="Apress.VisualCSharpRecipes.Chapter10.IEmployeeService" />
        <endpoint address="http://localhost:8000/EmployeeService/mex"
                  binding="mexHttpBinding"
                  contract="IMetadataExchange" />
        <host>
          <baseAddresses>
            <add baseAddress="http://localhost:8000/" />
          </baseAddresses>
        </host>
      </service>
    </services>
  </system.serviceModel>
</configuration>
```

Finally, the following simple client code demonstrates how to interact with the service via a proxy:

```
using System;
using Apress.VisualCSharpRecipes.Chapter10.Services;

namespace Apress.VisualCSharpRecipes.Chapter10
{
    class Recipe10_13Client
    {
        private static string FormatEmployee(Employee emp)
        {
```

```
            return String.Format("ID:{0}, NAME:{1}, DOB:{2}",
                emp.Id, emp.Name, emp.DateOfBirth);
        }

        static void Main(string[] args)
        {
            // Create a service proxy.
            using (EmployeeServiceClient employeeService
                = new EmployeeServiceClient())
            {
                // Create a new Employee.
                Employee emp = new Employee()
                {
                    DateOfBirth = DateTime.Now,
                    Name = "Allen Jones"
                };

                // Call the EmployeeService to create a new Employee record.
                emp = employeeService.CreateEmployee(emp);

                Console.WriteLine("Created employee record - {0}",
                    FormatEmployee(emp));

                // Update the existing Employee.
                emp.DateOfBirth = new DateTime(1950, 10, 13);
                emp = employeeService.UpdateEmployee(emp);

                Console.WriteLine("Updated employee record - {0}",
                    FormatEmployee(emp));

                // Wait to continue.
                Console.WriteLine(Environment.NewLine);
                Console.WriteLine("Main method complete. Press Enter");
                Console.ReadLine();
            }
        }
    }
}
```

10-14. Call a WCF Service Using a Dynamically Generated Service Proxy

Problem

You need to call the methods of a WCF service but can't or don't want to generate a static proxy class as described in recipe 10-13.

Solution

If you have access to classes that represent the service and data contracts exposed by the service, you can create a dynamic service proxy using the `System.ServiceModel.ChannelFactory` class.

How It Works

The `ChannelFactory` class is a generic class that allows you to create proxies dynamically based on WCF service contracts. When instantiating a `ChannelFactory`, in addition to identifying the type of the service proxy you want to create, you must provide details of the WCF endpoint to which you want to connect. This includes the binding you want to use and the address of the service you want to communicate with.

Once you have instantiated a properly configured `ChannelFactory`, you call its `CreateChannel` method, which will return a service proxy in the form of an instance of the service contract type. You can then use this proxy to make calls against the service endpoint identified in the `ChannelFactory` constructor.

The Code

The following code demonstrates the use of a dynamic service proxy to communicate with a WCF service. The service used in this example is basically the same as that used in recipe 10-13. Instead of using Visual Studio to generate a proxy class, the client project contains a reference to the service project. The reference gives the client code access to the service and data contract classes of the service, enabling the use of the `ChannelFactory` to create dynamic service proxies at runtime.

```
using System;
using System.ServiceModel;

namespace Apress.VisualCSharpRecipes.Chapter10
{
    class Recipe10_14Client
    {
        static void Main(string[] args)
        {
            string serviceUri = "http://localhost:8000/EmployeeService";

            // Create the ChannelFactory that is used to generate service
            // proxies.
            using (ChannelFactory<IEmployeeService> channelFactory =
                new ChannelFactory<IEmployeeService>(new WSHttpBinding(), serviceUri))
            {
                // Create a dynamic proxy for IEmployeeService.
                IEmployeeService proxy = channelFactory.CreateChannel();

                // Create a new Employee.
                Employee emp = new Employee()
                {
                    DateOfBirth = DateTime.Now,
                    Name = "Allen Jones"
                };
```

```
                // Call the EmployeeService to create a new Employee record.
                emp = proxy.CreateEmployee(emp);

                Console.WriteLine("Created employee record - {0}", emp);

                // Update an existing Employee record.
                emp.DateOfBirth = new DateTime(1950, 10, 13);
                emp = proxy.UpdateEmployee(emp);

                Console.WriteLine("Updated employee record - {0}", emp);

                // Wait to continue.
                Console.WriteLine(Environment.NewLine);
                Console.WriteLine("Main method complete. Press Enter");
                Console.ReadLine();
            }
        }
    }
}
```

10-15. Process the Content of an Atom or RSS Feed

Problem

You need to process the content of an Atom 1.0 or RSS 2.0 feed to extract details of the feed, or the items it contains.

Solution

Parse the feed data using one of the format-specific classes derived from `System.ServiceModel.Syndication.SyndicationFeedFormatter`. Once parsed, the `SyndicationFeedFormatter.Feed` property returns a `System.ServiceModel.Syndication.SyndicationFeed` object whose properties provide access to the attributes of the feed and the items it contains. Use the `SyndicationFeedFormatter.Items` property to access a collection of `System.ServiceModel.Syndication.SyndicationItem` objects that represent the items in the feed. The properties of each `SyndicationItem` object expose the attributes of the individual feed items.

How It Works

The `SyndicationFeed` and `SyndicationFeedItem` classes provide a generic abstraction of Atom 1.0 and RSS 2.0 feeds and feed items, and present a common interface to simplify the processing of both feed types. The `Rss20FeedFormatter` class allows you to create a `SyndicationFeed` object from an RSS 2.0 feed, and the `Atom10FeedFormatter` class provides equivalent support for Atom 1.0 feeds. Both classes are members of the `System.ServiceModel.Syndication` namespace.

To load feed data for processing, use the `SyndicationFeedFormatter.ReadFrom` method and pass it a `System.Xml.XmlReader` that provides access to the feed data. Once loaded with feed data, the `SyndicationFeedFormatter.Feed` property provides access to a `SyndicationFeed` object allowing you to use the properties listed in Table 10-5 to access the feed attributes.

Table 10-5. Properties of the SyndicatedFeed Class

Property	Description
`Authors`	Gets a collection of authors from the feed
`BaseUri`	Gets the base URI from the feed
`Categories`	Gets a collection of categories from the feed
`Description`	Gets the description from the feed
`Id`	Gets the ID from the feed
`ImageUrl`	Gets the image URL from the feed
`Items`	Gets the collection of items contained in the feed
`Language`	Gets the language from the feed
`LastUpdatedTime`	Gets the last updated time from the feed
`Links`	Gets a collection of links associated with the feed
`Title`	Gets the title from the feed

The `SyndicationFeed.Items` property provides access to the set of items contained in the feed. Each item is represented by a `SyndicationItem`. Table 10-6 lists the properties that provide access to the attributes of a feed item.

Table 10-6. Properties of the SyndicationItem Class

Property	Description
`Authors`	Gets a collection of authors from the feed item
`BaseUri`	Gets the base URI from the feed item
`Categories`	Gets a collection of categories from the feed item
`Content`	Gets the content from the feed item
`Id`	Gets the ID from the feed item
`Language`	Gets the language from the feed item
`LastUpdatedTime`	Gets the last updated time from the feed item
`Links`	Gets a collection of links associated with the feed
`Summary`	Gets the summary from the feed item
`Title`	Gets the title from the feed item

The Code

The following example takes the URL of a feed as a command-line argument, downloads the feed, determines whether it is an RSS or Atom feed, and parses it using the appropriate `SyndicationFeedFormatter`. The output from running the example contains the title and description of the overall feed, and then the title, summary, and publication date of each item in the feed.

```
using System;
using System.Net;
using System.ServiceModel.Syndication;
using System.Xml.Linq;

namespace Apress.VisualCSharpRecipes.Chapter10
{
    class Recipe10_15
    {
        static void Main(string[] args)
        {
            Uri feedUrl = null;
```

```
if (args.Length == 0 || String.IsNullOrEmpty(args[0])
    || !Uri.TryCreate(args[0], UriKind.RelativeOrAbsolute,
        out feedUrl))
{
    // Error and wait to continue.
    Console.WriteLine("Invalid feed URL. Press Enter.");
    Console.ReadLine();
    return;
}

// Create the web request based on the URL provided for the feed.
WebRequest req = WebRequest.Create(feedUrl);

// Get the data from the feed.
WebResponse res = req.GetResponse();

// Simple test for the type of feed: Atom 1.0 or RSS 2.0.
SyndicationFeedFormatter formatter = null;
XElement feed = XElement.Load(res.GetResponseStream());

if (feed.Name.LocalName == "rss")
{
    formatter = new Rss20FeedFormatter();
}
else if (feed.Name.LocalName == "feed")
{
    formatter = new Atom10FeedFormatter();
}
else
{
    // Error and wait to continue.
    Console.WriteLine("Unsupported feed type: "
        + feed.Name.LocalName);
    Console.ReadLine();
    return;
}

// Read the feed data into the formatter.
formatter.ReadFrom(feed.CreateReader());

// Display feed level data:
Console.WriteLine("Title: " + formatter.Feed.Title.Text);
Console.WriteLine("Description: "
    + formatter.Feed.Description.Text);
Console.Write(Environment.NewLine);
Console.WriteLine("Items: ");
```

```
            // Display the item data.
            foreach (var item in formatter.Feed.Items)
            {
                Console.WriteLine("\tTitle: " + item.Title.Text);
                Console.WriteLine("\tSummary: " + item.Summary.Text);
                Console.WriteLine("\tPublish Date: " + item.PublishDate);
                Console.Write(Environment.NewLine);
            }

            // Wait to continue.
            Console.WriteLine(Environment.NewLine);
            Console.WriteLine("Main method complete. Press Enter.");
            Console.ReadLine();
        }
    }
}
```

10-16. Manipulate URIs

Problem

You need to construct a well-formed URI or extract the component parts of a provided URI.

Solution

Use the `System.Uri` class to extract the component parts of an existing URI and the `System.UriBuilder` class to construct a new well-formed URI.

How It Works

When doing web or network programming, you will regularly need to manipulate URIs and their closely related derivatives: URNs and URLs. For example, you may need to construct URLs that represent servers and network resources you want to access, or extract information like the host, port, or protocol specified in an externally provided URI.

The `System.Uri` class provides an object representation of a URI and implements properties that allow you to extract the various elements that constitute the URI. To create a `Uri`, pass the string representing the URI you want to parse to the `Uri` constructor. A number of constructor overloads allow you to handle both absolute and relative URIs. However, if the URI string is invalid, the constructor will throw a `System.UriFormatException`. To avoid this, you can use the static method `Uri.TryCreate`, which returns `true` if the parse was successful and `false` otherwise.

Once you have a `Uri` object, you can use its properties to extract specific components of the URI. Table 10-7 contains some commonly used properties of the `Uri` class.

Table 10-7. Commonly Used Members of the Uri Class

Property	Description
`AbsolutePath`	Gets a `string` that contains the absolute path of the URI
`AbsoluteUri`	Gets a `string` representation of the full URI as an absolute address
`Host`	Gets a `string` containing the host name specified in the URI
`IsDefaultPort`	Gets a `bool` indicating whether the specified port is the default port for the URI scheme
`OriginalString`	Gets the original `string` used to construct the `Uri`
`Port`	Gets an `int` containing the port number specified in the URI
`Query`	Gets a `string` containing the query string specified in the URI
`Scheme`	Gets a `string` containing the scheme specified in the URI

The `Uri` class is read-only, so if you want to create a new well-formed URI, you should use the `UriBuilder` class. You can specify the key elements of the URI in various overloads of the `UriBuilder` constructor, or you can configure a new `UriBuilder` object via its properties. Table 10-8 describes the properties of the `UriBuilder` class.

Table 10-8. Properties of the UriBuilder Class

Property	Description
`Fragment`	Gets or sets a `string` specifying the fragment element of the URI. This is the part after the hash symbol (#) found at the end of URLs.
`Host`	Gets or sets a `string` specifying the host element of the URI.
`Password`	Gets or sets a `string` specifying the password to use with the URI.
`Path`	Gets or sets a `string` specifying the path element of the URI.
`Port`	Gets or sets an `int` specifying the port element of the URI.
`Query`	Gets or sets a `string` specifying the query string element of the URI.

Property	Description
Scheme	Gets or sets a string specifying the scheme element of the URI.
UserName	Gets or sets a string containing the username to use with the URI.

Once you have configured the UriBuilder, you obtain an appropriately configured Uri object representing the URI via the UriBuilder.Uri property. Many methods that require URIs take Uri instances, but if you need a string representation of the URI you can use the Uri.AbsolutePath property.

The Code

The following code demonstrates the use of the Uri and UriBuilder classes.

```
using System;
using System.Collections.Generic;
using System.Linq;
using System.Text;

namespace Apress.VisualCSharpRecipes.Chapter10
{
    class Recipe10_16
    {
        private static string defualtUrl
            = "http://www.apress.com:80/book/view/9781430225256";

        static void Main(string[] args)
        {
            Uri uri = null;

            // Extract information from a string URL passed as a
            // command line argument or use the default URL.
            string strUri = defualtUrl;

            if (args.Length > 0 && !String.IsNullOrEmpty(args[0]))
            {
                strUri = args[0];
            }

            // Safely parse the url
            if (Uri.TryCreate(strUri, UriKind.RelativeOrAbsolute, out uri))
            {
                Console.WriteLine("Parsed URI: " + uri.OriginalString);
                Console.WriteLine("\tScheme: " + uri.Scheme);
                Console.WriteLine("\tHost: " + uri.Host);
                Console.WriteLine("\tPort: " + uri.Port);
                Console.WriteLine("\tPath and Query: " + uri.PathAndQuery);
            }
```

```
            else
            {
                Console.WriteLine("Unable to parse URI: " + strUri);
            }

            // Create a new URI.
            UriBuilder newUri = new UriBuilder();
            newUri.Scheme = "http";
            newUri.Host = "www.apress.com";
            newUri.Port = 80;
            newUri.Path = "book/view/9781430225256";

            Console.WriteLine(Environment.NewLine);
            Console.WriteLine("Created URI: " + newUri.Uri.AbsoluteUri);

            // Wait to continue.
            Console.WriteLine(Environment.NewLine);
            Console.WriteLine("Main method complete. Press Enter.");
            Console.ReadLine();
        }
    }
}
```

CHAPTER 11

Security and Cryptography

Prior to version 4.0, the .NET Framework incorporated two complementary security models that addressed user and code security: role-based security (RBS) and code access security (CAS). With version 4.0, CAS has been deprecated. The previous edition of this book included a number of CAS recipes (11-1 through to 11-7), and we have included them in this new version because of the number of developers still using .NET 3.5 or earlier, where CAS still has a significant function. The C# compiler will show deprecation warnings if you use CAS in a project. You can prevent these errors by targeting your project at an earlier version of the .NET Framework on the Application tab. You can enable CAS in your .NET 4.0 projects with the `NetFx40_LegacySecurityPolicy` configuration element in the `app.config` file—for example:

```
<?xml version="1.0"?>
<configuration>
  <runtime>
    <NetFx40_LegacySecurityPolicy enabled="true"/>
  </runtime>
</configuration>
```

RBS remains current in .NET 4.0 and allows you to make runtime decisions based on the identity and roles of the user on whose behalf an application is running. On the Windows operating system, this equates to making decisions based on the Windows username and the Windows groups to which that user belongs. However, RBS provides a generic security mechanism that is independent of the underlying operating system, allowing you (with some development) to integrate with any user account system.

An important aspect of the security features provided by the .NET Framework is *cryptography*. Cryptography is one of the most complex aspects of software development that any developer will use. The theory of modern cryptographic techniques is extremely difficult to understand and requires a level of mathematical knowledge that relatively few people have or need. Fortunately, the Microsoft .NET Framework class library provides easy-to-use implementations of the most commonly used cryptographic techniques and support for the most popular and well-understood algorithms.

This chapter provides a wide variety of recipes that cover some of the more commonly used security capabilities provided by the .NET Framework. As you read the recipes in this chapter and think about how to apply the techniques to your own code, keep in mind that individual security features are rarely effective when implemented in isolation. In particular, cryptography does not equal security; the use of cryptography is merely one small element of creating a secure solution.

The recipes in this chapter describe how to do the following:

- Develop strongly named assemblies that can still be called by partially trusted code (recipe 11-1)
- Configure the .NET Framework security policy to turn off CAS completely or turn off only execution permission checks (recipes 11-2 and 11-3)
- Request specific code access permissions for your assemblies, determine at runtime what permissions the current assembly has, and inspect third-party assemblies to determine what permissions they need in order to run correctly (recipes 11-4, 11-5, 11-6, and 11-7)
- Control inheritance and member overrides using CAS (recipe 11-8)
- Inspect the evidence presented by an assembly to the runtime when the assembly is loaded (recipe 11-9)
- Integrate with Windows security to determine if a user is a member of a specific Windows group, restrict which users can execute your code, and impersonate other Windows users (recipes 11-10, 11-11, and 11-12)
- Generate random numbers that are nondeterministic and are suitable for use in security-sensitive applications (recipe 11-13)
- Use hash codes and keyed hash codes to store user passwords and determine if files have changed (recipes 11-14, 11-15, 11-16, and 11-17)
- Use encryption to protect sensitive data both in memory and when it is stored to disk (recipes 11-18 and 11-19)

11-1. Allow Partially Trusted Code to Use Your Strongly Named Assembly

Problem

You need to write a shared assembly that is accessible to partially trusted code. (By default, the runtime does not allow partially trusted code to access the types and members contained in a strongly named assembly.)

Solution

Apply the assembly-level attribute `System.Security.AllowPartiallyTrustedCallersAttribute` to your shared assembly.

■ **Note** CAS is deprecated in .NET 4.0.

How It Works

To minimize the security risks posed by malicious code, the runtime does not allow assemblies granted only partial trust to access strongly named assemblies. This restriction dramatically reduces the opportunity for malicious code to attack your system, but the reasoning behind such a heavy-handed approach requires some explanation.

Assemblies that contain important functionality that is shared between multiple applications are usually strongly named and are often installed in the Global Assembly Cache (GAC). This is particularly true of the assemblies that constitute the .NET Framework class library. Other strongly named assemblies from well-known and widely distributed products are in the GAC and accessible to managed applications. The high chance that certain assemblies will be present in the GAC, their easy accessibility, and their importance to many different applications make strongly named assemblies the most likely target for any type of subversive activity by malicious managed code.

Generally, the code most likely to be malicious is that which is loaded from remote locations over which you have little or no control (such as over the Internet). Under the default security policy of the .NET Framework, all code run from the local machine has full trust, whereas code loaded from remote locations has only partial trust. Stopping partially trusted code from accessing strongly named assemblies means that partially trusted code has no opportunity to use the features of the assembly for malicious purposes, and cannot probe and explore the assembly to find exploitable holes. Of course, this theory hinges on the assumption that you correctly administer your security policy. If you simply assign all code full trust, not only will any assembly be able to access your strongly named assembly, but the code will also be able to access all of the functionality of the .NET Framework and even Win32 or any COM object through P/Invoke and COM Interop. That would be a security disaster!

■ **Note** If you design, implement, and test your shared assembly correctly using CAS to restrict access to important members, you do not need to impose a blanket restriction to prevent partially trusted code from using your assembly. However, for an assembly of any significance, it's impossible to prove there are no security holes that malicious code can exploit. Therefore, you should carefully consider the need to allow partially trusted code to access your strongly named assembly before applying `AllowPartiallyTrustedCallersAttribute`. However, you might have no choice. If you are exposing public classes that provide events, you must apply this attribute. If you do not, an assembly that is not strongly named will be allowed to register a handler for one of your events, but when it is called, a security exception will be thrown. Code in an assembly that is not strongly named is not allowed to call code in a strongly named assembly.

The runtime stops partially trusted code from accessing strongly named assemblies by placing an implicit `LinkDemand` for the `FullTrust` permission set on every public and protected member of every publicly accessible type defined in the assembly. This means that only assemblies granted the permissions equivalent to the `FullTrust` permission set are able to access the types and members from the strongly named assembly. Applying `AllowPartiallyTrustedCallersAttribute` to your strongly named assembly signals the runtime to not enforce the `LinkDemand` on the contained types and members.

■ **Note** The runtime is responsible for enforcing the implicit `LinkDemand` security actions required to protect strongly named assemblies. The C# assembler does not generate declarative `LinkDemand` statements at compile time.

The Code

The following code fragment shows the application of the attribute `AllowPartiallyTrustedCallersAttribute`. Notice that you must prefix the attribute with `assembly:` to signal to the compiler that the target of the attribute is the assembly (also called a *global attribute*). In addition, you do not need to include the `Attribute` part of the attribute name, although you can if you want to add it. Because you target the assembly, the attribute must be positioned after any top-level `using` statements, but before any namespace or type declarations.

```
using System.Security;

[assembly:AllowPartiallyTrustedCallers]

namespace Apress.VisualCSharpRecipes.Chapter11
{
    public class Recipe11-01 {

        // Implementation code . . .
    }
}
```

■ **Tip** It's common practice to contain all global attributes in a file separate from the rest of your application code. Microsoft Visual Studio uses this approach, creating a file named `AssemblyInfo.cs` to contain all global attributes.

Notes

If, after applying `AllowPartiallyTrustedCallersAttribute` to your assembly, you want to restrict partially trusted code from calling only specific members, you should implement a `LinkDemand` for the `FullTrust` permission set on the necessary members, as shown in the following code fragment:

```
[System.Security.Permissions.PermissionSetAttribute
    (System.Security.Permissions.SecurityAction.LinkDemand, Name="FullTrust")]

public void SomeMethod() {
    // Method code . . .
}
```

11-2. Disable Code Access Security

Problem

You need to turn off all CAS checks.

Solution

Use the Code Access Security Policy tool (`Caspol.exe`) and execute the command `caspol -s off` from the command line to temporarily disable code access security checks.

■ **Note** This recipe only applies to .NET version 3.5 and earlier.

How It Works

Although CAS was implemented with performance in mind and has been used prudently throughout the .NET class library, some overhead is associated with each security demand and resulting stack walk that the runtime must execute to check every caller in the chain of execution.

You can temporarily disable CAS and remove the overhead and possible interference caused by code-level security checks. Turning off CAS has the effect of giving all code the ability to perform any action supported by the .NET Framework (equivalent to the `FullTrust` permission set). This includes the ability to load other code, call native libraries, and use pointers to access memory directly.

`Caspol.exe` is a utility provided with the .NET Framework that allows you to configure all aspects of your code access security policy from the command line. When you enter the command `caspol -s off` from the command line, you will see the following message indicating that CAS has been temporarily disabled:

```
Microsoft (r) .NET Framework CasPol 2.0.50727.42
Copyright (c) Microsoft Corporation. Al rights reserved.

CAS enforcement is being turned off temporarily. Press <enter> when you want to
restore the setting back on.
```

As the message states, CAS enforcement is off until you press Enter, or until the console in which `Caspol.exe` is running terminates.

11-3. Disable Execution Permission Checks

Problem

You need to load assemblies at runtime without the runtime checking them for execution permission.

Solution

In code, set the property `CheckExecutionRights` of the class `System.Security.SecurityManager` to `false` and persist the change by calling `SecurityManager.SavePolicy`. Alternatively, use the Code Access Security Policy tool (`Caspol.exe`), and execute the command `caspol -e off` from the command line.

■ **Note** This recipe only applies to .NET version 3.5 and earlier.

How It Works

As the runtime loads each assembly, it ensures that the assembly's grant set (the permissions assigned to the assembly based on the security policy) includes the `Execution` element of `SecurityPermission`. The runtime implements a lazy policy resolution process, meaning that the grant set of an assembly is not calculated until the first time a security demand is made against the assembly. Not only does execution permission checking force the runtime to check that every assembly has the execution permission, but it also indirectly causes policy resolution for every assembly loaded, effectively negating the benefits of lazy policy resolution. These factors can introduce a noticeable delay as assemblies are loaded, especially when the runtime loads a number of assemblies together, as it does at application startup.

In many situations, simply allowing code to load and run is not a significant risk, as long as all other important operations and resources are correctly secured using CAS and operating system security. The `SecurityManager` class contains a set of static methods that provide access to critical security functionality and data. This includes the `CheckExecutionRights` property, which turns on and off execution permission checks.

To modify the value of `CheckExecutionRights`, your code must have the `ControlPolicy` element of `SecurityPermission`. The change will affect the current process immediately, allowing you to load assemblies at runtime without the runtime checking them for execution permission. However, the change will not affect other existing processes. You must call the `SavePolicy` method to persist the change to the Windows registry for it to affect new processes.

The Code

The following example contains two methods (`ExecutionCheckOn` and `ExecutionCheckOff`) that demonstrate the code required to turn execution permission checks on and off and persist the configuration change. You may need to run the example with administrator privileges.

```
using System;
using System.Security;

namespace Apress.VisualCSharpRecipes.Chapter11
{
    class Recipe11_03
    {
        // A method to turn on execution permission checking
        // and persist the change.
        public void ExecutionCheckOn()
        {
            // Turn on execution permission checks.
            SecurityManager.CheckExecutionRights = true;

            // Persist the configuration change.
            SecurityManager.SavePolicy();
        }

        // A method to turn off execution permission checking
        // and persist the change.
        public void ExecutionCheckOff()
        {
            // Turn off execution permission checks.
            SecurityManager.CheckExecutionRights = false;

            // Persist the configuration change.
            SecurityManager.SavePolicy();
        }
    }
}
```

Notes

The .NET runtime allows you to turn off the automatic checks for execution permissions from within code or by using `Caspol.exe`. When you enter the command `caspol -e off` or its counterpart `caspol -e on` from the command line, the `Caspol.exe` utility actually sets the `CheckExecutionRights` property of the `SecurityManager` class before calling `SecurityManager.SavePolicy`.

11-4. Ensure the Runtime Grants Specific Permissions to Your Assembly

Problem

You need to ensure that the runtime grants your assembly those code access permissions that are critical to the successful operation of your application.

Solution

In your assembly, use permission requests to specify the code access permissions that your assembly must have. You declare permission requests using assembly-level code access permission attributes.

■ **Note** CAS is deprecated in .NET 4.0.

How It Works

The name *permission request* is a little misleading given that the runtime will never grant permissions to an assembly unless security policy dictates that the assembly should have those permissions. However, naming aside, permission requests serve an essential purpose, and although the way the runtime handles permission requests might initially seem strange, the nature of CAS does not allow for any obvious alternative.

Permission requests identify permissions that your code must have to function. For example, if you wrote a movie player that your customers could use to download and view movies from your web server, it would be disastrous if the user's security policy did not allow your player to open a network connection to your media server. Your player would load and run, but as soon as the user tried to connect to your server to play a movie, the application would crash with the exception `System.Security.SecurityException`. The solution is to include in your assembly a permission request for the code access permission required to open a network connection to your server (`System.Net.WebPermission` or `System.Net.SocketPermission`, depending on the type of connection you need to open).

The runtime honors permission requests using the premise that it's better that your code never load than to load and fail sometime later when it tries to perform an action that it does not have permission to perform. Therefore, if after security policy resolution the runtime determines that the grant set of your assembly does not satisfy the assembly's permission requests, the runtime will fail to load the assembly and will instead throw the exception `System.Security.Policy.PolicyException`. Since your own code failed to load, the runtime will handle this security exception during the assembly loading and transform it into a `System.IO.FileLoadException` exception that will terminate your program.

When you try to load an assembly from within code (either automatically or manually), and the loaded assembly contains permission requests that the security policy does not satisfy, the method you use to load the assembly will throw a `PolicyException` exception, which you must handle appropriately.

To declare a permission request, you must use the attribute counterpart of the code access permission that you need to request. All code access permissions have an attribute counterpart that you use to construct declarative security statements, including permission requests. For example, the attribute counterpart of `SocketPermission` is `SocketPermissionAttribute`, and the attribute counterpart of `WebPermission` is `WebPermissionAttribute`. All permissions and their attribute counterparts follow the same naming convention and are members of the same namespace.

When making a permission request, it's important to remember the following:

- You must declare the permission request after any top-level `using` statements but before any namespace or type declarations.
- The attribute must target the assembly, so you must prefix the attribute name with `assembly`.

- You do not need to include the `Attribute` portion of an attribute's name, although you can.
- You must specify `SecurityAction.RequestMinimum` as the first positional argument of the attribute. This value identifies the statement as a permission request.
- You must configure the attribute to represent the code access permission you want to request using the attribute's properties. Refer to the .NET Framework SDK documentation for details of the properties implemented by each code access security attribute.
- The permission request statements do not end with a semicolon (`;`).
- To make more than one permission request, simply include multiple permission request statements.

The Code

The following example is a console application that includes two permission requests: one for `SocketPermission` and the other for `SecurityPermission`. If you try to execute the `PermissionRequestExample` application and your security policy does not grant the assembly the requested permissions, you will get a `PolicyException`, and the application will not execute. Using the default security policy, this will happen if you run the assembly from a network share, because assemblies loaded from the intranet zone are not granted `SocketPermission`.

```
using System;
using System.Net;
using System.Security.Permissions;

// Permission request for a SocketPermission that allows the code to open
// a TCP connection to the specified host and port.
[assembly:SocketPermission(SecurityAction.RequestMinimum,
    Access = "Connect", Host = "www.fabrikam.com",
    Port = "3538", Transport = "Tcp")]

// Permission request for the UnmanagedCode element of SecurityPermission,
// which controls the code's ability to execute unmanaged code.
[assembly:SecurityPermission(SecurityAction.RequestMinimum,
    UnmanagedCode = true)]

namespace Apress.VisualCSharpRecipes.Chapter11
{
    class Recipe11_04
    {
        public static void Main()
        {
            // Do something . . .
```

```
            // Wait to continue.
            Console.WriteLine("Main method complete. Press Enter.");
            Console.ReadLine();
        }
    }
}
```

11-5. Limit the Permissions Granted to Your Assembly

Problem

You need to restrict the code access permissions granted to your assembly, ensuring that people and other software can never use your code as a mechanism through which to perform undesirable or malicious actions.

Solution

Use declarative security statements to specify optional permission requests and permission refusal requests in your assembly. Optional permission requests define the maximum set of permissions that the runtime will grant to your assembly. Permission refusal requests specify particular permissions that the runtime should not grant to your assembly.

■ **Note** CAS is deprecated in .NET 4.0.

How It Works

In the interest of security, it's ideal if your code has only those code access permissions required to perform its function. This minimizes the opportunities for people and other code to use your code to carry out malicious or undesirable actions. The problem is that the runtime resolves an assembly's permissions using security policy, which a user or an administrator configures. Security policy could be different in every location where your application is run, and you have no control over what permissions the security policy assigns to your code.

Although you cannot control security policy in all locations where your code runs, the .NET Framework provides two mechanisms through which you can reject permissions granted to your assembly:

- *Refuse request*: This allows you to identify specific permissions that you do not want the runtime to grant to your assembly. After policy resolution, if the final grant set of an assembly contains any permission specified in a refuse request, the runtime removes that permission.
- *Optional permission request*: This defines the maximum set of permissions that the runtime can grant to your assembly. If the final grant set of an assembly contains any permissions other than those specified in the optional permission request, the runtime removes those permissions. Unlike as with a minimum permission request (discussed in recipe 11-4), the runtime will not refuse to load your assembly if it cannot grant all of the permissions specified in the optional request.

You can think of a refuse request and an optional request as alternative ways to achieve the same result. The approach you use depends on how many permissions you want to reject. If you want to reject only a handful of permissions, a refuse request is easier to code. However, if you want to reject a large number of permissions, it's easier to code an optional request for the few permissions you want, which will automatically reject the rest.

You include optional and refuse requests in your code using declarative security statements with the same syntax as the minimum permission requests discussed in recipe 11-4. The only difference is the value of the `System.Security.Permissions.SecurityAction` that you pass to the permission attribute's constructor. Use `SecurityAction.RequestOptional` to declare an optional permission request and `SecurityAction.RequestRefuse` to declare a refuse request. As with minimal permission requests, you must declare optional and refuse requests as global attributes by beginning the permission attribute name with the prefix `assembly`. In addition, all requests must appear after any top-level `using` statements but before any namespace or type declarations.

The Code

The code shown here demonstrates an optional permission request for the Internet permission set. The Internet permission set is a named permission set defined by the default security policy. When the runtime loads the example, it will not grant the assembly any permission that is not included within the Internet permission set. (Consult the .NET Framework SDK documentation for details of the permissions contained in the Internet permission set.)

```
using System.Security.Permissions;

[assembly:PermissionSet(SecurityAction.RequestOptional, Name = "Internet")]

namespace Apress.VisualCSharpRecipes.Chapter11
{
    class Recipe11_05_OptionalRequest
    {
        // Class implementation . . .
    }
}
```

In contrast to the preceding example, the following example uses a refuse request to single out the permission System.Security.Permissions.FileIOPermission—representing write access to the C: drive—for refusal.

```
using System.Security.Permissions;

[assembly:FileIOPermission(SecurityAction.RequestRefuse, Write = @"C:\")]

namespace Apress.VisualCSharpRecipes.Chapter11
{
    class Recipe11_05_RefuseRequest
    {
        // Class implementation . . .
    }
}
```

11-6. View the Permissions Required by an Assembly

Problem

You need to view the permissions that an assembly must be granted in order to run correctly.

Solution

Use the Permissions Calculator (Permcalc.exe) supplied with the .NET Framework SDK version 3.5 or earlier.

■ **Note** CAS is deprecated in .NET 4.0.

How It Works

To configure security policy correctly, you need to know the code access permission requirements of the assemblies you intend to run. This is true of both executable assemblies and libraries that you access from your own applications. With libraries, it's also important to know which permissions the assembly refuses so that you do not try to use the library to perform a restricted action, which would result in a System.Security.SecurityException exception.

The Permissions Calculator (Permcalc.exe) supplied with the .NET Framework SDK version overcomes this limitation. Permcalc.exe walks through an assembly and provides an estimate of the permissions the assembly requires to run, regardless of whether they are declarative or imperative.

The Code

The following example shows a class that declares a minimum, optional, and refusal request, as well as a number of imperative security demands:

```
using System;
using System.Net;
using System.Security.Permissions;

// Minimum permission request for SocketPermission.
[assembly: SocketPermission(SecurityAction.RequestMinimum,
    Unrestricted = true)]

// Optional permission request for IsolatedStorageFilePermission.
[assembly: IsolatedStorageFilePermission(SecurityAction.RequestOptional,
    Unrestricted = true)]

// Refuse request for ReflectionPermission.
[assembly: ReflectionPermission(SecurityAction.RequestRefuse,
    Unrestricted = true)]

namespace Apress.VisualCSharpRecipes.Chapter11
{
    class Recipe11_06
    {
        public static void Main()
        {
            // Create and configure a FileIOPermission object that represents
            // write access to the C:\Data folder.
            FileIOPermission fileIOPerm =
                new FileIOPermission(FileIOPermissionAccess.Write, @"C:\Data");

            // Make the demand.
            fileIOPerm.Demand();

            // Do something . . .

            // Wait to continue.
            Console.WriteLine("Main method complete. Press Enter.");
            Console.ReadLine();
        }
    }
}
```

Usage

Executing the command `permview Recipe11-06.exe` will generate the following output. Although this output is not particularly user-friendly, you can decipher it to determine the declarative permission requests made by an assembly. Each of the three types of permission requests—minimum, optional, and refused—is listed under a separate heading and is structured as the XML representation of a `System.Security.PermissionSet` object.

```
Microsoft (R) .NET Framework Permission Request Viewer.

Version 1.1.4322.573

Copyright (C) Microsoft Corporation 1998-2002. All rights reserved.



minimal permission set:

<PermissionSet class=System.Security.PermissionSet" version="1">

  <IPermission class="System.Net.SocketPermission, System, Version=1.

0.5000.0, Culture=neutral, PublicKeyToken=b77a5c561934e089" version="

1" Unrestricted="true"/>

</PermissionSet>



optional permission set:

<PermissionSet class="System.Security.PermissionSet" version="1">

  <IPermission class="System.Security.Permissions.IsolatedStorageFilePermission,

mscorlib, Version=1.0.5000.0, Culture=neutral, PublicKeyToken=b77a5c5

61934e089" version="1" Unrestricted="true"/>

</PermissionSet>
```

```
refused permission set:
<PermissionSet class="System.Security.PermissionSet" version="1">
  <IPermission class="System.Security.Permissions.ReflectionPermission,
mscorlib, Version=1.0.5000.0, Culture=neutral, PublicKeyToken=b77a5c5
61934e089" version="1" Unrestricted="true"/>
</PermissionSet>
```

Executing the command `permcalc -sandbox Recipe11-06.exe` will generate a file named `sandbox.PermCalc.xml` that contains XML representations of the permissions required by the assembly. Where the exact requirements of a permission cannot be determined (because it is based on runtime data), `Permcalc.exe` reports that unrestricted permissions of that type are required. You can instead default to the Internet zone permissions using the `-Internet` flag. Here are the contents of `sandbox.PermCalc.xml` when run against the sample code:

```
<?xml version="1.0"?>
<Sandbox>
  <PermissionSet version="1" class="System.Security.PermissionSet">
    <IPermission Write="C:\Data" version="1"
        class="System.Security.Permissions.FileIOPermission, mscorlib,
        Version=2.0.0.0, Culture=neutral,
        PublicKeyToken=b77a5c561934e089" />
    <IPermission version="1" class="System.Security.Permissions.SecurityPermission,
        mscorlib, Version=2.0.0.0, Culture=neutral,
        PublicKeyToken=b77a5c561934e089" Flags="Execution" />
    <IPermission version="1" class="System.Security.Permissions.UIPermission,
        mscorlib, Version=2.0.0.0, Culture=neutral,
        PublicKeyToken=b77a5c561934e089" Unrestricted="true" />
```

```
    <IPermission version="1" class="System.Net.SocketPermission, System,
         Version=2.0.0.0, Culture=neutral, PublicKeyToken=b77a5c561934e089"
         Unrestricted="true" />
  </PermissionSet>
</Sandbox>
```

11-7. Determine at Runtime If Your Code Has a Specific Permission

Problem

You need to determine at runtime if your assembly has a specific permission.

Solution

Instantiate and configure the permission you want to test for, and then pass it as an argument to the static method `IsGranted` of the class `System.Security.SecurityManager`.

■ **Note** CAS is deprecated in .NET 4.0.

How It Works

Using minimum permission requests, you can ensure that the runtime grants your assembly a specified set of permissions. As a result, when your code is running, you can safely assume that it has the requested minimum permissions. However, you might want to implement opportunistic functionality that your application offers only if the runtime grants your assembly appropriate permissions. This approach is partially formalized using optional permission requests, which allow you to define a set of permissions that your code could use if the security policy granted them, but are not essential for the successful operation of your code. (Recipe 11-5 provides more details on using optional permission requests.)

The problem with optional permission requests is that the runtime has no ability to communicate to your assembly which of the requested optional permissions it has granted. You can try to use a protected operation and fail gracefully if the call results in the exception `System.Security.SecurityException`. However, it's more efficient to determine in advance whether you have the necessary permissions. You can then build logic into your code to avoid invoking secured members that will cause stack walks and raise security exceptions.

■ **Note** `IsGranted` checks the grant set only of the calling assembly. It does not do a full stack walk to evaluate the grant set of other assemblies on the call stack.

The Code

The following example demonstrates how to use the **IsGranted** method to determine if the assembly has write permission to the directory **C:\Data**. You could make such a call each time you needed to test for the permission, but it's more efficient to use the returned Boolean value to set a configuration flag indicating whether to allow users to save files.

```
using System.Security;
using System.Security.Permissions;

namespace Apress.VisualCSharpRecipes.Chapter11
{
    class Recipe11_07
    {
        // Define a variable to indicate whether the assembly has write
        // access to the C:\Data folder.
        private bool canWrite = false;

        public Recipe11_07()
        {
            // Create and configure a FileIOPermission object that represents
            // write access to the C:\Data folder.
            FileIOPermission fileIOPerm =
                new FileIOPermission(FileIOPermissionAccess.Write, @"C:\Data");

            // Test if the current assembly has the specified permission.
            canWrite = SecurityManager.IsGranted(fileIOPerm);
        }
    }
}
```

11-8. Restrict Who Can Extend Your Classes and Override Class Members

Problem

You need to control what code can extend your classes through inheritance and which class members a derived class can override.

Solution

Use declarative security statements to apply `SecurityAction.InheritanceDemand` to the declarations of the classes and members that you need to protect.

How It Works

Language modifiers such as `sealed`, `public`, `private`, and `virtual` give you a level of control over the ability of classes to inherit from your class and override its members. However, these modifiers are inflexible, providing no selectivity in restricting what code can extend a class or override its members. For example, you might want to allow only code written by your company or department to extend business-critical classes. By applying an `InheritanceDemand` attribute to your class or member declaration, you can specify runtime permissions that a class must have to extend your class or override particular members. Remember that the permissions of a class are the permissions of the assembly in which the class is declared.

Although you can demand any permission or permission set in your `InheritanceDemand`, it's more common to demand identity permissions. Identity permissions represent evidence presented to the runtime by an assembly. If an assembly presents certain types of evidence at load time, the runtime will automatically assign the assembly the appropriate identity permission. Identity permissions allow you to use regular imperative and declarative security statements to base security decisions directly on code identity, without the need to evaluate evidence objects directly. Table 11-1 lists the type of identity permission generated for each type of evidence. (Evidence types are members of the `System.Security.Policy` namespace, and identity permission types are members of the `System.Security.Permissions` namespace.)

Table 11-1. *Evidence Classes That Generate Identity Permissions*

Evidence Class	Identity Permission
`ApplicationDirectory`	None
`Hash`	None
`Publisher`	`PublisherIdentityPermission`
`Site`	`SiteIdentityPermission`
`StrongName`	`StrongNameIdentityPermission`
`Url`	`UrlIdentityPermission`
`Zone`	`ZoneIdentityPermission`

■ **Note** The runtime assigns identity permissions to an assembly based on the evidence presented by the assembly. You cannot assign additional identity permissions to an assembly through the configuration of security policy.

You must use declarative security syntax to implement an InheritanceDemand, and so you must use the attribute counterpart of the permission class that you want to demand. All permission classes, including InheritanceDemand, have an attribute counterpart that you use to construct declarative security statements. For example, the attribute counterpart of PublisherIdentityPermission is PublisherIdentityPermissionAttribute, and the attribute counterpart of StrongNameIdentityPermission is StrongNameIdentityPermissionAttribute. All permissions and their attribute counterparts follow the same naming convention and are members of the same namespace.

To control which code can extend your class, apply the InheritanceDemand to the class declaration using one of the permissions listed in Table 11-1. To control which code can override specific members of a class, apply the InheritanceDemand to the member declaration.

The Code

The following example demonstrates the use of an InheritanceDemand attribute on both a class and a method. Applying a PublisherIdentityPermissionAttribute to the Recipe11_08 class means that only classes in assemblies signed by the publisher certificate contained in the pubcert.cer file (or assemblies granted FullTrust) can extend the class. The contents of the pubcert.cer file are read at compile time, and the necessary certificate information is built into the assembly metadata. To demonstrate that other permissions can also be used with an InheritanceDemand, the PermissionSetAttribute is used to allow only classes granted the FullTrust permission set to override the method SomeProtectedMethod.

```
using System.Security.Permissions;

namespace Apress.VisualCSharpRecipes.Chapter11
{
    [PublisherIdentityPermission(SecurityAction.InheritanceDemand,
        CertFile = "pubcert.cer")]
    public class Recipe11_08
    {
        [PermissionSet(SecurityAction.InheritanceDemand, Name="FullTrust")]
        public void SomeProtectedMethod ()
        {
            // Method implementation . . .
        }
    }
}
```

11-9. Inspect an Assembly's Evidence

Problem

You need to inspect the evidence that the runtime assigned to an assembly.

Solution

Obtain a `System.Reflection.Assembly` object that represents the assembly in which you are interested. Get the `System.Security.Policy.Evidence` collection from the `Evidence` property of the `Assembly` object, and access the contained evidence objects using the `GetEnumerator`, `GetHostEnumerator`, or `GetAssemblyEnumerator` method of the `Evidence` class.

How It Works

The `Evidence` class represents a collection of evidence objects. The read-only `Evidence` property of the `Assembly` class returns an `Evidence` collection object that contains all of the evidence objects that the runtime assigned to the assembly as the assembly was loaded.

The `Evidence` class actually contains two collections, representing different types of evidence:

- *Host evidence* includes those evidence objects assigned to the assembly by the runtime or the trusted code that loaded the assembly.
- *Assembly evidence* represents custom evidence objects embedded into the assembly at build time.

The `Evidence` class implements three methods for enumerating the evidence objects it contains: `GetEnumerator`, `GetHostEnumerator`, and `GetAssemblyEnumerator`. The `GetHostEnumerator` and `GetAssemblyEnumerator` methods return a `System.Collections.IEnumerator` instance that enumerates only those evidence objects from the appropriate collection. The `GetEnumerator` method returns an `IEnumerator` instance that enumerates *all* of the evidence objects contained in the `Evidence` collection.

■ **Note** Evidence classes do not extend a standard base class or implement a standard interface. Therefore, when working with evidence programmatically, you need to test the type of each object and know what particular types you are seeking. (See recipe 3-11 for details on how to test the type of an object at runtime.)

The Code

The following example demonstrates how to display the host and assembly evidence of an assembly to the console. The example relies on the fact that all standard evidence classes override the `Object.ToString` method to display a useful representation of the evidence object's state. Although interesting, this example does not always show the evidence that an assembly would have when loaded from within your program. The runtime host (such as the Microsoft ASP.NET or Internet Explorer runtime host) is free to assign additional host evidence as it loads an assembly.

```
using System;
using System.Reflection;
using System.Collections;
using System.Security.Policy;

namespace Apress.VisualCSharpRecipes.Chapter11
{
    public class Recipe11_09
    {
        public static void Main(string[] args)
        {
            // Load the specified assembly.
            Assembly a = Assembly.LoadFrom(args[0]);

            // Get the Evidence collection from the
            // loaded assembly.
            Evidence e = a.Evidence;

            // Display the host evidence.
            IEnumerator x = e.GetHostEnumerator();
            Console.WriteLine("HOST EVIDENCE COLLECTION:");
            while(x.MoveNext())
            {
                Console.WriteLine(x.Current.ToString());
                Console.WriteLine("Press Enter to see next evidence.");
                Console.ReadLine();
            }

            // Display the assembly evidence.
            x = e.GetAssemblyEnumerator();
            Console.WriteLine("ASSEMBLY EVIDENCE COLLECTION:");
            while(x.MoveNext())
            {
                Console.WriteLine(x.Current.ToString());
                Console.WriteLine("Press Enter to see next evidence.");
                Console.ReadLine();
            }

            // Wait to continue.
            Console.WriteLine("Main method complete. Press Enter.");
            Console.ReadLine();
        }
    }
}
```

11-10. Determine If the Current User Is a Member of a Specific Windows Group

Problem

You need to determine if the current user of your application is a member of a specific Windows user group.

Solution

Obtain a `System.Security.Principal.WindowsIdentity` object representing the current Windows user by calling the static method `WindowsIdentity.GetCurrent`. Create a `System.Security.Principal.WindowsPrincipal` class using the `WindowsIdentity` class, and then call the method `IsInRole` of the `WindowsPrincipal` object.

How It Works

The RBS mechanism of the .NET Framework abstracts the user-based security features of the underlying operating system through the following two key interfaces:

- The `System.Security.Principal.IIdentity` interface, which represents the entity on whose behalf code is running; for example, a user or service account.
- The `System.Security.Principal.IPrincipal` interface, which represents the entity's `IIdentity` and the set of roles to which the entity belongs. A *role* is simply a categorization used to group entities with similar security capabilities, such as a Windows user group.

To integrate RBS with Windows user security, the .NET Framework provides the following two Windows-specific classes that implement the `IIdentity` and `IPrincipal` interfaces:

- `System.Security.Principal.WindowsIdentity`, which implements the `IIdentity` interface and represents a Windows user.
- `System.Security.Principal.WindowsPrincipal`, which implements `IPrincipal` and represents the set of Windows groups to which the user belongs.

Because .NET RBS is a generic solution designed to be platform-independent, you have no access to the features and capabilities of the Windows user account through the `IIdentity` and `IPrincipal` interfaces, and you must frequently use the `WindowsIdentity` and `WindowsPrincipal` objects directly.

To determine if the current user is a member of a specific Windows group, you must first call the static method `WindowsIdentity.GetCurrent`. The `GetCurrent` method returns a `WindowsIdentity` object that represents the Windows user on whose behalf the current thread is running. An overload of the `GetCurrent` method takes a `bool` argument and allows you to control what is returned by `GetCurrent` if the current thread is impersonating a user different from the one associated with the process. If the argument is `true`, then `GetCurrent` returns a `WindowsIdentity` representing the impersonated user, and it returns `null` if the thread is not impersonating a user. If the argument is `false`, then `GetCurrent` returns the `WindowsIdentity` of the thread if it is not impersonating a user, and it returns the `WindowsIdentity` of the process if the thread is currently impersonating a user.

■ **Note** The `WindowsIdentity` class provides overloaded constructors that, when running on Microsoft Windows Server 2003 or later platforms, allow you to obtain a `WindowsIdentity` object representing a named user. You can use this `WindowsIdentity` object and the process described in this recipe to determine whether that user is a member of a specific Windows group. If you try to use one of these constructors when running on an earlier version of Windows, the `WindowsIdentity` constructor will throw an exception. On Windows platforms preceding Windows Server 2003, you must use native code to obtain a Windows access token representing the desired user. You can then use this access token to instantiate a `WindowsIdentity` object. Recipe 11-12 explains how to obtain Windows access tokens for specific users.

Once you have a `WindowsIdentity`, instantiate a new `WindowsPrincipal` object, passing the `WindowsIdentity` object as an argument to the constructor. Finally, call the `IsInRole` method of the `WindowsPrincipal` object to test if the user is in a specific group (role). `IsInRole` returns `true` if the user is a member of the specified group; otherwise, it returns `false`. The `IsInRole` method provides four overloads:

- The first overload takes a `string` containing the name of the group for which you want to test. The group name must be of the form `[`*`DomainName`*`]\[`*`GroupName`*`]` for domain-based groups and `[`*`MachineName`*`]\[`*`GroupName`*`]` for locally defined groups. If you want to test for membership of a standard Windows group, use the form `BUILTIN\[`*`GroupName`*`]` or the other overload that takes a value from the `System.Security.Principal.WindowsBuiltInRole` enumeration. `IsInRole` performs a case-insensitive test for the specified group name.
- The second `IsInRole` overload accepts an `int`, which specifies a Windows role identifier (RID). RIDs provide a mechanism that is independent of language and localization to identify groups.
- The third `IsInRole` overload accepts a member of the `System.Security.Principal.WindowsBuiltInRole` enumeration. The `WindowsBuiltInRole` enumeration defines a set of members that represent each of the built-in Windows groups.
- The fourth `IsInRole` overload accepts a `System.Security.Principal.SecurityIdentifier` object that represents the security identifier (SID) of the group for which you want to test.

Table 11-2 lists the name, RID, and `WindowsBuiltInRole` value for each of the standard Windows groups.

Table 11-2. Windows Built-In Account Names and Identifiers

Account Name	RID (Hex)	WindowsBuiltInRole Value
BUILTIN\Account Operators	0x224	AccountOperator
BUILTIN\Administrators	0x220	Administrator
BUILTIN\Backup Operators	0x227	BackupOperator
BUILTIN\Guests	0x222	Guest
BUILTIN\Power Users	0x223	PowerUser
BUILTIN\Print Operators	0x226	PrintOperator
BUILTIN\Replicators	0x228	Replicator
BUILTIN\Server Operators	0x225	SystemOperator
BUILTIN\Users	0x221	User

■ **Note** Membership of the `BUILTIN\Administrators` group under Windows 7 will depend on the whether your process is running with elevated privileges. If the current user is an administrator but your process is running without elevated privileges, checking membership of `BUILTIN\Administrators` will return `false`. See Chapter 14 for recipes relating to elevated privileges.

The Code

The following example demonstrates how to test whether the current user is a member of a set of named "Windows groups." You specify the groups that you want to test for as command-line arguments. Remember to prefix the group name with the machine or domain name, or `BUILTIN` for standard Windows groups.

```
using System;
using System.Security.Principal;

namespace Apress.VisualCSharpRecipes.Chapter11
{
    class Recipe11_10
    {
        public static void Main (string[] args)
        {
```

```
            if (args.Length == 0)
            {
                Console.WriteLine(
                    "Please provide groups to check as command line arguments");
            }

            // Obtain a WindowsIdentity object representing the currently
            // logged-on Windows user.
            WindowsIdentity identity = WindowsIdentity.GetCurrent();

            // Create a WindowsPrincipal object that represents the security
            // capabilities of the specified WindowsIdentity; in this case,
            // the Windows groups to which the current user belongs.
            WindowsPrincipal principal = new WindowsPrincipal(identity);

            // Iterate through the group names specified as command-line
            // arguments and test to see if the current user is a member of
            // each one.
            foreach (string role in args)
            {
                Console.WriteLine("Is {0} a member of {1}? = {2}",
                    identity.Name, role, principal.IsInRole(role));
            }

            // Wait to continue.
            Console.WriteLine("\nMain method complete. Press Enter.");
            Console.ReadLine();
        }
    }
}
```

Usage

If you run this example as a user named Darryl on a computer named MACHINE using this command:

```
Recipe11-10 BUILTIN\Administrators BUILTIN\Users MACHINE\Accountants
```

you will see console output similar to the following:

```
Is MACHINE\Darryl a member of BUILTIN\Administrators? = False

Is MACHINE\Darryl a member of BUILTIN\Users? = True

Is MACHINE\Darryl a member of MACHINE\Accountants? = True
```

11-11. Restrict Which Users Can Execute Your Code

Problem

You need to restrict which users can execute elements of your code based on the user's name or the roles of which the user is a member.

Solution

Use the permission class `System.Security.Permissions.PrincipalPermission` and its attribute counterpart `System.Security.Permissions.PrincipalPermissionAttribute` to protect your program elements with RBS demands.

How It Works

The .NET Framework supports both imperative and declarative RBS demands. The class `PrincipalPermission` provides support for imperative security statements, and its attribute counterpart `PrincipalPermissionAttribute` provides support for declarative security statements. RBS demands use the same syntax as CAS demands, but RBS demands specify the name the current user must have, or more commonly, the roles of which the user must be a member. An RBS demand instructs the runtime to look at the name and roles of the current user, and if that user does not meet the requirements of the demand, the runtime throws a `System.Security.SecurityException` exception.

To make an imperative security demand, you must first create a `PrincipalPermission` object specifying the username and role name you want to demand, and then you must call its `Demand` method. You can specify only a single username and role name per demand. If either the username or the role name is `null`, any value will satisfy the demand. Unlike with code access permissions, an RBS demand does not result in a stack walk; the runtime evaluates only the username and roles of the current user.

To make a declarative security demand, you must annotate the class or member you want to protect with a correctly configured `PrincipalPermissionAttribute` attribute. Class-level demands apply to all members of the class, unless a member-specific demand overrides the class demand.

Generally, you are free to choose whether to implement imperative or declarative demands. However, imperative security demands allow you to integrate RBS demands with code logic to achieve more sophisticated demand behavior. In addition, if you do not know the role or usernames to demand at compile time, you must use imperative demands. Declarative demands have the advantage that they are separate from code logic and easier to identify. In addition, you can view declarative demands using the `Permview.exe` tool (discussed in recipe 11-6). Whether you implement imperative or declarative demands, you must ensure that the runtime has access to the name and roles for the current user to evaluate the demand correctly.

The `System.Threading.Thread` class represents an operating system thread running managed code. The static property `CurrentPrincipal` of the `Thread` class contains an `IPrincipal` instance representing the user on whose behalf the managed thread is running. At the operating system level, each thread also has an associated Windows access token, which represents the Windows account on whose behalf the thread is running. The `IPrincipal` instance and the Windows access token are two separate entities. Windows uses its access token to enforce operating system security, whereas the .NET runtime uses its `IPrincipal` instance to evaluate application-level RBS demands. Although they may, and often do, represent the same user, this is by no means always the case.

The benefit of this approach is that you can implement a user and an RBS model within your application using a proprietary user accounts database, without the need for all users to have Windows user accounts. This is a particularly useful approach in large-scale, publicly accessible Internet applications.

By default, the `Thread.CurrentPrincipal` property is undefined. Because obtaining user-related information can be time-consuming, and only a minority of applications use this information, the .NET designers opted for lazy initialization of the `CurrentPrincipal` property. The first time code gets the `Thread.CurrentPrincipal` property, the runtime assigns an `IPrincipal` instance to the property using the following logic:

- If the application domain in which the current thread is executing has a default principal, the runtime assigns this principal to the `Thread.CurrentPrincipal` property. By default, application domains do not have default principals. You can set the default principal of an application domain by calling the `SetThreadPrincipal` method on a `System.AppDomain` object that represents the application domain you want to configure. Code must have the `ControlPrincipal` element of `SecurityPermission` to call `SetThreadPrincipal`. You can set the default principal only once for each application domain; a second call to `SetThreadPrincipal` results in the exception `System.Security.Policy.PolicyException`.

- If the application domain does not have a default principal, the application domain's principal policy determines which `IPrincipal` implementation to create and assign to `Thread.CurrentPrincipal`. To configure principal policy for an application domain, obtain an `AppDomain` object that represents the application domain and call the object's `SetPrincipalPolicy` method. The `SetPrincipalPolicy` method accepts a member of the enumeration `System.Security.Principal.PrincipalPolicy`, which specifies the type of `IPrincipal` object to assign to `Thread.CurrentPrincipal`. Code must have the `ControlPrincipal` element of `SecurityPermission` to call `SetPrincipalPolicy`. Table 11-3 lists the available `PrincipalPolicy` values; the default value is `UnauthenticatedPrincipal`.

- If your code has the `ControlPrincipal` element of `SecurityPermission`, you can instantiate your own `IPrincipal` object and assign it to the `Thread.CurrentPrincipal` property directly. This will prevent the runtime from assigning default `IPrincipal` objects or creating new ones based on principal policy.

Table 11-3. Members of the PrincipalPolicy Enumeration

Member Name	Description
`NoPrincipal`	No `IPrincipal` object is created. `Thread.CurrentPrincipal` returns a `null` reference.
`UnauthenticatedPrincipal`	An empty `System.Security.Principal.GenericPrincipal` object is created and assigned to `Thread.CurrentPrincipal`.
`WindowsPrincipal`	A `WindowsPrincipal` object representing the currently logged-on Windows user is created and assigned to `Thread.CurrentPrincipal`.

Whatever method you use to establish the `IPrincipal` for the current thread, you must do so before you use RBS demands, or the correct user (`IPrincipal`) information will not be available for the runtime to process the demand. Normally, when running on the Windows platform, you would set the principal policy of an application domain to `PrincipalPolicy.WindowsPrincipal` (as shown here) to obtain Windows user information.

```
// Obtain a reference to the current application domain.
AppDomain appDomain = System.AppDomain.CurrentDomain;

// Configure the current application domain to use Windows-based principals.
appDomain.SetPrincipalPolicy(
    System.Security.Principal.PrincipalPolicy.WindowsPrincipal);
```

The Code

The following example demonstrates the use of imperative and declarative RBS demands. The example shows three methods protected using imperative RBS demands (`Method1`, `Method2`, and `Method3`), and then three other methods protected using the equivalent declarative RBS demands (`Method4`, `Method5`, and `Method6`).

```
using System;
using System.Security.Permissions;

namespace Apress.VisualCSharpRecipes.Chapter11
{
    class Recipe11_11
    {
        public static void Method1()
        {
            // An imperative role-based security demand for the current principal
            // to represent an identity with the name Anya. The roles of the
            // principal are irrelevant.
            PrincipalPermission perm =
                new PrincipalPermission(@"MACHINE\Anya", null);
```

```
        // Make the demand.
        perm.Demand();
    }

    public static void Method2()
    {
        // An imperative role-based security demand for the current principal
        // to be a member of the roles Managers OR Developers. If the
        // principal is a member of either role, access is granted. Using the
        // PrincipalPermission, you can express only an OR-type relationship.
        // This is because the PrincipalPolicy.Intersect method always
        // returns an empty permission unless the two inputs are the same.
        // However, you can use code logic to implement more complex
        // conditions. In this case, the name of the identity is irrelevant.
        PrincipalPermission perm1 =
            new PrincipalPermission(null, @"MACHINE\Managers");

        PrincipalPermission perm2 =
            new PrincipalPermission(null, @"MACHINE\Developers");

        // Make the demand.
        perm1.Union(perm2).Demand();
    }

    public static void Method3()
    {
        // An imperative role-based security demand for the current principal
        // to represent an identity with the name Anya AND be a member of the
        // Managers role.
        PrincipalPermission perm =
            new PrincipalPermission(@"MACHINE\Anya", @"MACHINE\Managers");

        // Make the demand.
        perm.Demand();
    }

    // A declarative role-based security demand for the current principal
    // to represent an identity with the name Anya. The roles of the
    // principal are irrelevant.
    [PrincipalPermission(SecurityAction.Demand, Name = @"MACHINE\Anya")]
    public static void Method4()
    {
        // Method implementation . . .
    }

    // A declarative role-based security demand for the current principal
    // to be a member of the roles Managers OR Developers. If the
    // principal is a member of either role, access is granted. You
    // can express only an OR type relationship, not an AND relationship.
    // The name of the identity is irrelevant.
    [PrincipalPermission(SecurityAction.Demand, Role = @"MACHINE\Managers")]
```

```
        [PrincipalPermission(SecurityAction.Demand, Role = @"MACHINE\Developers")]
        public static void Method5()
        {
            // Method implementation . . .
        }

        // A declarative role-based security demand for the current principal
        // to represent an identity with the name Anya AND be a member of the
        // Managers role.
        [PrincipalPermission(SecurityAction.Demand, Name = @"MACHINE\Anya",
            Role = @"MACHINE\Managers")]
        public static void Method6()
        {
            // Method implementation . . .
        }
    }
}
```

11-12. Impersonate a Windows User

Problem

You need your code to run in the context of a Windows user other than the currently active user account.

Solution

Obtain a `System.Security.Principal.WindowsIdentity` object representing the Windows user you need to impersonate, and then call the `Impersonate` method of the `WindowsIdentity` object.

How It Works

Every Windows thread has an associated *access token*, which represents the Windows account on whose behalf the thread is running. The Windows operating system uses the access token to determine whether a thread has the appropriate permissions to perform protected operations on behalf of the account, such as read and write files, reboot the system, and change the system time.

By default, a managed application runs in the context of the Windows account that executed the application. This is normally desirable behavior, but sometimes you will want to run an application in the context of a different Windows account. This is particularly true in the case of server-side applications that process transactions on behalf of the users remotely connected to the server.

It's common for a server application to run in the context of a Windows account created specifically for the application—a service account. This service account will have minimal permissions to access system resources. Enabling the application to operate as though it were the connected user permits the application to access the operations and resources appropriate to that user's security clearance. When an application assumes the identity of another user, it's known as *impersonation*. Correctly implemented, impersonation simplifies security administration and application design while maintaining user accountability.

■ **Note** As discussed in recipe 11-11, a thread's Windows access token and its .NET principal are separate entities and can represent different users. The impersonation technique described in this recipe changes only the Windows access token of the current thread; it does not change the thread's principal. To change the thread's principal, code must have the `ControlPrincipal` element of `SecurityPermission` and assign a new `System.Security.Principal.IPrincipal` object to the `CurrentPrincipal` property of the current `System.Threading.Thread`.

The `System.Security.Principal.WindowsIdentity` class provides the functionality through which you invoke impersonation. However, the exact process depends on which version of Windows your application is running. If it's running on Windows Server 2003 or later, the `WindowsIdentity` class supports constructor overloads that create `WindowsIdentity` objects based on the account name of the user you want to impersonate. On all previous versions of Windows, you must first obtain a `System.IntPtr` containing a reference to a Windows access token that represents the user to impersonate. To obtain the access token reference, you must use a native method such as the `LogonUser` function from the Win32 API.

Once you have a `WindowsIdentity` object representing the user you want to impersonate, call its `Impersonate` method. From that point on, all actions your code performs occur in the context of the impersonated Windows account. The `Impersonate` method returns a `System.Security.Principal.WindowsSecurityContext` object, which represents the active account prior to impersonation. To revert to the original account, call the `Undo` method of this `WindowsSecurityContext` object.

The Code

The following example demonstrates impersonation of a Windows user. The example uses the `LogonUser` function of the Win32 API to obtain a Windows access token for the specified user, impersonates the user, and then reverts to the original user context.

```
using System;
using System.IO;
using System.Security.Principal;
using System.Security.Permissions;
using System.Runtime.InteropServices;

// Ensure the assembly has permission to execute unmanaged code
// and control the thread principal.
[assembly:SecurityPermission(SecurityAction.RequestMinimum,
    UnmanagedCode=true, ControlPrincipal=true)]

namespace Apress.VisualCSharpRecipes.Chapter11
{
    class Recipe11_12
    {
```

```
// Define some constants for use with the LogonUser function.
const int LOGON32_PROVIDER_DEFAULT = 0;
const int LOGON32_LOGON_INTERACTIVE = 2;

// Import the Win32 LogonUser function from advapi32.dll. Specify
// "SetLastError = true" to correctly support access to Win32 error
// codes.
[DllImport("advapi32.dll", SetLastError=true, CharSet=CharSet.Unicode)]
static extern bool LogonUser(string userName, string domain,
    string password, int logonType, int logonProvider,
    ref IntPtr accessToken);

public static void Main(string[] args)
{
    // Create a new IntPtr to hold the access token returned by the
    // LogonUser function.
    IntPtr accessToken = IntPtr.Zero;

    // Call LogonUser to obtain an access token for the specified user.
    // The accessToken variable is passed to LogonUser by reference and
    // will contain a reference to the Windows access token if
    // LogonUser is successful.
    bool success = LogonUser(
        args[0],                     // Username to log on.
        ".",                         // Use the local account database.
        args[1],                     // User's password.
        LOGON32_LOGON_INTERACTIVE,   // Create an interactive login.
        LOGON32_PROVIDER_DEFAULT,    // Use the default logon provider.
        ref accessToken              // Receives access token handle.
    );

    // If the LogonUser return code is zero, an error has occurred.
    // Display the error and exit.
    if (!success)
    {
        Console.WriteLine("LogonUser returned error {0}",
            Marshal.GetLastWin32Error());
    }
    else
    {
        // Create a new WindowsIdentity from the Windows access token.
        WindowsIdentity identity = new WindowsIdentity(accessToken);

        // Display the active identity.
        Console.WriteLine("Identity before impersonation = {0}",
            WindowsIdentity.GetCurrent().Name);

        // Impersonate the specified user, saving a reference to the
        // returned WindowsImpersonationContext, which contains the
        // information necessary to revert to the original user
        // context.
```

```
                WindowsImpersonationContext impContext =
                    identity.Impersonate();

                // Display the active identity.
                Console.WriteLine("Identity during impersonation = {0}",
                    WindowsIdentity.GetCurrent().Name);

                // ****************************************
                // Perform actions as the impersonated user.
                // ****************************************

                // Revert to the original Windows user using the
                // WindowsImpersonationContext object.
                impContext.Undo();

                // Display the active identity.
                Console.WriteLine("Identity after impersonation  = {0}",
                    WindowsIdentity.GetCurrent().Name);

                // Wait to continue.
                Console.WriteLine("\nMain method complete. Press Enter.");
                Console.ReadLine();
            }
        }
    }
}
```

Usage

The example expects two command-line arguments: the account name of the user on the local machine to impersonate and the account's password. For example, the command `Recipe11-12 Bob password` impersonates the user Bob, as long as that user exists in the local accounts database and his password is "password."

11-13. Create a Cryptographically Random Number

Problem

You need to create a random number that is suitable for use in cryptographic and security applications.

Solution

Use a cryptographic random number generator such as the `System.Security.Cryptography.RNGCryptoServiceProvider` class.

How It Works

The System.Random class is a pseudorandom number generator that uses a mathematical algorithm to simulate the generation of random numbers. In fact, the algorithm it uses is deterministic, meaning that you can always calculate what the next number will be based on the previously generated number. This means that numbers generated by the Random class are unsuitable for use in situations in which security is a priority, such as generating encryption keys and passwords.

When you need a nondeterministic random number for use in cryptographic or security-related applications, you must use a random number generator derived from the class System.Security.Cryptography.RandomNumberGenerator. The RandomNumberGenerator class is an abstract class from which all concrete .NET random number generator classes should inherit. Currently, the RNGCryptoServiceProvider class is the only concrete implementation provided. The RNGCryptoServiceProvider class provides a managed wrapper around the CryptGenRandom function of the Win32 CryptoAPI, and you can use it to fill byte arrays with cryptographically random byte values.

■ **Note** The numbers produced by the RNGCryptoServiceProvider class are not truly random. However, they are sufficiently random to meet the requirements of cryptography and security applications in most commercial and government environments.

As is the case with many of the .NET cryptography classes, the RandomNumberGenerator base class is a factory for the concrete implementation classes that derive from it. Calling RandomNumberGenerator.Create("System.Security.Cryptography.RNGCryptoServiceProvider") will return an instance of RNGCryptoServiceProvider that you can use to generate random numbers. In addition, because RNGCryptoServiceProvider is the only concrete implementation provided, it's the default class created if you call the Create method without arguments, as in RandomNumberGenerator.Create().

Once you have a RandomNumberGenerator instance, the method GetBytes fills a byte array with random byte values. As an alternative, you can use the GetNonZeroBytes method if you need random data that contains no zero values.

The Code

The following example instantiates an RNGCryptoServiceProvider object and uses it to generate random values.

```
using System;
using System.Security.Cryptography;

namespace Apress.VisualCSharpRecipes.Chapter11
{
    class Recipe11_13
    {
        public static void Main() {

            // Create a byte array to hold the random data.
            byte[] number = new byte[32];
```

```
            // Instantiate the default random number generator.
            RandomNumberGenerator rng = RandomNumberGenerator.Create();

            // Generate 32 bytes of random data.
            rng.GetBytes(number);

            // Display the random number.
            Console.WriteLine(BitConverter.ToString(number));

            // Wait to continue.
            Console.WriteLine("\nMain method complete. Press Enter.");
            Console.ReadLine();
        }
    }
}
```

■ **Note** The computational effort required to generate a random number with `RNGCryptoServiceProvider` is significantly greater than that required by `Random`. For everyday purposes, the use of `RNGCryptoServiceProvider` is overkill. You should consider the quantity of random numbers you need to generate and the purpose of the numbers before deciding to use `RNGCryptoServiceProvider`. Excessive and unnecessary use of the `RNGCryptoServiceProvider` class could have a noticeable effect on application performance if many random numbers are generated.

11-14. Calculate the Hash Code of a Password

Problem

You need to store a user's password securely so that you can use it to authenticate the user in the future.

Solution

Create and store a cryptographic hash code of the password using a hashing algorithm class derived from the `System.Security.Cryptography.HashAlgorithm` class. On future authentication attempts, generate the hash of the password entered by the user and compare it to the stored hash code.

■ **Caution** You should never store a user's plain text password, because it is a major security risk and one that most users would not appreciate, given that many of them will use the same password to access multiple systems.

How It Works

Hashing algorithms are one-way cryptographic functions that take plain text of variable length and generate a fixed-size numeric value. They are *one-way* because it's nearly impossible to derive the original plain text from the hash code. Hashing algorithms are deterministic; applying the same hashing algorithm to a specific piece of plain text always generates the same hash code. This makes hash codes useful for determining if two blocks of plain text (passwords in this case) are the same. The design of hashing algorithms ensures that the chance of two different pieces of plain text generating the same hash code is extremely small (although not impossible). In addition, there is no correlation between the similarity of two pieces of plain text and their hash codes; minor differences in the plain text cause significant differences in the resulting hash codes.

When using passwords to authenticate a user, you are not concerned with the content of the password that the user enters. You need to know only that the entered password matches the password that you have recorded for that user in your accounts database.

The nature of hashing algorithms makes them ideal for storing passwords securely. When the user provides a new password, you must create the hash code of the password and store it, and then discard the plain text password. Each time the user tries to authenticate with your application, calculate the hash code of the password that user provides and compare it with the hash code you have stored.

■ **Note** People regularly ask how to obtain a password from a hash code. The simple answer is that you cannot. The whole purpose of a hash code is to act as a token that you can freely store without creating security holes. If a user forgets a password, you cannot derive it from the stored hash code. Rather, you must either reset the account to some default value or generate a new password for the user.

Generating hash codes is simple in the .NET Framework. The abstract class `HashAlgorithm` provides a base from which all concrete hashing algorithm implementations derive. The .NET Framework class library includes the seven hashing algorithm implementations listed in Table 11-4; each implementation class is a member of the `System.Security.Cryptography` namespace. The classes with names ending in `CryptoServiceProvider` wrap functionality provided by the native Win32 CryptoAPI, whereas those with names ending in `Managed` are fully implemented in managed code.

Table 11-4. Hashing Algorithm Implementations

Algorithm Name	Class Name	Hash Code Size (in Bits)
MD5	`MD5CryptoServiceProvider`	128
RIPEMD160 or RIPEMD-160	`RIPEMD160Managed`	160
SHA or SHA1	`SHA1CryptoServiceProvider`	160
SHA1Managed	`SHA1Managed`	160
SHA256 or SHA-256	`SHA256Managed`	256
SHA384 or SHA-384	`SHA384Managed`	384
SHA512 or SHA-512	`SHA512Managed`	512

Although you can create instances of the hashing algorithm classes directly, the `HashAlgorithm` base class is a factory for the concrete implementation classes that derive from it. Calling the static method `HashAlgorithm.Create` will return an object of the specified type. Using the factory approach allows you to write generic code that can work with any hashing algorithm implementation. Note that unlike in recipe 11-13, you do not pass the class name as parameter to the factory; instead, you pass the algorithm name.

Once you have a `HashAlgorithm` object, its `ComputeHash` method accepts a `byte` array argument containing plain text and returns a new `byte` array containing the generated hash code. Table 11-4 shows the size of hash code (in bits) generated by each hashing algorithm class.

■ **Note** The SHA1Managed algorithm cannot be implemented using the factory approach. It must be instantiated directly.

The Code

The example shown here demonstrates the creation of a hash code from a string, such as a password. The application expects two command-line arguments: the name of the hashing algorithm to use and the string from which to generate the hash. Because the `HashAlgorithm.ComputeHash` method requires a byte array, you must first byte-encode the input string using the class `System.Text.Encoding`, which provides mechanisms for converting strings to and from various character-encoding formats.

```
using System;
using System.Text;
using System.Security.Cryptography;
```

```
namespace Apress.VisualCSharpRecipes.Chapter11
{
    class Recipe11_14
    {
        public static void Main(string[] args)
        {
            // Create a HashAlgorithm of the type specified by the first
            // command-line argument.
            HashAlgorithm hashAlg = null;
            if (args[0].CompareTo("SHA1Managed") == 0)
            {
                hashAlg = new SHA1Managed();
            }
            else
            {
                hashAlg = HashAlgorithm.Create(args[0]);
            }

            using (hashAlg)
            {
                // Convert the password string, provided as the second
                // command-line argument, to an array of bytes.
                byte[] pwordData = Encoding.Default.GetBytes(args[1]);

                // Generate the hash code of the password.
                byte[] hash = hashAlg.ComputeHash(pwordData);

                // Display the hash code of the password to the console.
                Console.WriteLine(BitConverter.ToString(hash));

                // Wait to continue.
                Console.WriteLine("\nMain method complete. Press Enter.");
                Console.ReadLine();
            }
        }
    }
}
```

Usage

Running the following command:

```
Recipe11-14 SHA1 ThisIsMyPassword
```

will display the following hash code to the console:

```
30-B8-BD-58-29-88-89-00-D1-5D-2B-BE-62-70-D9-BC-65-B0-70-2F
```

In contrast, executing this command:

```
Recipe11-14 RIPEMD-160 ThisIsMyPassword
```

will display the following hash code:

```
0C-39-3B-2E-8A-4E-D3-DD-FB-E3-C8-05-E4-62-6F-6B-76-7C-7A-49
```

11-15. Calculate the Hash Code of a File

Problem

You need to determine whether the contents of a file have changed over time.

Solution

Create a cryptographic hash code of the file's contents using the `ComputeHash` method of the `System.Security.Cryptography.HashAlgorithm` class. Store the hash code for future comparison against newly generated hash codes.

How It Works

As well as allowing you to store passwords securely (discussed in recipe 11-14), hash codes provide an excellent means of determining if a file has changed. By calculating and storing the cryptographic hash of a file, you can later recalculate the hash of the file to determine if the file has changed in the interim. A hashing algorithm will produce a very different hash code even if the file has been changed only slightly, and the chances of two different files resulting in the same hash code are extremely small.

■ **Caution** Standard hash codes are not suitable for sending with a file to ensure the integrity of the file's contents. If someone intercepts the file in transit, that person can easily change the file and recalculate the hash code, leaving the recipient none the wiser. Recipe 11-17 discusses a variant of the hash code—a keyed hash code—that is suitable for ensuring the integrity of a file in transit.

The `HashAlgorithm` class makes it easy to generate the hash code of a file. First, instantiate one of the concrete hashing algorithm implementations derived from the `HashAlgorithm` class. To instantiate the desired hashing algorithm class, pass the name of the hashing algorithm to the `HashAlgorithm.Create` method, as described in recipe 11-14. See Table 11-4 for a list of valid hashing algorithm names. Then, instead of passing a byte array to the `ComputeHash` method, you pass a `System.IO.Stream` object representing the file from which you want to generate the hash code. The `HashAlgorithm` object handles the process of reading data from the `Stream` and returns a byte array containing the hash code for the file.

The Code

The example shown here demonstrates the generation of a hash code from a file. The application expects two command-line arguments: the name of the hashing algorithm to use and the name of the file from which the hash is calculated.

```
using System;
using System.IO;
using System.Security.Cryptography;
namespace Apress.VisualCSharpRecipes.Chapter11
{
    class Recipe11_15
    {
        public static void Main(string[] args)
        {
            // Create a HashAlgorithm of the type specified by the first
            // command-line argument.
            using (HashAlgorithm hashAlg = HashAlgorithm.Create(args[0]))
            {
                // Open a FileStream to the file specified by the second
                // command-line argument.
                using (Stream file =
                    new FileStream(args[1], FileMode.Open, FileAccess.Read))
                {
                    // Generate the hash code of the file's contents.
                    byte[] hash = hashAlg.ComputeHash(file);

                    // Display the hash code of the file to the console.
                    Console.WriteLine(BitConverter.ToString(hash));
                }

                // Wait to continue.
                Console.WriteLine("\nMain method complete. Press Enter.");
                Console.ReadLine();
            }
        }
    }
}
```

Usage

Running this command:

```
Recipe11-15 SHA1 Recipe11-15.exe
```

will display the following hash code to the console:

```
CA-67-A5-2D-EC-E9-FC-45-AE-97-E9-E1-38-CB-17-86-BB-17-EE-30
```

In contrast, executing this command:

```
Recipe11-15 RIPEMD-160 Recipe11-15.exe
```

will display the following hash code:

```
E1-6E-FA-BB-89-BA-DA-83-20-D5-CA-EC-FC-3D-52-13-86-B9-41-7C
```

11-16. Verify a Hash Code

Problem

You need to verify a password or confirm that a file remains unchanged by comparing two hash codes.

Solution

Convert both the old and the new hash codes to hexadecimal code strings, Base64 strings, or byte arrays, and compare them.

How It Works

You can use hash codes to determine if two pieces of data (such as passwords or files) are the same, without the need to store or even maintain access to the original data. To determine if data changes over time, you must generate and store the original data's hash code. Later, you can generate another hash code for the data and compare the old and new hash codes, which will show whether any change has occurred. The format in which you store the original hash code will determine the most appropriate way to verify a newly generated hash code against the stored one.

■ **Note** The recipes in this chapter use the `ToString` method of the class `System.BitConverter` to convert byte arrays to hexadecimal string values for display. Although easy to use and appropriate for display purposes, you might find this approach inappropriate for use when storing hash codes, because it places a hyphen (-) between each byte value (for example, 4D-79-3A-C9- . . .). In addition, the `BitConverter` class does not provide a method to parse such a string representation back into a byte array.

Hash codes are often stored in text files, either as hexadecimal strings (for example, `89D22213170A9CFF09A392F00E2C6C4EDC1B0EF9`) or as Base64-encoded strings (for example, `idIiExcKnP8Jo5LwDixsTtwbDvk=`). Alternatively, hash codes may be stored in databases as raw byte values. Regardless of how you store your hash code, the first step in comparing old and new hash codes is to get them both into a common form.

The Code

This following example contains three methods that use different approaches to compare hash codes:

- `VerifyHexHash`: This method converts a new hash code (a byte array) to a hexadecimal string for comparison to an old hash code. Other than the `BitConverter.ToString` method, the .NET Framework class library does not provide an easy method to convert a byte array to a hexadecimal string. You must program a loop to step through the elements of the byte array, convert each individual byte to a string, and append the string to the hexadecimal string representation of the hash code. The use of `System.Text.StringBuilder` avoids the unnecessary creation of new strings each time the loop appends the next byte value to the result string. (See recipe 2-1 for more details.)
- `VerifyB64Hash`: This method takes a new hash code as a byte array and the old hash code as a Base64-encoded string. The method encodes the new hash code as a Base64 string and performs a straightforward string comparison of the two values.
- `VerifyByteHash`: This method compares two hash codes represented as byte arrays. The .NET Framework class library does not include a method that performs this type of comparison, and so you must program a loop to compare the elements of the two arrays. This code uses a few time-saving techniques, namely ensuring that the byte arrays are the same length before starting to compare them and returning `false` on the first difference found.

```
using System;
using System.Text;

namespace Apress.VisualCSharpRecipes.Chapter11
{
    class Recipe11_16
    {
        // A method to compare a newly generated hash code with an
        // existing hash code that's represented by a hex code string.
        public static bool VerifyHexHash(byte[] hash, string oldHashString)
        {
            // Create a string representation of the hash code bytes.
            StringBuilder newHashString = new StringBuilder(hash.Length);
```

```
            // Append each byte as a two-character uppercase hex string.
            foreach (byte b in hash)
            {
                newHashString.AppendFormat("{0:X2}", b);
            }

            // Compare the string representations of the old and new hash
            // codes and return the result.
            return (oldHashString == newHashString.ToString());
        }

        // A method to compare a newly generated hash code with an
        // existing hash code that's represented by a Base64-encoded string.
        private static bool VerifyB64Hash(byte[] hash, string oldHashString)
        {
            // Create a Base64 representation of the hash code bytes.
            string newHashString = Convert.ToBase64String(hash);

            // Compare the string representations of the old and new hash
            // codes and return the result.
            return (oldHashString == newHashString);
        }

        // A method to compare a newly generated hash code with an
        // existing hash code represented by a byte array.
        private static bool VerifyByteHash(byte[] hash, byte[] oldHash)
        {
            // If either array is null or the arrays are different lengths,
            // then they are not equal.
            if (hash == null || oldHash == null || hash.Length != oldHash.Length)
                return false;

            // Step through the byte arrays and compare each byte value.
            for (int count = 0; count < hash.Length; count++)
            {
                if (hash[count] != oldHash[count]) return false;
            }

            // Hash codes are equal.
            return true;
        }
    }
}
```

11-17. Ensure Data Integrity Using a Keyed Hash Code

Problem

You need to transmit a file to someone and provide the recipient with a means to verify the integrity of the file and its source.

Solution

Share a secret key with the intended recipient. This key would ideally be a randomly generated number, but it could also be a phrase that you and the recipient agree to use. Use the key with one of the keyed hashing algorithm classes derived from the `System.Security.Cryptography.KeyedHashAlgorithm` class to create a keyed hash code. Send the hash code with the file. On receipt of the file, the recipient will generate the keyed hash code of the file using the shared secret key. If the hash codes are equal, the recipient knows that the file is from you and that it has not changed in transit.

How It Works

Hash codes are useful for comparing two pieces of data to determine if they are the same, even if you no longer have access to the original data. However, you cannot use a hash code to reassure the recipient of data as to the data's integrity. If someone could intercept the data, that person could replace the data and generate a new hash code. When the recipient verifies the hash code, it will seem correct, even though the data is actually nothing like what you sent originally.

A simple and efficient solution to the problem of data integrity is a *keyed hash code*. A keyed hash code is similar to a normal hash code (discussed in recipes 11-14 and 11-15); however, the keyed hash code incorporates an element of secret data—a *key*—known only to the sender and the receiver. Without the key, a person cannot generate the correct hash code from a given set of data. When you successfully verify a keyed hash code, you can be certain that only someone who knows the secret key could generate the hash code.

■ **Caution** The secret key must remain secret. Anyone who knows the secret key can generate valid keyed hash codes, meaning that you would be unable to determine whether someone else who knew the key had changed the content of a document. For this reason, you should not transmit or store the secret key with the document whose integrity you are trying to protect.

Generating keyed hash codes is similar to generating normal hash codes. The abstract class `System.Security.Cryptography.KeyedHashAlgorithm` extends the class `System.Security.Cryptography.HashAlgorithm` and provides a base class from which all concrete keyed hashing algorithm implementations must derive. The .NET Framework class library includes the seven keyed hashing algorithm implementations listed in Table 11-5. Each implementation is a member of the namespace `System.Security.Cryptography`.

Table 11-5. Keyed Hashing Algorithm Implementations

Algorithm/Class Name	Key Size (in Bits)	Hash Code Size (in Bits)
HMACMD5	Any	128
HMACRIPEMD160	Any	160
HMACSHA1	Any	160
HMACSHA256	Any	256
HMACSHA384	Any	384
HMACSHA512	Any	512
MACTripleDES	128, 192	64

As with the standard hashing algorithms, you can either create keyed hashing algorithm objects directly or use the static factory method `KeyedHashAlgorithm.Create` and pass the algorithm name as an argument. Using the factory approach allows you to write generic code that can work with any keyed hashing algorithm implementation, but as shown in Table 11-5, `MACTripleDES` supports fixed key lengths that you must accommodate in generic code.

If you use constructors to instantiate a keyed hashing object, you can pass the secret key to the constructor. Using the factory approach, you must set the key using the `Key` property inherited from the `KeyedHashAlgorithm` class. Then call the `ComputeHash` method and pass either a byte array or a `System.IO.Stream` object. The keyed hashing algorithm will process the input data and return a byte array containing the keyed hash code. Table 11-5 shows the size of the hash code generated by each keyed hashing algorithm.

The Code

The following example demonstrates the generation of a keyed hash code from a file. The example uses the given class to generate the keyed hash code, and then displays it to the console. The example requires three command-line arguments: the name of the file from which the hash is calculated, the name of the class to instantiate, and the key to use when calculating the hash.

```
using System;
using System.IO;
using System.Text;
using System.Security.Cryptography;

namespace Apress.VisualCSharpRecipes.Chapter11
{
    class Recipe11_17
    {
```

```
        public static void Main(string[] args)
        {
            // Create a byte array from the key string, which is the
            // second command-line argument.
            byte[] key = Encoding.Unicode.GetBytes(args[2]);

            // Create a KeyedHashAlgorithm-derived object to generate the keyed
            // hash code for the input file. Pass the byte array representing the
            // key to the constructor.
            using (KeyedHashAlgorithm hashAlg = KeyedHashAlgorithm.Create(args[1]))
            {
                // Assign the key.
                hashAlg.Key = key;

                // Open a FileStream to read the input file. The file name is
                // specified by the first command-line argument.
                using (Stream file =
                    new FileStream(args[0], FileMode.Open, FileAccess.Read))
                {
                    // Generate the keyed hash code of the file's contents.
                    byte[] hash = hashAlg.ComputeHash(file);

                    // Display the keyed hash code to the console.
                    Console.WriteLine(BitConverter.ToString(hash));
                }
            }

            // Wait to continue.
            Console.WriteLine("\nMain method complete. Press Enter.");
            Console.ReadLine();
        }
    }
}
```

Usage

Executing the following command:

```
Recipe11-17 Recipe11-17.exe HMACSHA1 secretKey
```

will display the following hash code to the console:

```
2E-5B-9B-2C-91-42-BA-4E-98-DF-39-F6-AE-89-B6-44-61-FB-32-E7
```

In contrast, executing this command:

```
Recipe11-17 Recipe11-17.exe HMACSHA1 anotherKey
```

will display the following hash code to the console:

```
EF-64-79-3A-3C-A4-44-01-AD-9E-94-2A-B4-58-CF-42-84-3E-27-91
```

11-18. Work with Security-Sensitive Strings in Memory

Problem

You need to work with sensitive string data, such as passwords or credit card numbers, in memory, and you need to minimize the risk of other people or processes accessing that data.

Solution

Use the class `System.Security.SecureString` to hold the sensitive data values in memory.

How It Works

Storing sensitive data such as passwords, personal details, and banking information in memory as `String` objects is insecure for many reasons, including the following:

- `String` objects are not encrypted.
- The immutability of `String` objects means that whenever you change the `String`, the old `String` value is left in memory until it is garbage-collected and later overwritten.
- Because the garbage collector is free to reorganize the contents of the managed heap, multiple copies of your sensitive data may be present on the heap.
- If part of your process address space is swapped to disk or a memory dump is written to disk, a copy of your data may be stored on the disk.

Each of these factors increases the opportunities for others to access your sensitive data. The .NET Framework includes the `SecureString` class to simplify the task of working with sensitive `string` data in memory.

You create a `SecureString` as either initially empty or from a pointer to a character (char) array. Then you manipulate the contents of the `SecureString` one character at a time using the methods `AppendChar`, `InsertAt`, `RemoveAt`, and `SetAt`. As you add characters to the `SecureString`, they are encrypted using the capabilities of the Data Protection API.

■ **Note** The `SecureString` class uses features of Data Protection API (DPAPI) and is available only on Windows 2000 SP3 and later operating system versions.

The SecureString class also provides a method named MakeReadOnly. As the name suggests, calling MakeReadOnly configures the SecureString to no longer allow its value to be changed. Attempting to modify a SecureString marked as read-only results in the exception System.InvalidOperationException being thrown. Once you have set the SecureString to read-only, it cannot be undone.

The SecureString class has a ToString method, but this does not retrieve a string representation of the contained data. Instead, the class System.Runtime.InteropServices.Marshal implements a number of static methods that take a SecureString object; decrypts it; converts it to a binary string, a block of ANSI, or a block of Unicode data; and returns a System.IntPtr object that points to the converted data.

At any time, you can call the SecureString.Clear method to clear the sensitive data, and when you have finished with the SecureString object, call its Dispose method to clear the data and free the memory. SecureString implements System.IDisposable.

■ **Note** Although it might seem that the benefits of the SecureString class are limited, because there is no way in Windows Forms applications to get such a secured string from the GUI without first retrieving an unsecured String through a TextBox or another control, it is likely that third parties and future additions to the .NET Framework will use the SecureString class to handle sensitive data. This is already the case in System.Diagnostics.ProcessStartInfo, where using a SecureString, you can set the Password property to the password of the user context in which the new process should be run.

The Code

The following example reads a username and password from the console and starts Notepad.exe as the specified user. The password is masked on input and stored in a SecureString in memory, maximizing the chances of the password remaining secret.

```
using System;
using System.Security;
using System.Diagnostics;

namespace Apress.VisualCSharpRecipes.Chapter11
{
    class Recipe11_18
    {
        public static SecureString ReadString()
        {
            // Create a new emtpty SecureString.
            SecureString str = new SecureString();

            // Read the string from the console one
            // character at a time without displaying it.
            ConsoleKeyInfo nextChar = Console.ReadKey(true);
```

```
        // Read characters until Enter is pressed.
        while (nextChar.Key != ConsoleKey.Enter)
        {
            if (nextChar.Key == ConsoleKey.Backspace)
            {
                if (str.Length > 0)
                {
                    // Backspace pressed, remove the last character.
                    str.RemoveAt(str.Length - 1);

                    Console.Write(nextChar.KeyChar);
                    Console.Write(" ");
                    Console.Write(nextChar.KeyChar);
                }
                else
                {
                    Console.Beep();
                }
            }
            else
            {
                // Append the character to the SecureString and
                // display a masked character.
                str.AppendChar(nextChar.KeyChar);
                Console.Write("*");
            }

            // Read the next character.
            nextChar = Console.ReadKey(true);
        }

        // String entry finished. Make it read-only.
        str.MakeReadOnly();
        return str;
    }

    public static void Main()
    {
        string user = "";

        // Get the username under which Notepad.exe will be run.
        Console.Write("Enter the user name: ");
        user = Console.ReadLine();

        // Get the user's password as a SecureString.
        Console.Write("Enter the user's password: ");
        using (SecureString pword = ReadString())
        {
```

```
                // Start Notepad as the specified user.
                ProcessStartInfo startInfo = new ProcessStartInfo();

                startInfo.FileName = "notepad.exe";
                startInfo.UserName = user;
                startInfo.Password = pword;
                startInfo.UseShellExecute = false;

                // Create a new Process object.
                using (Process process = new Process())
                {
                    // Assign the ProcessStartInfo to the Process object.
                    process.StartInfo = startInfo;

                    try
                    {
                        // Start the new process.
                        process.Start();
                    }
                    catch (Exception ex)
                    {
                        Console.WriteLine("\n\nCould not start Notepad process.");
                        Console.WriteLine(ex);
                    }
                }
            }

            // Wait to continue.
            Console.WriteLine("\n\nMain method complete. Press Enter.");
            Console.ReadLine();
        }
    }
}
```

11-19. Encrypt and Decrypt Data Using the Data Protection API

Problem

You need a convenient way to securely encrypt data without the headache associated with key management.

Solution

Use the `ProtectedData` and `ProtectedMemory` classes of the `System.Security.Cryptography` namespace to access the encryption and key management capabilities provided by the Data Protection API (DPAPI).

How It Works

Given that the .NET Framework provides you with well-tested implementations of the most widely used and trusted encryption algorithms, the biggest challenge you face when using cryptography is key management, namely the effective generation, storage, and sharing of keys to facilitate the use of cryptography. In fact, key management is the biggest problem facing most people when they want to securely store or transmit data using cryptographic techniques. If implemented incorrectly, key management can easily render useless all of your efforts to encrypt your data.

DPAPI provides encryption and decryption services without the need for you to worry about key management. DPAPI automatically generates keys based on Windows user credentials, stores keys securely as part of your profile, and even provides automated key expiry without losing access to previously encrypted data.

■ **Note** DPAPI is suitable for many common uses of cryptography in Windows applications, but will not help you in situations that require you to distribute or share secret or public keys with other users.

The .NET Framework contains two classes in `System.Security.dll` that provide easy access to the encryption and decryption capabilities of DPAPI: `ProtectedData` and `ProtectedMemory`. Both classes allow you to encrypt a byte array by passing it to the static method `Protect`, and decrypt a byte array of encrypted data by passing it the static method `Unprotect`. The difference in the classes is in the scope that they allow you to specify when you encrypt and decrypt data.

■ **Caution** You must use `ProtectedData` if you intend to store encrypted data and reboot your machine before decrypting it. `ProtectedMemory` will be unable to decrypt data that was encrypted before a reboot.

When you call `ProtectedData.Protect`, you specify a value from the enumeration `System.Security.Cryptography.DataProtectionScope`. The following are the possible values:

- `CurrentUser`, which means that only code running in the context of the current user can decrypt the data
- `LocalMachine`, which means that any code running on the same computer can decrypt the data

When you call `ProtectedMemory.Protect`, you specify a value from the enumeration `System.Security.Cryptography.MemoryProtectionScope`. The possible values are as follows:

- `CrossProcess`, which means that any code in any process can decrypt the encrypted data
- `SameLogon`, which means that only code running in the same user context can decrypt the data

- `SameProcess`, which means that only code running in the same process can decrypt the data

Both classes allow you to specify additional data (*entropy*) when you encrypt your data. Entropy makes certain types of cryptographic attacks less likely to succeed. If you choose to use entropy when you protect data, you must use the same entropy value when you unprotect the data. It is not essential that you keep the entropy data secret, so it can be stored freely without encryption.

The Code

The following example demonstrates the use of the `ProtectedData` class to encrypt a string entered at the console by the user. Note that you need to reference the `System.Security.dll` assembly.

```
using System;
using System.Text;
using System.Security.Cryptography;

namespace Apress.VisualCSharpRecipes.Chapter11
{
    class Recipe11_19
    {
        public static void Main()
        {
            // Read the string from the console.
            Console.Write("Enter the string to encrypt: ");
            string str = Console.ReadLine();

            // Create a byte array of entropy to use in the encryption process.
            byte[] entropy = { 0, 1, 2, 3, 4, 5, 6, 7, 8 };

            // Encrypt the entered string after converting it to
            // a byte array. Use LocalMachine scope so that only
            // the current user can decrypt the data.
            byte[] enc = ProtectedData.Protect(Encoding.Unicode.GetBytes(str),
                entropy, DataProtectionScope.LocalMachine);

            // Display the encrypted data to the console.
            Console.WriteLine("\nEncrypted string = {0}",
                BitConverter.ToString(enc));

            // Attempt to decrypt the data using CurrentUser scope.
            byte[] dec = ProtectedData.Unprotect(enc,
                entropy, DataProtectionScope.CurrentUser);

            // Display the data decrypted using CurrentUser scope.
            Console.WriteLine("\nDecrypted data using CurrentUser scope = {0}",
                Encoding.Unicode.GetString(dec));
```

```
            // Wait to continue.
            Console.WriteLine("\nMain method complete. Press Enter.");
            Console.ReadLine();
        }
    }
}
```

CHAPTER 12

Unmanaged Code Interoperability

The Microsoft .NET Framework is an extensive platform. However, despite having reached version 4.0, it still does not duplicate all the features that are available in unmanaged code. Currently, the .NET Framework does not include every function that is available in the Win32 API, and many businesses use proprietary solutions that they have built in native code or as COM or ActiveX components.

Fortunately, the .NET Framework is equipped with interoperability features that allow you to use native code from .NET Framework applications as well as access .NET assemblies as though they were COM components. The recipes in this chapter describe how to do the following:

- Call functions defined in a DLL, get the handles for a control or window, invoke an unmanaged function that uses a structure, invoke unmanaged callback functions, and retrieve unmanaged error information (recipes 12-1 through 12-5)
- Use COM components from .NET Framework applications, release COM components, and use optional parameters (recipes 12-6 through 12-8)
- Use ActiveX controls from .NET Framework applications (recipe 12-9)
- Expose the functionality of a .NET assembly as a COM component (recipe 12-10)

Note The web site PInvoke.net (`http://pinvoke.net`) is an invaluable resource when trying to use PInvoke to call Win32 API functions. It provides predefined method signatures for most if not all of the Win32 API functions, as well as usage examples and tips for many of the functions.

12-1. Call a Function in an Unmanaged DLL

Problem

You need to call a function exported by a native DLL. This function might be a part of the Win32 API or your own native code library.

Solution

Declare a method in your C# code that you will use to access the unmanaged function. Declare this method as both `extern` and `static`, and apply the attribute `System.Runtime.InteropServices.DllImportAttribute` to specify the DLL file and the name of the unmanaged function.

How It Works

To use a native function contained in an external library, all you need to do is declare a method with the appropriate signature—the Common Language Runtime (CLR) automatically handles the rest, including loading the DLL into memory when the function is called and marshaling the parameters from .NET data types to native data types. The .NET service that supports this cross-platform execution is named PInvoke (Platform Invoke), and the process is usually seamless. Occasionally, you will need to do a little more work, such as when you need to support in-memory structures, callbacks, or mutable strings.

PInvoke is often used to access functionality in the Win32 API, particularly Win32 features that are not present in the set of managed classes that make up the .NET Framework. Three core libraries make up the Win32 API:

- `Kernel32.dll` includes operating system–specific functionality such as process loading, context switching, and file and memory I/O.
- `User32.dll` includes functionality for manipulating windows, menus, dialog boxes, icons, and so on.
- `GDI32.dll` includes graphical capabilities for drawing directly on windows, menus, and control surfaces, as well as for printing.

As an example, consider the Win32 API functions used for writing and reading INI files, such as `GetPrivateProfileString` and `WritePrivateProfileString`, in `Kernel32.dll`. The .NET Framework does not include any classes that wrap this functionality. However, you can import these functions using the attribute `DllImportAttribute`, like this:

```
[DllImport("kernel32.DLL", EntryPoint="WritePrivateProfileString")]
private static extern bool WritePrivateProfileString(string lpAppName,
  string lpKeyName, string lpString, string lpFileName);
```

The arguments specified in the signature of the `WritePrivateProfileString` method must match the DLL method or a runtime error will occur when you attempt to invoke it. Remember that you do not define any method body, because the declaration refers to a method in the DLL. The `EntryPoint` portion of the attribute `DllImportAttribute` is optional in this example. You do not need to specify the `EntryPoint` when the declared function name matches the function name in the external library.

The Code

The following is an example of using some Win32 API functions to get INI file information. It declares the unmanaged functions used and exposes `public` methods to call them. (Other Win32 API functions for getting INI file information not shown in this example include those that retrieve all the sections in an INI file.) The code first displays the current value of a key in the INI file, modifies it, retrieves the new value, and then writes the default value.

```
using System;
using System.Runtime.InteropServices;
using System.Text;
using System.IO;

namespace Apress.VisualCSharpRecipes.Chapter12
{
    class Recipe12_01
    {
        // Declare the unmanaged functions.
        [DllImport("kernel32.dll", EntryPoint = "GetPrivateProfileString")]
        private static extern int GetPrivateProfileString(string lpAppName,
          string lpKeyName, string lpDefault, StringBuilder lpReturnedString,
          int nSize, string lpFileName);

        [DllImport("kernel32.dll", EntryPoint = "WritePrivateProfileString")]
        private static extern bool WritePrivateProfileString(string lpAppName,
          string lpKeyName, string lpString, string lpFileName);

        static void Main(string[] args)
        {
            // Must use full path or Windows will try to write the INI file
            // to the Windows folder, causing issues on Vista and Windows 7.
            string iniFileName = Path.Combine(Directory.GetCurrentDirectory(),
                "Recipe12-01.ini");

            string message = "Value of LastAccess in [SampleSection] is: {0}";

            // Write a new value to the INI file.
            WriteIniValue("SampleSection", "LastAccess",
                DateTime.Now.ToString(), iniFileName);

            // Obtain the value contained in the INI file.
            string val = GetIniValue("SampleSection", "LastAccess", iniFileName);
            Console.WriteLine(message, val ?? "???");

            // Wait to continue.
            Console.WriteLine(Environment.NewLine);
            Console.WriteLine("Press Enter to continue the example.");
            Console.ReadLine();

            // Update the INI file.
            WriteIniValue("SampleSection", "LastAccess",
                DateTime.Now.ToString(), iniFileName);

            // Obtain the new value.
            val = GetIniValue("SampleSection", "LastAccess", iniFileName);
            Console.WriteLine(message, val ?? "???");
```

```
            // Wait to continue.
            Console.WriteLine(Environment.NewLine);
            Console.WriteLine("Main method complete. Press Enter.");
            Console.ReadLine();
        }

        public static string GetIniValue(string section, string key,
            string filename)
        {
            int chars = 256;
            StringBuilder buffer = new StringBuilder(chars);
            string sDefault = "";
            if (GetPrivateProfileString(section, key, sDefault,
              buffer, chars, filename) != 0)
            {
                return buffer.ToString();
            }
            else
            {
                // Look at the last Win32 error.
                int err = Marshal.GetLastWin32Error();
                return null;
            }
        }

        public static bool WriteIniValue(string section, string key,
            string value, string filename)
        {
            return WritePrivateProfileString(section, key, value, filename);
        }
    }
}
```

■ **Note** The `GetPrivateProfileString` method is declared with one `StringBuilder` parameter (`lpReturnedString`). This is because this string must be mutable; when the call completes, it will contain the returned INI file information. Whenever you need a mutable string, you must substitute `StringBuilder` in place of the `String` class. Often, you will need to create the `StringBuilder` object with a character buffer of a set size, and then pass the size of the buffer to the function as another parameter. You can specify the number of characters in the `StringBuilder` constructor. See recipe 2-1 for more information about using the `StringBuilder` class.

12-2. Get the Handle for a Control, Window, or File

Problem

You need to call an unmanaged function that requires the handle for a control, a window, or a file.

Solution

Many classes, including all `Control`-derived classes and the `FileStream` class, return the handle of the unmanaged Windows object they are wrapping as an `IntPtr` through a property named `Handle`. Other classes also provide similar information; for example, the `System.Diagnostics.Process` class provides a `Process.MainWindowHandle` property in addition to the `Handle` property.

How It Works

The .NET Framework does not hide underlying details such as the operating system handles used for controls and windows. Although you usually will not use this information, you can retrieve it if you need to call an unmanaged function that requires it. Many Microsoft Windows API functions, for example, require control or window handles.

The Code

As an example, consider the Windows-based application shown in Figure 12-1. It consists of a single window that always stays on top of all other windows regardless of focus. (This behavior is enforced by setting the `Form.TopMost` property to `true`.) The form also includes a timer that periodically calls the unmanaged `GetForegroundWindow` and `GetWindowText` WinAPI functions to determine which window is currently active.

One additional detail in this example is that the code also uses the `Form.Handle` property to get the handle of the main application form. It then compares with the handle of the active form to test if the current application has focus. The following is the complete code for this form:

```
using System;
using System.Windows.Forms;
using System.Runtime.InteropServices;
using System.Text;

namespace Apress.VisualCSharpRecipes.Chapter12
{
    public partial class ActiveWindowInfo : Form
    {
        public ActiveWindowInfo()
        {
            InitializeComponent();
        }
```

```
            // Declare external functions.
            [DllImport("user32.dll")]
            private static extern IntPtr GetForegroundWindow();

            [DllImport("user32.dll")]
            private static extern int GetWindowText(IntPtr hWnd,
                StringBuilder text, int count);

            private void tmrRefresh_Tick(object sender, EventArgs e)
            {
                int chars = 256;
                StringBuilder buff = new StringBuilder(chars);

                // Obtain the handle of the active window.
                IntPtr handle = GetForegroundWindow();

                // Update the controls.
                if (GetWindowText(handle, buff, chars) > 0)
                {
                    lblCaption.Text = buff.ToString();
                    lblHandle.Text = handle.ToString();
                    if (handle == this.Handle)
                    {
                        lblCurrent.Text = "True";
                    }
                    else
                    {
                        lblCurrent.Text = "False";
                    }
                }
            }
        }
    }
```

■ **Caution** The Windows Forms infrastructure manages window handles for forms and controls transparently. Changing some of their properties can force the CLR to create a new native window behind the scenes, and the new window gets assigned a different handle. For that reason, you should always retrieve the handle before you use it (rather than storing it in a member variable for a long period of time).

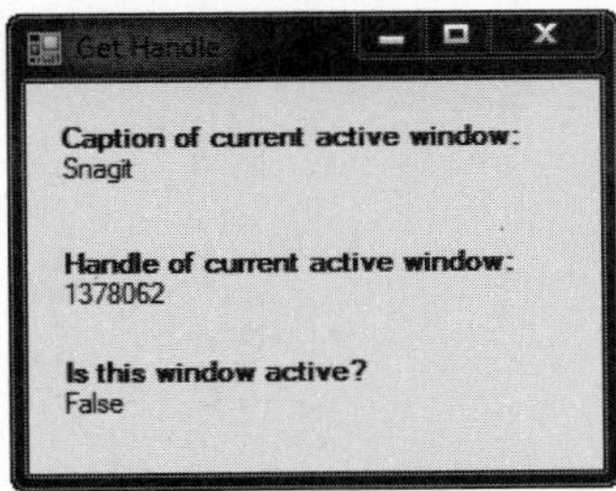

Figure 12-1. Retrieving information about the active window

12-3. Call an Unmanaged Function That Uses a Structure

Problem

You need to call an unmanaged function that accepts a structure as a parameter.

Solution

Define the structure in your C# code. Use the attribute `System.Runtime.InteropServices.StructLayoutAttribute` to configure how the structure fields are laid out in memory. Use the static `SizeOf` method of the `System.Runtime.Interop.Marshal` class if you need to determine the size of the unmanaged structure in bytes.

How It Works

In pure C# code, you are not able to directly control how type fields are laid out once the memory is allocated. Instead, the CLR is free to arrange fields to optimize performance, especially in the context of moving memory around during garbage collection. This can cause problems when interacting with native functions that expect structures to be laid out sequentially in memory as defined in include files. Fortunately, the .NET Framework allows you to solve this problem by using the attribute `StructLayoutAttribute`, which lets you specify how the members of a given class or structure should be arranged in memory.

The Code

As an example, consider the unmanaged `GetVersionEx` function implemented in the `Kernel32.dll` file. This function accepts a pointer to an `OSVERSIONINFO` structure and uses it to return information about the current operating system version. To use the `OSVERSIONINFO` structure in C# code, you must define it with the attribute `StructLayoutAttribute`, as shown here:

```
[StructLayout(LayoutKind.Sequential)]
public class OSVersionInfo {

    public int dwOSVersionInfoSize;
    public int dwMajorVersion;
    public int dwMinorVersion;
    public int dwBuildNumber;
    public int dwPlatformId;
    [MarshalAs(UnmanagedType.ByValTStr, SizeConst=128)]
    public String szCSDVersion;
}
```

Notice that this structure also uses the attribute `System.Runtime.InteropServices.MarshalAsAttribute`, which is required for fixed-length strings. In this example, `MarshalAsAttribute` specifies that the string will be passed by value and will contain a buffer of exactly 128 characters, as specified in the `OSVERSIONINFO` structure. This example uses sequential layout, which means that the data types in the structure are laid out in the order they are listed in the class or structure. When using sequential layout, you can also configure the packing for the structure by specifying a named `Pack` field in the `StructLayoutAttribute` constructor. The default is 8, which means the structure will be packed on 8-byte boundaries.

Instead of using sequential layout, you could use `LayoutKind.Explicit`; in which case, you must define the byte offset of each field using `FieldOffsetAttribute`. This layout is useful when dealing with an irregularly packed structure or one where you want to omit some of the fields that you do not want to use. Here is an example that defines the `OSVersionInfo` class with explicit layout:

```
[StructLayout(LayoutKind.Explicit)]
public class OSVersionInfo {

    [FieldOffset(0)]public int dwOSVersionInfoSize;
    [FieldOffset(4)]public int dwMajorVersion;
    [FieldOffset(8)]public int dwMinorVersion;
    [FieldOffset(12)]public int dwBuildNumber;
    [FieldOffset(16)]public int dwPlatformId;
    [MarshalAs(UnmanagedType.ByValTStr, SizeConst=128)]
    [FieldOffset(20)]public String szCSDVersion;
}
```

Now that you've defined the structure used by the `GetVersionEx` function, you can declare the function and then use it. The following console application shows all the code you will need. Notice that `InAttribute` and `OutAttribute` are applied to the `OSVersionInfo` parameter to indicate that marshaling should be performed on this structure when it is passed to the function and when it is returned from the function. In addition, the code uses the `Marshal.SizeOf` method to calculate the size the marshaled structure will occupy in memory.

```
using System;
using System.Runtime.InteropServices;

namespace Apress.VisualCSharpRecipes.Chapter12
{
    class Recipe12_03
    {
```

```
        // Declare the external function.
        [DllImport("kernel32.dll")]
        public static extern bool GetVersionEx([In, Out] OSVersionInfo osvi);

        static void Main(string[] args)
        {
            OSVersionInfo osvi = new OSVersionInfo();
            osvi.dwOSVersionInfoSize = Marshal.SizeOf(osvi);

            // Obtain the OS version information.
            GetVersionEx(osvi);

            // Display the version information.
            Console.WriteLine("Class size: " + osvi.dwOSVersionInfoSize);
            Console.WriteLine("Major Version: " + osvi.dwMajorVersion);
            Console.WriteLine("Minor Version: " + osvi.dwMinorVersion);
            Console.WriteLine("Build Number: " + osvi.dwBuildNumber);
            Console.WriteLine("Platform Id: " + osvi.dwPlatformId);
            Console.WriteLine("CSD Version: " + osvi.szCSDVersion);
            Console.WriteLine("Platform: " + Environment.OSVersion.Platform);
            Console.WriteLine("Version: " + Environment.OSVersion.Version);

            // Wait to continue.
            Console.WriteLine(Environment.NewLine);
            Console.WriteLine("Main method complete. Press Enter.");
            Console.ReadLine();
        }
    }

    // Define the structure and specify the layout type as sequential.
    [StructLayout(LayoutKind.Sequential)]
    public class OSVersionInfo
    {
        public int dwOSVersionInfoSize;
        public int dwMajorVersion;
        public int dwMinorVersion;
        public int dwBuildNumber;
        public int dwPlatformId;
        [MarshalAs(UnmanagedType.ByValTStr, SizeConst = 128)]
        public String szCSDVersion;
    }
}
```

If you run this application on a Windows 7 system, you will see information such as this:

```
Class size: 148

Major Version: 6

Minor Version: 1

Build Number: 7600

Platform Id: 2

CSD Version:

Platform: Win32NT

Version: 6.1.7600.0
```

12-4. Call an Unmanaged Function That Uses a Callback

Problem

You need to call an unmanaged function and allow it to call a method in your code.

Solution

Create a delegate that has the required signature for the callback. Use this delegate when defining and using the unmanaged function.

How It Works

Many of the Win32 API functions use callbacks. For example, if you want to retrieve the name of all the top-level windows that are currently open, you can call the unmanaged `EnumWindows` function in the `User32.dll` file. When calling `EnumWindows`, you need to supply a pointer to a function in your code. The Windows operating system will then call this function repeatedly—once for each top-level window that it finds—and pass the window handle to your code.

The .NET Framework allows you to handle callback scenarios like this without resorting to pointers and unsafe code blocks. Instead, you can define and use a delegate that points to your callback function. When you pass the delegate to the `EnumWindows` function, for example, the CLR will automatically marshal the delegate to the expected unmanaged function pointer.

The Code

Following is a console application that uses EnumWindows with a callback to display the name of every open window:

```
using System;
using System.Text;
using System.Runtime.InteropServices;

namespace Apress.VisualCSharpRecipes.Chapter12
{
    class Recipe12_04
    {
        // The signature for the callback method.
        public delegate bool CallBack(IntPtr hwnd, int lParam);

        // The unmanaged function that will trigger the callback
        // as it enumerates the open windows.
        [DllImport("user32.dll")]
        public static extern int EnumWindows(CallBack callback, int param);

        [DllImport("user32.dll")]
        public static extern int GetWindowText(IntPtr hWnd,
            StringBuilder lpString, int nMaxCount);

        static void Main(string[] args)
        {
            // Request that the operating system enumerate all windows,
            // and trigger your callback with the handle of each one.
            EnumWindows(new CallBack (DisplayWindowInfo), 0);

            // Wait to continue.
            Console.WriteLine(Environment.NewLine);
            Console.WriteLine("Main method complete. Press Enter.");
            Console.ReadLine();
        }

        // The method that will receive the callback. The second
        // parameter is not used, but is needed to match the
        // callback's signature.
        public static bool DisplayWindowInfo(IntPtr hWnd, int lParam)
        {
            int chars = 100;
            StringBuilder buf = new StringBuilder(chars);
            if (GetWindowText(hWnd, buf, chars) != 0)
            {
                Console.WriteLine(buf);
            }
```

```
            return true;
        }
    }
}
```

12-5. Retrieve Unmanaged Error Information

Problem

You need to retrieve error information (either an error code or a text message) explaining why a Win32 API call failed.

Solution

On the declaration of the unmanaged method, set the `SetLastError` field of the `DllImportAttribute` to `true`. If an error occurs when you execute the method, call the `static Marshal.GetLastWin32Error` method to retrieve the error code. To get a text description for a specific error code, use the unmanaged `FormatMessage` function.

How It Works

You cannot retrieve error information directly using the unmanaged `GetLastError` function. The problem is that the error code returned by `GetLastError` might not reflect the error caused by the unmanaged function you are using. Instead, it might be set by other .NET Framework classes or the CLR. You can retrieve the error information safely using the static `Marshal.GetLastWin32Error` method. This method should be called immediately after the unmanaged call, and it will return the error information only once. (Subsequent calls to `GetLastWin32Error` will simply return the error code 127.) In addition, you must specifically set the `SetLastError` field of the `DllImportAttribute` to `true` to indicate that errors from this function should be cached, as shown here:

```
[DllImport("user32.dll", SetLastError=true)]
```

You can extract additional information from the Win32 error code using the unmanaged `FormatMessage` function from the `Kernel32.dll` file.

The Code

The following console application attempts to show a message box, but submits an invalid window handle. The error information is retrieved with `Marshal.GetLastWin32Error`, and the corresponding text information is retrieved using `FormatMessage`.

```
using System;
using System.Runtime.InteropServices;

namespace Apress.VisualCSharpRecipes.Chapter12
{
    class Recipe12_05
    {
        // Declare the unmanaged functions.
        [DllImport("kernel32.dll")]
        private static extern int FormatMessage(int dwFlags, int lpSource,
          int dwMessageId, int dwLanguageId, ref String lpBuffer, int nSize,
          int Arguments);

        [DllImport("user32.dll", SetLastError = true)]
        public static extern int MessageBox(IntPtr hWnd, string pText,
          string pCaption, int uType);

        static void Main(string[] args)
        {
            // Invoke the MessageBox function passing an invalid
            // window handle and thus force an error.
            IntPtr badWindowHandle = (IntPtr)453;
            MessageBox(badWindowHandle, "Message", "Caption", 0);

            // Obtain the error information.
            int errorCode = Marshal.GetLastWin32Error();
            Console.WriteLine(errorCode);
            Console.WriteLine(GetErrorMessage(errorCode));

            // Wait to continue.
            Console.WriteLine(Environment.NewLine);
            Console.WriteLine("Main method complete. Press Enter.");
            Console.ReadLine();
        }

        // GetErrorMessage formats and returns an error message
        // corresponding to the input errorCode.
        public static string GetErrorMessage(int errorCode)
        {
            int FORMAT_MESSAGE_ALLOCATE_BUFFER = 0x00000100;
            int FORMAT_MESSAGE_IGNORE_INSERTS = 0x00000200;
            int FORMAT_MESSAGE_FROM_SYSTEM = 0x00001000;

            int messageSize = 255;
            string lpMsgBuf = "";
            int dwFlags = FORMAT_MESSAGE_ALLOCATE_BUFFER |
              FORMAT_MESSAGE_FROM_SYSTEM | FORMAT_MESSAGE_IGNORE_INSERTS;
```

```
            int retVal = FormatMessage(dwFlags, 0, errorCode, 0,
              ref lpMsgBuf, messageSize, 0);

            if (0 == retVal)
            {
                return null;
            }
            else
            {
                return lpMsgBuf;
            }
        }
    }
}
```

Here is the output generated by the preceding program:

```
1400

Invalid window handle.
```

12-6. Use a COM Component in a .NET Client

Problem

You need to use a COM component in a .NET client.

Solution

Use a Primary Interop Assembly (PIA) supplied by the COM object publisher, if one is available. Otherwise, generate a runtime callable wrapper (RCW) using the Type Library Importer (`Tlbimp.exe`) or the Add Reference feature in Visual Studio .NET.

How It Works

Because of the continuing importance of COM objects in Windows-based software development, the .NET Framework includes extensive support for COM interoperability. To allow .NET clients to interact with a COM component, .NET uses an RCW—a special .NET proxy class that sits between your managed .NET code and the unmanaged COM component. The RCW handles all the details of communicating between .NET code and COM objects, including marshaling data types, using the traditional COM interfaces, and handling COM events.

You have the following three options for using an RCW:

- Obtain an RCW from the author of the original COM component. In this case, the RCW is created from a PIA provided by the publisher, as Microsoft does for Microsoft Office.
- Generate an RCW using the `Tlbimp.exe` command-line utility or Visual Studio .NET.
- Create your own RCW using the types in the `System.Runtime.InteropServices` namespace. (This can be an extremely tedious and complicated process.)

If you want to use Visual Studio .NET to generate an RCW, you simply need to right-click your project in Solution Explorer and click Add Reference in the context menu, and then select the appropriate component from the COM tab. When you click OK, the RCW will be generated and added to your project references. After that, you can use the Object Browser to inspect the namespaces and classes that are available.

If you are not using Visual Studio .NET, you can create a wrapper assembly using the `Tlbimp.exe` command-line utility that is included with the .NET Framework. The only mandatory piece of information is the filename that contains the COM component. For example, the following statement creates an RCW with the default filename and namespace, assuming that the `MyCOMComponent.dll` file is in the current directory.

```
tlbimp MyCOMComponent.dll
```

Assuming that `MyCOMComponent` has a type library named `MyClasses`, the generated RCW file will have the name `MyClasses.dll` and will expose its classes through a namespace named `MyClasses`. You can also configure these options with command-line parameters, as described in the MSDN reference. For example, you can use `/out:[Filename]` to specify a different assembly file name and `/namespace:[Namespace]` to set a different namespace for the generated classes. You can also specify a key file using `/keyfile[keyfilename]` so that the component will be signed and given a strong name, allowing it to be placed in the Global Assembly Cache (GAC). Use the `/primary` parameter to create a PIA.

If possible, you should always use a PIA instead of generating your own RCW. PIAs are more likely to work as expected, because they are created by the original component publisher. They might also include additional .NET refinements or enhancements. If a PIA is registered on your system for a COM component, Visual Studio .NET will automatically use that PIA when you add a reference to the COM component. For example, the .NET Framework includes an `adodb.dll` assembly that allows you to use the ADO classic COM objects. If you add a reference to the Microsoft ActiveX Data Objects component, this PIA will be used automatically; no new RCW will be generated. Similarly, Microsoft Office provides a PIA that improves .NET support for Office automation. However, you must download this assembly from the MSDN web site.

The Code

The following example shows how you can use COM Interop, in the form of the Microsoft Office PIAs, to access Office automation functionality from a .NET Framework application. As you can see, the code is like any other .NET code—the key is the need to add the appropriate reference to the COM wrapper, which handles the communication between your code and the COM component. The example code also highlights (using the `Workbooks.Open` method) the significant syntax simplification enabled by .NET 4.0 when calling Interop methods that contain many optional parameters—something discussed further in recipe 12-8.

```
using System;
using System.IO;
using System.Runtime.InteropServices;
using Excel = Microsoft.Office.Interop.Excel;

namespace Apress.VisualCSharpRecipes.Chapter12
{
    class Recipe12_06
    {
        static void Main()
        {
            string fileName =
                Path.Combine(Directory.GetCurrentDirectory(),
                "Ranges.xlsx");

            // Create an instance of Excel.
            Console.WriteLine("Creating Excel instance...");
            Console.WriteLine(Environment.NewLine);
            Excel.Application excel = new Excel.Application();

            // Open the required file in Excel.
            Console.WriteLine("Opening file: {0}", fileName);
            Console.WriteLine(Environment.NewLine);

            // Open the specified file in Excel using .NET 4.0 optional
            // and named argument capabilities.
            Excel.Workbook workbook =
                excel.Workbooks.Open(fileName, ReadOnly: true);

            /* Pre-.NET 4.0 syntax required to open Excel file:
            Excel.Workbook workbook =
                excel.Workbooks.Open(fileName, Type.Missing,
                false, Type.Missing, Type.Missing, Type.Missing,
                Type.Missing, Type.Missing, Type.Missing, Type.Missing,
                Type.Missing, Type.Missing, Type.Missing, Type.Missing,
                Type.Missing); */

            // Display the list of named ranges from the file.
            Console.WriteLine("Named ranges:");
            foreach (Excel.Name name in workbook.Names)
            {
                Console.WriteLine("  {0} ({1})",name.Name,name.Value);
            }
            Console.WriteLine(Environment.NewLine);

            // Close the workbook.
            workbook.Close();

            /* Pre-.NET 4.0 syntax required to close Excel file:
            workbook.Close(Type.Missing, Type.Missing, Type.Missing); */
```

```
            // Terminate Excel instance.
            Console.WriteLine("Closing Excel instance...");
            excel.Quit();
            Marshal.ReleaseComObject(excel);
            excel = null;

            // Wait to continue.
            Console.WriteLine(Environment.NewLine);
            Console.WriteLine("Main method complete. Press Enter.");
            Console.ReadLine();
        }
    }}
```

12-7. Release a COM Component Quickly

Problem

You need to ensure that a COM component is removed from memory immediately, without waiting for garbage collection to take place, or you need to make sure that COM objects are released in a specific order.

Solution

Release the reference to the underlying COM object using the static `Marshal.FinalReleaseComObject` method and passing the appropriate RCW.

How It Works

COM uses reference counting to determine when objects should be released. When you use an RCW, the reference will be held to the underlying COM object even when the object variable goes out of scope. The reference will be released only when the garbage collector disposes of the RCW object. As a result, you cannot control when or in what order COM objects will be released from memory.

To get around this limitation, you usually use the `Marshal.ReleaseComObject` method. However, if the COM object's pointer is marshaled several times, you need to repeatedly call this method to decrease the count to zero. However, the `FinalReleaseComObject` method allows you to release all references in one go, by setting the reference count of the supplied RCW to zero. This means that you do not need to loop and invoke `ReleaseComObject` to completely release an RCW.

For example, in the Excel example in recipe 12-6, you could release all references to the Excel Application component using this code:

```
System.Runtime.InteropServices.Marshal.FinalReleaseComObject(excel);
```

■ **Note** The `ReleaseComObject` method does not actually release the COM object; it just decrements the reference count. If the reference count reaches zero, the COM object will be released. `FinalReleaseComObject` works by setting the reference count of an RCW to zero. It thus bypasses the internal count logic and releases all references.

12-8. Use Optional Parameters

Problem

You need to call a method in a COM component without supplying all the required parameters.

Solution

Prior to .NET 4.0, you would need to use the `Type.Missing` field. As of .NET 4.0, you can simply omit unused optional parameters and use named parameters for those values you do want to provide.

How It Works

The .NET Framework is designed with a heavy use of method overloading. Many methods are overloaded several times so that you can call the version that requires only the parameters you choose to supply. COM, on the other hand, does not support method overloading. Instead, COM components usually implement methods with a long list of optional parameters.

Prior to .NET 4.0, C# (unlike Visual Basic .NET) did not support optional parameters, which meant C# developers were forced to supply numerous additional or irrelevant values when calling a method on a COM component. And because COM parameters are often passed by reference, code could not simply pass a `null` reference. Instead, it had to declare an object variable and then pass that variable. This resulted in code that used the `Type.Missing` field whenever there was an unused optional parameter. In Office automation code, it is not unusual to see method calls with 10 or 15 `Type.Missing` parameters with 1 or 2 real values scattered among them. The optional and named parameter features included in .NET mean that COM Interop code becomes much cleaner and easier to understand. Instead of providing `Type.Missing` references for optional parameters you do not use, you can simply ignore them. And for those few parameters that you do need to provide, you can use named parameter syntax.

The Code

The following code snippet, taken from recipe 12-6, illustrates the improved clarity achieved using the optional and named parameter support added in .NET 4.0. In the example, the `fileName` parameter is not named as it is in the correct position (first), whereas `ReadOnly` would actually be the third parameter if it were not identified by name.

```
        // Open the specified file in Excel using .NET 4.0 optional
        // and named argument capabilities.
        Excel.Workbook workbook =
            excel.Workbooks.Open(fileName, ReadOnly: true);

        /* Pre-.NET 4.0 syntax required to open Excel file:
        Excel.Workbook workbook =
            excel.Workbooks.Open(fileName, Type.Missing,
            false, Type.Missing, Type.Missing, Type.Missing,
            Type.Missing, Type.Missing, Type.Missing, Type.Missing,
            Type.Missing, Type.Missing, Type.Missing, Type.Missing,
            Type.Missing); */
}
```

12-9. Use an ActiveX Control in a .NET Client

Problem

You need to place an ActiveX control on a form or a user control in a .NET Framework application.

Solution

Use an RCW exactly as you would with an ordinary COM component (see recipe 12-6). To work with the ActiveX control at design time, add it to the Visual Studio .NET Toolbox.

How It Works

The .NET Framework includes the same support for all COM components, including ActiveX controls. The key difference is that the RCW class for an ActiveX control derives from the special .NET Framework type `System.Windows.Forms.AxHost`. You add the `AxHost` control to your form, and it communicates with the ActiveX control behind the scenes. Because `AxHost` derives from `System.Windows.Forms.Control`, it provides the standard .NET control properties, methods, and events, such as `Location`, `Size`, `Anchor`, and so on. In the case of an autogenerated RCW, the `AxHost` classes will always begin with the letters `Ax`.

You can create an RCW for an ActiveX control as you would for any other COM component, as described in recipe 12-6: use the Type Library Importer (`Tlbimp.exe`) command-line utility or use the Add Reference feature in Visual Studio .NET and create the control programmatically. However, an easier approach in Visual Studio .NET is to add the ActiveX control to the toolbox. To add a control to the toolbox, in Visual Studio, open the Tools menu and click the Choose Toolbox Items menu option. Choose the COM Components tab and either select an item that is already listed or click the Browse button to locate a new control.

Nothing happens to your project when you add an ActiveX control to the toolbox. However, you can use the Toolbox icon to add an instance of the control to your form. The first time you do this, Visual Studio .NET will create the Interop assembly and add it to your project. For example, if you add the Microsoft Masked Edit control, Visual Studio .NET creates an RCW assembly with a name such as `AxInterop.MSMask.dll`. Here is the code you might expect to see in the hidden designer region that creates the control instance and adds it to the form:

```
this.axMaskEdBox1 = new AxMSMask.AxMaskEdBox();
((System.ComponentModel.ISupportInitialize)(this.axMaskEdBox1)).BeginInit();

//
// axMaskEdBox1
//
this.axMaskEdBox1.Location = new System.Drawing.Point(16, 12);
this.axMaskEdBox1.Name = "axMaskEdBox1";
this.axMaskEdBox1.OcxState = ((System.Windows.Forms.AxHost.State)
  (resources.GetObject("axMaskEdBox1.OcxState")));

this.axMaskEdBox1.Size = new System.Drawing.Size(112, 20);
this.axMaskEdBox1.TabIndex = 0;

this.Controls.Add(this.axMaskEdBox1);
```

Notice that the custom properties for the ActiveX control are not applied directly through property `set` statements. Instead, they are restored as a group when the control sets its persisted `OcxState` property. However, your code can use the control's properties directly.

12-10. Expose a .NET Component Through COM

Problem

You need to create a .NET component that can be called by a COM client.

Solution

Create an assembly that follows certain restrictions identified in this recipe. Export a type library for this assembly using the Type Library Exporter (`Tlbexp.exe`) command-line utility.

How It Works

The .NET Framework includes support for COM clients to use .NET components. When a COM client needs to create a .NET object, the CLR creates the managed object and a COM callable wrapper (CCW) that wraps the object. The COM client interacts with the managed object through the CCW. The runtime creates only one CCW for a managed object, regardless of how many COM clients are using it.

Types that need to be accessed by COM clients must meet certain requirements:

- The managed type (class, interface, struct, or enum) must be public.
- If the COM client needs to create the object, it must have a public default constructor. COM does not support parameterized constructors.
- The members of the type that are being accessed must be public instance members. Private, protected, internal, and static members are not accessible to COM clients.

In addition, you should consider the following recommendations:

- You should not create inheritance relationships between classes, because these relationships will not be visible to COM clients (although .NET will attempt to simulate this by declaring a shared base class interface).
- The classes you are exposing should implement an interface. For added versioning control, you can use the attribute `System.Runtime.InteropServices.GuidAttribute` to specify the GUID that should be assigned to an interface.
- Ideally, you should give the managed assembly a strong name so that it can be installed into the GAC and shared among multiple clients.

In order for a COM client to create the .NET object, it requires a type library (a TLB file). The type library can be generated from an assembly using the `Tlbexp.exe` command-line utility. Here is an example of the syntax you use:

```
tlbexp ManagedLibrary.dll
```

Once you generate the type library, you can reference it from the unmanaged development tool. With Visual Basic 6, you reference the TLB file from the Project References dialog box. In Visual C++, you can use the `#import` statement to import the type definitions from the type library.

CHAPTER 13

■ ■ ■

Commonly Used Interfaces and Patterns

The recipes in this chapter show you how to implement patterns you will use frequently during the development of Microsoft .NET Framework applications. Some of these patterns are formalized using interfaces defined in the .NET Framework class library. Others are less rigid, but still require you to take specific approaches to their design and implementation of your types. The recipes in this chapter describe how to do the following:

- Create custom serializable types that you can easily store to disk, send across the network, or pass by value across application domain boundaries (recipe 13-1)
- Provide a mechanism that creates accurate and complete copies (clones) of objects (recipe 13-2)
- Implement types that are easy to compare and sort (recipe 13-3)
- Support the enumeration of the elements contained in custom collections using a default or custom iterator (recipes 13-4 and 13-5)
- Ensure that a type that uses unmanaged resources correctly releases those resources when they are no longer needed (recipe 13-6)
- Display string representations of objects that vary based on format specifiers (recipe 13-7)
- Correctly implement custom exception and event argument types, which you will use frequently in the development of your applications (recipes 13-8 and 13-9)
- Implement the commonly used Singleton and Observer design patterns using the built-in features of C# and the .NET Framework class library (recipes 13-10 and 13-11)
- Implement the producer/consumer pattern to coordinate multiple threads or tasks safely (recipe 13-12)
- Defer initialization of a type until the first time it is used (recipe 13-13)
- Define a method that has optional parameters with default values (recipe 13-14).

- Define an extension method (recipe 13-15)
- Invoke type members dynamically and without static checking (recipe 13-16)
- Create variant generic types (recipe 13-18)

13-1. Implement a Custom Serializable Type

Problem

You need to implement a custom type that is serializable, allowing you to do the following:

- Store instances of the type to persistent storage (for example, a file or a database)
- Transmit instances of the type across a network
- Pass instances of the type by value across application domain boundaries

Solution

For serialization of simple types, apply the attribute `System.SerializableAttribute` to the type declaration. For types that are more complex, or to control the content and structure of the serialized data, implement the interface `System.Runtime.Serialization.ISerializable`.

How It Works

Recipe 2-13 showed how to serialize and deserialize an object using the formatter classes provided with the .NET Framework class library. However, types are not serializable by default. To implement a custom type that is serializable, you must apply the attribute `SerializableAttribute` to your type declaration. As long as all of the data fields in your type are serializable types, applying `SerializableAttribute` is all you need to do to make your custom type serializable. If you are implementing a custom class that derives from a base class, the base class must also be serializable.

■ **Caution** Classes that derive from a serializable type don't inherit the attribute `SerializableAttribute`. To make derived types serializable, you must explicitly declare them as serializable by applying the `SerializableAttribute` attribute.

Each formatter class contains the logic necessary to serialize types decorated with `SerializableAttribute`, and will correctly serialize all public, protected, and private fields. You can exclude specific fields from serialization by applying the attribute `System.NonSerializedAttribute` to those fields. As a rule, you should exclude the following fields from serialization:

- Fields that contain unserializable data types
- Fields that contain values that might be invalid when the object is deserialized, such as database connections, memory addresses, thread IDs, and unmanaged resource handles
- Fields that contain sensitive or secret information, such as passwords, encryption keys, and the personal details of people and organizations
- Fields that contain data that is easily re-creatable or retrievable from other sources, especially if there is a lot of data

---

■ **Note** See Recipe 2-14 for an example of using a slightly different method to exclude members from serialization when using the JSON format.

If you exclude fields from serialization, you must implement your type to compensate for the fact that some data will not be present when an object is deserialized. Unfortunately, you cannot create or retrieve the missing data fields in an instance constructor, because formatters do not call constructors during the process of deserializing objects. The best approach for achieving fine-grained control of the serialization of your custom types is to use the attributes from the `System.Runtime.Serialization` namespace described in Table 13-1. These attributes allow you to identify methods of the serializable type that the serialization process should execute before and after serialization and deserialization. Any method annotated with one of these attributes must take a single `System.Runtime.Serialization.StreamingContext` argument, which contains details about the source or intended destination of the serialized object so that you can determine what to serialize. For example, you might be happy to serialize secret data if it's destined for another application domain in the same process, but not if the data will be written to a file.

***Table 13-1.** Attributes to Customize the Serialization and Deserialization Processs*

Attribute	Description
`OnSerializingAttribute`	Apply this attribute to a method to have it executed before the object is serialized. This is useful if you need to modify object state before it is serialized. For example, you may need to convert a `DateTime` field to UTC time for storage.
`OnSerializedAttribute`	Apply this attribute to a method to have it executed after the object is serialized. This is useful in case you need to revert the object state to what it was before the method annotated with `OnSerializingAttribute` was run.
`OnDeserializingAttribute`	Apply this attribute to a method to have it executed before the object is deserialized. This is useful if you need to modify the object state prior to deserialization.

Attribute	Description
OnDeserializedAttribute	Apply this attribute to a method to have it executed after the object is deserialized. This is useful if you need to re-create additional object state that depends on the data that was deserialized with the object or modify the deserialized state before the object is used.

As types evolve, you often add new member variables to support new features. This new state causes a problem when deserializing old objects because the new member variables are not part of the serialized object. The.NET Framework supports the attribute `System.Runtime.Serialization.OptionalFieldAttribute`. When you create a new version of a type and add data members, annotate them with `OptionalFieldAttribute`, and the deserialization process will not fail if they are not present. You can then use a method annotated with `OnDeserializedAttribute` (see Table 13-1) to configure the new member variables appropriately.

For the majority of custom types, the mechanisms described will be sufficient to meet your serialization needs. If you require more control over the serialization process, you can implement the interface `ISerializable`. The formatter classes use different logic when serializing and deserializing instances of types that implement `ISerializable`. To implement `ISerializable` correctly, you must do the following:

- Declare that your type implements `ISerializable`
- Apply the attribute `SerializableAttribute` to your type declaration as just described. Do not use `NonSerializedAttribute`, because it will have no effect.
- Implement the `ISerializable.GetObjectData` method (used during serialization), which takes the argument types `System.Runtime.Serialization.SerializationInfo` and `System.Runtime.Serialization.StreamingContext`.
- Implement a nonpublic constructor (used during deserialization) that accepts the same arguments as the `GetObjectData` method. Remember that if you plan to derive classes from your serializable class, you should make the constructor protected.

During serialization, the formatter calls the `GetObjectData` method and passes it `SerializationInfo` and `StreamingContext` references as arguments. Your type must populate the `SerializationInfo` object with the data you want to serialize.

If you are creating a serializable class from a base class that also implements `ISerializable`, your type's `GetObjectData` method and deserialization constructor must call the equivalent method and constructor in the parent class.

The `SerializationInfo` class acts as a list of field/value pairs and provides the `AddValue` method to let you store a field with its value. In each call to `AddValue`, you must specify a name for the field/value pair; you use this name during deserialization to retrieve the value of each field. The `AddValue` method has 16 overloads that allow you to add values of different data types to the `SerializationInfo` object.

The `StreamingContext` object, as described earlier, provides information about the purpose and destination of the serialized data, allowing you to choose which data to serialize.

When a formatter deserializes an instance of your type, it calls the deserialization constructor, again passing a `SerializationInfo` and a `StreamingContext` reference as arguments. Your type must extract the serialized data from the `SerializationInfo` object using one of the `SerializationInfo.Get*` methods; for example, using `GetString`, `GetInt32`, or `GetBoolean`. During deserialization, the `StreamingContext` object provides information about the source of the serialized data, allowing you to mirror the logic you implemented for serialization.

The Code

This following example demonstrates a serializable `Employee` class that implements the `ISerializable` interface. In this example, the `Employee` class does not serialize the `address` field if the provided `StreamingContext` object specifies that the destination of the serialized data is a file. The `Main` method demonstrates the serialization and deserialization of an `Employee` object.

```
using System;
using System.IO;
using System.Text;
using System.Runtime.Serialization;
using System.Runtime.Serialization.Formatters.Binary;

namespace Apress.VisualCSharpRecipes.Chapter13
{
    [Serializable]
    public class Employee : ISerializable
    {
        private string name;
        private int age;
        private string address;

        // Simple Employee constructor.
        public Employee(string name, int age, string address)
        {
            this.name = name;
            this.age = age;
            this.address = address;
        }

        // Constructor required to enable a formatter to deserialize an
        // Employee object. You should declare the constructor private or at
        // least protected to ensure it is not called unnecessarily.
        private Employee(SerializationInfo info, StreamingContext context)
        {
            // Extract the name and age of the employee, which will always be
            // present in the serialized data regardless of the value of the
            // StreamingContext.
            name = info.GetString("Name");
            age = info.GetInt32("Age");

            // Attempt to extract the employee's address and fail gracefully
            // if it is not available.
            try
            {
                address = info.GetString("Address");
            }
```

```
        catch (SerializationException)
        {
            address = null;
        }
    }

    // Public property to provide access to employee's name.
    public string Name
    {
        get { return name; }
        set { name = value; }
    }

    // Public property to provide access to employee's age.
    public int Age
    {
        get { return age; }
        set { age = value; }
    }

    // Public property to provide access to employee's address.
    // Uses lazy initialization to establish address because
    // a deserialized object will not have an address value.
    public string Address
    {
        get
        {
            if (address == null)
            {
                // Load the address from persistent storage.
                // In this case, set it to an empty string.
                address = String.Empty;
            }
            return address;
        }

        set
        {
            address = value;
        }
    }

    // Declared by the ISerializable interface, the GetObjectData method
    // provides the mechanism with which a formatter obtains the object
    // data that it should serialize.
    public void GetObjectData(SerializationInfo inf, StreamingContext con)
    {
        // Always serialize the employee's name and age.
        inf.AddValue("Name", name);
        inf.AddValue("Age", age);
```

```
        // Don't serialize the employee's address if the StreamingContext
        // indicates that the serialized data is to be written to a file.
        if ((con.State & StreamingContextStates.File) == 0)
        {
            inf.AddValue("Address", address);
        }
    }

    // Override Object.ToString to return a string representation of the
    // Employee state.
    public override string ToString()
    {
        StringBuilder str = new StringBuilder();

        str.AppendFormat("Name: {0}\r\n", Name);
        str.AppendFormat("Age: {0}\r\n", Age);
        str.AppendFormat("Address: {0}\r\n", Address);

        return str.ToString();
    }
}

// A class to demonstrate the use of Employee.
public class Recipe13_01
{
    public static void Main(string[] args)
    {
        // Create an Employee object representing Roger.
        Employee roger = new Employee("Roger", 56, "London");

        // Display Roger.
        Console.WriteLine(roger);

        // Serialize Roger specifying another application domain as the
        // destination of the serialized data. All data including Roger's
        // address is serialized.
        Stream str = File.Create("roger.bin");
        BinaryFormatter bf = new BinaryFormatter();
        bf.Context =
            new StreamingContext(StreamingContextStates.CrossAppDomain);
        bf.Serialize(str, roger);
        str.Close();

        // Deserialize and display Roger.
        str = File.OpenRead("roger.bin");
        bf = new BinaryFormatter();
        roger = (Employee)bf.Deserialize(str);
        str.Close();
        Console.WriteLine(roger);
```

```
            // Serialize Roger specifying a file as the destination of the
            // serialized data. In this case, Roger's address is not included
            // in the serialized data.
            str = File.Create("roger.bin");
            bf = new BinaryFormatter();
            bf.Context = new StreamingContext(StreamingContextStates.File);
            bf.Serialize(str, roger);
            str.Close();

            // Deserialize and display Roger.
            str = File.OpenRead("roger.bin");
            bf = new BinaryFormatter();
            roger = (Employee)bf.Deserialize(str);
            str.Close();
            Console.WriteLine(roger);

            // Wait to continue.
            Console.WriteLine(Environment.NewLine);
            Console.WriteLine("Main method complete. Press Enter");
            Console.ReadLine();
        }
    }
}
```

13-2. Implement a Cloneable Type

Problem

You need to create a custom type that provides a simple mechanism for programmers to create copies of type instances.

Solution

Implement the `System.ICloneable` interface.

How It Works

When you assign one value type to another, you create a copy of the value. No link exists between the two values—a change to one will not affect the other. However, when you assign one reference type to another (excluding strings, which receive special treatment by the runtime), you do not create a new copy of the reference type. Instead, both reference types refer to the same object, and changes to the value of the object are reflected in both references. To create a true copy of a reference type, you must *clone* the object to which it refers.

The `ICloneable` interface identifies a type as cloneable and declares the `Clone` method as the mechanism through which you obtain a clone of an object. The `Clone` method takes no arguments, and returns a `System.Object`, regardless of the implementing type. This means that once you clone an object, you must explicitly cast the clone to the correct type.

The approach you take to implement the `Clone` method for a custom type depends on the data members declared within the type. If the custom type contains only value-type data members (`int`, `byte`, and so on) and `System.String` data members, you can implement the `Clone` method by instantiating a new object and setting its data members to the same values as the current object. The `Object` class (from which all types derive) includes the protected method `MemberwiseClone`, which automates this process.

If your custom type contains reference-type data members, you must decide whether your `Clone` method will perform a shallow copy or a deep copy. A *shallow copy* means that any reference-type data members in the clone will refer to the same objects as the equivalent reference-type data members in the original object. A *deep copy* means that you must create clones of the entire object graph so that the reference-type data members of the clone refer to physically independent copies (clones) of the objects referenced by the original object.

A shallow copy is easy to implement using the `MemberwiseClone` method just described. However, a deep copy is often what programmers expect when they first clone an object, but it's rarely what they get. This is especially true of the collection classes in the `System.Collections` namespace, which all implement shallow copies in their `Clone` methods. Although it would often be useful if these collections implemented a deep copy, there are two key reasons why types (especially generic collection classes) do not implement deep copies:

- Creating a clone of a large object graph is processor-intensive and memory-intensive.
- General-purpose collections can contain wide and deep object graphs consisting of any type of object. Creating a deep-copy implementation to cater to such variety is not feasible because some objects in the collection might not be cloneable, and others might contain circular references, which would send the cloning process into an infinite loop.

For strongly typed collections in which the nature of the contained elements are understood and controlled, a deep copy can be a very useful feature; for example, `System.Xml.XmlNode` implements a deep copy in its `Clone` method. This allows you to create true copies of entire XML object hierarchies with a single statement.

■ **Tip** If you need to clone an object that does not implement `ICloneable` but is serializable, you can often serialize and then deserialize the object to achieve the same result as cloning. However, be aware that the serialization process might not serialize all data members (as discussed in recipe 13-1). Likewise, if you create a custom serializable type, you can potentially use the serialization process just described to perform a deep copy within your `ICloneable.Clone` method implementation. To clone a serializable object, use the class `System.Runtime.Serialization.Formatters.Binary.BinaryFormatter` to serialize the object to, and then deserialize the object from a `System.IO.MemoryStream` object.

The Code

The following example demonstrates various approaches to cloning. The simple class **Employee** contains only **string** and **int** members, and so relies on the inherited **MemberwiseClone** method to create a clone. The **Team** class contains an implementation of the **Clone** method that performs a deep copy. The **Team** class contains a collection of **Employee** objects, representing a team of people. When you call the **Clone** method of a **Team** object, the method creates a clone of every contained **Employee** object and adds it to the cloned **Team** object. The **Team** class provides a private constructor to simplify the code in the **Clone** method. The use of constructors is a common approach to simplifying the cloning process.

```
using System;
using System.Text;
using System.Collections.Generic;

namespace Apress.VisualCSharpRecipes.Chapter13
{
    public class Employee : ICloneable
    {
        public string Name;
        public string Title;
        public int Age;

        // Simple Employee constructor.
        public Employee(string name, string title, int age)
        {
            Name = name;
            Title = title;
            Age = age;
        }

        // Create a clone using the Object.MemberwiseClone method because the
        // Employee class contains only string and value types.
        public object Clone()
        {
            return MemberwiseClone();
        }

        // Returns a string representation of the Employee object.
        public override string ToString()
        {
            return string.Format("{0} ({1}) - Age {2}", Name, Title, Age);
        }
    }

    public class Team : ICloneable
    {
        // A List to hold the Employee team members.
        public List<Employee> TeamMembers =
            new List<Employee>();
```

```
    public Team()
    {
    }

    // Private constructor called by the Clone method to create a new Team
    // object and populate its List with clones of Employee objects from
    // a provided List.
    private Team(List<Employee> members)
    {
        foreach (Employee e in members)
        {
            // Clone the individual employee objects and
            // add them to the List.
            TeamMembers.Add((Employee)e.Clone());
        }
    }

    // Adds an Employee object to the Team.
    public void AddMember(Employee member)
    {
        TeamMembers.Add(member);
    }

    // Override Object.ToString to return a string representation of the
    // entire Team.
    public override string ToString()
    {
        StringBuilder str = new StringBuilder();

        foreach (Employee e in TeamMembers)
        {
            str.AppendFormat("  {0}\r\n", e);
        }

        return str.ToString();
    }

    // Implementation of ICloneable.Clone.
    public object Clone()
    {
        // Create a deep copy of the team by calling the private Team
        // constructor and passing the ArrayList containing team members.
        return new Team(this.TeamMembers);

        // The following command would create a shallow copy of the Team.
        // return MemberwiseClone();
    }
}
```

```
    // A class to demonstrate the use of Employee.
    public class Recipe13_02
    {
        public static void Main()
        {
            // Create the original team.
            Team team = new Team();
            team.AddMember(new Employee("Frank", "Developer", 34));
            team.AddMember(new Employee("Kathy", "Tester", 78));
            team.AddMember(new Employee("Chris", "Support", 18));

            // Clone the original team.
            Team clone = (Team)team.Clone();

            // Display the original team.
            Console.WriteLine("Original Team:");
            Console.WriteLine(team);

            // Display the cloned team.
            Console.WriteLine("Clone Team:");
            Console.WriteLine(clone);

            // Make change.
            Console.WriteLine("*** Make a change to original team ***");
            Console.WriteLine(Environment.NewLine);
            team.TeamMembers[0].Name = "Luke";
            team.TeamMembers[0].Title = "Manager";
            team.TeamMembers[0].Age = 44;

            // Display the original team.
            Console.WriteLine("Original Team:");
            Console.WriteLine(team);

            // Display the cloned team.
            Console.WriteLine("Clone Team:");
            Console.WriteLine(clone);

            // Wait to continue.
            Console.WriteLine(Environment.NewLine);
            Console.WriteLine("Main method complete. Press Enter");
            Console.ReadLine();
        }
    }
}
```

13-3. Implement a Comparable Type

Problem

You need to provide a mechanism that allows you to compare custom types, enabling you to easily sort collections containing instances of those types.

Solution

To provide a standard comparison mechanism for a type, implement the generic `System.IComparable<T>` interface. To support the comparison of a type based on more than one characteristic, create separate types that implement the generic `System.Collections.Generic.IComparer<T>` interface.

How It Works

If you need to sort your type into only a single order, such as ascending ID number, or alphabetically based on surname, you should implement the `IComparable<T>` interface. `IComparable<T>` defines a single method named `CompareTo`, shown here:

```
int CompareTo(T other);
```

The value returned by `CompareTo` should be calculated as follows:

- If the current object is less than `other`, return less than zero (for example,`-1`).
- If the current object has the same value as `other`, return zero.
- If the current object is greater than `other`, return greater than zero (for example, `1`).

What these comparisons mean depends on the type implementing the `IComparable` interface. For example, if you were sorting people based on their surname, you would do a `String` comparison on this field. However, if you wanted to sort by birthday, you would need to perform a comparison of the corresponding `System.DateTime` fields.

To support a variety of sort orders for a particular type, you must implement separate helper types that implement the `IComparer<T>` interface, which defines the `Compare` method shown here:

```
int Compare(T x, T y);
```

These helper types must encapsulate the necessary logic to compare two objects and return a value based on the following logic:

- If `x` is less than `y`, return less than zero (for example, `-1`).
- If `x` has the same value as `y`, return zero.
- If `x` is greater than `y`, return greater than zero (for example, `1`).

The Code

The Newspaper class listed here demonstrates the implementation of both the IComparable and IComparer interfaces. The Newspaper.CompareTo method performs a case-insensitive comparison of two Newspaper objects based on their name fields. A private nested class named AscendingCirculationComparer implements IComparer and compares two Newspaper objects based on their circulation fields. An AscendingCirculationComparer object is obtained using the static Newspaper.CirculationSorter property.

The Main method shown here demonstrates the comparison and sorting capabilities provided by implementing the IComparable and IComparer interfaces. The method creates a System.Collections.ArrayList collection containing five Newspaper objects. Main then sorts the ArrayList twice using the ArrayList.Sort method. The first Sort operation uses the default Newspaper comparison mechanism provided by the IComparable.CompareTo method. The second Sort operation uses an AscendingCirculationComparer object to perform comparisons through its implementation of the IComparer.Compare method.

```
using System;
using System.Collections.Generic;

namespace Apress.VisualCSharpRecipes.Chapter13
{
    public class Newspaper : IComparable<Newspaper>
    {
        private string name;
        private int circulation;

        private class AscendingCirculationComparer : IComparer<Newspaper>
        {
            // Implementation of IComparer.Compare. The generic definition of
            // IComparer allows us to ensure both arguments are Newspaper
            // objects.
            public int Compare(Newspaper x, Newspaper y)
            {
                // Handle logic for null reference as dictated by the
                // IComparer interface. Null is considered less than
                // any other value.
                if (x == null && y == null) return 0;
                else if (x == null) return -1;
                else if (y == null) return 1;

                // Short-circuit condition where x and y are references
                // to the same object.
                if (x == y) return 0;

                // Compare the circulation figures. IComparer dictates that:
                //      return less than zero if x < y
                //      return zero if x = y
                //      return greater than zero if x > y
```

```
            // This logic is easily implemented using integer arithmetic.
            return x.circulation - y.circulation;
        }
    }

    // Simple Newspaper constructor.
    public Newspaper(string name, int circulation)
    {
        this.name = name;
        this.circulation = circulation;
    }

    // Declare a read-only property that returns an instance of the
    // AscendingCirculationComparer.
    public static IComparer<Newspaper> CirculationSorter
    {
        get { return new AscendingCirculationComparer(); }
    }

    // Override Object.ToString.
    public override string ToString()
    {
        return string.Format("{0}: Circulation = {1}", name, circulation);
    }

    // Implementation of IComparable.CompareTo. The generic definition
    // of IComparable allows us to ensure that the argument provided
    // must be a Newspaper object. Comparison is based on a
    // case-insensitive comparison of the Newspaper names.
    public int CompareTo(Newspaper other)
    {
        // IComparable dictates that an object is always considered greater
        // than null.
        if (other == null) return 1;

        // Short-circuit the case where the other Newspaper object is a
        // reference to this one.
        if (other == this) return 0;

        // Calculate return value by performing a case-insensitive
        // comparison of the Newspaper names.

        // Because the Newspaper name is a string, the easiest approach
        // is to rely on the comparison capabilities of the String
        // class, which perform culture-sensitive string comparisons.
        return string.Compare(this.name, other.name, true);
    }
}
```

```
    // A class to demonstrate the use of Newspaper.
    public class Recipe13_03
    {
        public static void Main()
        {
            List<Newspaper> newspapers = new List<Newspaper>();

            newspapers.Add(new Newspaper("The Echo", 125780));
            newspapers.Add(new Newspaper("The Times", 55230));
            newspapers.Add(new Newspaper("The Gazette", 235950));
            newspapers.Add(new Newspaper("The Sun", 88760));
            newspapers.Add(new Newspaper("The Herald", 5670));

            Console.Clear();
            Console.WriteLine("Unsorted newspaper list:");
            foreach (Newspaper n in newspapers)
            {
                Console.WriteLine("  " + n);
            }

            Console.WriteLine(Environment.NewLine);
            Console.WriteLine("Newspaper list sorted by name (default order):");
            newspapers.Sort();
            foreach (Newspaper n in newspapers)
            {
                Console.WriteLine("  " + n);
            }

            Console.WriteLine(Environment.NewLine);
            Console.WriteLine("Newspaper list sorted by circulation:");
            newspapers.Sort(Newspaper.CirculationSorter);
            foreach (Newspaper n in newspapers)
            {
                Console.WriteLine("  " + n);
            }

            // Wait to continue.
            Console.WriteLine(Environment.NewLine);
            Console.WriteLine("Main method complete. Press Enter");
            Console.ReadLine();
        }
    }
}
```

Usage

Running the example will produce the results shown here. The first list of newspapers is unsorted, the second is sorted using the `IComparable` interface, and the third is sorted using a comparer class that implements `IComparer`.

```
Unsorted newspaper list:
  The Echo: Circulation = 125780
  The Times: Circulation = 55230
  The Gazette: Circulation = 235950
  The Sun: Circulation = 88760
  The Herald: Circulation = 5670

Newspaper list sorted by name (default order):
  The Echo: Circulation = 125780
  The Gazette: Circulation = 235950
  The Herald: Circulation = 5670
  The Sun: Circulation = 88760
  The Times: Circulation = 55230

Newspaper list sorted by circulation:
  The Herald: Circulation = 5670
  The Times: Circulation = 55230
  The Sun: Circulation = 88760
  The Echo: Circulation = 125780
  The Gazette: Circulation = 235950
```

13-4. Implement an Enumerable Collection

Problem

You need to create a collection type whose contents you can enumerate using a `foreach` statement.

Solution

Implement the generic interface `System.Collections.Generic.IEnumerable<T>` on your collection type. The `GetEnumerator` method of the `IEnumerable` interface returns an *enumerator*, which is an object that implements the interface `System.Collections.Generic.IEnumerator<T>`. Within the `GetEnumerator` method, traverse the items in the collection using whatever logic is appropriate to your data structure and return the next value using the `yield return` statement. The C# compiler will automatically generate the necessary code to enable enumeration across the contents of your type.

How It Works

A numeric indexer allows you to iterate through the elements of most standard collections using a `for` loop. However, this technique does not always provide an appropriate abstraction for nonlinear data structures, such as trees and multidimensional collections. The `foreach` statement provides an easy-to-use and syntactically elegant mechanism for iterating through a collection of objects, regardless of their internal structures.

In order to support `foreach` semantics, the type containing the collection of objects should implement the `IEnumerable<T>` interface. The `IEnumerable<T>` interface declares a single method named `GetEnumerator`, which takes no arguments and returns an object that implements `IEnumerator<T>`. All you need to do in your `GetEnumerator` method is write the code necessary to iterate through the items in your collection using logic appropriate to the data structure. Each time you want to return an item, call the `yield return` statement and specify the value to return. The compiler generates code that returns the specified value and maintains appropriate state for the next time a value is requested. If you need to stop partway through the enumeration, call the `yield break` statement instead, and the enumeration will terminate as if it had reached the end of the collection.

■ **Tip** You do not actually need to explicitly implement `IEnumerable` on your type to make it enumerable. As long as it has a `GetEnumerator` method that returns an `IEnumerator` instance, the compiler will allow you to use the type in a `foreach` statement. However, it is always good practice to explicitly declare the capabilities of a type by declaring the interfaces it implements, as it allows users of your class to more easily understand its capabilities and purpose.

The `GetEnumerator` method is used automatically whenever you use an instance of your collection type in a `foreach` statement. However, if you want to provide multiple ways to enumerate the items in your collection, you can implement multiple methods or properties that are declared to return

IEnumerable<T> instances. Within the body of the member, use the **yield return** statement just mentioned, and the C# compiler will generate the appropriate code automatically. To use one of the alternative enumerations from a **foreach** statement, you must directly reference the appropriate member, as in this example:

```
foreach (node n in Tree.BreadthFirst)
```

The Code

The following example demonstrates the creation of an enumerable collection using the **IEnumerable<T>** and IEnumerator<T> interfaces in conjunction with the **yield return** and **yield break** statements. The Team class, which represents a team of people, is a collection of enumerable TeamMember objects.

```
using System;
using System.Collections.Generic;

namespace Apress.VisualCSharpRecipes.Chapter13
{
    // The TeamMember class represents an individual team member.
    public class TeamMember
    {
        public string Name;
        public string Title;

        // Simple TeamMember constructor.
        public TeamMember(string name, string title)
        {
            Name = name;
            Title = title;
        }

        // Returns a string representation of the TeamMember.
        public override string ToString()
        {
            return string.Format("{0} ({1})", Name, Title);
        }
    }

    // Team class represents a collection of TeamMember objects.
    public class Team
    {
        // A List to contain the TeamMember objects.
        private List<TeamMember> teamMembers = new List<TeamMember>();
```

```
        // Implement the GetEnumerator method, which will support
        // iteration across the entire team member List.
        public IEnumerator<TeamMember> GetEnumerator()
        {
            foreach (TeamMember tm in teamMembers)
            {
                yield return tm;
            }
        }

        // Implement the Reverse method, which will iterate through
        // the team members in alphabetical order.
        public IEnumerable<TeamMember> Reverse
        {
            get
            {
                for (int c = teamMembers.Count - 1; c >= 0; c--)
                {
                    yield return teamMembers[c];
                }
            }
        }

        // Implement the FirstTwo method, which will stop the iteration
        // after only the first two team members.
        public IEnumerable<TeamMember> FirstTwo
        {
            get
            {
                int count = 0;

                foreach (TeamMember tm in teamMembers)
                {
                    if (count >= 2)
                    {
                        // Terminate the iterator.
                        yield break;
                    }
                    else
                    {
                        // Return the TeamMember and maintain the iterator.
                        count++;
                        yield return tm;
                    }
                }
            }
        }
```

```
        // Adds a TeamMember object to the Team.
        public void AddMember(TeamMember member)
        {
            teamMembers.Add(member);
        }
    }

    // A class to demonstrate the use of Team.
    public class Recipe13_04
    {
        public static void Main()
        {
            // Create and populate a new Team.
            Team team = new Team();
            team.AddMember(new TeamMember("Curly", "Clown"));
            team.AddMember(new TeamMember("Nick", "Knife Thrower"));
            team.AddMember(new TeamMember("Nancy", "Strong Man"));

            // Enumerate the entire Team using the default iterator.
            Console.Clear();
            Console.WriteLine("Enumerate using default iterator:");
            foreach (TeamMember member in team)
            {
                Console.WriteLine("  " + member.ToString());
            }

            // Enumerate the first two Team members only.
            Console.WriteLine(Environment.NewLine);
            Console.WriteLine("Enumerate using the FirstTwo iterator:");
            foreach (TeamMember member in team.FirstTwo)
            {
                Console.WriteLine("  " + member.ToString());
            }

            // Enumerate the entire Team in reverse order.
            Console.WriteLine(Environment.NewLine);
            Console.WriteLine("Enumerate using the Reverse iterator:");
            foreach (TeamMember member in team.Reverse)
            {
                Console.WriteLine("  " + member.ToString());
            }

            // Wait to continue.
            Console.WriteLine(Environment.NewLine);
            Console.WriteLine("Main method complete. Press Enter");
            Console.ReadLine();
        }
    }
}
```

13-5. Implement an Enumerable Type Using a Custom Iterator

Problem

You need to create an enumerable type but do not want to rely on the built-in iterator support provided by the .NET Framework (described in recipe 13-4).

Solution

Implement the interface `System.Collections.IEnumerable` on your collection type. The `GetEnumerator` method of the `IEnumerable` interface returns an *enumerator*, which is an object that implements the interface `System.Collections.IEnumerator`. The `IEnumerator` interface defines the methods used by the `foreach` statement to enumerate the collection.

Implement a private inner class within the enumerable type that implements the interface `IEnumerator` and can iterate over the enumerable type while maintaining appropriate state information. In the `GetEnumerator` method of the enumerable type, create and return an instance of the iterator class.

How It Works

The automatic iterator support built into C# is very powerful and will be sufficient in the majority of cases. However, in some cases you may want to take direct control of the implementation of your collection's iterators. For example, you may want an iterator that supports changes to the underlying collection during enumeration.

Whatever your reason, the basic model of an enumerable collection is the same as that described in recipe 13-4. Your enumerable type should implement the `IEnumerable` interface, which requires you to implement a method named `GetEnumerator`. However, instead of using the `yield return` statement in `GetEnumerator`, you must instantiate and return an object that implements the `IEnumerator` interface. The `IEnumerator` interface provides a read-only, forward-only cursor for accessing the members of the underlying collection. Table 13-2 describes the members of the `IEnumerator` interface. The `IEnumerator` instance returned by `GetEnumerator` is your custom iterator—the object that actually supports enumeration of the collection's data elements.

Table 13-2. Members of the IEnumerator Interface

Member	Description
`Current`	Property that returns the current data element. When the enumerator is created, `Current` refers to a position preceding the first data element. This means you must call `MoveNext` before using `Current`. If `Current` is called and the enumerator is positioned before the first element or after the last element in the data collection, `Current` must throw a `System.InvalidOperationException`.
`MoveNext`	Method that moves the enumerator to the next data element in the collection. Returns `true` if there are more elements; otherwise, it returns `false`. If the underlying source of data changes during the life of the enumerator, `MoveNext` must throw an `InvalidOperationException`.
`Reset`	Method that moves the enumerator to a position preceding the first element in the data collection. If the underlying source of data changes during the life of the enumerator, `Reset` must throw an `InvalidOperationException`.

If your collection class contains different types of data that you want to enumerate separately, implementing the `IEnumerable` interface on the collection class is insufficient. In this case, you would implement a number of properties that return different `IEnumerator` instances.

The Code

The `TeamMember`, `Team`, and `TeamMemberEnumerator` classes in the following example demonstrate the implementation of a custom iterator using the `IEnumerable` and `IEnumerator` interfaces. The `TeamMember` class represents a member of a team. The `Team` class, which represents a team of people, is a collection of `TeamMember` objects. `Team` implements the `IEnumerable` interface and declares a separate class, named `TeamMemberEnumerator`, to provide enumeration functionality. `Team` implements the Observer pattern using delegate and event members to notify all `TeamMemberEnumerator` objects if their underlying `Team` changes. (See recipe 13-11 for a detailed description of the Observer pattern.) The `TeamMemberEnumerator` class is a private nested class, so you cannot create instances of it other than through the `Team.GetEnumerator` method.

```
using System;
using System.Collections;

namespace Apress.VisualCSharpRecipes.Chapter13
{
    // TeamMember class represents an individual team member.
    public class TeamMember
    {
        public string Name;
        public string Title;
```

```
        // Simple TeamMember constructor.
        public TeamMember(string name, string title)
        {
            Name = name;
            Title = title;
        }

        // Returns a string representation of the TeamMember.
        public override string ToString()
        {
            return string.Format("{0} ({1})", Name, Title);
        }
    }

    // Team class represents a collection of TeamMember objects. Implements
    // the IEnumerable interface to support enumerating TeamMember objects.
    public class Team : IEnumerable
    {
        // TeamMemberEnumerator is a private nested class that provides
        // the functionality to enumerate the TeamMembers contained in
        // a Team collection. As a nested class, TeamMemberEnumerator
        // has access to the private members of the Team class.
        private class TeamMemberEnumerator : IEnumerator
        {
            // The Team that this object is enumerating.
            private Team sourceTeam;

            // Boolean to indicate whether underlying Team has changed
            // and so is invalid for further enumeration.
            private bool teamInvalid = false;

            // Integer to identify the current TeamMember. Provides
            // the index of the TeamMember in the underlying ArrayList
            // used by the Team collection. Initialize to -1, which is
            // the index prior to the first element.
            private int currentMember = -1;

            // Constructor takes a reference to the Team that is the source
            // of enumerated data.
            internal TeamMemberEnumerator(Team team)
            {
                this.sourceTeam = team;

                // Register with sourceTeam for change notifications.
                sourceTeam.TeamChange +=
                    new TeamChangedEventHandler(this.TeamChange);
            }
```

```
// Implement the IEnumerator.Current property.
public object Current
{
    get
    {
        // If the TeamMemberEnumerator is positioned before
        // the first element or after the last element, then
        // throw an exception.
        if (currentMember == -1 ||
            currentMember > (sourceTeam.teamMembers.Count - 1))
        {
            throw new InvalidOperationException();
        }

        //Otherwise, return the current TeamMember.
        return sourceTeam.teamMembers[currentMember];
    }
}

// Implement the IEnumerator.MoveNext method.
public bool MoveNext()
{
    // If underlying Team is invalid, throw exception.
    if (teamInvalid)
    {
        throw new InvalidOperationException("Team modified");
    }

    // Otherwise, progress to the next TeamMember.
    currentMember++;

    // Return false if we have moved past the last TeamMember.
    if (currentMember > (sourceTeam.teamMembers.Count - 1))
    {
        return false;
    }
    else
    {
        return true;
    }
}

// Implement the IEnumerator.Reset method.
// This method resets the position of the TeamMemberEnumerator
// to the beginning of the TeamMembers collection.
public void Reset()
{
```

```
            // If underlying Team is invalid, throw exception.
            if (teamInvalid)
            {
                throw new InvalidOperationException("Team modified");
            }

            // Move the currentMember pointer back to the index
            // preceding the first element.
            currentMember = -1;
        }

        // An event handler to handle notifications that the underlying
        // Team collection has changed.
        internal void TeamChange(Team t, EventArgs e)
        {
            // Signal that the underlying Team is now invalid.
            teamInvalid = true;
        }
    }

    // A delegate that specifies the signature that all team change event
    // handler methods must implement.
    public delegate void TeamChangedEventHandler(Team t, EventArgs e);

    // An ArrayList to contain the TeamMember objects.
    private ArrayList teamMembers;

    // The event used to notify TeamMemberEnumerators that the Team
    // has changed.
    public event TeamChangedEventHandler TeamChange;

    // Team constructor.
    public Team()
    {
        teamMembers = new ArrayList();
    }

    // Implement the IEnumerable.GetEnumerator method.
    public IEnumerator GetEnumerator()
    {
        return new TeamMemberEnumerator(this);
    }

    // Adds a TeamMember object to the Team.
    public void AddMember(TeamMember member)
    {
        teamMembers.Add(member);
```

```
            // Notify listeners that the list has changed.
            if (TeamChange != null)
            {
                TeamChange(this, null);
            }
        }
    }

    // A class to demonstrate the use of Team.
    public class Recipe13_05
    {
        public static void Main()
        {
            // Create a new Team.
            Team team = new Team();
            team.AddMember(new TeamMember("Curly", "Clown"));
            team.AddMember(new TeamMember("Nick", "Knife Thrower"));
            team.AddMember(new TeamMember("Nancy", "Strong Man"));

            // Enumerate the Team.
            Console.Clear();
            Console.WriteLine("Enumerate with foreach loop:");
            foreach (TeamMember member in team)
            {
                Console.WriteLine(member.ToString());
            }

            // Enumerate using a While loop.
            Console.WriteLine(Environment.NewLine);
            Console.WriteLine("Enumerate with while loop:");
            IEnumerator e = team.GetEnumerator();
            while (e.MoveNext())
            {
                Console.WriteLine(e.Current);
            }

            // Enumerate the Team and try to add a Team Member.
            // (This will cause an exception to be thrown.)
            Console.WriteLine(Environment.NewLine);
            Console.WriteLine("Modify while enumerating:");
            foreach (TeamMember member in team)
            {
                Console.WriteLine(member.ToString());
                team.AddMember(new TeamMember("Stumpy", "Lion Tamer"));
            }
```

```
            // Wait to continue.
            Console.WriteLine(Environment.NewLine);
            Console.WriteLine("Main method complete. Press Enter");
            Console.ReadLine();
        }
    }
}
```

The example enumerates through the data with `foreach` and `while` loops and then attempts to modify the data during an enumeration, resulting in an exception. The output from the example is as follows:

```
Enumerate with foreach loop:

Curly (Clown)

Nick (Knife Thrower)

Nancy (Strong Man)




Enumerate with while loop:

Curly (Clown)

Nick (Knife Thrower)

Nancy (Strong Man)




Modify while enumerating:

Curly (Clown)
```

```
Unhandled Exception: System.InvalidOperationException: Team modified

   at Apress.VisualCSharpRecipes.Chapter13.Team.TeamMemberEnumerator.MoveNext() in

C:\Users\Adam\Documents\Work\C# Cookbook\Repository\CSHARPRECIPES\SourceCode

   \Chapter13\Recipe13-05\Recipe13-05.cs:line 85

   at Apress.VisualCSharpRecipes.Chapter13.Recipe13_05.Main() in C:\Users\Adam\

    Documents\Work\C# Cookbook\Repository\CSH

ARPRECIPES\SourceCode\Chapter13\Recipe13-05\Recipe13-05.cs:line 195

Press any key to continue . . .
```

13-6. Implement a Disposable Class

Problem

You need to create a class that references unmanaged resources and provide a mechanism for users of the class to free those unmanaged resources deterministically.

Solution

Implement the `System.IDisposable` interface and release the unmanaged resources when client code calls the `IDisposable.Dispose` method.

How It Works

An unreferenced object continues to exist on the managed heap and consume resources until the garbage collector releases the object and reclaims the resources. The garbage collector will automatically free managed resources (such as memory), but it will not free unmanaged resources (such as file handles and database connections) referenced by managed objects. If an object contains data members that reference unmanaged resources, the object must free those resources explicitly.

One solution is to declare a destructor—or finalizer—for the class (*destructor* is a C++ term equivalent to the more general .NET term *finalizer*). Prior to reclaiming the memory consumed by an instance of the class, the garbage collector calls the object's finalizer. The finalizer can take the necessary steps to release any unmanaged resources. Unfortunately, because the garbage collector uses a single thread to execute all finalizers, use of finalizers can have a detrimental effect on the efficiency of the garbage collection process, which will affect the performance of your application. In addition, you cannot control when the runtime frees unmanaged resources because you cannot call an object's finalizer directly, and you have only limited control over the activities of the garbage collector using the `System.GC` class.

As a complementary mechanism to using finalizers, the .NET Framework defines the *Dispose pattern* as a means to provide deterministic control over when to free unmanaged resources. To implement the Dispose pattern, a class must implement the `IDisposable` interface, which declares a single method named `Dispose`. In the `Dispose` method, you must implement the code necessary to release any unmanaged resources and remove the object from the list of objects eligible for finalization if a finalizer has been defined.

Instances of classes that implement the Dispose pattern are called *disposable objects*. When code has finished with a disposable object, it calls the object's `Dispose` method to free all resources and make it unusable, but still relies on the garbage collector to eventually release the object memory. It's important to understand that the runtime does not enforce disposal of objects; it's the responsibility of the client to call the `Dispose` method. However, because the .NET Framework class library uses the Dispose pattern extensively, C# provides the `using` statement to simplify the correct use of disposable objects. The following code shows the structure of a `using` statement:

```
using (FileStream fileStream = new FileStream("SomeFile.txt", FileMode.Open)) {
    // Do something with the fileStream object.
}
```

When the code reaches the end of the block in which the disposable object was declared, the object's `Dispose` method is automatically called, even if an exception is raised. Here are some points to consider when implementing the Dispose pattern:

- Client code should be able to call the `Dispose` method repeatedly with no adverse effects.
- In multithreaded applications, it's important that only one thread execute the `Dispose` method at a time. It's normally the responsibility of the client code to ensure thread synchronization, although you could decide to implement synchronization within the `Dispose` method.
- The `Dispose` method should not throw exceptions.
- Because the `Dispose` method does all necessary cleaning up, you do not need to call the object's finalizer. Your `Dispose` method should call the `GC.SuppressFinalize` method to ensure that the finalizer is not called during garbage collection.
- Implement a finalizer that calls the unmanaged cleanup part of your `Dispose` method as a safety mechanism in case client code does not call `Dispose` correctly. However, avoid referencing managed objects in finalizers, because you cannot be certain of the object's state.
- If a disposable class extends another disposable class, the `Dispose` method of the child must call the `Dispose` method of its base class. Wrap the child's code in a `try` block and call the parent's `Dispose` method in a `finally` clause to ensure execution.
- Other instance methods and properties of the class should throw a `System.ObjectDisposedException` exception if client code attempts to execute a method on an already disposed object.

The Code

The following example demonstrates a common implementation of the Dispose pattern.

```
using System;

namespace Apress.VisualCSharpRecipes.Chapter13
{
    // Implement the IDisposable interface.
    public class DisposeExample : IDisposable
    {
        // Private data member to signal if the object has already been
        // disposed.
        bool isDisposed = false;

        // Private data member that holds the handle to an unmanaged resource.
        private IntPtr resourceHandle;

        // Constructor.
        public DisposeExample()
        {
            // Constructor code obtains reference to unmanaged resource.
            resourceHandle = default(IntPtr);
        }

        // Destructor/finalizer. Because Dispose calls GC.SuppressFinalize,
        // this method is called by the garbage collection process only if
        // the consumer of the object does not call Dispose as it should.
        ~DisposeExample()
        {
            // Call the Dispose method as opposed to duplicating the code to
            // clean up any unmanaged resources. Use the protected Dispose
            // overload and pass a value of "false" to indicate that Dispose is
            // being called during the garbage collection process, not by
            // consumer code.
            Dispose(false);
        }

        // Public implementation of the IDisposable.Dispose method, called
        // by the consumer of the object in order to free unmanaged resources
        // deterministically.
        public void Dispose()
        {
            // Call the protected Dispose overload and pass a value of "true"
            // to indicate that Dispose is being called by consumer code, not
            // by the garbage collector.
            Dispose(true);

            // Because the Dispose method performs all necessary cleanup,
            // ensure the garbage collector does not call the class destructor.
            GC.SuppressFinalize(this);
        }
```

```
        // Protected overload of the Dispose method. The disposing argument
        // signals whether the method is called by consumer code (true), or by
        // the garbage collector (false). Note that this method is not part of
        // the IDisposable interface because it has a different signature to the
        // parameterless Dispose method.
        protected virtual void Dispose(bool disposing)
        {
            // Don't try to dispose of the object twice.
            if (!isDisposed)
            {
                // Determine if consumer code or the garbage collector is
                // calling. Avoid referencing other managed objects during
                // finalization.
                if (disposing)
                {
                    // Method called by consumer code. Call the Dispose method
                    // of any managed data members that implement the
                    // IDisposable interface.
                    // ...
                }

                // Whether called by consumer code or the garbage collector,
                // free all unmanaged resources and set the value of managed
                // data members to null.
                // Close(resourceHandle);

                // In the case of an inherited type, call base.Dispose(disposing).
            }

            // Signal that this object has been disposed.
            isDisposed = true;
        }

        // Before executing any functionality, ensure that Dispose has not
        // already been executed on the object.
        public void SomeMethod()
        {
            // Throw an exception if the object has already been disposed.
            if (isDisposed)
            {
                throw new ObjectDisposedException("DisposeExample");
            }

            // Execute method functionality.
            // . . .
        }
    }

    // A class to demonstrate the use of DisposeExample.
    public class Recipe13_06
    {
```

```
        public static void Main()
        {
            // The using statement ensures the Dispose method is called
            // even if an exception occurs.
            using (DisposeExample d = new DisposeExample())
            {
                // Do something with d.
            }

            // Wait to continue.
            Console.WriteLine(Environment.NewLine);
            Console.WriteLine("Main method complete. Press Enter");
            Console.ReadLine();
        }
    }
}
```

13-7. Implement a Formattable Type

Problem

You need to implement a type that can create different string representations of its content based on the use of format specifiers, for use in formatted strings.

Solution

Implement the `System.IFormattable` interface.

How It Works

The following code fragment demonstrates the use of format specifiers in the `WriteLine` method of the `System.Console` class. The format specifiers are inside the braces (shown in bold in the example).

```
double a = 345678.5678;
uint b = 12000;
byte c = 254;
Console.WriteLine("a = {0}, b = {1}, and c = {2}", a, b, c);
Console.WriteLine("a = {0:c0}, b = {1:n4}, and c = {2,10:x5}", a, b, c);
```

When run on a machine configured with English (UK) regional settings, this code will result in the output shown here:

```
a = 345678.5678, b = 12000, and c = 254

a = £345,679, b = 12,000.0000, and c =      000fe
```

As you can see, changing the contents of the format specifiers changes the format of the output significantly, even though the data has not changed. To enable support for format specifiers in your own types, you must implement the `IFormattable` interface. `IFormattable` declares a single method named `ToString` with the following signature:

```
string ToString(string format, IFormatProvider formatProvider);
```

The `format` argument is a `System.String` containing a *format string*. The format string is the portion of the format specifier that follows the colon. For example, in the format specifier `{2,10:x5}` used in the previous example, `x5` is the format string. The format string contains the instructions that the `IFormattable` instance should use when it's generating the string representation of its content. The .NET Framework documentation for `IFormattable` states that types that implement `IFormattable` must support the `G` (general) format string, but that the other supported format strings depend on the implementation. The `format` argument will be `null` if the format specifier does not include a format string component; for example, `{0}` or `{1,20}`.

The `formatProvider` argument is a reference to an instance of a type that implements `System.IFormatProvider`, and that provides access to information about the cultural and regional preferences to use when generating the string representation of the `IFormattable` object. This information includes data such as the appropriate currency symbol or number of decimal places to use. By default, `formatProvider` is `null`, which means you should use the current thread's regional and cultural settings, available through the static method `CurrentCulture` of the `System.Globalization.CultureInfo` class. Some methods that generate formatted strings, such as `String.Format`, allow you to specify an alternative `IFormatProvider` to use such as `CultureInfo`, `DateTimeFormatInfo`, or `NumberFormatInfo`.

The .NET Framework uses `IFormattable` primarily to support the formatting of value types, but it can be used to good effect with any type.

The Code

The following example contains a class named `Person` that implements the `IFormattable` interface. The `Person` class contains the title and names of a person and will render the person's name in different formats depending on the format strings provided. The `Person` class does not make use of regional and cultural settings provided by the `formatProvider` argument. The `Main` method demonstrates how to use the formatting capabilities of the `Person` class.

```
using System;

namespace Apress.VisualCSharpRecipes.Chapter13
{
    public class Person : IFormattable
    {
```

```
// Private members to hold the person's title and name details.
private string title;
private string[] names;

// Constructor used to set the person's title and names.
public Person(string title, params string[] names)
{
    this.title = title;
    this.names = names;
}

// Override the Object.ToString method to return the person's
// name using the general format.
public override string ToString()
{
    return ToString("G", null);
}

// Implementation of the IFormattable.ToString method to return the
// person's name in different forms based on the format string
// provided.
public string ToString(string format, IFormatProvider formatProvider)
{
    string result = null;

    // Use the general format if none is specified.
    if (format == null) format = "G";

    // The contents of the format string determine the format of the
    // name returned.
    switch (format.ToUpper()[0])
    {
        case 'S':
            // Use short form - first initial and surname.
            result = names[0][0] + ". " + names[names.Length - 1];
            break;

        case 'P':
            // Use polite form - title, initials, and surname.
            // Add the person's title to the result.
            if (title != null && title.Length != 0)
            {
                result = title + ". ";
            }
            // Add the person's initials and surname.
            for (int count = 0; count < names.Length; count++)
            {
                if (count != (names.Length - 1))
                {
                    result += names[count][0] + ". ";
                }
```

```
                    else
                    {
                        result += names[count];
                    }
                }
                break;

            case 'I':
                // Use informal form - first name only.
                result = names[0];
                break;

            case 'G':
            default:
                // Use general/default form - first name and surname.
                result = names[0] + " " + names[names.Length - 1];
                break;
        }
        return result;
    }
}

// A class to demonstrate the use of Person.
public class Recipe13_07
{
    public static void Main()
    {
        // Create a Person object representing a man with the name
        // Mr. Richard Glen David Peters.
        Person person =
            new Person("Mr", "Richard", "Glen", "David", "Peters");

        // Display the person's name using a variety of format strings.
        System.Console.WriteLine("Dear {0:G},", person);
        System.Console.WriteLine("Dear {0:P},", person);
        System.Console.WriteLine("Dear {0:I},", person);
        System.Console.WriteLine("Dear {0},", person);
        System.Console.WriteLine("Dear {0:S},", person);

        // Wait to continue.
        Console.WriteLine(Environment.NewLine);
        Console.WriteLine("Main method complete. Press Enter");
        Console.ReadLine();
    }
}
}
```

Usage

When executed, the preceding example produces the following output:

```
Dear Richard Peters,

Dear Mr. R. G. D. Peters,

Dear Richard,

Dear Richard Peters,

Dear R. Peters,
```

13-8. Implement a Custom Exception Class

Problem

You need to create a custom exception class so that you can use the runtime's exception-handling mechanism to handle application-specific exceptions.

Solution

Create a serializable class that extends the `System.Exception` class. Add support for any custom data members required by the exception, including constructors and properties required to manipulate the data members.

How It Works

Exception classes are unique in the fact that you do not declare new classes solely to implement new or extended functionality. The runtime's exception-handling mechanism—exposed by the C# statements `try`, `catch`, and `finally`—works based on the *type* of exception thrown, not the functional or data members implemented by the thrown exception.

If you need to throw an exception, you should use an existing exception class from the .NET Framework class library, if a suitable one exists. For example, some useful exceptions include the following:

- `System.ArgumentNullException`, when code passes a `null` argument value that does not support `null` arguments to your method
- `System.ArgumentOutOfRangeException`, when code passes an inappropriately large or small argument value to your method

- `System.FormatException`, when code attempts to pass your method a `String` argument containing incorrectly formatted data

If none of the existing exception classes meet your needs, or you feel your application would benefit from using application-specific exceptions, it's a simple matter to create your own exception class. In order to integrate your custom exception with the runtime's exception-handling mechanism and remain consistent with the pattern implemented by .NET Framework–defined exception classes, you should do the following:

- Give your exception class a meaningful name ending in the word `Exception`, such as `TypeMismatchException` or `RecordNotFoundException`.
- Mark your exception class as `sealed` if you do not intend other exception classes to extend it.
- Implement additional data members and properties to support custom information that the exception class should provide.
- Implement three public constructors with the signatures shown here and ensure that they call the base class constructor:

```
public CustomException() : base() {}
public CustomException(string msg): base(msg) {}
public CustomException(string msg, Exception inner) : base(msg, inner) {}
```

- Make your exception class serializable so that the runtime can marshal instances of your exception across application domain and machine boundaries. Applying the attribute `System.SerializableAttribute` is sufficient for exception classes that do not implement custom data members. However, because `Exception` implements the interface `System.Runtime.Serialization.ISerializable`, if your exception declares custom data members, you must override the `ISerializable.GetObjectData` method of the `Exception` class as well as implement a deserialization constructor with this signature. If your exception class is sealed, mark the deserialization constructor as `private`; otherwise, mark it as `protected`. The `GetObjectData` method and deserialization constructor must call the equivalent base class method to allow the base class to serialize and deserialize its data correctly. (See recipe 13-1 for details on making classes serializable.)

■ **Tip** In large applications, you will usually implement quite a few custom exception classes. It pays to put significant thought into how you organize your custom exceptions and how code will use them. Generally, avoid creating new exception classes unless code will make specific efforts to catch that exception; use data members to achieve informational granularity, not additional exception classes. In addition, avoid deep class hierarchies when possible in favor of broad, shallow hierarchies.

The Code

The following example is a custom exception named CustomException that extends Exception and declares two custom data members: a string named stringInfo and a bool named booleanInfo.

```
using System;
using System.Runtime.Serialization;

namespace Apress.VisualCSharpRecipes.Chapter13
{
    // Mark CustomException as Serializable.
    [Serializable]
    public sealed class CustomException : Exception
    {
        // Custom data members for CustomException.
        private string stringInfo;
        private bool booleanInfo;

        // Three standard constructors and simply call the base class.
        // constructor (System.Exception).
        public CustomException() : base() { }

        public CustomException(string message) : base(message) { }

        public CustomException(string message, Exception inner)
            : base(message, inner) { }

        // The deserialization constructor required by the ISerialization
        // interface. Because CustomException is sealed, this constructor
        // is private. If CustomException were not sealed, this constructor
        // should be declared as protected so that derived classes can call
        // it during deserialization.
        private CustomException(SerializationInfo info,
            StreamingContext context) : base(info, context)
        {
            // Deserialize each custom data member.
            stringInfo = info.GetString("StringInfo");
            booleanInfo = info.GetBoolean("BooleanInfo");
        }

        // Additional constructors to allow code to set the custom data
        // members.
        public CustomException(string message, string stringInfo,
            bool booleanInfo) : this(message)
        {
            this.stringInfo = stringInfo;
            this.booleanInfo = booleanInfo;
        }
```

```
        public CustomException(string message, Exception inner,
            string stringInfo, bool booleanInfo): this(message, inner)
        {
            this.stringInfo = stringInfo;
            this.booleanInfo = booleanInfo;
        }

        // Read-only properties that provide access to the custom data members.
        public string StringInfo
        {
            get { return stringInfo; }
        }

        public bool BooleanInfo
        {
            get { return booleanInfo; }
        }

        // The GetObjectData method (declared in the ISerializable interface)
        // is used during serialization of CustomException. Because
        // CustomException declares custom data members, it must override the
        // base class implementation of GetObjectData.
        public override void GetObjectData(SerializationInfo info,
            StreamingContext context)
        {
            // Serialize the custom data members.
            info.AddValue("StringInfo", stringInfo);
            info.AddValue("BooleanInfo", booleanInfo);

            // Call the base class to serialize its members.
            base.GetObjectData(info, context);
        }

        // Override the base class Message property to include the custom data
        // members.
        public override string Message
        {
            get
            {
                string message = base.Message;
                if (stringInfo != null)
                {
                    message += Environment.NewLine +
                        stringInfo + " = " + booleanInfo;
                }
                return message;
            }
        }
    }
```

```
    // A class to demonstrate the use of CustomException.
    public class Recipe13_08
    {
        public static void Main()
        {
            try
            {
                // Create and throw a CustomException object.
                throw new CustomException("Some error",
                    "SomeCustomMessage", true);
            }
            catch (CustomException ex)
            {
                Console.WriteLine(ex.Message);
            }

            // Wait to continue.
            Console.WriteLine(Environment.NewLine);
            Console.WriteLine("Main method complete. Press Enter");
            Console.ReadLine();
        }
    }
}
```

13-9. Implement a Custom Event Argument

Problem

When you raise an event, you need to pass an event-specific state to the event handlers.

Solution

Create a custom event argument class derived from the `System.EventArg` class. When you raise the event, create an instance of your event argument class and pass it to the event handlers.

How It Works

When you declare your own event types, you will often want to pass event-specific state to any listening event handlers. To create a custom event argument class that complies with the Event pattern defined by the .NET Framework, you should do the following:

- Derive your custom event argument class from the `EventArgs` class. The `EventArgs` class contains no data and is used with events that do not need to pass event state.
- Give your event argument class a meaningful name ending in `EventArgs`, such as `DiskFullEventArgs` or `MailReceivedEventArgs`.

- Mark your argument class as `sealed` if you do not intend other event argument classes to extend it.
- Implement additional data members and properties that you need to pass to event handlers to support event state. It's best to make event state immutable, so you should use private `readonly` data members and public properties to provide read-only access to the data members.
- Implement a public constructor that allows you to set the initial configuration of the event state.
- Make your event argument class serializable so that the runtime can marshal instances of it across application domain and machine boundaries. Applying the attribute `System.SerializableAttribute` is usually sufficient for event argument classes. However, if your class has special serialization requirements, you must also implement the interface `System.Runtime.Serialization.ISerializable`. (See recipe 13-1 for details on making classes serializable.)

The Code

The following example demonstrates the implementation of an event argument class named `MailReceivedEventArgs`. Theoretically, an e-mail server passes instances of the `MailReceivedEventArgs` class to event handlers in response to the receipt of an e-mail message. The `MailReceivedEventArgs` class contains information about the sender and subject of the received e-mail message.

```
using System;

namespace Apress.VisualCSharpRecipes.Chapter13
{
    [Serializable]
    public sealed class MailReceivedEventArgs : EventArgs
    {
        // Private read-only members that hold the event state that is to be
        // distributed to all event handlers. The MailReceivedEventArgs class
        // will specify who sent the received mail and what the subject is.
        private readonly string from;
        private readonly string subject;

        // Constructor, initializes event state.
        public MailReceivedEventArgs(string from, string subject)
        {
            this.from = from;
            this.subject = subject;
        }

        // Read-only properties to provide access to event state.
        public string From { get { return from; } }
        public string Subject { get { return subject; } }
    }
```

```
    // A class to demonstrate the use of MailReceivedEventArgs.
    public class Recipe13_09
    {
        public static void Main()
        {
            MailReceivedEventArgs args =
                new MailReceivedEventArgs("Danielle", "Your book");

            Console.WriteLine("From: {0}, Subject: {1}", args.From, args.Subject);

            // Wait to continue.
            Console.WriteLine(Environment.NewLine);
            Console.WriteLine("Main method complete. Press Enter");
            Console.ReadLine();
        }
    }
}
```

13-10. Implement the Singleton Pattern

Problem

You need to ensure that only a single instance of a type exists at any given time and that the single instance is accessible to all elements of your application.

Solution

Implement the type using the Singleton pattern.

How It Works

Of all the identified patterns, the Singleton pattern is perhaps the most widely known and commonly used. The purposes of the Singleton pattern are to ensure that only one instance of a type exists at a given time and to provide global access to the functionality of that single instance. You can implement the type using the Singleton pattern by doing the following:

- Implement a private static member within the type to hold a reference to the single instance of the type.
- Implement a publicly accessible static property in the type to provide read-only access to the singleton instance.
- Implement only a private constructor so that code cannot create additional instances of the type.

The Code

The following example demonstrates an implementation of the Singleton pattern for a class named SingletonExample:

```
using System;

namespace Apress.VisualCSharpRecipes.Chapter13
{
    public class SingletonExample
    {
        // A static member to hold a reference to the singleton instance.
        private static SingletonExample instance;

        // A static constructor to create the singleton instance. Another
        // alternative is to use lazy initialization in the Instance property.
        static SingletonExample()
        {
            instance = new SingletonExample();
        }

        // A private constructor to stop code from creating additional
        // instances of the singleton type.
        private SingletonExample() { }

        // A public property to provide access to the singleton instance.
        public static SingletonExample Instance
        {
            get { return instance; }
        }

        // Public methods that provide singleton functionality.
        public void SomeMethod1() { /*..*/ }
        public void SomeMethod2() { /*..*/ }
    }
}
```

Usage

To invoke the functionality of the SingletonExample class, you can obtain a reference to the singleton using the Instance property and then call its methods. Alternatively, you can execute members of the singleton directly through the Instance property. The following code shows both approaches.

```
// Obtain reference to singleton and invoke methods
SingletonExample s = SingletonExample.Instance;
s.SomeMethod1();

// Execute singleton functionality without a reference
SingletonExample.Instance.SomeMethod2();
```

13-11. Implement the Observer Pattern

Problem

You need to implement an efficient mechanism for an object (the subject) to notify other objects (the observers) about changes to its state.

Solution

Implement the Observer pattern using delegate types as type-safe function pointers and event types to manage and notify the set of observers.

How It Works

The traditional approach to implementing the Observer pattern is to implement two interfaces: one to represent an observer (`IObserver`) and the other to represent the subject (`ISubject`). Objects that implement `IObserver` register with the subject, indicating that they want to be notified of important events (such as state changes) affecting the subject. The subject is responsible for managing the list of registered observers and notifying them in response to events affecting the subject. The subject usually notifies observers by calling a `Notify` method declared in the `IObserver` interface. The subject might pass data to the observer as part of the `Notify` method, or the observer might need to call a method declared in the `ISubject` interface to obtain additional details about the event.

Although you are free to implement the Observer pattern in C# using the approach just described, the Observer pattern is so pervasive in modern software solutions that C# and the .NET Framework include event and delegate types to simplify its implementation. The use of events and delegates means that you do not need to declare `IObserver` and `ISubject` interfaces. In addition, you do not need to implement the logic necessary to manage and notify the set of registered observers—the area where most coding errors occur.

The .NET Framework uses one particular implementation of the event-based and delegate-based Observer pattern so frequently that it has been given its own name: the Event pattern. (Pattern purists might prefer the name *Event idiom*, but *Event pattern* is the name most commonly used in Microsoft documentation.)

The Code

The example for this recipe contains a complete implementation of the Event pattern, which includes the following types:

- `Thermostat` class (the subject of the example), which keeps track of the current temperature and notifies observers when a temperature change occurs
- `TemperatureChangeEventArgs` class, which is a custom implementation of the `System.EventArgs` class used to encapsulate temperature change data for distribution during the notification of observers

- `TemperatureEventHandler` delegate, which defines the signature of the method that all observers of a `Thermostat` object must implement and that a `Thermostat` object will call in the event of temperature changes
- `TemperatureChangeObserver` and `TemperatureAverageObserver` classes, which are observers of the `Thermostat` class

The `TemperatureChangeEventArgs` class (in the following listing) derives from the class `System.EventArgs`. The custom event argument class should contain all of the data that the subject needs to pass to its observers when it notifies them of an event. If you do not need to pass data with your event notifications, you do not need to define a new argument class; simply pass `EventArgs.Empty` or `null` as the argument when you raise the event. (See recipe 13-9 for details on implementing custom event argument classes.)

```
namespace Apress.VisualCSharpRecipes.Chapter13
{
    // An event argument class that contains information about a temperature
    // change event. An instance of this class is passed with every event.
    public class TemperatureChangedEventArgs : EventArgs
    {
        // Private data members contain the old and new temperature readings.
        private readonly int oldTemperature, newTemperature;

        // Constructor that takes the old and new temperature values.
        public TemperatureChangedEventArgs(int oldTemp, int newTemp)
        {
            oldTemperature = oldTemp;
            newTemperature = newTemp;
        }

        // Read-only properties provide access to the temperature values.
        public int OldTemperature { get { return oldTemperature; } }
        public int NewTemperature { get { return newTemperature; } }
    }
}
```

The following code shows the declaration of the `TemperatureEventHandler` delegate. Based on this declaration, all observers must implement a method (the name is unimportant) that returns `void` and takes two arguments: an `Object` instance as the first argument and a `TemperatureChangeEventArgs` object as the second. During notification, the `Object` argument is a reference to the `Thermostat` object that raises the event, and the `TemperatureChangeEventArgs` argument contains data about the old and new temperature values.

```
namespace Apress.VisualCSharpRecipes.Chapter13
{
    // A delegate that specifies the signature that all temperature event
    // handler methods must implement.
    public delegate void TemperatureChangedEventHandler(Object sender,
        TemperatureChangedEventArgs args);
}
```

For the purpose of demonstrating the Observer pattern, the example contains two different observer types: TemperatureAverageObserver and TemperatureChangeObserver. Both classes have the same basic implementation. TemperatureAverageObserver keeps a count of the number of temperature change events and the sum of the temperature values, and displays an average temperature when each event occurs. TemperatureChangeObserver displays information about the change in temperature each time a temperature change event occurs.

The following listing shows the TemperatureChangeObserver and TemperatureAverageObserver classes. Notice that the constructors take references to the Thermostat object that the TemperatureChangeObserver or TemperatureAverageObserver object should observe. When you instantiate an observer, pass it a reference to the subject. The observer must create a delegate instance containing a reference to the observer's event-handler method. To register as an observer, the observer object must then add its delegate instance to the subject using the subject's public event member. This is made even easier with the simplified delegate syntax provided by C#, where it is no longer required to explicitly instantiate a delegate to wrap the listening method.

Once the TemperatureChangeObserver or TemperatureAverageObserver object has registered its delegate instance with the Thermostat object, you need to maintain a reference to this Thermostat object only if you want to stop observing it later on. In addition, you do not need to maintain a reference to the subject, because a reference to the event source is included as the first argument each time the Thermostat object raises an event through the TemperatureChange method.

```
namespace Apress.VisualCSharpRecipes.Chapter13
{
    // A Thermostat observer that displays information about the change in
    // temperature when a temperature change event occurs.
    public class TemperatureChangeObserver
    {
        // A constructor that takes a reference to the Thermostat object that
        // the TemperatureChangeObserver object should observe.
        public TemperatureChangeObserver(Thermostat t)
        {
            // Create a new TemperatureChangedEventHandler delegate instance and
            // register it with the specified Thermostat.
            t.TemperatureChanged += this.TemperatureChange;
        }

        // The method to handle temperature change events.
        public void TemperatureChange(Object sender,
            TemperatureChangedEventArgs temp)
        {
            Console.WriteLine ("ChangeObserver: Old={0}, New={1}, Change={2}",
                temp.OldTemperature, temp.NewTemperature,
                temp.NewTemperature - temp.OldTemperature);
        }
    }

    // A Thermostat observer that displays information about the average
    // temperature when a temperature change event occurs.
    public class TemperatureAverageObserver
    {
```

```
        // Sum contains the running total of temperature readings.
        // Count contains the number of temperature events received.
        private int sum = 0, count = 0;

        // A constructor that takes a reference to the Thermostat object that
        // the TemperatureAverageObserver object should observe.
        public TemperatureAverageObserver(Thermostat t)
        {
            // Create a new TemperatureChangedEventHandler delegate instance and
            // register it with the specified Thermostat.
            t.TemperatureChanged += this.TemperatureChange;
        }

        // The method to handle temperature change events.
        public void TemperatureChange(Object sender,
            TemperatureChangedEventArgs temp)
        {
            count++;
            sum += temp.NewTemperature;

            Console.WriteLine
                ("AverageObserver: Average={0:F}", (double)sum / (double)count);
        }
    }
}
```

Finally, the `Thermostat` class is the observed object in this Observer (Event) pattern. In theory, a monitoring device sets the current temperature by calling the `Temperature` property on a `Thermostat` object. This causes the `Thermostat` object to raise its `TemperatureChange` event and send a `TemperatureChangeEventArgs` object to each observer.

The example contains a `Recipe13_11` class that defines a `Main` method to drive the example. After creating a `Thermostat` object and two different observer objects, the `Main` method repeatedly prompts you to enter a temperature. Each time you enter a new temperature, the `Thermostat` object notifies the listeners, which display information to the console. The following is the code for the `Thermostat` class:

```
namespace Apress.VisualCSharpRecipes.Chapter13
{
    // A class that represents a Thermostat, which is the source of temperature
    // change events. In the Observer pattern, a Thermostat object is the
    // subject that Observers listen to for change notifications.
    public class Thermostat
    {
        // Private field to hold current temperature.
        private int temperature = 0;

        // The event used to maintain a list of observer delegates and raise
        // a temperature change event when a temperature change occurs.
        public event TemperatureChangedEventHandler TemperatureChanged;

        // A protected method used to raise the TemperatureChanged event.
        // Because events can be triggered only from within the containing
```

```
    // type, using a protected method to raise the event allows derived
    // classes to provide customized behavior and still be able to raise
    // the base class event.
    virtual protected void OnTemperatureChanged
        (TemperatureChangedEventArgs args)
    {
        // Notify all observers. A test for null indicates whether any
        // observers are registered.
        if (TemperatureChanged != null)
        {
            TemperatureChanged(this, args);
        }
    }

    // Public property to get and set the current temperature. The "set"
    // side of the property is responsible for raising the temperature
    // change event to notify all observers of a change in temperature.
    public int Temperature
    {
        get { return temperature; }

        set
        {
            // Create a new event argument object containing the old and
            // new temperatures.
            TemperatureChangedEventArgs args =
                new TemperatureChangedEventArgs(temperature, value);

            // Update the current temperature.
            temperature = value;

            // Raise the temperature change event.
            OnTemperatureChanged(args);
        }
    }
}

// A class to demonstrate the use of the Observer pattern.
public class Recipe13_11
{
    public static void Main()
    {
        // Create a Thermostat instance.
        Thermostat t = new Thermostat();

        // Create the Thermostat observers.
        new TemperatureChangeObserver(t);
        new TemperatureAverageObserver(t);
```

```
            // Loop, getting temperature readings from the user.
            // Any noninteger value will terminate the loop.
            do
            {
                Console.WriteLine(Environment.NewLine);
                Console.Write("Enter current temperature: ");

                try
                {
                    // Convert the user's input to an integer and use it to set
                    // the current temperature of the Thermostat.
                    t.Temperature = Int32.Parse(Console.ReadLine());
                }
                catch (Exception)
                {
                    // Use the exception condition to trigger termination.
                    Console.WriteLine("Terminating Observer Pattern Example.");

                    // Wait to continue.
                    Console.WriteLine(Environment.NewLine);
                    Console.WriteLine("Main method complete. Press Enter");
                    Console.ReadLine();
                    return;
                }
            } while (true);
        }
    }
}
```

Usage

The following listing shows the kind of output you should expect if you build and run the previous example. The bold values show your input.

```
Enter current temperature: 50

ChangeObserver: Old=0, New=50, Change=50

AverageObserver: Average=50.00



Enter current temperature: 20

ChangeObserver: Old=50, New=20, Change=-30

AverageObserver: Average=35.00
```

```
Enter current temperature: 40

ChangeObserver: Old=20, New=40, Change=20

AverageObserver: Average=36.67
```

13-12. Implement a Parallel Producer-Consumer Pattern

Problem

You need to coordinate several threads using a collection, such that one or more producer threads places items into the collection as one or more consumer threads removes items from it.

Solution

Use the `System.Collections.Concurrent.BlockingCollection` class.

How It Works

The `BlockingCollection` is a wrapper class that provides the foundation for the parallel producer-consumer pattern. Consumer threads are blocked when trying to take data from the collection until there are data items available. Optionally, producer threads are blocked when trying to add data to the collection if there are too many items already in the collection.

`BlockingCollection` wraps around collections classes that implement the `System.Collections.Concurrent.IProducerConsumerCollection` interface—this includes the `ConcurrentQueue`, `ConcurrentStack`, and `ConcurrentBag` collections in the `System.Collections.Concurrent` namespace.

To create a new instance of `BlockingCollection`, pass in an instance of the collection that you want to wrap and, if required, the maximum number of items you wish to be in the collection before producers will block when adding. For example, the following statement creates a new instance wrapped around a `ConcurrentQueue` with a size limit of three pending items:

```
new BlockingCollection<string>(new ConcurrentStack<string>(), 3);
```

The default constructor for `BlockingCollection` (which takes no arguments) uses the `ConcurrentQueue` class as the underlying collection, and uses no size limit—meaning that items will be taken out of the collection in the same order in which they were added, and also that producer threads will not block when adding items, irrespective of how many items are in the collection.

There are two ways for consumers to take items out of the collection. If you have one consumer thread, then the simplest way is to call the `GetConsumingEnumerable` method and use the resulting `IEnumerable` in a `foreach` loop. The loop will block when there are no items in the collection to be consumed. If you have multiple consumers, then they should call the `Take` method, which will return an item if one is available in the collection or block until such time as one becomes available.

If you don't want your producers and consumers to block, you can use the `BlockingCollection.TryAdd` and `BlockingCollection.TryTake` methods. These methods won't block, regardless of the state of the collection, and they return a `bool` to indicate whether the add or take operations succeeded.

When using this pattern, there often comes a point when your producers have added all of the items that you require and their tasks or threads have completed. However, your consumers will still be blocking because they continue to wait for new items to arrive in the collection. To avoid this situation, you should call the `BlockingCollection.CompleteAdding` instance method, which stops the methods the consumers are using from blocking—see the following code example for an illustration of this.

The Code

The following example creates a `BlockingCollection` using a `ConcurrentQueue` as the underlying collection. Using the .NET parallel programming features (see Chapter 15 for further information about parallel programming), a single consumer reads items from the collection while four producers add items. The main application thread waits for the producers to add their items and finish, before calling `CompleteAdding` on the collection. This causes the consumer's `foreach` method to stop blocking when all of the items are read from the collection.

```
using System;
using System.Collections.Generic;
using System.Linq;
using System.Text;
using System.Collections.Concurrent;
using System.Threading.Tasks;

namespace Apress.VisualCSharpRecipes.Chapter13
{
    class Recipe13_12
    {
        static void Main(string[] args)
        {
            // Create the collection.
            BlockingCollection<string> bCollection
                = new BlockingCollection<string>(new ConcurrentQueue<string>(), 3);

            // Start the consumer.
            Task consumerTask = Task.Factory.StartNew(
                () => performConsumerTasks(bCollection));
            // Start the producers.
            Task producer0 = Task.Factory.StartNew(
                () => performProducerTasks(bCollection, 0));
            Task producer1 = Task.Factory.StartNew(
                () => performProducerTasks(bCollection, 1));
            Task producer2 = Task.Factory.StartNew(
                () => performProducerTasks(bCollection, 2));
            Task producer3 = Task.Factory.StartNew(
                () => performProducerTasks(bCollection, 3));

            // Wait for the producers to complete.
            Task.WaitAll(producer0, producer1, producer2, producer3);
            Console.WriteLine("Producer tasks complete.");
```

```
            // Indicate that we will not add anything further.
            bCollection.CompleteAdding();

            // Wait for the consumer task to complete.
            consumerTask.Wait();

            // Wait to continue.
            Console.WriteLine(Environment.NewLine);
            Console.WriteLine("Main method complete. Press Enter");
            Console.ReadLine();
        }

        static void performConsumerTasks(BlockingCollection<string> collection)
        {
            Console.WriteLine("Consumer started");
            foreach (string collData in collection.GetConsumingEnumerable())
            {
                // Write out the data.
                Console.WriteLine("Consumer got message {0}", collData);
            }
            Console.WriteLine("Consumer completed");
        }

        static void performProducerTasks(BlockingCollection<string> collection,
            int taskID)
        {
            Console.WriteLine("Producer started");
            for (int i = 0; i < 100; i++)
            {
                // Put something into the collection.
                collection.Add("TaskID " + taskID + " Message" + i++);
                Console.WriteLine("Task {0} wrote message {1}", taskID, i);
            }
        }
    }
}
```

13-13. Perform Lazy Object Initialization

Problem

You want to defer instantiating an object until it is used for the first time.

Solution

Use the `System.Lazy` class to wrap the creation of your data type and call the `Lazy.Value` instance method to access the type instance—the type will not be initialized until `Lazy.Value` is first called.

How It Works

The .NET Framework performs eager initialization by default, which means that types are initialized as soon as they are created. By contrast, lazy initialization lets you defer object initialization until you need to access one of the members of your type. Eager initialization tends to create applications that create lots of objects when they start, even though the objects themselves may not be used for some time—this can consume resources unnecessarily and slow down your application, at least until all of the objects are created. To use lazy initialization, you simply pass your normal object instantiation as a delegate argument to the constructor of the `System.Lazy` class, so that

```
MyDataType mytype = new MydataType();
```

becomes

```
Lazy<MyDataType> myType = new Lazy<MyDataType<(() => new MyDataType());
```

In order to access the type within the `Lazy` instance, you call the `Value` property—the first time that `Value` is called, the type will be initialized—in this way, you can defer initializing your object until you need to use it.

The Code

The following example defines a type called `MyDataType`, which has a constructor and a method called `sayHello`. The `Main` method called when the application starts creates an instance of `MyDataType` using eager initialization, prints out a message simulating performing other tasks, and then calls `sayHello`. This process is then repeated using lazy initialization. The result is that the constructor is called as soon as the object reference is created using eager initialization, whereas the constructor is not called until the `sayHello` method is invoked when using lazy initialization.

```
using System;
using System.Collections.Generic;
using System.Linq;
using System.Text;

namespace Apress.VisualCSharpRecipes.Chapter13
{
    class Recipe13_13
    {
        static void Main(string[] args)
        {
            // Create an instance using eager initialization.
            MyDataType eagerInstance = new MyDataType(false);
            Console.WriteLine("...do other things...");
            eagerInstance.sayHello();

            Lazy<MyDataType> lazyInstance = new Lazy<MyDataType>(()
               => new MyDataType(true));
            Console.WriteLine("...do other things...");
            lazyInstance.Value.sayHello();
```

```
            // Wait to continue.
            Console.WriteLine(Environment.NewLine);
            Console.WriteLine("Main method complete. Press Enter");
            Console.ReadLine();
        }
    }

    class MyDataType
    {
        public MyDataType(bool lazy)
        {
            Console.WriteLine("Initializing MyDataType - lazy instance: {0}", lazy);
        }

        public void sayHello()
        {
            Console.WriteLine("MyDataType Says Hello");
        }
    }
}
```

13-14. Use Optional Parameters

Problem

You need to define a method with optional parameters.

Solution

Supply a default value for the parameters you wish to make optional when defining your method.

How It Works

The optional parameters feature allows you to simplify a common programming pattern, where several slightly different methods exist to allow a caller to use default values, such as the following:

```
void printMessage()
{
    printMessage("Adam");
}

void printMessage(string from)
{
    printMessage(from, "Hello");
}
```

```
void printMessage(string from, string message)
{
    printMessage(from, message, false);
}

void printMessage(string from, string message, bool urgent)
{
    // Do something.
}
```

This approach allows callers of the method to rely on default values—this helps to simplify the code of the calling classes. C# supports optional parameters so that you can achieve the same effect with only one method in your class—you do this by setting the default values when defining the parameters—for example:

```
void printMessage(string from = "Adam", string message = "Hello",
    bool urgent = false)
```

Optional parameters must be defined after normal parameters.

The Code

The following example defines a method with three optional parameters:

```
using System;
using System.Collections.Generic;
using System.Linq;
using System.Text;

namespace Apress.VisualCSharpRecipes.Chapter13
{
    class Recipe13_14
    {
        static void Main(string[] args)
        {
            printMessage();
            printMessage("Allen");
            printMessage("Bob", "Goodbye");
            printMessage("Joe", "Help", true);

            // Wait to continue.
            Console.WriteLine(Environment.NewLine);
            Console.WriteLine("Main method complete. Press Enter");
            Console.ReadLine();
        }

        static void printMessage(string from = "Adam", string message = "Hello",
                bool urgent = false)
        {
```

```
            Console.WriteLine("From: {0}, Urgent: {1}, Message: {2}",
                from, message, urgent);
        }
    }
}
```

13-15. Add a Method to a Type Without Modifying It

Problem

You want to add a method to a type without modifying it, most likely because you didn't write the type you want to modify.

Solution

Implement and call a custom extension method.

How It Works

Extension types allow you to extend a type by providing new methods in a separate class file and associating them with the type you wish to apply them to. The main need for this C# feature is when you want to associate new features with a type that you didn't write—one from the .NET Framework class library, for example. To create an extension method, start by creating a static class—a static class has the keyword `static` before `class` in the declaration. A static class is like a regular class, except the class cannot be instantiated and all of the methods must be static.

Add a static method to the static class with the name and result type you require. The first parameter of the method must be of the type that you wish to extend and be prefaced with the word `this`.

Implement the method body, performing the tasks you require. The parameter you prefaced with `this` represents the instance of the type you have extended on which your method has been invoked. For example, suppose we define an extension for `string` like this:

```
public static int countVowels(this string str)
```

The `str` parameter is the `string` instance that the extension has been invoked to process. To use an extension method, you must ensure that the namespace in which you created the static class is available to the calling class with the `using` keyword, just as you would for any other namespace. Then you simply call the extension method as though it is an instance method of the type you have extended—for example:

```
String mystring = "Hello";
Mystring.countVowels();
```

Note that you don't need to provide the first argument you declared for your extension method (the one prefaced with `this`).

The Code

The following example defines two extension methods for the `string` type in the namespace `Apress.VisualCSharpRecipes.Chapter13.Extensions`:

```
using System;
using System.Collections.Generic;
using System.Linq;
using System.Text;
using Apress.VisualCSharpRecipes.Chapter13.Extensions;

namespace Apress.VisualCSharpRecipes.Chapter13.Extensions
{
    public static class MyStringExtentions
    {
        public static string toMixedCase(this String str)
        {
            StringBuilder builder = new StringBuilder(str.Length);
            for (int i = 0; i < str.Length; i += 2)
            {
                builder.Append(str.ToLower()[i]);
                builder.Append(str.ToUpper()[i + 1]);
            }
            return builder.ToString();
        }

        public static int countVowels(this String str)
        {
            char[] vowels = { 'a', 'e', 'i', 'o', 'u' };
            int vowelcount = 0;
            foreach (char c in str)
            {
                if (vowels.Contains(c))
                {
                    vowelcount++;
                }
            }
            return vowelcount;
        }
    }
}

namespace Apress.VisualCSharpRecipes.Chapter13
{
    class Recipe13_15
    {
        static void Main(string[] args)
        {
            string str = "The quick brown fox jumped over the...";
            Console.WriteLine(str.toMixedCase());
            Console.WriteLine("There are {0} vowels", str.countVowels());
```

```
            // Wait to continue.
            Console.WriteLine(Environment.NewLine);
            Console.WriteLine("Main method complete. Press Enter");
            Console.ReadLine();
        }
    }
}
```

13-16. Call an Object Member Dynamically

Problem

You need to call a method or property dynamically.

Solution

Use the `dynamic` keyword to disable static checking for an object instance.

How It Works

Usually, the C# compiler checks to see that calls you make to type members are valid—that they exist, that they are accessible to the type you are calling from, that you have supplied the right number of arguments, that the arguments are of the right type, and so on.

C# also supports dynamic calls to type members in which these checks are not performed until the program is running and the call needs to be made. In order to take advantage of this feature, you declare an instance of `dynamic`—for example:

```
dynamic myobject = new MyObject();
```

You can then use the object reference you have created as you would normally—however, the calls you make against the dynamic instance are not checked by the compiler, and errors will not be detected until the calls are executed at runtime.

The Code

The following example defines a type. The program `Main` method creates a dynamic instance of that type and calls `countVowels`, which exists, and `thisMethodDoesNotExist`, which does not.

```
using System;
using System.Collections.Generic;
using System.Linq;
using System.Text;
using System.Dynamic;
```

```
namespace Apress.VisualCSharpRecipes.Chapter13
{
    class myType
    {
        public myType(string strval)
        {
            str = strval;
        }

        public string str {get; set;}

        public int countVowels()
        {
            char[] vowels = { 'a', 'e', 'i', 'o', 'u' };
            int vowelcount = 0;
            foreach (char c in str)
            {
                if (vowels.Contains(c))
                {
                    vowelcount++;
                }
            }
            return vowelcount;
        }
    }

    class Recipe13_16
    {
        static void Main(string[] args)
        {
            // create a dynamic type
            dynamic dynInstance
                = new myType("The quick brown fox jumped over the...");
            // call the countVowels method
            int vowels = dynInstance.countVowels();
            Console.WriteLine("There are {0} vowels", vowels);
            // call a method that does not exist
            dynInstance.thisMethodDoesNotExist();
        }
    }
}
```

The code compiles, even though we have called a method that does not exist. When we execute the program, we get the following output:

```
There are 10 vowels


Unhandled Exception: Microsoft.CSharp.RuntimeBinder.RuntimeBinderException:
 'Apress.VisualCSharpRecipes.Chapter13.myType
' does not contain a definition for 'thisMethodDoesNotExist'
   at CallSite.Target(Closure , CallSite , Object )
   at System.Dynamic.UpdateDelegates.UpdateAndExecuteVoid1[T0](
      CallSite site, T0 arg0)
   at Apress.VisualCSharpRecipes.Chapter13.Recipe13_16.Main(String[] args) in
C:\Users\Adam\Documents\Work\C# Cookbook\Chapter13\Recipe13-16\
    Recipe13-16.cs:line 44
Press any key to continue . . .
```

13-17. Create a Variant Generic Type

Problem

You need to treat a generic interface of one type as a generic interface of a type it derives from.

Solution

Apply the `in` or `out` modifiers to your generic interface definition.

How It Works

Generic types allow you to provide strict controls on types that collections and classes will accept, but can create some unexpected behaviors. For example, suppose we define two classes, one of which derives from the other, and a generic interface, as follows:

```
class BaseType
{
}

class DerivedType : BaseType
{
}

public interface IMyInterface<T>
{
        T getValue();
}
```

The following program illustrates the problem—the compiler won't allow us to treat a `IMyInterface<DerivedType>` as a `IMyInterface<BaseType>` so that we can call the `processData` method:

```
class Recipe13_17
{
    static void Main(string[] args)
    {
        IMyInterface<DerivedType> variant = // implementation class //;
        processData(variant);
    }

    static void processData(IMyInterface<BaseType> data)
    {
        ...do something...
    }
}
```

Covariance allows you to change this behavior when there is no possibility of breaking type safety. You use covariance by applying the `out` keyword to your interface definition, such as `public interface IMyInterface<out T>`

Now the preceding code will work. Covariance can only be used for interfaces that only contain methods that return the generic type—if you define a method that accepts the type as a parameter, the compiler will generate an error. *Contravariance* is the complement to covariance—in order to handle parameters, you must use the `in` keyword, either in a separate interface or as a different type in the same interface—for example:

```
public interface IMyInterface<out T1, in T2 >
```

■ **Note** The generic interfaces in the .NET Framework class library have been updated in .NET 4.0 to use variance so that you can perform safe conversion using those types.

The Code

The following example is similar to the fragments shown preceding, and contains two types (one derived from the other) and a covariant generic interface. In the `Main` method, we create an implementation of the interface that is typed using the derived class, and then call a method that requires an implementation of the interface that is typed using the base class.

```
using System;

namespace Apress.VisualCSharpRecipes.Chapter13
{
    class Recipe13_17
    {
        static void Main(string[] args)
        {
            // Create an implementation of the interface that is typed
            // (and contains) the derived type.
            IMyInterface<DerivedType> variant
                = new ImplClass<DerivedType>(new DerivedType());
            // Call a method that accepts an instance of the interface typed.
            // with the base type - if the interface has been
            // defined with the out keyword
            // This will work; otherwise, the compiler will report an error.m
            processData(variant);
        }

        static void processData(IMyInterface<BaseType> data)
        {
            data.getValue().printMessage();
        }
    }

    class BaseType
    {
        public virtual void printMessage()
        {
            Console.WriteLine("BaseType Message");
        }
    }

    class DerivedType : BaseType
    {
        public override void printMessage()
        {
            Console.WriteLine("DerivedType Message");
        }
    }
```

```
    public interface IMyInterface<out T>
    {
        T getValue();
    }

    public class ImplClass<T> : IMyInterface<T>
    {
        private T value;
        public ImplClass(T val)
        {
            value = val;
        }

        public T getValue()
        {
            return value;
        }
    }
}
```

CHAPTER 14

■ ■ ■

Windows Integration

The Microsoft .NET Framework is intended to run on a wide variety of operating systems to improve code mobility and simplify cross-platform integration. At the time this book was written, versions of the .NET Framework were available for various operating systems, including Microsoft Windows, FreeBSD, Linux, and Mac OS X. However, many of these implementations have yet to be widely adopted. Microsoft Windows is currently the operating system on which the .NET Framework is most commonly installed. Therefore, the recipes in this chapter describe how to perform the following tasks, specific to the Windows operating system:

- Retrieve runtime environment information (recipes 14-1 and 14-2)
- Write to the Windows event log (recipe 14-3)
- Read, write, and search the Windows registry (recipe 14-4 and 14-5)
- Create and install Windows services (recipes 14-6 and 14-7)
- Create a shortcut on the Windows Start menu or desktop (recipe 14-8)
- Create Windows 7 Jump Lists (recipe 14-9)
- Use the Windows Search service (recipe 14-10)
- Check Internet connectivity (recipe 14-11)
- Display a task dialog (recipe 14-12)
- Read and write performance counters (recipes 14-13 and 14-14)
- Obtain elevated privileges (recipe 14-15)

■ **Note** The majority of functionality discussed in this chapter is protected by code access security permissions enforced by the Common Language Runtime (CLR). See the .NET Framework software development kit (SDK) documentation for the specific permissions required to execute each member.

14-1. Access Runtime Environment Information

Problem

You need to access information about the runtime environment in which your application is running.

Solution

Use the members of the `System.Environment` class.

How It Works

The static `Environment` class provides a set of static members that you can use to obtain (and in some cases modify) information about the environment in which an application is running. Table 14-1 describes some of the most commonly used `Environment` members.

Table 14-1. Commonly Used Members of the Environment Class

Member	Description
Properties	
`CommandLine`	Gets a `string` containing the command line used to execute the current application, including the application name. See recipe 1-5 for details.
`CurrentDirectory`	Gets and sets a `string` containing the current application directory. Initially, this property will contain the name of the directory in which the application was started.
`HasShutdownStarted`	Gets a `bool` that indicates whether the CLR has started to shut down or the current application domain has started unloading.
`MachineName`	Gets a `string` containing the name of the machine.
`OSVersion`	Gets a `System.OperatingSystem` object that contains information about the platform and version of the underlying operating system. See the discussion of this topic in this recipe for more details.
`ProcessorCount`	Gets the number of processors on the machine.
`SystemDirectory`	Gets a `string` containing the fully qualified path of the system directory—that is, the `system32` subdirectory of the `Windows` folder.

Member	Description
`TickCount`	Gets an `int` representing the number of milliseconds that have elapsed since the system was started.
`UserDomainName`	Gets a `string` containing the Windows domain name to which the current user belongs. This will be the same as `MachineName` if the user has logged in on a machine account instead of a domain account.
`UserInteractive`	Gets a `bool` indicating whether the application is running in user interactive mode; in other words, its forms and message boxes will be visible to the logged-on user. `UserInteractive` will return `false` when the application is running as a service or is a web application.
`UserName`	Gets a `string` containing the name of the user that started the current thread, which can be different from the logged-on user in case of impersonation.
`Version`	Gets a `System.Version` object that contains information about the version of the CLR.
Methods	
`ExpandEnvironmentVariables`	Replaces the names of environment variables in a `string` with the value of the variable. See recipe 14-2 for details.
`GetCommandLineArgs`	Returns a `string` array containing all elements of the command line used to execute the current application, including the application name. See recipe 1-5 for details.
`GetEnvironmentVariable`	Returns a `string` containing the value of a specified environment variable. See recipe 14-2 for details.
`GetEnvironmentVariables`	Returns an object implementing `System.Collections.IDictionary`, which contains all environment variables and their values. See recipe 14-2 for details.
`GetFolderPath`	Returns a `string` containing the path to a special system folder specified using the `System.Environment.SpecialFolder` enumeration. This includes folders for the Internet cache, cookies, history, desktop, and favorites; see the .NET Framework SDK documentation for a complete list of values.
`GetLogicalDrives`	Returns a `string` array containing the names of all logical drives, including network-mapped drives. Note that each drive has the following syntax: `<drive letter>:\`.

The `System.OperatingSystem` object returned by `OSVersion` contains four properties:

- The `Platform` property returns a value of the `System.PlatformID` enumeration identifying the current operating system; valid values are `Unix`, `Win32NT`, `Win32S`, `Win32Windows`, and `WinCE`.
- The `ServicePack` property returns a `string` identifying the service pack level installed on the computer. If no service packs are installed, or service packs are not supported, an empty `string` is returned.
- The `Version` property returns a `System.Version` object that identifies the specific operating system version.
- The `VersionString` property returns a concatenated string summary of the `Platform`, `ServicePack`, and `Version` properties.

To determine the operating system on which you are running, you must use both the platform and the version information, as detailed in Table 14-2.

Table 14-2. Determining the Current Operating System

PlatformID	Major Version	Minor Version	Operating System
`Win32Windows`	4	10	Windows 98
`Win32Windows`	4	90	Windows Me
`Win32NT`	4	0	Windows NT 4
`Win32NT`	5	0	Windows 2000
`Win32NT`	5	1	Windows XP
`Win32NT`	5	2	Windows Server 2003
`Win32NT`	6	0	Windows Vista, Windows Server 2008
`Win32NT`	6	1	Windows 7, Windows Server 2008 R2

The Code

The following example uses the `Environment` class to display information about the current environment to the console:

```
using System;

namespace Apress.VisualCSharpRecipes.Chapter14
{
    class Recipe14_01
    {
        public static void Main()
        {
            // Command line.
            Console.WriteLine("Command line : " + Environment.CommandLine);

            // OS and CLR version information.
            Console.WriteLine(Environment.NewLine);
            Console.WriteLine("OS PlatformID : " +
                Environment.OSVersion.Platform);
            Console.WriteLine("OS Major Version : " +
                Environment.OSVersion.Version.Major);
            Console.WriteLine("OS Minor Version : " +
                Environment.OSVersion.Version.Minor);
            Console.WriteLine("CLR Version : " + Environment.Version);

            // User, machine, and domain name information.
            Console.WriteLine(Environment.NewLine);
            Console.WriteLine("User Name : " + Environment.UserName);
            Console.WriteLine("Domain Name : " + Environment.UserDomainName);
            Console.WriteLine("Machine name : " + Environment.MachineName);

            // Other environment information.
            Console.WriteLine(Environment.NewLine);
            Console.WriteLine("Is interactive? : "
                + Environment.UserInteractive);
            Console.WriteLine("Shutting down? : "
                + Environment.HasShutdownStarted);
            Console.WriteLine("Ticks since startup : "
                + Environment.TickCount);

            // Display the names of all logical drives.
            Console.WriteLine(Environment.NewLine);
            foreach (string s in Environment.GetLogicalDrives())
            {
                Console.WriteLine("Logical drive : " + s);
            }

            // Standard folder information.
            Console.WriteLine(Environment.NewLine);
            Console.WriteLine("Current folder : "
                + Environment.CurrentDirectory);
            Console.WriteLine("System folder : "
                + Environment.SystemDirectory);
```

```
            // Enumerate all special folders and display them.
            Console.WriteLine(Environment.NewLine);
            foreach (Environment.SpecialFolder s in
                Enum.GetValues(typeof(Environment.SpecialFolder)))
            {
                Console.WriteLine("{0} folder : {1}",
                    s, Environment.GetFolderPath(s));
            }

            // Wait to continue.
            Console.WriteLine(Environment.NewLine);
            Console.WriteLine("Main method complete. Press Enter.");
            Console.ReadLine();
        }
    }
}
```

14-2. Retrieve the Value of an Environment Variable

Problem

You need to retrieve the value of an environment variable for use in your application.

Solution

Use the `GetEnvironmentVariable`, `GetEnvironmentVariables`, and `ExpandEnvironmentVariables` methods of the `Environment` class.

How It Works

The `GetEnvironmentVariable` method allows you to retrieve a string containing the value of a single named environment variable, whereas the `GetEnvironmentVariables` method returns an object implementing `IDictionary` that contains the names and values of all environment variables as strings. The .NET Framework includes an overload of the `GetEnvironmentVariables` method that takes a `System.EnvironmentVariableTarget` argument, allowing you to specify a subset of environment variables to return based on the target of the variable: `Machine`, `Process`, or `User`.

The `ExpandEnvironmentVariables` method provides a simple mechanism for substituting the value of an environment variable into a string by including the variable name enclosed in percent signs (%) within the string.

The Code

Here is an example that demonstrates how to use all three methods:

```
using System;
using System.Collections;

namespace Apress.VisualCSharpRecipes.Chapter14
{
    class Recipe14_02
    {
        public static void Main()
        {
            // Retrieve a named environment variable.
            Console.WriteLine("Path = " +
                Environment.GetEnvironmentVariable("Path"));
            Console.WriteLine(Environment.NewLine);

            // Substitute the value of named environment variables.
            Console.WriteLine(Environment.ExpandEnvironmentVariables(
                    "The Path on %computername% is %Path%"));
            Console.WriteLine(Environment.NewLine);

            // Retrieve all environment variables targeted at the process and
            // display the values of all that begin with the letter U.
            IDictionary vars = Environment.GetEnvironmentVariables(
                EnvironmentVariableTarget.Process);

            foreach (string s in vars.Keys)
            {
                if (s.ToUpper().StartsWith("U"))
                {
                    Console.WriteLine(s + " = " + vars[s]);
                }
            }

            // Wait to continue.
            Console.WriteLine(Environment.NewLine);
            Console.WriteLine("Main method complete. Press Enter.");
            Console.ReadLine();
        }
    }
}
```

14-3. Write an Event to the Windows Event Log

Problem

You need to write an event to the Windows event log.

Solution

Use the members of the `System.Diagnostics.EventLog` class to create a log (if required), register an event source, and write events.

How It Works

You can write to the Windows event log using the static methods of the `EventLog` class, or you can create an `EventLog` object and use its members. Whichever approach you choose, before writing to the event log you must decide which log you will use and register an event source against that log. The event source is simply a string that uniquely identifies your application. An event source may be registered against only one log at a time.

By default, the event log contains three separate logs: Application, System, and Security. Usually, you will write to the Application log, but you might decide your application warrants a custom log in which to write events. You do not need to explicitly create a custom log; when you register an event source against a log, if the specified log doesn't exist, it's created automatically.

■ **Tip** You must have administrator privileges to create an event source—this is because the .NET Framework checks all of the event logs to ensure that the source name is unique and this means being able to read the security log.

Once you have decided on the destination log and registered an event source, you can start to write event log entries using the `WriteEntry` method. `WriteEntry` provides a variety of overloads that allow you to specify some or all of the following values:

- A `string` containing the event source for the log entry (static versions of `WriteEntry` only).
- A `string` containing the message for the log entry.
- A value from the `System.Diagnostics.EventLogEntryType` enumeration, which identifies the type of log entry. Valid values are `Error`, `FailureAudit`, `Information`, `SuccessAudit`, and `Warning`.
- An `int` that specifies an application-specific event ID for the log entry.

- A `short` that specifies an application-specific subcategory for the log entry.
- A `byte` array containing any raw data to associate with the log entry.

■ **Note** The methods of the `EventLog` class also provide overloads that support the writing of events to the event log of remote machines; see the .NET Framework SDK documentation for more information.

The Code

The following example demonstrates how to use the static members of the `EventLog` class to write an entry to the event log of the local machine. You must run the example as administrator in order to create the event source—if you do not, a security exception will be thrown.

```
using System;
using System.Diagnostics;

namespace Apress.VisualCSharpRecipes.Chapter14
{
    class Recipe14_03
    {
        public static void Main ()
        {
            // If it does not exist, register an event source for this
            // application against the Application log of the local machine.
            // Trying to register an event source that already exists on the
            // specified machine will throw a System.ArgumentException.
            if (!EventLog.SourceExists("Visual C# Recipes"))
            {
                EventLog.CreateEventSource("Visual C# Recipes",
                    "Application");
            }

            // Write an event to the event log.
            EventLog.WriteEntry(
                "Visual C# Recipes",      // Registered event source
                "A simple test event.",        // Event entry message
                EventLogEntryType.Information, // Event type
                1,                             // Application-specific ID
                0,                             // Application-specific category
                new byte[] {10, 55, 200}       // Event data
            );
```

```
            // Wait to continue.
            Console.WriteLine(Environment.NewLine);
            Console.WriteLine("Main method complete. Press Enter.");
            Console.ReadLine();
        }
    }
}
```

14-4. Read and Write to the Windows Registry

Problem

You need to read information from or write information to the Windows registry.

Solution

Use the methods `GetValue` and `SetValue` of the `Microsoft.Win32.Registry` class.

■ **Tip** The `GetValue` and `SetValue` methods open a registry key, get or set its value, and close the key each time they are called. This means they are inefficient when used to perform many read or write operations. The `GetValue` and `SetValue` methods of the `Microsoft.Win32.RegistryKey` class discussed in recipe 14-5 will provide better performance if you need to perform many read or write operations on the registry.

How It Works

The `GetValue` and `SetValue` methods allow you to read and write named values in named registry keys. `GetValue` takes three arguments:

- A `string` containing the fully qualified name of the key you want to read. The key name must start with one of the following root key names:
  - `HKEY_CLASSES_ROOT`
  - `HKEY_CURRENT_CONFIG`
  - `HKEY_CURRENT_USER`
  - `HKEY_DYN_DATA`
  - `HKEY_LOCAL_MACHINE`
  - `HKEY_PERFORMANCE_DATA`
  - `HKEY_USERS`

- A `string` containing the name of the value in the key you want to read.
- An `object` containing the default value to return if the named value is not present in the key.

`GetValue` returns an `object` containing either the data read from the registry or the default value specified as the third argument if the named value is not found. If the specified key does not exist, `GetValue` returns `null`.

`SetValue` offers two overloads. The most functional expects the following arguments:

- A `string` containing the fully qualified name of the key you want to write. The key must start with one of the root key names specified previously.
- A `string` containing the name of the value in the key you want to write.
- An `object` containing the value to write.
- An element of the `Microsoft.Win32.RegistyValueKind` enumeration that specifies the registry data type that should be used to hold the data.

If the registry key specified in the `SetValue` call does not exist, it is automatically created.

The Code

The following example demonstrates how to use `GetValue` and `SetValue` to read from and write to the registry. Every time the example is run, it reads usage information from the registry and displays it to the screen. The example also updates the stored usage information, which you can see the next time you run the example.

```
using System;
using Microsoft.Win32;

namespace Apress.VisualCSharpRecipes.Chapter14
{
    class Recipe14_04
    {
        public static void Main(String[] args)
        {
            // Variables to hold usage information read from registry.
            string lastUser;
            string lastRun;
            int runCount;

            // Read the name of the last user to run the application from the
            // registry. This is stored as the default value of the key and is
            // accessed by not specifying a value name. Cast the returned Object
            // to a string.
            lastUser = (string)Registry.GetValue(
                @"HKEY_CURRENT_USER\Software\Apress\Visual C# Recipes",
                "", "Nobody");
```

```
// If lastUser is null, it means that the specified registry key
// does not exist.
if (lastUser == null)
{
    // Set initial values for the usage information.
    lastUser = "Nobody";
    lastRun = "Never";
    runCount = 0;
}
else
{
    // Read the last run date and specify a default value of
    // "Never". Cast the returned Object to string.
    lastRun = (string)Registry.GetValue(
        @"HKEY_CURRENT_USER\Software\Apress\Visual C# Recipes",
        "LastRun", "Never");

    // Read the run count value and specify a default value of
    // 0 (zero). Cast the Object to Int32 and assign to an int.
    runCount = (Int32)Registry.GetValue(
        @"HKEY_CURRENT_USER\Software\Apress\Visual C# Recipes",
        "RunCount", 0);
}

// Display the usage information.
Console.WriteLine("Last user name: " + lastUser);
Console.WriteLine("Last run date/time: " + lastRun);
Console.WriteLine("Previous executions: " + runCount);

// Update the usage information. It doesn't matter if the registry
// key exists or not, SetValue will automatically create it.

// Update the "last user" information with the current username.
// Specify that this should be stored as the default value
// for the key by using an empty string as the value name.
Registry.SetValue(
    @"HKEY_CURRENT_USER\Software\Apress\Visual C# Recipes",
    "", Environment.UserName, RegistryValueKind.String);

// Update the "last run" information with the current date and time.
// Specify that this should be stored as a string value in the
// registry.
Registry.SetValue(
    @"HKEY_CURRENT_USER\Software\Apress\Visual C# Recipes",
    "LastRun", DateTime.Now.ToString(), RegistryValueKind.String);

// Update the usage count information. Specify that this should
// be stored as an integer value in the registry.
Registry.SetValue(
    @"HKEY_CURRENT_USER\Software\Apress\Visual C# Recipes",
    "RunCount", ++runCount, RegistryValueKind.DWord);
```

```
            // Wait to continue.
            Console.WriteLine(Environment.NewLine);
            Console.WriteLine("Main method complete. Press Enter.");
            Console.ReadLine();
        }
    }
}
```

14-5. Search the Windows Registry

Problem

You need to search the Windows registry for a key that contains a specific value or content.

Solution

Use the `Microsoft.Win32.Registry` class to obtain a `Microsoft.Win32.RegistryKey` object that represents the root key of a registry hive you want to search. Use the members of this `RegistryKey` object to navigate through and enumerate the registry key hierarchy, as well as to read the names and content of values held in the keys.

How It Works

You must first obtain a `RegistryKey` object that represents a base-level key and navigate through the hierarchy of `RegistryKey` objects as required. The `Registry` class implements a set of seven static fields that return `RegistryKey` objects representing base-level registry keys; Table 14-3 describes the registry location to where each of these fields maps.

Table 14-3. *Static Fields of the Registry Class*

Field	Registry Mapping
`ClassesRoot`	HKEY_CLASSES_ROOT
`CurrentConfig`	HKEY_CURRENT_CONFIG
`CurrentUser`	HKEY_CURRENT_USER
`DynData`	HKEY_DYN_DATA
`LocalMachine`	HKEY_LOCAL_MACHINE
`PerformanceData`	HKEY_PERFORMANCE_DATA
`Users`	HKEY_USERS

■ **Tip** The static method `RegistryKey.OpenRemoteBaseKey` allows you to open a registry base key on a remote machine. See the .NET Framework SDK documentation for details of its use.

Once you have the base-level `RegistryKey` object, you must navigate through its child subkeys recursively. To support navigation, the `RegistryKey` class allows you to do the following:

- Get the number of immediate subkeys using the `SubKeyCount` property.
- Get a `string` array containing the names of all subkeys using the `GetSubKeyNames` method.
- Get a `RegistryKey` reference to a subkey using the `OpenSubKey` method. The `OpenSubKey` method provides two overloads: the first opens the named key as read-only; the second accepts a `bool` argument that, if `true`, will open a writable `RegistryKey` object.

Once you obtain a `RegistryKey`, you can create, read, update, and delete subkeys and values using the methods listed in Table 14-4. Methods that modify the contents of the key require you to have a writable `RegistryKey` object.

Table 14-4. *RegistryKey Methods to Create, Read, Update, and Delete Registry Keys and Values*

Method	Description
`CreateSubKey`	Creates a new subkey with the specified name and returns a writable `RegistryKey` object. If the specified subkey already exists, `CreateSubKey` will return a writable reference to the existing subkey.
`DeleteSubKey`	Deletes the subkey with the specified name, which must be empty of subkeys (but not values); otherwise, a `System.InvalidOperationException` is thrown.
`DeleteSubKeyTree`	Deletes the subkey with the specified name along with all of its subkeys.
`DeleteValue`	Deletes the value with the specified name from the current key.
`GetValue`	Returns the value with the specified name from the current key. The value is returned as an `object`, which you must cast to the appropriate type. The simplest form of `GetValue` returns `null` if the specified value doesn't exist. An overload allows you to specify a default value to return (instead of `null`) if the named value doesn't exist.
`GetValueKind`	Returns the registry data type of the value with the specified name in the current key. The value is returned as a member of the `Microsoft.Win32.RegistryValueKind` enumeration.

Method	Description
GetValueNames	Returns a string array containing the names of all values in the current registry key.
SetValue	Creates (or updates) the value with the specified name. In 2.0, you can specify the data type used to store the value with the overload that takes a RegistryValueKind as last parameter. If you don't provide such a value kind, one will be calculated automatically, based on the managed type of the object you pass as value to set.

■ **Tip** On 64-bit versions of Windows, separate portions of the registry exist for 32-bit and 64-bit applications. The RegistryView enumeration can be used as an argument to the static OpenBaseKey method of RegistryKey to specify which portion of the registry is accessed. See the .NET Framework SDK documentation for further details.

The RegistryKey class implements IDisposable; you should call the IDisposable.Dispose method to free operating system resources when you have finished with the RegistryKey object.

The Code

The following example takes a single command-line argument and recursively searches the CurrentUser hive of the registry looking for keys with names matching the supplied argument. When the example finds a match, it displays all string type values contained in the key to the console.

```
using System;
using Microsoft.Win32;

namespace Apress.VisualCSharpRecipes.Chapter14
{
    class Recipe14_05
    {
        public static void SearchSubKeys(RegistryKey root, String searchKey)
        {
            try
            {
                // Get the subkeys contained in the current key.
                string[] subkeys = root.GetSubKeyNames();

                // Loop through all subkeys contained in the current key.
                foreach (string keyname in subkeys)
                {
                    try
                    {
                        using (RegistryKey key = root.OpenSubKey(keyname))
                        {
```

```
                    if (keyname == searchKey) PrintKeyValues(key);
                    SearchSubKeys(key, searchKey);
                }
            }
            catch (System.Security.SecurityException)
            {
                // Ignore SecurityException for the purpose of the example.
                // Some subkeys of HKEY_CURRENT_USER are secured and will
                // throw a SecurityException when opened.
            }
        }
    }
    catch (UnauthorizedAccessException)
    {
        // Ignore UnauthorizedAccessException for the purpose of the example
        // - this exception is thrown if the user does not have the
        // rights to read part of the registry.
    }

}

public static void PrintKeyValues(RegistryKey key)
{
    // Display the name of the matching subkey and the number of
    // values it contains.
    Console.WriteLine("Registry key found : {0} contains {1} values",
        key.Name, key.ValueCount);

    // Loop through the values and display.
    foreach (string valuename in key.GetValueNames())
    {
        if (key.GetValue(valuename) is String)
        {
            Console.WriteLine("  Value : {0} = {1}",
                valuename, key.GetValue(valuename));
        }
    }
}

public static void Main(String[] args)
{
    if (args.Length > 0)
    {
        // Open the CurrentUser base key.
        using (RegistryKey root = Registry.CurrentUser)
        {
            // Search recursively through the registry for any keys
            // with the specified name.
            SearchSubKeys(root, args[0]);
        }
    }
```

```
            // Wait to continue.
            Console.WriteLine(Environment.NewLine);
            Console.WriteLine("Main method complete. Press Enter.");
            Console.ReadLine();
        }
    }
}
```

Usage

Running the example using the command `Recipe14-05 Environment` will display output similar to the following when executed using the command on a machine running Windows 7:

```
Registry key found : HKEY_CURRENT_USER\Environment contains 2 values

  Value : TEMP = C:\Users\Adam\AppData\Local\Temp

  Value : TMP = C:\Users\Adam\AppData\Local\Temp
```

14-6. Create a Windows Service

Problem

You need to create an application that will run as a Windows service.

Solution

Create a class that extends `System.ServiceProcess.ServiceBase`. Use the inherited properties to control the behavior of your service, and override inherited methods to implement the functionality required. Implement a `Main` method that creates an instance of your service class and passes it to the static `ServiceBase.Run` method.

■ **Note** The `ServiceBase` class is defined in the `System.Serviceprocess.dll` assembly, so you must include a reference to this assembly when you build your service class.

How It Works

To create a Windows service manually, you must implement a class derived from the `ServiceBase` class. The `ServiceBase` class provides the base functionality that allows the Windows Service Control Manager

(SCM) to configure the service, operate the service as a background task, and control the life cycle of the service. The SCM also controls how other applications can control the service programmatically.

■ **Tip** If you are using Microsoft Visual Studio, you can use the Windows Service project template to create a Windows service. The template provides the basic code infrastructure required by a Windows service class, which you can extend with your custom functionality.

To control your service, the SCM uses the eight protected methods inherited from the `ServiceBase` class described in Table 14-5. You should override these virtual methods to implement the functionality and behavior required by your service. Not all services must support all control messages. The `Can`*`XXX`* properties inherited from the `ServiceBase` class declare to the SCM which control messages your service supports; Table 14-5 specifies the property that controls each operation.

Table 14-5. *Methods That Control the Operation of a Service*

Method	Description
`OnStart`	All services must support the `OnStart` method, which the SCM calls to start the service. The SCM passes a `string` array containing arguments specified for the service. These arguments can be specified when the `ServiceController.Start` method is called, and are usually configured in the service's property window in the Windows Control Panel. However, they are rarely used, because it is better for the service to retrieve its configuration information directly from the Windows registry. The `OnStart` method must normally return within 30 seconds, or else the SCM will abort the service. Your service must call the `RequestAdditionalTime` method of the `ServiceBase` class if it requires more time; specify the additional milliseconds required as an `int`.
`OnStop`	Called by the SCM to stop a service—the SCM will call `OnStop` only if the `CanStop` property is set to `true`.
`OnPause`	Called by the SCM to pause a service—the SCM will call `OnPause` only if the `CanPauseAndContinue` property is set to `true`.
`OnContinue`	Called by the SCM to continue a paused service—the SCM will call `OnContinue` only if the `CanPauseAndContinue` property is set to `true`.
`OnShutdown`	Called by the SCM when the system is shutting down—the SCM will call `OnShutdown` only if the `CanShutdown` property is set to `true`.
`OnPowerEvent`	Called by the SCM when a system-level power status change occurs, such as a laptop going into suspend mode. The SCM will call `OnPowerEvent` only if the `CanHandlePowerEvent` property is set to `true`.

Method	Description
`OnCustomCommand`	Allows you to extend the service control mechanism with custom control messages; see the .NET Framework SDK documentation for more details.
`OnSessionChange`	Called by the SCM when a change event is received from the Terminal Services session or when users log on and off on the local machine. A `System.ServiceProcess.SessionChangeDescription` object passed as an argument by the SCM contains details of what type of session change occurred. The SCM will call `OnSessionChange` only if the `CanHandleSessionChangeEvent` property is set to `true`. This method is new in the .NET Framework 2.0.

As mentioned in Table 14-5, the `OnStart` method is expected to return within 30 seconds, so you should not use `OnStart` to perform lengthy initialization tasks if possible. A service class should implement a constructor that performs initialization, including configuring the inherited properties of the `ServiceBase` class. In addition to the properties that declare the control messages supported by a service, the `ServiceBase` class implements three other important properties:

- `ServiceName` is the name used internally by the SCM to identify the service and must be set before the service is run.
- `AutoLog` controls whether the service automatically writes entries to the event log when it receives any of the `OnStart`, `OnStop`, `OnPause`, or `OnContinue` control messages from Table 14-5.
- `EventLog` provides access to an `EventLog` object that's preconfigured with an event source name that's the same as the `ServiceName` property registered against the Application log. (See recipe 14-3 for more information about the `EventLog` class.)

The final step in creating a service is to implement a static `Main` method. The `Main` method must create an instance of your service class and pass it as an argument to the static method `ServiceBase.Run`.

The Code

The following Windows service example uses a configurable `System.Timers.Timer` to write an entry to the Windows event log periodically. You can start, pause, and stop the service using the Services application in the Control Panel.

```
using System;
using System.Timers;
using System.ServiceProcess;

namespace Apress.VisualCSharpRecipes.Chapter14
{
    class Recipe14_06 : ServiceBase
    {
        // A Timer that controls how frequently the example writes to the
        // event log.
        private System.Timers.Timer timer;
```

```
        public Recipe14_06()
        {
            // Set the ServiceBase.ServiceName property.
            ServiceName = "Recipe 14_06 Service";

            // Configure the level of control available on the service.
            CanStop = true;
            CanPauseAndContinue = true;
            CanHandleSessionChangeEvent = true;

            // Configure the service to log important events to the
            // Application event log automatically.
            AutoLog = true;
        }

        // The method executed when the timer expires and writes an
        // entry to the Application event log.
        private void WriteLogEntry(object sender, ElapsedEventArgs e)
        {
            // Use the EventLog object automatically configured by the
            // ServiceBase class to write to the event log.
            EventLog.WriteEntry("Recipe14_06 Service active : " + e.SignalTime);
        }

        protected override void OnStart(string[] args)
        {
            // Obtain the interval between log entry writes from the first
            // argument. Use 5000 milliseconds by default and enforce a 1000
            // millisecond minimum.
            double interval;

            try
            {
                interval = Double.Parse(args[0]);
                interval = Math.Max(1000, interval);
            }
            catch
            {
                interval = 5000;
            }

            EventLog.WriteEntry(String.Format("Recipe14_06 Service starting. " +
                "Writing log entries every {0} milliseconds...", interval));

            // Create, configure, and start a System.Timers.Timer to
            // periodically call the WriteLogEntry method. The Start
            // and Stop methods of the System.Timers.Timer class
            // make starting, pausing, resuming, and stopping the
            // service straightforward.
            timer = new Timer();
            timer.Interval = interval;
```

```
            timer.AutoReset = true;
            timer.Elapsed += new ElapsedEventHandler(WriteLogEntry);
            timer.Start();
        }

        protected override void OnStop()
        {
            EventLog.WriteEntry("Recipe14_06 Service stopping...");
            timer.Stop();

            // Free system resources used by the Timer object.
            timer.Dispose();
            timer = null;
        }

        protected override void OnPause()
        {
            if (timer != null)
            {
                EventLog.WriteEntry("Recipe14_06 Service pausing...");
                timer.Stop();
            }
        }

        protected override void OnContinue()
        {
            if (timer != null)
            {
                EventLog.WriteEntry("Recipe14_06 Service resuming...");
                timer.Start();
            }
        }

        protected override void OnSessionChange(SessionChangeDescription change)
        {
            EventLog.WriteEntry("Recipe14_06 Session change..." +
                change.Reason);
        }

        public static void Main()
        {
            // Create an instance of the Recipe14_06 class that will write
            // an entry to the Application event log. Pass the object to the
            // static ServiceBase.Run method.
            ServiceBase.Run(new Recipe14_06());
        }
    }
}
```

Usage

If you want to run multiple services in a single process, you must create an array of `ServiceBase` objects and pass it to the `ServiceBase.Run` method. Although service classes have a `Main` method, you can't execute service code directly or run a service class directly. Recipe 14-7 describes what you must do to install your service before it will execute.

14-7. Create a Windows Service Installer

Problem

You have created a Windows service application and need to install it.

Solution

Add a new class to your Windows service project that extends the `System.Configuration.Install.Installer` class to create an installer class containing the information necessary to install and configure your service class. Use the Installer tool (`Installutil.exe`) to perform the installation, which is installed as part of the .NET Framework.

■ **Note** You must create the installer class in the same assembly as the service class for the service to install and function correctly.

How It Works

As recipe 14-6 points out, you cannot run service classes directly. The high level of integration with the Windows operating system and the information stored about the service in the Windows registry means services require explicit installation.

If you have Microsoft Visual Studio .NET, you can create an installation component for your service automatically by right-clicking in the design view of your service class and selecting Add Installer from the context menu. You can call this installation component by using deployment projects or by using the Installer tool to install your service. You can also create installer components for Windows services manually by following these steps:

1. In your project, create a class derived from the `Installer` class.
2. Apply the attribute `System.ComponentModel.RunInstallerAttribute(true)` to the installer class.
3. In the constructor of the installer class, create a single instance of the `System.ServiceProcess.ServiceProcessInstaller` class. Set the `Account`, `User`, and `Password` properties of `ServiceProcessInstaller` to configure the account under which your service will run. This account must already exist.

4. In the constructor of the installer class, create one instance of the `System.ServiceProcess.ServiceInstaller` class for each individual service you want to install. Use the properties of the `ServiceInstaller` objects to configure information about each service, including the following:

   - `ServiceName`, which specifies the name Windows uses internally to identify the service. This must be the same as the value assigned to the `ServiceBase.ServiceName` property.
   - `DisplayName`, which provides a user-friendly name for the service.
   - `StartType`, which uses values of the `System.ServiceProcess.ServiceStartMode` enumeration to control whether the service is started automatically or manually, or is disabled.
   - `ServiceDependsUpon`, which allows you to provide a string array containing a set of service names that must be started before this service can start.

5. Add the `ServiceProcessInstaller` object and all `ServiceInstaller` objects to the `System.Configuration.Install.InstallerCollection` object accessed through the `Installers` property, which is inherited by your installer class from the `Installer` base class.

The Code

The following example is an installer for the `Recipe14_06` Windows service created in recipe 14-6. The sample project contains the code from recipe 14-6 and for the installer class. This is necessary for the service installation to function correctly. To compile the example, you must reference two additional assemblies: `System.Configuration.Install.dll` and `System.ServiceProcess.dll`.

```
using System.Configuration.Install;
using System.ServiceProcess;
using System.ComponentModel;

namespace Apress.VisualCSharpRecipes.Chapter14
{
    [RunInstaller(true)]
    public class Recipe14_07 : Installer
    {
        public Recipe14_07()
        {
            // Instantiate and configure a ServiceProcessInstaller.
            ServiceProcessInstaller ServiceExampleProcess =
                new ServiceProcessInstaller();
            ServiceExampleProcess.Account = ServiceAccount.LocalSystem;

            // Instantiate and configure a ServiceInstaller.
            ServiceInstaller ServiceExampleInstaller =
                new ServiceInstaller();
            ServiceExampleInstaller.DisplayName =
                "Visual C# Recipes Service Example";
```

```
            ServiceExampleInstaller.ServiceName = "Recipe 14_06 Service";
            ServiceExampleInstaller.StartType = ServiceStartMode.Automatic;

            // Add both the ServiceProcessInstaller and ServiceInstaller to
            // the Installers collection, which is inherited from the
            // Installer base class.
            Installers.Add(ServiceExampleInstaller);
            Installers.Add(ServiceExampleProcess);
        }
    }
}
```

Usage

To install the `Recipe14_06` service, build the project, navigate to the directory where `Recipe14-07.exe` is located (`bin\debug` by default), and execute the command `Installutil Recipe14-07.exe`—you will need to do this as an administrator. You can then see and control the Visual C# Recipes Service Example service using the Windows Computer Management console. However, even though you have specified a `StartType` of `Automatic`, the service is initially installed without being started; you must start the service manually (or restart your computer) before the service will write entries to the event log. Once the service is running, you can view the entries it writes to the Application event log using the Event Viewer application. To uninstall the `Recipe14_06` service, add the `/u` switch to the `Installutil` command, as follows: `Installutil /u Recipe14-07.exe`.

■ **Note** If you have the Service application from the Control Panel open when you uninstall the service, the service will not uninstall completely until you close the Service application. Once you close the Service application, you can reinstall the service; otherwise, you will get an error telling you that the installation failed because the service is scheduled for deletion.

14-8. Create a Shortcut on the Desktop or Start Menu

Problem

You need to create a shortcut on the user's Windows desktop or Start menu.

Solution

Use COM Interop to access the functionality of the Windows Script Host. Create and configure an `IWshShortcut` instance that represents the shortcut. The folder in which you save the shortcut determines whether it appears on the desktop or in the Start menu.

How It Works

The .NET Framework class library does not include the functionality to create desktop or Start menu shortcuts; however, this is relatively easy to do using the Windows Script Host component accessed through COM Interop. Chapter 15 describes how to create an Interop assembly that provides access to a COM component. If you are using Visual Studio, add a reference to the Windows Script Host object model, listed on the COM tab of the Add Reference dialog box. If you don't have Visual Studio .NET, use the Type Library Importer (`Tlbimp.exe`) to create an Interop assembly for the `wshom.ocx` file, which is usually located in the `Windows\System32` folder. (You can obtain the latest version of the Windows Script Host from `http://msdn.microsoft.com/scripting`.)

Once you have generated the Interop assembly and imported it into your project, follow these steps to create a desktop or Start menu shortcut.

1. Instantiate a `WshShell` object, which provides access to the Windows shell.
2. Use the `SpecialFolders` property of the `WshShell` object to determine the correct path of the folder where you want to put the shortcut. You must specify the name of the folder you want as an index to the `SpecialFolders` property. For example, to create a desktop shortcut, specify the value `Desktop`, and to create a Start menu shortcut, specify `StartMenu`. Using the `SpecialFolders` property, you can obtain the path to any of the special system folders. If the specified folder does not exist on the platform you are running on, `SpecialFolders` returns an empty `string`. Other commonly used values include `AllUsersDesktop` and `AllUsersStartMenu`; you can find the full list of special folder names in the section on the `SpecialFolders` property in the Windows Script Host documentation.
3. Call the `CreateShortcut` method of the `WshShell` object, and provide the fully qualified file name of the shortcut file you want to create. The file should have the extension `.lnk`. `CreateShortcut` will return an `IWshShortcut` instance.
4. Use the properties of the `IWshShortcut` instance to configure the shortcut. You can configure properties such as the executable that the shortcut references, a description for the shortcut, a hotkey sequence, and the icon displayed for the shortcut.
5. Call the `Save` method of the `IWshShortcut` instance to write the shortcut to disk. The shortcut will appear either on the desktop or in the Start menu (or elsewhere), depending on the path specified when the `IWshShortcut` instance was created.

The Code

The following example class creates a shortcut to `Notepad.exe` on both the desktop and Start menu of the current user. The example creates both shortcuts by calling the `CreateShortcut` method and specifying a different destination folder for each shortcut file. This approach makes it possible to create the shortcut file in any of the special folders returned by the `WshShell.SpecialFolders` property.

```
using System;
using System.IO;
using IWshRuntimeLibrary;

namespace Apress.VisualCSharpRecipes.Chapter14
{
    class Recipe14_08
    {
        public static void CreateShortcut(string destination)
        {
            // Create a WshShell instance through which to access the
            // functionality of the Windows shell.
            WshShell wshShell = new WshShell();

            // Assemble a fully qualified name that places the Notepad.lnk
            // file in the specified destination folder. You could use the
            // System.Environment.GetFolderPath method to obtain a path, but
            // the WshShell.SpecialFolders method provides access to a wider
            // range of folders. You need to create a temporary object reference
            // to the destination string to satisfy the requirements of the
            // Item method signature.
            object destFolder = (object)destination;
            string fileName = Path.Combine(
                (string)wshShell.SpecialFolders.Item(ref destFolder),
                "Notepad.lnk"
            );

            // Create the shortcut object. Nothing is created in the
            // destination folder until the shortcut is saved.
            IWshShortcut shortcut =
                (IWshShortcut)wshShell.CreateShortcut(fileName);

            // Configure the fully qualified name to the executable.
            // Use the Environment class for simplicity.
            shortcut.TargetPath = Path.Combine(
                Environment.GetFolderPath(Environment.SpecialFolder.System),
                "notepad.exe"
            );

            // Set the working directory to the Personal (My Documents) folder.
            shortcut.WorkingDirectory =
                Environment.GetFolderPath(Environment.SpecialFolder.Personal);

            // Provide a description for the shortcut.
            shortcut.Description = "Notepad Text Editor";

            // Assign a hotkey to the shortcut.
            shortcut.Hotkey = "CTRL+ALT+N";

            // Configure Notepad to always start maximized.
            shortcut.WindowStyle = 3;
```

```
            // Configure the shortcut to display the first icon in Notepad.exe.
            shortcut.IconLocation = "notepad.exe, 0";

            // Save the configured shortcut file.
            shortcut.Save();
        }

        public static void Main()
        {
            // Create the Notepad shortcut on the desktop.
            CreateShortcut("Desktop");

            // Create the Notepad shortcut on the Windows Start menu of
            // the current user.
            CreateShortcut("StartMenu");

            // Wait to continue.
            Console.WriteLine(Environment.NewLine);
            Console.WriteLine("Main method complete. Press Enter.");
            Console.ReadLine();
        }
    }
}
```

14-9. Create a Windows 7 Jump List

Problem

You need to create a Windows 7 Jump List for your application.

Solution

Use the features of Windows API CodePack for Microsoft .NET Framework. Create and configure a `JumpList` instance for your application. The items that you add to the `JumpList` define the tasks, documents, and categories that appear in the Windows taskbar.

How It Works

Windows API CodePack for Microsoft .NET Framework is a source code library published by Microsoft to simplify integration with Windows using managed code. One feature of the CodePack is support for the Windows 7 taskbar. There is nothing in the CodePack that you could not write yourself, but using the CodePack is simpler and quicker, and provides a consistent API that Microsoft will support across Windows versions. (You can download the CodePack from

`http://code.msdn.microsoft.com/WindowsAPICodePack`).

Once you have compiled the library, reference the `Microsoft.WindowsAPICodePack.dll` and `Microsoft.WindowsAPICodePack.Shell.dll` assemblies (these files will be in `Shell\bin\debug` folder within the CodePack directory) and follow these steps to create and populate a Jump List:

1. Import the `Microsoft.WindowsAPICodePack.Shell` and `Microsoft.WindowsAPICodePack.Taskbar` namespaces with the `using` directive.
2. Add an event handler to the `Shown` member of your application class.
3. Within the event handler, call the static method `JumpList.CreateJumpList` to create a new `JumpList` instance for your application.
4. Create instances of `JumpListLink` to represent tasks and documents and add them to the `JumpList` instance using the `AddUserTasks` method.

■ **Note** The `JumpList` class can also be used to display recently used documents, but only if your application is registered as a handler for the document types you display. See the Windows API CodePack for details and example code to handle document type registration.

The Code

The following example uses the `Microsoft.WindowsAPICodePack.Taskbar.JumpList` class to populate the Windows 7 Jump List with three items. The first item opens a command prompt. The second item opens Notepad and displays the Notepad icon in the Jump List. The third item shows how to open another application's file using a Jump List. To compile the example, you must build the Windows API CodePack for .NET Framework and reference the `Microsoft.WindowsAPICodePack.dll` and `Microsoft.WindowsAPICodePack.Shell.dll` assemblies.

```
using System;
using System.Collections.Generic;
using System.ComponentModel;
using System.Data;
using System.Drawing;
using System.Linq;
using System.Text;
using System.IO;
using System.Windows.Forms;

using Microsoft.WindowsAPICodePack.Shell;
using Microsoft.WindowsAPICodePack.Taskbar;

namespace Recipe14_09
{
    public partial class Form1 : Form
    {
        public Form1()
        {
```

```
            // Call the default intializer.
            InitializeComponent();

            // Register an event handler for when the windows is shown.
            this.Shown += new EventHandler(onWindowShown);
        }

        void onWindowShown(object sender, EventArgs e)
        {
            // Create a new Jump List.
            JumpList jumpList = JumpList.CreateJumpList();

            // Create a user task.
            jumpList.AddUserTasks(
                new JumpListLink("cmd.exe", "Open Command Prompt"));

            // Create a user task with an icon.
            jumpList.AddUserTasks(new JumpListLink("notepad.exe", "Open Notepad")
            {
                IconReference = new IconReference("notepad.exe", 0)
            });

            // Create a user task with a document.
            jumpList.AddUserTasks(
                new JumpListLink(@"C:\Users\Adam\Desktop\test.txt",
                  "Open Text File"));

        }
    }
}
```

14-10. Use Windows Search

Problem

You need to search the Windows file system.

Solution

Use Microsoft Windows API CodePack for .NET Framework to access the Windows Search feature. Create one or more `Microsoft.WindowsAPICodePack.Shell.SearchConditions` to define the constraints for your search and pass them to an instance of `Microsoft.WindowsAPICodePack.Shell.ShellSearchFolder`. The `ShellSearchFolder` acts as a collection whose members represent the results of your search. The Windows API CodePack for .NET Framework is a source code library published by Microsoft to simplify integration with Windows using managed code. (You can download the CodePack from `http://code.msdn.microsoft.com/WindowsAPICodePack`).

How It Works

The search model is built around conditions and locations. *Conditions* are the individual aspects of a file that match your search—for example, if you needed to find files text files that have "windows" in the file name, the constrains would be:

1. Files that have the `.txt` extension
2. Files that have the word *windows* in the file name.

Locations are where you want the search to be conducted and can include Windows 7 libraries. When using the CodePack, searches are created and performed as follows:

1. Create one or more instances of `SearchCondition` using the `SearchConditionFactory.CreateLeafCondition` method. The `CreateLeafCondition` method accepts three parameters:
   - A property of the `SystemProperties.System` class. The `System` class contains properties for all of the attributes you can search for—some of the most commonly used are described in Table 14-6.
   - The data value to match when searching. This must match the data type of the preceding attribute.
   - A value from the `SearchConditionOperation` enumeration. This value specifies the way in which the data value is matched (equals, greater than, less than, etc.). Commonly used members are described in Table 14-7.
2. If you have created more than one `SearchCondition`, you must combine them with the `SearchConditionFactory.CreateAndOrCondition` method. This method takes a value from the `SearchConditionType` enumeration (`And`, `Or`, `Not`) that specifies how the individual conditions are combined.
3. Create a new instance of the `ShellSearchFolder` class, using the `SearchCondition` you previously created and one or more locations as constructor parameters. The CodePack includes the `KnownFolders` enumeration, whose members reference useful directories and libraries.
4. Treat the `ShellSearchFolder` as a collection. Enumerating the contents will return the results of your search, with each file represented by an instance of `ShellObject`.

■ **Tip** Your search is not performed until you try to access the members of the `ShellSearchFolder` collection—at which point the current thread is blocked until the search has completed. Perform the search in a background thread to avoid an unresponsive application.

Table 14-6. Commonly Used Members of the SystemProperties.System Class

Property	Data Type	Description
`DateModified`	`DateTime`	The last time that the file was changed
`DateCreated`	`DateTime`	The time the file was created
`FileExtention`	`String`	The extension for the file, including the period
`FileName`	`String`	The name of the file, including the file extension
`FileOwner`	`String`	The owner of the file

Table 14-7. Commonly Used Members of the SearchConditionOperation Class

Member	Description
`Equal`	The file attribute and the target value are the same.
`NotEqual`	The file attribute and the target value are different.
`ValueContains`	The file attribute contains the target value (for example, "windows" contains "win").
`ValueStartsWith`	The file attribute starts with the target value (for example, "windows" starts with "win").
`ValueEndsWith`	The file attribute ends with the target value (for example, "Microsoft" ends with "soft").
`ValueNotContains`	The file attribute does not contains the target value (for example, "Microsoft" does not contain "win").
`LessThan`	The file attribute is less than the target value.
`GreaterThan`	The file attribute is greater than the target value.

The Code

The following example is a Windows Forms application that uses the `FileExtension` and `FileName` attributes to search for files in the current user's directories. The user interface, built using the Visual Studio designer, is shown in Figure 14-1. To compile the example, you must build Windows API CodePack for Microsoft .NET Framework and reference the `Microsoft.WindowsAPICodePack.dll` and `Microsoft.WindowsAPICodePack.Shell.dll` assemblies.

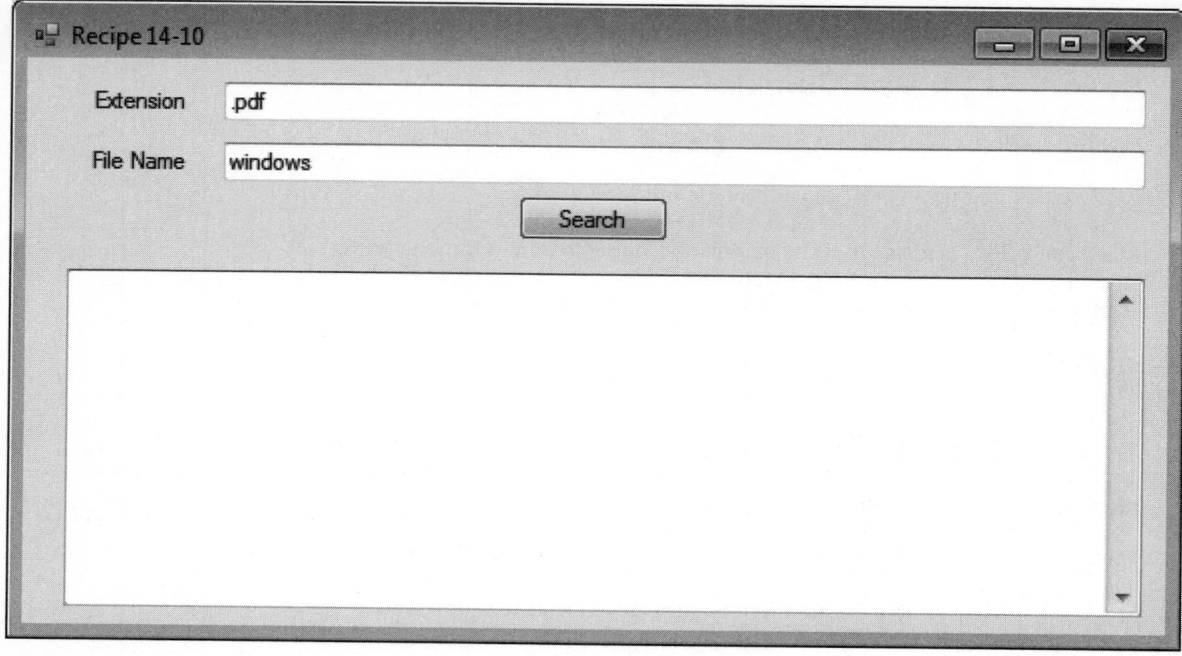

Figure 14-1. Example search application

The `button1_Click` method is called when the Search button is pressed. A `SearchCondition` is created using the values that the user has entered for the file name and extension, and combined using the `SearchConditionType.And` enumeration value. The search results are read from the `ShellSearchFolder` and name of each file found is added to the large text box.

```
using System;
using System.Collections.Generic;
using System.ComponentModel;
using System.Data;
using System.Drawing;
using System.Linq;
using System.Text;
using System.Windows.Forms;
using Microsoft.WindowsAPICodePack.Shell;
using Microsoft.WindowsAPICodePack.Shell.PropertySystem;

namespace Recipe14_10
{
    public partial class Recipe14_10 : Form
    {
```

```
        public Recipe14_10()
        {
            InitializeComponent();
        }

        private void button1_Click(object sender, EventArgs e)
        {
            // Create the leaf condition for the file extension.
            SearchCondition fileExtCondition =
                SearchConditionFactory.CreateLeafCondition(
                SystemProperties.System.FileExtension, textBox1.Text,
                SearchConditionOperation.Equal);

            // Create the leaf condition for the file name.
            SearchCondition fileNameCondition =
                SearchConditionFactory.CreateLeafCondition(
                SystemProperties.System.FileName, textBox2.Text,
                SearchConditionOperation.ValueContains);

            // Combine the two leaf conditions.
            SearchCondition comboCondition =
                SearchConditionFactory.CreateAndOrCondition(
                SearchConditionType.And,
                false, fileExtCondition, fileNameCondition);

            // Create the search folder.
            ShellSearchFolder searchFolder = new ShellSearchFolder(
                comboCondition, (ShellContainer)KnownFolders.UsersFiles);

            // Clear the result text box.
            textBox3.Clear();
            textBox3.AppendText("Processing search results...\n");

            // Run through each search result.
            foreach (ShellObject shellObject in searchFolder)
            {
                textBox3.AppendText("Result: "
                    + shellObject.ParsingName + "\n");
            }

            // Display a final message to the user.
            textBox3.AppendText("All results processed\n");

        }
    }
}
```

14-11. Check Internet Connectivity

Problem

You need to check that the computer has Internet access.

Solution

Use the Windows API CodePack for Microsoft .NET Framework to access to enumerate the available network connections and determine which, if any, are connected to the Internet. The Windows API CodePack for Microsoft .NET Framework is a source code library published by Microsoft to simplify integration with Windows using managed code. (You can download the CodePack from `http://code.msdn.microsoft.com/WindowsAPICodePack`).

How It Works

The `Microsoft.WindowsAPICodePack.Net.NetworkListManager` class contains the `IsConnectedToInternet` property. If this returns `true`, the `GetNetworks` method can be used to obtain a collection of connected networks, each of which is represented by the `Microsoft.WindowsAPICodePack.Net.Network` class.

The Code

The following example uses the `IsConnectedToInternet` property of the `Microsoft.WindowsAPICodePack.Net.NetworkListManager` class, and if the result is positive, gets the list of network connections and writes out the name of those that are connected. To compile the example, you must build Windows API CodePack for Microsoft .NET Framework and reference the `Microsoft.WindowsAPICodePack.dll` assembly.

```
using System;
using Microsoft.WindowsAPICodePack.Net;

namespace Recipe14_11
{
    class Recipe14_11
    {
        static void Main(string[] args)
        {
            // Check the internet connection state.
            bool isInternetConnected =
                NetworkListManager.IsConnectedToInternet;

            Console.WriteLine("Machine connected to Internet: {0}",
                isInternetConnected);

            if (isInternetConnected)
            {
```

```
                // Get the list of all network connections.
                NetworkCollection netCollection =
                    NetworkListManager.GetNetworks(
                       NetworkConnectivityLevels.Connected);

                // Work through the set of connections and write out the
                // name of those that are connected to the internet.
                foreach (Network network in netCollection)
                {
                    if (network.IsConnectedToInternet)
                    {
                        Console.WriteLine(
                            "Connection {0} is connected to the internet",
                            network.Name);
                    }
                }
            }

            Console.WriteLine("\nMain method complete. Press Enter.");
            Console.ReadLine();
        }
    }
}
```

14-12. Display a Task Dialog

Problem

You need to display a task dialog—a standard Windows-specific dialog box, such as an elevated task request.

Solution

Use Windows API CodePack for Microsoft .NET Framework to create and display task dialogs. Windows API CodePack for Microsoft .NET Framework is a source code library published by Microsoft to simplify integration with Windows using managed code—it contains extensive support for Windows-specific dialog boxes, which allow your application to better integrate with the platform. (You can download the CodePack from `http://code.msdn.microsoft.com/WindowsAPICodePack`).

How It Works

Create an instance of the `Microsoft.WindowsAPICodePack.Dialogs.TaskDialog` class and use the class properties to configure the task dialog. Add event handlers so that you are notified when buttons are pressed and then call the `Show` method to display the dialog. Some of the most useful properties of the `TaskDialog` class are shown in Table 14-8.

Table 14-8. Selected Properties of the TaskDialog Class

Property	Description
`Cancelable`	Determines if the user can dismiss the dialog.
`Controls`	The set of controls embedded within the task dialog. See the recipe code for an example.
`InstructionText`	The summary text displayed in the dialog.
`StandardButtons`	The standard buttons for the dialog. Set with the values of the `TaskDialogStandardButtons` enumeration. See the recipe code for an example.
`Text`	The detailed text, displayed below the `InstructionText`.

The Code

The following example is a Windows Forms application comprising a button and a text area. To compile the example, you must build the Windows API CodePack for Microsoft .NET Framework and reference the `Microsoft.WindowsAPICodePack.dll` assembly. The user interface is shown in Figure 14-2. We have added an event handler such that the `showElevatedTaskRequest` method is called when the button is clicked.

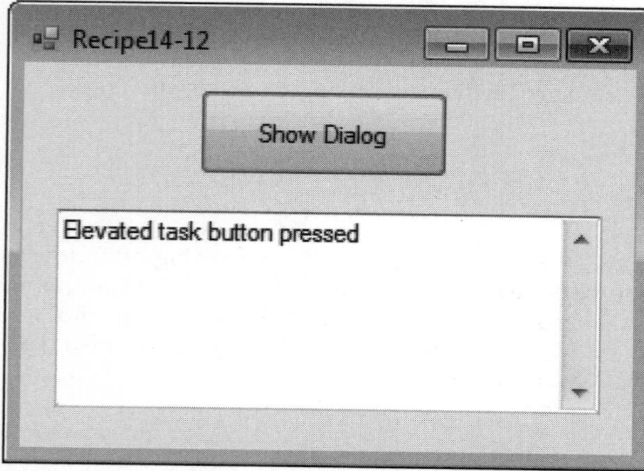

Figure 14-2. Windows Forms interface

When the button is clicked, we create a new instance of `TaskDialog` and configure the basic settings, allowing the user to cancel the dialog and specifying which buttons should be displayed at the bottom of the dialog window. We then create an instance of `TaskDialogCommandLink`, using sample text as the constructor parameters and add it to the `TaskDialog.Controls` property. We register an event handler so that we can add a line of text to the text box on the main window when the elevated task button is clicked. The dialog interface is shown in Figure 14-3.

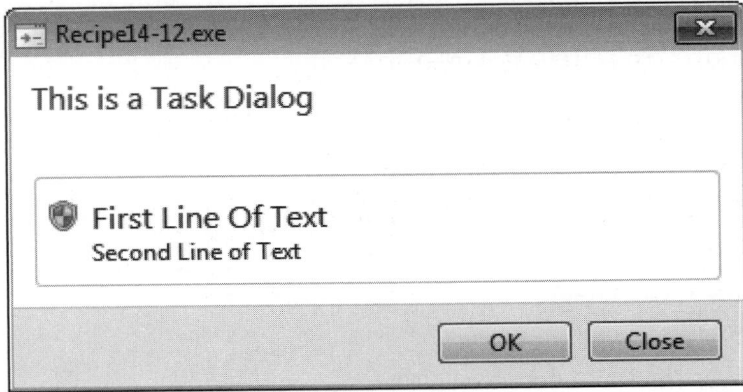

Figure 14-3. *Elevated task dialog*

■ **Note** Using the task dialog to allow your application to indicate to a user that a particular task requires elevated privileges does not elevate the privilege level for your application. See recipe 14-15 for details of how to perform an elevated task.

```
using System;
using System.Collections.Generic;
using System.ComponentModel;
using System.Data;
using System.Drawing;
using System.Linq;
using System.Text;
using System.Windows.Forms;
using Microsoft.WindowsAPICodePack.Dialogs;

namespace Recipe14_12
{
    public partial class Form1 : Form
    {
```

```
        public Form1()
        {
            InitializeComponent();
        }

        void showElevatedTaskRequest(object sender, EventArgs args)
        {
            // Create the TaskDialog and configure the basics.
            TaskDialog taskDialog = new TaskDialog();
            taskDialog.Cancelable = true;
            taskDialog.InstructionText = "This is a Task Dialog";
            taskDialog.StandardButtons =
                TaskDialogStandardButtons.Ok | TaskDialogStandardButtons.Close;

            // Create the control that will represent the elevated task.
            TaskDialogCommandLink commLink = new TaskDialogCommandLink(
                "adminTask", "First Line Of Text", "Second Line of Text");
            commLink.ShowElevationIcon = true;

            // Add the control to the task dialog.
            taskDialog.Controls.Add(commLink);

            // Add an event handler to the command link so that
            // we are notified when the user presses the button.
            commLink.Click += new EventHandler(performElevatedTask);

            // display the task dialog
            taskDialog.Show();
        }

        void performElevatedTask(object sender, EventArgs args)
        {
            textBox1.AppendText("Elevated task button pressed\n");
        }
    }
}
```

14-13. Write Custom Performance Counters

Problem

You need to create and write to performance counters to instrument your application.

Solution

To set up the counters, add one or more instances of `System.Diagnostics.CounterCreateData`, add them to an instance of `System.Diagnostics.CounterCreationDataCollection`, and pass the collection as an argument to the `Create` method of the `System.Diagnostics.PerformanceCounterCategory` class.

■ **Note** Creating new counters requires administrator privileges.

To write to a counter, create an instance of `System.Diagnostics.PerformanceCounter` using the same details you specified when creating the corresponding `CounterCreateData` instance. Ensure that the `ReadOnly` property is `false`. Use the `Increment`, `IncrementBy`, `Decrement`, and `DecrementBy` methods to change the value of the counter.

How It Works

Counters are grouped together in categories. You can determine if a category already exists by using the `PerformanceCategory.Exists` method—an exception will be thrown if you try to create a category that already exists. An individual counter is created using the `CounterCreationData` class. The three key properties are `CounterName` (the name of the counter), `CounterHelp` (a descriptive string that can be displayed to the user), and `CounterType`, which defines the kind of counter that will be created. There are many kinds of counters available, ranging from simple 32- and 64-bit values to pairs of counters that must be created together so that Windows can calculate rate information (see the recipe code for an example of this). The range of counter types available is described in the `System.Diagnostic.PerformanceCounterType` enumeration.

Writing to performance counters uses a different set of classes. To write to a counter, create an instance of the `PerformanceCounter` class, setting the `CategoryName` property and `CounterName` properties to those you used when creating the category and counters. `PerformanceCounter` values can be incremented using the `Increment` and `IncrementBy` methods, decremented using the `Decrement` and `DecrementBy` methods, and set to a specific value using the `RawValue` property.

The Code

The following example creates a new performance counter category called `Recipe 14-13 Performance Counters` and populates it with three counters: `NumberOfItems32`, `AverageTimer32`, and `AverageBase`.

Two of the counters are closely related. When creating a counter of the `AverageTimer32` type, the next counter that is created must be of the `AverageBase` type. The two counters are used together to report the number of occurrences of an operation over time. We update the `AverageBase` value to report how many operations have been performed and the `AverageTimer32` value to report how many ticks have passed since you last updated the `AverageBase` value.

Having created the category and counters, we then create three instance of `PerformanceCounter` and enter a loop so that the counter values are updated randomly.

■ **Caution** `AverageTimer32` should be updated with the number of ticks reported by the Windows high-resolution performance counter. The counter value is not available through a managed library, and must be obtained using the `QueryPerformanceCounter` method `in Kernel32.dll`. You can see how the DLL is imported and used in the example.

```
using System;
using System.Security.Principal;
using System.Diagnostics;
using System.Runtime.InteropServices;

namespace Recipe14_13
{
    class Recipe14_13
    {

        [DllImport("Kernel32.dll")]
        public static extern void QueryPerformanceCounter(ref long ticks);

        static void Main(string[] args)
        {

            if (!checkElevatedPrivilege())
            {
                Console.WriteLine("This recipe requires administrator rights");
                Console.ReadLine();
                Environment.Exit(1);
            }

            // Define the category name for the performance counters.
            string categoryName = "Recipe 14-13 Performance Counters";

            if (!PerformanceCounterCategory.Exists(categoryName))
            {
                Console.WriteLine("Creating counters.");

                // We need to create the category.
                CounterCreationDataCollection counterCollection
                    = new CounterCreationDataCollection();

                // Create the individual counters.
                CounterCreationData counter1 = new CounterCreationData();
                counter1.CounterType = PerformanceCounterType.NumberOfItems32;
                counter1.CounterName = "Number of Items Counter";
                counter1.CounterHelp = "A sample 32-bit number counter";

                CounterCreationData counter2 = new CounterCreationData();
                counter2.CounterType = PerformanceCounterType.AverageTimer32;
```

```
        counter2.CounterName = "Average Timer Counter";
        counter2.CounterHelp = "A sample average timer counter";

        CounterCreationData counter3 = new CounterCreationData();
        counter3.CounterType = PerformanceCounterType.AverageBase;
        counter3.CounterName = "Average Base Counter";
        counter3.CounterHelp = "A sample average base counter";

        // Add the counters to the collection.
        counterCollection.Add(counter1);
        counterCollection.Add(counter2);
        counterCollection.Add(counter3);

        // Create the counters category.
        PerformanceCounterCategory.Create(categoryName,
            "Category for Visual C# Recipe 14-13",
            PerformanceCounterCategoryType.SingleInstance,
            counterCollection);
    }
    else
    {
        Console.WriteLine("Counters already exist.");
    }

    // Open the counters for reading.
    PerformanceCounter perfCounter1 = new PerformanceCounter();
    perfCounter1.CategoryName = categoryName;
    perfCounter1.CounterName = "Number of Items Counter";
    perfCounter1.ReadOnly = false;

    PerformanceCounter perfCounter2 = new PerformanceCounter();
    perfCounter2.CategoryName = categoryName;
    perfCounter2.CounterName = "Average Timer Counter";
    perfCounter2.ReadOnly = false;

    PerformanceCounter perfCounter3 = new PerformanceCounter();
    perfCounter3.CategoryName = categoryName;
    perfCounter3.CounterName = "Average Base Counter";
    perfCounter3.ReadOnly = false;

    // Create a number generator to produce values.
    Random numberGenerator = new Random();

    // Enter a loop to update the values every second.
    long startTickCount = 0, endTickCount = 0;
    while (true)
    {
        // Get the high-frequency tick count.
        QueryPerformanceCounter(ref startTickCount);
        // put the thread to sleep for up to a second
        System.Threading.Thread.Sleep(numberGenerator.Next(1000));
```

```
                // Get the high-frequency tick count again.
                QueryPerformanceCounter(ref endTickCount);

                Console.WriteLine("Updating counter values.");
                perfCounter1.Increment();
                perfCounter2.IncrementBy(endTickCount - startTickCount);
                perfCounter3.Increment();
            }
        }

        static bool checkElevatedPrivilege()
        {
            WindowsIdentity winIdentity = WindowsIdentity.GetCurrent();
            WindowsPrincipal winPrincipal = new WindowsPrincipal(winIdentity);
            return winPrincipal.IsInRole(WindowsBuiltInRole.Administrator);
        }
    }
}
```

14-14. Read Performance Counters

Problem

You need to read performance counter values.

Solution

Create an instance of the `System.Diagnostics.PerformanceCounter` class for each counter that you want to read, specifying the counter category and name as constructor arguments. Read data values by calling the `NextValue` method.

How It Works

The process for reading performance counter values is very similar to that for writing values, except that instead of using the `Increment` and `Decrement` methods, the `NextSample` method is called to return data points as `float` values.

■ **Note** Administrator privileges are required to read performance counters.

The Code

The following example reads values from the counters that we created in the previous recipe. In the previous recipe, we noted that two of the counters were related. When reading data from such a pair, you only read values from the first counter—Windows returns the calculated value (the number of operations/second). If you need to access the underlying data, then consult the .NET documentation for details of the `System.Diagnostics.CounterSample` class, instances of which can be obtained from the `PerformanceCounter.NextSample` method. You must run the previous example at the same time as this example; otherwise, you will only be able to read zeros from the counters, as no updates will be generated.

```
using System;
using System.Collections.Generic;
using System.Linq;
using System.Text;
using System.Diagnostics;
using System.Security.Principal;

namespace Recipe14_14
{
    class Recipe14_14
    {
        static void Main(string[] args)
        {

            if (!checkElevatedPrivilege())
            {
                Console.WriteLine("This recipe requires administrator rights");
                Console.ReadLine();
                Environment.Exit(1);
            }

            // Define the category name for the performance counters.
            string categoryName = "Recipe 14-13 Performance Counters";

            // Open the counters for reading.
            PerformanceCounter perfCounter1 = new PerformanceCounter();
            perfCounter1.CategoryName = categoryName;
            perfCounter1.CounterName = "Number of Items Counter";

            PerformanceCounter perfCounter2 = new PerformanceCounter();
            perfCounter2.CategoryName = categoryName;
            perfCounter2.CounterName = "Average Timer Counter";

            while (true)
            {
                float value1 = perfCounter1.NextValue();
                Console.WriteLine("Value for first counter: {0}", value1);
                float value2 = perfCounter2.NextValue();
                Console.WriteLine("Value for second counter: {0}", value2);
```

```
                // Put the thread to sleep for a second.
                System.Threading.Thread.Sleep(1000);
            }
        }

        static bool checkElevatedPrivilege()
        {
            WindowsIdentity winIdentity = WindowsIdentity.GetCurrent();
            WindowsPrincipal winPrincipal = new WindowsPrincipal(winIdentity);
            return winPrincipal.IsInRole(WindowsBuiltInRole.Administrator);
        }
    }
}
```

14-15. Obtain Elevated Privileges

Problem

You need elevated (administrator) privileges for part of your application's functionality.

Solution

Use the `runas` command to start a second instance of your application with elevated privileges using a command-line argument to indicate that the privileged operations should be performed.

How It Works

Windows doesn't support temporarily elevating privileges for a process. If your application needs elevated privileges for specific tasks, create a second process that starts your application with elevated privileges and use command-line arguments to indicate that elevated tasks should be performed.

To execute a process with elevated privileges, create a new instance of the `System.Diagnostics.ProcessStartInfo` class, set the `Verb` property to `runas` and the `Arguments` property to be a string that represents a request for elevated actions (we use `elevated` in the following example). Pass the `ProcessStartInfo` instance to the static `System.Diagnostics.Process.Start` method. In your application's `Main` method, check the arguments to determine whether you should perform the elevated tasks or run normally. Encapsulate the tasks that require elevated privileges in separate methods and invoke them when your application is started using the command-line argument.

■ **Tip** If your application needs to perform different sets of elevated tasks, use an additional argument to indicate which set should be executed.

The Code

In the following example, the performNormalTasks method represents normal operation and the performElevatedTasks method represents the tasks that require elevation. When the example is started, the Main method is called and the arguments are checked to determine which of these methods should be called.

The checkElevatedPrivilege method uses the System.Security.Principal.WindowsIdentity and System.Security.Principal.WindowsPrincipal classes to establish our privilege level. We don't want to start a new process if the application has been started with elevated privileges, so the performNormalTasks method checks the elevation level before calling the startElevatedInstance method.

Starting the example normally will result in an elevated process being started with the elevated argument. The new process will perform the elevated task and then exit. Starting the process as administrator will result in the elevated tasks being performed within the same process.

```
using System;
using System.Collections.Generic;
using System.Linq;
using System.Text;
using System.Security.Principal;
using System.Diagnostics;


namespace Recipe14_15
{
    class Program
    {
        static void Main(string[] args)
        {
            // Check to see if the first argument is "elevated".
            if (args.Length > 0 && args[0] == "elevated")
            {
                Console.WriteLine("Started with command line argument");
                performElevatedTasks();
            }
            else
            {
                Console.WriteLine("Started without command line argument");
                performNormalTasks();
            }
        }

        static void performNormalTasks()
        {

            Console.WriteLine("Press return to perform elevated tasks");
            Console.ReadLine();
            // Check to see if we have been started with elevated privileges.
            if (checkElevatedPrivilege())
            {
```

```
                // We already have privileges - perform the tasks.
                performElevatedTasks();
            }
            else
            {
                // We need to start an elevated instance.
                startElevatedInstance();
            }
        }

        static void performElevatedTasks()
        {
            // Check to see that we have elevated privileges.
            if (checkElevatedPrivilege())
            {
                // perform the elevated task
                Console.WriteLine("Elevated tasks performed");
            }
            else
            {
                // We are not able to perform the elevated tasks.
                Console.WriteLine("Cannot perform elevated tasks");
            }
            Console.WriteLine("Press return to exit");
            Console.ReadLine();
        }

        static bool checkElevatedPrivilege()
        {
            WindowsIdentity winIdentity = WindowsIdentity.GetCurrent();
            WindowsPrincipal winPrincipal = new WindowsPrincipal(winIdentity);
            return winPrincipal.IsInRole (WindowsBuiltInRole.Administrator);
        }

        static void startElevatedInstance()
        {
            ProcessStartInfo procstartinf = new ProcessStartInfo("Recipe14-15.exe");
            procstartinf.Arguments = "elevated";
            procstartinf.Verb = "runas";
            Process.Start(procstartinf).WaitForExit();
        }
    }
}
```

CHAPTER 15

■ ■ ■

Parallel Programming

With version 4.0 of the .NET Framework, Microsoft introduced a new model for writing applications that need to perform multiple simultaneous tasks—that model is known as *parallel programming*, and the implementation is called the *Task Parallel Library*. Unlike the traditional approach to multitasking, where you create and manage a set of threads in your code, the new parallel programming model lets you focus on the tasks you need to accomplish and allows the runtime to create and manage the threads on your behalf.

There key advantage of this approach is that your code is focused on the tasks you need to perform, not the way in which they will be performed. The main disadvantage is that you give up direct control of the behavior of your application—so, for many applications, the new parallel programming model will be ideal, but for those applications that require careful control and management (and for those programmers who cannot let go), we refer you to Chapter 4, which covers the traditional threading approach. The recipes in this chapter describe how to perform the following tasks:

- Performing simple parallel tasks (recipe 15-1)
- Writing more complex tasks (recipes 15-2, 15-6, and 15-7)
- Managing tasks (recipes 15-3, 15-5 and 15-8)
- Working in parallel with data (recipes 15-4 and 15-9)

15-1. Perform Simple Parallel Tasks

Problem

You need to perform simple tasks simultaneously.

Solution

Use the `Invoke` method of the `System.Threading.Parallel` class, passing in an instance of the `System.Action` delegate for each method you wish to run.

How It Works

The `Invoke` method of the `Parallel` class is the simplest way to add multitasking to your application. You simply provide a set of `Action` delegates, each of which wraps around a method you wish to invoke. The .NET Framework takes care of the rest—threads are created and managed automatically on your behalf.

■ **Note** The `Parallel.Invoke` method can only be used to invoke methods that do not return a result. See the other recipes in this chapter for more complex examples.

The Code

The following example invokes three methods concurrently, each of which writes a series of messages to the console. In order to simulate a time-intensive task, these methods call `Thread.Sleep` to slow down the progress of the application—something that you would not do with a real application.

We have created the `Action` delegates explicitly to make the example as clear as possible, but a more elegant approach is to use lambda expressions, so that

```
Parallel.Invoke(
    new Action(writeDays),
    new Action(writeMonths),
    new Action(writeCities)
);
```

would be written as

```
Parallel.Invoke(
    () => writeDays(),
    () => writeMonths(),
    () => writeCities()
);
```

The remaining recipes in this chapter use lambda expressions.

```
using System;
using System.Threading;
using System.Threading.Tasks;

namespace Recipe15_01
{
    class Recipe15_01
    {
        static void Main(string[] args)
        {
            Console.WriteLine("Press enter to start");
            Console.ReadLine();
```

```
            // Invoke the methods we want to run.
            Parallel.Invoke(
                new Action(writeDays),
                new Action(writeMonths),
                new Action(writeCities)
            );

            // Wait to continue.
            Console.WriteLine("\nMain method complete. Press Enter");
            Console.ReadLine();
        }

        static void writeDays()
        {
            string[] daysArray = { "Monday", "Tuesday", "Wednesday",
                "Thursday", "Friday", "Saturday", "Sunday" };
            foreach (string day in daysArray)
            {
                Console.WriteLine("Day of the Week: {0}", day);
                Thread.Sleep(500);
            }
        }

        static void writeMonths()
        {
            string[] monthsArray = { "Jan", "Feb", "Mar", "Apr",
                                       "May", "Jun", "Jul",
                                       "Aug", "Sep", "Oct", "Nov", "Dec" };
            foreach (string month in monthsArray)
            {
                Console.WriteLine("Month: {0}", month);
                Thread.Sleep(500);
            }
        }

        static void writeCities()
        {
            string[] citiesArray = { "London", "New York", "Paris", "Tokyo",
                "Sydney" };
            foreach (string city in citiesArray)
            {
                Console.WriteLine("City: {0}", city);
                Thread.Sleep(500);
            }

        }
    }
}
```

15-2. Return a Result from a Task

Problem

You need to perform concurrent tasks that return results.

Solution

Create typed instances of the `Task` class by passing function delegates to the generic-typed static `System.Threading.Task<>.Factory.StartNew` method. Use the `Task.Result` property to obtain the result from your task.

How It Works

For anything other than simple tasks, such as those in the previous recipe, you use the `Task` class to write parallel applications. New tasks are created (and automatically started) when you call the `Task<>.Factory.StartNew` method, passing in a function delegate as the argument. You obtain the result of your task through the `Task.Result` property.

■ **Tip** The `StartNew` method creates and starts a new task in one step. If you need to create tasks and start them later, you can create instances of `Task` directly with the class constructors and start them running using the `Start` method.

The Code

The following example modifies the task methods from the previous recipe to return how many items have been printed out. We call the `Result` property for each task and write it to the console. Notice that when running the example, the results are intermingled with the output from the tasks themselves, as shown following:

```
. . .
Month: Jul
Day of the Week: Sunday
Month: Aug
7 days were written
Month: Sep
Month: Oct
Month: Nov
Month: Dec
12 months were written
5 cities were written
. . .
```

This happens because the Result property blocks until the task has completed. See the following recipes for different ways to wait for tasks to complete.

```
using System;
using System.Threading;
using System.Threading.Tasks;

namespace Recipe15_02
{
    class Recipe15_02
    {
        static void Main(string[] args)
        {

            Console.WriteLine("Press enter to start");
            Console.ReadLine();

            // Create the tasks.
            Task<int> task1 = Task<int>.Factory.StartNew(() => writeDays());
            Task<int> task2 = Task<int>.Factory.StartNew(() => writeMonths());
            Task<int> task3 = Task<int>.Factory.StartNew(() => writeCities());

            // Get the results and write them out.
            Console.WriteLine("{0} days were written", task1.Result);
            Console.WriteLine("{0} months were written", task2.Result);
            Console.WriteLine("{0} cities were written", task3.Result);

            // Wait to continue.
            Console.WriteLine("\nMain method complete. Press Enter");
            Console.ReadLine();
        }

        static int writeDays()
        {
            string[] daysArray = { "Monday", "Tuesday", "Wednesday",
                                   "Thursday", "Friday",
                                   "Saturday", "Sunday" };
            foreach (string day in daysArray)
            {
                Console.WriteLine("Day of the Week: {0}", day);
                Thread.Sleep(500);
            }
            return daysArray.Length;
        }

        static int writeMonths()
        {
            string[] monthsArray = { "Jan", "Feb", "Mar", "Apr",
                                     "May", "Jun", "Jul",
                                     "Aug", "Sep", "Oct", "Nov", "Dec" };
```

```
            foreach (string month in monthsArray)
            {
                Console.WriteLine("Month: {0}", month);
                Thread.Sleep(500);
            }
            return monthsArray.Length;
        }

        static int writeCities()
        {
            string[] citiesArray = { "London", "New York", "Paris",
                                     "Tokyo", "Sydney" };
            foreach (string city in citiesArray)
            {
                Console.WriteLine("City: {0}", city);
                Thread.Sleep(500);
            }
            return citiesArray.Length;
        }
    }
}
```

15-3. Wait for Tasks to Complete

Problem

You need to wait for one or more tasks to complete.

Solution

Use the `Wait`, `WaitAll`, or `WaitAny` methods of the `System.Threading.Task` class.

How It Works

The `Wait` method is called on a `Task` instance and blocks until the task is complete. The static `WaitAll` and `WaitAny` methods take an array of tasks as parameters—the `WaitAll` method blocks until all of the `Tasks` in the array have completed, and the `WaitAny` method blocks until any one of the `Tasks` is finished. These methods also accept an `int` argument that will block for the specific number of milliseconds and then continue regardless of whether the task or tasks have completed. The `IsCompleted` property of the `Task` class is used to determine whether a task has finished.

The Code

This example changes the code from the previous recipe to wait for all of the tasks we created using the `WaitAll` method. In the previous example, the results of the tasks were reported as each result we requested became available—this example waits for all of the tasks to complete before obtaining the results.

```
using System;
using System.Threading;
using System.Threading.Tasks;

namespace Recipe15_03
{
    class Recipe15_03
    {
        static void Main(string[] args)
        {

            Console.WriteLine("Press enter to start");
            Console.ReadLine();

            // Create the tasks.
            Task<int> task1 = Task<int>.Factory.StartNew(() => writeDays());
            Task<int> task2 = Task<int>.Factory.StartNew(() => writeMonths());
            Task<int> task3 = Task<int>.Factory.StartNew(() => writeCities());

            // Wait for all of the tasks to complete.
            Task.WaitAll(task1, task2, task3);

            // Get the results and write them out.
            Console.WriteLine("{0} days were written", task1.Result);
            Console.WriteLine("{0} months were written", task2.Result);
            Console.WriteLine("{0} cities were written", task3.Result);

            // Wait to continue.
            Console.WriteLine("\nMain method complete. Press Enter");
            Console.ReadLine();
        }

        static int writeDays()
        {
            string[] daysArray = { "Monday", "Tuesday", "Wednesday",
                                   "Thursday", "Friday",
                                   "Saturday", "Sunday" };
            foreach (string day in daysArray)
            {
                Console.WriteLine("Day of the Week: {0}", day);
                Thread.Sleep(500);
            }
            return daysArray.Length;
        }
```

```
        static int writeMonths()
        {
            string[] monthsArray = { "Jan", "Feb", "Mar", "Apr",
                                     "May", "Jun", "Jul",
                                     "Aug", "Sep", "Oct", "Nov", "Dec" };
            foreach (string month in monthsArray)
            {
                Console.WriteLine("Month: {0}", month);
                Thread.Sleep(500);
            }
            return monthsArray.Length;
        }

        static int writeCities()
        {
            string[] citiesArray = { "London", "New York", "Paris",
                                     "Tokyo", "Sydney" };
            foreach (string city in citiesArray)
            {
                Console.WriteLine("City: {0}", city);
                Thread.Sleep(500);
            }
            return citiesArray.Length;
        }
    }
}
```

15-4. Parallel Process a Collection

Problem

You need to parallel process each element in a collection.

Solution

Use the `System.Threading.Parallel.ForEach` method to create a new task to process each of the elements in a collection. Optionally, use `System.Threading.ParallelOptions` to limit the degree of parallelism that will be used.

How It Works

The static `Parallel.ForEach` method accepts a collection, a function delegate, and an optional instance of `ParallelOptions` as arguments. A new task is created to process each element in the collection using the function referenced by the delegate. The number of concurrent tasks is controlled by the `ParallelOptions.MaxDegreeOfParallelism` property—a value of `-1` means that the degree of parallelism will be determined by the runtime, whereas a value of `1` or more limits the number of tasks that will run at the same time (a value of `0` will throw an exception).

The Code

The following example creates tasks to process each element of a simple array using the `printNumbers` method. We have called `Thread.Sleep` in this method to slow down the processing so that the example is clearer. We use the `MaxDegreeOfParallelism` property of `ParallelOptions` to ensure that at most two tasks are performed simultaneously—when running the example, notice that the output from the first two tasks is intermingled and then followed by the output from the third task.

```
using System;
using System.Threading;
using System.Threading.Tasks;

namespace Recipe15_04
{
    class Recipe15_04
    {
        static void Main(string[] args)
        {
            Console.WriteLine("Press enter to start");
            Console.ReadLine();

            // Define the data we want to process.
            int[] numbersArray = { 100, 200, 300 };

            // Configure the options.
            ParallelOptions options = new ParallelOptions();
            options.MaxDegreeOfParallelism = 2;

            // Process each data element in parallel.
            Parallel.ForEach(numbersArray, options, baseNumber =>
                printNumbers(baseNumber));

            Console.WriteLine("Tasks Completed.  Press Enter");
            Console.ReadLine();
        }

        static void printNumbers(int baseNumber)
        {
            for (int i = baseNumber, j = baseNumber + 10; i < j; i++)
            {
                Console.WriteLine("Number: {0}", i);
                Thread.Sleep(100);
            }
        }
    }
}
```

15-5. Chain Tasks Together

Problem

You need to perform several tasks in sequence.

Solution

Create an instance of `Task` for the initial activity using the class constructors (as shown in the previous recipes in this chapter), and then call the `ContinueWith` method to create a `Task` instance representing the next activity in the sequence. When you have created all of the `Task` instances you require, call the `Start` method on the first in the sequence.

How It Works

The `Task.ContinueWith` and `Task.ContinueWith<>` methods create a new task that will continue upon completion of the `Task` instance on which they are invoked. The previous task (known as the antecedent) is provided as an input parameter to the lambda expression in the `ContinueWith` method—this can be used to check the states or get the result of the previous task, as shown in the following example.

The Code

The example for this recipe chains three tasks together. The first task adds some integer values. The second obtains the result from the first and prints it out, and the third task simply writes a message without reference to the previous tasks at all.

```
using System;
using System.Threading;
using System.Threading.Tasks;

namespace Recipe15_05
{
    class Recipe15_05
    {
        static void Main(string[] args)
        {
            Console.WriteLine("Press enter to start");
            Console.ReadLine();

            // Create the set of tasks.
            Task<int> firstTask = new Task<int>(() => sumAndPrintNumbers(100));
            Task secondTask = firstTask.ContinueWith(parent => printTotal(parent));
            Task thirdTask = secondTask.ContinueWith(parent => printMessage());
```

```
            // Start the first task.
            firstTask.Start();

            // Read a line to keep the process alive.
            Console.WriteLine("Press enter to finish");
            Console.ReadLine();
        }

        static int sumAndPrintNumbers(int baseNumber)
        {
            Console.WriteLine("sum&print called for {0}", baseNumber);
            int total = 0;
            for (int i = baseNumber, j = baseNumber + 10; i < j; i++)
            {
                Console.WriteLine("Number: {0}", i);
                total += i;
            }
            return total;
        }

        static void printTotal(Task<int> parentTask)
        {
            Console.WriteLine("Total is {0}", parentTask.Result);
        }

        static void printMessage()
        {
            Console.WriteLine("Message from third task");
        }
    }
}
```

15-6. Write a Cooperative Algorithm

Problem

You need to write a parallel algorithm with multiple phases, each of which must be completed before the next can begin.

Solution

Create an instance of the `System.Threading.Barrier` class and call the `SignalAndWait` method from your `Task` code at the end of each algorithm phase.

How It Works

The Barrier class allows you to wait for a set of tasks to complete one part of an algorithm before moving onto the next. This is useful when the overall results from the one phase are required by all tasks in order to complete a subsequent phase. When creating an instance of Barrier, you specify an integer as a constructor argument. In your Task code, you call the SignalAndWait method when you have reached the end of a phase—your Task will block until the specified number of Tasks is waiting, at which point the Barrier allows all of the waiting tasks to continue into the next phase. It is up to you to determine what constitutes each phase of your algorithm and to specify how many Tasks must reach the barrier before the next phase can begin.

You can also specify an action to be performed when each phase is completed (i.e., after the required number of tasks have called the SignalAndWait method, but before the tasks are allowed to continue to the next phase—the example for this recipe demonstrates how to do this with a lambda function.

■ **Note** It is important to ensure that you set the Barrier instance to expect the correct number of tasks at each stage of your algorithm. If you tell the Barrier to expect too few tasks, one phase may not have completed before the next begins. If you tell the Barrier to expect too many tasks, a phase will never start, even though all of your tasks have completed the earlier phase. You can change the number of tasks a Barrier will wait for by using the AddParticipant, AddParticipants, RemoveParticipant, and RemoveParticipants methods.

The Code

The following example shows a simple two-phase cooperative algorithm, performed by three tasks. When all of the tasks reach the barrier at the end of each phase, the notifyPhaseEnd method is called.

```
using System;
using System.Threading;
using System.Threading.Tasks;

namespace Recipe15_06
{
    class Recipe15_06
    {
        static void Main(string[] args)
        {
            // Create the barrier.
            Barrier myBarrier = new Barrier(3,
                (barrier) => notifyPhaseEnd(barrier));

            Task task1 = Task.Factory.StartNew(
                () => cooperatingAlgorithm(1, myBarrier));
            Task task2 = Task.Factory.StartNew(
                () => cooperatingAlgorithm(2, myBarrier));
```

```
            Task task3 = Task.Factory.StartNew(
                () => cooperatingAlgorithm(3, myBarrier));

            // Wait for all of the tasks to complete.
            Task.WaitAll(task1, task2, task3);

            // Wait to continue.
            Console.WriteLine("\nMain method complete. Press Enter");
            Console.ReadLine();
        }

        static void cooperatingAlgorithm(int taskid, Barrier barrier)
        {
            Console.WriteLine("Running algorithm for task {0}", taskid);

            // Perform phase one and wait at the barrier.
            performPhase1(taskid);
            barrier.SignalAndWait();

            // Perform phase two and wait at the barrier.
            performPhase2(taskid);
            barrier.SignalAndWait();
        }

        static void performPhase1(int taskid)
        {
            Console.WriteLine("Phase one performed for task {0}", taskid);
        }

        static void performPhase2(int taskid)
        {
            Console.WriteLine("Phase two performed for task {0}", taskid);
        }

        static void notifyPhaseEnd(Barrier barrier)
        {
            Console.WriteLine("Phase has concluded");
        }
    }
}
```

15-7. Handle Exceptions in Tasks

Problem

You need to catch and process exceptions thrown by a Task.

Solution

Call the Task.Wait or Task.WaitAll methods within a try...catch block to catch the System.AggregateException exception. Call the Handle method of AggregateException with a function delegate—the delegate will receive each exception that has been thrown by the Tasks. Your function should return true if the exception can be handled, and false otherwise.

How It Works

Catching AggregateException as it is thrown from Task.Wait or Task.WaitAll allows you to be notified of exceptions that are unhandled by your Task. If an error has occurred, then you will catch a single instance of System.AggregateException representing all of the exceptions that have been thrown.

You process each individual exception by calling the AggregateException.Handle method, which accepts a function delegate (usually specified using a lambda expression)—the delegate will be called once for each exception that has been thrown by your task or tasks. Bear in mind that several threads may have encountered the same problem, and that you are likely to have to process the same exception type more than once. If you can handle the exception, your function delegate should return true—returning false will cause your application to terminate.

■ **Tip** If you do not catch exceptions from Wait or WaitAll, then any exception thrown by a Task will be considered unhandled and terminate your application.

The Code

The following example demonstrates how use the AggregateException.Handle method to implement a custom exception handler function:

```
using System;
using System.Collections.Generic;
using System.Linq;
using System.Text;
using System.Threading;
using System.Threading.Tasks;

namespace Recipe15_07
{
    class Recipe15_07
    {
        static void Main(string[] args)
        {
            // Create two tasks, one with a null param.
            Task goodTask = Task.Factory.StartNew(() => performTask("good"));
            Task badTask = Task.Factory.StartNew(() => performTask("bad"));
```

```
            try
            {
                Task.WaitAll(goodTask, badTask);
            }
            catch (AggregateException aggex)
            {
                aggex.Handle(ex => handleException(ex));
            }

            // Wait to continue.
            Console.WriteLine("\nMain method complete. Press Enter");
            Console.ReadLine();
        }

        static bool handleException(Exception exception)
        {
            Console.WriteLine("Processed Exception");
            Console.WriteLine(exception);
            // Return true to indicate we have handled the exception.
            return true;
        }

        static void performTask(string label)
        {
            if (label == "bad")
            {
                Console.WriteLine("About to throw exception.");
                throw new ArgumentOutOfRangeException("label");
            }
            else
            {
                Console.WriteLine("performTask for label: {0}", label);
            }
        }
    }
}
```

15-8. Cancel a Task

Problem

You need to cancel a Task while it is running.

Solution

Create an instance of System.Threading.CancellationTokenSource and call the Token property to obtain a System.Threading.CancellationToken. Pass a function delegate that calls the Cancel method of your Task to the Register method of CancellationToken. Cancel your Task by calling the Cancel method of CancellationTokenSource.

How It Works

The System.Threading.CancellationTokenSource class provides a mechanism to cancel one or more tasks. CancellationTokenSource is a factory for System.Threading.CancellationToken.

CancallationToken has the property IsCancellationRequested, which returns true when the Cancel method is called on the CancellationTokenSource that produced the token. You can also use the Register method to specify one or more functions to be called when the Cancel method is called. The sequence for handling cancellation is as follows:

1. Create an instance of CancellationTokenSource.
2. Create one or more Tasks to handle your work, passing CancellationToken as a constructor parameter.
3. For each Task you have created, obtain a CancellationToken by calling Token on the CancellationTokenSource created in step 1.
4. Check the IsCancellationRequested property of the token in your Task body—if the property returns true, then release any resources and throw an instance of OperationCanceledException.
5. When you are ready to cancel, call the Cancel method on the CancellationTokenSource from step 1.

Note that you must throw an instance of OperationCanceledException to acknowledge the task cancellation request.

The Code

The following example creates a CancellationToken that is used to create an instance of Task. A method to be called when the CancellationTokenSource is canceled is registered with the Register method. When CancellationTokenSource.Cancel is called, the Task is stopped and a message is written to the console.

```
using System;
using System.Threading;
using System.Threading.Tasks;

namespace Recipe15_08
{
    class Recipe15_08
    {
        static void Main(string[] args)
        {
            // Create the token source.
            CancellationTokenSource tokenSource = new CancellationTokenSource();
            // create the cancellation token
            CancellationToken token = tokenSource.Token;
```

```
            // Create the task.
            Task task = Task.Factory.StartNew(() => printNumbers(token), token);
            // register the task with the token
            token.Register(() => notifyTaskCanceled ());

            // Wait for the user to request cancellation.
            Console.WriteLine("Press enter to cancel token");
            Console.ReadLine();

            // Canceling.
            tokenSource.Cancel();
        }

        static void notifyTaskCanceled()
        {
            Console.WriteLine("Task cancellation requested");
        }

        static void printNumbers(CancellationToken token)
        {
            int i = 0;
            while (!token.IsCancellationRequested)
            {
                Console.WriteLine("Number {0}", i++);
                Thread.Sleep(500);
            }
            throw new OperationCanceledException(token);
        }
    }
}
```

15-9. Share Data Between Tasks

Problem

You need to share data safely between `Tasks`.

Solution

Use the collection classes in the `System.Collections.Concurrent` namespace.

How It Works

One of the biggest problems when writing parallel or threaded code is ensuring that data is shared safely. Microsoft has introduced new classes in .NET 4.0 that are designed to be more efficient than using synchronization around the default collection classes, which we demonstrated in Chapter 4. The techniques demonstrated in Chapter 4 will work with the .NET parallel programming model, but the new collection classes may be more efficient for large-scale applications. Table 15-1 lists the most useful classes from the `System.Collections.Concurrent` namespace.

Table 15-1. Useful System.Collections.Concurrent Classes

Class	Description
`ConcurrentBag`	A thread-safe collection of objects where no typing or ordering is assumed
`ConcurrentDictionary`	A key/value pair collection
`ConcurrentQueue`	A first in, first out (FIFO) queue
`ConcurrentStack`	A last in, first out (LIFO) stack

These new collections take care of managing data automatically—you do not have to use synchronization techniques in your code.

The Code

The following example creates a `ConcurrentStack`, which is then used by three `Tasks`.

```
using System;
using System.Collections.Generic;
using System.Linq;
using System.Text;
using System.Threading;
using System.Threading.Tasks;
using System.Collections.Concurrent;

namespace Recipe15_9
{
    class Recipe15_9
    {
        static void Main(string[] args)
        {
            // Create a concurrent collection.
            ConcurrentStack<int> cStack = new ConcurrentStack<int>();

            // create tasks that will use the stack
            Task task1 = Task.Factory.StartNew(
                () => addNumbersToCollection(cStack));
            Task task2 = Task.Factory.StartNew(
                () => addNumbersToCollection(cStack));
            Task task3 = Task.Factory.StartNew(
                () => addNumbersToCollection(cStack));
```

```
            // Wait for all of the tasks to complete.
            Task.WaitAll(task1, task2, task3);

            // Report how many items there are in the stack.
            Console.WriteLine("There are {0} items in the collection",
                cStack.Count);

            // Wait to continue.
            Console.WriteLine("\nMain method complete. Press Enter");
            Console.ReadLine();
        }

        static void addNumbersToCollection(ConcurrentStack<int> stack)
        {
            for (int i = 0; i < 1000; i++)
            {
                stack.Push(i);
            }
        }
    }
}
```

CHAPTER 16

■ ■ ■

Using LINQ

In some of the previous chapters, we illustrated how to use LINQ to perform queries on different types of data. Chapter 2 showed how to query collections and arrays, Chapter 6 to query XML trees, and Chapter 9 to query databases. This chapter shows you how to build on those simple examples to exploit the full flexibility of LINQ.

One of the best features of LINQ is that you can perform the same kinds of queries whatever the data source is. Each of the recipes in this chapter uses an array or a collection as the data source, but the same techniques can be applied equally to XML or databases. The recipes in this chapter are all self-contained and illustrate different LINQ features—but part of the allure of LINQ is that you will be able to combine these techniques to create complex and powerful queries. The recipes in this chapter describe how to perform the following tasks:

- Filter elements in a data source (recipes 16-1, 16-2, and 16-3)
- Create anonymous types in results (recipe 16-4)
- Work with multiple data sources in queries (recipes 16-6, 16-7, ad 16-8)
- Grouping, sorting, comparing, and aggregating data (recipes 16-9 through to 16-12)
- Sharing interim results across query clauses (recipe 16-13)
- Extending LINQ with custom extension methods (recipe 16-14)
- Converting LINQ results into other types (recipe 16-15)

16-1. Perform a Simple LINQ Query

Problem

You need to select all items from a collection, database, or XML document.

Solution

Use the `from` and `select` keywords.

How It Works

The most basic LINQ query selects all of the items contained in a data source. The most powerful aspect of LINQ is that you can apply the same query approach to any data source and get consistent, predictable results. Microsoft has embedded LINQ support throughout the .NET Framework so that you can use arrays, collections, XML documents and databases in the same way.

To select all of the items in a data source is a simple two-step process

1. Start a new LINQ query using the `from` keyword, providing an element variable name that you will use to refer to elements that LINQ finds (for example, `from e in datasource`).
2. Indicate what will be added to the result set from each matching element using the `select` keyword.

For the basic "select all" query used in this recipe, we simply define the element variable name in the first step and use it as the basis for the second step, as follows:

```
IEnumerable<myType> myEnum = from e in datasource select e;
```

The type that you use for the `datasource` reference must implement the `System.Collections.Generic.IEnumerable<>` interface. If you are using an array or a generic collection, then you can simply use the references to your instance as the data source because arrays and all standard generic collections implement `IEnumerable<>`, as follows:

```
IEnumerable<myType> myEnum = from e in myarray select e;
IEnumerable<myType> myEnum = from e in mycollection select e;
```

If you are using an XML tree, you can get an `IEnumerable` from the root `XElement` by calling the `Elements` method; and for a `DataTable`, you can get an `IEnumerable` by calling the `AsEnumerable` method, as follows:

```
IEnumerable<XElement> myEnum = from e in root.Elements() select e;
IEnumerable<DataRow> myEnum = from e in table.AsEnumerable() select e;
```

Notice that the generic type of the result is dependent on the data source. For an array or collection, the result will be an `IEnumerable` of the data contained in the array—`string` for `string[]` and `IList<string>`, for example. LINQ queries of `DataTables` return an `IEnumerable<DataRow>`, and queries of an XML tree return `IEnumerable<XElement>`.

If you want to select a value contained within a data source element (for example, if `myType` had a property called `Name` that returned a `string`), then you simply specify the value you want after the `select` keyword—for example:

```
IEnumerable<string> myEnum = from e in datasource select e.Name;
```

Notice that the generic type of the result has changed—we are querying a data source that contains myType instances, but selecting a string property—therefore, the result is an IEnumerable<string>.

IEnumerable<> can be used with a foreach loop to enumerate the results of a query, but because LINQ queries return instances of IEnumerable<> and LINQ data sources must implement IEnumerable<>, you can also use the result of one query as the data source for another.

The Code

The following example performs a basic LINQ query on a string array, a collection, an XML tree, and a DataTable, and prints out the results in each case:

```
using System;
using System.Collections.Generic;
using System.Linq;
using System.Text;
using System.Xml.Linq;
using System.Data;

namespace Apress.VisualCSharpRecipes.Chapter16
{
    class Recipe16_01
    {
        static void Main(string[] args)
        {
            Console.WriteLine("Using an array source");
            // Create the source.
            string[] array = createArray();
            // Perform the query.
            IEnumerable<string> arrayEnum = from e in array select e;
            // Write out the elements.
            foreach (string str in arrayEnum)
            {
                Console.WriteLine("Element {0}", str);
            }

            Console.WriteLine("\nUsing a collection source");
            // Create the source.
            ICollection<string> collection = createCollection();
            // Perform the query.
            IEnumerable<string> collEnum = from e in collection select e;
            // Write out the elements.
            foreach (string str in collEnum)
            {
                Console.WriteLine("Element {0}", str);
            }

            Console.WriteLine("\nUsing an xml source");
            // Create the source.
            XElement xmltree = createXML();
```

```
            // Perform the query.
            IEnumerable<XElement> xmlEnum = from e in xmltree.Elements() select e;
            // Write out the elements.
            foreach (string str in xmlEnum)
            {
                Console.WriteLine("Element {0}", str);
            }

            Console.WriteLine("\nUsing a data table source");
            // Create the source.
            DataTable table = createDataTable();

            // Perform the query.
            IEnumerable<string> dtEnum = from e in table.AsEnumerable()
                select e.Field<string>(0);
            // Write out the elements.
            foreach (string str in dtEnum)
            {
                Console.WriteLine("Element {0}", str);
            }

            // Wait to continue.
            Console.WriteLine("\nMain method complete. Press Enter");
            Console.ReadLine();
        }

        static string[] createArray()
        {
            return new string[] { "apple", "orange", "grape", "fig",
                "plum", "banana", "cherry" };
        }

        static IList<string> createCollection()
        {
            return new List<string>() { "apple", "orange", "grape", "fig",
                "plum", "banana", "cherry" };
        }

        static XElement createXML()
        {
            return new XElement("fruit",
                new XElement("name", "apple"),
                new XElement("name", "orange"),
                new XElement("name", "grape"),
                new XElement("name", "fig"),
                new XElement("name", "plum"),
                new XElement("name", "banana"),
                new XElement("name", "cherry")
            );
        }
```

```
        static DataTable createDataTable()
        {
            DataTable table = new DataTable();
            table.Columns.Add("name", typeof(string));
            string[] fruit = { "apple", "orange", "grape", "fig", "plum",
                "banana", "cherry" };
            foreach (string name in fruit)
            {
                table.Rows.Add(name);
            }
            return table;
        }
    }
}
```

Running the example produces the following result:

```
Using an array source

Element apple

Element orange

Element grape

Element fig

Element plum

Element banana

Element cherry



Using a collection source

Element apple

Element orange

Element grape

Element fig

Element plum

Element banana
```

```
Element cherry

Using an xml source
Element apple
Element orange
Element grape
Element fig
Element plum
Element banana
Element cherry

Using a data table source
Element apple
Element orange
Element grape
Element fig
Element plum
Element banana
Element cherry

Main method complete. Press Enter
```

16-2. Filter Items from a Data Source

Problem

You need to filter the contents of a LINQ data source to select specific items.

Solution

Use the `where` keyword.

How It Works

Using the `where` keyword in conjunction with the basic LINQ query covered in recipe 16-1 allows you to specify criteria that will be used to filter the contents of a data source. You supply an expression that will be evaluated for each element in the data source— an element will be included in the results if your expression returns `true` and excluded if your expression returns `false`. You can use the element variable declared with the `from` keyword to refer to the current element.

For example, the following fragment uses the element variable to filter only string elements whose first character is `t`:

```
string[] array = { "one", "two", "three", "four" };
IEnumerable<string> result = from e in array where e[0] == 't' select e;
```

You can make your filter expressions as complex as required and also call methods that return a `bool`. A LINQ query can have multiple filters, such that the two LINQ queries in the following fragment are equivalent:

```
string[] array = { "one", "two", "three", "four" };
IEnumerable<string> result1
    = from e in array where e[0] == 't' where e[1] == 'w' select e;
IEnumerable<string> result2
    = from e in array where e[0] == 't' && e[1] == 'w' select e;
```

The Code

The following example creates a collection of a type `Fruit` and then filters the data using the LINQ `where` operator using a string comparison and an arithmetic operator:

```
using System;
using System.Collections.Generic;
using System.Linq;
using System.Text;
using System.Data;
using System.Xml.Linq;
```

```
namespace Apress.VisualCSharpRecipes.Chapter16
{
    class Recipe16_02
    {
        static void Main(string[] args)
        {
            // Create the data.
            IList<Fruit> datasource = createData();

            // Filter based on a single characteristic.
            IEnumerable<string> result1 = from e in datasource
                                          where e.Color == "green" select e.Name;
            Console.WriteLine("Filter for green fruit");
            foreach (string str in result1)
            {
                Console.WriteLine("Fruit {0}", str);
            }

            // Filter based using > operator.
            IEnumerable<Fruit> result2 = from e in datasource
                                         where e.ShelfLife > 5 select e;
            Console.WriteLine("\nFilter for life > 5 days");
            foreach (Fruit fruit in result2)
            {
                Console.WriteLine("Fruit {0}", fruit.Name);
            }

            // Filter using two characteristics.
            IEnumerable<string> result3 = from e in datasource
                                          where e.Color == "green"
                                              && e.ShelfLife > 5
                                          select e.Name;
            Console.WriteLine("\nFilter for green fruit and life > 5 days");
            foreach (string str in result3)
            {
                Console.WriteLine("Fruit {0}", str);
            }

            // Wait to continue.
            Console.WriteLine("\nMain method complete. Press Enter");
            Console.ReadLine();
        }

        static IList<Fruit> createData()
        {
            return new List<Fruit>()
            {
                new Fruit("apple", "green", 7),
                new Fruit("orange", "orange", 10),
                new Fruit("grape", "green", 4),
                new Fruit("fig", "brown", 12),
```

```
                new Fruit("plum", "red", 2),
                new Fruit("banana", "yellow", 10),
                new Fruit("cherry", "red", 7)
            };
        }
    }
    class Fruit
    {
        public Fruit(string namearg, string colorarg, int lifearg)
        {
            Name = namearg;
            Color = colorarg;
            ShelfLife = lifearg;
        }
        public string Name { get; set;}
        public string Color { get; set;}
        public int ShelfLife { get; set;}
    }
}
```

16-3. Filter a Data Source by Type

Problem

You need to select all of the elements in a data source that are of a given type.

Solution

Use the LINQ `OfType` extension method.

How It Works

C# has keywords for many LINQ features, but they are mappings to extension methods in the `System.Linq` namespace—the keywords exist to simplify your code. See recipe 13-15 for a recipe to create and use an extension method. Keywords do not exist for all of the LINQ functions—some features are only available using extension methods directly. In order to filter a data source for all objects of a given type, you call the `OfType<>` method, specifying the type that you are looking for, as the following code fragment shows:

```
IEnumerable <string> stringData = mixedData.OfType<string>();
```

The fragment filters the data source for all string instances and will omit any other type from the results. Notice that the result of calling `OfType<>` is an `IEnumeration<>`, which can be used as the data source for a further LINQ query, as shown by the following fragment, which filters a data source for all string instances and then filters the results for strings with the first character of `c`:

```
IEnumerable<string> stringData = from e in mixedData.OfType<string>()
                                 where e[0] == 'c' select e;
```

■ **Note** You must import the `System.Linq` namespace before you can use the LINQ extension methods with the `using System.Linq` statement.

The Code

The following example creates a collection of mixed.
types and then filters the elements using the `OfType<>` extension method:

```
using System;
using System.Collections.Generic;
using System.Linq;
using System.Text;

namespace Apress.VisualCSharpRecipes.Chapter16
{
    class Recipe16_03
    {
        static void Main(string[] args)
        {
            IList<object> mixedData = createData();
            IEnumerable <string> stringData = mixedData.OfType<string>();
            foreach (string str in stringData)
            {
                Console.WriteLine(str);
            }

            // Wait to continue.
            Console.WriteLine("\nMain method complete. Press Enter");
            Console.ReadLine();
        }

        static IList<object> createData()
        {
            return new List<object>()
            {
                "this is a string",
                23,
                9.2,
                "this is another string"
            };
        }
    }
}
```

16-4. Filter Ranges of Elements

Problem

You need to apply a LINQ query to part of a data source.

Solution

Use the `Skip<>`, `Take<>`, and `Range<>` extension methods.

How It Works

The `Skip<>` extension method omits the specified number of elements, starting at the beginning of the set of elements in the data source, and includes the remaining elements. The `Take<>` extension method does the opposite—it includes the specified number of elements and omits the rest. As with all of the LINQ extension methods, you must supply a generic type annotation when calling the method—this determines the type of `IEnumeration<>` that will be returned. The `Range<>` extension method takes a start index and a count as method parameters and returns a subset of the elements in the data source.

`Skip<>`, `Take<>`, and `Range<>` all return `IEnumeration<>`, so the results from these methods can be used either to enumerate the results or as the data source for another LINQ query.

The Code

The following example creates a `string` array and uses it as the data source for `Take` and `Skip` filters:

```
using System;
using System.Collections.Generic;
using System.Linq;
using System.Text;

namespace Apress.VisualCSharpRecipes.Chapter16
{
    class Recipe16_04
    {
        static void Main(string[] args)
        {
            string[] array = { "one", "two", "three", "four", "five" };

            IEnumerable<string> skipresult
                = from e in array.Skip<string>(2) select e;
            foreach (string str in skipresult)
            {
                Console.WriteLine("Result from skip filter: {0}", str);
            }
```

```
            IEnumerable<string> takeresult
                = from e in array.Take<string>(2) select e;
            foreach (string str in takeresult)
            {
                Console.WriteLine("Result from take filter: {0}", str);
            }

            // Wait to continue.
            Console.WriteLine("\nMain method complete. Press Enter");
            Console.ReadLine();

        }
    }
}
```

Running the example program gives the following results:

```
Result from skip filter: three

Result from skip filter: four

Result from skip filter: five

Result from take filter: one

Result from take filter: two


Main method complete. Press Enter
```

16-5. Select Multiple Member Values

Problem

You need to select the values returned by more than one member of a data element.

Solution

Use the `new` keyword in your `select` statement to create an anonymous type.

How It Works

If you want to create a LINQ result that contains the values from more than one member of a data element, you can use the new keyword after the select keyword to create an anonymous type. An anonymous type doesn't have a name (hence "anonymous") and is made up of just the values that you specify.

You reference the result from the query using the special var type, as shown in the example code.

The Code

The following example creates a collection of the Fruit type and then performs a LINQ query that returns an anonymous type containing the Name and Color properties from each Fruit element:

```
using System;
using System.Collections.Generic;
using System.Linq;
using System.Text;

namespace Apress.VisualCSharpRecipes.Chapter16
{
    class Recipe16_05
    {
        static void Main(string[] args)
        {
            IList<Fruit> sourcedata = createData();
            var result = from e in sourcedata
                         select new
                         {
                             e.Name,
                             e.Color
                         };
            foreach (var element in result)
            {
                Console.WriteLine("Result: {0} {1}", element.Name, element.Color);
            }

            // Wait to continue.
            Console.WriteLine("\nMain method complete. Press Enter");
            Console.ReadLine();
        }

        static IList<Fruit> createData()
        {
            return new List<Fruit>()
            {
                new Fruit("apple", "green", 7),
                new Fruit("orange", "orange", 10),
                new Fruit("grape", "green", 4),
                new Fruit("fig", "brown", 12),
                new Fruit("plum", "red", 2),
```

```
                new Fruit("banana", "yellow", 10),
                new Fruit("cherry", "red", 7)
            };
        }
    }
    class Fruit
    {
        public Fruit(string namearg, string colorarg, int lifearg)
        {
            Name = namearg;
            Color = colorarg;
            ShelfLife = lifearg;
        }
        public string Name { get; set; }
        public string Color { get; set; }
        public int ShelfLife { get; set; }
    }
}
```

16-6. Filter and Select from Multiple Data Sources

Problem

You need to create an anonymous type that contains values from multiple data sources with common keys.

Solution

Use the `join...in...on...equals...` keyword sequence.

How It Works

If you have two data sources that share a common key, you can combine them in a LINQ query using the `join...in...on...equals...` keywords. The following fragment demonstrates how to do this:

```
from e in firstDataSource join f in secondDataSource
    on e.CommonKey equals f.CommonKey
```

LINQ will arrange the data so that your filter and `select` statements are called once per common key. You can refer to the individual elements using the variable names you have defined—in the fragment, we have used `e` and `f`. You can join as many data sources as you wish in a LINQ query, as long as they share a common key.

The Code

The following example creates two data sources that share a common key, and uses the `join` keyword to combine them in a LINQ query in order to create an anonymous result type that contains elements from both data sources:

```
using System;
using System.Collections.Generic;
using System.Linq;
using System.Text;

namespace Apress.VisualCSharpRecipes.Chapter16
{
    class Recipe16_6
    {
        static void Main(string[] args)
        {
            // Create the data sources.
            IList<FruitColor> colorsource = createColorData();
            IList<FruitShelfLife> shelflifesource = createShelfLifeData();

            // Perform the LINQ query with a join.
            var result = from e in colorsource
                         join f in shelflifesource on e.Name equals f.Name
                         where e.Color == "green"
                         select new
                         {
                             e.Name,
                             e.Color,
                             f.Life
                         };

            // Write out the results.
            foreach (var element in result)
            {
                Console.WriteLine("Name: {0}, Color: {1}, Shelf Life: {2} days",
                    element.Name, element.Color, element.Life);
            }

            // Wait to continue.
            Console.WriteLine("\nMain method complete. Press Enter");
            Console.ReadLine();
        }

        static IList<FruitColor> createColorData()
        {
            return new List<FruitColor>()
            {
                new FruitColor("apple", "green"),
                new FruitColor("orange", "orange"),
                new FruitColor("grape", "green"),
```

```
                new FruitColor("fig", "brown"),
                new FruitColor("plum", "red"),
                new FruitColor("banana", "yellow"),
                new FruitColor("cherry", "red")
            };
        }

        static IList<FruitShelfLife> createShelfLifeData()
        {
            return new List<FruitShelfLife>()
            {
                new FruitShelfLife("apple", 7),
                new FruitShelfLife("orange", 10),
                new FruitShelfLife("grape", 4),
                new FruitShelfLife("fig", 12),
                new FruitShelfLife("plum", 2),
                new FruitShelfLife("banana", 10),
                new FruitShelfLife("cherry",  7)
            };
        }
    }

    class FruitColor
    {
        public FruitColor(string namearg, string colorarg)
        {
            Name = namearg;
            Color = colorarg;
        }
        public string Name { get; set; }
        public string Color { get; set; }
    }

    class FruitShelfLife
    {
        public FruitShelfLife(string namearg, int lifearg)
        {
            Name = namearg;
            Life = lifearg;
        }
        public string Name { get; set; }
        public int Life{ get; set; }
    }
}
```

Running the example gives the following results:

```
Name: apple Color green Shelf Life: 7 days

Name: grape Color green Shelf Life: 4 days


Main method complete. Press Enter
```

16-7. Use Permutations of Data Sources

Problem

You need to enumerate all permutations of two or more data sources.

Solution

Include more than one `from` statement in your LINQ query.

How It Works

You can enumerate through the permutations of multiple data sources by using more than one `from` keyword in your LINQ query. The query will be applied to every permutation of every element in each data source. The following fragment illustrates a query that uses `from` twice:

```
string[] datasource1 = { "apple", "orange",};
int[]    datasource2 = { 21, 42 };

var result = from e in datasource1
   from f in datasource2
   select new
   {
      e,
      f
   };
```

The `select` part of the query (and any filters that we might have applied) will be called for every combination of element from the two data sources—`apple` and `21`, `apple` and `42`, `orange` and `21`, and `orange` and `42`.

The Code

The following example creates two arrays and uses them as data sources for a LINQ query with multiple from keywords. The result is an anonymous type containing the elements from both sources, and each element in the result is printed to the console.

```
using System;
using System.Collections.Generic;
using System.Linq;
using System.Text;

namespace Apress.VisualCSharpRecipes.Chapter16
{
    class Recipe16_7
    {
        static void Main(string[] args)
        {
            // Create the data sources.
            string[] datasource1 = { "apple", "orange", "cherry", "pear" };
            int[]    datasource2 = { 21, 42, 37 };

            // Perform the LINQ query.
            var result = from e in datasource1
                         from f in datasource2
                         select new
                         {
                             e,
                             f
                         };

            // Print the results.
            foreach (var element in result)
            {
                Console.WriteLine("{0}, {1}", element.e, element.f);
            }

            // Wait to continue.
            Console.WriteLine("\nMain method complete. Press Enter");
            Console.ReadLine();
        }
    }
}
```

Running the program produces the following results:

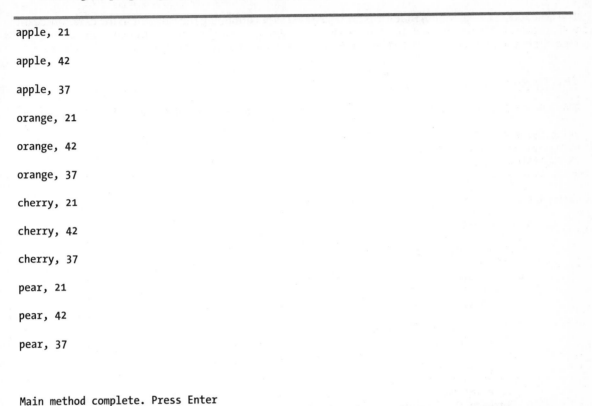

```
apple, 21
apple, 42
apple, 37
orange, 21
orange, 42
orange, 37
cherry, 21
cherry, 42
cherry, 37
pear, 21
pear, 42
pear, 37

Main method complete. Press Enter
```

16-8. Concatenate Data Sources

Problem

You need to combine one or more data sources.

Solution

Use the `Concat<>` extension method to combine multiple sources into a sequence that LINQ will process as a single data source.

How It Works

The **Concat<>** extension method returns an **IEnumeration<>** containing the element in the data source on which you call the method and the elements in the data source you pass as a method parameter. The type annotation you pass to the **Concat<>** method must match the element types in the data sources.

The Code

The following example concatenates two arrays of strings to form a single data source for a LINQ query:

```
using System;
using System.Collections.Generic;
using System.Linq;
using System.Text;

namespace Apress.VisualCSharpRecipes.Chapter16
{
    class Recipe16_08
    {
        static void Main(string[] args)
        {
            // Create the data sources.
            string[] datasource1 = { "apple", "orange", "cherry", "pear" };
            string[] datasource2 = { "banana", "kiwi", "fig" };

            // Perform the LINQ query.
            IEnumerable<string> result
                = from e in datasource1.Concat<string>(datasource2)
                select e;

            // Print the results.
            foreach (string element in result)
            {
                Console.WriteLine(element);
            }

            // Wait to continue.
            Console.WriteLine("\nMain method complete. Press Enter");
            Console.ReadLine();
        }
    }
}
```

Running the example produces the following result:

```
apple

orange

cherry

pear

banana

kiwi

fig


Main method complete. Press Enter
```

16-9. Group Result Elements by Attribute

Problem

You need to order the result of a LINQ query so that elements that share a common attribute are grouped together.

Solution

Use the `group...by...` keywords.

How It Works

The `group...by...` keywords allow you to create a result where elements that share a member value are grouped together. Using `group...by...` in a query results in a fragment such as this:

```
IEnumerable<IGrouping<T1, T2>> result
    = from e in datasource group e.FirstMember by e.SecondMember;
```

The result from this query in an instance of `System.Linq.IGrouping<T1, T2>`, where `T1` is the type of `e.SecondMember` and `T2` is the type of `e.FirstMember`. All of the elements in the data source that have the same value of `e.SecondMember` will appear in the same `IGrouping<>`, and there will be an instance of `IGrouping<>` contained in the `IEnumeration<>` for each distinct value of `e.SecondMember` that LINQ finds in the data source. The easiest way to understand these keywords is to review and run the example program that follows.

You can get the value that the elements contained in an `IGrouping<>` share by calling the `Key` property. `IGrouping<>` extends `IEnumerable<>`, so you can enumerate the values of a group using a `foreach` loop or use an `IGrouping<>` as the data source for a LINQ query.

You can access each individual group as it is created by LINQ using the `order...by...into...` keywords. The addition of `into` allows you to define a variable that will contain the `IGrouping<>` instance—see the example program for this recipe to see an example of using `into` to create an anonymous type.

The Code

The following example uses a collection of the type `Fruit` as the data source for two LINQ queries. The first uses a standard `group...by...` format to create an `IEnumerable<IGrouping<string, Fruit>>` result, which is then enumerated by group and the elements in each group. The second query uses `group...by...into...` in order to create an anonymous type containing the `Key` value of the group and the set of matching `Fruit` instances, which are then printed out.

```
using System;
using System.Collections.Generic;
using System.Linq;
using System.Text;

namespace Apress.VisualCSharpRecipes.Chapter16
{
    class Recipe16_09
    {
        static void Main(string[] args)
        {
            // Create the data source.
            IList<Fruit> datasource = createData();

            Console.WriteLine("Perfoming group...by... query");
            // Perform a query with a basic grouping.
            IEnumerable<IGrouping<string, Fruit>> result =
                from e in datasource group e by e.Color;

            foreach (IGrouping<string, Fruit> group in result)
            {
                Console.WriteLine("\nStart of group for {0}", group.Key);
                foreach (Fruit fruit in group)
                {
                    Console.WriteLine("Name: {0} Color: {1} Shelf Life: {2} days.",
                        fruit.Name, fruit.Color, fruit.ShelfLife);
                }
            }
```

```
            Console.WriteLine("\n\nPerfoming group...by...into query");
            // Use the group...by...into... keywords.
            var result2 = from e in datasource
                          group e by e.Color into g
                          select new
                          {
                             Color = g.Key,
                             Fruits = g
                          };

            foreach (var element in result2)
            {
                Console.WriteLine("\nElement for color {0}", element.Color);
                foreach (var fruit in element.Fruits)
                {
                    Console.WriteLine("Name: {0} Color: {1} Shelf Life: {2} days.",
                        fruit.Name, fruit.Color, fruit.ShelfLife);
                }
            }

            // Wait to continue.
            Console.WriteLine("\nMain method complete. Press Enter");
            Console.ReadLine();
        }

        static IList<Fruit> createData()
        {
            return new List<Fruit>()
            {
                new Fruit("apple", "green", 7),
                new Fruit("orange", "orange", 10),
                new Fruit("grape", "green", 4),
                new Fruit("fig", "brown", 12),
                new Fruit("plum", "red", 2),
                new Fruit("banana", "yellow", 10),
                new Fruit("cherry", "red", 7)
            };
        }
    }
    class Fruit
    {
        public Fruit(string namearg, string colorarg, int lifearg)
        {
            Name = namearg;
            Color = colorarg;
            ShelfLife = lifearg;
        }
```

```
        public string Name { get; set; }
        public string Color { get; set; }
        public int ShelfLife { get; set; }
    }
}
```

Running the example program produces the following results:

```
Perfoming order...by... query



Start of group for green

Name: apple Color: green Shelf Life: 7 days.

Name: grape Color: green Shelf Life: 4 days.



Start of group for orange

Name: orange Color: orange Shelf Life: 10 days.



Start of group for brown

Name: fig Color: brown Shelf Life: 12 days.



Start of group for red

Name: plum Color: red Shelf Life: 2 days.

Name: cherry Color: red Shelf Life: 7 days.
```

```
Start of group for yellow
Name: banana Color: yellow Shelf Life: 10 days.

Perfoming order...by...into query

Element for color green
Name: apple Color: green Shelf Life: 7 days.
Name: grape Color: green Shelf Life: 4 days.

Element for color orange
Name: orange Color: orange Shelf Life: 10 days.

Element for color brown
Name: fig Color: brown Shelf Life: 12 days.

Element for color red
Name: plum Color: red Shelf Life: 2 days.
Name: cherry Color: red Shelf Life: 7 days.

Element for color yellow
Name: banana Color: yellow Shelf Life: 10 days.

Main method complete. Press Enter
```

16-10. Sort Query Results

Problem

You need to sort the results of a LINQ query.

Solution

Use the orderby keyword.

How It Works

The orderby keyword sorts the result elements of a LINQ query by the member you specify. You can sort on several members by using the orderby keyword more than once—see the example code for this recipe for an illustration. By default, LINQ will sort the elements in ascending order (the smallest value will come first in the results)—you can use the descending keyword after the member you want to use for sorting to get the reverse effect.

The Code

The following example creates a collection containing the Fruit type and uses it as the basis for a LINQ query that orders the results by the Color property in descending order and then the Name property in ascending order.

```
using System;
using System.Collections.Generic;
using System.Linq;
using System.Text;

namespace Apress.VisualCSharpRecipes.Chapter16
{
    class Recipe16_10
    {
        static void Main(string[] args)
        {
            // Create the data source.
            IList<Fruit> datasource = createData();

            IEnumerable<Fruit> result = from e in datasource
                                        orderby e.Name
                                        orderby e.Color descending
                                        select e;

            foreach (Fruit fruit in result)
            {
```

```
                Console.WriteLine("Name: {0} Color: {1} Shelf Life: {2} days.",
                    fruit.Name, fruit.Color, fruit.ShelfLife);
            }

            // Wait to continue.
            Console.WriteLine("\nMain method complete. Press Enter");
            Console.ReadLine();
        }

        static IList<Fruit> createData()
        {
            return new List<Fruit>()
            {
                new Fruit("apple", "red", 7),
                new Fruit("apple", "green", 7),
                new Fruit("orange", "orange", 10),
                new Fruit("grape", "green", 4),
                new Fruit("fig", "brown", 12),
                new Fruit("plum", "red", 2),
                new Fruit("banana", "yellow", 10),
                new Fruit("cherry", "red", 7)
            };
        }
    }
    class Fruit
    {
        public Fruit(string namearg, string colorarg, int lifearg)
        {
            Name = namearg;
            Color = colorarg;
            ShelfLife = lifearg;
        }
        public string Name { get; set; }
        public string Color { get; set; }
        public int ShelfLife { get; set; }
    }
}
```

Running the program gives the following results:

```
Name: apple Color: red Shelf Life: 7 days.

Name: apple Color: green Shelf Life: 7 days.

Name: banana Color: yellow Shelf Life: 10 days.

Name: cherry Color: red Shelf Life: 7 days.

Name: fig Color: brown Shelf Life: 12 days.
```

```
Name: grape Color: green Shelf Life: 4 days.

Name: orange Color: orange Shelf Life: 10 days.

Name: plum Color: red Shelf Life: 2 days.


Main method complete. Press Enter
```

16-11. Compare Data Sources

Problem

You need to determine whether two data sources contain the same elements.

The Solution

Use the `SequenceEquals<>` extension method.

How It Works

The `SequenceEquals<>` extension method compares two data sources and returns `true` if both data sources contain the same number of elements and the individual elements in each position in each data source are the same. You can specify your own code to assess element equality by implementing the `System.Collections.Generic.IEqualityComparer<>` interface and supplying an instance of the implementation as an argument to `SequenceEquals<>`.

The Code

The following example creates four data sources. The first contains a list of names of fruit. The second contains the same names in the same order. The third contains the same names in a different order, and the last contains different names, but with the same first letters as the names in the first list. Comparisons are then performed using the default `IEqualityComparer` and a custom `IEqualityComparer` that treats strings with the same first character as being equal.

```
using System;
using System.Collections.Generic;
using System.Linq;
using System.Text;
```

```
namespace Apress.VisualCSharpRecipes.Chapter16
{
    class Recipe16_11
    {
        static void Main(string[] args)
        {
            // Create the first data source.
            string[] ds1 = { "apple", "cherry", "pear" };
            // Create a data source with the same elements
            // in the same order.
            string[] ds2 = { "apple", "cherry", "pear" };
            // Create a data source with the
            // same elements in a different order.
            string[] ds3 = { "pear", "cherry", "apple" };
            // Create a data source with different elements.
            string[] ds4 = { "apricot", "cranberry", "plum" };

            // Perform the comparisons.
            Console.WriteLine("Using standard comparer");
            Console.WriteLine("DS1 == DS2? {0}", ds1.SequenceEqual(ds2));
            Console.WriteLine("DS1 == DS3? {0}", ds1.SequenceEqual(ds3));
            Console.WriteLine("DS1 == DS4? {0}", ds1.SequenceEqual(ds4));

            // Create the custom comparer.
            MyComparer comparer = new MyComparer();

            Console.WriteLine("\nUsing custom comparer");
            Console.WriteLine("DS1 == DS2? {0}", ds1.SequenceEqual(ds2, comparer));
            Console.WriteLine("DS1 == DS3? {0}", ds1.SequenceEqual(ds3, comparer));
            Console.WriteLine("DS1 == DS4? {0}", ds1.SequenceEqual(ds4, comparer));

            // Wait to continue.
            Console.WriteLine("\nMain method complete. Press Enter");
            Console.ReadLine();
        }
    }
    class MyComparer : IEqualityComparer<string>
    {
        public bool Equals(string first, string second)
        {
            return first[0] == second[0];
        }

        public int GetHashCode(string str)
        {
            return str[0].GetHashCode();
        }
    }
}
```

Running the program gives the following results:

```
Using standard comparer

DS1 == DS2? True

DS1 == DS3? False

DS1 == DS4? False


Using custom comparer

DS1 == DS2? True

DS1 == DS3? False

DS1 == DS4? True


Main method complete. Press Enter
```

16-12. Aggregate Data Sources

Problem

You need to aggregate the values in a data source.

Solution

Use the `Average<>`, `Count<>`, `Max<>`, `Min<>`, or `Sum<>` extension methods for standard aggregations, or the `Aggregate<>` extension method to perform a custom aggregation.

How It Works

The standard aggregation extension methods process the elements in a data source to perform useful calculations. `Average<>` calculates the mean value, `Count<>` returns the number of elements in the data source, `Min<>` and `Max<>` return the smallest and largest elements, and `Sum<>` totals the elements.

You can perform custom aggregation operations using the `Aggregate<>` method. The example code demonstrates two custom aggregation operations. The expression receives two arguments—the first is the aggregate value so far and the second is the current element to process. The parameters and return value are of the same type as the data source type—that is, if you are aggregating an `IEnumeration<string>`, you will receive two `strings` as arguments and must return a `string` as your aggregate result.

The Code

The following example creates a data source of integers and calls each of the standard aggregation methods. The same data source is used to demonstrate a custom aggregation method that totals the individual elements (equivalent to the `Sum<>` method). Finally, a `string` array is used as a data source for a custom aggregation that concatenates the individual elements.

```
using System;
using System.Collections.Generic;
using System.Linq;
using System.Text;

namespace Apress.VisualCSharpRecipes.Chapter16
{
    class Recipe16_12
    {
        static void Main(string[] args)
        {
            // Define a numeric data source.
            int[] ds1 = { 1, 23, 37, 49, 143 };

            // Use the standard aggregation methods.
            Console.WriteLine("Standard aggregation methods");
            Console.WriteLine("Average: {0}", ds1.Average());
            Console.WriteLine("Count: {0}", ds1.Count());
            Console.WriteLine("Max: {0}", ds1.Max());
            Console.WriteLine("Min: {0}", ds1.Min());
            Console.WriteLine("Sum: {0}", ds1.Sum());

            // Perform our own sum aggregation.
            Console.WriteLine("\nCustom aggregation");
            Console.WriteLine(ds1.Aggregate((total, elem) => total += elem));

            // Define a string data source.
            string[] ds2 = { "apple", "pear", "cherry" };

            // Perform a concat aggregation.
            Console.WriteLine("\nString concatenation aggregation");
            Console.WriteLine(ds2.Aggregate((len, elem) => len += elem));
```

```
            // Wait to continue.
            Console.WriteLine("\nMain method complete. Press Enter");
            Console.ReadLine();
        }
    }
}
```

The program gives the following results:

```
Standard aggregation methods

Average: 50.6

Count: 5

Max: 143

Min: 1

Sum: 253


Custom aggregation

253


String concatenation aggregation

applepearcherry


Main method complete. Press Enter
```

16-13. Share Values Within a Query

Problem

You need to perform an operation on an element or a data source only once in a query.

Solution

Use the let keywords.

How It Works

If you need to perform the same operation in different parts of your query, you can store the result of an expression and use it several times. The example for this recipe demonstrates using the Sum aggregate method and using the result in both the where and select clauses of the query. Without the use of the let keyword, we would have to perform the aggregation in each clause. You can use let multiple times in a query.

The Code

The following example demonstrates how to use the let keyword to obtain the sum of the elements in a data source consisting of integers and use the result in the where and select sections of the same LINQ query.

```
using System;
using System.Collections.Generic;
using System.Linq;
using System.Text;

namespace Apress.VisualCSharpRecipes.Chapter16
{
    class Recipe16_13
    {
        static void Main(string[] args)
        {
            // Define a numeric data source.
            int[] ds1 = { 1, 23, 37, 49, 143 };

            // Perform a query that shares a calculated value.
            IEnumerable<double> result1 = from e in ds1
                                          let avg = ds1.Average()
                                          where (e < avg)
                                          select (e + avg);

            Console.WriteLine("Query using shared value");
            foreach (double element in result1)
            {
                Console.WriteLine("Result element {0}", element);
            }
```

```
            // Wait to continue.
            Console.WriteLine("\nMain method complete. Press Enter");
            Console.ReadLine();
        }
    }
}
```

Running the program gives the following results:

```
Query using shared value

Result element 51.6

Result element 73.6

Result element 87.6

Result element 99.6


Main method complete. Press Enter
```

16-14. Create Custom LINQ Extension Methods

Problem

You need to create a custom extension method that you can apply to LINQ data sources.

Solution

Create an extension method that works on instances of `IEnumerable<>`.

How It Works

Recipe 13-15 demonstrates how to create and use an extension method. The process for a LINQ extension method is the same, except that you specify the type to operate on as `IEnumerable<>`. All LINQ data sources implement `IEnumerable<>` or have a member that returns `IEnumerable<>`, so once you have defined your extension method, you will be able to apply it to any data source that contains elements of the type you have specified.

The Code

The following example demonstrates creating a customer LINQ extension method that removes the first and last element from string data sources:

```
using System;
using System.Collections.Generic;
using System.Linq;
using System.Text;

namespace Apress.VisualCSharpRecipes.Chapter16
{
    static class LINQExtensions
    {
        public static IEnumerable<string> RemoveFirstAndLast(
            this IEnumerable<string> source)
        {
            return source.Skip(1).Take(source.Count() - 2);
        }
    }

    class Recipe16_14
    {
        static void Main(string[] args)
        {
            // Create the data sources.
            string[] ds1 = {"apple", "banana", "pear", "fig"};
            IList<string> ds2 = new List<string>
                { "apple", "banana", "pear", "fig" };

            Console.WriteLine("Extension method used on string[]");
            IEnumerable<string> result1 = ds1.RemoveFirstAndLast();
            foreach (string element in result1)
            {
                Console.WriteLine("Result: {0}", element);
            }

            Console.WriteLine("\nExtension method used on IList<string>");
            IEnumerable<string> result2 = ds1.RemoveFirstAndLast();
            foreach (string element in result2)
            {
                Console.WriteLine("Result: {0}", element);
            }

            // Wait to continue.
            Console.WriteLine("\nMain method complete. Press Enter");
            Console.ReadLine();
        }
    }
}
```

Running the sample program gives the same result for the differing data sources:

```
Extension method used on string[]
Result: banana
Result: pear

Extension method used on IList<string>
Result: banana
Result: pear

Main method complete. Press Enter
```

16-15. Convert from IEnumerable<>

Problem

You want to use the results of a LINQ query in a form other than an enumeration.

Solution

Use one of the LINQ convenience extension methods to convert your result.

How It Works

It is not always convenient to have the results of a query as an `IEnumerable`. LINQ provides a series of extension methods that you can use to convert a query result into different types.

The Code

The following example creates a data source containing instances of the type `Fruit`, performs a LINQ query to select those with a short shelf life, and then converts the result to an array, a `Dictionary`, a `List`, and a `Lookup`, printing out the contents of each:

```
using System;
using System.Collections.Generic;
using System.Linq;
using System.Text;

namespace Apress.VisualCSharpRecipes.Chapter16
{
    class Recipe16_15
    {
        static void Main(string[] args)
        {
            // Create the data sources.
            IEnumerable<Fruit> datasource = createData();

            // Perform a query.
            IEnumerable<Fruit> result = from e in datasource
                                        where e.ShelfLife <= 7
                                        select e;

            // Enumerate the result elements.
            Console.WriteLine("Results from enumeration");
            foreach (Fruit fruit in result)
            {
                Console.WriteLine("Name: {0} Color: {1} Shelf Life: {2} days.",
                    fruit.Name, fruit.Color, fruit.ShelfLife);
            }

            // Convert the IEnumerable to an array.
            Fruit[] array = result.ToArray<Fruit>();
            // print out the contents of the array
            Console.WriteLine("\nResults from array");
            for (int i = 0; i < array.Length; i++)
            {
                Console.WriteLine("Name: {0} Color: {1} Shelf Life: {2} days.",
                                  array[i].Name,
                                  array[i].Color, array[i].ShelfLife);
            }

            // Convert the IEnumerable to a dictionary indexed by name.
            Dictionary<string, Fruit> dictionary = result.ToDictionary(e => e.Name);
            // print out the contents of the dictionary
            Console.WriteLine("\nResults from dictionary");
            foreach (KeyValuePair<string, Fruit> kvp in dictionary)
            {
                Console.WriteLine("Name: {0} Color: {1} Shelf Life: {2} days.",
                    kvp.Key, kvp.Value.Color, kvp.Value.ShelfLife);
            }
```

```
            // Convert the IEnumerable to a list.
            IList<Fruit> list = result.ToList<Fruit>();
            // print out the contents of the list
            Console.WriteLine("\nResults from list");
            foreach (Fruit fruit in list)
            {
                Console.WriteLine("Name: {0} Color: {1} Shelf Life: {2} days.",
                    fruit.Name, fruit.Color, fruit.ShelfLife);
            }

            // Convert the IEnumerable to a lookup, indexed by color.
            ILookup<string, Fruit> lookup = result.ToLookup(e => e.Color);
            // Print out the contents of the list.
            Console.WriteLine("\nResults from lookup");
            IEnumerator<IGrouping<string, Fruit>> groups = lookup.GetEnumerator();
            while (groups.MoveNext())
            {
                IGrouping<string, Fruit> group = groups.Current;
                Console.WriteLine("Group for {0}", group.Key);
                foreach (Fruit fruit in group)
                {
                    Console.WriteLine("Name: {0} Color: {1} Shelf Life: {2} days.",
                        fruit.Name, fruit.Color, fruit.ShelfLife);
                }
            }

            // Wait to continue.
            Console.WriteLine("\nMain method complete. Press Enter");
            Console.ReadLine();
        }

        static IList<Fruit> createData()
        {
            return new List<Fruit>()
            {
                new Fruit("apple", "red", 7),
                new Fruit("orange", "orange", 10),
                new Fruit("grape", "green", 4),
                new Fruit("fig", "brown", 12),
                new Fruit("plum", "red", 2),
                new Fruit("banana", "yellow", 10),
                new Fruit("cherry", "red", 7)
            };
        }
    }
    class Fruit
    {
```

```
        public Fruit(string namearg, string colorarg, int lifearg)
        {
            Name = namearg;
            Color = colorarg;
            ShelfLife = lifearg;
        }
        public string Name { get; set; }
        public string Color { get; set; }
        public int ShelfLife { get; set; }
    }
}
```

Running the program gives the following results:

```
Results from enumeration

Name: apple Color: red Shelf Life: 7 days.

Name: grape Color: green Shelf Life: 4 days.

Name: plum Color: red Shelf Life: 2 days.

Name: cherry Color: red Shelf Life: 7 days.


Results from array

Name: apple Color: red Shelf Life: 7 days.

Name: grape Color: green Shelf Life: 4 days.

Name: plum Color: red Shelf Life: 2 days.

Name: cherry Color: red Shelf Life: 7 days.


Results from dictionary

Name: apple Color: red Shelf Life: 7 days.

Name: grape Color: green Shelf Life: 4 days.

Name: plum Color: red Shelf Life: 2 days.

Name: cherry Color: red Shelf Life: 7 days.
```

```
Results from list
Name: apple Color: red Shelf Life: 7 days.
Name: grape Color: green Shelf Life: 4 days.
Name: plum Color: red Shelf Life: 2 days.
Name: cherry Color: red Shelf Life: 7 days.

Results from lookup
Group for red
Name: apple Color: red Shelf Life: 7 days.
Name: plum Color: red Shelf Life: 2 days.
Name: cherry Color: red Shelf Life: 7 days.
Group for green
Name: grape Color: green Shelf Life: 4 days.

Main method complete. Press Enter
```

CHAPTER 17

■ ■ ■

Windows Presentation Foundation

Windows Presentation Foundation (WPF), introduced in the .NET Framework 3.0, provides an alternative to Windows Forms (see Chapter 7) for the development of highly functional rich client applications. The WPF development model is radically different than that of Windows Forms and can be difficult to adjust to—especially for experienced Windows Forms developers. However, WPF is incredibly flexible and powerful, and taking the time to learn it can be lots of fun and immensely rewarding. WPF enables the average developer to create user interfaces that incorporate techniques previously accessible only to highly specialized graphics developers and take a fraction of the time to develop that they would have once taken.

The capabilities offered by WPF are immense, so it is not possible to provide full coverage here. A far more extensive set of recipes about WPF is provided in *WPF Recipes in C# 2010* (Apress, 2010), of which the recipes in the chapter are a much simplified subset. Thanks to Sam Bourton and Sam Noble for the original work on some of the recipes in this chapter. The recipes in this chapter describe how to do the following:

- Create and use a dependency and attached properties (recipes 17-1 and 17-2)
- Define and use application-wide resources (recipe 17-3)
- Debug data bindings (recipes 17-4 and 17-5)
- Control the position of UI elements using layout containers (recipes 17-6 through 17-9)
- Get rich text input from the user (recipe 17-10)
- Display a control rotated (recipe 17-11)
- Create and configure user controls (recipes 17-12 through 17-14)
- Create two-way and command bindings (recipes 17-15 and 17-16)
- Use data templates to display bound data (recipe 17-17)
- Bind controls to a master-detail collection (recipe 17-18)
- Change a control's appearance when the mouse goes over it (recipe 17-19)

- Make alternate items in a list look different (recipe 17-20)
- Allow the user to drag items from a list and position them on a canvas (recipe 17-21)
- Show progress and allow cancellation of a long-running process (recipe 17-22)
- Draw and reuse two-dimensional shapes (recipes 17-23 and 17-24)
- Fill shapes with colors, gradients, images, and textures (recipes 17-25 through 17-28)
- Animate the properties of a control (recipes 17-29 through 17-32)
- Play a media file (recipe 17-33)
- Query the state of the keyboard (recipe 17-34)

17-1. Create and Use a Dependency Property

Problem

You need to add a property to a class that derives from `System.Windows.DependencyObject` to provide support for any or all of the following:

- Data bindings
- Animation
- Setting with a dynamic resource reference
- Automatically inheriting a property value from a superclass
- Setting in a style
- Using property value inheritance
- Notification through callbacks on property value changes

Solution

Register a `System.Windows.DependencyProperty` to use as the backing store for the required property on your class.

How It Works

A dependency property is implemented using a standard Common Language Runtime (CLR) property, but instead of using a private field to back the property, you use a `DependencyProperty`. A `DependencyProperty` is instantiated using the static method `DependencyProperty.Register(string name, System.Type propertyType, Type ownerType)`, which returns a `DependencyProperty` instance that is stored using a static, read-only field. There are also two overrides that allow you to specify metadata that defines behavior and a callback for validation.

The first argument passed to the `DependencyProperty.Register` method specifies the name of the dependency property being registered. This name must be unique within registrations that occur in the owner type's namespace. The next two arguments give the type of property being registered and the class against which the dependency property is being defined. It is important to note that the owning type must derive from `DependencyObject`; otherwise, an exception is raised when you initialize the dependency property.

The first override for the `Register` method allows a `System.Windows.PropertyMetadata` object, or one of the several derived types, to be specified for the property. Property metadata is used to define characteristics of a dependency property, allowing for greater richness than simply using reflection or common CLR characteristics. The use of property metadata can be broken down into three areas:

- Specifying a default value for the property
- Providing callback implementations for property changes and value coercion
- Reporting framework-level characteristics used in layout, inheritance, and so on

---

■ **Caution** Because values for dependency properties can be set in several places, a set of rules define the precedence of these values and any default value specified in property metadata. These rules are beyond the scope of this recipe; for more information, you can look at the subject of dependency property value precedence at `http://msdn.microsoft.com/en-us/library/ms743230(VS.100).aspx`.

In addition to specifying a default value, property-changed callbacks, and coercion callbacks, the `System.Windows.FrameworkPropertyMetadata` object allows you to specify various options given by the `System.Windows.FrameworkPropertyMetadataOptions` enumeration. You can use as many of these options as required, combining them as flags. Table 17-1 details the values defined in the `FrameworkPropertyMetadataOptions` enumeration.

Table 17-1. Values for the FrameworkPropertyMetadataOptions Class

Property	Description
`None`	The property will adopt the default behavior of the WPF property system.
`AffectsMeasure`	Changes to the dependency property's value affect the owning control's measure.
`AffectsArrange`	Changes to the dependency property's value affect the owning control's arrangement.
`AffectsParentMeasure`	Changes to the dependency property's value affect the parent of the owning control's measure.
`AffectsParentArrange`	Changes to the dependency property's value affect the parent of the owning control's arrangement.
`AffectsRender`	Changes to the dependency property's value affect the owning control's render or layout composition.
`Inherits`	The value of the dependency property is inherited by any child elements of the owning type.
`OverridesInheritanceBehavior`	The value of the dependency property spans disconnected trees in the context of property value inheritance.
`NotDataBindable`	Binding operations cannot be performed on this dependency property.
`BindsTwoWayByDefault`	When used in data bindings, the `System.Windows.BindingMode` is `TwoWay` by default.
`Journal`	The value of the dependency property is saved or restored through any journaling processes or URI navigations.
`SubPropertiesDoNotAffectRender`	Properties of the value of the dependency property do not affect the owning type's rendering in any way.

■ **Caution** When implementing a dependency property, it is important to use the correct naming convention. The identifier used for the dependency property must be the same as the identifier used to name the CLR property it is registered against, appended with `Property`. For example, if you were defining a property to store the velocity of an object, the CLR property would be named `Velocity`, and the dependency property field would be named `VelocityProperty`. If a dependency property isn't implemented in this fashion, you may experience strange behavior with property system–style applications and some visual designers not correctly reporting the property's value.

Value coercion plays an important role in dependency properties and comes into play when the value of a dependency property is set. By supplying a `CoerceValueCallback` argument, it is possible to alter the value to which the property is being set. An example of value coercion is when setting the value of the `System.Windows.Window.RenderTransform` property. It is not valid to set the `RenderTransform` property of a window to anything other than an identity matrix. If any other value is used, an exception is thrown. It should be noted that any coercion callback methods are invoked before any `System.Windows.ValidateValueCallback` methods.

The Code

The following example demonstrates the definition of a custom `DependencyProperty` on a simple `System.Windows.Controls.UserControl` (`MyControl`, defined in `MyControl.xaml`). The `UserControl` contains two text blocks: one set by the control's code-behind, and the other bound to a dependency property defined in the control's code-behind.

```
<UserControl
    x:Class="Apress.VisualCSharpRecipes.Chapter17.MyControl"
    xmlns="http://schemas.microsoft.com/winfx/2006/xaml/presentation"
    xmlns:x="http://schemas.microsoft.com/winfx/2006/xaml">
    <Grid>
        <Grid.RowDefinitions>
            <RowDefinition Height="20" />
            <RowDefinition Height="*" />
        </Grid.RowDefinitions>

        <TextBlock x:Name="txblFontWeight" Text="FontWeight set to: Normal."  />

        <Viewbox Grid.Row="1">
            <TextBlock Text="{Binding Path=TextContent}"
                FontWeight="{Binding Path=TextFontWeight}" />
        </Viewbox>
    </Grid>
</UserControl>
```

The following code block details the code-behind for the previous markup (`MyControl.xaml.cs`):

```
using System.Windows;
using System.Windows.Controls;

namespace Apress.VisualCSharpRecipes.Chapter17
{
    public partial class MyControl : UserControl
    {
        public MyControl()
        {
            InitializeComponent();
            DataContext = this;
        }

        public FontWeight TextFontWeight
        {
            get { return (FontWeight)GetValue(TextFontWeightProperty); }
            set { SetValue(TextFontWeightProperty, value); }
        }

        public static readonly DependencyProperty TextFontWeightProperty =
            DependencyProperty.Register(
                "TextFontWeight",
                typeof(FontWeight),
                typeof(MyControl),
                new FrameworkPropertyMetadata(FontWeights.Normal,
                             FrameworkPropertyMetadataOptions.AffectsArrange
                             & FrameworkPropertyMetadataOptions.AffectsMeasure
                             & FrameworkPropertyMetadataOptions.AffectsRender,
                             TextFontWeight_PropertyChanged,
                             TextFontWeight_CoerceValue));

        public string TextContent
        {
            get { return (string)GetValue(TextContentProperty); }
            set { SetValue(TextContentProperty, value); }
        }

        public static readonly DependencyProperty TextContentProperty =
            DependencyProperty.Register(
                "TextContent",
                typeof(string),
                typeof(MyControl),

                new FrameworkPropertyMetadata(
                   "Default Value",
                   FrameworkPropertyMetadataOptions.AffectsArrange
                   & FrameworkPropertyMetadataOptions.AffectsMeasure
                   & FrameworkPropertyMetadataOptions.AffectsRender));
```

```
        private static object TextFontWeight_CoerceValue(DependencyObject d,
                object value)
        {
            FontWeight fontWeight = (FontWeight)value;

            if (fontWeight == FontWeights.Bold
                || fontWeight == FontWeights.Normal)
            {
                return fontWeight;
            }

            return FontWeights.Normal;
        }

        private static void TextFontWeight_PropertyChanged(DependencyObject d,
                                DependencyPropertyChangedEventArgs e)
        {
            MyControl myControl = d as MyControl;

            if (myControl != null)
            {
                FontWeight fontWeight = (FontWeight)e.NewValue;
                string fontWeightName;

                if (fontWeight == FontWeights.Bold)
                    fontWeightName = "Bold";
                else
                    fontWeightName = "Normal";

                myControl.txblFontWeight.Text =
                        string.Format("Font weight set to: {0}.", fontWeightName);
            }
        }
    }
}
```

17-2. Create and Use an Attached Property

Problem

You need to add a dependency property to a class but are not able to access the class in a way that would allow you to add the property, or you want to use a property that can be set on any child objects of the type.

Solution

Create an attached property by registering a System.Windows.DependencyProperty using the static DependencyProperty.RegisterAttached method.

How It Works

You can think of an attached property as a special type of dependency property (see Recipe 17-1) that doesn't get exposed using a CLR property wrapper. Common examples of attached properties include System.Windows.Controls.Canvas.Top, System.Windows.Controls.DockPanel.Dock, and System.Windows.Controls.Grid.Row.

As attached properties are registered in a similar way to dependency properties, you are still able to provide metadata for handling property changes, and so on. In addition to metadata, it is possible to enable property value inheritance on attached properties.

Attached properties are not set like dependency properties using a CLR wrapper property; they are instead accessed through a method for getting and setting their values. These methods have specific signatures and naming conventions so that they can be matched up to the correct attached property. The signatures for the property's getter and setter methods can be found in the following code listing.

The Code

The following code defines a simple System.Windows.Window that contains a few controls. The window's code-behind defines an attached property named RotationProperty with SystemWindows.UIElement as the target type. The window's markup defines four controls, three of which have the value of MainWindow.Rotation set in XAML. The button's value for this property is not set and will therefore return the default value for the property—0 in this case.

```
<Window
    x:Class=" Apress.VisualCSharpRecipes.Chapter17.MainWindow"
    xmlns="http://schemas.microsoft.com/winfx/2006/xaml/presentation"
    xmlns:x="http://schemas.microsoft.com/winfx/2006/xaml"
    xmlns:local="clr-namespace:Apress.VisualCSharpRecipes.Chapter17"
    Title="Recipe17_02" Height="350" Width="350">
    <UniformGrid>
        <Button Content="Click me!"  Click="UIElement_Click" Margin="10" />

        <Border MouseLeftButtonDown="UIElement_Click"
             BorderThickness="1" BorderBrush="Black" Background="Transparent"
             Margin="10" local:MainWindow.Rotation="3.14" />

        <ListView PreviewMouseLeftButtonDown="UIElement_Click"
            Margin="10" local:MainWindow.Rotation="1.57">
            <ListViewItem Content="Item 1" />
            <ListViewItem Content="Item 1" />
            <ListViewItem Content="Item 1" />
            <ListViewItem Content="Item 1" />
        </ListView>
```

```
        <local:UserControl1 Margin="10" local:MainWindow.Rotation="1.0" />
    </UniformGrid>
</Window>

using System.Windows;
using System.Windows.Controls;

namespace Apress.VisualCSharpRecipes.Chapter17
{
    /// <summary>
    /// Interaction logic for MainWindow.xaml
    /// </summary>
    public partial class MainWindow : Window
    {
        public MainWindow()
        {
            InitializeComponent();
        }

        private void UIElement_Click(object sender, RoutedEventArgs e)
        {
            UIElement uiElement = (UIElement)sender;

            MessageBox.Show("Rotation = " + GetRotation(uiElement), "Recipe17_02");
        }

        public static readonly DependencyProperty RotationProperty =
            DependencyProperty.RegisterAttached("Rotation",
                                                typeof(double),
                                                typeof(MainWindow),
                                                new FrameworkPropertyMetadata(
                                0d, FrameworkPropertyMetadataOptions.AffectsRender));

        public static void SetRotation(UIElement element, double value)
        {
            element.SetValue(RotationProperty, value);
        }

        public static double GetRotation(UIElement element)
        {
            return (double)element.GetValue(RotationProperty);
        }
    }
}
```

The following markup and code-behind define a simple `System.Windows.Controls.UserControl` that demonstrates the use of the custom attached property in code:

```
<UserControl
    x:Class=" Apress.VisualCSharpRecipes.Chapter17.UserControl1"
    xmlns="http://schemas.microsoft.com/winfx/2006/xaml/presentation"
    xmlns:x="http://schemas.microsoft.com/winfx/2006/xaml"
    MouseLeftButtonDown="UserControl_MouseLeftButtonDown"
    Background="Transparent">
    <Viewbox>
        <TextBlock Text="I'm a UserControl" />
    </Viewbox>
</UserControl>
```

```
using System.Windows;
using System.Windows.Controls;

namespace Apress.VisualCSharpRecipes.Chapter17
{
    /// <summary>
    /// Interaction logic for UserControl1.xaml
    /// </summary>
    public partial class UserControl1 : UserControl
    {
        public UserControl1()
        {
            InitializeComponent();
        }

        private void UserControl_MouseLeftButtonDown(object sender,
                                                     RoutedEventArgs e)
        {
            UserControl1 uiElement = (UserControl1)sender;

            MessageBox.Show("Rotation = " + MainWindow.GetRotation(uiElement),
                            "Recipe17_02");
        }
    }
}
```

Figure 17-1 shows the result of clicking the button. A value for the `MainWindow.Rotation` property is not explicitly set on the button; therefore, it is displaying the default value.

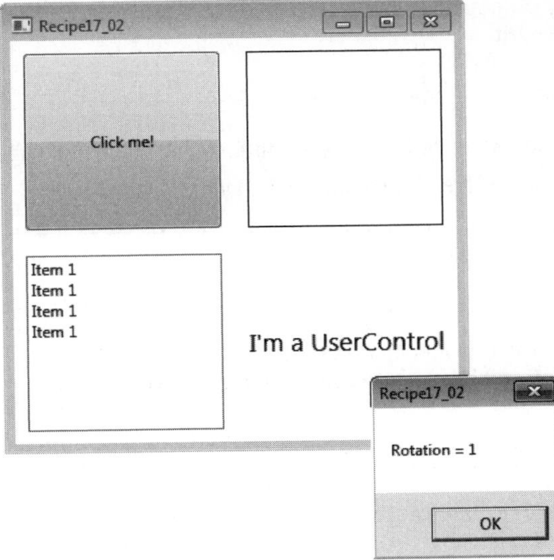

Figure 17-1. The result of clicking the button

17-3. Define Application-Wide Resources

Problem

You have several resources that you want to make available throughout your application.

Solution

Merge all the required `System.Windows.ResourceDictionary` objects into the application's `ResourceDictionary`.

How It Works

`ResourceDictionary` objects are by default available to all objects that are within the scope of the application. This means that some `System.Windows.Controls.Control` that is placed within a `System.Windows.Window` will be able to reference objects contained within any of the `ResourceDictionary` objects referenced at the application level. This ensures the maintainability of your styles because you will need to update the objects in a single place.

It is important to know that each time a `ResourceDictionary` is referenced by a `System.Windows.Controls.Control`, a local copy of that `ResourceDictionary` is made for each instance of the control. This means that if you have several large ResourceDictionary objects that are referenced by a control that is instantiated several times, you may notice a performance hit.

■ **Note** System.Windows.Controls.ToolTip styles need to be referenced once per control. If several controls all use a ToolTip style referenced at the application level, you will observe strange behavior in your tooltips.

The Code

The following example demonstrates the content of an application's App.xaml. Two System.Windows.Media.SolidColorBrush resources are defined that are referenced in other parts of the application.

```
<Application
  x:Class="Apress.VisualCSharpRecipes.Chapter17.App"
  xmlns="http://schemas.microsoft.com/winfx/2006/xaml/presentation"
  xmlns:x="http://schemas.microsoft.com/winfx/2006/xaml"
  StartupUri="MainWindow.xaml">
  <Application.Resources>
    <SolidColorBrush x:Key="FontBrush" Color="#FF222222" />
    <SolidColorBrush x:Key="BackgroundBrush" Color="#FFDDDDDD" />
  </Application.Resources>
</Application>
```

The following example demonstrates the content of the application's MainWindow.xaml file. The two resources that were defined in the application's resources are used by controls in the System.Windows.Window. The first resource is used to set the background property of the outer System.Windows.Controls.Grid, and the second resource is used to set the foreground property of a System.Windows.Controls.TextBlock (see Figure 17-2).

```
<Window
    x:Class="Apress.VisualCSharpRecipes.Chapter17.MainWindow"
    xmlns="http://schemas.microsoft.com/winfx/2006/xaml/presentation"
    xmlns:x="http://schemas.microsoft.com/winfx/2006/xaml"
    Title="Recipe17_03" Height="100" Width="300">
    <Grid Background="{StaticResource BackgroundBrush}">
        <Viewbox>
            <TextBlock Text="Some Text" Margin="5"
                Foreground="{StaticResource FontBrush}" />
        </Viewbox>
    </Grid>
</Window>
```

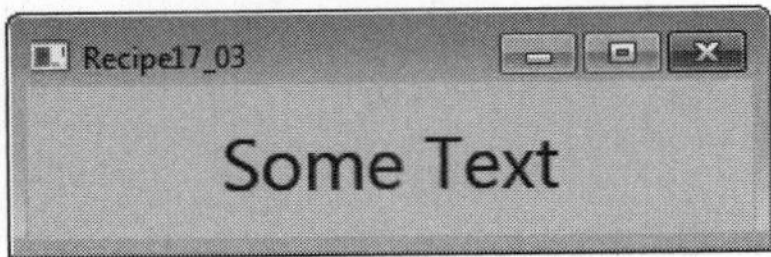

Figure 17-2. Using an application-level resource to set properties on controls

17-4. Debug Data Bindings Using an IValueConverter

Problem

You need to debug a binding that is not working as expected and want to make sure the correct values are going in.

Solution

Create a converter class that implements `System.Windows.Data.IValueConverter` and simply returns the value it receives for conversion, setting a breakpoint or tracepoint within the converter.

How It Works

Debugging a data binding can be quite tricky and consume a lot of time. Because data bindings are generally defined in XAML, you don't have anywhere you can set a breakpoint to make sure things are working as you intended. In some cases, you will be able to place a breakpoint on a property of the object that is being bound, but that option isn't always available, such as when binding to a property of some other control in your application. This is where a converter can be useful.

When using a simple converter that returns the argument being passed in, unchanged, you immediately have code on which you can place a breakpoint or write debugging information to the Output window or log. This can tell you whether the value coming in is the wrong type, is in a form that means it is not valid for the binding, or has a strange value. You'll also soon realize whether the binding is not being used, because the converter will never be hit.

The Code

The following example demonstrates a `System.Windows.Window` that contains a `System.Windows.Controls.Grid`. Inside the `Grid` are a `System.Windows.Controls.CheckBox` and a `System.Windows.Controls.Expander`. The `IsExpanded` property of the `Expander` is bound to the `IsChecked` property of the `CheckBox`. This is a very simple binding, but it gives an example where you are able to place a breakpoint in code.

```
<Window
    x:Class="Apress.VisualCSharpRecipes.Chapter17.MainWindow"
    xmlns="http://schemas.microsoft.com/winfx/2006/xaml/presentation"
    xmlns:x="http://schemas.microsoft.com/winfx/2006/xaml"
    xmlns:local="clr-namespace:Apress.VisualCSharpRecipes.Chapter17"
    Title="Recipe17_04" Width="200" Height="200">
    <Window.Resources>
        <local:DebugConverter x:Key="DebugConverter" />
    </Window.Resources>
    <Grid>
        <Grid.RowDefinitions>
            <RowDefinition Height="0.5*" />
            <RowDefinition Height="0.5*"/>
        </Grid.RowDefinitions>

        <CheckBox x:Name="chkShouldItBeOpen" Margin="10"
            IsChecked="False" Content="Open Expander" />

        <Expander IsExpanded="{Binding
            ElementName=chkShouldItBeOpen, Path=IsChecked,
            Converter={StaticResource DebugConverter}}"
            Grid.Row="1" Background="Black" Foreground="White"
            Margin="10" VerticalAlignment="Center"
            HorizontalAlignment="Center" Header="I'm an Expander!">
                <TextBlock Text="Expander Open" Foreground="White"/>
        </Expander>
    </Grid>
</Window>
```

The following code defines the code-behind for the previous XAML:

```
using System.Windows;

namespace Apress.VisualCSharpRecipes.Chapter17
{
    /// <summary>
    /// Interaction logic for MainWindow.xaml
    /// </summary>
    public partial class MainWindow : Window
    {
        public MainWindow()
        {
            InitializeComponent();
        }
    }
}
```

The following code defines a converter class that simply returns the value passed to it unchanged. However, you can place breakpoints on these lines of code to see what data is flowing through the converter:

```
using System;
using System.Globalization;
using System.Windows.Data;

namespace Apress.VisualCSharpRecipes.Chapter17
{
    public class DebugConverter : IValueConverter
    {
        public object Convert(object value,
                              Type targetType,
                              object parameter,
                              CultureInfo culture)
        {
            return value;
        }

        public object ConvertBack(object value,
                                  Type targetType,
                                  object parameter,
                                  CultureInfo culture)
        {
            return value;
        }
    }
}
```

17-5. Debug Bindings Using Attached Properties

Problem

You need to debug a binding that is not working as expected and want to make sure the correct values are going in. Using a converter is either undesired or not feasible.

Solution

Use the `System.Diagnostics.PresentationTraceSources.TraceLevel` attached property defined in the `WindowsBase` assembly, setting the level of detail required. If the data binding is defined in code, use the static method `PresentationTraceLevel.SetTraceLevel`.

■ **Caution** Using the `PresentationTraceSources.TraceLevel` attached property can affect the performance of a WPF application and should be removed as soon as it is no longer required.

How It Works

The `PresentationTraceSources.TraceLevel` attached property allows you to specify the level of information written to the Output window for data bindings, on a per-binding basis. The higher the `System.Diagnostics.PresentationTraceLevel` value that is used, the more information that will be generated. The `PresentationTraceSources.TraceLevel` can be used on the following object types:

- `System.Windows.Data.BindingBase`
- `System.Windows.Data.BindingExpressionBase`
- `System.Windows.Data.ObjectDataProvider`
- `System.Windows.Data.XmlDataProvider`

It is important to remember to remove any trace-level attached properties from your code once you are finished debugging a binding; otherwise, your Output window will continue to be filled with binding information. Table 17-2 details the values of the `PresentationTraceSource.TraceLevel` enumeration.

Table 17-2. *Values for PresentationTraceSources.TraceLevel*

Property	Description
`None`	Generates no additional information.
`Low`	Generates some information about binding failures. This generally details the target and source properties involved and any exception that is thrown. No information is generated for bindings that work properly.
`Medium`	Generates a medium amount of information about binding failures and a small amount of information for valid bindings. When a binding fails, information is generated for the source and target properties, some of the transformations that are applied to the value, any exceptions that occur, the final value of the binding, and some of the steps taken during the whole process. For valid bindings, information logging is light.
`High`	Generates the most binding state information for binding failures and valid bindings. When a binding fails, a great deal of information about the binding process is logged, covering all the previous data in a more verbose manner.

The Code

The following markup demonstrates how to use the `PresentationTraceSource.TraceLevel` property in two different bindings. One of the bindings is valid and binds the value of the text block to the width of the parent grid; the other is invalid and attempts to bind the width of the parent grid to the height of the text block. Set the values of the `PresentatonTraceSource.TraceLevel` attached properties to see how they behave.

```
<Window
    x:Class="Apress.VisualCSharpRecipes.Chapter17.MainWindow"
    xmlns="http://schemas.microsoft.com/winfx/2006/xaml/presentation"
    xmlns:x="http://schemas.microsoft.com/winfx/2006/xaml"
    xmlns:diagnostics="clr-namespace:System.Diagnostics;assembly=WindowsBase"
    Title="Recipe17_05" Height="300" Width="300">
    <Grid x:Name="gdLayoutRoot">
        <Viewbox>
            <TextBlock x:Name="tbkTextBlock">
                <TextBlock.Text>
                  <Binding ElementName="gdLayoutRoot" Path="ActualWidth"
                  diagnostics:PresentationTraceSources.TraceLevel="High" />
                </TextBlock.Text>
                <TextBlock.Height>
                  <Binding ElementName="gdLayoutRoot" Path="Name"
                  diagnostics:PresentationTraceSources.TraceLevel="High" />
                </TextBlock.Height>
            </TextBlock>
        </Viewbox>
    </Grid>
</Window>
```

17-6. Arrange UI Elements in a Horizontal or Vertical Stack

Problem

You need to arrange a group of UI elements in a horizontal or vertical stack.

Solution

Place the UI elements in a `System.Windows.Controls.StackPanel`. Use the `Orientation` property of the `StackPanel` to control the flow of the stacking (vertical or horizontal).

How It Works

The `StackPanel` arranges the elements it contains in a horizontal or vertical stack. The order of the elements is determined by the order in which they are declared in the XAML (that is, the order in which they occur in the `Children` collection of the `StackPanel`). By default, the `StackPanel` will arrange the elements vertically (one under another). You can control the direction of the stack using the Orientation property. To stack the elements horizontally (next to each other), set the Orientation property to the value Horizontal.

■ **Note** If the StackPanel is smaller than the space required to display its content, the content is visually cropped. However, you can still interact with visual elements that are cropped by using keyboard shortcuts or by tabbing to the control and pressing Enter.

The default height and width of elements in a StackPanel depend on the type of element and the orientation of the StackPanel. When the Orientation property of the StackPanel has the value Vertical, text is left justified, but buttons are stretched to the width of the StackPanel. You can override this default behavior by directly configuring the width of the element or by setting the HorizontalAlignment property of the contained element to the value Left, Center, or Right. These values force the element to take a width based on its content and position it in the left, center, or right of the StackPanel.

Similarly, when the Orientation property of the StackPanel has the value Horizontal, the text is top justified, but the height of buttons is stretched to fill the height of the StackPanel. You can override this behavior by directly configuring the height of the element or by setting the VerticalAlignment property of the contained element to the value Top, Center, or Bottom. These values force the element to take a height based on its content and position it in the top, center, or bottom of the StackPanel.

The Code

The following XAML demonstrates how to use three StackPanel panels. An outer StackPanel allows you to stack two inner StackPanel panels vertically. The first inner StackPanel has a horizontal orientation and contains a set of System.Windows.Controls.Button controls. The Button controls show the effects of the various VerticalAlignment property values on the positioning of the controls. This panel also shows the cropping behavior of the StackPanel on the elements it contains (see Figure 17-3). You can see that Button 4 is partially cropped and that Button 5 is not visible at all. However, you can still tab to and interact with Button 5.

The second inner StackPanel has a vertical orientation and also contains a set of Button controls. These buttons show the effects of the various HorizontalAlignment property values on the positioning of a control in the StackPanel.

```
<Window x:Class="Apress.VisualCSharpRecipes.Chapter17.MainWindow"
    xmlns="http://schemas.microsoft.com/winfx/2006/xaml/presentation"
    xmlns:x="http://schemas.microsoft.com/winfx/2006/xaml"
    Title="Recipe17_06" Height="240" Width="250">
    <StackPanel Width="200">
        <StackPanel Height="50" Margin ="5" Orientation="Horizontal">
            <Button Content="Button _1" Margin="2" />
            <Button Content="Button _2" Margin="2"
                    VerticalAlignment="Top"/>
            <Button Content="Button _3" Margin="2"
                    VerticalAlignment="Center"/>
```

```
            <Button Content="Button _4" Margin="2"
                    VerticalAlignment="Bottom"/>
            <Button Content="Button _5" Margin="2" />
        </StackPanel>
        <Separator />
        <StackPanel Margin="5" Orientation="Vertical">
            <Button Content="Button _A" Margin="2" />
            <Button Content="Button _B" Margin="2"
                    HorizontalAlignment="Left" />
            <Button Content="Button _C" Margin="2"
                    HorizontalAlignment="Center" />
            <Button Content="Button _D" Margin="2"
                    HorizontalAlignment="Right" />
            <Button Content="Button _E" Margin="2" />
        </StackPanel>
    </StackPanel>
</Window>
```

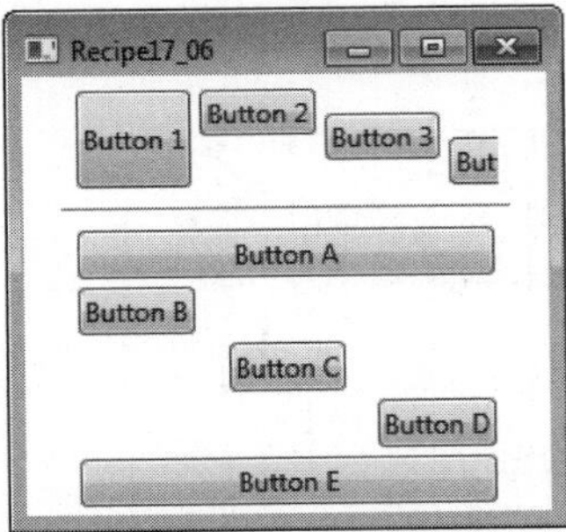

Figure 17-3. *Using a StackPanel to control the layout of UI elements*

17-7. Dock UI Elements to the Edges of a Form

Problem

You need to dock UI elements to specific edges of a form.

Solution

Place the UI elements in a `System.Windows.Controls.DockPanel`. Use the `DockPanel.Dock` attached property on each element in the `DockPanel` to position the element on a particular edge.

How It Works

The DockPanel allows you to arrange UI elements (including other panels) along its edges. This is very useful in achieving the basic window layout common to many Windows applications with menus and toolbars along the top of the window and control panels along the sides.

When you apply the DockPanel.Dock attached property to the elements contained in a DockPanel, the DockPanel places the UI element along the specified edge: Left, Right, Top, or Bottom. The DockPanel assigns the elements' positions in the same order they are declared in the XAML (that is, in the order in which they occur in the Children collection of the DockPanel).

As each element is placed on an edge, it takes up all the space available along that edge. This means you must consider the layout you want when ordering the contained elements. Also, if there are multiple elements on a given edge, the DockPanel stacks them in order.

By default, the last element added to the DockPanel fills all the remaining space in the panel regardless of its DockPanel.Dock property value. You can stop this behavior by setting the LastChildFill property of the DockPanel to False. The DockPanel places any elements without a DockPanel.Dock property value along the left edge.

Figure 17-4 provides examples of the different layouts you can achieve by declaring elements in different orders. The third example also shows how the DockPanel stacks elements when specified on a common edge.

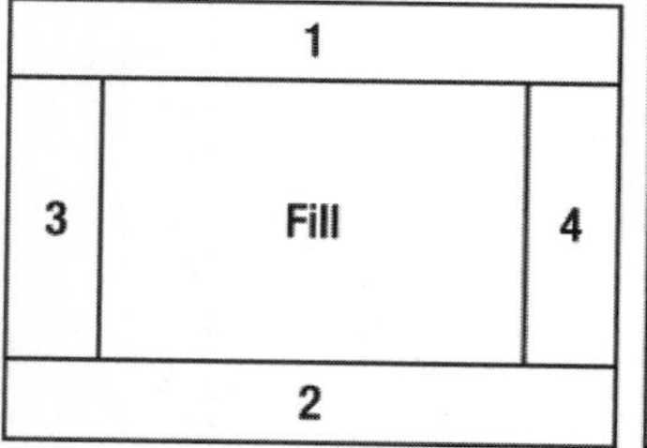

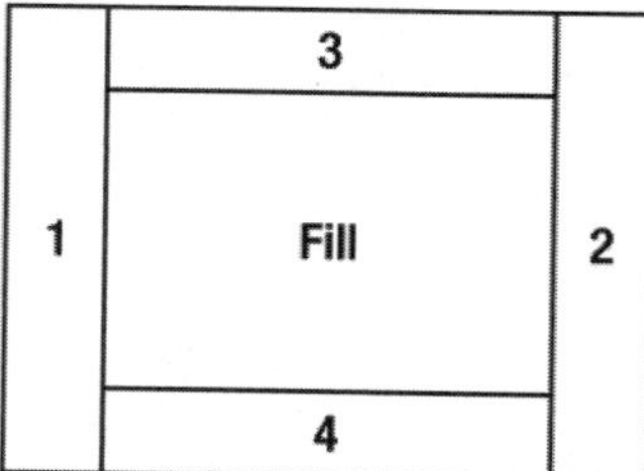

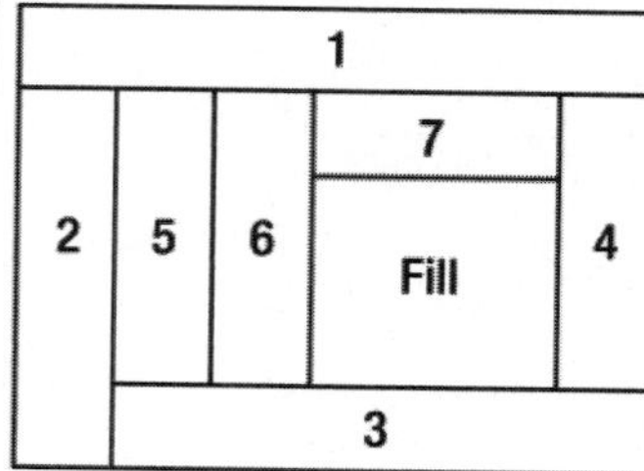

Figure 17-4. Layout examples using a DockPanel

The Code

The following XAML demonstrates how to use a DockPanel to dock a System.Windows.Controls.StackPanel containing a set of System.Windows.Controls.Button controls along its top edge and another along its left edge. The final Button added to the DockPanel stretches to fill all the remaining space in the panel (see Figure 17-5).

```
<Window x:Class="Apress.VisualCSharpRecipes.Chapter17.MainWindow"
    xmlns="http://schemas.microsoft.com/winfx/2006/xaml/presentation"
    xmlns:x="http://schemas.microsoft.com/winfx/2006/xaml"
    Title="Recipe17_07" Height="200" Width="300">
    <DockPanel >
        <StackPanel DockPanel.Dock="Top" Orientation="Horizontal">
            <Button Content="Button 1" Margin="2" />
            <Button Content="Button 2" Margin="2" />
```

```
            <Button Content="Button 3" Margin="2" />
            <Button Content="Button 4" Margin="2" />
            <Button Content="Button 5" Margin="2" />
        </StackPanel>
        <StackPanel DockPanel.Dock="Left">
            <Button Content="Button A" Margin="2" />
            <Button Content="Button B" Margin="2" />
            <Button Content="Button C" Margin="2" />
            <Button Content="Button D" Margin="2" />
            <Button Content="Button E" Margin="2" />
        </StackPanel>
        <Button Content="Fill Button" />
    </DockPanel>
</Window>
```

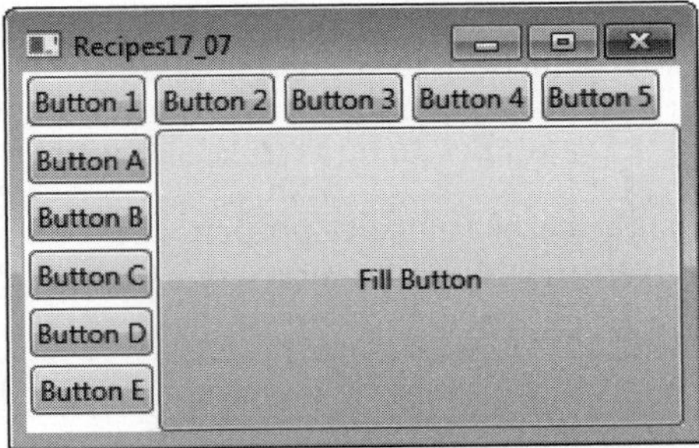

Figure 17-5. Arranging UI elements in a DockPanel

17-8. Arrange UI Elements in a Grid

Problem

You need to arrange a group of UI elements in a two-dimensional grid layout.

Solution

Place the UI elements in a `System.Windows.Controls.Grid`. Define the number of rows and columns in the `Grid`. For each UI element in the `Grid`, define its row and column coordinates using the `Grid.Row` and `Grid.Column` attached properties.

How It Works

To define the number of rows in a Grid panel, you must include a Grid.RowDefinitions element inside the Grid. Within the Grid.RowDefinitions element, you declare one RowDefintion element for each row you need. You must do the same thing for columns, but you use elements named Grid.ColumnDefinitions and ColumnDefinition.

■ **Tip** Although you will rarely want it in live production code, it is often useful during development to be able to see where the row and column boundaries are within your Grid panel. Setting the ShowGridLines property of the Grid panel to True will turn visible grid lines on.

Using the Height property of the RowDefinition element and the Width property of the ColumnDefinition, you have fine-grained control over the layout of a Grid. Both the Height and Width properties can take absolute values if you require fixed sizes. You must define the size of the column or row as a number and an optional unit identifier. By default, the unit is assumed to be px (pixels) but can also be in (inches), cm (centimeters), or pt (points).

If you do not want fixed sizes, you can assign the value Auto to the Height or Width property, in which case the Grid allocates only the amount of space required by the elements contained in the row or column.

If you do not specify absolute or auto values, the Grid will divide its horizontal space equally between all columns and its vertical space equally between all rows. You can override this default behavior and change the proportions of available space assigned to each row or column using an asterisk (*) preceded by the relative weighting the Grid should give the row or column. For example, a RowDefinition element with the Height property of 3* will get three times as much space allocated to it as a RowDefinition element with a Height property of *. Most often, you will use a mix of auto and proportional sizing.

Once you have defined the structure of your Grid, you specify where in the Grid each element should go using the Grid.Row and Grid.Column attached properties. Both the Grid.Row and Grid.Column properties are zero-based and default to zero if you do not define them for an element contained within the Grid.

If you want elements in the Grid that span multiple rows or columns, you can assign them Grid.RowSpan and Grid.ColumnSpan attached properties that specify the number of rows or columns that the element should span.

The Code

The following XAML demonstrates how to use a three-by-three Grid to lay out a set of System.Windows.Controls.Button controls. The Grid uses a mix of fixed, auto, and proportional row and column sizing, and the Grid lines are turned on so that you can see (in Figure 17-6) the resulting Grid structure. The top-left Button controls span multiple rows or columns, and the leftmost Button is rotated (see recipe 17-11 for details on how to do this).

```
<Window x:Class="Apress.VisualCSharpRecipes.Chapter17.MainWindow"
    xmlns="http://schemas.microsoft.com/winfx/2006/xaml/presentation"
```

```
    xmlns:x="http://schemas.microsoft.com/winfx/2006/xaml"
    Title="Recipe17_08" Height="200" Width="250">
    <Grid ShowGridLines="True">
        <Grid.RowDefinitions>
            <RowDefinition MinHeight="50" />
            <RowDefinition Height="2*" />
            <RowDefinition Height="*" />
        </Grid.RowDefinitions>
        <Grid.ColumnDefinitions>
            <ColumnDefinition Width="50" />
            <ColumnDefinition Width="2*" />
            <ColumnDefinition Width="3*" />
        </Grid.ColumnDefinitions>
        <Button Content="Button spanning 3 rows" Grid.RowSpan="3">
            <Button.LayoutTransform>
                <RotateTransform Angle="90" />
            </Button.LayoutTransform>
        </Button>
        <Button Content="Button spanning 2 columns" Grid.Column="1"
                Grid.Row="0" Grid.ColumnSpan="2" />
        <Button Content="Button" Grid.Column="2" Grid.Row="2"/>
    </Grid>
</Window>
```

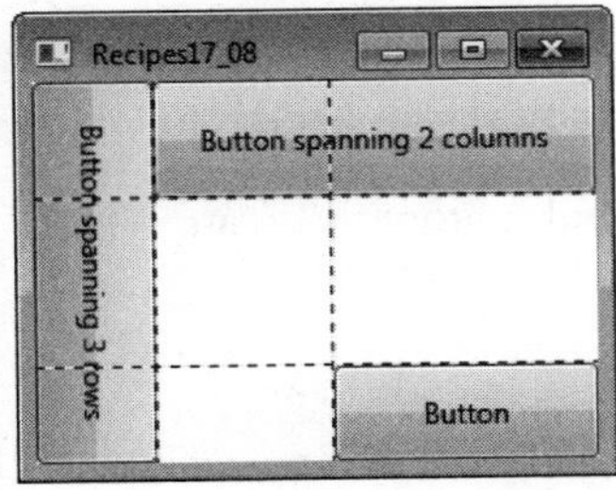

Figure 17-6. *Arranging UI elements in a Grid*

17-9. Position UI Elements Using Exact Coordinates

Problem

You need complete control over the positioning of the UI elements in a form.

Solution

Place the UI elements in a System.Windows.Controls.Canvas panel. Use the Canvas.Top, Canvas.Bottom, Canvas.Left, and Canvas.Right attached properties to define the position of each element.

How It Works

The Canvas panel allows you to place UI elements using exact coordinates. Unlike other layout panels, the Canvas does not provide special layout logic to position and size the elements it contains based on the space it has available. Instead, the Canvas simply places each element at its specified location and gives it the exact dimensions it requires. This does not facilitate maintainable user interfaces that are easy to localize, but in certain circumstances (such as drawing and graphical design applications) it may be necessary.

By default, the Canvas positions the elements it contains in its top-left corner. To position an element elsewhere in the Canvas, you can define the Canvas.Top, Canvas.Bottom, Canvas.Left, and Canvas.Right attached properties on the element. Each property takes a number and an optional unit identifier. By default, the unit is assumed to be px (pixels), but can also be in (inches), cm (centimeters), or pt (points). The value can even be negative, which allows the Canvas to draw elements outside its own visual boundaries.

If you define both Canvas.Top and Canvas.Bottom on an element, the Canvas ignores the Canvas.Bottom value. Similarly, if you define both Canvas.Left and Canvas.Right on an element, the Canvas ignores the Canvas.Right value.

Because you have complete control over element position when using a Canvas, it is easy to get elements that overlap. The Canvas draws the elements in the same order they are declared in the XAML (that is, the order in which they occur in the Children collection of the Canvas). So, elements declared later are visible on top of elements declared earlier. You can override this default stacking order (referred to as the *z-order*) by defining the Canvas.ZIndex attached property on the element. The default Canvas.ZIndex is zero, so by assigning a higher integer value to the Canvas.ZIndex property on an element, the Canvas will draw that element over the top of elements with a lower value.

The Code

The following XAML demonstrates how to use a Canvas to lay out a set of System.Windows.Controls.Button controls. In Figure 17-7, the shaded area shows the boundary of the Canvas. You can see how using negative position values for Button 1 and Button 5 place them wholly or partially outside the boundary of the Canvas. Despite Button 4 being declared after Button 2, the higher Canvas.ZIndex assigned on Button 2 forces the Canvas to draw Button 2 over the top of Button 4.

```
<Window x:Class="Apress.VisualCSharpRecipes.Chapter17.MainWindow"
    xmlns="http://schemas.microsoft.com/winfx/2006/xaml/presentation"
    xmlns:x="http://schemas.microsoft.com/winfx/2006/xaml"
    Title="Recipe17_09" Height="300" Width="300">
    <Canvas Background="LightGray" Margin="1cm">
        <Button Content="Button _1" Canvas.Top="-1cm" Canvas.Left="1cm" />
        <Button Content="Button _2" Canvas.Bottom="1cm" Canvas.Left="1cm"
                Canvas.ZIndex="1"/>
        <Button Content="Button _3" Canvas.Top="1cm" Canvas.Right="1cm" />
        <Button Content="Button _4" Canvas.Bottom="1.2cm" Canvas.Left="1.5cm" />
```

```
        <Button Content="Button _5" Canvas.Bottom="1cm" Canvas.Right="-1cm" />
    </Canvas>
</Window>
```

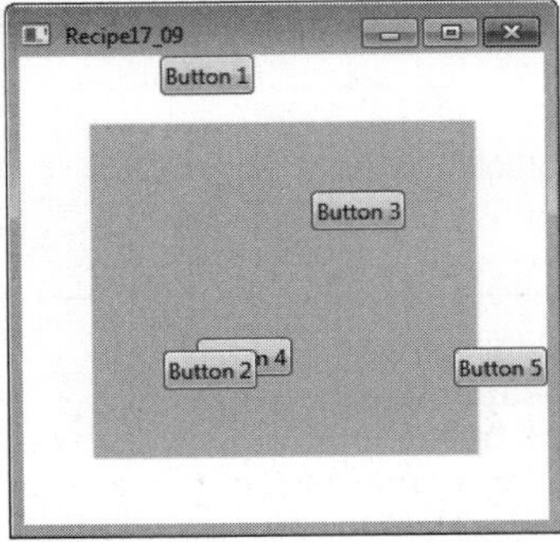

Figure 17-7. Arranging UI elements using a Canvas

17-10. Get Rich Text Input from a User

Problem

You need to allow the user to edit large amounts of text and give them fine-grained control over the formatting of text they enter.

Solution

Use the `System.Windows.Controls.RichTextBox` control.

How It Works

The `RichTextBox` is a sophisticated and highly functional control designed to allow you to display and edit `System.Windows.Documents.FlowDocument` objects. The combination of the `RichTextBox` and `FlowDocument` objects provides the user with access to advanced document-editing capabilities that you do not get in a `System.Windows.Controls.TextBox` control. These features include mixed text formatting, hyphenation, tables, lists, paragraphs, and embedded images.

To populate the content of a `RichTextBox` statically, you include a `FlowDocument` element as the content of the `RichTextBox` XAML declaration. Within the `FlowDocument` element, you can define richly formatted content using elements of the flow document content model. Key structural elements of this content model include `Figure`, `Hyperlink`, `List`, `ListItem`, `Paragraph`, `Section`, and `Table`.

To populate the `RichTextBox` in code, you must work with a `FlowDocument` object directly. You can either create a new `FlowDocument` object or obtain one currently in a `RichTextBox` through the `RichTextBox.Document` property.

You manipulate the content of the FlowDocument by selecting portions of its content using a System.Windows.Documents.TextSelection object. The TextSelection object contains two properties, Start and End, which identify the beginning and end positions of the FlowDocument content you want to manipulate. Once you have a suitable TextSelection object, you can manipulate its content using the TextSelection members.

■ **Note** For detailed information about flow content, see the .NET Framework documentation at http://msdn.microsoft.com/en-us/library/ms753113(VS.100).aspx.

To simplify the manipulation of FlowDocument objects, the RichTextBox supports standard commands defined by the ApplicationCommands and EditingCommands classes from the System.Windows.Input namespace. The RichTextBox also supports standard key combinations to execute basic text-formatting operations such as applying bold, italic, and underline formats to text, as well as cutting, copying, and pasting selected content. Table 17-3 summarizes some of the more commonly used members of the RichTextBox control.

Table 17-3. *Commonly Used Members of the RichTextBox Control*

Member	Summary
Properties	
AcceptsTab	Controls whether the user can insert tab characters in the RichTextBox content or whether pressing Tab takes the user out of the RichTextBox and moves to the next control marked as a tab stop.
CaretPostion	Gets or sets the current insertion position index of the RichTextBox.
Document	Gets or sets the FlowDocument object that represents the RichTextBox content.
HorizontalScrollBarVisibility	Determines whether the RichTextBox displays a horizontal scroll bar.
IsReadOnly	Controls whether the RichTextBox is read-only or whether the user can also edit the content of the TextBox. Even if IsReadOnly is set to True, you can still programmatically change the content of the RichTextBox.
Selection	Gets a System.Windows.Documents.TextSelection object representing the current selection in the RichTextBox.
VerticalScrollBarVisibility	Determines whether the RichTextBox displays a vertical scroll bar.

Member	Summary
Methods	
AppendText	Appends text to the existing content of the RichTextBox.
Copy	Copies the currently selected RichTextBox content to the clipboard.
Cut	Cuts the currently selected RichTextBox content and places it in the clipboard.
Paste	Pastes the current content of the clipboard over the currently selected RichTextBox content or inserts it at the cursor position if nothing is selected.
SelectAll	Selects the entire content of the RichTextBox control.
Undo	Undoes the most recent undoable action on the RichTextBox control.
Events	
TextChanged	The event fired when the text in a RichTextBox changes.

The Code

The following code provides a simple example of a RichTextBox used to edit a FlowDocument. The XAML defines a static FlowDocument that contains a variety of structural and formatting elements. The user interface provides a set of buttons to manipulate the RichTextBox content. The buttons rely on the application and editing command support provided by the RichTextBox control and use a style to make the RichTextBox the target of the button's command.

```
<Window x:Class="Apress.VisualCSharpRecipes.Chapter17.MainWindow"
    xmlns="http://schemas.microsoft.com/winfx/2006/xaml/presentation"
    xmlns:x="http://schemas.microsoft.com/winfx/2006/xaml"
    Title="Recipe17_10" Height="350" Width="500">
    <DockPanel>
        <StackPanel DockPanel.Dock="Top" Orientation="Horizontal">
            <StackPanel.Resources>
                <Style TargetType="{x:Type Button}">
                    <Setter Property="CommandTarget"
                            Value="{Binding ElementName=rtbTextBox1}" />
                </Style>
            </StackPanel.Resources>
```

```
        <Button Content="Clear" Name="btnClear" Click="btnClear_Click" />
        <Separator Margin="5"/>
        <Button Content="Cu_t" Command="ApplicationCommands.Cut" />
        <Button Content="_Copy" Command="ApplicationCommands.Copy" />
        <Button Content="_Paste" Command="ApplicationCommands.Paste" />
        <Separator Margin="5"/>
        <Button Content="_Undo" Command="ApplicationCommands.Undo" />
        <Button Content="_Redo" Command="ApplicationCommands.Redo" />
        <Separator Margin="5"/>
        <Button Content="_Bold" Command="EditingCommands.ToggleBold" />
        <Button Content="_Italic" Command="EditingCommands.ToggleItalic" />
        <Button Content="Underline"
                Command="EditingCommands.ToggleUnderline" />
        <Separator Margin="5"/>
        <Button Content="_Right" Command="EditingCommands.AlignRight" />
        <Button Content="C_enter" Command="EditingCommands.AlignCenter" />
        <Button Content="_Left" Command="EditingCommands.AlignLeft" />
    </StackPanel>
    <RichTextBox DockPanel.Dock="Bottom" Name="rtbTextBox1"
                 HorizontalScrollBarVisibility="Visible"
                 VerticalScrollBarVisibility="Visible">
        <FlowDocument>
            <Paragraph FontSize="12">
                Lorem ipsum dolor sit amet, consectetuer adipiscing elit,
                sed diam nonummy nibh euismod tincidunt ut laoreet dolore
                magna aliquam erat volutpat.
            </Paragraph>
            <Paragraph FontSize="15">
                Ut wisi enim ad minim veniam, quis nostrud exerci tation
                ullamcorper suscipit lobortis nisl ut aliquip ex ea
                commodo consequat. Duis autem vel eum iriure.
            </Paragraph>

            <Paragraph FontSize="18">A List</Paragraph>

            <List>
                <ListItem>
                    <Paragraph>
                        <Bold>Bold List Item</Bold>
                    </Paragraph>
                </ListItem>
                <ListItem>
                    <Paragraph>
                        <Italic>Italic List Item</Italic>
                    </Paragraph>
                </ListItem>
                <ListItem>
                    <Paragraph>
                        <Underline>Underlined List Item</Underline>
                    </Paragraph>
                </ListItem>
```

```
                </List>
            </FlowDocument>
        </RichTextBox>
    </DockPanel>
</Window>
```

The following code-behind contains the event handler that handles the Clear button provided on the user interface defined earlier:

```
using System.Windows;

namespace Apress.VisualCSharpRecipes.Chapter17
{
    /// <summary>
    /// Interaction logic for MainWindow.xaml
    /// </summary>
    public partial class MainWindow : Window
    {
        public MainWindow()
        {
            InitializeComponent();
        }

        // Handles Clear button click event.
        private void btnClear_Click(object sender, RoutedEventArgs e)
        {
            // Select all the text in the FlowDocument and cut it.
            rtbTextBox1.SelectAll();
            rtbTextBox1.Cut();
        }
    }
}
```

Figure 17-8 shows what the RichTextBox looks like when the example is first run.

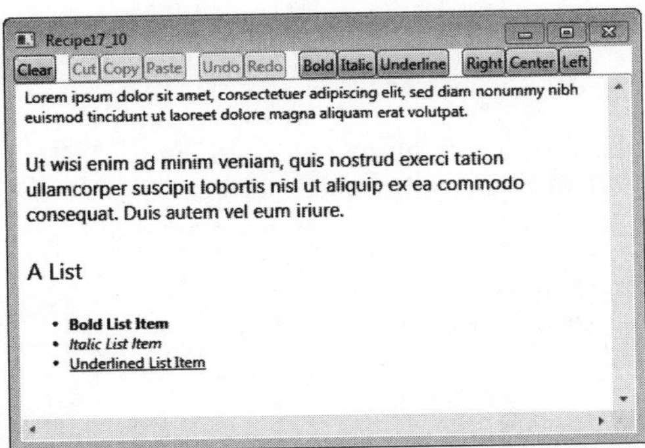

Figure 17-8. Using a RichTextBox to edit a FlowDocument

17-11. Display a Control Rotated

Problem

You need to display a control rotated from its normal horizontal or vertical axis.

Solution

Apply a `LayoutTransform` or a `RenderTransform` to the control.

How It Works

WPF makes many things trivial that are incredibly complex to do in Windows Forms programming. One of those things is the ability to rotate controls to any orientation yet still have them appear and function as normal. Admittedly, it is not every day you need to display a rotated control, but when you do, you will appreciate how easy it is in WPF. Most frequently, the ability to rotate controls becomes important when you start to customize the appearance of standard controls using templates or when you create custom controls.

Both the `LayoutTransform` and `RenderTransform` have a `RotateTransform` property, in which you specify in degrees the angle you want your control rotated by. Positive values rotate the control clockwise and negative values rotate the control counterclockwise. The rotation occurs around the point specified by the `CenterX` and `CenterY` properties. These properties refer to the coordinate space of the control that is being transformed, with (0,0) being the upper-left corner. Alternatively, you can use the `RenderTransformOrigin` property on the control you are rotating; this allows you to specify a point a relative distance from the origin using values between 0 and 1, which WPF automatically converts to specific values.

The difference between the `LayoutTransform` and `RenderTransform` is the order in which WPF executes the transformation. WPF executes the `LayoutTransform` as part of the layout processing, so the rotated position of the control affects the layout of controls around it. The `RenderTransform`, on the other hand, is executed after layout is determined, which means the rotated control does not affect the positioning of other controls and can therefore end up appearing partially over or under other controls.

The Code

The following XAML demonstrates a variety of rotated controls, and the output is shown in Figure 17-9. Figure 17-9 shows the difference in behavior between a `LayoutTransform` (bottom left) and a `RenderTransform` (bottom-right).

```
<Window x:Class="Apress.VisualCSharpRecipes.Chapter17.MainWindow"
    xmlns="http://schemas.microsoft.com/winfx/2006/xaml/presentation"
    xmlns:x="http://schemas.microsoft.com/winfx/2006/xaml"
    Title="Recipe17_11" Height="350" Width="400">
    <Grid ShowGridLines="True">
        <Grid.RowDefinitions>
            <RowDefinition MinHeight="140" />
            <RowDefinition MinHeight="170" />
```

```
        </Grid.RowDefinitions>
        <Grid.ColumnDefinitions>
            <ColumnDefinition />
            <ColumnDefinition />
        </Grid.ColumnDefinitions>
        <TextBox Grid.Row="0" Grid.Column="0" Height="23"
                 HorizontalAlignment="Center" Text="An upside down TextBox."
                 Width="140">
            <TextBox.LayoutTransform>
                <RotateTransform Angle="180"/>
            </TextBox.LayoutTransform>
        </TextBox>
        <Button Content="A rotated Button" Grid.Row="0" Grid.Column="1"
                Height="23" Width="100">
            <Button.LayoutTransform>
                <RotateTransform Angle="-120"/>
            </Button.LayoutTransform>
        </Button>
        <StackPanel Grid.Row="1" Grid.Column="0" >
            <TextBlock HorizontalAlignment="Center" Margin="5">
                Layout Tranform
            </TextBlock>
            <Button Margin="5" Width="100">Top Button</Button>
            <Button Content="Middle Button" Margin="5" Width="100">
                <Button.LayoutTransform>
                    <RotateTransform Angle="30" />
                </Button.LayoutTransform>
            </Button>
            <Button Margin="5" Width="100">Bottom Button</Button>
        </StackPanel>
        <StackPanel Grid.Row="1" Grid.Column="1" >
            <TextBlock HorizontalAlignment="Center" Margin="5">
                Render Tranform
            </TextBlock>
            <Button Margin="5" Width="100">Top Button</Button>
            <Button Content="Middle Button" Margin="5"
                    RenderTransformOrigin="0.5, 0.5" Width="100">
                <Button.RenderTransform>
                    <RotateTransform Angle="30" />
                </Button.RenderTransform>
            </Button>
            <Button Margin="5" Width="100">Bottom Button</Button>
        </StackPanel>
    </Grid>
</Window>
```

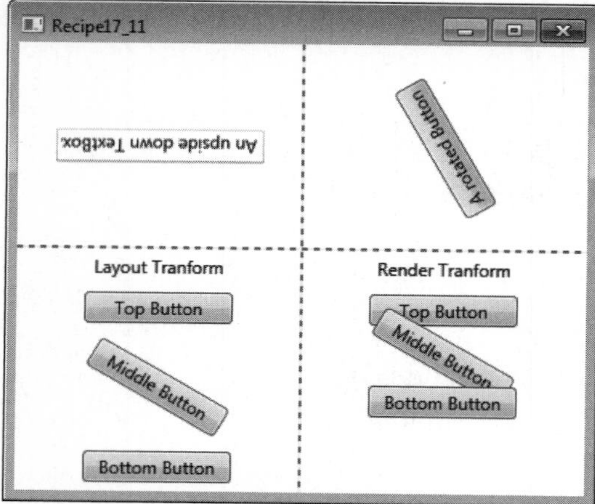

Figure 17-9. *A set of rotated controls*

17-12. Create a User Control

Problem

You need to create a user control to reuse part of the UI in different contexts within your application, without duplicating appearance or behavior logic.

Solution

Create a class that derives from `System.Windows.Controls.UserControl` or `System.Windows.Controls.ContentControl`, and place the visual elements you need in your reusable component in the XAML for the user control. Put custom logic in the code-behind for the `UserControl` to control custom behavior and functionality.

■ **Tip** A control that derives from `UserControl` is useful for creating a reusable component within an application but is less useful if the control must be shared by other applications, software teams, or even companies. This is because a control that derives from `UserControl` cannot have its appearance customized by applying custom styles and templates in the consumer. If this is needed, then you need to use a custom control, which is a control that derives from `System.Windows.UIElement.FrameworkElement` or `System.Windows.Controls.Control`.

How It Works

User controls provide a simple development model that is similar to creating WPF elements in standard windows. They are ideal for composing reusable UI controls out of existing components or elements, provided you do not need to allow them to be extensively customized by consumers of your control. If you do want to provide full control over the visual appearance of your control, or allow it to be a container for other controls, then a custom control is more suitable. Custom controls are covered in recipe 17-14.

To create a user control, right-click your project in Visual Studio, click Add, and then click the User Control option in the submenu. This creates a new XAML file and a corresponding code-behind file. The root element of the new XAML file is a `System.Windows.Controls.UserControl` class. Inside this XAML file, you can create the UI elements that compose your control.

The Code

The following example demonstrates how to create a `FileInputControl`, a custom reusable user control to encapsulate the functionality of browsing for a file and displaying the selected file name. This user control is then used in a window, as shown in Figure 17-10. The XAML for the `FileInputControl` is as follows:

```
<UserControl x:Class="Apress.VisualCSharpRecipes.Chapter17.FileInputControl"
    xmlns="http://schemas.microsoft.com/winfx/2006/xaml/presentation"
    xmlns:x="http://schemas.microsoft.com/winfx/2006/xaml">
    <DockPanel>
        <Button DockPanel.Dock="Right" Margin="2,0,0,0" Click="BrowseButton_Click">
            Browse...
        </Button>
        <TextBox x:Name="txtBox" IsReadOnly="True" />
    </DockPanel>
</UserControl>
```

The code-behind for the control is as follows:

```
using System.Windows.Controls;
using Microsoft.Win32;

namespace Apress.VisualCSharpRecipes.Chapter17
{
    public partial class FileInputControl : UserControl
    {
        public FileInputControl()
        {
            InitializeComponent();
        }

        private void BrowseButton_Click(
            object sender,
            System.Windows.RoutedEventArgs e)
        {
            OpenFileDialog dlg = new OpenFileDialog();
```

```
                if(dlg.ShowDialog() == true)
                {
                    this.FileName = dlg.FileName;
                }
            }

            public string FileName
            {
                get
                {
                    return txtBox.Text;
                }
                set
                {
                    txtBox.Text = value;
                }
            }
        }
    }
```

The XAML for the window that consumes this user control is as follows:

```
<Window x:Class="Apress.VisualCSharpRecipes.Chapter17.MainWindow"
    xmlns="http://schemas.microsoft.com/winfx/2006/xaml/presentation"
    xmlns:x="http://schemas.microsoft.com/winfx/2006/xaml"
    xmlns:local="clr-namespace:Apress.VisualCSharpRecipes.Chapter17;assembly="
     Title="Recipe17_12" Height="80" Width="300">
    <Grid>
        <local:FileInputControl Margin="8" />
    </Grid>
</Window>
```

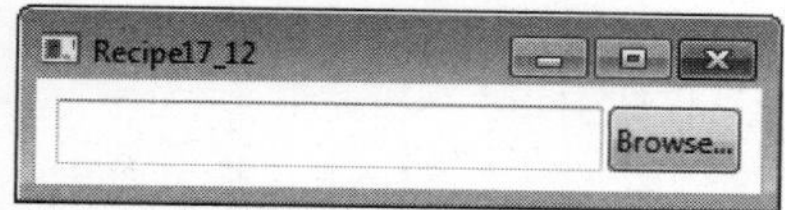

Figure 17-10. *Creating and using a FileInput user control*

17-13. Support Application Commands in a User Control

Problem

You need to support common application commands in your `System.Windows.Controls.UserControl`, such as Undo, Redo, Open, Copy, Paste, and so on, so that your control can respond to a command without needing any external code.

Solution

Use the `System.Windows.Input.CommandManager` to register an instance of the `System.Windows.Input.CommandBinding` class for each member of `System.Windows.Input.ApplicationCommands` that you need to support in your user control. The `CommandBinding` specifies the type of command you want to receive notification of, specifies a `CanExecute` event handler to determine when the command can be executed, and specifies an `Executed` event handler to be called when the command is executed.

How It Works

There are many predefined commands in WPF to support common scenarios. These commands are grouped as static properties on five different classes, mostly in the `System.Windows.Input` namespace, as shown in Table 17-4.

Table 17-4. *Predefined Common Commands*

Value	Description
`ApplicationCommands`	Common commands for an application; for example, `Copy`, `Paste`, `Undo`, `Redo`, `Find`, `Open`, `SaveAs`, and `Print`
`ComponentCommands`	Common commands for user interface components; for example, `MoveLeft`, `MoveToEnd`, and `ScrollPageDown`
`MediaCommands`	Common commands used for multimedia; for example, `Play`, `Pause`, `NextTrack`, `IncreaseVolume`, and `ToggleMicrophoneOnOff`
`NavigationCommands`	A set of commands used for page navigation; for example, `BrowseBack`, `GoToPage`, `NextPage`, `Refresh`, and `Zoom`
`EditingCommands`	A set of commands for editing documents; for example, `AlignCenter`, `IncreaseFontSize`, `EnterParagraphBreak`, and `ToggleBold`

Each command has a `System.Windows.Input.InputGestureCollection` that specifies the possible mouse or keyboard combinations that trigger the command. These are defined by the command itself, which is why you are able to register to receive these automatically by registering a `CommandBinding` for a particular command.

A `CommandBinding` for a particular command registers the `CanExecute` and `Executed` handlers so that the execution and the validation of the execution of the command are routed to these event handlers.

The Code

The following example creates a `UserControl` called `FileInputControl` that can be used to browse to a file using `Microsoft.Win32.OpenFileDialog` and display the file name in a `System.Windows.Controls.TextBox`.

It registers a CommandBinding for two application commands, Open and Find. When the user control has focus and the keyboard shortcuts for the Open and Find commands (Ctrl+O and Ctrl+F, respectively) are used, the Executed event handler for the respective command is invoked.

The Executed event handler for the Find command launches the OpenFileDialog, as if the user has clicked the Browse button. This command can always be executed, so the CanExecute event handler simply sets the CanExecute property of System.Windows.Input.CanExecuteRoutedEventArgs to True.

The Executed event handler for the Open command launches the file that is currently displayed in the TextBox. Therefore, the CanExecute event handler for this command sets the CanExecuteRoutedEventArgs to True only if there is a valid FileName. The XAML for the FileInputControl is as follows:

```
<UserControl x:Class=" Apress.VisualCSharpRecipes.Chapter17.FileInputControl"
    xmlns="http://schemas.microsoft.com/winfx/2006/xaml/presentation"
    xmlns:x="http://schemas.microsoft.com/winfx/2006/xaml">
    <DockPanel>
        <Button DockPanel.Dock="Right" Margin="2,0,0,0" Click="BrowseButton_Click">
            Browse...
        </Button>
        <TextBox x:Name="txtBox" />
    </DockPanel>
</UserControl>
```

The code-behind for the FileInputControl is as follows:

```
using System.Diagnostics;
using System.IO;
using System.Windows.Controls;
using System.Windows.Input;
using Microsoft.Win32;

namespace Apress.VisualCSharpRecipes.Chapter17
{
    public partial class FileInputControl : UserControl
    {
        public FileInputControl()
        {
            InitializeComponent();

            // Register command bindings

            // ApplicationCommands.Find
            CommandManager.RegisterClassCommandBinding(
                typeof(FileInputControl),
                new CommandBinding(
                    ApplicationCommands.Find,
                    FindCommand_Executed,
                    FindCommand_CanExecute));

            // ApplicationCommands.Open
            CommandManager.RegisterClassCommandBinding(
                typeof(FileInputControl),
                new CommandBinding(
```

```
            ApplicationCommands.Open,
            OpenCommand_Executed,
            OpenCommand_CanExecute));
}

#region Find Command

private void FindCommand_CanExecute(
    object sender,
    CanExecuteRoutedEventArgs e)
{
    e.CanExecute = true;
}

private void FindCommand_Executed(
    object sender,
    ExecutedRoutedEventArgs e)
{
    DoFindFile();
}

#endregion

#region Open Command

private void OpenCommand_CanExecute(
    object sender,
    CanExecuteRoutedEventArgs e)
{
    e.CanExecute =
        !string.IsNullOrEmpty(this.FileName)
        && File.Exists(this.FileName);
}

private void OpenCommand_Executed(
    object sender,
    ExecutedRoutedEventArgs e)
{
    Process.Start(this.FileName);
}

#endregion

private void BrowseButton_Click(
    object sender,
    System.Windows.RoutedEventArgs e)
{
    DoFindFile();
}
```

```
        private void DoFindFile()
        {
            OpenFileDialog dlg = new OpenFileDialog();
            if(dlg.ShowDialog() == true)
            {
                this.FileName = dlg.FileName;
            }
        }

        public string FileName
        {
            get
            {
                return txtBox.Text;
            }

            set
            {
                txtBox.Text = value;
            }
        }
    }
}
```

The following XAML shows how to use the FileInputControl in a window. If the TextBox has the focus, then pressing the keyboard shortcut Ctrl+F will automatically open the OpenFileDialog. If a file is selected and a valid file name appears in the TextBox, then the shortcut Ctrl+O will launch it.

```
<Window x:Class="Apress.VisualCSharpRecipes.Chapter17.MainWindow"
    xmlns="http://schemas.microsoft.com/winfx/2006/xaml/presentation"
    xmlns:x="http://schemas.microsoft.com/winfx/2006/xaml"
    xmlns:local="clr-namespace:Apress.VisualCSharpRecipes.Chapter17;assembly="
    Title="Recipe17_13" Height="80" Width="300">
    <Grid>
        <local:FileInputControl Margin="8"/>
    </Grid>
</Window>
```

17-14. Create a Lookless Custom Control

Problem

You need to create a custom control that encapsulates functionality and behavior logic but can have its visual appearance changed by consumers. For example, you need consumers to be able to change the style, template, or visual theme of your control for a particular context, application, or operating system theme.

Solution

Create a lookless custom control class that contains interaction and behavior logic but little or no assumptions about its visual implementation. Then declare the default visual elements for it in a control template within a default style.

■ **Tip** When creating the code for a custom control, you need to ensure it is lookless and assumes as little as possible about the actual implementation of the visual elements in the control template, because it could be different across different consumers. This means ensuring that the UI is decoupled from the interaction logic by using commands and bindings, avoiding event handlers, and referencing elements in the `ControlTemplate` whenever possible.

How It Works

The first step in creating a lookless custom control is choosing which control to inherit from. You could derive from the most basic option available to you, because it provides the minimum required functionality and gives the control consumer the maximum freedom. On the other hand, it also makes sense to leverage as much built-in support as possible by deriving from an existing WPF control if it possesses similar behavior and functionality to your custom control. For example, if your control will be clickable, then it might make sense to inherit from the `Button` class. If your control is not only clickable but also has the notion of being in a selected or unselected state, then it might make sense to inherit from `ToggleButton`.

Some of the most common base classes you will derive from are listed in Table 17-5.

Table 17-5. Common Base Classes for Creating a Custom Control

Name	Description
`FrameworkElement`	This is usually the most basic element from which you will derive. Use this when you need to draw your own element by overriding the `OnRender` method and explicitly defining the component visuals. `FrameworkElement` classes tend not to interact with the user; for example, the WPF `Image` and `Border` controls are `FrameworkElement` classes.
`Control`	`Control` is the base class used by most of the existing WPF controls. It allows you to define its appearance by using control templates, and it adds properties for setting the background and foreground, font, padding, tab index, and alignment of content. It also supports double-clicking through the `MouseDoubleClick` and `PreviewMouseDoubleClick` events.

Name	Description
ContentControl	This inherits from Control and adds a Content property that provides the ability to contain a single piece of content, which could be a string or another visual element. For example, a button ultimately derives from ContentControl, which is why it has the ability to contain any arbitrary visual element such as an image. Use this as your base class if you need your control to contain other objects defined by the control consumer.
Panel	This has a property called Children that contains a collection of System.Windows.UIElements, and it provides the layout logic for positioning these children within it.
Decorator	This wraps another control to decorate it with a particular visual effect or feature. For example, the Border is a Decorator control that draws a line around an element.

After choosing an appropriate base class for your custom control, you can create the class and put the logic for the interaction, functionality, and behavior of your control in the custom control class.

However, don't define your visual elements in a XAML file for the class, like you would with a user control. Instead, put the default definition of visual elements in a System.Windows.ControlTemplate, and declare this ControlTemplate in a default System.Windows.Style.

The next step is to specify that you will be providing this new style; otherwise, your control will continue to use the default template of its base class. You specify this by calling the OverrideMetadata method of DefaultStyleKeyProperty in the static constructor for your class.

Next, you need to place your style in the Generic.xaml resource dictionary in the Themes subfolder of your project. This ensures it is recognized as the default style for your control. You can also create other resource dictionaries in this subfolder, which enables you to target specific operating systems and give your custom controls a different visual appearance for each one.

■ **Tip** When a custom control library contains several controls, it is often better the keep their styles separate instead of putting them all in the same Generic.xaml resource dictionary. You can use resource dictionary merging to keep each style in a separate resource dictionary file and then merge them into the main Generic.xaml one.

The custom style and template for your control must use the System.Type.TargetType attribute to attach it to the custom control automatically.

■ **Tip** In Visual Studio, when you add a new WPF custom control to an existing project, it does a number of the previous steps for you. It automatically creates a code file with the correct call to `DefaultStyleKeyproperty.OverrideMetadata`. It creates the `Themes` subfolder and `Generic.xaml` resource dictionary if they don't already exist, and it defines a placeholder `Style` and `ControlTemplate` in there.

When creating your custom control class and default control template, you have to remember to make as few assumptions as possible about the actual implementation of the visual elements. This is in order to make the custom control as flexible as possible and to give control consumers as much freedom as possible when creating new styles and control templates. You can enable this separation between the interaction logic and the visual implementation of your control in a number of ways.

First, when binding a property of a visual element in the default `ControlTemplate` to a dependency property of the control, use the `System.Windows.Data.RelativeSource` property instead of naming the element and referencing it via the `ElementName` property.

Second, instead of declaring event handlers in the XAML for the template—for example, for the `Click` event of a `Button`—either add the event handler programmatically in the control constructor or bind to commands. If you choose to use event handlers and bind them programmatically, override the `OnApplyTemplate` method and locate the controls dynamically.

Furthermore, give names only to those elements without which the control would not be able to function as intended. By convention, give these intrinsic elements the name PART_*ElementName* so that they can be identified as part of the public interface for your control. For example, it is intrinsic to a `ProgressBar` that it has a visual element representing the total value at completion and a visual element indicating the relative value of the current progress. The default `ControlTemplate` for the `System.Windows.Controls.ProgressBar` therefore defines two named elements, `PART_Track` and `PART_Indicator`. These happen to be `Border` controls in the default template, but there is no reason why a control consumer could not provide a custom template that uses different controls to display these functional parts.

■ **Tip** If your control requires named elements, as well as using the previously mentioned naming convention, apply the `System.Windows.TemplatePart` attribute to your control class, which documents and signals this requirement to users of your control and to design tools such as Expression Blend.

The following code example demonstrates how to separate the interaction logic and the visual implementation using these methods.

The Code

The following example demonstrates how to create a lookless custom control to encapsulate the functionality of browsing to a file and displaying the file name. Figure 17-11 shows the control in use.

The `FileInputControl` class derives from `Control` and uses the `TemplatePart` attribute to signal that it expects a `Button` control called `PART_Browse`. It overrides the `OnApplyTemplate` method and calls

GetTemplateChild to find the button defined by its actual template. If this exists, it adds an event handler to the button's Click event. The code for the control is as follows:

```
using System.Windows;
using System.Windows.Controls;
using System.Windows.Markup;
using Microsoft.Win32;

namespace Apress.VisualCSharpRecipes.Chapter17
{
    [TemplatePart(Name = "PART_Browse", Type = typeof(Button))]
    [ContentProperty("FileName")]
    public class FileInputControl : Control
    {
        static FileInputControl()
        {
            DefaultStyleKeyProperty.OverrideMetadata(
                typeof(FileInputControl),
                new FrameworkPropertyMetadata(
                    typeof(FileInputControl)));
        }

        public override void OnApplyTemplate()
        {
            base.OnApplyTemplate();

            Button browseButton = base.GetTemplateChild("PART_Browse") as Button;

            if (browseButton != null)
                browseButton.Click += new RoutedEventHandler(browseButton_Click);
        }

        void browseButton_Click(object sender, RoutedEventArgs e)
        {
            OpenFileDialog dlg = new OpenFileDialog();
            if (dlg.ShowDialog() == true)
            {
                this.FileName = dlg.FileName;
            }
        }

        public string FileName
        {
            get
            {
                return (string)GetValue(FileNameProperty);
            }
```

```
            set
            {
                SetValue(FileNameProperty, value);
            }
        }

        public static readonly DependencyProperty FileNameProperty =
            DependencyProperty.Register( "FileName", typeof(string),
typeof(FileInputControl));
    }
}
```

The default style and control template for FileInputControl is in a ResourceDictionary in the Themes subfolder and is merged into the Generic ResourceDictionary. The XAML for this style is as follows:

```
<ResourceDictionary
    xmlns="http://schemas.microsoft.com/winfx/2006/xaml/presentation"
    xmlns:x="http://schemas.microsoft.com/winfx/2006/xaml"
    xmlns:local="clr-namespace:Apress.VisualCSharpRecipes.Chapter17;assembly=">

    <Style TargetType="{x:Type local:FileInputControl}">
        <Setter Property="Template">
            <Setter.Value>
                <ControlTemplate
                      TargetType="{x:Type local:FileInputControl}">
                    <Border Background="{TemplateBinding Background}"
                            BorderBrush="{TemplateBinding BorderBrush}"
                            BorderThickness="{TemplateBinding BorderThickness}">
                        <DockPanel>
                            <Button x:Name="PART_Browse" DockPanel.Dock="Right"
                                Margin="2,0,0,0">
                                Browse...
                            </Button>
                            <TextBox IsReadOnly="True"
                                Text="{Binding Path=FileName,
                                    RelativeSource=
                                       {RelativeSource TemplatedParent}}" />
                        </DockPanel>
                    </Border>
                </ControlTemplate>
            </Setter.Value>
        </Setter>
    </Style>
</ResourceDictionary>
```

The XAML for the window that consumes this custom control is as follows:

```
<Window x:Class="Apress.VisualCSharpRecipes.Chapter17.MainWindow"
    xmlns="http://schemas.microsoft.com/winfx/2006/xaml/presentation"
    xmlns:x="http://schemas.microsoft.com/winfx/2006/xaml"
    xmlns:local="clr-namespace:Apress.VisualCSharpRecipes.Chapter17;assembly="
```

```
    Title="Recipe17_14" Height="200" Width="300">
     <StackPanel>
       <StackPanel.Resources>
         <Style x:Key="fileInputStyle">
           <Setter Property="Control.Height" Value="50" />
           <Setter Property="Control.FontSize" Value="20px" />
           <Setter Property="Control.BorderBrush" Value="Blue" />
           <Setter Property="Control.BorderThickness" Value="2" />
           <Style.Triggers>
             <Trigger Property="Control.IsMouseOver" Value="True">
               <Setter Property="Control.BorderThickness" Value="3" />
               <Setter Property="Control.BorderBrush" Value="RoyalBlue" />
             </Trigger>
           </Style.Triggers>
         </Style>
         <ControlTemplate x:Key="fileInputTemplate"
               TargetType="{x:Type local:FileInputControl}">
           <Border Background="{TemplateBinding Background}"
                   BorderBrush="{TemplateBinding BorderBrush}"
                   BorderThickness="{TemplateBinding BorderThickness}">
             <DockPanel>
               <Button x:Name="PART_Browse" DockPanel.Dock="Left"
                       Background="Lightgreen">
                 <TextBlock FontSize="20px" Padding="3px" FontFamily="Arial" Text="Open..."/>
               </Button>
               <TextBlock x:Name="PART_Text" VerticalAlignment="Center"
                   Margin="5, 0, 0, 0" FontSize="16px" FontWeight="Bold"
                   Text="{Binding Path=FileName,
                                  RelativeSource=
                                  {RelativeSource TemplatedParent}}" />
             </DockPanel>
           </Border>
         </ControlTemplate>
       </StackPanel.Resources>
       <!-- Use the default appearance -->
       <local:FileInputControl Margin="8" />
       <!-- Applying a style to the control -->
       <local:FileInputControl Margin="8" Style="{StaticResource fileInputStyle}" />
       <!-- Applying a template to the control -->
       <local:FileInputControl Margin="8" Template="{StaticResource fileInputTemplate}" />
     </StackPanel>
</Window>
```

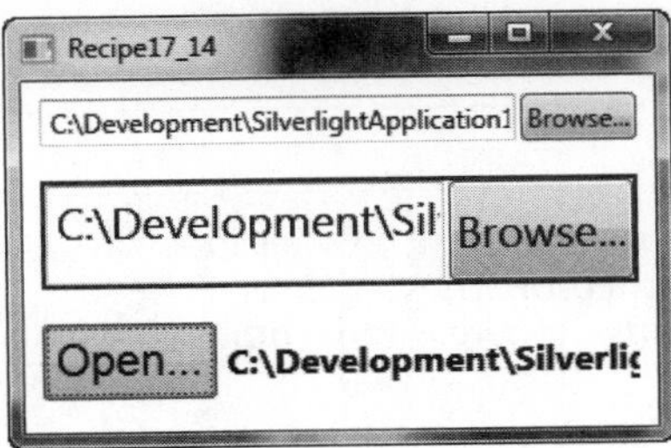

Figure 17-11. Creating and using a FileInput custom control

17-15. Create a Two-Way Binding

Problem

You need to create a two-way binding so that when the value of either property changes, the other one automatically updates to reflect it.

Solution

Use the `System.Windows.Data.Binding` markup extension, and set the `Mode` attribute to `System.Windows.Data.BindingMode.TwoWay`. Use the `UpdateSourceTrigger` attribute to specify when the binding source should be updated.

How It Works

The data in a binding can flow from the source property to the target property, from the target property to the source property, or in both directions. For example, suppose the `Text` property of a `System.Windows.Controls.TextBox` control is bound to the `Value` property of a `System.Windows.Controls.Slider` control. In this case, the `Text` property of the `TextBox` control is the target of the binding, and the `Value` property of the `Slider` control is the binding source. The direction of data flow between the target and the source can be configured in a number of different ways. It could be configured such that when the `Value` of the `Slider` control changes, the `Text` property of the `TextBox` is updated. This is called a *one-way binding*. Alternatively, you could configure the binding so that when the `Text` property of the `TextBox` changes, the `Slider` control's `Value` is automatically updated to reflect it. This is called a *one-way binding to the source*. A *two-way binding* means that a change to either the source property or the target property automatically updates the other. This type of binding is useful for editable forms or other fully interactive UI scenarios.

It is the `Mode` property of a `Binding` object that configures its data flow. This stores an instance of the `System.Windows.Data.BindingMode` enumeration and can be configured with the values listed in Table 17-6.

Table 17-6. BindingMode Values for Configuring the Data Flow in a Binding

Value	Description
`Default`	The `Binding` uses the default `Mode` value of the binding target, which varies for each dependency property. In general, user-editable control properties, such as those of text boxes and check boxes, default to two-way bindings, whereas most other properties default to one-way bindings.
`OneTime`	The target property is updated when the control is first loaded or when the data context changes. This type of binding is appropriate if the data is static and won't change once it has been set.
`OneWay`	The target property is updated whenever the source property changes. This is appropriate if the target control is read-only, such as a `System.Windows.Controls.Label` or `System.Windows.Controls.TextBlock`. If the target property does change, the source property will not be updated.
`OneWayToSource`	This is the opposite of `OneWay`. The source property is updated when the target property changes.
`TwoWay`	Changes to either the target property or the source automatically update the other.

Bindings that are `TwoWay` or `OneWayToSource` listen for changes in the target property and update the source. It is the `UpdateSourceTrigger` property of the binding that determines when this update occurs. For example, suppose you created a `TwoWay` binding between the `Text` property of a `TextBox` control and the `Value` property of a `Slider` control. You could configure the binding so that the slider is updated either as soon as you type text into the `TextBox` or when the `TextBox` loses its focus. Alternatively, you could specify that the `TextBox` is updated only when you explicitly call the `UpdateSource` property of the `System.Windows.Data.BindingExpression` class. These options are configured by the `Binding`'s `UpdateSourceTrigger` property, which stores an instance of the `System.Windows.Data.UpdateSourceTrigger` enumeration. Table 17-7 lists the possible values of this enumeration.

Therefore, to create a two-way binding that updates the source as soon as the target property changes, you need to specify `TwoWay` as the value of the `Binding`'s `Mode` attribute and `PropertyChanged` for the `UpdateSourceTrigger` attribute.

■ **Note** To detect source changes in `OneWay` and `TwoWay` bindings, if the source property is not a `System.Windows.DependencyProperty`, it must implement `System.ComponentModel.INotifyPropertyChanged` to notify the target that its value has changed.

Table 17-7. UpdateSourceTrigger Values for Configuring When the Binding Source Is Updated

Value	Description
`Default`	The `Binding` uses the default `UpdateSourceTrigger` of the binding target property. For most dependency properties, this is `PropertyChanged`, but for the `TextBox.Text` property, it is `LostFocus`.
`Explicit`	Updates the binding source only when you call the `System.Windows.Data.BindingExpression.UpdateSource` method.
`LostFocus`	Updates the binding source whenever the binding target element loses focus.
`PropertyChanged`	Updates the binding source immediately whenever the binding target property changes.

The Code

The following example demonstrates a window containing a `System.Windows.Controls.Slider` control and a `System.Windows.Controls.TextBlock` control. The XAML statement for the `Text` property of the `TextBlock` specifies a `Binding` statement that binds it to the `Value` property of the `Slider` control. In the binding statement, the `Mode` attribute is set to `TwoWay`, and the `UpdateSourceTrigger` attribute is set to `PropertyChanged`. This ensures that when a number from 1 to 100 is typed into the `TextBox`, the `Slider` control immediately updates its value to reflect it. The XAML for the window is as follows:

```
<Window x:Class="Apress.VisualCSharpRecipes.Chapter17.MainWindow"
    xmlns="http://schemas.microsoft.com/winfx/2006/xaml/presentation"
    xmlns:x="http://schemas.microsoft.com/winfx/2006/xaml"
     Title="Recipe17_15" Height="100" Width="260">
    <StackPanel>
        <Slider Name="slider" Margin="4" Interval="1"
                TickFrequency="1" IsSnapToTickEnabled="True"
                Minimum="0" Maximum="100"/>
        <StackPanel Orientation="Horizontal" >
            <TextBlock Width="Auto" HorizontalAlignment="Left"
                       VerticalAlignment="Center" Margin="4"
                       Text="Gets and sets the value of the slider:" />
            <TextBox Width="40" HorizontalAlignment="Center" Margin="4"
                 Text="{Binding
                        ElementName=slider,
                        Path=Value,
                        Mode=TwoWay,
                        UpdateSourceTrigger=PropertyChanged}" />
        </StackPanel>
    </StackPanel>
</Window>
```

Figure 17-12 shows the resulting window.

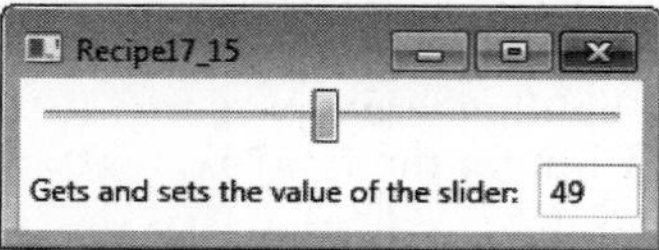

Figure 17-12. *Creating a two-way binding*

17-16. Bind to a Command

Problem

You need to bind a `System.Windows.Controls.Button` control directly to a `System.Windows.Input.ICommand`. This enables you to execute custom logic when the `Button` is clicked, without having to handle its `Click` event and call a method. You can also bind the `IsEnabled` property of the `Button` to the `ICommand` object's `CanExecute` method.

Solution

Create a class that implements `ICommand`, and expose an instance of it as a property on another class or business object. Bind this property to a `Button` control's `Command` property.

How It Works

The `Button` control derives from the `System.Windows.Controls.Primitives.ButtonBase` class. This implements the `System.Windows.Input.ICommandSource` interface and exposes an `ICommand` property called `Command`. The `ICommand` interface encapsulates a unit of functionality. When its `Execute` method is called, this functionality is executed. The `CanExecute` method determines whether the `ICommand` can be executed in its current state. It returns `True` if the `ICommand` can be executed and returns `False` if not.

To execute custom application logic when a `Button` is clicked, you would typically attach an event handler to its `Click` event. However, you can also encapsulate this custom logic in a command and bind it directly to the `Button` control's `Command` property. This approach has several advantages. First, the `IsEnabled` property of the `Button` will automatically be bound to the `CanExecute` method of the `ICommand`. This means that when the `CanExecuteChanged` event is fired, the `Button` will call the command's `CanExecute` method and refresh its own `IsEnabled` property dynamically. Second, the application functionality that should be executed when the `Button` is clicked does not have to reside in the code-behind for the window. This enables greater separation of presentation and business logic, which is always desirable in object-oriented programming in general, and even more so in WPF development, because it makes it easier for UI designers to work alongside developers without getting in each other's way.

To bind the Command property of a Button to an instance of an ICommand, simply set the Path attribute to the name of the ICommand property, just as you would any other property. You can also optionally specify parameters using the CommandParameter attribute. This in turn can be bound to the properties of other elements and is passed to the Execute and CanExecute methods of the command.

The Code

The following example demonstrates a window containing three System.Windows.Controls.TextBox controls. These are bound to the FirstName, LastName, and Age properties of a custom Person object. The Person class also exposes an instance of the AddPersonCommand and SetOccupationCommand as read-only properties. There are two Button controls on the window that have their Command attribute bound to these command properties. Custom logic in the CanExecute methods of the commands specifies when the Buttons should be enabled or disabled. If the ICommand can be executed and the Button should therefore be enabled, the code in the CanExecute method returns True. If it returns False, the Button will be disabled. The Set Occupation Button control also binds its CommandParameter to the Text property of a System.Windows.Controls.ComboBox control. This demonstrates how to pass parameters to an instance of an ICommand. Figure 17-13 shows the resulting window. The XAML for the window is as follows:

```
<Window x:Class="Apress.VisualCSharpRecipes.Chapter17.MainWindow"
   xmlns="http://schemas.microsoft.com/winfx/2006/xaml/presentation"
   xmlns:x="http://schemas.microsoft.com/winfx/2006/xaml"
   Title="Recipe17_16" Height="233" Width="300">
    <Grid>
        <Grid.ColumnDefinitions>
            <ColumnDefinition Width="70"/>
            <ColumnDefinition Width="*"/>
        </Grid.ColumnDefinitions>

        <Grid.RowDefinitions>
            <RowDefinition Height="30"/>
            <RowDefinition Height="30"/>
            <RowDefinition Height="30"/>
            <RowDefinition Height="40"/>
            <RowDefinition Height="34"/>
            <RowDefinition Height="30"/>
        </Grid.RowDefinitions>

        <TextBlock Margin="4" Text="First Name" VerticalAlignment="Center"/>
        <TextBox Text="{Binding Path=FirstName}" Margin="4" Grid.Column="1"/>
```

```
        <TextBlock Margin="4" Text="Last Name" Grid.Row="1"
            VerticalAlignment="Center"/>
        <TextBox Margin="4" Text="{Binding Path=LastName}"
            Grid.Column="1" Grid.Row="1"/>

        <TextBlock Margin="4" Text="Age" Grid.Row="2"
            VerticalAlignment="Center"/>
        <TextBox Margin="4" Text="{Binding Path=Age}"
            Grid.Column="1" Grid.Row="2"/>

        <!-- Bind the Button to the Add Command -->
        <Button Command="{Binding Path=Add}" Content="Add"
            Margin="4" Grid.Row="3" Grid.Column="2"/>

        <StackPanel Orientation="Horizontal"
            Grid.Column="2" Grid.Row="4">

        <ComboBox x:Name="cboOccupation" IsEditable="False"
            Margin="4" Width="100">
             <ComboBoxItem>Student</ComboBoxItem>
             <ComboBoxItem>Skilled</ComboBoxItem>
             <ComboBoxItem>Professional</ComboBoxItem>
        </ComboBox>

         <Button Command="{Binding Path=SetOccupation}"
            CommandParameter="{Binding ElementName=cboOccupation, Path=Text}"
            Content="Set Occupation" Margin="4" />
        </StackPanel>

        <TextBlock Margin="4" Text="Status"
            Grid.Row="5" VerticalAlignment="Center"/>
        <TextBlock Margin="4"
            Text="{Binding Path=Status, UpdateSourceTrigger=PropertyChanged}"
            VerticalAlignment="Center" FontStyle="Italic" Grid.Column="1"
            Grid.Row="5"/>
    </Grid>
</Window>
```

The code-behind for the window sets its `DataContext` property to a new `Person` object. The code for this is as follows:

```
using System.Windows;

namespace Apress.VisualCSharpRecipes.Chapter17
{
    public partial class MainWindow : Window
    {
        public MainWindow()
        {
            InitializeComponent();
```

```
            // Set the DataContext to a Person object
            this.DataContext = new Person()
                {
                    FirstName = "Zander",
                    LastName = "Harris"
                };
        }
    }
}
```

The code for the Person, AddPersonCommand, and SetOccupationCommand classes are as follows:

```
using System;
using System.ComponentModel;
using System.Windows.Input;

namespace Apress.VisualCSharpRecipes.Chapter17
{
    public class Person : INotifyPropertyChanged
    {
        private string firstName;
        private int age;
        private string lastName;
        private string status;
        private string occupation;

        private AddPersonCommand addPersonCommand;
        private SetOccupationCommand setOccupationCommand;

        public string FirstName
        {
            get
            {
                return firstName;
            }
            set
            {
                if(firstName != value)
                {
                    firstName = value;
                    OnPropertyChanged("FirstName");
                }
            }
        }

        public string LastName
        {
            get
            {
                return lastName;
            }
```

```
        set
        {
            if(this.lastName != value)
            {
                this.lastName = value;
                OnPropertyChanged("LastName");
            }
        }
    }

    public int Age
    {
        get
        {
            return age;
        }
        set
        {
            if(this.age != value)
            {
                this.age = value;
                OnPropertyChanged("Age");
            }
        }
    }

    public string Status
    {
        get
        {
            return status;
        }
        set
        {
            if(this.status != value)
            {
                this.status = value;
                OnPropertyChanged("Status");
            }
        }
    }

    public string Occupation
    {
        get
        {
            return occupation;
        }
        set
        {
```

```
            if(this.occupation != value)
            {
                this.occupation = value;
                OnPropertyChanged("Occupation");
            }
        }
    }

    /// Gets an AddPersonCommand for data binding
    public AddPersonCommand Add
    {
        get
        {
            if(addPersonCommand == null)
                addPersonCommand = new AddPersonCommand(this);

            return addPersonCommand;
        }
    }

    /// Gets a SetOccupationCommand for data binding
    public SetOccupationCommand SetOccupation
    {
        get
        {
            if(setOccupationCommand == null)
                setOccupationCommand = new SetOccupationCommand(this);

            return setOccupationCommand;
        }
    }

    #region INotifyPropertyChanged Members

    /// Implement INotifyPropertyChanged to notify the binding
    /// targets when the values of properties change.
    public event PropertyChangedEventHandler PropertyChanged;

    private void OnPropertyChanged(string propertyName)
    {
        if(this.PropertyChanged != null)
        {
            this.PropertyChanged(
                this, new PropertyChangedEventArgs(propertyName));
        }
    }

    #endregion
}
```

```
public class AddPersonCommand : ICommand
{
    private Person person;

    public AddPersonCommand(Person person)
    {
        this.person = person;

        this.person.PropertyChanged +=
            new PropertyChangedEventHandler(person_PropertyChanged);
    }

    // Handle the PropertyChanged event of the person to raise the
    // CanExecuteChanged event
    private void person_PropertyChanged(
        object sender, PropertyChangedEventArgs e)
    {
        if(CanExecuteChanged != null)
        {
            CanExecuteChanged(this, EventArgs.Empty);
        }
    }

    #region ICommand Members

    /// The command can execute if there are valid values
    /// for the person's FirstName, LastName, and Age properties
    /// and if it hasn't already been executed and had its
    /// Status property set.
    public bool CanExecute(object parameter)
    {
        if(!string.IsNullOrEmpty(person.FirstName))
            if(!string.IsNullOrEmpty(person.LastName))
                if(person.Age > 0)
                    if(string.IsNullOrEmpty(person.Status))
                        return true;

        return false;
    }

    public event EventHandler CanExecuteChanged;

    /// When the command is executed, update the
    /// status property of the person.
    public void Execute(object parameter)
    {
        person.Status =
            string.Format("Added {0} {1}",
                          person.FirstName, person.LastName);
    }
```

```
    #endregion
}

public class SetOccupationCommand : ICommand
{
    private Person person;

    public SetOccupationCommand(Person person)
    {
        this.person = person;

        this.person.PropertyChanged +=
            new PropertyChangedEventHandler(person_PropertyChanged);
    }

    // Handle the PropertyChanged event of the person to raise the
    // CanExecuteChanged event
    private void person_PropertyChanged(
        object sender, PropertyChangedEventArgs e)
    {
        if(CanExecuteChanged != null)
        {
            CanExecuteChanged(this, EventArgs.Empty);
        }
    }

    #region ICommand Members

    /// The command can execute if the person has been added,
    /// which means its Status will be set, and if the occupation
    /// parameter is not null
    public bool CanExecute(object parameter)
    {
        if(!string.IsNullOrEmpty(parameter as string))
            if(!string.IsNullOrEmpty(person.Status))
                return true;

        return false;
    }

    public event EventHandler CanExecuteChanged;

    /// When the command is executed, set the Occupation
    /// property of the person, and update the Status.
    public void Execute(object parameter)
    {
        // Get the occupation string from the command parameter
        person.Occupation = parameter.ToString();
```

```
            person.Status =
                string.Format("Added {0} {1}, {2}",
                              person.FirstName, person.LastName, person.Occupation);
        }
        #endregion
    }
}
```

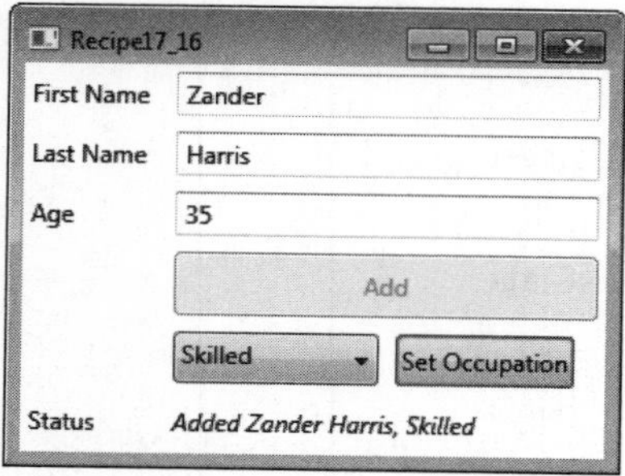

Figure 17-13. Binding to a command

17-17. Use Data Templates to Display Bound Data

Problem

You need to specify a set of UI elements to use to visualize your bound data objects.

Solution

Create a `System.Windows.DataTemplate` to define the presentation of your data objects. This specifies the visual structure of UI elements to use to display your data.

How It Works

When you bind to a data object, the binding target displays a string representation of the object by default. Internally, this is because without any specific instructions the binding mechanism calls the `ToString` method of the binding source when binding to it. Creating a `DataTemplate` enables you to specify a different visual structure of UI elements when displaying your data object. When the binding mechanism is asked to display a data object, it will use the UI elements specified in the `DataTemplate` to render it.

The Code

The following example demonstrates a window that contains a `System.Windows.Controls.ListBox` control. The `ItemsSource` property of the `ListBox` is bound to a collection of `Person` objects. The `Person` class is defined in the `Data.cs` file and exposes `FirstName`, `LastName`, `Age`, and `Photo` properties. It also overrides the `ToString` method to return the full name of the person it represents. Without a `DataTemplate`, the `ListBox` control would just display this list of names. Figure 17-14 shows what this would look like.

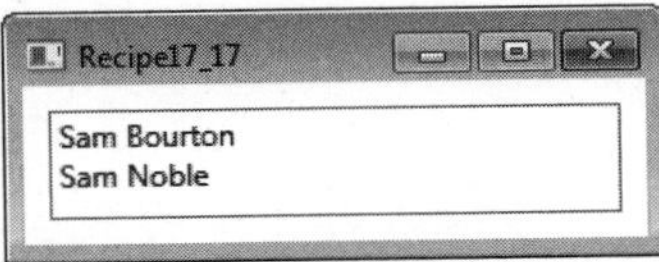

Figure 17-14. *Binding to a list of data objects without specifying a DataTemplate*

However, the `ItemTemplate` property of the `ListBox` is set to a static resource called `personTemplate`. This is a `DataTemplate` resource defined in the window's `System.Windows.ResourceDictionary`. The `DataTemplate` creates a `System.Windows.Controls.Grid` control inside a `System.Windows.Controls.Border` control. Inside the `Grid`, it defines a series of `System.Windows.Controls.TextBlock` controls and a `System.Windows.Controls.Image` control. These controls have standard binding statements that bind their properties to properties on the `Person` class. When the window opens and the `ListBox` binds to the collection of `Person` objects, the binding mechanism uses the set of UI elements in the `DataTemplate` to display each item. Figure 17-15 shows the same `ListBox` as in Figure 17-14 but with its `ItemTemplate` property set to the `DataTemplate`.

The XAML for the window is as follows:

```
<Window
    x:Class="Apress.VisualCSharpRecipes.Chapter17.MainWindow"
    xmlns="http://schemas.microsoft.com/winfx/2006/xaml/presentation"
    xmlns:x="http://schemas.microsoft.com/winfx/2006/xaml"
    xmlns:local="clr-namespace:Apress.VisualCSharpRecipes.Chapter17"
    Title="Recipe17_17" Height="298" Width="260">

    <Window.Resources>

        <!-- Creates the local data source for binding -->
        <local:PersonCollection x:Key="people"/>

        <!-- Styles used by the UI elements in the DataTemplate -->
        <Style
            x:Key="lblStyle"
            TargetType="{x:Type TextBlock}">
            <Setter Property="FontFamily" Value="Tahoma"/>
            <Setter Property="FontSize" Value="11pt"/>
            <Setter Property="VerticalAlignment" Value="Center"/>
```

```
    <Setter Property="Margin" Value="2"/>
    <Setter Property="Foreground" Value="Red"/>
</Style>

<Style
    x:Key="dataStyle"
    TargetType="{x:Type TextBlock}"
    BasedOn="{StaticResource lblStyle}">
    <Setter Property="Margin" Value="10,2,2,2"/>
    <Setter Property="Foreground" Value="Blue"/>
    <Setter Property="FontStyle" Value="Italic"/>
</Style>

<!-- DataTemplate to use for displaying each Person item -->
<DataTemplate x:Key="personTemplate">
    <Border
        BorderThickness="1"
        BorderBrush="Gray"
        Padding="4"
        Margin="4"
        Height="Auto"
        Width="Auto">
        <Grid>
            <Grid.ColumnDefinitions>
                <ColumnDefinition Width="80"/>
                <ColumnDefinition Width="*"/>
            </Grid.ColumnDefinitions>

            <StackPanel>
                <TextBlock
                    Style="{StaticResource lblStyle}"
                    Text="First Name" />
                <TextBlock
                    Style="{StaticResource dataStyle}"
                    Text="{Binding Path=FirstName}"/>

                <TextBlock
                    Style="{StaticResource lblStyle}"
                    Text="Last Name" />
                <TextBlock
                    Style="{StaticResource dataStyle}"
                    Text="{Binding Path=LastName}" />

                <TextBlock
                    Style="{StaticResource lblStyle}"
                    Text="Age" />
                <TextBlock
                    Style="{StaticResource dataStyle}"
                    Text="{Binding Path=Age}" />
            </StackPanel>
```

```
                <Image
                    Margin="4"
                    Grid.Column="1"
                    Width="96"
                    Height="140"
                    Source="{Binding Path=Photo}"/>
            </Grid>
        </Border>
    </DataTemplate>


</Window.Resources>

<Grid>
    <!-- The ListBox binds to the people collection, and sets the -->
    <!-- DataTemplate to use for displaying each item -->
    <ListBox
        Margin="10"
        ItemsSource="{Binding Source={StaticResource people}}"
        ItemTemplate="{StaticResource personTemplate}"/>

    <!-- Without specifying a DataTemplate, the ListBox just -->
    <!-- displays a list of names. -->
    <!--<ListBox
        Margin="10"
        ItemsSource="{Binding Source={StaticResource people}}"/>-->
</Grid>
</Window>
```

Figure 17-15. Binding to a list of data objects and specifying a DataTemplate

17-18. Bind to a Collection with the Master-Detail Pattern

Problem

You need to bind to the items in a data collection and display more information about the selected item. For example, you might display a list of product names and prices on one side of the screen and a more detailed view of the selected product on the other side.

Solution

Bind a data collection to the `ItemsSource` property of a `System.Windows.Controls.ItemsControl` such as a `System.Windows.Controls.ListBox`, `System.Windows.Controls.ListView`, or `System.Windows.Controls.TreeView`. Implement `System.Collections.Specialized.INotifyCollectionChanged` on the data collection to ensure that insertions or deletions in the collection update the UI automatically. Implement the master-detail pattern by binding a `System.Windows.Controls.ContentControl` to the same collection.

How It Works

To bind an `ItemsControl` to a collection object, set its `ItemsSource` property to an instance of a collection class. This is a class that implements the `System.Collections.IEnumerable` interface, such as `System.Collections.Generic.List<T>` or `System.Collections.ObjectModel.Collection<T>`, or the `System.Collections.IList` and `System.Collections.ICollection` interfaces. However, if you bind to any of these objects, the binding will be one-way and read-only. To set up dynamic bindings so that insertions or deletions in the collection update the UI automatically, the collection must implement the `System.Collections.Specialized.INotifyCollectionChanged` interface. This interface provides the mechanism for notifying the binding target of changes to the source collection, in much the same way as the `System.ComponentModel.INotifyPropertyChanged` interface notifies bindings of changes to properties in single objects.

`INotifyCollectionChanged` exposes an event called `CollectionChanged` that should be raised whenever the underlying collection changes. When you raise this event, you pass in an instance of the `System.Collections.Specialized.NotifyCollectionChangedEventArgs` class. This contains properties that specify the action that caused the event—for example, whether items were added, moved, or removed from the collection and the list of affected items. The binding mechanism listens for these events and updates the target UI element accordingly.

You do not need to implement `INotifyCollectionChanged` on your own collection classes. WPF provides the `System.Collections.ObjectModel.ObservableCollection<T>` class, which is a built-in implementation of a data collection that exposes `INotifyCollectionChanged`. If your collection classes are instances of the `ObservableCollection<T>` class or they inherit from it, you will get two-way dynamic data binding for free.

■ **Note** To fully support transferring data values from source objects to targets, each object in your collection that supports bindable properties must also implement the `INotifyPropertyChanged` interface. It is common practice to create a base class for all your custom business objects that implements `INotifyPropertyChanged` and a base collection class for collections of these objects that inherits from `ObservableCollection<T>`. This automatically enables all your custom objects and collection classes for data binding.

To implement the master-detail scenario of binding to a collection, you simply need to bind two or more controls to the same `System.Windows.Data.CollectionView` object. A `CollectionView` represents a wrapper around a binding source collection that allows you to navigate, sort, filter, and group the collection, without having to manipulate the underlying source collection itself. When you bind to any class that implements `IEnumerable`, the WPF binding engine creates a default `CollectionView` object automatically behind the scenes. So if you bind two or more controls to the same `ObservableCollection<T>` object, you are in effect binding them to the same default `CollectionView` class. If you want to implement custom sorting, grouping, and filtering of your collection, you will need to define a `CollectionView` explicitly yourself. You do this by creating a `System.Windows.Data.CollectionViewSource` class in your XAML. This approach is demonstrated in the next few recipes in this chapter. However, for the purpose of implementing the master-detail pattern, you can simply bind directly to an `ObservableCollection<T>` and accept the default `CollectionView` behind the scenes.

To display the master aspect of the pattern, simply bind your collection to the `ItemsSource` property of an `ItemsControl`, such as a `System.Windows.Controls.ListBox`, `System.Windows.Controls.ListView`, or `System.Windows.Controls.TreeView`. If you do not specify a `DataTemplate` for the `ItemTemplate` property of the `ItemsControl`, you can use the `DisplayMemberPath` property to specify the name of the property the `ItemsControl` should display. If you do not support a value for `DisplayMemberPath`, it will display the value returned by the `ToString` method of each data item in the collection.

To display the detail aspect of the pattern for the selected item, simply bind a singleton object to the collection, such as a `ContentControl`. When a singleton object is bound to a `CollectionView`, it automatically binds to the `CurrentItem` of the view.

If you are explicitly creating a `CollectionView` using a `CollectionViewSource` object, it will automatically synchronize currency and selection between the binding source and targets. However, if you are bound directly to an `ObservableCollection<T>` or other such `IEnumerable` object, then you will need to set the `IsSynchronizedWithCurrentItem` property of your `ListBox` to `True` for this to work. Setting the `IsSynchronizedWithCurrentItem` property to `True` ensures that the item selected always corresponds to the `CurrentItem` property in the `ItemCollection`. For example, suppose there are two `ListBox` controls with their `ItemsSource` property bound to the same `ObservableCollection<T>`. If you set `IsSynchronizedWithCurrentItem` to `True` on both `ListBox` controls, the selected item in each will be the same.

The Code

The following example demonstrates a window that data-binds to an instance of the `PersonCollection` class in its constructor. The `PersonCollection` class is an `ObservableCollection<T>` of `Person` objects. Each `Person` object exposes name, age, and occupation data, as well as a description.

In the top half of the window, a `ListBox` is bound to the window's `DataContext`. This is assigned an instance of the `PersonCollection` in the code-behind for the window. The `ItemTemplate` property of the

ListBox references a DataTemplate called masterTemplate defined in the window's Resources collection. This shows the value of the Description property for each Person object in the collection. It sets the UpdateSourceTrigger attribute to System.Windows.Data.UpdateSourceTrigger.PropertyChanged. This ensures that the text in the ListBox item is updated automatically and immediately when the Description property of a Person changes. In the bottom half of the window, a ContentControl binds to the same collection. Because it is a singleton UI element and does not display a collection of items, it automatically binds to the current item in the PersonCollection class. Because the IsSynchronizedWithCurrentItem property of the ListBox is set to True, this corresponds to the selected item in the ListBox. The ContentControl uses a DataTemplate called detailTemplate to display the full details of the selected Person.

When the data displayed in the details section is changed, it automatically updates the corresponding description in the master section above it. This is made possible for two reasons. First, the System.Windows.Controls.TextBox controls in the details section specify a System.Windows.Data.Binding.BindingMode of TwoWay, which means that when new text is input, it is automatically marshaled to the binding source. Second, the Person class implements the INotifyPropertyChanged interface. This means that when a value of a property changes, the binding target is automatically notified.

At the bottom of the window, there is a System.Windows.Controls.Button control marked Add Person. When this button is clicked, it adds a new Person object to the collection. Because the PersonCollection class derives from ObservableCollection<T>, which in turn implements INotifyCollectionChanged, the master list of items automatically updates to show the new item.

The XAML for the window is as follows:

```
<Window x:Class="Apress.VisualCSharpRecipes.Chapter17.MainWindow"
    xmlns="http://schemas.microsoft.com/winfx/2006/xaml/presentation"
    xmlns:x="http://schemas.microsoft.com/winfx/2006/xaml"
    Title="Recipe17_18" Height="380" Width="280">
    <Window.Resources>

        <DataTemplate
            x:Key="masterTemplate">
            <TextBlock
                Margin="4"
                Text="{Binding
                       Path=Description,
                       UpdateSourceTrigger=PropertyChanged}"/>
        </DataTemplate>

        <DataTemplate x:Key="detailTemplate">
            <Border
                BorderBrush="LightBlue"
                BorderThickness="1">
                <Grid Margin="10">
                    <Grid.ColumnDefinitions>
                        <ColumnDefinition Width="74"/>
                        <ColumnDefinition Width="*"/>
                    </Grid.ColumnDefinitions>

                    <Grid.RowDefinitions>
                        <RowDefinition Height="30"/>
                        <RowDefinition Height="30"/>
```

```
                <RowDefinition Height="30"/>
                <RowDefinition Height="30"/>
            </Grid.RowDefinitions>

            <TextBlock
    Margin="4"
    Text="First Name"
    VerticalAlignment="Center"/>
<TextBox
    Text="{Binding Path=FirstName, Mode=TwoWay}"
    Margin="4" Grid.Column="1"/>

<TextBlock
    Margin="4"
    Text="Last Name"
    Grid.Row="1"
    VerticalAlignment="Center"/>
<TextBox
    Margin="4"
    Text="{Binding Path=LastName, Mode=TwoWay}"
    Grid.Column="1" Grid.Row="1"/>

<TextBlock
    Margin="4"
    Text="Age"
    Grid.Row="2"
    VerticalAlignment="Center"/>
<TextBox
    Margin="4"
    Text="{Binding Path=Age, Mode=TwoWay}"
    Grid.Column="1"
    Grid.Row="2"/>

 <TextBlock
    Margin="4"
    Text="Occupation"
    Grid.Row="3"
    VerticalAlignment="Center"/>

 <ComboBox
    x:Name="cboOccupation"
    IsEditable="False"
    Grid.Column="1"
    Grid.Row="3"
    HorizontalAlignment="Left"
    Text="{Binding Path=Occupation, Mode=TwoWay}"
    Margin="4" Width="140">
     <ComboBoxItem>Student</ComboBoxItem>
     <ComboBoxItem>Engineer</ComboBoxItem>
     <ComboBoxItem>Professional</ComboBoxItem>
</ComboBox>
```

```
        </Grid>
            </Border>
        </DataTemplate>
    </Window.Resources>

    <StackPanel Margin="5">

        <TextBlock
            VerticalAlignment="Center"
            FontSize="14"
            Margin="4"
            Text="People"/>

        <!-- The ItemsControls binds to the collection. -->
        <ListBox
            ItemsSource="{Binding}"
            ItemTemplate="{StaticResource masterTemplate}"
            IsSynchronizedWithCurrentItem="True" />

        <TextBlock
            VerticalAlignment="Center"
            FontSize="14"
            Margin="4"
            Text="Details"/>

        <!-- The ContentControl binds to the CurrentItem of the collection. -->
        <ContentControl
          Content="{Binding}"
          ContentTemplate="{StaticResource detailTemplate}" />

        <!-- Add a new person to the collection. -->
        <Button
            Margin="4"
            Width="100"
            Height="34"
            HorizontalAlignment="Right"
            Click="AddButton_Click">
            Add Person
        </Button>
    </StackPanel>
</Window>
```

The code-behind for the window is as follows:

```
using System.Windows;

namespace Apress.VisualCSharpRecipes.Chapter17
{
    public partial class MainWindow : Window
    {
        // Create an instance of the PersonCollection class
```

```
        PersonCollection people =
            new PersonCollection();

        public MainWindow()
        {
            InitializeComponent();

            // Set the DataContext to the PersonCollection
            this.DataContext = people;
        }

        private void AddButton_Click(
            object sender, RoutedEventArgs e)
        {
            people.Add(new Person()
                           {
                               FirstName = "Simon",
                               LastName = "Williams",
                               Age = 39,
                               Occupation = "Professional"
                           });
        }
    }
}
```

The code for the Person class is omitted for brevity. The code for the PersonCollection class is as follows:

```
using System.Collections.ObjectModel;

namespace Apress.VisualCSharpRecipes.Chapter17
{
    public class PersonCollection
        : ObservableCollection<Person>
    {
        public PersonCollection()
        {
            this.Add(new Person()
                         {
                             FirstName = "Sam",
                             LastName = "Bourton",
                             Age = 33,
                             Occupation = "Engineer"
                         });
            this.Add(new Person()
                         {
                             FirstName = "Adam",
                             LastName = "Freeman",
                             Age = 37,
                             Occupation = "Professional"
                         });
```

```
            this.Add(new Person()
                        {
                            FirstName = "Sam",
                            LastName = "Noble",
                            Age = 24,
                            Occupation = "Engineer"
                        });
        }
    }
}
```

Figure 17-16 shows the resulting window.

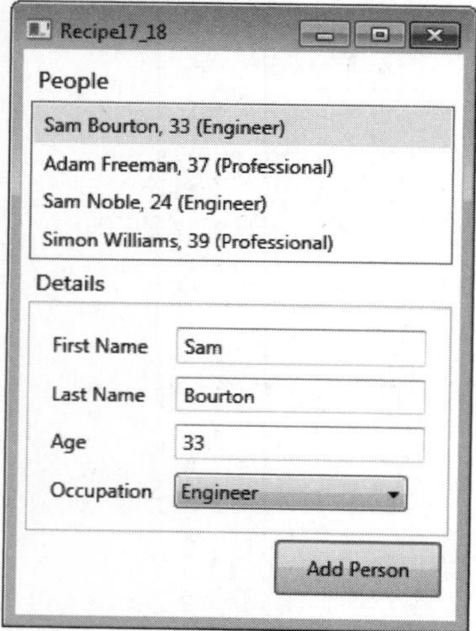

Figure 17-16. *Binding to a collection using the master-detail pattern*

17-19. Change a Control's Appearance on Mouseover

Problem

You need to change the appearance of a control when the mouse moves over it.

Solution

Create a `System.Windows.Style` resource for the `System.Windows.Controls.Control`, and use a property trigger to change the properties of the `Style` when the `IsMouseOver` property is `True`.

How It Works

Every control ultimately inherits from `System.Windows.UIElement`. This exposes a dependency property called `IsMouseOverProperty`. A `System.Windows.Trigger` can be defined in the `Style` of the control, which receives notification when this property changes and can subsequently change the control's `Style`. When the mouse leaves the control, the property is set back to `False`, which notifies the trigger, and the control is automatically set back to the default state.

The Code

The following example demonstrates a window with a `Style` resource and two `System.Windows.Controls.Button` controls. The `Style` uses a `Trigger` to change the `System.Windows.FontWeight` and `BitmapEffect` properties of the `Button` controls when the mouse is over them. The XAML for the window is as follows:

```
<Window x:Class="Apress.VisualCSharpRecipes.Chapter17.MainWindow"
    xmlns="http://schemas.microsoft.com/winfx/2006/xaml/presentation"
    xmlns:x="http://schemas.microsoft.com/winfx/2006/xaml"
    Title="Recipe17_19" Height="120" Width="240">

    <Window.Resources>
        <Style TargetType="{x:Type Button}">
            <Style.Triggers>
                <Trigger Property="IsMouseOver" Value="True">
                    <Setter Property="FontWeight" Value="Bold" />
                    <Setter Property="BitmapEffect">
                        <Setter.Value>
                            <DropShadowEffect BlurRadius="15"
                                Color="Orange" ShadowDepth="0" />
                        </Setter.Value>
                    </Setter>
                </Trigger>
            </Style.Triggers>
        </Style>
    </Window.Resources>

    <StackPanel Margin="8">
        <Button Height="25" Width="100" Margin="4">
            Mouse Over Me!
        </Button>
        <Button Height="25" Width="100" Margin="4">
            Mouse Over Me!
        </Button>
    </StackPanel>
</Window>
```

Figure 17-17 shows the resulting window.

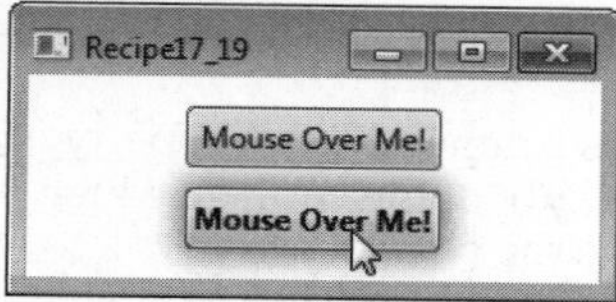

Figure 17-17. Changing a control's appearance on mouseover

17-20. Change the Appearance of Alternate Items in a List

Problem

You need to give a different appearance to items in alternate rows of a `System.Windows.Controls.ListBox`.

Solution

Create a `System.Windows.Controls.StyleSelector` class, and override the `SelectStyle` method.

How It Works

When you set the `ItemContainerStyleSelector` property of a `ListBox` to a `StyleSelector`, it will evaluate each item and apply the correct `Style`. This allows you to specify custom logic to vary the appearance of items based on any particular value or criteria.

The Code

The following example demonstrates a window that displays a list of country names in a `ListBox`. In the XAML for the `ListBox`, its `ItemContainerStyleSelector` property is set to a local `StyleSelector` class called `AlternatingRowStyleSelector`. This class has a property called `AlternateStyle`, which is set to a `Style` resource that changes the `Background` property of a `ListBoxItem`.

The `AlternatingRowStyleSelector` class overrides the `SelectStyle` property and returns either the default or the alternate `Style`, based on a Boolean flag. The XAML for the window is as follows:

```
<Window x:Class="Apress.VisualCSharpRecipes.Chapter17.MainWindow"
    xmlns="http://schemas.microsoft.com/winfx/2006/xaml/presentation"
    xmlns:x="http://schemas.microsoft.com/winfx/2006/xaml"
    xmlns:local="clr-namespace:Apress.VisualCSharpRecipes.Chapter17;assembly="
    Title="Recipe17_20" Height="248" Width="200">
```

```
    <Window.Resources>
        <local:Countries x:Key="countries"/>
        <Style x:Key="AlternateStyle">
            <Setter Property="ListBoxItem.Background" Value="LightGray"/>
        </Style>
    </Window.Resources>

    <Grid Margin="4">
        <ListBox
            DisplayMemberPath="Name"
            ItemsSource="{Binding Source={StaticResource countries}}" >

            <ListBox.ItemContainerStyleSelector>
                <local:AlternatingRowStyleSelector
                    AlternateStyle="{StaticResource AlternateStyle}" />
            </ListBox.ItemContainerStyleSelector>
        </ListBox>
    </Grid>
</Window>
```

The code for the StyleSelector is as follows:

```
using System.Windows;
using System.Windows.Controls;

namespace Apress.VisualCSharpRecipes.Chapter17
{
    public class AlternatingRowStyleSelector : StyleSelector
    {
        // Flag to track the alternate rows
        private bool isAlternate = false;

        public Style DefaultStyle {  get; set; }
        public Style AlternateStyle { get; set; }

        public override Style SelectStyle(object item, DependencyObject container)
        {
            // Select the style, based on the value of isAlternate
            Style style = isAlternate ? AlternateStyle : DefaultStyle;

            // Invert the flag
            isAlternate = !isAlternate;

            return style;
        }
    }
}
```

Figure 17-18 shows the resulting window.

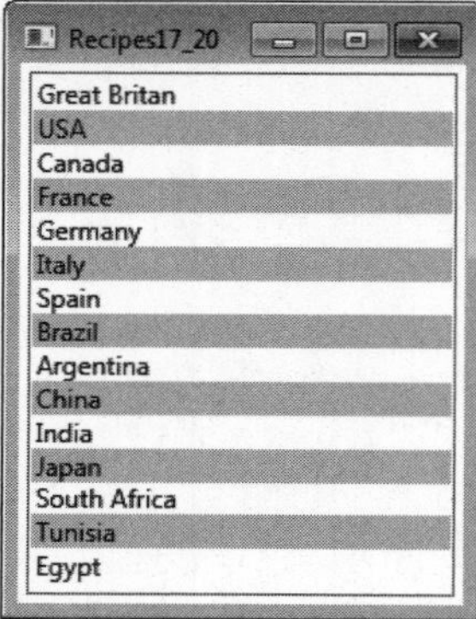

Figure 17-18. *Changing the appearance of alternate rows*

17-21. Drag Items from a List and Drop Them on a Canvas

Problem

You need to allow the user to drag items from a `System.Windows.Controls.ListBox` to a `System.Windows.Controls.Canvas`.

■ **Note** Drag-and-drop is relatively simple to implement in WPF, but contains a lot of variations depending on what you are trying to do and what content you are dragging. This example focuses on dragging content from a `ListBox` to a `Canvas`, but the principles are similar for other types of drag-and-drop operations and can be adapted easily.

Solution

On the `ListBox` or `ListBoxItem`, handle the `PreviewMouseLeftButtonDown` event to identify the start of a possible drag operation and identify the `ListBoxItem` being dragged. Handle the `PreviewMouseMove` event to determine whether the user is actually dragging the item, and if so, set up the drop operation using the static `System.Windows.DragDrop` class. On the `Canvas` (the target for the drop operation), handle the `DragEnter` and `Drop` events to support the dropping of dragged content.

How It Works

The static `DragDrop` class provides the functionality central to making it easy to execute drag-and-drop operations in WPF. First, however, you must determine that the user is actually trying to drag something.

There is no single best way to do this, but usually you will need a combination of handling MouseLeftButtonDown or PreviewMouseLeftButtonDown events to know when the user clicks something, and MouseMove or PreviewMouseMove events to determine whether the user is moving the mouse while holding the left button down. Also, you should use the SystemParameters.MinimumHorizontalDragDistance and SystemParameters.MinimumVerticalDragDistance properties to make sure the user has dragged the item a sufficient distance to be considered a drag operation; otherwise, the user will often get false drag operations starting as they click items.

Once you are sure the user is trying to drag something, you configure the DragDrop object using the DoDragDrop method. You must pass the DoDragDrop method a reference to the source object being dragged, a System.Object containing the data that the drag operation is taking with it, and a value from the System.Windows.DragDropEffects enumeration representing the type of drag operation being performed. Commonly used values of the DragDropEffects enumeration are Copy, Move, and Link. The type of operation is often driven by special keys being held down at the time of clicking—for example, holding the Ctrl key signals the user's intent to copy (see recipe 17-34 for information on how to query keyboard state).

On the target of the drop operation, implement event handlers for the DragEnter and Drop events. The DragEnter handler allows you to control the behavior seen by the user as the mouse pointer enters the target control. This usually indicates whether the control is a suitable target for the type of content the user is dragging. The Drop event signals that the user has released the left mouse button and indicates that the content contained in the DragDrop object should be retrieved (using the Data.GetData method of the DragEventArgs object passed to the Drop event handler) and inserted into the target control.

The Code

The following XAML demonstrates how to set up a ListBox with ListBoxItem objects that support drag-and-drop operations (see Figure 17-19):

```
<Window x:Class="Apress.VisualCSharpRecipes.Chapter17.MainWindow"
    xmlns="http://schemas.microsoft.com/winfx/2006/xaml/presentation"
    xmlns:x="http://schemas.microsoft.com/winfx/2006/xaml"
    Title="Recipe17_21" Height="300" Width="300">
    <DockPanel LastChildFill="True" >
        <ListBox DockPanel.Dock="Left" Name="lstLabels">
            <ListBox.Resources>
                <Style TargetType="{x:Type ListBoxItem}">
                    <Setter Property="FontSize" Value="14" />
                    <Setter Property="Margin" Value="2" />
                    <EventSetter Event="PreviewMouseLeftButtonDown"
                       Handler="ListBoxItem_PreviewMouseLeftButtonDown"/>
                    <EventSetter Event="PreviewMouseMove"
                                 Handler="ListBoxItem_PreviewMouseMove"/>
                </Style>
            </ListBox.Resources>
            <ListBoxItem IsSelected="True">Allen</ListBoxItem>
            <ListBoxItem>Andy</ListBoxItem>
            <ListBoxItem>Antoan</ListBoxItem>
            <ListBoxItem>Bruce</ListBoxItem>
            <ListBoxItem>Ian</ListBoxItem>
            <ListBoxItem>Matthew</ListBoxItem>
```

```
            <ListBoxItem>Sam</ListBoxItem>
            <ListBoxItem>Simon</ListBoxItem>
        </ListBox>
        <Canvas AllowDrop="True" Background="Transparent"
                DragEnter="cvsSurface_DragEnter" Drop="cvsSurface_Drop"
                Name="cvsSurface" >
        </Canvas>
    </DockPanel>
</Window>
```

The following code-behind contains the event handlers that allow the example to identify the ListBoxItem that the user is dragging, determine whether a mouse movement constitutes a drag operation, and allow the Canvas to receive the dragged ListBoxItem content.

```
using System;
using System.Windows;
using System.Windows.Controls;
using System.Windows.Input;

namespace Apress.VisualCSharpRecipes.Chapter17
{
    /// <summary>
    /// Interaction logic for MainWindow.xaml
    /// </summary>
    public partial class MainWindow : Window
    {
        private ListBoxItem draggedItem;
        private Point startDragPoint;

        public MainWindow()
        {
            InitializeComponent();
        }

        // Handles the DragEnter event for the Canvas. Changes the mouse
        // pointer to show the user that copy is an option if the drop
        // text content is over the Canvas.
        private void cvsSurface_DragEnter(object sender, DragEventArgs e)
        {
            if (e.Data.GetDataPresent(DataFormats.Text))
            {
                e.Effects = DragDropEffects.Copy;
            }
            else
            {
                e.Effects = DragDropEffects.None;
            }
        }

        // Handles the Drop event for the Canvas. Creates a new Label
        // and adds it to the Canvas at the location of the mouse pointer.
```

```
        private void cvsSurface_Drop(object sender, DragEventArgs e)
        {
            // Create a new Label.
            Label newLabel = new Label();
            newLabel.Content = e.Data.GetData(DataFormats.Text);
            newLabel.FontSize = 14;

            // Add the Label to the Canvas and position it.
            cvsSurface.Children.Add(newLabel);
            Canvas.SetLeft(newLabel, e.GetPosition(cvsSurface).X);
            Canvas.SetTop(newLabel, e.GetPosition(cvsSurface).Y);
        }

        // Handles the PreviewMouseLeftButtonDown event for all ListBoxItem
        // objects. Stores a reference to the item being dragged and the
        // point at which the drag started.
        private void ListBoxItem_PreviewMouseLeftButtonDown(object sender,
            MouseButtonEventArgs e)
        {
            draggedItem = sender as ListBoxItem;
            startDragPoint = e.GetPosition(null);
        }

        // Handles the PreviewMouseMove event for all ListBoxItem objects.
        // Determines whether the mouse has been moved far enough to be
        // considered a drag operation.
        private void ListBoxItem_PreviewMouseMove(object sender,
            MouseEventArgs e)
        {
            if (e.LeftButton == MouseButtonState.Pressed)
            {
                Point position = e.GetPosition(null);

                if (Math.Abs(position.X - startDragPoint.X) >
                        SystemParameters.MinimumHorizontalDragDistance ||
                    Math.Abs(position.Y - startDragPoint.Y) >
                        SystemParameters.MinimumVerticalDragDistance)
                {
                    // User is dragging, set up the DragDrop behavior.
                    DragDrop.DoDragDrop(draggedItem, draggedItem.Content,
                        DragDropEffects.Copy);
                }
            }
        }
    }
}
```

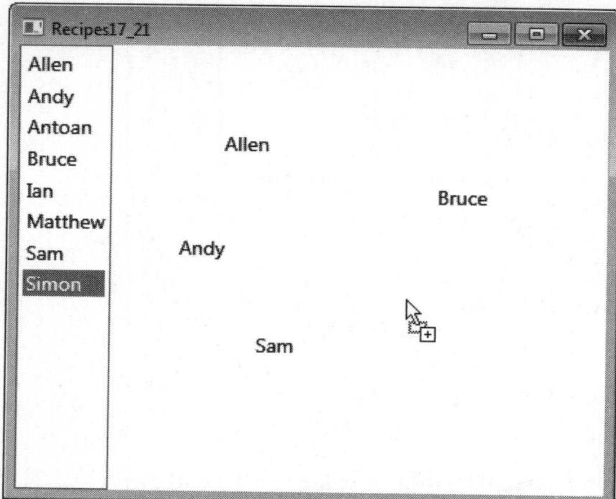

Figure 17-19. Dragging items from a ListBox and dropping them on a Canvas

17-22. Display the Progress of a Long-Running Operation and Allow the User to Cancel It

Problem

You need to execute a method asynchronously on a background thread, show a `System.Windows.Controls.ProgressBar` while the process is executing, and allow the user to cancel the background operation before completion.

Solution

Create an instance of the `System.ComponentModel.BackgroundWorker` class and attach event handlers to its `DoWork` and `RunWorkerCompleted` events. To report progress, set its `WorkerReportsProgress` property to `True`, and add an event handler to its `ProgressChanged` event. Call the `ReportProgress` method of the `BackgroundWorker` while processing the operation on the background thread, and in the code for this ProgressChanged event handler, update the Value property of a ProgressBar.

To support cancellation, set its `WorkerSupportsCancellation` property to `True` and call the `CancelAsync` method when the user wants to cancel the operation. In the `DoWork` event handler, check the `CancellationPending` property, and if this is `True`, use the `Cancel` property of `System.ComponentModel.DoWorkEventArgs` to notify the `RunWorkerCompleted` event handler that the operation was cancelled.

How It Works

The BackgroundWorker component gives you the ability to execute time-consuming operations asynchronously. It automatically executes the operation on a different thread to the one that created it and then automatically returns control to the calling thread when it is completed.

The BackgroundWorker's DoWork event specifies the delegate to execute asynchronously. It is this delegate that is executed on a background thread when the RunWorkerAsync method is called. When it has completed the operation, it calls the RunWorkerCompleted event and executes the attached delegate on the same thread that was used to create it. If the BackgroundWorker object is created on the UI thread—for example, in the constructor method for a window or control—then you can access and update the UI in the RunWorkerCompleted event without having to check that you are on the UI thread again. The BackgroundWorker object handles all the thread marshaling for you.

The DoWork method takes an argument of type System.ComponentModel.DoWorkEventArgs, which allows you to pass an argument to the method. The RunWorkerCompleted event is passed an instance of the System.ComponentModel.RunWorkerCompletedEventArgs class, which allows you to receive the result of the background process and any error that might have been thrown during processing.

The BackgroundWorker class has a Boolean property called WorkerReportsProgress, which indicates whether the BackgroundWorker can report progress updates. It is set to False by default. When this is set to True, calling the ReportProgress method will raise the ProgressChanged event. The ReportProgress method takes an integer parameter specifying the percentage of progress completed by the BackgroundWorker. This parameter is passed to the ProgressChanged event handler via the ProgressPercentage property of the System.ComponentModel.ProgressChangedEventArgs class. The ProgressBar control sets the default value for its Maximum property to 100, which lends itself perfectly and automatically to receive the ProgressPercentage as its Value property.

The BackgroundWorker class has a Boolean property called WorkerSupportsCancellation, which when set to True allows the CancelAsync method to interrupt the background operation. It is set to False by default. In the RunWorkerCompleted event handler, you can use the Cancelled property of the RunWorkerCompletedEventArgs to check whether the BackgroundWorker was cancelled.

The Code

The following example demonstrates a window that declares a ProgressBar control and a Button. An instance of the BackgroundWorker class is created in the window's constructor, and its WorkerSupportsCancellation property is set to True.

When the Button is clicked, the code in the Click handler runs the BackgroundWorker asynchronously and changes the text of the Button from Start to Cancel. If it is clicked again, the IsBusy property of the BackgroundWorker returns True, and the code calls the CancelAsync method to cancel the operation.

In the RunWorkerCompleted event handler, a System.Windows.MessageBox is shown if the Cancelled property of the RunWorkerCompletedEventArgs parameter is True. The XAML for the window is as follows:

```
<Window x:Class="Apress.VisualCSharpRecipes.Chapter17.MainWindow"
        xmlns="http://schemas.microsoft.com/winfx/2006/xaml/presentation"
        xmlns:x="http://schemas.microsoft.com/winfx/2006/xaml"
        Title="Recipe17_22" Height="100" Width="250">
    <Grid>
```

```
        <Grid.RowDefinitions>
            <RowDefinition/>
            <RowDefinition/>
        </Grid.RowDefinitions>

        <ProgressBar Name="progressBar" Margin="4"/>

        <Button Name="button" Grid.Row="1" Click="button_Click"
            HorizontalAlignment="Center" Margin="4" Width="60">
            Start
        </Button>
    </Grid>
</Window>
```

The code-behind for the window is as follows:

```
using System.ComponentModel;
using System.Threading;
using System.Windows;
using System.Windows.Input;

namespace Apress.VisualCSharpRecipes.Chapter17
{
    /// <summary>
    /// Interaction logic for MainWindow.xaml
    /// </summary>
    public partial class MainWindow : Window
    {
        private BackgroundWorker worker;

        public MainWindow()
        {
            InitializeComponent();

            // Create a Background Worker
            worker = new BackgroundWorker();
            worker.WorkerReportsProgress = true;

            // Enable support for cancellation
            worker.WorkerSupportsCancellation = true;

            // Attach the event handlers
            worker.DoWork +=
                new DoWorkEventHandler(worker_DoWork);
            worker.RunWorkerCompleted +=
                new RunWorkerCompletedEventHandler(worker_RunWorkerCompleted);
            worker.ProgressChanged +=
                worker_ProgressChanged;
        }
```

```
private void button_Click(
    object sender, RoutedEventArgs e)
{
    if(!worker.IsBusy)
    {
        this.Cursor = Cursors.Wait;

        // Start the Background Worker
        worker.RunWorkerAsync();
        button.Content = "Cancel";
    }
    else
    {
        // Cancel the Background Worker
        worker.CancelAsync();
    }
}

private void worker_RunWorkerCompleted(
    object sender, RunWorkerCompletedEventArgs e)
{
    this.Cursor = Cursors.Arrow;

    if(e.Cancelled)
    {
        // The user cancelled the operation
        MessageBox.Show("Operation was cancelled");
    }
    else if(e.Error != null)
    {
        MessageBox.Show(e.Error.Message);
    }

    button.Content = "Start";
}

private void worker_DoWork(
    object sender, DoWorkEventArgs e)
{
    for(int i = 1; i <= 100; i++)
    {
        // Check if the BackgroundWorker
        // has been cancelled
        if(worker.CancellationPending)
        {
            // Set the Cancel property
            e.Cancel = true;
            return;
        }
```

```
                // Simulate some processing by sleeping
                Thread.Sleep(100);
                worker.ReportProgress(i);
            }
        }

        private void worker_ProgressChanged(
            object sender, ProgressChangedEventArgs e)
        {
            progressBar.Value = e.ProgressPercentage;
        }
    }
}
```

Figure 17-20 shows the resulting window.

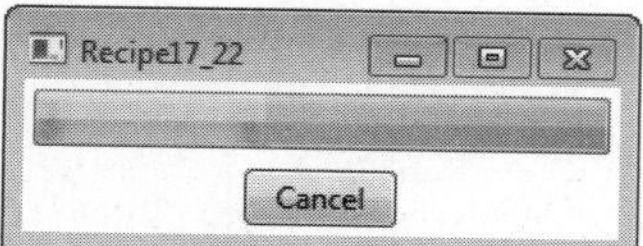

***Figure 17-20.** Executing a method asynchronously using a background thread*

17-23. Draw Two-Dimensional Shapes

Problem

You need to draw shapes such as circles, rectangles, polygons, or more complex shapes constructed from a combination of simpler shapes with straight and curved lines.

Solution

Draw simple shapes using the `Ellipse`, `Rectangle`, or `Polygon` classes from the `System.Windows.Shapes` namespace. For complex shapes, use a `System.Windows.Shapes.Path` element to represent the overall shape. In the `Data` property of the `Path` object, include a `GeometryGroup` element containing one or more `EllipseGeometry`, `LineGeometry`, `PathGeometry`, or `RectangleGeometry` elements that together describe your shape. `GeometryGroup`, `EllipseGeometry`, `LineGeometry`, `PathGeometry`, and `RectangleGeometry` are all classes from the `System.Windows.Media` namespace.

■ **Tip** Defining complex shapes manually can be time-consuming, error prone, and frustrating. For complex shapes, you should consider using a visual design tool (such as Microsoft Expression Design) that generates XAML to draw the shape and then use the output of the tool in your application.

How It Works

The `Ellipse`, `Rectangle`, and `Polygon` classes all derive from the `System.Windows.Shapes.Shape` class and provide a quick and easy way to draw simple shapes. To use an `Ellipse` or `Rectangle` element, you need only specify a `Height` property and a `Width` property to control the basic size of the shape. The values are assumed to be `px` (pixels) but can also be `in` (inches), `cm` (centimeters), or `pt` (points). For the `Rectangle` element, you can also specify values for the `RadiusX` and `RadiusY` properties, which set the radius of the ellipse used to round the corners of the rectangle.

The `Polygon` allows you to create shapes with as many sides as you require by constructing a shape from a sequence of connected lines. To do this, you specify the sequence of points you want connected by lines to form your shape. The `Polygon` automatically draws a final line segment from the final point back to the first point to ensure the shape is closed.

You can declare the points for the `Polygon` statically by specifying a sequence of coordinate pairs in the `Points` property of the `Polygon` element. Each of these coordinate pairs represents the x and y offset of a point from the base position of the `Polygon` within its container (see recipes 17-6 through 17-9 for details on how to position UI elements in the various types of containers provided by WPF). For clarity, you should separate the x and y coordinates of a pair with a comma and separate each coordinate pair with a space (for example, `x1,y1 x2,y2 x3,y3`, and so on). To configure the points of a `Polygon` programmatically, you need to add `System.Windows.Point` objects to the `System.Windows.Media.PointsCollection` collection contained in the `Points` property of the `Polygon` object.

Although the `Polygon` class allows you to create somewhat complex shapes easily, it allows you to use only straight edges on those shapes. `Polygon` also includes significant overhead because of all the functionality inherited from the `System.Windows.Shapes.Shape` class.

For complex and lightweight shapes over which you have more control, use a `Path` element to represent the overall shape. `Path` defines the settings—such as color and thickness—used to actually draw the line and also implements events for handling mouse and keyboard interaction with the line. You must then construct the desired shape using the classes derived from the `System.Windows.Media.Geometry` class, including `PathGeometry`, `EllipseGeometry`, `LineGeometry`, and `RectangleGeometry`. To make shapes that consist of multiple simpler shapes, you must encapsulate the collection of simpler shapes in a `GeometryGroup` element within the `Data` property of the `Path`.

The `EllipseGeometry`, `LineGeometry`, and `RectangleGeometry` elements are lighter-weight equivalents of the `Ellipse`, `Line`, and `Rectangle` classes from the `System.Windows.Shapes` namespace, intended for use when creating more complex shapes. To draw an ellipse with the `EllipseGeometry` class, position the ellipse using the `Center` property, and specify the width and height of the ellipse using the `RadiusX` and `RadiusY` properties. To draw a line with the `LineGeometry` class, specify the starting point of the line using the `StartPoint` property and the end of the line using the `EndPoint` property. To draw a rectangle with the `RectangleGeometry` class, specify the position of the top-left corner of the rectangle as well as the width and height of the rectangle using the `Rect` property. You can also specify values for the `RadiusX` and `RadiusY` properties, which set the radius of the ellipse used to round the corners of the rectangle. All coordinates are relative to the root position of the `Path` element within its container.

Drawing curved lines in WPF is not as simple as you would hope. Unlike with lines, ellipses, and rectangles, there is no simple class that draws a curved line for you. However, at the expense of a little complexity, you get a great deal of flexibility and control, which is what you really want if you need to draw all but the simplest curved lines. To draw a curved line, you must use a `PathGeometry` element. The `PathGeometry` element can define multiple lines, so you must declare each line inside the `PathGeometry` element within its own `PathFigure` element. The `StartPoint` property of the `PathFigure` element defines the point where WPF will start to draw your line. The `StartPoint` property takes a pair of `System.Double` values representing the x and y offsets from the root position of the `Path` element within its container.

Within the `PathFigure` element, you finally get to define what your line is going to look like using one or more `ArcSegment`, `LineSegment`, and `BezierSegment` elements. When rendered, each segment defines how your line continues from the point where the previous segment ended (or the `StartPoint` of the `PathFigure` if it is the first segment).

A `LineSegment` defines a straight line drawn from the end of the last segment to the point defined in its `Point` property. The `Point` property takes a pair of `Double` values representing the x and y offsets from the root position of the `Path` element.

An `ArcSegment` defines an elliptical arc drawn between the end of the last segment and the point defined in its `Point` property. The `Point` property takes a pair of `Double` values representing the x and y offsets from the root position of the `Path` element. Table 17-8 defines the properties of the `ArcSegment` class that let you configure the shape of the curved line it defines.

Table 17-8. *Properties of the ArcSegment Class*

Value	Description
`IsLargeArc`	Specifies whether the line drawn between the start and end of the `ArcSegment` is the small or large section of the ellipse used to calculate the arc.
`IsSmoothJoin`	A `Boolean` that defines whether the join between the previous line and the `ArcSegment` should be treated as a corner. This determines how the `StrokeLineJoin` property of the `Path` element affects the rendering of the join.
`RotationAngle`	A `double` that defines the amount in degrees by which the ellipse (from which the arc is taken) is rotated about the x axis.
`Size`	A pair of `Double` values that specify the x and y radii of the ellipse used to calculate the arc.
`SweepDirection`	Defines the direction in which WPF draws the `ArcSegment`; available values are `Clockwise` and `Counterclockwise`.

A `BezierSegment` defines a Bezier curve drawn between the end of the last segment and the point defined in its `Point3` property. The `Point3` property takes a pair of `Double` values representing the x and y offsets from the root position of the `Path` element. The `Point1` and `Point2` properties of the `BezierSegment` define the control points of the Bezier curve that exert a "pull" on the line, causing it to create a curve. You can read more about Bezier curves at `http://en.wikipedia.org/wiki/Bezier_curves`.

■ **Note** WPF defines a minilanguage that provides a concise syntax by which you can define complex geometries. Because it is terse and difficult to read, this language is primarily intended for tools that generate geometry definitions automatically, but can also be used in manual definitions. A discussion of this minilanguage is beyond the scope of this book. To find out more, read the MSDN article at `http://msdn.microsoft.com/en-us/library/ms752293(VS.100).aspx`.

The Code

The following XAML demonstrates how to use the various drawing elements mentioned previously to draw a wide variety of two-dimensional shapes in a `System.Windows.Controls.Canvas` (see Figure 17-21).

```
<Window x:Class="Apress.VisualCSharpRecipes.Chapter17.MainWindow"
    xmlns="http://schemas.microsoft.com/winfx/2006/xaml/presentation"
    xmlns:x="http://schemas.microsoft.com/winfx/2006/xaml"
    Title="Recipe17_23" Height="350" Width="450">
    <Canvas>
        <Canvas.Resources>
            <Style TargetType="Ellipse">
                <Setter Property="Stroke" Value="Black" />
                <Setter Property="StrokeThickness" Value="3" />
            </Style>
            <Style TargetType="Polygon">
                <Setter Property="Stroke" Value="Black" />
                <Setter Property="StrokeThickness" Value="3" />
            </Style>
            <Style TargetType="Rectangle">
                <Setter Property="Stroke" Value="Black" />
                <Setter Property="StrokeThickness" Value="3" />
            </Style>
        </Canvas.Resources>
        <Rectangle Canvas.Top="20" Canvas.Left="10"
                   Height="60" Width="90" />
        <Rectangle Canvas.Top="20" Canvas.Left="120"
                   Height="100" Width="70"
                   RadiusX="10" RadiusY="10"/>
        <Rectangle Canvas.Top="20" Canvas.Left="220"
                   Height="70" Width="70"
                   RadiusX="5" RadiusY="30"/>
        <Ellipse Canvas.Top="100" Canvas.Left="20"
                 Height="100" Width="70"/>
        <Ellipse Canvas.Top="130" Canvas.Left="110"
                 Height="50" Width="90"/>
        <Ellipse Canvas.Top="120" Canvas.Left="220"
                 Height="70" Width="70"/>
        <Polygon Canvas.Top="200" Canvas.Left="10"
                 Margin="5" Points="40,10 70,80 10,80"/>
```

```
        <Polygon Canvas.Top="200" Canvas.Left="110"
                 Margin="5" Points="20,0 60,0 80,20 80,60 60,80
                 20,80 0,60 0,20"/>
        <Polygon Canvas.Top="200" Canvas.Left="210"
                 Margin="5" Points="20,0 50,10 50,50 80,60 60,80 0,20"/>
        <Path Canvas.Top="60" Canvas.Left="320"
              Stroke="Black" StrokeThickness="3" >
            <Path.Data>
                <GeometryGroup>
                    <!--Head and hat-->
                    <PathGeometry>
                        <PathFigure IsClosed="True" StartPoint="40,0">
                            <LineSegment Point="70,100" />
                            <ArcSegment Point="70,110" IsLargeArc="True"
                                    Size="10,10" SweepDirection="Clockwise"/>
                            <ArcSegment Point="10,110" Size="30,30"
                                    SweepDirection="Clockwise"/>

                            <ArcSegment Point="10,100" IsLargeArc="True"
                                    Size="10,10" SweepDirection="Clockwise"/>
                        </PathFigure>
                    </PathGeometry>
                    <!--Hat buttons-->
                    <EllipseGeometry Center="40,40" RadiusX="2" RadiusY="2"/>
                    <EllipseGeometry Center="40,50" RadiusX="2" RadiusY="2"/>
                    <EllipseGeometry Center="40,60" RadiusX="2" RadiusY="2"/>
                    <!--Eyes-->
                    <EllipseGeometry Center="30,100" RadiusX="3" RadiusY="2"/>
                    <EllipseGeometry Center="50,100" RadiusX="3" RadiusY="2"/>
                    <!--Nose-->
                    <EllipseGeometry Center="40,110" RadiusX="3" RadiusY="3"/>
                    <!--Mouth-->
                    <RectangleGeometry Rect="30,120 20,10"/>
                </GeometryGroup>
            </Path.Data>
        </Path>
    </Canvas>
</Window>
```

Figure 17-21. Examples of simple and complex shapes on a canvas

17-24. Create Reusable Shapes

Problem

You need to create a shape that you can use many times without having to define it each time.

Solution

Define the geometry of the shape as a static resource, and give it a `Key`. You can then use binding syntax to reference the geometry from the `Data` property of a `System.Windows.Shapes.Path` element wherever you need it.

How It Works

Geometries describing complex shapes can be long and complicated, so you will not want to repeat the geometry description in multiple places. Instead, you can define the geometry once as a static resource and refer to the resource wherever you would normally use that geometry.

You can declare instances of any of the classes that inherit from the `System.Windows.Media.Geometry` class in the resource dictionary of a suitable container. This includes the `PathGeometry`, `EllipseGeometry`, `LineGeometry`, `RectangleGeometry`, and `GeometryGroup` classes from the `System.Windows.Media` namespace. The only special action you need to take is to give the geometry resource a name by assigning a value to the `x:Key` property.

Once defined, refer to the geometry resource from the `Data` property of a `Path` element using the following syntax:

```
... Data="{StaticResource GeometryKey}" ...
```

The Code

The following XAML demonstrates how to create a `System.Windows.Media.GeometryGroup` static resource with the key `Clown`, and its subsequent use to display a clown shape multiple times in a `System.Windows.Controls.UniformGrid`. Each clown displayed uses the same underlying geometry but different stroke settings to change the color and format of the lines (see Figure 17-22).

```
<Window x:Class="Apress.VisualCSharpRecipes.Chapter17.MainWindow"
    xmlns="http://schemas.microsoft.com/winfx/2006/xaml/presentation"
    xmlns:x="http://schemas.microsoft.com/winfx/2006/xaml"
    Title="Recipe17_24" Height="350" Width="300">
    <Window.Resources>
        <GeometryGroup x:Key="Clown">
            <!--Head and hat-->
            <PathGeometry>
                <PathFigure IsClosed="True" StartPoint="40,0">
                    <LineSegment Point="70,100" />
                    <ArcSegment Point="70,110" IsLargeArc="True"
                                Size="10,10" SweepDirection="Clockwise"/>
                    <ArcSegment Point="10,110" Size="30,30"
                                SweepDirection="Clockwise"/>
                    <ArcSegment Point="10,100" IsLargeArc="True"
                                Size="10,10" SweepDirection="Clockwise"/>
                </PathFigure>
            </PathGeometry>

            <!--Hat buttons-->
            <EllipseGeometry Center="40,40" RadiusX="2" RadiusY="2"/>
            <EllipseGeometry Center="40,50" RadiusX="2" RadiusY="2"/>
            <EllipseGeometry Center="40,60" RadiusX="2" RadiusY="2"/>
            <!--Eyes-->
            <EllipseGeometry Center="30,100" RadiusX="3" RadiusY="2"/>
            <EllipseGeometry Center="50,100" RadiusX="3" RadiusY="2"/>
            <!--Nose-->
            <EllipseGeometry Center="40,110" RadiusX="3" RadiusY="3"/>
            <!--Mouth-->
            <RectangleGeometry Rect="30,120 20,10"/>
        </GeometryGroup>
    </Window.Resources>
    <UniformGrid Columns="2" Rows="2">
        <Path HorizontalAlignment="Center" Data="{StaticResource Clown}"
              Stroke="Black" StrokeThickness="1" Margin="5" Fill="BurlyWood"/>
        <Path HorizontalAlignment="Center" Data="{StaticResource Clown}"
              Stroke="Blue" StrokeThickness="5" Margin="5" />
        <Path HorizontalAlignment="Center" Data="{StaticResource Clown}"
              Stroke="Red" StrokeThickness="3"  StrokeDashArray="1 1"/>
        <Path HorizontalAlignment="Center" Data="{StaticResource Clown}"
              Stroke="Green" StrokeThickness="4" StrokeDashArray="2 1"/>
    </UniformGrid>
</Window>
```

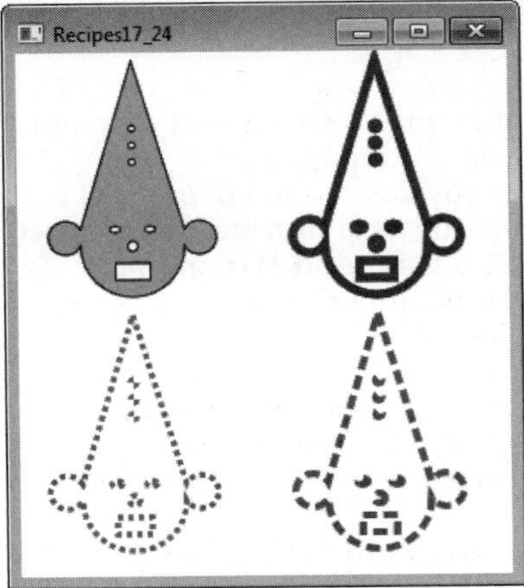

Figure 17-22. Using static geometry resources to create reusable shapes

17-25. Draw or Fill a Shape Using a Solid Color

Problem

You need to draw or fill a shape using a solid color.

Solution

For shapes derived from `System.Windows.Shapes.Shape`, set the `Stroke` or `Fill` property to an instance of `System.Windows.Media.SolidColorBrush` configured with the color you want to use.

How It Works

The `SolidColorBrush` class represents a brush with a single solid color that you can use to draw or fill shapes. To draw a shape derived from `Shape` using a solid color, assign an instance of a `SolidColorBrush` to the `Stroke` property of the `Shape`. To fill a shape derived from `Shape` using a solid color, assign an instance of a `SolidColorBrush` to the `Fill` property of the `Shape`.

There are a variety of ways to obtain `SolidColorBrush` objects in both XAML and code, but you need to understand how WPF represents color to best understand how to create and use `SolidColorBrush` objects.

WPF represents color with the `System.Windows.Media.Color` structure, which uses four channels to define a color: alpha, red, green, and blue. Alpha defines the amount of transparency the color has, and the red, green, and blue channels define how much of that primary color is included in the aggregate color.

The `Color` structure supports two common standards for defining the values for these channels: RGB and scRGB. The RGB standard uses 8-bit values for each channel, and you use a number between 0 and 255 to specify the value. This gives you 32 bits of color information, which is usually sufficient when displaying graphics on a computer screen.

However, when you are creating images for printing or further digital processing, a wider range of colors is required. The scRGB standard uses 16-bit values for each channel, and you use a floating-point number between 0 and 1 to specify the value. This gives you 64 bits of color information.

To support both the RGB and scRGB standards, the `Color` structure provides two sets of properties to represent the alpha, red, green, and blue channels of a color. The properties that provide RGB support are named `A`, `R`, `G`, and `B`, and take `System.Byte` values. The properties that provide scRGB support are named `ScA`, `ScR`, `ScG`, and `ScB`, and take `System.Single` values. The two sets of properties are synchronized, so, for example, if you change the `A` property of a `Color` object, the `ScA` property changes to the equivalent value on its own scale.

To obtain a `Color` object in code, you can use the static properties of the `System.Windows.Media.Colors` class, which provide access to more than 140 predefined `Color` objects. To create a custom `Color` object, call the static `FromArgb`, `FromAValues`, `FromRgb`, `FromScRgb`, or `FromValues` methods of the `Color` structure.

Once you have a `Color` object, you can pass it as an argument to the `SolidColorBrush` constructor and obtain a `SolidColorBrush` instance that will draw or fill your shape with that color. You can also obtain a `SolidColorBrush` instance preconfigured with current system colors using the static properties of the `System.Windows.SystemColors` class.

XAML provides flexible syntax support to allow you to specify the color of a `SolidColorBrush` within the `Stroke` or `Fill` property of a shape. You can use RGB syntax, scRGB syntax, or the names of the colors defined in the `Colors` class.

If you want to reuse a specific `SolidColorBrush`, you can declare it as a resource within the resources collection of a suitable container and assign it a key. Once defined, refer to the `SolidColorBrush` resource from the `Fill` or `Stroke` property of a `Shape` element using the following syntax:

```
... Fill="{StaticResource SolidColorBrushKey}" ...
```

The Code

The following XAML uses a set of `Rectangle`, `Ellipse`, and `Line` objects (from the `System.Windows.Shapes` namespace) to demonstrate how to use `SolidColorBrush` objects to draw and fill shapes (see Figure 17-23). The XAML demonstrates how to use named colors, RGB syntax, and scRGB syntax, as well as how to create and use a static `SolidColorBrush` resource.

```
<Window x:Class="Apress.VisualCSharpRecipes.Chapter17.MainWindow"
    xmlns="http://schemas.microsoft.com/winfx/2006/xaml/presentation"
    xmlns:x="http://schemas.microsoft.com/winfx/2006/xaml"
    Title="Recipe17_25" Height="300" Width="300">
    <Canvas Margin="5">
        <Canvas.Resources>
            <!--scRGB semi-transparent color-->
            <SolidColorBrush Color="sc# 0.8,0.3,0.9,0.25" x:Key="Brush1" />
        </Canvas.Resources>

        <!--SolidColorBrush resource-->
        <Rectangle Fill="{StaticResource Brush1}" Height="180" Width="80" />
        <!--Named color-->
```

```
        <Rectangle Canvas.Top="10" Canvas.Left="50"
            Fill="RoyalBlue" Height="70" Width="220" />
        <!--RGB semi-transparent color-->
        <Ellipse Canvas.Top="30" Canvas.Left="90"
            Fill="#72ff8805" Height="150" Width="100" />
        <!--RGB solid color-->
        <Ellipse Canvas.Top="150" Canvas.Left="70"
            Fill="#ff0000" Height="100" Width="200" />
        <!--scRGB semi-transparent color-->
        <Line X1="20" X2="260" Y1="200" Y2="50"
                Stroke="sc# 0.6,0.8,0.3,0.0" StrokeThickness="40"/>
        <!--scRGB solid color-->
        <Line X1="20" X2="270" Y1="240" Y2="240"
                Stroke="sc# 0.1,0.5,0.1" StrokeThickness="20"/>
    </Canvas>
</Window>
```

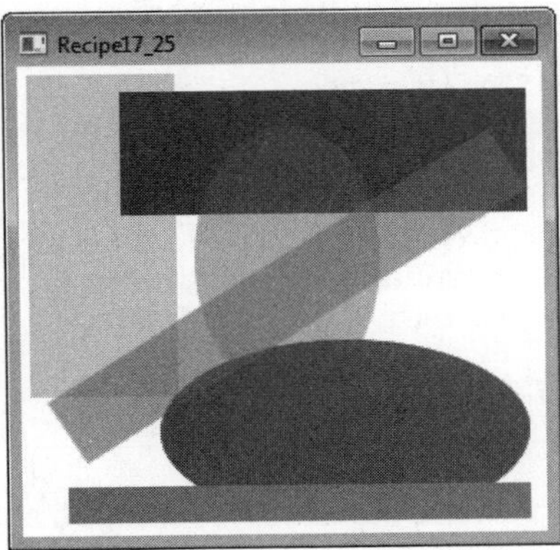

Figure 17-23. Drawing and filling shapes with solid colors

17-26. Fill a Shape with a Linear or Radial Color Gradient

Problem

You need to draw or fill a shape with a linear or radial color gradient (that is, a fill that transitions smoothly between two or more colors).

Solution

For shapes derived from `System.Windows.Shapes.Shape`, to use a linear gradient, set the `Fill` or `Stroke` property to an instance of `System.Windows.Media.LinearGradientBrush`. To use a radial gradient, set the `Fill` or `Stroke` property to an instance of `System.Windows.Media.RadialGradientBrush`.

How It Works

The `LinearGradientBrush` and `RadialGradientBrush` classes allow you to create a blended fill or stroke that transitions from one color to another. It is also possible to transition through a sequence of colors.

A `LinearGradientBrush` represents a sequence of linear color transitions that occur according to a set of gradient stops you define along a gradient axis. The gradient axis is an imaginary line that by default connects the top-left corner of the area being painted with its bottom-right corner. You define gradient stops using `GradientStop` elements inside the `LinearGradientBrush` element.

To position gradient stops along the gradient axis, you assign a `System.Double` value between 0 and 1 to the `Offset` property of a `GradientStop`. The `Offset` value represents the percentage distance along the gradient axis at which the gradient stop occurs. So, for example, 0 represents the start of the gradient axis, 0.5 represents halfway, and 0.75 represents 75 percent along the gradient axis. You specify the color associated with a gradient stop using the `Color` property of the `GradientStop` element.

You can change the position and orientation of the gradient axis using the `StartPoint` and `EndPoint` properties of the `LinearGradientBrush`. Each of the `StartPoint` and `EndPoint` properties takes a pair of `Double` values that allow you to position the point using a coordinate system relative to the area being painted. The point `0,0` represents the top left of the area, and the point `1,1` represents the bottom right. So, to change the gradient axis from its default diagonal orientation to a horizontal one, set `StartPoint` to the value `0,0.5` and `EndPoint` to the value `1,0.5`; to make the gradient axis vertical, set `StartPoint` to the value `0.5,0` and `EndPoint` to the value `0.5,1`.

■ **Note** By setting the `MappingMode` property of the `LinearGradientBrush` to the value `Absolute`, you change the coordinate system used by the `StartPoint` and `EndPoint` properties from being one relative to the area being filled to being one expressed as device-independent pixels. For details, refer to the MSDN documentation on the `MappingMode` property, at `http://msdn.microsoft.com/en-us/library/system.windows.media.gradientbrush.mappingmode.aspx`.

Using the `StartPoint` and `EndPoint` properties of the `LinearGradientBrush`, you can assign negative numbers or numbers greater than 1 to create a gradient axis that starts or ends outside the area being filled. You can also define a gradient axis that starts or ends somewhere inside the body of the area being filled.

Where the gradient axis does not start and end on the boundary of the area being painted, WPF calculates the gradient as specified but does not paint anything that lies outside the area. Where the gradient does not completely fill the area, WPF by default fills the remaining area with the final color in the gradient. You can change this behavior using the `SpreadMethod` property of the `LinearGradientBrush` element. Table 17-9 lists the possible values of the `SpreadMethod` property.

Table 17-9. Possible Values of the SpreadMethod Property

Value	Description
`Pad`	The default value. The last color in the gradient fills all remaining area.
`Reflect`	The gradient is repeated in reverse order.
`Repeat`	The gradient is repeated in the original order.

The `RadialGradientBrush` is similar in behavior to the `LinearGradientBrush` except that it has an elliptical gradient axis that radiates out from a defined focal point. You still use `GradientStop` elements in the `RadialGradientBrush` to define the position and color of transitions, but you use the `RadiusX` and `RadiusY` properties to define the size of the elliptical area covered by the gradient and the `Center` property to position the ellipse within the area being painted. You then use the `GradientOrigin` property to specify the location from where the sequence of gradient stops and starts within the gradient ellipse. As with the `LinearGradientBrush`, all of these properties' values are relative to the area being painted.

■ **Tip** If you want to reuse `LinearGradientBrush` or `RadialGradientBrush` elements, you can declare them as a resource within the resources collection of a suitable container and assign them a key. Once defined, refer to the gradient resource from the `Fill` or `Stroke` property of the `Shape` element using the following syntax:

```
... Fill="{StaticResource GradientKey}" ...
```

The Code

The following XAML uses a set of `Rectangle`, `Ellipse`, and `Line` objects (from the `System.Windows.Shapes` namespace) to demonstrate how to use `LinearGradientBrush` and `RadialGradientBrush` objects to draw and fill shapes (see Figure 17-24). The XAML also demonstrates how to create and use static `LinearGradientBrush` and `RadialGradientBrush` resources.

```
<Window x:Class="Apress.VisualCSharpRecipes.Chapter17.MainWindow"
    xmlns="http://schemas.microsoft.com/winfx/2006/xaml/presentation"
    xmlns:x="http://schemas.microsoft.com/winfx/2006/xaml"
    Title="Recipe17_26" Height="300" Width="300">
    <Canvas Margin="5">
        <Canvas.Resources>
            <!--Vertical reflected LinearGradientBrush static resource-->
            <LinearGradientBrush x:Key="LGB1" SpreadMethod="Reflect"
                                 StartPoint="0.5,-0.25" EndPoint="0.5,.5">
                <GradientStop Color="Aqua" Offset="0.5" />
                <GradientStop Color="Navy" Offset="1.0" />
            </LinearGradientBrush>
```

```
            <!--Centered RadialGradientBrush static resource-->
            <RadialGradientBrush Center="0.5,0.5" RadiusX=".8" RadiusY=".5"
                                 GradientOrigin="0.5,0.5" x:Key="RGB1">
                <GradientStop Color="BlanchedAlmond" Offset="0" />
                <GradientStop Color="DarkGreen" Offset=".7" />
            </RadialGradientBrush>
        </Canvas.Resources>

        <!--Fill with LinearGradientBrush static resource-->
        <Rectangle Canvas.Top="5" Canvas.Left="5"
            Fill="{StaticResource LGB1}" Height="180" Width="80" />
        <!--Fill with RadialGradientBrush static resource-->
        <Rectangle Canvas.Top="10" Canvas.Left="50"
                   Fill="{StaticResource RGB1}" Height="70" Width="230" />
        <!--Fill with offset RadialGradientBrush-->
        <Ellipse Canvas.Top="130" Canvas.Left="30" Height="100" Width="230">
            <Ellipse.Fill>
                <RadialGradientBrush RadiusX=".8" RadiusY="1"
                                     Center="0.5,0.5" GradientOrigin="0.05,0.5">
                    <GradientStop Color="#ffffff" Offset="0.1" />
                    <GradientStop Color="#ff0000" Offset="0.5" />
                    <GradientStop Color="#880000" Offset="0.8" />
                </RadialGradientBrush>
            </Ellipse.Fill>
        </Ellipse>
        <!--Fill with diagonal LinearGradientBrush-->
        <Ellipse Canvas.Top="30" Canvas.Left="110" Height="150" Width="150">
            <Ellipse.Fill>
                <LinearGradientBrush StartPoint="1,1" EndPoint="0,0">
                    <GradientStop Color="#DDFFFFFF" Offset=".2" />
                    <GradientStop Color="#FF000000" Offset=".8" />
                </LinearGradientBrush>
            </Ellipse.Fill>
        </Ellipse>

        <!--Stroke with horizontal multi-color LinearGradientBrush-->
        <Line X1="20" X2="280" Y1="240" Y2="240" StrokeThickness="30">
            <Line.Stroke>
                <LinearGradientBrush StartPoint="0,0.5" EndPoint="1,0.5">
                    <GradientStop Color="Red" Offset="0.15" />
                    <GradientStop Color="Orange" Offset="0.2" />
                    <GradientStop Color="Yellow" Offset="0.35" />
                    <GradientStop Color="Green" Offset="0.5" />
                    <GradientStop Color="Blue" Offset="0.65" />
                    <GradientStop Color="Indigo" Offset="0.75" />
                    <GradientStop Color="Violet" Offset="0.9" />
                </LinearGradientBrush>
            </Line.Stroke>
        </Line>
    </Canvas>
</Window>
```

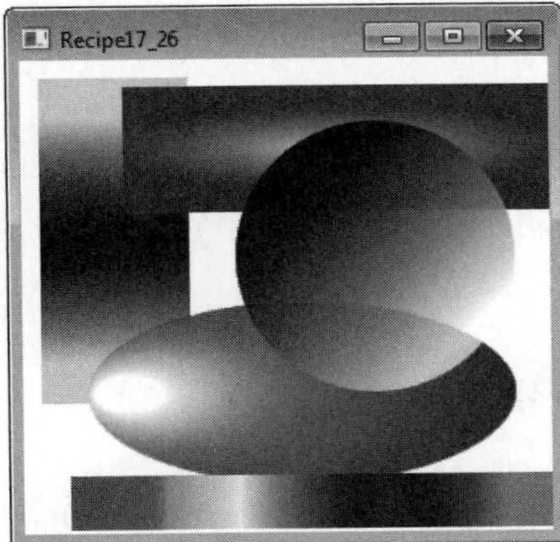

Figure 17-24. Filling and drawing shapes with linear and radial gradients

17-27. Fill a Shape with an Image

Problem

You need to fill a shape derived from `System.Windows.Shapes.Shape` with an image.

Solution

Assign an instance of `System.Windows.Media.ImageBrush` to the `Fill` property of the `Shape`. Use the `Stretch`, `AlignmentX`, `AlignmentY`, and `ViewBox` properties of the `ImageBrush` element to control the way the image fills the shape.

How It Works

The abstract `System.Windows.Media.TileBrush` class contains the functionality required to use a graphical image to paint a specified area. Classes derived from `TileBrush` include `ImageBrush`, `DrawingBrush`, and `VisualBrush` (all from the `System.Windows.Media` namespace). Each `TileBrush` subclassallows you to specify a different source for the graphics used to fill the area: `ImageBrush` lets you use a graphics file, `DrawingBrush` lets you use a drawing object, and `VisualBrush` lets you use an existing screen element.

To use an image to fill a shape, you simply assign an `ImageBrush` element to the `Fill` property of the `Shape` you want to fill. You specify the name of the source image file using the `Source` property of the `ImageBrush`. You can use a local file name or a URL. The image can be loaded from any of the following image formats:

- .bmp
- .gif
- .ico
- .jpg
- .png
- .wdp
- .tiff

The default ImageBrush behavior (inherited from TileBrush) is to stretch the source image to completely fill the shape. This does not maintain the aspect ratios of the source image and will result in a stretched and distorted image if the source image is not the same size as the shape. You can override this behavior using the Stretch property of the ImageBrush. Table 17-10 lists the possible values you can assign to the Stretch property and describes their effect.

Table 17-10. *Possible Values of the Stretch Property*

Value	Description
None	Don't scale the image at all. If the image is smaller than the area of the shape, the rest of the area is left empty (transparent fill). If the image is larger than the shape, the image is cropped.
Uniform	Scale the source image so that it all fits in the shape while still maintaining the original aspect ratio of the image. This will result in some parts of the shape being left transparent unless the source image and shape have the same aspect ratios.
UniformToFill	Scale the source image so that it fills the shape completely while still maintaining the original aspect ratio of the image. This will result in some parts of the source image being cropped unless the source image and shape have the same aspect ratios.
Fill	The default behavior. Scale the image to fit the shape exactly without maintaining the original aspect ratio of the source image.

When using None, Uniform, and UniformToFill values for the Stretch property, you will want to control the positioning of the image within the shape. ImageBrush will center the image by default, but you can change this with the AlignmentX and AlignmentY properties of the ImageBrush element. Valid values for the AlignmentX property are Left, Center, and Right. Valid values for the AlignmentY property are Top, Center, and Bottom.

You can also configure the ImageBrush to use only a rectangular subsection of the source image as the brush instead of the whole image. You do this with the Viewbox property of the ImageBrush element. Viewbox takes four comma-separated System.Double values that identify the coordinates of the upper-left and lower-right corners of the image subsection relative to the original image. The point 0,0 represents the top left of the original image, and the point 1,1 represents the bottom right. If you want to use absolute pixel values to specify the size of the `Viewbox`, set the `ViewboxUnits` property of the `ImageBrush` to the value `Absolute`.

The Code

The following XAML uses a set of `Rectangle`, `Ellipse`, `Polygon`, and `Line` objects (from the `System.Windows.Shapes` namespace) to demonstrate how to use `ImageBrush` objects to fill shapes with an image (see Figure 17-25). The XAML also demonstrates how to create and use a static `ImageBrush` resource.

```
<Window x:Class="Apress.VisualCSharpRecipes.Chapter17.MainWindow"
    xmlns="http://schemas.microsoft.com/winfx/2006/xaml/presentation"
    xmlns:x="http://schemas.microsoft.com/winfx/2006/xaml"
    Title="Recipe17_27" Height="300" Width="300">
    <Canvas Margin="5">
        <!--Define a static ImageBrush resource-->
        <Canvas.Resources>
            <ImageBrush x:Key="IB1" ImageSource="WeeMee.jpg" />
        </Canvas.Resources>

        <!--Fill ellipse using static ImageBrush resource-->
        <Ellipse Height="160" Width="160"
                 Canvas.Top="0" Canvas.Left="110"
                 Stroke="Black" StrokeThickness="1"
                 Fill="{StaticResource IB1}" />
        <!--Fill rectangle with UniformToFill ImageBrush-->
        <Rectangle Height="180" Width="50"
                   Canvas.Top="5" Canvas.Left="5"
                   Stroke="Black" StrokeThickness="1" >
            <Rectangle.Fill>
                <ImageBrush ImageSource="WeeMee.jpg" Stretch="UniformToFill"/>
            </Rectangle.Fill>
        </Rectangle>
        <!--Fill Polygon with Left aligned Uniform ImageBrush-->
        <Polygon Canvas.Top="110" Canvas.Left="45"
                 Points="40,0 150,100 10,100"
                 Stroke="Black" StrokeThickness="1">

            <Polygon.Fill>
                <ImageBrush ImageSource="WeeMee.jpg" Stretch="Uniform"
                            AlignmentX="Left" />
            </Polygon.Fill>
        </Polygon>
```

```
        <!--Draw a line using a part of the source image-->
        <Line X1="20" X2="280" Y1="240" Y2="240" StrokeThickness="30">
            <Line.Stroke>
                <ImageBrush ImageSource="WeeMee.jpg"
                            Viewbox="30,46,42,15" ViewboxUnits="Absolute" />
            </Line.Stroke>
        </Line>
    </Canvas>
</Window>
```

Figure 17-25. *Filling and drawing shapes with images*

17-28. Fill a Shape with a Pattern or Texture

Problem

You need to fill a shape with a repeating pattern or texture.

Solution

To fill shapes derived from `System.Windows.Shapes.Shape`, assign an instance of `System.Windows.Media.ImageBrush` to the `Fill` property of the `Shape`. Use the `Stretch`, `TileMode`, `ViewBox`, and `ViewPort` properties of the `ImageBrush` element to control the way WPF uses the image to fill the shape.

How It Works

Recipe 17-27 describes how to fill a shape with an image using an `ImageBrush`. To fill a shape with a pattern or texture, you typically load some abstract graphic or texture from a file and apply it repeatedly to cover the entire area of a given shape. You do this using the same techniques discussed in recipe 17-27, but you use a number of additional `ImageBrush` properties (inherited from `TileBrush`) to completely fill the shape by drawing the image repeatedly instead of once.

The first step is to define the tile that the `ImageBrush` will use to fill the shape. The `ImageBrush` uses the concept of a viewport to represent the tile. By default, the viewport is a rectangle with dimensions equal to those of the image that the `ImageBrush` would normally use to fill the shape. Normally the viewport would be completely filled with the source image, but you can define what proportion of the viewport is filled by the source image using the `Viewport` property of the `ImageBrush`.

The `Viewport` property takes four comma-separated `System.Double` values that identify the coordinates of the upper-left and lower-right corners of the rectangle within the viewport where you want the `ImageBrush` to insert the source image. So, for example, you can take the original image and configure it to cover only a fraction of the viewport. The point 0,0 represents the top-left corner of the viewport, and the point 1,1 represents the bottom-right corner.

With your base tile defined, you use the `TileMode` property of the `ImageBrush` to define how the `ImageBrush` fills the shape using the tile defined by the viewport. Table 17-11 lists the possible values of the `TileMode` property you can assign and describes their effect.

Table 17-11. *Possible Values of the TileMode Property*

Value	Description
`None`	The default value. The base tile is drawn but not repeated. You get a single image, and the rest of the shape is empty (transparent fill).
`Tile`	The base tile is used repeatedly to fill the shape. Each tile is placed next to the other using the same orientation.
`FlipX`	The base tile is used repeatedly to fill the shape, except that the tiles in alternate columns are flipped horizontally.
`FlipY`	The base tile is used repeatedly to fill the shape, except that the tiles in alternate rows are flipped vertically.
`FlipXY`	The base tile is used repeatedly to fill the shape, except that the tiles in alternate columns are flipped horizontally and the tiles in alternate rows are flipped vertically.

The Code

The following XAML uses a set of `Rectangle`, `Ellipse`, and `Line` objects (from the `System.Windows.Shapes` namespace) to demonstrate how to use `ImageBrush` objects to fill shapes with repeating patterns loaded from image files (see Figure 17-26). The XAML also demonstrates how to create and use static `ImageBrush` resources for the purpose of tiling.

```
<Window x:Class="Apress.VisualCSharpRecipes.Chapter17.MainWindow"
    xmlns="http://schemas.microsoft.com/winfx/2006/xaml/presentation"
    xmlns:x="http://schemas.microsoft.com/winfx/2006/xaml"
    Title="Recipe17_28" Height="300" Width="380">
    <StackPanel Orientation="Horizontal">
```

```
<StackPanel Margin="10">
    <StackPanel.Resources>
        <!--Style for the tile swabs-->
        <Style TargetType="{x:Type Image}">
            <Setter Property="Margin" Value="5"/>
            <Setter Property="MaxHeight" Value="50"/>
        </Style>
    </StackPanel.Resources>
    <!--Display the basic tiles used in the example-->
    <TextBlock Text="Tiles:" />
    <Image Source="bubble_dropper.jpg" />
    <Image Source="mini_mountains.jpg" />
    <Image Source="fly_larvae.jpg" />
    <Image Source="fishy_rainbow.jpg" />
</StackPanel>
<Canvas Margin="5">
    <Canvas.Resources>
        <!--Define static ImageBrush resource with TileMode FlipXY-->
        <ImageBrush x:Key="IB1" ImageSource="bubble_dropper.jpg"
                    Stretch="UniformToFill" TileMode="FlipXY"
                    Viewport="0,0,0.2,0.2" />
        <!--Define static ImageBrush resource with TileMode FlipX-->
        <ImageBrush x:Key="IB2" ImageSource="mini_mountains.jpg"
                    Stretch="UniformToFill" TileMode="FlipX"
                    Viewport="0,0,0.5,0.2" />
    </Canvas.Resources>

    <!--Fill Rectangles with static ImageBrush resources-->
    <Rectangle Canvas.Top="5" Canvas.Left="5"
               Height="180" Width="80"
               Fill="{StaticResource IB1}" />
    <Rectangle Canvas.Top="10" Canvas.Left="50"
               Height="70" Width="230"
               Fill="{StaticResource IB2}" />
    <!--Fill Ellipse with custom ImageBrush - TileMode Tile-->
    <Ellipse Canvas.Top="130" Canvas.Left="30"
             Height="100" Width="230">

        <Ellipse.Fill>
            <ImageBrush ImageSource="fishy_rainbow.jpg"
                        Stretch="Fill" TileMode="Tile"
                        Viewport="0,0,0.25,0.5" />
        </Ellipse.Fill>
    </Ellipse>
```

```
            <!--Fill with custom ImageBrush - TileMode Tile-->
            <Ellipse Canvas.Top="30" Canvas.Left="110"
                     Height="150" Width="150">
                <Ellipse.Fill>
                    <ImageBrush ImageSource="fly_larvae.jpg" Opacity=".7"
                                Stretch="Uniform" TileMode="Tile"
                                Viewport="0,0,0.5,.5" />
                </Ellipse.Fill>
            </Ellipse>
            <!--Draw Stroke with tiled ImageBrush - TileMode Tile-->
            <Line X1="20" X2="280" Y1="240" Y2="240" StrokeThickness="30">
                <Line.Stroke>
                    <ImageBrush ImageSource="ApressLogo.gif"
                                Stretch="UniformToFill" TileMode="Tile"
                                Viewport="0,0,0.25,1" />
                </Line.Stroke>
            </Line>
        </Canvas>
    </StackPanel>
</Window>
```

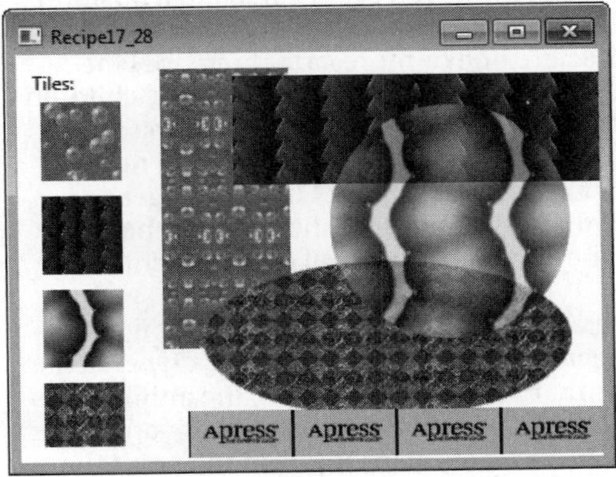

Figure 17-26. Filling and drawing shapes with patterns

17-29. Animate the Property of a Control

Problem

You need to change the value of a property on a control with respect to time. This could be the opacity of a button, the color of a rectangle, or the height of an expander, for example.

Solution

Animate the value of the property using one or more `System.Windows.Media.Animation.Timeline` objects in a `System.Windows.Media.Animation.Storyboard`.

How It Works

Owing to the richness of WPF's animation framework, there are myriad options when it comes to animating something. In essence, you are able to animate just about any `System.Windows.DependencyProperty` of an object that derives from `System.Windows.Media.Animation.Animatable`. Couple that with the range of types for which `Timeline` objects already exist, and you find yourself in a position of endless possibilities.

To animate the property of a control, you will generally declare one or more `AnimationTimeline` objects that target the data type of the property being animated. These timelines are defined as children of a `System.Windows.Media.Animation.Storyboard`, with the root `Storyboard` being activated by a `System.Windows.Media.Animation.BeginStoryboard` when used in markup. It is also possible to nest `Storyboard` objects and `ParallelTimeline` objects as children. Each `AnimationTimeline` can target a different property of a different object, a different property of the same object, or the same property of the same object. The target object or target property can also be defined at the level of the parent `ParallelTimeline` or `Storyboard`.

For each data type that WPF supports, there exists an `AnimationTimeline`. Each timeline will be named *`<Type>Animation`*, possibly with several variants for special types of `Timeline`, where *`<Type>`* is the target data type of the `Timeline`. With the exception of a few `AnimationTimeline` objects, the animation's effect on a target property is defined by specifying values for one or more of the `To`, `From`, or `By` properties. If the `From` property of an `AnimationTimeline` is not specified, the value of the property at the point the timeline's clock is applied will be used. This is useful because it means you do not need to worry about storing a property's initial value and then restoring it at a later date. If a value for the `From` property is specified, the property will be set with that value when the `Timeline` is applied. Again, the original value of the property will be restored when the timeline's clock is removed.

The abstract `Timeline` class, from which all `AnimationTimeline`, `Storyboard`, and `ParallelTimeline` objects derive, defines several properties that allow you to define the characteristics of an animation. Table 17-12 describes these properties of the `Timeline` class.

Table 17-12. Commonly Used Properties of the Timeline Class

Property	Description
AccelerationRatio	Used to specify a percentage of the timeline's duration that should be used to accelerate the speed of the animation from 0 to the animation's maximum rate. The value should be a System.Double ranging between 0 and 1, inclusive, and is 0 by default. The sum of a timeline's AccelerationRatio and DecelerationRatio must not be greater than 1.
AutoReverse	A System.Boolean property that specifies whether the Timeline should play back to the beginning once the end has been reached.
BeginTime	A System.Nullable(TimeSpan) that specifies when a timeline should become active, relative to its parent's BeginTime. For a root Timeline, the offset is taken from the time that it becomes active. This value can be negative and will start the Timeline from the specified offset, giving the appearance that the Timeline has already been playing for the given time. The SpeedRatio of a Timeline has no effect on its BeginTime value, although it is affected by its parent SpeedRatio. If the property is set to null, the Timeline will never begin.
DecelerationRatio	Used to specify a percentage of the timeline's duration that should be used to reduce the speed of the animation from the maximum rate to 0. The value should be a System.Double ranging between 0 and 1, inclusive, and is 0 by default. The sum of a timeline's AccelerationRatio and DecelerationRatio must not be greater than 1.
Duration	A nullable System.Windows.Duration specifying the length of time the animation should take to play from beginning to end. For Storyboard and ParallelTimeline objects, this value will default to the longest duration of its children. For a basic AnimationTimeline object—for example, System.Windows.Media.Animation.DoubleAnimation—this value will default to 1 second, and a keyframe-based animation will have a value equal to the sum of System.Windows.Media.Animation.KeyTime values for each keyframe.
FillBehavior	A value of the System.Windows.Media.Animation.FillBehavior enumeration is used to define an animation's behavior once it has completed, but its parent is still active, or its parent is in its hold period. The FillBehavior.HoldEnd value is used when an animation should hold its final value for a property until its parent is no longer active or outside of its hold period. The FillBehavior.Stop value will cause the timeline to not hold its final value for a property once it completes, regardless of whether its parent is still active.

Property	Description
RepeatBehavior	A System.Windows.Media.Animation.RepeatBehavior value indicating whether and how an animation is repeated.
SpeedRatio	A property of type System.Double that is used as a multiplier to alter the playback speed of an animation. A speed ratio of 0.25 will slow the animation down such that it runs at a quarter of its normal speed. A value of 2 will double the speed of the animation, and a speed ratio of 1 means the animation will play back at normal speed. Note that this will affect the actual duration of an animation.

The Code

The following example demonstrates some of the functionality available with animations. Properties of various controls are animated using different values for the previously discussed properties to give an example of their effect.

```
<Window x:Class="Apress.VisualCSharpRecipes.Chapter17.MainWindow"
    xmlns="http://schemas.microsoft.com/winfx/2006/xaml/presentation"
    xmlns:x="http://schemas.microsoft.com/winfx/2006/xaml"
    Title="Recipe17_29" Height="300" Width="300">
    <Window.Resources>
        <Storyboard x:Key="ellipse1Storyboard"
                    Storyboard.TargetName="ellipse1">
            <ParallelTimeline>
                <DoubleAnimation
                    To="50"
                    Duration="0:0:5"
                    AccelerationRatio="0.25"
                    DecelerationRatio="0.25"
                    Storyboard.TargetProperty="Width"
                    RepeatBehavior="5x" />
                <DoubleAnimation
                    To="50"
                    Duration="0:0:5"
                    AccelerationRatio="0.5"
                    DecelerationRatio="0.25"
                    Storyboard.TargetProperty="Height"
                    RepeatBehavior="5x"
                    SpeedRatio="4" />
            </ParallelTimeline>
        </Storyboard>

        <Storyboard x:Key="rect1Storyboard"
            Storyboard.TargetName="rect1">
            <ParallelTimeline>
                <DoubleAnimation
                    To="50"
                    Duration="0:0:10"
```

```
                FillBehavior="Stop"
                Storyboard.TargetProperty="Width" />
            <DoubleAnimation
                To="50"
                Duration="0:0:5"
                FillBehavior="HoldEnd"
                AccelerationRatio="0.5"
                DecelerationRatio="0.25"
                Storyboard.TargetProperty="Height" />
        </ParallelTimeline>
    </Storyboard>
</Window.Resources>

<Window.Triggers>
    <EventTrigger
    RoutedEvent="Ellipse.Loaded"
    SourceName="ellipse1">
    <BeginStoryboard
    Storyboard="{DynamicResource ellipse1Storyboard}" />
    </EventTrigger>
    <EventTrigger
    RoutedEvent="Rectangle.Loaded"
    SourceName="rect1">
    <BeginStoryboard
    Storyboard="{StaticResource rect1Storyboard}" />
    </EventTrigger>
</Window.Triggers>

<Grid>
    <Grid.ColumnDefinitions>
        <ColumnDefinition Width="0.5*" />
        <ColumnDefinition Width="0.5*" />
    </Grid.ColumnDefinitions>
    <Ellipse x:Name="ellipse1" Margin="10" Width="100" Height="100"
             Fill="CornflowerBlue" />
    <Rectangle x:Name="rect1" Margin="10" Width="100" Height="100"
               Fill="Firebrick" Grid.Column="1" />
</Grid>
</Window>
```

17-30. Animate Several Properties in Parallel

Problem

You need to animate several properties of a control at the same time—for example, its height, width, and color.

Solution

Define your animations as discussed in Recipe 17-29, but make them children of a System.Windows.Media.Animation.ParallelTimeline.

How It Works

The ParallelTimeline is a special type of System.Windows.Media.Animation.Timeline that allows for one or more child Timeline objects to be defined as its children, with each child Timeline being run in parallel. Because ParallelTimeline is a Timeline object, it can be used like any other Timeline object. Unlike a Storyboard, where animations are activated based on the order in which its child Timeline objects are declared, a ParallelTimeline will activate its children based on the value of their BeginTime properties. If any of the animations overlap, they will run in parallel.

The Storyboard class actually inherits from ParallelTimeline, and simply gives each child a BeginTime based on where in the list of child objects a Timeline is declared and the cumulative Duration and BeginTime values of each preceding Timeline. The Storyboard class goes further to extend the ParallelTimeline class by adding a number of methods for controlling the processing of its child Timeline objects. Because ParallelTimeline is the ancestor of a Storyboard, ParallelTimeline objects are more suited to nesting because they are much slimmer objects.

Like other Timeline objects, the ParallelTimeline has a BeginTime property. This allows you to specify an offset from the start of the owning Storyboard to the activation of the ParallelTimeline. As a result, if a value for BeginTime is given by the ParallelTimeline, its children's BeginTime will work relative to this value, as opposed to being relative to the Storyboard.

It is important to note that a Storyboard.Completed event will not be raised on the owning Storyboard until the last child Timeline in the ParallelTimeline finishes. This is because a ParallelTimeline can contain Timeline objects with different BeginTime and Duration values, meaning they won't all necessarily finish at the same time.

The Code

The following example defines a System.Windows.Window that contains a single System.Windows.Shapes.Rectangle. When the mouse is placed over the rectangle, the Rectangle.Height, Rectangle.Width, and Rectangle.Fill properties are animated. The animation continues until the mouse is moved out of the rectangle.

```
<Window x:Class="Apress.VisualCSharpRecipes.Chapter17.MainWindow"
    xmlns="http://schemas.microsoft.com/winfx/2006/xaml/presentation"
    xmlns:x="http://schemas.microsoft.com/winfx/2006/xaml"
    Title="Recipe17_30" Height="300" Width="300">
    <Grid>
        <Rectangle Height="100" Width="100" Fill="Firebrick"
            Stroke="Black" StrokeThickness="1">
            <Rectangle.Style>
                <Style TargetType="Rectangle">
                    <Style.Triggers>
```

```
                    <EventTrigger
                        RoutedEvent="Rectangle.MouseEnter">
                        <BeginStoryboard>
                            <Storyboard>
                            <ParallelTimeline
                            RepeatBehavior="Forever"
                            AutoReverse="True">
                            <DoubleAnimation
                            Storyboard.TargetProperty="Width"
                            To="150" />
                            <DoubleAnimation
                            Storyboard.TargetProperty="Height"
                            To="150" />
                            <ColorAnimation
                            Storyboard.TargetProperty="Fill.Color"
                            To="Orange" />
                            </ParallelTimeline>
                            </Storyboard>
                        </BeginStoryboard>
                    </EventTrigger>
                    <EventTrigger
                        RoutedEvent="Rectangle.MouseLeave">
                        <BeginStoryboard>
                            <Storyboard>
                            <ParallelTimeline>
                            <DoubleAnimation
                            Storyboard.TargetProperty="Width"
                            To="100" />
                            <DoubleAnimation
                            Storyboard.TargetProperty="Height"
                            To="100" />
                            <ColorAnimation
                            Storyboard.TargetProperty="Fill.Color"
                            To="Firebrick" />
                            </ParallelTimeline>
                            </Storyboard>
                        </BeginStoryboard>
                    </EventTrigger>
                </Style.Triggers>
            </Style>
        </Rectangle.Style>
    </Rectangle>
  </Grid>
</Window>
```

17-31. Create a Keyframe-Based Animation

Problem

You need to create an animation that uses keyframes to specify key points in the animation.

Solution

Use a keyframe-based animation such as `System.Windows.Media.Animation.DoubleAnimationUsingKeyFrames`. You can then use several `System.Windows.Media.Animation.IKeyFrame` objects to define the keyframes in your animation.

How It Works

Keyframes allow you to specify key points in an animation where the object being animated needs to be at a required position or in a required state. The frames in between are then interpolated between these two keyframes, effectively filling in the blanks in the animation. This process of interpolating the in-between frames is often referred to as *tweening*.

When defining an animation using keyframes, you will need to specify one or more keyframes that define the animation's flow. These keyframes are defined as children of your keyframe animation. It is important to note that the target type of the keyframe must match that of the parent animation. For example, if you are using a `System.Windows.Media.Animation.DoubleAnimationUsingKeyFrames`, any keyframes must be derived from the abstract class `System.Windows.Media.Animation.DoubleKeyFrame`.

You will be pleased to hear that a good number of types have keyframe objects, from `System.Int` to `System.String` and `System.Windows.Thickness` to `System.Windows.Media.Media3D.Quarternion`. (For a more complete list of the types covered, please see `http://msdn.microsoft.com/en-us/library/ms742524(VS.100).aspx`.) All but a few of the types covered by animations have a choice of interpolation methods, allowing you to specify how the frames between two keyframes are generated. Each interpolation method is defined as a prefix to the keyframe's class name, and is listed in Table 17-13.

***Table 17-13.** Interpolation Methods for Keyframe Animation*

Type	Description
`Discrete`	A discrete keyframe will not create any frames between it and the following keyframe. Once the discrete keyframe's duration has elapsed, the animation will jump to the value specified in the following keyframe.
`Linear`	Linear keyframes will create a smooth transition between it and the following frame. The generated frames will animate the value steadily at a constant rate to its endpoint.
`Spline`	Spline keyframes allow you to vary the speed at which a property is animated using the shape of a Bezier curve. The curve is described by defining its control points in unit coordinate space. The gradient of the curve defines the speed or rate of change in the animation.

Although keyframes must match the type of the owning animation, it is possible to mix the different types of interpolation, offering variable speeds throughout.

The Code

The following XAML demonstrates how to use linear and double keyframes to animate the `Height` and `Width` properties of a `System.Windows.Shapes.Ellipse` control (see Figure 17-27). The animation is triggered when the `System.Windows.Controls.Button` is clicked.

```
<Window x:Class="Apress.VisualCSharpRecipes.Chapter17.MainWindow"
    xmlns="http://schemas.microsoft.com/winfx/2006/xaml/presentation"
    xmlns:x="http://schemas.microsoft.com/winfx/2006/xaml"
    Title="Recipe17_31" Height="300" Width="300">
    <Window.Resources>
        <Storyboard x:Key="ResizeEllipseStoryboard">
            <ParallelTimeline>
                <DoubleAnimationUsingKeyFrames
                  Storyboard.TargetName="ellipse"
                  Storyboard.TargetProperty="Height">
                  <LinearDoubleKeyFrame Value="150" KeyTime="0:0:1" />
                  <LinearDoubleKeyFrame Value="230" KeyTime="0:0:2" />
                  <LinearDoubleKeyFrame Value="150" KeyTime="0:0:2.5" />
                  <LinearDoubleKeyFrame Value="230" KeyTime="0:0:5" />
                  <LinearDoubleKeyFrame Value="40" KeyTime="0:0:9" />
                </DoubleAnimationUsingKeyFrames>
                <DoubleAnimationUsingKeyFrames
                  Storyboard.TargetName="ellipse"
                  Storyboard.TargetProperty="Width">
                  <DiscreteDoubleKeyFrame Value="150" KeyTime="0:0:1" />
                  <DiscreteDoubleKeyFrame Value="230" KeyTime="0:0:2" />
                  <DiscreteDoubleKeyFrame Value="150" KeyTime="0:0:2.5" />
                  <DiscreteDoubleKeyFrame Value="230" KeyTime="0:0:5" />
                  <DiscreteDoubleKeyFrame Value="40" KeyTime="0:0:9" />
                </DoubleAnimationUsingKeyFrames>
            </ParallelTimeline>
        </Storyboard>
    </Window.Resources>

    <Grid>
        <Grid.RowDefinitions>
            <RowDefinition />
            <RowDefinition Height="40" />
        </Grid.RowDefinitions>

        <Ellipse Height="40" Width="40" x:Name="ellipse"
            HorizontalAlignment="Center" VerticalAlignment="Center">
            <Ellipse.Fill>
                <RadialGradientBrush GradientOrigin="0.75,0.25">
                    <GradientStop Color="Yellow" Offset="0.0" />
                    <GradientStop Color="Orange" Offset="0.5" />
```

```
                        <GradientStop Color="Red" Offset="1.0" />
                    </RadialGradientBrush>
                </Ellipse.Fill>
            </Ellipse>

            <Button Content="Start..." Margin="10" Grid.Row="1">
                <Button.Triggers>
                    <EventTrigger RoutedEvent="Button.Click">
                        <BeginStoryboard
                            Storyboard="{DynamicResource ResizeEllipseStoryboard}" />
                    </EventTrigger>
                </Button.Triggers>
            </Button>
        </Grid>
    </Window>
```

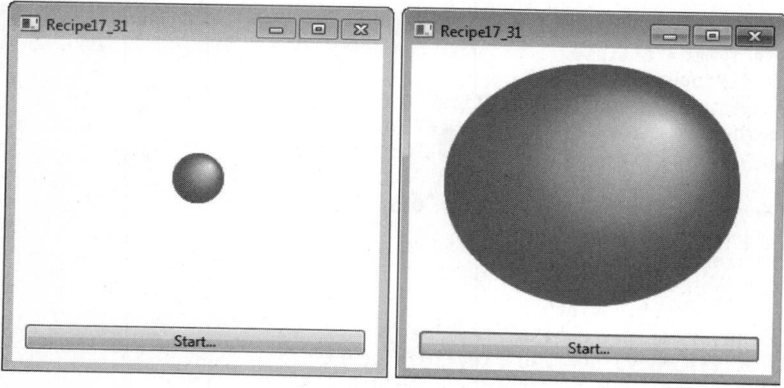

Figure 17-27. *An animated ellipse in its initial state (left) and after several seconds have passed (right)*

17-32. Animate an Object Along a Path

Problem

You need to animate some control so that it moves along a path.

Solution

Use one of the three available path animation timeline objects.

How It Works

WPF kindly provides you with three ways of animating an object along a path. Each of these methods takes a `System.Windows.Media.PathGeometry` as its input, defining the shape of the path that the object will follow, and produces some kind of output, depending on the timeline's target type. All three timelines generate their output values by linearly interpolating between the values of the input path. Table 17-14 describes each of these three methods.

Table 17-14. *Path Animation Types*

Type	Description
`DoubleAnimationUsingPath`	Outputs a single `System.Double` value, generated from the input `PathGeometry`. Unlike the other two path-based timelines, the `DoubleAnimationUsingPath` also exposes a `Source` property that is a `System.Windows.Media.Animation.PathAnimationSource`. Table 17-15 describes the value of this enumeration.
`PointAnimationUsingPath`	Generates a series of `System.Windows.Point` objects, describing a position along the input `PathGeometry`, based on the current time of the animation. `PointAnimationUsingPath` is the only timeline of the three that does not provide any values for the angle of rotation to the tangent of the path at the current point.
`MatrixAnimationUsingPath`	Generates a series of `System.Windows.Media.Matrix` objects describing a translation matrix relating to a point in the input path. If the `DoesRotateWithTangent` property of a `MatrixAnimationUsingPath` timeline is set to `True`, the output matrix is composed of a translation and rotation matrix, allowing both the position and orientation of the target to be animated with a single animation.

Table 17-15. *Values of the PathAnimationSource Enumeration*

Value	Description
`X`	Values output by the `DoubleAnimationUsingPath` correspond to the interpolated x component of the current position along the input path.
`Y`	Values output by the `DoubleAnimationUsingPath` correspond to the interpolated y component of the current position along the input path.
`Angle`	Values output by the `DoubleAnimationUsingPath` correspond to the angle of rotation to the tangent of the line at the current point along the input path.

It should be clear that each of the path timelines has a specific use and offers different levels of functionality. The `MatrixAnimationUsingPath` provides the neatest method for animating both the position and the orientation of an object. The same effect is not possible using a

PointAnimationUsingPath, and would require three DoubleAnimationUsingPath timelines, each with a different PathAnimationSource value for the Source property.

When using a value of PathAnimationSource.Angle for the Source property of a DoubleAnimationUsingPath timeline or setting the DoesRotateWithTangent property of a MatrixAnimationUsingPath timeline to True, you ensure that the object being animated is correctly rotated so that it follows the gradient of the path. If an arrow is translated using a path-driven animation, its orientation will remain the same throughout the timeline's duration. If, however, the arrow's orientation is animated to coincide with the path, the arrow will be rotated relative to its initial orientation, based on the gradient of the path. If you have a path defining a circle and the arrow initially points in to the center of the circle, the arrow will continue to point into the center of the circle as it moves around the circle's circumference.

Although the MatrixAnimationUsingPath has the most compact output, controls will rarely expose a Matrix property that you can directly animate. The target property of a MatrixAnimationUsingPath timeline will most commonly be the Matrix property of a System.Windows.Media.MatrixTransform, where the MatrixTransform is used in the render transform or layout transform of the control you want to animate. In a similar fashion, DoubleAnimationUsingPath can be used to animate the properties of a System.Windows.Media.TranslateTransform and System.Windows.Media.RotateTransform, or just about any System.Double property of the target control.

The Code

The following XAML demonstrates how to use a MatrixAnimationUsingPath, where a System.Windows.Controls.Border is translated and rotated according to the shape of the path. The path is also drawn on the screen so you can better visualize the motion of the border (see Figure 17-28).

```
<Window x:Class="Apress.VisualCSharpRecipes.Chapter17.MainWindow"
    xmlns="http://schemas.microsoft.com/winfx/2006/xaml/presentation"
    xmlns:x="http://schemas.microsoft.com/winfx/2006/xaml"
    Title="Recipe17_32" Height="300" Width="550">
    <Window.Resources>
        <PathGeometry x:Key="AnimationPathGeometry"
        Figures="M 50,150 C 100,-200 500,400 450,100 400,-100 285,400 50,150" />

        <Storyboard x:Key="MatrixAnimationStoryboard">
            <MatrixAnimationUsingPath
            RepeatBehavior="Forever"
            Duration="0:0:5"
            AutoReverse="True"
            Storyboard.TargetName="BorderMatrixTransform"
            Storyboard.TargetProperty="Matrix"
            DoesRotateWithTangent="True"
            PathGeometry="{StaticResource AnimationPathGeometry}" />
        </Storyboard>
    </Window.Resources>

    <Grid>
        <Path
        Stroke="Black"
        StrokeThickness="1"
        Data="{StaticResource AnimationPathGeometry}" />
```

```
        <Border HorizontalAlignment="Left" VerticalAlignment="Top"
            Width="100" Height="50" CornerRadius="5" BorderBrush="Black"
            BorderThickness="1" RenderTransformOrigin="0,0">
            <Border.Background>
                <LinearGradientBrush StartPoint="0.5,0" EndPoint="0.5,1">
                    <GradientStop Color="CadetBlue" Offset="0" />
                    <GradientStop Color="CornflowerBlue" Offset="1" />
                </LinearGradientBrush>
            </Border.Background>
            <Border.RenderTransform>
                <MatrixTransform x:Name="BorderMatrixTransform" />
            </Border.RenderTransform>
            <Border.Triggers>
                <EventTrigger RoutedEvent="Border.Loaded">
                <BeginStoryboard
                  Storyboard="{StaticResource MatrixAnimationStoryboard}"/>
                </EventTrigger>
            </Border.Triggers>
            <TextBlock Text="^ This way up ^" HorizontalAlignment="Center"
                VerticalAlignment="Center" />
        </Border>
    </Grid>
</Window>
```

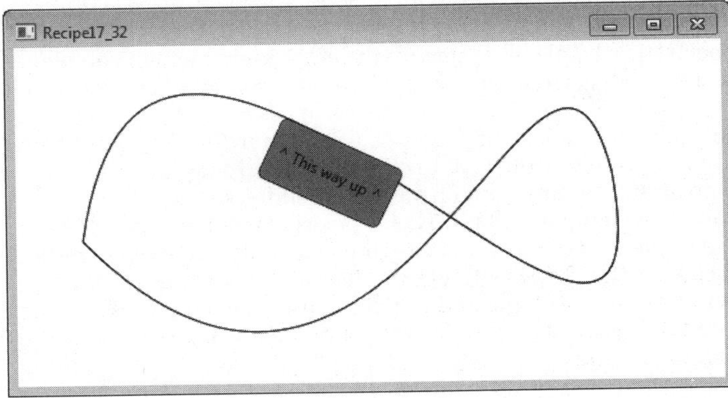

Figure 17-28. A control midway through a path animation. Notice how the control is oriented such that it follows a tangent to the gradient of the curve.

17-33. Play a Media File

Problem

You need to play a sound or music file and allow the user to control the progress of the playback, volume, or balance.

Solution

Use a `System.Windows.Controls.MediaElement` to handle the playback of the media file. Use a `System.Windows.Media.MediaTimeline` to control the playback of the desired media through the `MediaElement`. Declare the set of controls that will enable the user to control the playback and associate triggers with the controls that start, stop, pause, and resume the animation controlling the `MediaTimeline`. For volume and balance, data-bind controls to the `Volume` and `Balance` properties of the `MediaElement`.

How It Works

A `MediaElement` performs the playback of a media file, and you control that playback via animation using a `MediaTimeline`. To control the playback, you use a set of `EventTrigger` elements to start, stop, pause, and resume the animation `Storyboard` containing the `MediaTimeline`.

You can either define the `EventTrigger` elements in the `Triggers` collection on the controls that control the playback or centralize their declaration by placing them on the container in which you place the controls. Within the `Actions` element of the `Triggers` collection, declare the `Storyboard` elements to control the `MediaTimeline`.

One complexity arises when you want a control such as a `System.Windows.Controls.Slider` to show the current position within the media file as well as allow the user to change the current play position. To update the display of the current play position, you must attach an event handler to the `MediaTimeline.CurrentTimeInvalidated` event, which updates the `Slider` position when it fires.

To move the play position in response to the `Slider` position changing, you attach an event handler to the `Slider.ValueChanged` property, which calls the `Stoyboard.Seek` method to change the current `MediaTimeline` play position. However, you must include logic in the event handlers to stop these events from triggering each other repeatedly as the user and `MediaTimeline` try to update the `Slider` position (and in turn the media play position) at the same time.

The Code

The following XAML demonstrates how to play an AVI file using a `MediaElement` and allow the user to start, stop, pause, and resume the playback. The user can also move quickly back and forth through the media file using a slider to position the current play position, as well as control the volume and balance of the audio (see Figure 17-29).

```
<Window x:Class="Apress.VisualCSharpRecipes.Chapter17.MainWindow"
    xmlns="http://schemas.microsoft.com/winfx/2006/xaml/presentation"
    xmlns:x="http://schemas.microsoft.com/winfx/2006/xaml"
    Title="Recipe17_33" Height="450" Width="300">
    <StackPanel x:Name="Panel">
        <StackPanel.Resources>
            <!-- Style all buttons the same. -->
            <Style TargetType="{x:Type Button}">
                <Setter Property="Height" Value="25" />
                <Setter Property="MinWidth" Value="50" />
            </Style>
        </StackPanel.Resources>
        <StackPanel.Triggers>
            <!-- Triggers for handling playback of media file. -->
            <EventTrigger RoutedEvent="Button.Click" SourceName="btnPlay">
                <EventTrigger.Actions>
                    <BeginStoryboard Name="ClockStoryboard">
                        <Storyboard x:Name="Storyboard"  SlipBehavior="Slip"
                                    CurrentTimeInvalidated="Storyboard_Changed">
                            <MediaTimeline BeginTime="0" Source="clock.avi"
                                Storyboard.TargetName="meMediaElement"
                                RepeatBehavior="Forever" />
                        </Storyboard>
                    </BeginStoryboard>
                </EventTrigger.Actions>
            </EventTrigger>
            <EventTrigger RoutedEvent="Button.Click" SourceName="btnPause">
                <EventTrigger.Actions>
                    <PauseStoryboard BeginStoryboardName="ClockStoryboard" />
                </EventTrigger.Actions>
            </EventTrigger>
            <EventTrigger RoutedEvent="Button.Click" SourceName="btnResume">
                <EventTrigger.Actions>
                    <ResumeStoryboard BeginStoryboardName="ClockStoryboard" />
                </EventTrigger.Actions>
            </EventTrigger>
            <EventTrigger RoutedEvent="Button.Click" SourceName="btnStop">
                <EventTrigger.Actions>
                    <StopStoryboard BeginStoryboardName="ClockStoryboard" />
                </EventTrigger.Actions>
            </EventTrigger>
            <EventTrigger RoutedEvent="Slider.PreviewMouseLeftButtonDown"
                          SourceName="sldPosition" >
                <PauseStoryboard BeginStoryboardName="ClockStoryboard" />
            </EventTrigger>
            <EventTrigger RoutedEvent="Slider.PreviewMouseLeftButtonUp"
                          SourceName="sldPosition" >
                <ResumeStoryboard BeginStoryboardName="ClockStoryboard" />
            </EventTrigger>
        </StackPanel.Triggers>
```

```
        <!-- Media element to play the sound, music, or video file. -->
        <MediaElement Name="meMediaElement" HorizontalAlignment="Center"
                      Margin="5" MinHeight="300" Stretch="Fill"
                      MediaOpened="MediaOpened" />

        <!-- Button controls for play, pause, resume, and stop. -->
        <StackPanel HorizontalAlignment="Center" Orientation="Horizontal">
            <Button Content="_Play" Name="btnPlay" />
            <Button Content="P_ause" Name="btnPause" />
            <Button Content="_Resume" Name="btnResume" />
            <Button Content="_Stop" Name="btnStop" />
        </StackPanel>

        <!-- Slider shows the position within the media. -->
        <Slider HorizontalAlignment="Center" Margin="5"
                Name="sldPosition" Width="250"
                ValueChanged="sldPosition_ValueChanged">
        </Slider>

        <!-- Sliders to control volume and balance. -->
        <Grid>
            <Grid.ColumnDefinitions>
                <ColumnDefinition Width="1*"/>
                <ColumnDefinition Width="4*"/>
            </Grid.ColumnDefinitions>
            <Grid.RowDefinitions>
                <RowDefinition />
                <RowDefinition />
            </Grid.RowDefinitions>
            <TextBlock Grid.Column="0" Grid.Row="0" Text="Volume:"
                       HorizontalAlignment="Right" VerticalAlignment="Center"/>
            <Slider Grid.Column="1" Grid.Row="0" Minimum="0" Maximum="1"
                    TickFrequency="0.1" TickPlacement="TopLeft"
Value="{Binding ElementName=meMediaElement, Path=Volume, Mode=TwoWay}" />
            <TextBlock Grid.Column="0" Grid.Row="1" Text="Balance:"
                       HorizontalAlignment="Right" VerticalAlignment="Center"/>
            <Slider Grid.Column="1" Grid.Row="1" Minimum="-1" Maximum="1"
                    TickFrequency="0.2" TickPlacement="TopLeft"
Value="{Binding ElementName=meMediaElement, Path=Balance, Mode=TwoWay}" />
        </Grid>
    </StackPanel>
</Window>
```

The following code-behind shows the event handlers that allow the user to set the current play position using a slider and update the position of the slider to reflect the current play position:

```
using System;
using System.Windows;
using System.Windows.Input;
using System.Windows.Media;
using System.Windows.Media.Animation;
```

```
namespace Apress.VisualCSharpRecipes.Chapter17
{
    /// <summary>
    /// Interaction logic for MainWindow.xaml
    /// </summary>
    public partial class MainWindow : Window
    {
        bool ignoreValueChanged = false;

        public MainWindow()
        {
            InitializeComponent();
        }

        // Handles the opening of the media file and sets the Maximum
        // value of the position slider based on the natural duration
        // of the media file.
        private void MediaOpened(object sender, EventArgs e)
        {
            sldPosition.Maximum =
                meMediaElement.NaturalDuration.TimeSpan.TotalMilliseconds;
        }

        // Updates the position slider when the media time changes.
        private void Storyboard_Changed(object sender, EventArgs e)
        {
            ClockGroup clockGroup = sender as ClockGroup;

            MediaClock mediaClock = clockGroup.Children[0] as MediaClock;

            if (mediaClock.CurrentProgress.HasValue)
            {
                ignoreValueChanged = true;
                sldPosition.Value = meMediaElement.Position.TotalMilliseconds;
                ignoreValueChanged = false;
            }
        }

        // Handles the movement of the slider and updates the position
        // being played.
        private void sldPosition_ValueChanged(object sender,
            RoutedPropertyChangedEventArgs<double> e)
        {
            if (ignoreValueChanged)
            {
                return;
            }
```

```
                Storyboard.Seek(Panel,
                    TimeSpan.FromMilliseconds(sldPosition.Value),
                    TimeSeekOrigin.BeginTime);
            }
        }
    }
```

Figure 17-29. Controlling the playback of media files

17-34. Query Keyboard State

Problem

You need to query the state of the keyboard to determine whether the user is pressing any special keys.

Solution

Use the `IsKeyDown` and `IsKeyToggled` methods of the static `System.Windows.Input.Keyboard` class.

How It Works

The static Keyboard class contains two methods that allow you to determine whether a particular key is currently pressed or whether keys that have a toggled state (for example, Caps Lock) are currently on or off.

To determine whether a key is currently pressed, call the IsKeyDown method and pass a member of the System.Windows.Input.Keys enumeration that represents the key you want to test. The method returns True if the key is currently pressed. To test the state of toggled keys, call the IsKeyToggled method, again passing a member of the Keys enumeration to identify the key to test.

The Code

The following XAML defines a set of CheckBox controls representing various special keys on the keyboard. When the key is pressed, the program uses the Keyboard class to test the state of each button and update the IsSelected property of the appropriate CheckBox (see Figure 17-30).

```
<Window x:Class="Apress.VisualCSharpRecipes.Chapter17.MainWindow"
    xmlns="http://schemas.microsoft.com/winfx/2006/xaml/presentation"
    xmlns:x="http://schemas.microsoft.com/winfx/2006/xaml"
    Title="Recipe17_34" Height="190" Width="210">
    <StackPanel HorizontalAlignment="Center">
        <UniformGrid Columns="2">
            <UniformGrid.Resources>
                <Style TargetType="{x:Type CheckBox}">
                    <Setter Property="IsHitTestVisible" Value="False" />
                    <Setter Property="Margin" Value="5" />
                </Style>
            </UniformGrid.Resources>
            <CheckBox Content="LeftShift" Name="chkLShift"/>
            <CheckBox Content="RightShift" Name="chkRShift"/>
            <CheckBox Content="LeftControl" Name="chkLControl"/>
            <CheckBox Content="RightControl" Name="chkRControl"/>
            <CheckBox Content="LeftAlt" Name="chkLAlt"/>
            <CheckBox Content="RightAlt" Name="chkRAlt"/>
            <CheckBox Content="CapsLock" Name="chkCaps"/>
            <CheckBox Content="NumLock" Name="chkNum"/>
        </UniformGrid>
        <Button Content="Check Keyboard" Margin="10" Click="Button_Click"/>
    </StackPanel>
</Window>
```

The following code-behind contains the Button.Click event that checks the keyboard and updates the CheckBox controls:

```
using System.Windows;
using System.Windows.Input;

namespace Apress.VisualCSharpRecipes.Chapter17
{
    /// <summary>
```

```
    /// Interaction logic for MainWindow.xaml
    /// </summary>
    public partial class MainWindow : Window
    {
        public MainWindow()
        {
            InitializeComponent();
            CheckKeyboardState();
        }

        // Handles the Click event on the Button.
        private void Button_Click(object sender, RoutedEventArgs e)
        {
            CheckKeyboardState();
        }

        // Checks the state of the keyboard and updates the check boxes.
        private void CheckKeyboardState()
        {
            // Control keys.
            chkLControl.IsChecked = Keyboard.IsKeyDown(Key.LeftCtrl);
            chkRControl.IsChecked = Keyboard.IsKeyDown(Key.RightCtrl);

            // Shift keys.
            chkLShift.IsChecked = Keyboard.IsKeyDown(Key.LeftShift);
            chkRShift.IsChecked = Keyboard.IsKeyDown(Key.RightShift);

            // Alt keys.
            chkLAlt.IsChecked = Keyboard.IsKeyDown(Key.LeftAlt);
            chkRAlt.IsChecked = Keyboard.IsKeyDown(Key.RightAlt);

            // Num Lock and Caps Lock.
            chkCaps.IsChecked = Keyboard.IsKeyToggled(Key.CapsLock);
            chkNum.IsChecked = Keyboard.IsKeyToggled(Key.NumLock);
        }
    }
}
```

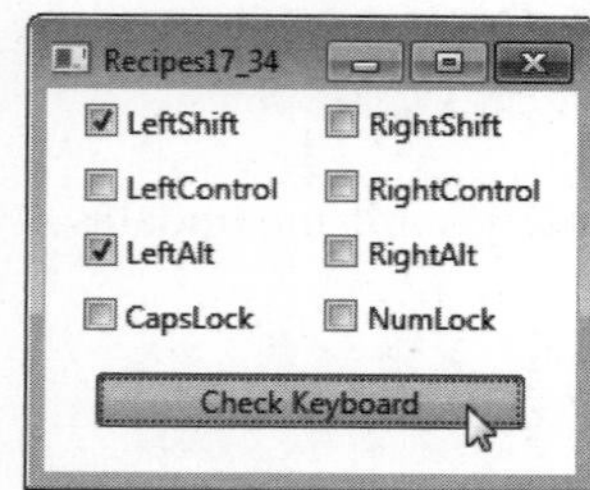

Figure 17-30. *Querying keyboard state*

Index

Numbers & Symbols

A

B

C

D

E

F

G

J

K

L

M

N

O

P

S

StructLayoutAttribute class, 603

T

X

Y

Z